ENCYCLOPEDIA
of the
HOLOCAUST

ENCYCLOPEDIA
of the
HOLOCAUST

Israel Gutman, Editor in Chief

Volume 2

Yad Vashem
The Holocaust Martyrs' and Heroes'
  Remembrance Authority
Jerusalem

Sifriat Poalim Publishing House
Tel Aviv

MACMILLAN PUBLISHING COMPANY
NEW YORK

Collier Macmillan Publishers
LONDON

Macmillan Publishing Company
866 Third Avenue
New York, New York 10022
Collier Macmillan Canada, Inc.
Library of Congress Catalog Card Number: 89-13466
Printed in the United States of America

printing number
2   3   4   5   6   7   8   9   10

Library of Congress Cataloging-in-Publication Data

Encyclopedia of the Holocaust / Israel Gutman, editor in chief.
p.   cm.
Includes bibliographical references.
ISBN 0−02−896090−4 (set)
Trade edition ISBN 0−02−546705−0 (set)
1. Holocaust, Jewish (1939−1945)—Dictionaries.   I. Gutman,
Israel.

| D804.3.E53 | 1990 | 89-13466 |
| 940.53'18'-03—dc20 | | CIP |

Acknowledgments of sources
and permissions to use previously published materials
are made in Acknowledgments, page xix.

E

EAST ASIA. *See* Japan; Rescue of Polish Jews via East Asia; Shanghai.

EASTERN BATTALIONS. *See* Ostbataillone.

EAST INDUSTRY, INC. *See* Ostindustrie GmbH.

EBENSEE, subcamp of the MAUTHAUSEN concentration camp, created on November 18, 1943, about 2.5 miles (4 km) from the town of Ebensee in the Salzkammergut district of Upper AUSTRIA, at the foot of the Alps. The purpose of the camp was to provide labor for the construction of a system of tunnels in the side of a mountain to house a rocket-research factory. The small section of the tunnels that was completed went down 76 feet (250 m) into the mountain, was coated with concrete, and was several stories high.

The camp consisted of thirty-two dwelling huts and service buildings, including a crematorium. Most of the prisoners arrived from the main Mauthausen camp and its other satellites. At the height of occupancy, there were 18,437 prisoners in Ebensee. The first camp commandant was SS-Obersturmführer Otto Riemer, who in May 1944, while drunk, fired on a group of prisoners returning from work, killing 9 of them. After his subsequent removal from office, the position was occupied by SS-Hauptsturmführer Anton Ganz. The *Lagerälteste* (camp elder) was a German crim-

inal offender named Magnus, who had occupied this office previously at the main Mauthausen camp. With his two assistants, also criminal offenders, he instituted a rule of terror among the prisoners. The camp registrar, who recorded the list of those who died at Ebensee, was Camille Scholtes, a prisoner from Luxembourg. The prisoners were of many nationalities, in particular Russian, Yugoslav, and French. Some staff positions were held by Germans, Spaniards, and Czechs.

In early June 1944 the first Jews arrived in Ebensee. As a result of the particularly difficult conditions and the cruel treatment meted out to them, their mortality rate was far higher than that of the non-Jewish prisoners. Early in 1945 the pace of work in digging the tunnels was intensified, and additional consignments of prisoners, including many Jews, were brought in. In mid-April of that year, inmates who had been transferred from the evacuated satellite camps to Mauthausen were sent to Ebensee; three consignments of 7,401 prisoners from MELK arrived.

The increased overcrowding in the camp brought with it a vast deterioration in the conditions of sanitation and a reduction in the food rations. In Block 23, where feeble prisoners were assembled, instances of cannibalism occurred. About eighty corpses were removed from that block daily. The mortality rate in the camp increased so greatly that the crematorium could not burn all the corpses. The sick were obliged to dig pits, into which the corpses were thrown; the bodies were then covered with a thin layer of earth. In April alone, 4,547 out of the 16,000 prisoners then in Ebensee died.

On April 30, most of the German prisoners were released and forced labor ended. At the roll call on May 5, the camp commandant, Ganz, asked the prisoners to go into Tunnel No. 5 so that they would not be wounded by the firing from the battles. When the prisoners refused, Ganz and his escort, followed by all the SS personnel, left the camp; its command was handed over to a local guard unit. On the following day, May 6, an American army unit arrived at Ebensee and the camp was liberated. At the entrance to Tunnel No. 5 a locomotive was found, with its water tank full of explosives. Apparently, it was intended to blow up the tunnel in which all the prisoners were to be assembled.

It is estimated that about eleven thousand persons died at Ebensee.

BIBLIOGRAPHY

Eckstein, B. *Mauthausen: Concentration and Annihilation Camp.* Jerusalem, 1984. (In Hebrew.)
Le Chêne, E. *Mauthausen: The History of a Death Camp.* London, 1971.
Marsalek, H., and K. Hacker. *Kurzgeschichte der Konzentrationslager Mauthausen und seiner drei grössten Nebenlager Gusen, Ebensee, und Melk.* Vienna, n.d.

BENYAMIN ECKSTEIN

ECLAIREURS ISRAÉLITES DE FRANCE

(French Jewish Scouts; EIF), pluralist and traditionalist scouting movement founded by Robert GAMZON in 1923. By 1939 the EIF was established in the Paris region, in the east of FRANCE, and in several other communities. From September 1939, it set up children's homes in the southwest of the country. After the armistice with Germany in June 1940, the movement redeployed in the unoccupied zone while continuing to function in Paris, despite the German prohibition against scouting. Together with the children's homes, which began to take in the children of Jews interned in camps, the movement organized in the south of France a number of rural groups made up partly of young foreign Jews.

Although the EIF was a full member of Scoutisme Français (the French scout movement), established under the auspices of the Vichy government in October 1940, it was nevertheless forced to join the southern branch (UGIF-South) of the UNION GÉNÉRALE DES ISRAÉLITES DE FRANCE, the compulsory Jewish organization, at the end of 1941. The position of the EIF was somewhat enhanced when Gamzon was appointed to the administrative council of the UGIF, and the Eclaireurs constituted the latter's Fourth Section, which dealt with issues concerning young people.

The first deportations of Jews from France in March 1942 and the massive roundups that summer led to the creation of EIF's social service, La Sixième (The Sixth). Originally under the cover of UGIF, and later functioning entirely in the underground, La Sixième developed a rescue network that provided, essentially for children, false identities, placement among non-Jews, and transportation across the French borders. Despite the dissolution of the Fourth Section by the COMMISSARIAT GÉNÉRALE AUX QUESTIONS JUIVES (General Office for Jewish Affairs) in January 1943, EIF's educational activities continued until the following autumn, when the centers began to disband. During that winter an EIF fighting underground came into being, called the Compagnie Marc Haguenau, after the leader of La Sixième, who had committed suicide when captured by the Gestapo. Incorporated into both the Organisation Juive de Combat (Jewish Fighting Organization) and the Armée Secrète (Gen. Charles de GAULLE's underground faction), the company took part in the liberation of the southwest of France. One hundred and fifty members of the EIF, chiefly in La Sixième, lost their lives. The organization succeeded in rescuing several thousand Jews.

BIBLIOGRAPHY

L'activité des organisations juives en France sous l'occupation. Paris, 1947.
Michel, A. *Les Eclaireurs Israélites de France pendant la Seconde Guerre Mondiale.* Paris, 1984.
Pougatch, I. *Un bâtisseur: Robert Gamzon.* Paris, 1971.

ALAIN MICHEL

ECONOMIC-ADMINISTRATIVE MAIN OFFICE. *See* Wirtschafts-Verwaltungshauptamt.

EDELMAN, MAREK (b. 1921), a commander of the WARSAW GHETTO UPRISING. A native of Warsaw, Edelman was a member of Zukunft, the youth movement affiliated with the Jewish Socialist party, the BUND, and was one of its activists in the ghetto underground. When the relative standing of the young people in the underground gained in strength, Edelman became a member of the Bund's central institutions. In November 1942 he joined the ŻYDOWSKA ORGANIZACJA BOJOWA (Jewish Fighting Organization; ŻOB) and shortly afterward was appointed as his movement's representative in the organization's command.

In the Warsaw ghetto uprising of April 1943, Edelman was at first in charge of the "Brushmakers" area in the ghetto; following the withdrawal of the ŻOB forces, he and his men joined the group centered on 30 Franciszkanska Street. Edelman was among the last group of fighters to hold out in the ŻOB headquarters at 18 Mila Street, and he then crossed over to the "Aryan" side of Warsaw by way of the sewers, on May 10. In August 1944 Edelman served in the ranks of the ŻOB company that took part in the WARSAW POLISH UPRISING.

After the war, in 1945, Edelman published *The Bund's Role in the Defense of the Warsaw Ghetto*, in Polish and Yiddish. He also published *The Ghetto Fights* (1946), a short history of the uprising, in Polish, Yiddish, and English. He studied medicine and practiced it, remaining in Poland. From the early 1980s he was active in the Solidarity trade union movement.

BIBLIOGRAPHY

Krall, H. *Shielding the Flame: An Intimate Conversation with Dr. Marek Edelman, the Last Surviving Leader of the Warsaw Ghetto Uprising.* New York, 1986.

ISRAEL GUTMAN

Marek Edelman.

EDELSTEIN, JACOB (1903–1944), chairman of the JUDENRAT (Jewish Council) in the THERESIENSTADT ghetto. Edelstein was born in Gorodenka, Galicia, and received a religious Zionist upbringing. During World War I his family moved to Brno (Ger., Brünn), the capital of Moravia, and from 1926 he was active in the Tekhelet-Lavan and He-Haluts Zionist youth movements. In 1929 he was elected Tekhelet-Lavan representative at the He-Haluts main office, and in 1933 he was appointed head of its Palestine Office in Prague. In the summer of 1937 Edelstein immigrated to Palestine and for three months worked there for Keren Hayesod (the Palestine Foundation Fund), but he was disappointed with that situation and decided to return to Prague, where he resumed his work as director of the Palestine Office.

On March 15, 1939, the day the Germans marched into Prague, the members of the Zionist leadership of Czechoslovakia held a meeting at which they decided that it was their duty to stay on and not abandon the Jewish population at a time of crisis. Edelstein became the leading personality in the

Jacob Edelstein.

Zionist leadership, was put in charge of emigration to Palestine, and before long became the official representative of the Jews in contacts with the Germans.

Until he was sent to Theresienstadt on December 4, 1941, Edelstein left the country for several trips abroad, with the Gestapo's permission, in order to look for ways and means to speed up the emigration of Jews. In May 1939 he visited Palestine, in November he was in Trieste, and at the end of that month he was in Vienna; in February 1940 he spent two days in Geneva and from there went to Berlin. He visited Bratislava in the fall of 1940, and in March 1941 he went to Amsterdam. In each of these places Edelstein met with the Jewish community leaders and the Zionist leadership, shared his information with them, and warned them of possible future developments. He had several opportunities to stay abroad rather than return to Czechoslovakia, but he always went back to Prague.

On October 18, 1939, Edelstein, with a group of a thousand men from Moravská Os-

trava, left for Nisko, on the San River, south of Lublin, in connection with a German plan for the "resettlement" of Jews in the Lublin district (*see* NISKO AND LUBLIN PLAN). This plan ended in failure, and some of the deportees were returned to their place of origin. Edelstein went back to Prague in November 1939. His Nisko experience gave him an idea of the conditions in the east and of what was happening there. He decided to do everything in his power to ensure that the Jews of Czechoslovakia would not be dispatched to Poland, since he doubted whether they could hold out in the harsh conditions prevailing in German-occupied Poland. It was now his major concern to persuade the Germans to let the Jews stay in the Protectorate of BOHEMIA AND MORAVIA and to utilize them as manpower. Jewish labor as a means of saving Jewish lives became the core of Edelstein's policy, and this prompted him time and again to make proposals for the German exploitation of Jewish manpower.

In October 1941 the Germans decided on the establishment of the Theresienstadt ghetto as a temporary solution for the Jews of the Protectorate and a base for their future deportation to the east. The Jewish leadership, with Edelstein at its head, saw in the founding of Theresienstadt a personal achievement and the success of their efforts to gain permission for the Jews to stay in the Protectorate. They did not know that Theresienstadt was only a temporary arrangement. Edelstein arrived at Theresienstadt on December 4, 1941, and became the first chairman of its Judenrat. He was assisted by a deputy, Otto Zucker, and a council of twelve. The emphasis in the ghetto was on education of the young and on making the ghetto into a productive establishment. In January of 1943 Edelstein was dismissed from his post, on the charge that there was a discrepancy between the registered population of the Theresienstadt ghetto and the actual figure. On December 18, 1943, he was deported to AUSCHWITZ, where he and his family were shot to death, on June 20, 1944.

Edelstein's activities in Theresienstadt have been the subject of dispute. Those who find fault with him charge him with cooperating with the Nazis and with misreading the facts of the situation; their criticism is directed at his policy, but no doubt has been cast on his personal honesty and integrity. Others regard Edelstein as a hero who sacrificed himself for the sake of his people.

BIBLIOGRAPHY

Adler, H. G. *Theresienstadt, 1941–1945; Das Antlitz einer Zwangsgemeinschaft: Geschichte, Soziologie, Psychologie.* Tübingen, 1960.
Bondy, R. *"Elder of the Jews": Jakob Edelstein of Theresienstadt.* New York, 1989.
Lederer, Z. *Ghetto Theresienstadt.* London, 1953.
Rothkirchen, L. "The Zionist Character of the Self-Government of Terezin (Theresienstadt): A Study in Historiography." *Yad Vashem Studies* 11 (1976): 56–90.

MICHAL UNGER

EDEN, SIR ANTHONY (1897–1977), British statesman. A member of the Conservative party, Eden held a number of ministerial posts during the 1930s, and in 1935, at the age of thirty-eight, he was appointed foreign secretary. Eden was a strong supporter of the League of Nations and the concept of collective security. He resigned from the government of Neville Chamberlain in 1938, primarily because he did not support the policy of appeasing Fascist Italy. In the months prior to the outbreak of World War II Eden was, together with Winston CHURCHILL, an opponent of the foreign policies of his own party in government. When war broke out, Eden was offered the post of secretary of state for the British dominions, although not a seat in the War Cabinet. In May 1940, when Churchill became prime minister, Eden was appointed secretary of state for war. That December he was appointed foreign secretary and began to play a central role in the conduct of the war.

Despite the potentially vast influence of his office, and regardless of his close relationship with Churchill, Eden made little personal contribution to British policy, either on Palestine or concerning the fate of European Jewry. He showed little interest in either problem, and faithfully adopted the policies of his senior advisers in the Foreign Office. The specific terms of the WHITE PAPER on Palestine of 1939 were of little interest to the Foreign Office, but the redirection of Palestine policy that it represented (against the growth of the Jewish national home and in favor of Arab demands on the future of the Palestine Mandate) was a major cornerstone of British Middle East policy. The internal British dissension during the war on the fate of the White Paper policy caused the Foreign Office to oppose any proposal, including relief and rescue plans, that would have singled out Jews as victims of Nazism. The Foreign Office feared that such measures would strengthen Jewish group identity and further the interests of the Zionists. According to Eden's private secretary, Oliver Harvey, the foreign secretary expressed on at least two occasions a definite dislike for Jews (and a strong preference for Arabs). But this attitude was so widespread within the Foreign Office that it is doubtful whether Eden personally contributed anything unique to the general indifference to the Holocaust. The exceptions were his statement in Parliament on December 17, 1942, which described and condemned Nazi atrocities against Jews and promised punishment of the perpetrators, and his endorsement, in July and August 1944, of Jewish Agency requests that Auschwitz be bombed (*see* AUSCHWITZ, BOMBING OF). However, Eden's staff managed to deflect his concern, and since he was distracted by other foreign-policy issues, he did not pursue the bombing proposal.

In his subsequent career, Eden was prime minister when the Anglo-French-Israeli Sinai campaign was undertaken in 1956.

BIBLIOGRAPHY

Carlton, D. *Anthony Eden: A Biography.* London, 1981.
James, R. R. *Anthony Eden.* London, 1986.
Wasserstein, B. *Britain and the Jews of Europe, 1939–1945.* Oxford, 1979.
Zweig, R. *Britain and Palestine during the Second World War.* London, 1986.

RONALD W. ZWEIG

EDINETI (Russ., Edintsy), town in northern BESSARABIA; site of a transit camp. On the eve of World War II, Edineti had a Jewish population of fifty-three hundred, 90 percent of the total. In June 1940 Edineti, with the rest of Bessarabia, became Soviet territory, but a year later, following the German invasion of the Soviet Union, the Romanian army reoccupied the area. Some one thousand Jews were killed by the Romanian troops, assisted by the local population; the rest were expelled to TRANSNISTRIA, after having wandered all over Bessarabia amid great suffering. Following the expulsion of the local Jewish population, Edineti became the site of a transit camp for Jews from BUKOVINA, pending their deportation, and Jews from Banila, Vaşcăuti, Jadova, Vizhnitsa (Vijniţa), Ciudei, and Lujeni, as well as from Herta in Moldavia, were sent there. These were remnants of the Jewish communities in those places, survivors of massacres conducted by the Romanian forces and by local Romanian and Ukrainian inhabitants; before being taken to Edineti they had been held in the Storojineti ghetto.

Also brought to Edineti were Jews from Bessarabia whose deportation to Transnistria, in August 1941, had been interdicted by the German authorities. The first of these groups of Jews arrived in Edineti on August 20, 1941. They were crowded into stables and cattle sheds, behind barbed-wire fences, many living without a roof over their heads. Except for small quantities of water, the Romanians did not supply the Jews with any rations, and every day seventy to one hundred of them died from starvation and exhaustion. Anyone trying to escape ran the risk of being put to death. The mayor of the town was bribed by some Jews, and permitted them to purchase food. A Romanian army medical officer was also bribed, and as a result twenty-five hundred Jewish prisoners in Edineti were allowed to move into abandoned Jewish school buildings situated outside the camp. All the male prisoners were put to work on road building.

More and more groups of deportees converged upon Edineti, their total number amounting to twenty-three thousand. Worst off were the Jews from Bessarabia, who had been on the road for a long time, had gone through much suffering, and were completely destitute. The mortality rate was extremely high, and in October 1941, 85 percent of the children in the camp died. A typhus epidemic broke out in the camp, and for lack of medicine and food many of the prisoners fell victim to the disease.

On October 11, 1941, the camp was evacuated. The prisoners were divided into two groups. The first was dispatched to MARCU-LEŞTI, Bessarabia, and from there to Transnistria, hundreds being murdered en route by their military escorts. The second group was left in a field out in the open, with no shelter from the rain and snow. Five hundred of that group, mostly women and children, died during the following night, and the rest were deported to Transnistria by way of the Atachi border post.

On the way to Atachi, all the Jews who could not keep up with the pace of the column were murdered on the spot. A total of eight hundred Jews perished in this second group.

The number of Jews who survived Edineti and the subsequent stay in Transnistria is not known. Most of the prisoners of the Edineti camp were killed either before its evacuation or on the way to Transnistria.

BIBLIOGRAPHY

Ancel, J., and T. Lavi, eds. *Rumania*, vol. 2. In *Pinkas Hakehillot; Encyclopaedia of Jewish Communities.* Jerusalem, 1980. (In Hebrew.)

Reicher, M., and Y. Magan-Shitz, eds. *Yad L'Yedinits: Memorial Book for the Jewish Community of Yedinits-Bessarabia.* Tel Aviv, 1979. (In Hebrew.)

JEAN ANCEL

EDUCATION ON THE HOLOCAUST. [*The attempt to translate the Holocaust experience into a teaching environment is the subject of this entry, which is divided into three articles:* Great Britain; United States and Israel; *and* West Germany.]

Great Britain

The tremendous interest manifested by the British in the history of modern wars beginning in the eighteenth century is hardly surprising, given Britain's role in most of them. There has been particular interest in World War II, its outcome having rightly been seen as decisive for the survival of the island kingdom in the twentieth century. This is reflected in the great demand for books, films, and television documentaries on all aspects of the war, especially where Britain was concerned in any way.

What is true in British society overall is similarly reflected in the educational system. The study of British history (including participation in the major international and imperial wars) takes priority at the primary (ages five to eleven) and secondary (ages eleven to sixteen, and up to eighteen) levels of education, and even at polytechnics and universities. The British approach to history (as to much else) can well be described as "insular."

It follows, then, that in Britain today the academic study of the Holocaust—at whatever level—is minimal, or even nonexistent. Whereas some small change has been noticeable at the end of the 1980s, there is little widespread interest in the Holocaust in British society, and, consequently, it is not studied systematically and in depth in the educational system as a whole.

British society's rejection of the subject is reflected in the academic response. Both seem to dislike intensely what they see as a Jewish "preoccupation" with the suffering endured by Jews during the war. Its extent is still acknowledged, but society and the academic world believe that it should be set within the wider context of the overall suffering that the war produced. Today, the Holocaust is regarded by most (but not all) British people and academics as being very largely a "Jewish" subject of interest.

One could argue that since so-called Christians committed the crime of the Holocaust, the subject actually "belongs" more to them than to the victimized Jews, since the burden of "coming to terms" with that deliberate and systematic exercise of terror is firmly in the Christian court. But in a supposedly Christian country like Britain, this approach causes tremendous religious and psychological problems. Yet that is only the half of it. At the heart of the Holocaust lie human prejudice and the practical execution of the murderous irrationality that is present in all human beings. As elsewhere in the world, in Britain people simply cannot face up to the uncomfortable question that any study of the Holocaust is bound to pose: was the Nazi experience really that "unique," given that the executioners were human beings and not monsters from another planet?

In Britain, the reservations and rejections concerning the Holocaust are rationalized thus: "Why don't the Jews forget all about it?"; "It all happened such a long time ago"; and—more perniciously, in the academic world, because historically incorrect—"The Holocaust does not deserve any special study since it was only a small part of the war."

A survey conducted in Great Britain in 1987 and 1988 under the auspices of the United Kingdom Yad Vashem Academic and Educational Sub-Committee (Fox, 1989) covered the teaching of the Holocaust at the university and polytechnic level, at teacher-training colleges, and at secondary schools in the state and private systems. The attitude of most respondents to the survey was rather positive, but less so in the case of the universities. Many replies from the latter were somewhat negative, and some verged on the hostile.

Where the replies were positive—in the sense that particular teachers or lecturers expressed regret that they were unable to devote more time to the subject—it was remarkable how often the diary of Anne FRANK (in book, film, or exhibit form) was quoted as having been the inspiration for their own interest and that of their students. Other sparks igniting interest were the American television series "Holocaust" and the British film series "The World at War."

Most of the negative replies objected to the Holocaust being studied as a special subject, that is, in depth and systematically, in its own right. The gist of the negative replies, mostly from the universities, was that any elevation of the subject to such a "special" status would tent to "distort" its role in the war. Yet Yehuda Bauer and Lucy S. Dawidowicz, among others, view the key to understanding Hitler's imperatives for war up to 1939 and beyond as his determination to exterminate Russian and then European Jewry, within the context of a war for *Lebensraum* in the east at Russia's expense. Given the pan-European nature of the Nazis' systematic collection and slaughter of Europe's Jews during the war, it is nonsense to suggest that the subject was of "secondary" importance at the time.

In Britain there are no university chairs in Holocaust studies (compared to the plethora of those in history), nor are there likely to be, because the general lack of interest is compounded by the total reluctance—of Jews and gentiles alike—to fund such professorships. Indeed, there is only one university, that of Leicester, which has actually presented a special course (as part of a bachelor's degree program) on the Holocaust. A Centre of Holocaust Studies has now been established there, with the aim of developing a wider interest in the subject.

But in most other British institutions of higher learning, the picture is a dismal one. In the main, the subject is touched upon in more general courses on twentieth-century European history, or in more specific courses on Nazi Germany. Again, in the above-mentioned survey, some replies asserted that there was so little time to cover everything that any more time devoted to the Holocaust would "distort" the history courses presented to the students. Given the almost total freedom that British universities and polytechnics have to devise their own courses, such an attitude is disappointing, the more so since present-day research and publications on the Holocaust in all its aspects far outnumber those on more "conventional" facets of World War II.

The situation is somewhat different, however, for the secondary schools. In British schools, when European or world history is dealt with, students are expected to have a much wider and more general education than at the post-secondary level. The schools, too, have virtually no freedom in devising examination syllabuses, which are determined largely by the examination boards throughout the country, although in 1989 the introduction by the government of a national curriculum was planned.

The lack of any specialized teaching on the Holocaust at the secondary level is, therefore, more understandable. On the other hand, it is encouraging that questions on Nazi Germany and, indeed, on the Holocaust, have begun to appear in some advanced-level (pre-university) examination papers. This forces teachers to pay more attention to the subject

in the classroom, generating—as many admitted in their replies to the survey—greater interest among pupils and students.

Not all the results of the survey were negative. It disclosed, for example, that many departments of religious studies—at schools, teacher-training colleges, and even polytechnics and universities—dealt with the subject of the Holocaust in one way or another. Even departments of psychology and sociology were prepared to confront issues lying at the heart of the Holocaust, especially if they had a contemporary relevance. This was found to be so more frequently at the school level, where often (it was admitted) the Holocaust was studied less for its own sake than as a means to promote antiracist education in Britain's increasingly multi-ethnic society.

This brings up the question of whether the Holocaust should be studied as a special subject in its own right, or subsumed within antiracial studies. One cannot entirely deny the validity of the second approach, which constitutes another way of keeping the subject of the Holocaust alive and generating interest in it. The latter point is especially important with regard to the education of sixteen-to-eighteen-year-olds, and even a single question on the Holocaust in their public examinations is a positive step forward in furthering their knowledge of it. Yet a more specialized historical approach seems desirable: not only is the Holocaust insufficiently known about in Britain and in the British educational system, but its intrinsic importance and the scholarly apparatus available for its close investigation make it imperative that it be studied more widely, in Britain as elsewhere.

BIBLIOGRAPHY

Fox, J. P. *Report on 1987 Survey of United Kingdom Teaching on "The Holocaust" or "Nazi Final Solution of the Jewish Question" and Related Subjects.* Leicester, England, 1989.

JOHN P. FOX

United States and Israel

Holocaust education encompasses a very diverse range of activities in formal and informal teaching environments where the history of the racist anti-Jewish ideology and mass murder of the Jews during World War II is presented, and lessons and meanings are drawn from it. Isolated pockets of teaching about the Holocaust exist in Europe, South America, Australia, and South Africa, many of them under the rubric of Jewish education in a particular institution or school. However, in relative terms these are quite limited. Holocaust education is most advanced and widespread in the United States and Canada, and in Israel.

United States. The underlying aim of Holocaust education in the United States is to direct students to confront the past in order to recognize their individual responsibilities to act morally. Therefore, educators generally give much weight to the issues that relate to the participants in murder and to the bystanders. The major questions raised in connection with the perpetrators—the Nazis and their helpers—are: How were intelligent and cultured people turned into mass murderers? Could a similar event happen again? Could it happen to us? What must I, personally, do in order to sensitize myself to this potential danger? As to the bystanders, the aim is to grapple with such questions as: How could the average good people of the world have done so little to stop these horrors? Did they not know? Did they not care? What role was played by the Allied governments, especially the United States administration? What did the churches do in response? What are the implications for today in the light of news reports about world events?

Teaching about the Holocaust and its background (such as antisemitism and the pre-Holocaust history of European Jewry) helps strengthen that part of America's civic legacy which stresses the values of democracy, pluralism, and the responsibility of the individual for shaping society. The methodologies used most commonly in American schools tend to rely heavily on literature (particularly fiction), film, open-ended discussions on how students feel as they "relate" to this material, and role-playing and other techniques from the social sciences.

Isolated public-school educators began teaching about the Holocaust during the late 1950s, but significant interest in the subject was first expressed only in the early 1970s. The treatment of Nazism and its vic-

tims in public-school textbooks, however, had been systematically observed for over three decades. The earliest studies, carried out in 1961, showed that the basic facts of the Holocaust were glossed over and Nazi persecution of the Jews was greatly minimized. If the Holocaust was mentioned, the few lines devoted to it often created a distorted and misleading picture. By 1978, the record had hardly improved.

Aside from any earlier initiatives undertaken by individual teachers in their classrooms, the first single official program of instruction on the Holocaust in a public-school setting was launched in 1972 in Barrington, Massachusetts. In 1975, Philadelphia and New York City became the first public-school systems to pioneer systemwide curricula. Several years later the Baltimore school system became the first to mandate teaching of the Holocaust. Not so long afterward, non-Jewish parochial schools began to incorporate Holocaust teaching into their school programs.

The development and spread of teaching programs did not proceed without resistance. Some American ethnic minorities feared that Holocaust teaching units would turn public opinion against their national groups. The New York Association of Black Educators argued the irrelevance of Holocaust studies for blacks. Even some Jews opposed its teaching in public schools, fearing trivialization of the subject and a possible upswing of antisemitism.

Holocaust curricula designed for public schools were conceptualized in accordance with the needs of the participating school or school district, or in response to larger trends in education and society. New York City's curriculum was developed against the background of ethnic tension between blacks and Jews. The study of the Holocaust was to be taught not as a period in Jewish history but as a case of monumental bigotry, and thus a key topic in values education. In a similar vein, the Baltimore school system developed its curriculum as part of a commitment to stressing multicultural realities with the aim of reducing prejudice.

The extent to which the subject is being introduced and taught within American public secondary schools today is difficult to determine. Individual states continue to pass laws mandating Holocaust instruction, and many city- and state-sponsored curricula are now being written. Still, with no central organ for the dissemination of materials, efforts to provide teachers with materials and training are haphazard. Despite growing public awareness, the advances do not appear to have spread uniformly across the nation. According to one survey in 1983, fewer than three hundred secondary schools out of thirty thousand in the United States incorporated Holocaust studies into their curricula. Another small-scale survey conducted the same year indicated that 95 percent of the administrators, teachers, and students interviewed from public and private schools believed adequate coverage of the Holocaust in their school curriculum was lacking.

In the United States, informal education on the Holocaust is, by its very nature, broader, and is consequently varied, fluid, and extremely uneven in quality. It includes a myriad of activities in community centers, synagogue groups, afternoon and Sunday schools, church programs, youth groups, and adult-education centers. The range and type of programs are limited only by the imagination of those who initiate them.

Jewish education in the United States followed its own path of development with regard to the teaching of the Holocaust. Whereas the EICHMANN TRIAL (1961–1962) marked a turning point in Holocaust awareness for Israeli educators, it was mainly the occasion of the twentieth anniversary of the WARSAW GHETTO UPRISING (1963) that brought the Holocaust into the consciousness of American Jewish educators. The National Council of Jewish Education at its 1963 conference discussed the subject. Some conference participants explained their avoidance of the Holocaust as a response to parental fears for their children's emotional well-being, while others held that Judaism should only be a joyful experience for the students. More prevalent was the anxiety of both parents and educators that children would develop feelings of insecurity and fear that they themselves might become victims.

As of 1964, throughout the United States only two local Jewish education agencies had prepared guidelines for teaching the Holocaust. Between 1964 and the end of the decade, outlines for teachers were produced by the Bureaus of Jewish Education in New York, Los Angeles, and Philadelphia.

Educators began articulating goals for teaching the Holocaust, but the content and tone of their discussions, particularly in the 1960s, emphasized the emotional meaning of the Holocaust for students. Since students had no personal experience or memory of the events themselves, one of the tasks of the educator was to employ an intensive educational program to evoke pain. This often entailed the use of simulations, or an emphasis on horrors and atrocities. Almost overnight, it seemed, educators went from an initial concern about the negative effects of the Holocaust on Jewish identity to making the strengthening of Jewish identity into a nearly universal article of faith for Holocaust education. It was hoped that studying the Holocaust, like other periods in Jewish history, would link students to the Jewish past and future; by remembering those who were lost in the Holocaust, students would develop a strengthened feeling of solidarity with other Jews and a deeper commitment to the survival of the Jewish people.

With few conceptual precedents to go on, Jewish educators in the United States had to construct their own frameworks from which to view and make meaning of the Holocaust. Perhaps the most natural response was to examine the event through the traditional lens of Jewish experience, by seeking to build the Holocaust into contemporary Jewish consciousness through language, ritual, and prayer. The Holocaust was also shown to be instructive for dealing with the issues of the day. Jews, knowing the dangers of RACISM and intolerance better than anyone, had a special responsibility to help advance the frontiers of civil rights and social equality. The ideals they espoused were universal, but the authority of the universal message was drawn from the Jewish historical experience.

By the mid-1970s, there was a discernible attempt to break the particularist view of the Holocaust held by Jews. Some teachers argued that unless political, theological, and philosophical issues were addressed by Holocaust curricula, the subject would never penetrate the public-school arena. The materials used and produced during this period reflect a trend toward viewing the Holocaust within a framework of universal values. Without excluding the goal of strengthening Jewish identity, the vision for Holocaust education in some sectors was broadened to include cultivation of a commitment to universal moral principles among both Jewish and non-Jewish students.

In the late 1970s some prominent American Jews began lamenting the exaggerated place of importance the Holocaust had assumed in Jewish life. They felt that the event was becoming the strongest focus of Jewish identity and was being substituted for real Jewish learning and identity. The more recent curricula reflect this new attitude, which defends the importance of teaching the Holocaust while recognizing the necessity of restoring it to its proper historical perspective. The impression of increased Holocaust coverage in Jewish schools is confirmed by the few systematic surveys available. A 1973 survey conducted in the United States and Canada found that 276 out of 354 schools taught about the Holocaust, and approximately a quarter of them offered it as a separate course. In 1981, a mini-survey conducted among Jewish educators indicated that almost all schools offered a Holocaust course of twenty-five to thirty hours of instruction.

Israel. The situation in Israeli schools is different in many respects. Since the autumn of 1982, the study of the Holocaust has been a compulsory subject in the history syllabus of government high schools (both state secular and state religious schools). It is mandated to be taught for thirty instructional hours in the eleventh or twelfth grade, depending on the preference of the local school. The methodological approach is historical. Primary sources are presented, and the instruction emphasizes factual information, the complexities of the historical situation, and the difficulties involved in attempting to arrive at generalizations or conclusions.

The focus of the subject matter is also different. While in the United States the issues seen to be most relevant are those related to the perpetrators and the bystanders, Israeli students concentrate their attention on the Jewish victims. The aim is to raise questions about the meaning of the Holocaust in the framework of Jewish history and as Jews living in Israel after the Holocaust: Why were the Jews murdered? Must they always be victims? What can the Jews do about their circumstances? In sharp contrast to the situation described above, where the meanings and implications of the Holocaust are mostly comprehended on an individual level, the most critical search for answers in Israel is a collective, national one: What is the central lesson of the Holocaust for Israeli society today? Is there a danger of Jews again becoming victims of genocidal slaughter? Or is the danger that Jews, forced to be militarily strong, are also becoming morally weak, and increasingly desensitized to the suffering of others?

These differences in what is seen to be the core of this history are significantly manifested in the controversy over the place and meaning of the Holocaust in human history. One extreme focuses on the evil that men do and places the context for the Holocaust in "man's inhumanity to man" and the universal lessons that can be learned from this extreme case study. Naturally, there is an emphasis on the parallels between this event and other examples of genocide and selective mass murder that have occurred in the past.

On the other extreme the focus is on the specific victims, the Jews, and the context is the long history of antisemitic persecutions, the particular situation of the Jews, and their unique position in this history (as compared with other victims of mass persecution). The emphasis is on those elements that distinguish the Holocaust from all other events in history. Between these extremes each educator finds his or her place.

Higher Education in the United States and Israel. Every tertiary institution in Israel that teaches the humanities offers an extensive range of courses on the Holocaust, either in a separate department or as part of a larger field of study, such as contemporary Jewish history or German history. To be certified to teach history in high school, education students must take at least one university course on the Holocaust.

The situation on American campuses is different. Naturally, Jewish history occupies a much more marginal place, and as a rule very few courses in it are offered at the average university. Nonetheless, in many places where little is taught about how Jews lived for thousands of years, there is an isolated course on how they were murdered in World War II. Teaching the Holocaust without the context of Jewish history may risk skewing the focus of the topic. Another serious problem is that alongside some highly qualified scholars who teach at North American universities, including two who hold full chairs in the field, a majority of those who teach Holocaust courses on the tertiary level are lecturers without specialized knowledge in this area of Jewish and general history who have transferred from another discipline in order to fill this gap.

BIBLIOGRAPHY

Friedlander, H. "Postscript: Towards a Methodology of Teaching about the Holocaust." In *The Holocaust—Ideology, Bureaucracy, and Genocide: The San Jose Papers*, pp. 323–345. Millwood, N.Y., 1981.
Gutman, Y., and C. Schatzker. *The Holocaust and Its Significance*. Jerusalem, 1984.
Pate, G. S. *The Treatment of the Holocaust in United States History Text Books*. New York, 1980.
Schatzker, C. "Teaching of the Holocaust: Dilemmas and Considerations." *Annals of the American Academy of Political and Social Science* 450 (July 1980): 218–226.
Strom, M. S., and W. Parsons. *Facing History and Ourselves: The Holocaust and Human Behavior*. Watertown, Mass., 1982.

ELLY DLIN and SHARON GILLERMAN

West Germany

When World War II ended, the schools in Germany were without history textbooks. The Allies who had occupied Germany and were administering the country had removed all books dating from the Nazi period, and it was about ten years before new history textbooks became available. Until the 1950s the Holocaust, and how to confront it, was not a subject raised in German schools.

A wave of swastika graffiti and desecration of synagogues that swept Germany toward the end of 1959 impelled the authorities, the churches, and the student and teachers' organizations to inquire about the extent to which the Holocaust was being taught in German schools, and how it was being presented in textbooks.

Each of the states comprising the Federal Republic of Germany has its own curricula and textbooks. Surveys, comparative studies, and other projects have considered the problems of teaching the Holocaust, and a German-Israeli conference was held that examined the history textbooks and submitted recommendations for improvements. However, no survey has been made of the actual teaching of the Holocaust in West Germany, and it is difficult to define how it is being taught, since every teacher is free to supplement or detract from the official curriculum or textbook contents as he or she sees fit.

In the chapters on Jewish history and the Holocaust in the West German history texts, it was found that three general approaches exist: (1) teaching the Holocaust as a moral obligation, in view of the crimes that were committed; (2) teaching the Holocaust as part of civic and political education; and (3) teaching the Holocaust as a basic element in history, indispensable for the study of Western civilization and German history. The Holocaust is described in detail in all the textbooks, and the charge that had been made, that knowledge of the Holocaust was being withheld, had no basis in fact.

On the other hand, most of the textbook descriptions of the Holocaust do not place it in the context of Jewish history, before or after the Holocaust, or in the continuity of European and German history. The majority of the textbooks limit themselves to a narrative description of the events, with expressions of dismay and shock added; no attempt is made to analyze the roots of antisemitism and its place in Nazi ideology and the Third Reich. Most of the books also avoid any serious in-depth consideration of the question of responsibility and culpability for the Holocaust, and of those who bore that responsibility, aside from mentioning Adolf Hitler, a handful of other leading figures, and the murderous personnel who perpetrated the actual killings. The greater part of the information and findings brought to light by Holocaust research in the past few decades has not found its way into the textbooks.

BIBLIOGRAPHY

Quenzer, W. "Young Germans' View of Auschwitz." *Patterns of Prejudice* 14/4 (October 1980): 10–17.

Renn, W. F. "Confronting Genocide: The Depiction of the Persecution of the Jews and the Holocaust in West German History Textbooks." In *Contemporary Views of the Holocaust*, edited by R. L. Braham, pp. 157–180. Boston, 1983.

Schatzker, C. "Die Juden in den deutschen Geschichtsbüchern: Schulbuchanalyse zur Darstellung der Juden, des Judentums und des Staates Israel." *Schriftenreihe der Bundeszentrale für Politische Bildung* 173 (1981): 1–188.

CHAIM SCHATZKER

Ilya Ehrenburg (center) with Jewish partisans from Vilna (1944).

EHRENBURG, ILYA GRIGORYEVICH

(1891–1967), Russian Jewish writer and journalist. Ehrenburg lived abroad for many years, mostly in Paris, and was a foreign correspondent for Soviet newspapers. After the German invasion of France in 1940, he returned to the Soviet Union. Although Ehrenburg was an assimilated Jew and was steeped in Russian culture, his writings often dealt with Jewish subjects. During World War II he became increasingly conscious of his Jewish identity and expressed these feelings in his publications. In *Padenie Parizha* (The Fall of Paris; 1941) he denounced fascism and antisemitism, and in a poem written in 1940 he lamented the Nazi persecution of the Jews. During the war years he was a correspondent for *Krasnaia Zvezda* (Red Star), the newspaper of the Red Army, and played a leading role in anti-Nazi propaganda in the Soviet Union and abroad.

Ehrenburg was one of the most prominent personalities to be appointed to the JEWISH ANTIFASCIST COMMITTEE. In the committee's meetings and consultations he stressed the need to publicize the Jewish role in the war effort against the Nazis, and openly criticized manifestations of antisemitism among the Soviet population. He was one of the first in the Soviet Union to encourage the collection of documentary evidence on the murder of the Jews and on active Jewish resistance to the Nazis. Ehrenburg was the editor of *Merder fun Felker* (Murderers of Peoples; 2 vols., 1944–

1945). Together with Vasily Grossman, he edited *Chernaya kniga* (The BLACK BOOK OF SOVIET JEWRY), a collection of documents on the Holocaust in the Soviet Union. He also co-sponsored *Krasnaya kniga* (The Red Book), which documented Jewish participation in the Red Army, the partisan movement, and the resistance to the Nazis in the ghettos. These books, however, were not released for publication, since it became Soviet policy to throw a veil over the Holocaust, a policy that became increasingly pronounced after the war. In the spring of 1945, official criticism was voiced against Ehrenburg's extreme anti-German stand.

The fate of the Jews during the war continued to preoccupy Ehrenburg in the postwar years. An abridged English translation of *Chernaya kniga* was published in New York in 1946, and the full version (which was smuggled out of the USSR), in 1980. Six volumes of his memoirs were serialized in the journal *Novyi Mir* between 1960 and 1965 under the title *Lyudi, gody, zhizn* (Men, Years, Life); at his death he was working on the concluding volumes. Ehrenburg bequeathed his entire archive to YAD VASHEM, including a complete, uncensored edition of *Chernaya kniga* and many personal letters from survivors.

BIBLIOGRAPHY

Goldberg, A. *Ilya Ehrenburg—Revolutionary, Novelist, Poet, War Correspondent, Propagandist: The*

Extraordinary Epic of a Russian Survivor. New York, 1984.

SHIMON REDLICH

EICHMANN, ADOLF (1906–1962), Nazi official who played a central role in organizing the anti-Jewish policies culminating in the "FINAL SOLUTION." Eichmann was born in Solingen, in the Rhineland; his father was an accountant. His mother died when he was eight years old, and the family—the father and five children—moved to Linz, Austria. Eichmann did not complete secondary school, nor did he finish the course in mechanics at the vocational school that he attended for two years. After holding several different jobs he became a traveling salesman for an American oil company, Vacuum Oil; using a motorcycle for his rounds, he had an accident in which he was seriously injured. In 1933 he was dismissed from his job. The previous year an acquaintance, Ernst KALTENBRUNNER, had persuaded Eichmann to join the Austrian National Socialist party, and eventually also the SS. When the latter was outlawed in Austria in 1933, Eichmann, now unemployed, moved to Germany. There he enlisted in the Austrian unit of the SS, where he also went through military training. He then served for a while in the DACHAU concentration camp.

In October 1934 Eichmann volunteered to work in the central office of the SD (Sicherheitsdienst; Security Service), then headed by Reinhard HEYDRICH, and moved to Berlin. At the time, Heinrich HIMMLER was chief of police in the SD. Eichmann first worked in the section that dealt with the FREEMASONS, and in 1935 he was moved to a new intelligence section, the Jewish section, then under Herbert Hagen. Henceforth Eichmann regarded the solution of the "Jewish question" in the Third Reich as his life mission.

Eichmann was now one of the chief planners of the anti-Jewish operations undertaken by the SS; before long, he was also responsible for their execution. At this time the SD and the Gestapo joined in an effort designed to speed up the emigration of the Jews from Germany, as part of which Hagen and Eichmann were sent in 1937 to Palestine and Egypt on a fact-finding mission. Eichmann's conclusion was that increased immigration of Jews into Palestine was not desirable, since the establishment of a Jewish state was not in the interest of the Third Reich.

Following the annexation of Austria to Germany in March 1938 (*see* ANSCHLUSS), Eichmann was sent to Vienna to organize the emigration of the Jews. It was here that he first revealed his organizational talent and his ability to put the anti-Jewish aims of the Nazis into practice. It was Eichmann who evolved a method of forced emigration, consisting of three elements: undermining the economic condition of the Jews by confiscation of their property; putting fear into their hearts by the use of terror; seizing control of Jewish communal institutions and forcing their leaders to cooperate (a foretaste of the JUDENRAT). In August 1938, in order to streamline the Jewish emigration process, Eichmann set up the ZENTRALSTELLE FÜR JÜDISCHE AUSWANDERUNG (Central Office for Jewish Emigration), whose purpose was to strip the Jews of all their belongings and leave them with no option but to seek emigration to some other country and to get there with the help of some Jewish organization (mainly the JOINT DISTRIBUTION COMMITTEE). Eichmann also took direct action to expel Jews, by pushing some of them into a no-man's-land across the Austrian border. Contrary to his previous reservations concerning Jewish immigration into Palestine, he now cooperated with the Jewish organizations that were running ALIYA BET ("illegal" immigration). When the Germans seized control of BOHEMIA AND MORAVIA, Eichmann introduced the system of forced emigration to PRAGUE, and, in the summer of 1939, he established in the Czech capital a Central Office for Jewish Emigration, on the model of the Vienna office. The pattern established by Eichmann had been adopted by the Reich leaders even earlier, in the wake of KRISTALLNACHT, and on January 24, 1939, on Hermann GÖRING's order, the Reichszentrale für Jüdische Auswanderung (Reich Central Office for Jewish Emigration) was set up in Germany under Heydrich in the Ministry of the Interior.

During 1938 and 1939, Eichmann's authority over Jewish policies grew rapidly; when war broke out, his area of operations was greatly widened and his own position strengthened. Following Himmler's creation in September 1939 of the REICHSSICHER-HEITSHAUPTAMT (Reich Security Main Office; RSHA), under Heydrich, Eichmann was appointed head of the Jewish section in the Gestapo, whose chief at the time was Heinrich MÜLLER. Eichmann's authority exceeded that of a section chief. In practice he came directly under Heydrich, but from time to time he was also called in by Himmler. In 1939 and 1940 Eichmann played the central role in the expulsion of Poles and Jews from the Polish areas that had been incorporated into the Reich (see DEPORTATIONS). By that time Eichmann had already established, in coordination with Müller, the pattern for the mass expulsion of Jews in an operation in which Jews from Vienna and Czechoslovakia were deported to Nisko (see NISKO AND LUBLIN PLAN). On the basis of this pattern, the methods were developed for mass deportations throughout the Nazi period. The Nisko operation served as a precedent for the attempt to concentrate all the Jews of the Reich in the Lublin Reservation—the first phase in the Nazi leaders' search for a total solution to the "Jewish question." After Nisko, further attempts were made, under Eichmann's supervision, to expel Jews from several places in Germany itself, but they met with opposition in Germany and elsewhere, and the Lublin Reservation plan was rescinded.

In October 1940, Eichmann in person led the expulsion of 6,500 Jews from Baden-Pfalz and the Saar district to the south of France. The operation may have been connected with the MADAGASCAR PLAN; while this plan was being prepared by the German Foreign Ministry, Eichmann was working out his own detailed program for the creation of a huge police-controlled ghetto on that tropical island off the coast of Africa. Eichmann was, by this time, in undisputed control of the Jewish populations of Germany, the Ostmark (Austria), and the Protectorate of Bohemia and Moravia. From time to time he summoned the leaders of these Jewish populations to his office in Berlin to give them his orders, especially concerning the issue of forced emigration—orders that were then carried out under the watchful eye of Eich-

mann's representatives in the respective capitals. He had a network of officials in most of the German-occupied countries and in the satellite states, where they served as "advisers" to the governments, their task being to promote the implementation of anti-Jewish policies. The more prominent of these representatives were Alois BRUNNER, Theodor DANNECKER, Dieter WISLICENY, and Rolf GÜNTHER (Eichmann's deputy).

A significant change in Eichmann's activities came with the decision to execute the "final solution of the Jewish question," together with the war against the Soviet Union. The final form of the Jewish section in the RSHA had been laid down in March 1941, and henceforth the section bore the designation IV B 4. Eichmann now gave orders on various occasions prohibiting the emigration of Jews from the European continent, and he ceased cooperating with the organizers of the "illegal" immigration into Palestine. His operations reached their full extent after Himmler's order of October 1941 prohibiting the emigration of Jews, which coincided with the start of transports of Jews from Germany to the east. Preparations for mass murder had begun even earlier, in the summer of 1941, at which time Eichmann, on Himmler's order, held talks with Rudolf HÖSS, the commandant of AUSCHWITZ, on the practical details of the mass murder.

In October 1941 Eichmann took part in more discussions on the subject, conducted by those charged with the implementation of the "Final Solution." At this point, he was promoted to *Obersturmbannführer* (lieutenant colonel). Since Eichmann was the officer in charge of transporting the Jews of Europe to the extermination sites, Heydrich asked him to prepare the WANNSEE CONFERENCE, where the implementation of the operation was outlined, with the participation of all government bodies that had a part in the "Final Solution." It was Eichmann who sent the invitations to the various officials, drafted Heydrich's address to the conference, and took down the minutes. Following the conference, he called in his representatives from the various countries to plan the operation. In 1942 and 1943, the years in which Jews from all over Europe were being deported to the extermination camps in Poland, it was from

Eichmann's office that the orders went out for the time and place of departure of the transports, the number of deportees, and so on. The schedules were coordinated with the railway authorities in each country; Eichmann was also in close contact with Martin LUTHER of the German Foreign Ministry. Rules were laid down on rounding up the Jews, seizing their homes, and confiscating their property; Eichmann saw to it that in Germany itself, his section would benefit from the booty.

Eichmann made every effort to solve problems in a way that ensured the maintenance of a regular timetable for the deportation trains going to the extermination camps. He made several visits to the camps and was well versed in the murder procedure. Eichmann was not directly involved in the extermination actions in Poland or the areas that had belonged to the Soviet Union, nor did he take any part in the EINSATZGRUPPEN operations, but through his representatives, he was active in all the other European countries from which Jews were being sent to their death. Only the Scandinavian countries—Denmark, Norway, and Finland—had no Eichmann representatives. One of the problems that confronted Eichmann and his associates was the treatment of the partners of mixed marriages and their progeny (*see* MISCHLINGE); there were many discussions on the subject, but the issue was never completely resolved.

A special place in Eichmann's actions was held by the THERESIENSTADT ghetto, which served first as a concentration camp for Jews from Czechoslovakia and Vienna, and later also for Jews of privileged status (mainly from Germany) and those over sixty, of whom it could not be said that they were being sent to the east to work. In practice, the "ghetto for the aged" was no more than a transit camp, from which a great many trains left for the extermination camps. Eichmann also tried to project Theresienstadt as a "model ghetto" by showing it to RED CROSS commissions—after first altering its appearance with temporary improvements—in order to refute published reports of the atrocities that the Nazis were committing.

Only in HUNGARY was Eichmann personally in charge of the deportations. Immediately after the occupation of the country by Ger-

man forces on March 19, 1944, Eichmann arrived in Hungary, accompanied by a large team of aides, which he had assembled at the MAUTHAUSEN camp in preparation for the invasion. In Hungary, Eichmann put to full use all the experience he had gained; within a short period—from May to early July—he succeeded in deporting some 440,000 Jews from all the provinces that were then part of Hungary. This was made possible by the cooperation of the Hungarian authorities. Even after the Hungarians stopped the deportations in early July, Eichmann tried, by deceptive tactics, to have additional thousands of Jews deported from Budapest. But it was only in October 1944, following the ARROW CROSS PARTY coup d'état in Hungary, that he was able to resume his murderous operations. By now it was no longer possible to send the Jews to Auschwitz by train, since the murders in the gas chambers there had stopped and the eastern front had drawn near. Eichmann's answer was to put 76,000 Jews on DEATH MARCHES to Austria, from where they were to be sent to forced-labor camps in Germany.

In Hungary, Eichmann encountered various efforts to rescue the Jews; among these was the rescue work carried out by Raoul WALLENBERG, in conjunction with other representatives of neutral countries, which persisted despite all that Eichmann tried to do to thwart it. Eichmann played a major role in the "Blood for Goods" plan, which led to the Joel BRAND mission to Istanbul, with a proposal to set Jews free in exchange for a supply of trucks and other goods needed by the Germans. He was also involved in the EUROPA PLAN conceived in Slovakia, according to which Jews were to be released in return for a large payment in United States dollars. On various occasions Eichmann intervened in order to foil opportunities that presented themselves for saving Jews and removing them from German control, as in negotiations with BULGARIA and ROMANIA. In two instances Eichmann was forced to agree to the liberation of some Jews: in the "Repatriation" plan, which primarily affected Jews of Spanish origin trapped in Greece, and in the program for the exchange of Jews and Germans (*see* EXCHANGE: JEWS AND GERMANS).

When the war ended, Eichmann went into hiding and then, like other SS men, fled to

Argentina with the help of the Vatican. He lived there with his family until May 1960, when he was captured by the Israeli Security Service and brought to Israel. In April 1961 he was put on trial before the district court in Jerusalem (*see* EICHMANN TRIAL). He was found guilty and sentenced to death; the Israeli Supreme Court, sitting as a court of appeals, upheld the sentence, and on June 1, 1962, Eichmann was executed by hanging. His body was cremated and the ashes scattered over the sea.

The trial engendered a debate about Eichmann's character. Some, headed by Hannah Arendt (*see* ARENDT CONTROVERSY), argued that Eichmann was a very ordinary individual, who was not motivated by any special hatred of Jews, and that all he did—as he himself claimed—was to carry out the orders received from his superiors, within the general framework of Nazi bureaucracy. Others believe that Eichmann was the personification of the spirit of inhumanity in Nazism, the regime that nurtured the rise of destructive drives and created the conditions for mass murder and the execution of the "Final Solution." What cannot be doubted is that Eichmann served the Nazi program for exterminating the Jewish people with zeal and efficiency.

BIBLIOGRAPHY

Arendt, H. *Eichmann in Jerusalem: A Report on the Banality of Evil.* New York, 1964.

Aronson, S. *Reinhard Heydrich und die Frühgeschichte von Gestapo und SD.* Stuttgart, 1971.

Harel, I. *The House on Garibaldi Street.* New York, 1975.

Kempner, R. M. W. *Eichmann und Kumplizen.* Zurich, 1961.

Levai, J. *Eichmann in Hungary: Documents.* Budapest, 1961.

Robinson, J. *And the Crooked Shall Be Made Straight: The Eichmann Trial, The Jewish Catastrophe, and Hannah Arendt's Narrative.* Philadelphia, 1965.

LENI YAHIL

EICHMANN TRIAL. The trial of Adolf EICHMANN, held in Jerusalem in 1961 and 1962, riveted the attention of the Israeli public and aroused great interest the world over. This was the first time that the Holocaust was presented to a competent judicial body in full detail, in all its stages and from all its aspects. Journalists from many countries converged upon Jerusalem to cover the trial, and international public opinion followed its course with concentration; the trial gave rise to discussions on a great variety of subjects, on the legal, social, educational, psychological, religious, and political levels.

In May 1960 Eichmann was kidnapped in Argentina by Israeli agents, taken to Israel, and handed over to the Israeli police. On May 23, 1960, the prime minister of Israel, David BEN-GURION, announced in the Knesset (the Israeli parliament): "Adolf Eichmann . . . is under arrest in Israel and will shortly be put on trial." A magistrate issued an order for Eichmann's arrest and remanded him for trial, the order being renewed from time to time. The police investigation was put into the hands of a special unit established for this purpose (Bureau 06), which took nine months to complete its task.

When the investigation was completed, on February 21, 1961, the attorney general, Gideon HAUSNER, signed the bill of indictment against Eichmann and submitted it to the district court in Jerusalem (which marked it Criminal File 40/61). The indictment consisted of fifteen counts of "crimes against the Jewish people," "crimes against humanity," "war crimes," and "membership in a hostile organization"—that is, the SS, SD (Sicherheitsdienst; Security Service), and GESTAPO, all three of which had been declared "criminal organizations" by the International Military Tribunal at the NUREMBERG TRIAL, in a judgment rendered on October 1, 1946.

The crimes against the Jewish people with which the accused was charged consisted of all aspects of the persecution of millions of Jews, including their arrest and imprisonment in concentration camps, their deportation to extermination camps, their murder, and the theft of their property. The charges did not, however, confine themselves to Eichmann's participation in crimes against the Jewish people; they also included crimes against other peoples, such as the mass expulsions of Poles and Slovenes; the seizure, deportation to extermination camps, and murder of tens of thousands of GYPSIES; and

The Eichmann trial. Supreme Court Justice Moshe Landau is at top center; Eichmann is in the questioning box. Robert Servatius, the defense attorney, is at the bottom, second from left, and Attorney General Gideon Hausner is third from left.

the deportation and murder of some one hundred children from the village of LIDICE in Czechoslovakia, in revenge for the killing of Reinhard HEYDRICH. All the counts related to offenses under the Nazis and Nazi Collaborators (Punishment) Law 5710-1950.

The trial, conducted by the District Court in Jerusalem, began on April 10, 1961. It took place in a Jerusalem community center that had been adapted for this special purpose. The court consisted of Supreme Court justice Moshe Landau (who presided), Jerusalem District Court president Benjamin Halevi, and Tel Aviv District Court judge Yitzhak Raveh.

The public prosecution was represented by a team headed by Attorney General Hausner, and the defense team was headed by Dr. Robert Servatius, a German lawyer who had served as attorney for the defense of several of the accused in the Nuremberg trials of major war criminals.

When the trial began, the defense lawyer raised several preliminary arguments, questioning the court's competence to try his client for the charges contained in the bill of indictment. His major arguments were: (1) there was reason to doubt whether the three judges, who were Jews and citizens of the state of Israel, were able to give the accused a fair trial; (2) the trial must not be held, because the accused had been kidnapped from his place of residence in Argentina and illegally taken to Israel; (3) the Nazis and Nazi Collaborators Law 5710-1950 was a *post factum* law and therefore wrong and unjust; and (4) the offenses listed in the bill of indictment had been committed outside the borders of the state of Israel and before the state's establishment.

All these arguments were rejected by the court. On the contention that the judges might lack objectivity, the court stated: "When a judge sits on a bench, he does not cease to be flesh and blood with human emotions; but he is bidden by law to overcome these emotions. If this were not so, no judge would ever be qualified to sit in judgment in a criminal case evoking strong disgust, such as a case of treason or murder or some other heinous offense."

Concerning the principle that no criminal laws should be passed that were of retroactive validity, the court stated that the principle was not legally binding; it was rather a principle of justice, since the natural sense of justice is generally outraged by a person's being punished for a deed that was not illegal at the time it was committed. The situation with regard to the offenses that were being charged in this case, however, was quite different: the Nazis and Nazi Collaborators Law (like similar laws enacted by various countries after the war) did not introduce new legal norms; all it did was to make it possible to bring persons to trial for committing offenses that were known to be against the law at the time they were committed, in every place in the world, including Germany—the illegality of which these persons were well aware. Owing to the illegal regime that was in power in Nazi Germany, the perpetrators of these crimes were not punished for them at the time; but it was precisely the sense of natural justice that called for the establishment of a forum where the persons suspected of these crimes could be brought to trial.

With regard to the argument concerning Eichmann's kidnapping in Argentina and the manner in which he was brought to Israel against his will, the court, quoting precedents of United States and British courts, found that jurisdiction to try an accused person depends only on the essence of the criminal law cited in the bill of indictment and its applicability to the offenses with which the accused is charged; a court is not entitled to examine in what manner an accused was brought into the sovereign territory of the state in which he is to stand trial.

The court further found that the date on which the state of Israel was established was of no relevance to the court's competence to try Eichmann; moreover, the plan for the destruction of the Jewish people was also meant to include Jews who at the time of World War II were residents of Palestine. Undoubtedly, there was a strong connection between the existence of the state of Israel and the objective of ensuring that persons who committed "crimes against the Jewish people" be brought to trial for those offenses.

After the court's rejection of the preliminary arguments, the accused was ordered to state how he pleaded on the counts as enumerated in the indictment. Eichmann's answer, on each count, was: "In the sense of the indictment, not guilty."

This was followed by the body of evidence being presented to the court. By means of more than one hundred witnesses and some sixteen hundred documents—many of them bearing Eichmann's own signature—the prosecution presented to the court the full account of all the events related to the Holocaust of European Jewry, or the "FINAL SOLUTION of the Jewish question," as the Nazis called it. In great detail the prosecution furnished the court with proof of the persecution of the Jews in all its stages: the anti-Jewish legislation; the incitement among the general population of hostility to the Jewish minority; the plunder of Jewish property; and, worst of all, the searching out of the Jews in every European country under German occupation and in the satellite states, their imprisonment, under inhuman conditions, in ghettos and concentration camps, where they were harassed and humiliated, and, finally, their systematic mass murder, with the aim of completely destroying the Jewish people. The prosecution demonstrated what had happened to the Jews of Europe, country by country and camp by camp; it proved the personal involvement of Eichmann, as the head of section IV B 4 (the Gestapo section for Jewish affairs), in every

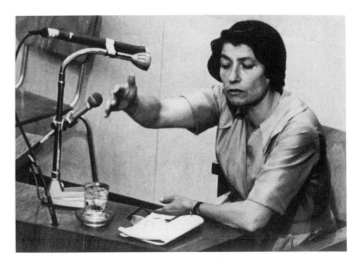

Zivia Lubetkin testifying at the Eichmann trial in Jerusalem (1961).

stage of the heinous operation, and that, in fact, Eichmann was in charge of all the steps taken to implement the plan for the "Final Solution."

The defense did not really question the facts related to these events, or challenge the authenticity of the documents proving Eichmann's involvement in the crimes. The systematic defense line was to play down Eichmann's role in the whole process by depicting him as a small cog in the machinery of murder, an underling who had no choice but to carry out the orders he was given by his superiors. The court rejected this claim. The trial proved that mentally and emotionally, Eichmann fully identified with his task; indeed, the evidence presented to the court—which included official documents from German sources—showed that in the final stages of the war, Eichmann's desire to come as close as possible to the complete and total destruction of the Jews became an obsession. This was demonstrated with particular force in Hungary, where Eichmann was sent by Heinrich HIMMLER in 1944 to take personal charge of the deportation of that country's Jews to the extermination camps in Poland.

The court also found that the claim made by the defense that Eichmann was only acting under orders was of no avail to him, from the legal standpoint; this claim was also disproved in fact, as the court was persuaded that Eichmann had done everything in his power to interpret and implement the orders he received in as extreme and harsh a manner as possible. Accordingly, the court found Eichmann guilty on all counts (with some unimportant changes) and, on December 15, 1961, sentenced him to death.

Eichmann lodged an appeal against the verdict that was heard by the supreme court sitting as a panel of five justices, with the president of the supreme court, Justice Yitzhak Olshan, presiding. On May 29, 1962, the supreme court announced its rejection of the appeal and confirmed the judgment of the lower court. Following the denial by the president of Israel, Itzhak Ben-Zvi, of Eichmann's request for clemency, Eichmann was executed by hanging at midnight between May 31 and June 1, 1962. It was the only instance in the annals of the state of Israel of a death sentence being carried out. Eich-

mann's body was cremated and the ashes scattered over the sea, beyond Israel's territorial waters.

In general, the trial was well received around the world and seen as the embodiment of historical justice. It also had various positive side effects. The citizens of Israel, particularly the youth, learned for the first time, from the mouths of numerous witnesses, how the brutal and inhuman methods employed by the Nazis made it possible for millions of people to be exterminated without having any chance of offering effective resistance, and they came to understand that there was no reason for this phenomenon to arouse in themselves feelings of guilt and inferiority. On the other hand, the heroism displayed by the Jews during the WARSAW GHETTO UPRISING and in other revolts evoked their admiration and pride.

The Eichmann trial also led to increased interest in Holocaust research and to a chain reaction in the investigation and trial of Nazi war criminals. In Germany particularly, the investigation of charges of complicity in Nazi crimes was intensified, and many of the trials that were subsequently held in Germany against Nazi criminals can be traced to the Eichmann trial and the shock it had upon the German people.

BIBLIOGRAPHY

Arendt, H. *Eichmann in Jerusalem: A Report on the Banality of Evil.* New York, 1964.

Harel, I. *The House on Garibaldi Street.* New York, 1975.

Hausner, G. *Justice in Jerusalem.* New York, 1966.

Kempner, R. M. W. *Eichmann und Komplizen.* Zurich, 1961.

Pearlman, M. *The Capture and Trial of Adolf Eichmann.* New York, 1963.

Robinson, J. *And the Crooked Shall Be Made Straight: The Eichmann Trial, The Jewish Catastrophe, and Hannah Arendt's Narrative.* Philadelphia, 1965.

Von Lang, J., ed. *Eichmann Interrogated.* New York, 1983.

GABRIEL BACH

EICKE, THEODOR (1892–1943), commandant of concentration camps and of SS

TOTENKOPFVERBÄNDE (Death's-Head Units). Born in Hüddingen, Eicke served in the German army from 1909 to the end of World War I and then became a police informant. He joined the Nazi party and the SA (Sturmabteilung; Storm Troopers) in 1928, and in 1930 transferred to the SS. Eicke was close to SS chief Heinrich HIMMLER and rose rapidly in the formation's chain of command. In June 1933 he was appointed commandant of the DACHAU concentration camp, with the rank of *Oberführer.* In this post he introduced his own methods in the administration of the camp, the torture of prisoners, and the manner in which the Totenkopfverbände camp guards conducted themselves. These methods, which were exceptionally cruel, became standard for all the concentration camps in Germany. Eicke played a key role in the "Night of the Long Knives" (*Nacht der langen Messer*) on June 30, 1934, when the top echelon of the SA was liquidated, and it was he who shot the SA chief, Ernst RÖHM, after the latter refused to commit suicide. The following month, Eicke was appointed chief of the concentration camps' administration and of the SS guard formations, and was promoted to the rank of *Brigadeführer.*

In November 1939 he became commander of the "Totenkopf" Division of the Waffen-SS. Under his command, it took part in the fighting in France and on the eastern front and had a great many crimes on its record; its first criminal action was the murder of some one hundred British prisoners of war in France on May 26, 1940. Eicke was killed on the eastern front on February 16, 1943, while serving as an SS-*Obergruppenführer* in the Waffen-SS.

BIBLIOGRAPHY

Berber, P. *Dachau.* London, 1975.
Krausnick, H., et al., eds. *Anatomy of the SS State.* London, 1968.
Sydnor, C. W., Jr. *Soldiers of Destruction: The SS Death's Head Division, 1933–1945.* Princeton, 1977.

SHMUEL KRAKOWSKI

EIF. *See* Eclaireurs Israélites de France.

EINSATZGRUPPEN (full name, Einsatzgruppen des Sicherheitsdienstes [SD] und der Sicherheitspolizei [Sipo]; Operational Squads of the Security Service and the Security Police), task force of mobile killing units operating in German-occupied territories during World War II. Einsatzgruppen made their first appearance during the ANSCHLUSS, the incorporation of Austria into the Reich in March 1938. These were intelligence units of the police accompanying the invading army; they reappeared in the invasion of Czechoslovakia, in March 1939, and of Poland, on September 1 of that year.

In the invasions of Austria and Czechoslovakia, the task of the Einsatzgruppen was to act as mobile offices of the SD and the Sipo until such time as these formations established their permanent offices; they were immediately behind the advancing military units, and, as in the Reich, they assumed responsibility for the security of the political regime. In the Sudetenland, the Einsatzgruppen, in close cooperation with the advancing military forces, lost no time in uncovering and imprisoning the "Marxist traitors" and other "enemies of the state" in the liberated areas.

Six Einsatzgruppen were organized on the eve of the Polish invasion; five were to accompany the invading German armies, and the sixth was to operate in the Poznań area, which was to be incorporated into the Reich as the WARTHEGAU. Each Einsatzgruppe was subdivided into several Einsatzkommandos, one each to an army corps. There were fifteen Einsatzkommandos, each with a complement of one hundred twenty to one hundred fifty men. Einsatzgruppe personnel were recruited from among the SD, Sipo, and SS, on a regional basis. During the invasion of Poland, the Einsatzgruppen were disposed as shown in Table 1.

The Einsatzgruppen did their work in accordance with policy lines for foreign operations issued by the Sipo and SD. These policy lines had been laid down as early as August 1939 by Reinhard HEYDRICH, head of the REICHSSICHERHEITSHAUPTAMT (Reich Security Main Office; RSHA), and by Generalquartiermeister Eduard Wagner, the Wehrmacht representative in that office. The basic instruction was to combat, in enemy countries, elements in the rear of the frontline units

TABLE 1.

EINSATZGRUPPE	COMMANDING OFFICER	ATTACHED TO ARMY	NUMBER OF COMMANDOS
I	Brigadeführer Bruno Streckenbach	Fourteenth	4
II	Obersturmbannführer Dr. Emanuel Schäfer	Tenth	2
III	Obersturmbannführer Dr. Ludwig Fischer	Eighth	2
IV	Brigadeführer Lothar Beutel	Fourth	2
V	Brigadeführer Ernst Damzog	Third	3
VI	Oberführer Erich Naumann	Posen	2

who were hostile to the Reich and to Germans.

A more detailed description of the Einsatzgruppen's mission is contained in an order of the day issued by the Eighth Corps: "To conduct counterespionage, to imprison political suspects, to confiscate arms, and to collect evidence that is of importance to police intelligence work." In practice, "combating hostile elements" was given a broad interpretation and became terror operations on a grand scale against Jews and the Polish intelligentsia, in which some fifteen thousand Jews and Poles were murdered.

On September 21, 1939, Heydrich sent a high-priority note to the Einsatzgruppe commanders giving instructions for the treatment of Jews in the conquered territories. The Jews were to be rounded up and concentrated in large communities situated on railway lines; Judenräte (Jewish councils; see JUDENRAT) were to be established; and operations against the Jews were to be coordinated with the civil administration and the military command.

On November 20 of that year, on orders from Berlin, the Einsatzgruppen's operations were terminated and their personnel were absorbed by the permanent SD and Sipo offices in occupied Poland. When the plans were drawn up for the attack on the Soviet Union, ample use was made of the experience these men had gained, and four Einsatzgruppen were reestablished as A, B, C, and D.

Invasion of the Soviet Union (June 1941). In briefing sessions with the German army commanders on the planned Operation "Barbarossa," Adolf Hitler emphasized that the impending war with the Soviet Union would

be a relentless struggle between two diametrically opposed ideologies. Its success would be determined not only by military victories, but also by the ability to root out and destroy the propagators of the rival ideology and its adherents. Hitler entrusted this job, of liquidating the personnel of the Soviet political and ideological apparatus, to Heinrich HIMMLER, chief of the SS and of all German police formations (Reichsführer-SS und Chef der Deutschen Polizei). Decree 21, Hitler's order for Operation "Barbarossa," in the section "Instructions for Special Areas," states:

In areas where military operations are being conducted, the Reichsführer-SS, in the name of the Führer, will assume the special duties required for setting up the political administration. . . . In the discharge of these duties the Reichsführer will operate independently and on his own authority. . . . The Reichsführer will ensure that the pursuit of his objectives will not interfere with military operations. Details will be worked out directly between the High Command and the Reichsführer-SS.

After consultations between Heydrich (acting as Himmler's representative) and Eduard Wagner, Gen. Walther von Brauchitsch, the commander in chief of the army, issued an order stating that for the fulfilling of special security police assignments that went beyond the scope of military operations, special units of the SD would be employed in the army's operational area. These units were to proceed according to the following guidelines: "The special units will operate in the rear of the fighting forces and their task will be to seize archives, to obtain lists of organizations and anti-German societies, and to look for individuals such as exiled former political leaders, saboteurs, and the like; they will uncover any existing anti-German movements and liquidate them; and they will coordinate their activities in these areas with the military field-security apparatus." The order adds that while the Sipo and the SD (including the Einsatzgruppen) would be operating on their own responsibility, as far as logistics were concerned they would be attached to the armed forces and would depend upon the latter for housing, rations, transport, communications, and other matters. To ensure the proper coordination, representatives of the SD and Sipo would be attached to corps and army headquarters. In its concluding section, the order provides that the special units were empowered to take administrative action against the civilian population, on their own responsibility but in cooperation with the military police, and with the approval of the local Wehrmacht commander. (For example, the extermination of the Kiev Jews at BABI YAR was decided on at a meeting held in the office of the military governor of the city, General Eberhardt, with the general attending and concurring in the decision.)

By this order, which faithfully reflects the agreement arrived at by Heydrich and Wagner, the Wehrmacht relieved itself of the task of carrying out mass murder, and restricted its involvement to logistics. However, under the conditions that developed in the occupied areas of the Soviet Union, the cooperation between the Wehrmacht and the Einsatzgruppen from time to time went beyond the provisions of the agreement, as when military units were deployed to stand guard over individuals or groups of persons who had been condemned to die, or over the area designated for their execution.

Organizing and Training the Einsatzgruppen. Early in May 1941, the men who had been chosen as candidates for the Einsatzgruppen were assembled in the training school of the German border guard in Pretzsch (a town on the Elbe River, northeast of Leipzig). The school did not have enough space to hold all the candidates, and some had to be quartered in the neighboring towns of Duben and Bad Schmiedeberg. Most of the candidates had come from the RSHA, whose manpower division had ordered the SD and

the Sipo to select suitable men for this purpose. Another group of candidates came from the Sipo senior officers' training school in Berlin; yet another group, of 100 men, had been attending an officer candidates' school of the KRIMINALPOLIZEI (Criminal Police), and were dispatched from there to join the Einsatzgruppe candidates at Pretzsch.

The commanding officers of the Einsatzgruppen, the Einsatzkommandos, and the Sonderkommandos were chosen by Himmler and Heydrich from a list prepared by Section I of the RSHA; most had been serving as senior officers of the SD (see Appendix, Volume 4). The technical staff of the Einsatzgruppen—radio operators, clerks, interpreters, drivers, and others—were recruited from among the staff of the RSHA and the SS. Three of the Einsatzgruppen—B, C, and D—had attached to them companies of Reserve Police Battalion No. 9, later replaced by men from Battalion No. 3, as well as companies of the Waffen-SS, for special duties.

Each of the reestablished Einsatzgruppen had sub-units, usually called Einsatzkommandos or Sonderkommandos. In theory, the Einsatzkommandos were to be attached to the armed forces behind the lines and the Sonderkommandos to those forces at the front. In practice, however, the Einsatzgruppen and their sub-units were deployed according to geographic sectors and not according to rear or frontline areas. The distinction between the Einsatzkommandos and the Sonderkommandos evaporated. Both the Einsatzkommandos and the Sonderkommandos also had temporary sub-units, usually referred to as Teilkommandos (lit., "part commandos"). When they were charged specifically with entering a town or city, they were sometimes called Vorkommandos (forward commandos).

The composition of the Einsatzgruppen was as follows:

1. Einsatzgruppe A consisted of Sonderkommandos SK1a, SK1b; and Einsatzkommandos EK2, EK3.
2. Einsatzgruppe B consisted of Sonderkommandos SK7a, SK7b; Einsatzkommandos EK8, EK9; and Vorkommando (V KO) Moskau (SK7c).
3. Einsatzgruppe C consisted of Sonderkom-

mandos SK4a, SK4b; and Einsatzkommandos EK5, EK6.
4. Einsatzgruppe D consisted of Sonderkommandos SK10a, SK10b; and Einsatzkommandos EK11a, EK11b, EK12.

The first commander of Einsatzgruppe A, SS-Standartenführer Dr. Franz Walter STAHLECKER, had about one thousand men at his disposal. Einsatzgruppe A was attached to Army Group North; its area of operations covered the Baltic states (LITHUANIA, LATVIA, and ESTONIA) and the territory between their eastern borders and the Leningrad district.

The first commander of Einsatzgruppe B, SS-Brigadeführer (later Gruppenführer) and Generalleutnant der Polizei Arthur NEBE, had 655 men under his command. The Einsatzgruppe was attached to Army Group Center, and its operational area extended over BELORUSSIA and the SMOLENSK district, up to the outskirts of Moscow. The sub-unit of Einsatzgruppe B that was deployed toward Moscow was called Vorkommando Moskau. When the German forces began their withdrawal from Moscow, the Vorkommando was disbanded.

The first commander of Einsatzgruppe C, SS-Standartenführer Dr. Emil Otto RASCH, had seven hundred men under his command; the Einsatzgruppe was attached to Army Group South and covered the southern and central Ukraine.

Einsatzgruppe D, commanded by SS-Standartenführer Professor Otto OHLENDORF, had a complement of six hundred men. It was attached to the Eleventh Army and operated in the southern Ukraine, the Crimea, and Ciscaucasia (the Krasnodar and Stavropol districts).

On the face of it, the units, relatively small in size, had a very large area to cover. However, when they were engaged in massmurder operations, the Einsatzgruppen were assisted by large forces of German police battalions and local auxiliary police battalions —Ukrainian, Belorussian, Latvian, or Lithuanian. At times they also had rear echelon troops at their disposal, such as garrison battalions, military gendarmeries, or even soldiers of the ORGANISATION TODT.

In early June 1941, Bruno Streckenbach, head of Branch I of the RSHA, came to Pretzsch in order to explain, on behalf of Himmler and Heydrich, Hitler's orders concerning the liquidation of the Jews. After the war, Ohlendorf gave evidence on the meeting with Streckenbach before the Nuremberg Military Tribunals, at the SUBSEQUENT NUREMBERG PROCEEDINGS, as did Dr. Walter Blume, who had been the commanding officer of Sonderkommando 7a. In his statement, Blume declared that in June 1941 Heydrich and Streckenbach had briefed them on their assignment of exterminating Jews, and had explained the ideological background. A large number of Einsatzgruppe, Einsatzkommando, and Sonderkommando commanders had taken part in the briefing sessions. Another such session, attended by the commanders of all units and sub-units, took place on June 17, 1941, in Heydrich's office in Berlin. At this time, Heydrich set out in detail the policy that was to guide the Einsatzgruppen in carrying out their assignments, among them the implementation of the Führer's order to liquidate the Jews. A third such meeting, also very close to the date of the invasion of the Soviet Union (June 22, 1941), was held in the office of the chief of the ORDNUNGSPOLIZEI, Kurt DALUEGE. It was attended by the senior SS and police officers who had been designated to act as Einsatzgruppe commanders in the various parts of the Soviet Union, when these were occupied by the German army. On July 2, 1941, these officers also received written instructions from Heydrich, which contained the following passage:

> The following is the gist of the highly important orders that I have issued to Einsatzkommandos of the Sipo and the SD, with which these two services are called upon to comply. . . .
> 4) *Executions.*
> The following categories are to be executed:
> Comintern officials (as well as all professional Communist politicians); party officials of all levels; and members of the central, provincial, and district committees;
> people's commissars;
> Jews in the party and state apparatus;
> and other extremist elements (saboteurs, propagandists, snipers, assassins, agitators, etc.).

The order affecting the "Jews in the party and state apparatus" encompassed, in prac-

EINSATZGRUPPEN

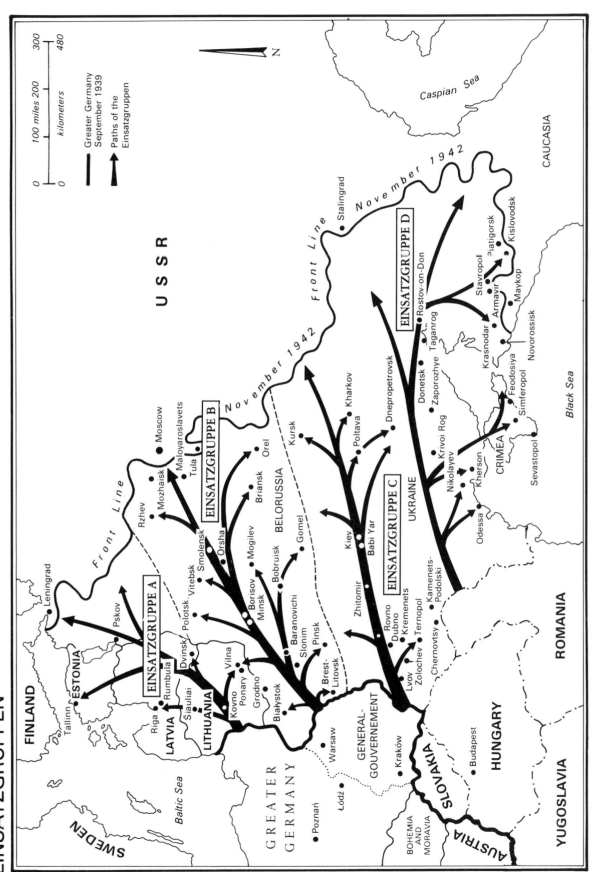

tice, all the Jews in the Soviet Union. Einsatzgruppe Report No. 111 of October 12, 1941, did in fact make it perfectly clear that the purpose was to kill all Jews.

The Einsatzgruppen's Itineraries. With these orders in mind, the Einsatzgruppen began their march into the Soviet Union, in the footsteps of the German army. Einsatzgruppe A started out from East Prussia, and its units—the Sonderkommandos and Einsatzkommandos—rapidly spread out across Lithuania, Latvia, and Estonia. On June 25, Einsatzgruppe A headquarters entered Kovno at the same time as the advance formations of the army, and at the beginning of July it moved to RIGA. The local auxiliary police (made up of Lithuanians or Latvians), together with the Einsatzgruppe's various units, embarked upon the massacre of Jews, mainly in VILNA (PONARY), KOVNO (the NINTH FORT), and Riga (RUMBULA), as well as in many other cities and towns. Next, Einsatzgruppe A and several of its sub-units advanced toward Leningrad, so as to be able to enter the city together with the "Totenkopf" Division of the Waffen-SS. When the Leningrad front stabilized, Einsatzgruppe A was for the most part disbanded, and some of its personnel were used to establish and staff the regional SD and Sipo offices. At the end of September 1941 Dr. Stahlecker, the Einsatzgruppe A commander, was also appointed SS and Sipo commander (*Befehlshaber der Sicherheitspolizei und des Sicherheitsdienstes*) of REICHSKOMMISSARIAT OSTLAND. Small and mobile sub-units of Sonderkommandos 1a and 1b continued to "clean up" the area between the Baltic states and the eastern front.

Einsatzgruppe B had WARSAW as its starting point; some of its units passed through Vilna and GRODNO on the way to MINSK, where they arrived on July 5, 1941. Other units belonging to Einsatzgruppe B passed through BREST-LITOVSK, SLONIM, BARANOVICHI, and Minsk, and from there proceeded to southern Belorussia: MOGILEV, Bobruisk, and GOMEL, advancing as far as Briansk, Kursk, Orel, and Tula. Along their route, in all the places through which they passed, they murdered masses of people—Jews, GYPSIES, Communist activists, and prisoners of war. At the beginning of August 1941, Einsatzgruppe B headquarters moved to Smolensk, and some of its units were deployed in northern Belorussia, in places such as Borisov, VITEBSK, and Orsha. Two months later the headquarters moved again, to Mozhaisk, while its special advance unit, Vorkommando Moskau, established itself in Maloyaroslavets; both expected to enter Moscow with the Fourth Panzer group of the German army.

Einsatzgruppe C made its way from Upper Silesia to the western Ukraine, by way of KRAKÓW. Two of its units, Einsatzkommandos 5 and 6, went to LVOV, where they organized a pogrom against the Jews with the participation of Ukrainian nationalists. Sonderkommando 4b organized the mass murders at TERNOPOL and ZOLOCHEV, and then continued on its way to the east. Einsatzgruppe C headquarters and Sonderkommando 4a went to ZHITOMIR, by way of Volhynia, with 4a carrying out massacres en route, in Dubno and Kremenets. On September 29 and 30, Sonderkommando 4a, commanded by Paul BLOBEL, perpetrated the mass slaughter of Kiev Jews at Babi Yar. This unit was also responsible for the murder of KHARKOV's Jews, in early January 1942. Einsatzkommando 6 marched to the east and undertook the liquidation of the Jews of Krivoi Rog, DNEPROPETROVSK, and Zaporozhye, proceeded to Stalino (Donetsk), and reached ROSTOV-ON-DON. Einsatzkommando 5 was then broken up into SD and Sipo teams to staff local offices of the two organizations in such cities as Kiev and ROVNO. In Rovno, the capital of REICHSKOMMISSARIAT UKRAINE, these teams launched a large-scale *Aktion* at the beginning of November 1941, in which most of the Jewish inhabitants were murdered.

Einsatzgruppe D, as mentioned, was attached to the Eleventh Army. During its advance it carried out massacres in the southern Ukraine (Nikolayev and KHERSON), in the Crimea (SIMFEROPOL, Sevastopol, Feodosiya, and other places), and in the KRASNODAR and Stavropol districts (Maykop, Novorossisk, Armavir, and Piatigorsk).

By the spring of 1943, when the Germans began their retreat from Soviet territory, the Einsatzgruppen had murdered 1.25 million Jews and hundreds of thousands of other Soviet nationals, including prisoners of war.

Jewish prisoners of war were separated from the rest and put to death at an early stage, in the advance transit camps. The method that the Einsatzgruppen employed was to shoot their victims in ravines, abandoned quarries, mines, antitank ditches, or huge trenches that had been dug for this purpose. The killing by shooting, especially of women and children, had a devastating effect on the murderers' mental state, which even heavy drinking of hard liquor (of which they were given a generous supply) could not suppress. This was among the primary factors that led the RSHA in Berlin, in August 1941, to look for an alternative method of execution. It was found in the form of GAS VANS—heavy trucks with hermetically sealed vans into which the trucks' exhaust fumes were piped. Within a short time these trucks were supplied to all the Einsatzgruppen.

The Einsatzgruppen performed their murderous work in broad daylight and in the presence of the local population; only when the Germans began their retreat was an effort made to erase the traces of their crimes. This was the job of Sonderkommando 1005 (see AKTION 1005): to open the mass graves, disinter the corpses, cremate them, and spread the ashes over the fields and streams.

In practice, the Einsatzgruppen left behind an immense record of their deeds, in the form of summary reports drawn up in Berlin on the basis of detailed reports submitted by the various units in the field. Among the most comprehensive of these summary reports was the *Ereignismeldung der UdSSR* (Report of Events in the USSR), which was first issued on June 23, 1941, and was continued until Report No. 195, dated April 24, 1942. Next, and in continuation, came the *Meldungen aus den besetzten Ostgebieten* (Reports from the Occupied Eastern Territories), which began on May 1, 1942, and were kept up until May 21, 1943. In addition, there were the reports on the operations and the situation of the SD and Sipo in the USSR, covering the period from June 22, 1941, to March 31, 1942.

After the war, the Einsatzgruppe leaders were tried at the SUBSEQUENT NUREMBERG PROCEEDINGS, in the ninth trial conducted by the Nuremberg Military Tribunals. The trial, *The United States of America* v. *Otto Ohlendorf et al.*, was presided over by Judge Michael A.

Musmanno. It began on July 3, 1947, and ended on April 10, 1948; there were twenty-four defendants. Fourteen of them were sentenced to death, seven to periods of imprisonment ranging from ten years to life, and one to the time already served; two were not tried or sentenced. Four of the defendants were actually executed, and sixteen had their sentences commuted or reduced to periods extending from the time already served to life imprisonment. One defendant was released, one died of natural causes, one committed suicide, and the execution of one was stayed because of the defendant's insanity.

Following the establishment of the Zentrale Stelle der Landesjustizverwaltungen (Central Office of the Judicial Administrations of the *Länder*) at Ludwigsburg, West Germany (*see* LUDWIGSBURGER ZENTRALSTELLE), over one hundred more indictments were handed down against Einsatzkommando commanders, officers, noncommissioned officers, and privates. In the ensuing trials no death sentences were passed, since the Federal Republic of Germany had abolished capital punishment.

[*See also* "Final Solution."]

BIBLIOGRAPHY

Hilberg, R. *The Destruction of the European Jews.* New York, 1985.

Krausnick, H., and H.-H. Wilhelm. *Die Truppe des Weltanschauungskrieges: Die Einsatzgruppen der Sicherheitspolizei und des SD 1938–1942.* Stuttgart, 1981.

Krausnick, H., et al. *Anatomy of the SS State.* London, 1968.

Lozowick, Y. "Rollbahn Mord: The Early Activities of Einsatzgruppe C." *Holocaust and Genocide Studies* 2/2 (1987): 221–241.

SHMUEL SPECTOR

EINSATZKOMMANDOS. *See* Einsatzgruppen.

EINSATZSTAB ROSENBERG (Operational Staff Rosenberg), organization for the plunder of the cultural and artistic treasures of the Jews, created by Alfred ROSENBERG in order to "secure ownerless cultural property of Jews." The unit's first activity of this kind was carried out in France by the Sonderstab Bildende Kunst (Special Operational Staff for the Arts), created by order of Hitler on September 17, 1940. Immediately after the occupation of France in June 1940, Hitler had expressed his desire to take possession of the artistic treasures of the Jews. Members of the unit carried out a thorough search operation in the collections of the Rothschild family and among the treasures of other Jewish collectors, in order to expropriate works of art remaining after the deportation or flight of their owners. They also attempted to discover storehouses and hiding places where works of art had been hidden, and searched the freight of overseas removal companies, claiming that they wished to prevent art treasures from being smuggled out of France. The operation was carried out with the aid of the French police and the German Sicherheitspolizei (Security Police), and with the active support of the German embassy in Paris.

Nonetheless, Rosenberg complained that the French authorities intrigued against the searches and that the French administrators responsible for Jewish property concealed works of art. According to the report summarizing the results of the operation in France between 1940 and 1944, the plundered works of art were transferred to Germany in twenty-nine consignments, in 137 freight cars holding 4,174 crates. They included nearly twenty-two thousand items: paintings, furniture—some antique—and objets d'art of all kinds from different periods, from all over the world. Besides the unique works of art that found their way to the homes of Hitler, Hermann Göring, and other leaders of the Third Reich, other items (principally furniture) were placed at the disposal of different Reich authorities, or were stored in different hiding places in Germany.

Concurrent with the activity in France, Einsatzstab Rosenberg carried out a furniture expropriation action (Möbel Aktion) in the Netherlands and in Belgium, such as that which Rosenberg had begun previously in Germany. Furniture was removed from tens of thousands of apartments of Jews who had emigrated or been deported to eastern Europe, and was given to Germans whose apart-

Some of the six hundred Torah scrolls plundered by the Nazis from synagogues in Germany.

Books and other archival material looted by the Nazis, later collected by the United States Army and brought to the Offenbach Archival Depot.

ments had been damaged by bombs. The property was transferred in 735 freight trains. Some of the pillage from the Netherlands, including clothing and linen, was transferred on rafts along the Rhine. On October 3, 1942, Rosenberg reported to Hitler that 40,000 tons of furnishings had been brought to Germany in the Möbel Aktion.

In eastern Europe the activity was less organized and controlled but no less comprehensive. In addition to the theft of works of art, there was large-scale plunder of ritual articles. In all the occupied countries, the Jewish libraries, including the ancient and valuable libraries of the Netherlands and Salonika, were looted. The plunder was one of the matters brought up on various occasions during the NUREMBERG TRIAL.

BIBLIOGRAPHY

Poliakov, L. *Harvest of Hate*. New York, 1979.

LENI YAHIL

EINSTEIN, ALBERT (1879–1955), physicist. Einstein was born at Ulm, Germany, of an assimilated Jewish family. While working in a patent office in Bern, Switzerland, he published in 1905 three revolutionary papers; one of them, on his special theory of relativity, gained him international fame. He then taught physics at the universities of Bern, Zurich, and Prague. In 1914, Einstein was appointed professor of physics at the Berlin Academy of Science and the Kaiser Wilhelm Institute of Physics, where he published in 1916 an extended version of the theory of relativity. In 1921, he was awarded the Nobel prize in physics. When Hitler came to power in 1933, Einstein happened to be out of Germany; he never set foot in that country again. He resigned from the Prussian Academy of Science and eventually emigrated to the United States, where he worked at the Institute for Advanced Studies in Princeton, New Jersey, for the rest of his life.

By his very nature Einstein was a fierce enemy of Nazism and all totalitarian regimes. Thus, in January 1933 he wrote: "My great fear is that this hate and power epidemic will spread throughout the world. It comes from below the surface like a flood, until the upper regions are isolated, terrified, and demoralized and then also submerged." The Nazis canceled his honorary citizenship (held from 1914, in addition to his Swiss citizenship), confiscated his property, and put a price of 50,000 reichsmarks on his head. In a statement to the Swiss press, he said: "As long as I have the choice, I shall live only in a land where political freedom, tolerance, and equality of all citizens reign."

In the United States, Einstein took part in Jewish rescue efforts, and in 1941 he tried in vain to influence President Franklin D. ROOSEVELT by writing to Eleanor Roosevelt, drawing her attention to the policy of the State Department, "which makes it all but impossible to give refuge in America to many worthy persons who are victims of the Fascist cruelty in Europe." Though Mrs. Roosevelt was ready to raise the issue with her husband, nothing came of it. After the war, Einstein also expressed criticism of SWITZERLAND's policy toward REFUGEES, stating that the country "behaved with unjust brutality . . . even towards those [refugees] whom it has allowed to enter its territory."

It was his hatred of Nazism that motivated Einstein, despite his pacifism, to warn Roosevelt, in August 1939, concerning the possibility that Germany might acquire sufficient quantities of uranium in the recently incorporated territory of Czechoslovakia to produce "extremely powerful bombs of a new type" that "might well destroy [a] whole port together with some surrounding territory." Einstein therefore recommended that the United States acquire uranium from the Belgian Congo. When the letter reached Roosevelt after the outbreak of the war, in October 1939, the National Research Defense Committee began to organize production of the atom bomb. In May 1946, after the war and the dropping of the first atom bombs, Einstein, presiding over the National Commission of Nuclear Scientists, declared: "The release of atom power has changed everything except our way of thinking, and thus we are being driven unarmed towards a catastrophe. . . . The solution of this problem lies in the heart of humankind."

BIBLIOGRAPHY

Clark, R. W. *Einstein: The Life and Times.* New York, 1971.

Frank, P. *Einstein: His Life and Times.* New York, 1948.

Seelig, K. *Albert Einstein: A Documentary Biography.* London, 1956.

ELIZABETH E. EPPLER

EISENHOWER, DWIGHT DAVID (1890–1969), military leader and thirty-fourth president of the United States. In World War II, Eisenhower was the architect and commander of the Allied invasion of Europe (June 6, 1944) and commander in chief of the Allied Expeditionary Forces in Europe up until the surrender of Germany (May 8, 1945). When the war ended, he became commander in chief of the American occupation forces in Europe until his appointment, later in 1945, as chairman of the United States Joint Chiefs of Staff, a post he held until 1948. From 1950 to 1952 he was commander in chief of the North Atlantic Treaty Organization (NATO). He served as president of the United States from 1953 to 1961.

The forces under Eisenhower's command liberated tens of thousands of Jews from concentration and forced-labor camps. Eisenhower himself visited several concentration camps as soon as they were liberated and, at news conferences and over the radio, expressed feelings of revulsion and shock at the atrocities that had been committed. He ordered that as many American soldiers as possible be taken to the camps to see for themselves the evidence of the unspeakable crimes that the Nazis had perpetrated.

Three years later, in his book *Crusade in Europe* (1948), Eisenhower recorded his impressions of his first visit to a concentration camp.

> The same day I saw my first horror camp. It was near the town of Gotha. I have never felt able to describe my emotional reactions when I first came face to face with Nazi brutality and ruthless disregard of every shred of decency. Up to that time I had known about it only generally or through secondary sources. I am certain, however, that I have never at any time experienced an equal sense of shock. I visited every nook and cranny of the camp because I felt it my duty to be in a position from then on to testify at first hand about these things in case there ever grew up at home the belief or assumption that "the stories of Nazi brutality were just propaganda."

To accelerate a solution to the problem of Jewish DISPLACED PERSONS (DPs), Eisenhower created the post of adviser on Jewish affairs to the supreme commander of the Allied forces. The first person to hold the post, army chaplain Rabbi Judah Nadich, made a deep

Gen. Dwight D. Eisenhower, commander in chief of the Allied forces in Europe, views the charred bodies of prisoners at the Ohrdruf camp in Germany (April 4, 1945). The camp was liberated by advance troops of the Fourth Armored Division of the Third Army. Second from the left is Gen. George S. Patton; at Eisenhower's left (arms akimbo) is Gen. Omar N. Bradley. [United States Army Signal Corps]

impression on Eisenhower; under his influence Eisenhower approved the establishment of separate Jewish DP camps in the American zone of Germany, in order both to keep the Jews apart from the many Nazi collaborators who had infiltrated the camps and to facilitate the physical, social, and moral rehabilitation of the survivors of the Holocaust. This action made it possible for the She'erit ha-Peletah (the "surviving remnant" of Europe's Jews) to organize as an autonomous body. Later, Eisenhower ordered the admission into the DP camps of the thousands of Holocaust survivors smuggled by the BERIḤA movement from eastern Europe into the American zone in Germany and Austria.

In October 1945, Eisenhower met with David BEN-GURION and agreed to his request that Hebrew teachers and agricultural instructors from Palestine be permitted to operate in the DP camps. This opened the door for the implementation of an extensive program of activities among the She'erit ha-Peletah by representatives of the YISHUV (the organized Jewish community of Palestine) and its underground armed force, the Hagana.

BIBLIOGRAPHY

Eisenhower, D. *Eisenhower: At War, 1943–1945.* New York, 1986.
Nadich, J. *Eisenhower and the Jews.* New York, 1953.

DAVID H. SHPIRO

ELKES, ELCHANAN (1879–1944), physician and chairman of the Ältestenrat (Council of Elders) in the KOVNO ghetto in Lithuania.

Elkes was born in the Lithuanian village of Kalvarija, close to the German border. He received a traditional Jewish and Hebrew education. While still a youngster, he was sent to Kovno to attend school. He completed his medical studies in Königsberg, Germany, and for seven years was village doctor in Berezino in Belorussia. During World War I, Elkes served as a medical officer in the Russian army, and he received numerous decorations. From the early 1920s, he headed the internal-medicine department in the Bikkur Holim Jewish hospital in Kovno. Reputed to be one of the best doctors in Lithuania, he numbered heads of state and diplomats among his patients.

Elkes was a Zionist, active on the Jewish cultural scene, and close to members of He-Haluts, the association of pioneering Zionist youth. During the period of Soviet rule (1940–1941), he used his contacts as physician to Moscow's representative in Lithuania to help obtain exit permits for thousands of Polish Jewish refugees who were stranded in Lithuania.

On June 24, 1941, the Germans captured Kovno, and thousands of Jews were arrested and murdered by the invaders and their

Elchanan Elkes (left), chairman of the Ältestenrat (Council of Elders) in the Kovno ghetto, with Dr. Moshe Berman. Berman was the head of the new hospital in the ghetto, opened at the end of 1941 after the Germans burned the old one in October. The photograph was taken by Zvi Kadushin, the Kovno photographer whose clandestine camera recorded life in the ghetto.

Lithuanian collaborators. The remaining thirty thousand Jews were ordered to move into a ghetto and to choose a head for the Ältestenrat. On August 4 an emergency meeting was called, and was attended by twenty-eight leading personalities from all walks of Jewish life in the city. At this meeting, the last of its kind in the Kovno Jewish community, Elkes was nominated unanimously for the position and, with a heavy heart, he accepted the nomination. He was sixty-two years old and in failing health.

Elkes headed the Ältestenrat from its establishment until it was disbanded. All who came into contact with him attested to his impressive moral stature and devotion to the Jewish cause, his courage and dignity in his dealings with Nazi officials, his simplicity of manner with his fellow Jews, and his modest way of life. This was in sharp contrast to the corruption and haughtiness manifested by some of the Ältestenrat personnel. For these qualities he was held in high regard by the Jewish ghetto population. Elkes looked favorably on the anti-Nazi underground activity in the Kovno ghetto. Despite the danger involved, he was asked to organize supplies for the members of the General Jewish Fighting Organization (Yidishe Algemeyne Kamfs Organizatsye; JFO) who left the ghetto to fight as partisans in the forests. He declared: "Every opportunity for resistance should be exploited, especially in matters of honor." Elkes's stand influenced other members of the Ältestenrat to support the JFO.

At the beginning of July 1944, with the Red Army not far from Kovno, the Nazis proceeded to liquidate the ghetto and transfer its inhabitants to Germany. Elkes, at the risk of his life, appeared before the ghetto commandant, Obersturmbannführer Wilhelm Göcke, and suggested that Göcke drop the transfer plan, saying that this act would be held to his credit. Göcke refused bluntly, but allowed Elkes to leave unharmed. A few days later the ghetto was evacuated, and Elkes was transferred, with many of the surviving Jews, to the Landsberg concentration camp in Germany, where he was put in charge of the hospital hut. Soon afterward he fell ill, and died on October 17, 1944.

On October 19, 1943, while still in the ghetto, Elkes sent his children in England a final testament in Hebrew. He wrote: "With my own ears I have heard the awful symphony of weeping, wailing, and screaming from tens of thousands of men, women, and children, which have rent the heavens. No one throughout the ages has heard such a sound. Along with many of these martyrs I have quarreled with my Creator, and with them I cried out from a broken heart, 'Who is as silent as you, O Lord' " (a bitter allusion to a well-known prayer, "Who can compare to you, O Lord").

BIBLIOGRAPHY

Garfunkel, L. *The Destruction of Kovno's Jewry.* Jerusalem, 1959. (In Hebrew.)
Gutman, Y., and C. Haft, eds. *Patterns of Jewish Leadership in Nazi Europe, 1933–1945.* Proceedings of the Third Yad Vashem International Historical Conference. Jerusalem, 1979. See pages 93–112.

DOV LEVIN

EMERGENCY COMMITTEE FOR ZIONIST AFFAIRS. *See* American Zionist Emergency Council.

EMIGRATION. *See* Aliya Bet; Beriha; Council for German Jewry; Haavara Agreement; HICEM; Hilfsverein der Deutschen Juden; Madagascar Plan; White Paper of 1939; Zentralstelle für Jüdische Auswanderung.

ENDLÖSUNG. *See* "Final Solution."

ENDRE, LÁSZLÓ (1895–1946), one of the leading figures of Hungarian Nazism. Endre played a prominent role in many ultrarightist organizations and was the founder of the "Race-protecting Socialist Party" (A Fajvédő Szocialista Párt). In 1919 he was appointed constable and in 1923 chief constable of Gödöllő, a position he held until the end of 1937, when he became deputy prefect of Pest county. He had intimate contacts with the German Nazis, and began a close personal relationship with Adolf EICHMANN after Hungary's occupation by the Germans on March

László Endre (left).

19, 1944. As undersecretary of state in the Döme SZTÓJAY puppet government's Ministry of the Interior, a position he held between April 9 and September 5, 1944, Endre was among those chiefly responsible for the destruction of Hungarian Jewry. He fled with the retreating Nazi forces, but was captured by the Americans and extradited to Hungary in October 1945. Tried as a war criminal, he was hanged on March 29, 1946.

BIBLIOGRAPHY

Katzburg, N. *Hungary and the Jews: Policy and Legislation, 1920–1943.* Ramat Gan, Israel, 1981.
Macartney, C. A. *October Fifteenth: A History of Hungary, 1929–1945.* New York, 1957.

RANDOLPH L. BRAHAM

ENGLAND. *See* Great Britain.

ENTERDUNGSAKTION. *See* Aktion 1005.

ENTJUDUNG (lit., "de-Judaization"), term put into use in Nazi ANTI-JEWISH LEGISLATION. It is found in Eugen Dühring's infamous work on the "Jewish question," *Die Judenfrage als Rassen- Sitten- und Kultur-Frage* (1881), in the chapter "Early Steps and Ultimate Goals," in which he speaks of the *Verjudung* ("Judaization," or "corruption by Jews") of the nations and all they stand for. "This," he writes, "is a fact; the challenge now is *Entjudung* ['removal of the Jews']." It was clear to Dühring that this challenge could not be met all at once, and he therefore recommended *Entjudungsprozeduren*—"procedures, ways and means, of getting rid of the Jews."

In the Nazi period the term was used exclusively in an economic context and meant the removal of the Jews from economic life. As such, it appears for the first time in Nazi legislation in a decree by the minister of the interior, dated February 6, 1939. This makes it possible to determine with a high degree of accuracy the emergence of the term in that sense. The need for it arose when the term ARISIERUNG ("Aryanization" [of Jewish businesses]) was found to be no longer suitable; that term had previously been used even in official communications, although the word *arisch*—"Aryan"—and its derivatives disappeared from the terminology of German legislation after the NUREMBERG LAWS. The new expression, with its negative connotation, put a greater emphasis on the desire to remove the Jews from the body politic.

The decree of February 6, 1939, was named *Einsatz des jüdischen Vermögens* (meaning, in effect, "confiscation of Jewish assets"), which was also the name under which its better-known predecessor (which it complemented), the decree of December 3, 1938, was known. It points out the earlier decree "complements in a decisive manner previous instructions concerning the *Entjudung*—the removal of the Jews—from the German economy and provides a comprehensive legal basis thereto." The important innovation is that, according to the decree, "henceforth, *Entjudungen* [the plural of *Entjudung*] may also be carried out by the use of force,"

although "for the time being there should be no forceful *Gesamtentjudung* [total de-Judaization] of real property that is not being used for agriculture or afforestation." The term *Entjudung* also appears in the other parts of that decree and its appendixes.

2. *Entjudung von gewerblichen Betrieben* (removal of Jews from industries);
3. *Entjudung des Grundbesitzes* (removal of Jews from the ownership of land);
4. *Erfassung ungerechtfertigter Entjudungsgewinne* (seizure of illegitimate profits derived from *Entjudung*);
5. *Beteiligung der Parteistellen an dem Entjudungsverfahren* (participation of Nazi party offices in the *Entjudung* process).

Later on, the *Entjudung* operation was referred to as the *Entjudungsgeschäft* ("de-Judaization business"). For example, on June 10, 1940, the Reich minister of economic affairs issued an "Order for the Investigation of *Entjudungsgeschäfte*" whose purpose was to reimburse the Reich (and not, of course, the original owners whose property had been confiscated) for "unreasonable profits" made on such transactions after January 30, 1933. Further instructions on this aspect were issued in 1941.

The term *Entjudung* also appears in a 1944 document containing a list of "privileged" Jews who were deported from the Netherlands to the "model camp" of THERESIENSTADT; listed among them are also "persons" (in a second document, "Jews") who had bought this status in the *Entjudung der Niederlande* ("removal of the Jews from the Netherlands").

BIBLIOGRAPHY

Esh, S. "Words and Their Meaning: Twenty-Five Examples of Nazi-Idiom." *Yad Vashem Studies* 5 (1963): 133–167.

SHAUL ESH

EPPSTEIN, PAUL (1901–1944), a leader of German Jewry under the Third Reich. Eppstein was born in Ludwigshafen, and he majored in sociology at Mannheim University, where his teachers were Max Weber, Karl Jaspers, and Karl Mannheim.

At the age of twenty-six he became a lecturer in sociology at the business college in Mannheim. In 1929 he was appointed principal of the city's adult education college (*Volkshochschule*), which in less than four years developed into one of the most important institutions of its kind in Germany. When Hitler came to power in 1933, the college was closed down. Eppstein was asked to come to Berlin to participate in community activities on behalf of German Jewry, activities that under the new circumstances were in need of expansion and reorganization. His first appointment was with the ZENTRALAUSSCHUSS DER DEUTSCHEN JUDEN FÜR HILFE UND AUFBAU (Central Committee of German Jews for Relief and Reconstruction) and the Union of Jewish Communities of Prussia.

That same year, Eppstein was invited to join the board of the REICHSVERTRETUNG DER DEUTSCHEN JUDEN (Reich Representation of German Jews), in which he was primarily occupied with administration and social activities. Following the KRISTALLNACHT pogrom in 1938, Eppstein was invited to England to lecture in sociology, but he refused to leave Germany so long as the remaining Jews were in need of his services. He kept up his work in the new Reichsvereinigung der Juden in Deutschland (Reich Association of Jews in Germany; 1939–1943); indeed, the scope of his responsibilities was enlarged, especially as regarded day-to-day contact with the authorities and his work in connection with emigration. As of the end of 1940, following the arrest of Otto HIRSCH, Eppstein was the organization's sole executive director, under its presiding officer, Rabbi Leo BAECK.

In the years that he worked for the Reichsvereinigung, Eppstein was arrested several times by the Gestapo. One such arrest took place in the summer of 1940. When he was released, in October of that year, the REICHS-SICHERHEITSHAUPTAMT (Reich Security Main Office; RSHA) ordered him to desist from any further activity related to emigration, and henceforth he concentrated on administrative affairs. Late in January 1943, about six months before the abolishment of the Reichsvereinigung, Eppstein was expelled to the THERESIENSTADT camp, together with Leo Baeck. On his arrival, he was appointed

Paul Eppstein (left) at Theresienstadt (1944). [Leo Baeck Institute, Jerusalem]

chairman of the Ältestenrat der Juden (Council of Jewish Elders), together with Jacob EDELSTEIN but in fact replacing him. Opinions vary on the way Eppstein carried out his task in Theresienstadt. In some quarters he has been criticized for not standing up to the German ghetto administration and for willingly submitting to its demands, as well as for alienating his fellow prisoners and standing aloof from them; others believe that he was a staunch spokesman for the Jews, both in Germany and in Theresienstadt. Eppstein was imprisoned in the summer of 1944, because (according to one version) the Germans found fault with a speech he had made before the ghetto prisoners. The day after the Day of Atonement, 1944, Eppstein was executed.

BIBLIOGRAPHY

Adler, H. G. *Theresienstadt, 1941–1945.* Tübingen, 1955.

Ehrmann, F., ed. *Terezin, 1941–1945.* London, 1965.

Lederer, Z. *Ghetto Theresienstadt.* London, 1953.

ESRIEL HILDESHEIMER

"ERNTEFEST" ("Harvest Festival"), code name for the operation to exterminate the last surviving Jews of the TRAWNIKI and PONIATOWA labor camps and the MAJDANEK concentration camp (all in the GENERALGOUVERNEMENT area of Poland). The date fixed for the operation (known as Aktion "Erntefest") was November 3, 1943, timing that was apparently influenced by the uprising of the Jewish prisoners in the SOBIBÓR extermination camp a few weeks earlier, on October 14. Heinrich HIMMLER, concerned that there might be more uprisings in the Generalgouvernement area, gave the order to kill all the Jews employed there on forced labor. The task of implementing the order was entrusted to Jacob SPORRENBERG, the *Höherer SS- und Polizeiführer* (Higher SS and Police Leader) of the Lublin district. "Erntefest" was carried out as a military operation, with thousands of SS and police, including Waffen-SS units, mobilized for it from all over the area. In order to forestall any acts of resistance, the operation was accomplished at top speed simultaneously in all three camps, and came as a complete surprise. On the eve of the operation, Poniatowa held some fifteen thousand Jews; Trawniki had eight thousand to ten thousand, including women and children, most of them brought there from the Warsaw ghetto, during and after its liquidation.

On November 3 at dawn, the Trawniki and Poniatowa camps were surrounded by SS and police forces. The Jews in the camps were taken out in groups and shot to death in pits that had been prepared for this purpose near each of the camps. In Trawniki the shooting was accompanied by background music blaring forth from loudspeakers, set up for this specific occasion in order to drown out the sound of the shooting. In Majdanek, the Jews were separated that day during the morning parade from the rest of the prisoners; they were then taken to pits that had been dug next to the camp's southern fence a few days earlier, and shot to death. Two powerful loudspeakers had been set up nearby to broadcast loud dance music. On the same day, Jews from other labor camps in Lublin —from the old airfield, the armament workshops, and elsewhere—were brought to Majdanek and shot to death next to the same pits. A total of seventeen thousand to eighteen thousand Jews were murdered in Majdanek on that day.

In Poniatowa, a Jewish underground group offered resistance when they were about to be taken to the pits, and set fire to some barracks. Their resistance was crushed. In all three camps Jews tried to take refuge in hiding places in the barracks, but they were all caught, either on November 3 or on the days that followed, and put to death. Hundreds of Jews were left behind in each camp in order to burn the bodies of the victims. They, too, were murdered when the job was done.

A total of forty-two thousand to forty-three thousand Jews were murdered in the "Erntefest" operation. This was the final *Aktion* to take place in the Generalgouvernement area, bringing AKTION REINHARD to an end.

BIBLIOGRAPHY

Arad, Y. *Belzec, Sobibor, Treblinka: Operation Reinhard Death Camps.* Bloomington, 1987.

YITZHAK ARAD

ESCAPE. *See* Beriḥa.

ESTONIA, Soviet republic in the northwestern USSR. Estonia is the northernmost of the three Baltic republics and the smallest; in 1939 its population was 1,133,917. At the end of 1917, after some two hundred years of Russian tsarist rule, Estonia declared its independence. Early in World War II it was forced to accept Soviet bases on its soil (September 29, 1939), and in August 1940 it was annexed to the USSR as a Soviet republic. In July 1941 the Germans, assisted by units of the Estonian nationalist group Omakaitse, conquered Estonia. During the three years of Nazi rule, Estonia was an administered area (Generalbezirk Estland) included in REICHSKOMMISSARIAT OSTLAND. The Estonians were granted self-rule under Hialmar Mae, leader of the extreme nationalist movement VAPS. When the Red Army returned in September 1944, Estonia once again became a Soviet republic.

Estonia's first Jewish communities arose in the middle of the nineteenth century. Between the two world wars, some forty-five hundred Jews (0.4 percent of the entire population) lived in Estonia, half of them in the capital city, TALLINN, and the rest in the towns of Tartu, Valga, Pärnu, Narva, Viljandi, Rakvere, Voru, and Nõmme, and in smaller settlements. Like the country's other national minorities, the Estonian Jews enjoyed broad cultural and educational autonomy, including the provision of Hebrew and Yiddish government schools. From the mid-1930s, as the extreme nationalist Omakaitse adherents gained power, demands increased to reduce the Jewish role in Estonia's economy and to limit the number of Jewish university students.

In the year of Soviet rule (1940–1941), the Jews' factories and businesses were nationalized along with those of the rest of the Estonians. Many Jewish breadwinners were absorbed into the nationalized economy, but the system of autonomy was canceled and the Jews' educational and religious activity curtailed. At the same time, however, Jews were appointed to government economic and security positions. During the waves of arrests visited on the Estonian population, the Jews suffered badly in proportion to their numbers because of economic activity discountenanced by the Soviet regime as well as Zionist political activity. On June 14, 1941, eight days before the German invasion of the Soviet Union, some ten thousand Estonians, including five hundred Jews (5 percent of the total), were exiled to Siberia. Most of the Jews managed to flee the country before the German conquest; some two hundred and fifty of them were conscripted into the Estonian Corps of the Red Army, where they constituted 0.8 percent of the soldiers; some one thousand Jews remained in Estonia under Nazi rule.

During the first weeks under the Germans, the Jews were subjected to many limitations and decrees. They were forced to wear the yellow badge (*see* BADGE, JEWISH) and forbidden to walk on sidewalks or use public transportation; their property was confiscated. The Jews of Estonia were in fact at that time already doomed. Sonderkommando 1a (SK1a; a division of Einsatzgruppe A), under SS-Obersturmbannführer Dr. Martin Sandberger, was placed in charge of their extermination. Omakaitse units assisted the Sonderkommando in the killing. First, the

ESTONIA on the Eve of WW II

Omakaitse arrested and murdered hundreds of youths and men aged sixteen and older. The remaining men, along with the women and children, were herded into school buildings; some were sent to perform forced labor. Later they were all interned at the Harka labor camp near Tallinn.

On October 12, Sandberger reported to his superiors that all Jewish men aged sixteen and over, except doctors and the "Jewish elders" appointed by the Germans, were being executed by the Estonian "self-defense" units, under the supervision of Sonderkommando 1a. They had already killed 440 Jews. The operation was continued in and around Tallinn, where Jews in hiding had not yet been captured. During the last weeks of 1941, the rest of the Jews, mostly women and children, were executed by the Sonderkommando and the Omakaitse. According to the report issued by Einsatzgruppe A, 936 Jews had been killed in Estonia by January 1942. On the regional map attached to that report, it was noted that Estonia was "free of Jews" (*judenfrei*). This fact was also announced at the WANNSEE CONFERENCE, held on January 20 of that year.

Starting in the fall of 1942, tens of thousands of Jews were sent to Estonia from other areas under Nazi rule: from THERESIENSTADT, from the Lithuanian ghettos of VILNA and KOVNO, Bistriţa in Transylvania, and the KAISERWALD camp in Latvia. They were concentrated in twenty labor camps and forced to mine oil shale for the production of synthetic fuel, dig antitank ditches, build bunkers, and perform other military work. The main camp was VAIVARA. When these Jews weakened and could no longer work, many of them were killed; others died of disease, hunger, and torture. In the fall of 1944, faced with the advance of the Red Army, the Germans hurriedly removed the remaining Jews from the camps and transported them across the Baltic Sea to the STUTTHOF concentration camp. On September 18 and 19, 1944, most of the Jews were killed in the Lagedi and KLOOGA camps. Fewer than ten survived.

Between 1944 and 1950 some fifteen hundred Estonian Jews—survivors of the thousands who had fled to the Soviet interior in 1941—returned to Estonia. Eventually, the survivors of the Siberian exile were also allowed to return.

BIBLIOGRAPHY

Dworzecki, M. *The Jewish Camps in Estonia, 1942–1944*. Jerusalem, 1970. (In Hebrew.)

Dworzecki, M. "Patterns in the Extermination of Estonian Jewry." *Yalkut Moreshet* 11 (November 1967): 135–147. (In Hebrew.)

Kruus, R. *People, Be Watchful*. Tallinn, 1962.

Levin, D. "Estonian Jews in the U.S.S.R., 1941–45." *Yad Vashem Studies* 11 (1976): 273–297.

Levin, D. "The Jews of Estonia in the First Year of the Soviet Regime (1940–1941)." *Behinot Studies on the Jews in the USSR and Eastern Europe* 7 (1976): 73–84. (In Hebrew.)

DOV LEVIN

ETHNIC GERMANS. *See* Volksdeutsche.

EUGENICS. *See* Anthropology and National Socialism.

EUROPA PLAN, plan devised by the PRACOVNÁ SKUPINA (Working Group) in SLOVAKIA for saving the Jews of Europe from extermination, by the payment of ransom.

In the summer of 1942, a group of activists within the ÚSTREDŇA ŽIDOV (Jewish Center) in Slovakia sought to end the deportation of Slovak Jews to extermination camps. One of the people the activists tried to influence was Dieter WISLICENY, the SS officer who served as adviser on Jewish affairs to the government of Slovakia, whom they planned to bribe with a substantial sum of United States dollars. The deportations did in fact come to an end after the group had reached agreement with Wisliceny on the sum to be paid (between $40,000 and $50,000). There is no evidence that it was Wisliceny's intervention that brought the deportations to an end, or that there was any such intervention on his part, but the members of the group believed that this was the case. Encouraged by what the group regarded as a success, one of its leading members, Rabbi Michael Dov WEISSMANDEL, suggested trying to end the extermination process in the camps in Poland, and to provide aid to the Jews who had already been deported. On the basis of ties that two members of the group —Gisi FLEISCHMANN and Andrej Steiner—had with Wisliceny, by way of Karol Hochberg, a plan was worked out. It was given various names: the Europa Plan, since it aimed to save the Jews of Europe; the Rabbis' Plan, because the letters dispatched to Jewish organizations abroad in relation to the plan were signed by two rabbis, Weissmandel and Armin-Abba Frieder, who was also a member of the Working Group; and the Great Plan, because it involved the rescue of Jews from all over Europe, compared with the Small Plan, which involved only the rescue of Slovak Jews. The substance of the plan was that in exchange for the Germans' bringing the deportations and exterminations to a stop, the Jews of the free world would pay them a large sum in hard currency—2 million to 3 million United States dollars, according to one version.

Negotiations on the plan continued for nearly a year, from the fall of 1942 until August 1943, when Wisliceny brought them to an end. In the course of the negotiations, the Working Group made attempts to save the Jews of Greece with the help of Wisliceny, and to establish contact between the SS and several leaders of Hungarian Jewry.

The Working Group members were convinced that the reason the Europa Plan failed was that the required funds were not provided. The replies received by the group from Jewish organizations and institutions in Switzerland and Istanbul stated that the money was not available, and that the transfer of funds to Axis countries was prohibited. The negotiations conducted by the Germans in Hungary concerning the rescue of Jews— "Blood for Goods" (see BRAND, JOEL)—were a direct sequel to the Europa Plan. To this day the plan has remained the subject of searching debate. No clearcut evidence has been found that would prove that the SS was indeed ready to make a deal with the Jews in exchange for money; all that exist are the testimonies given by the Working Group members and by Wisliceny. On the other hand, the appeals and entreaties of the group were sometimes met with disdain, derision, and callousness. Subsequently, the surviving members of the Working Group smarted under feelings of frustration and bitterness.

BIBLIOGRAPHY

Bauer, Y. *American Jewry and the Holocaust: The American Jewish Joint Distribution Committee, 1939–1945.* Detroit, 1981.
Bauer, Y. *The Jewish Emergence from Powerlessness.* Toronto, 1979.
Fuchs, A. *The Unheeded Cry.* New York, 1986.

YESHAYAHU JELINEK

EUTHANASIA PROGRAM. The term "euthanasia" is generally used to describe "mercy killings," but it was employed by the Nazis to describe their systematic killing of various groups of individuals.

Before 1933, a certain tradition appears to have existed in Germany of helping to bring about death in certain borderline cases, especially in hospitals and nursing institutions. Doctors and nurses with strong conservative-nationalist or religious convictions ignored the unequivocal provisions of criminal law and "assisted death," and not just in rare cases.

When Hitler came to power in 1933, it was soon apparent that what the Nazis had in mind when they used terms like "the nation's health" and "racial hygiene" was the creation of a homogeneous *Herrenvolk* (master race), exuding health, and superior in mind and body to all other peoples: a people that had the right to claim world rule for itself for all time to come. This goal was to be achieved by multiplying those who belonged to the *Volksgemeinschaft* ("folk community") and were regarded as healthy and racially superior, and by getting rid, as fast as possible, of all those who belonged to foreign races, those who were not needed for the superior development of the German people, and of the sick and weak. Hitler wanted the Hitler Youth to be "as hard as steel, as strong and pliant as leather, and as fast as greyhounds." He was less concerned about the mental superiority of the "people of poets and thinkers" presumably because he regarded it as a natural attribute of the Germans, and therefore allowed himself, now and then, to ridicule the "decadent intellectualism" of German intellectuals.

As long as the Nazis confined themselves to the forced sterilization of "Rhineland bastards" (the children fathered by black troops serving in the post–World War I occupation forces), the "hereditary diseased," and "habitual criminals," the resistance they encountered was remarkably small. Neither was there any objection to the forcible confinement of "asocial elements," the disabled, "idiots," and "shirkers." When the war broke out there was no protest against the field hospital that military doctors were setting up to filter "war neurotics," or against the formation of battalions made up exclusively of persons suffering from diseases of the ear, the heart, or the kidneys. "Malingerers" were threatened by doctors that they would be put into concentration camps or "probation units" (made up of convicted criminals who had been pardoned so that they could be sent to the front). Such threats were actually carried out. When the battle of Stalingrad was drawing to its end, only front-line troops had food rations delivered to them, and some thirty thousand to forty thousand wounded and sick troops were not given medical treatment.

The critical point came when doctors and medical aides were asked, unequivocally, to participate in the murder of at least some of their patients. This was the meaning of the Euthanasia Program that Hitler entrusted to Reichsleiter Philip Bouhler, Dr. Karl Brandt, and doctors of their choice, for implementation in the late fall of 1939, with retroactive authorization as of September 1, 1939. "Manslaughter on request" accounted for very few of the killings performed under the Euthanasia Program; this was Social Darwinism on a grand scale, carried out without constraints in the T4 institutions. (T4 was the code name of the Nazis' "euthanasia" killing measures, derived from the address in Berlin—Tiergartenstrasse 4—where the Euthanasia Program, under the aegis of the Reich Chancellery, had its headquarters.) Later, in 1941 and 1942, the T4 specialists were transferred to the east, where they could practice the skills they had acquired in gassing and other forms of mass murder, on a truly immense scale in the extermination of Jews.

The Euthanasia Program, to judge by available records, encountered astonishingly few misgivings on religious, moral, or legal grounds. This may well have been due to a sophisticated personnel policy, the cunning *modus operandi*, and the mentality of the men in charge of the institutions, who were not inclined to lodge public protests or to take part personally in the operation. Disciplinary problems were avoided by spreading the assignments over a relatively large number of staff. There was ample opportunity for relaxation and entertainment to enable staff members to take their mind off their work, and a strong effort was made to keep the operation secret. To blunt any remaining humane feelings, hard liquor was always available in ample quantities. Frequent vacations were granted at choice resorts in Austria, free of charge, for the staff members together with their families; there were special allowances and bonuses and various other perquisites. The result was that the turnover of personnel in the T4 institutions was extraordinarily small, and no serious conflict ever developed between management and staff. Institutions whose managements were loath to cooperate in the operation had their patients transferred elsewhere, where no such difficulties were encountered.

The Euthanasia Program, even under the conditions prevailing at the time, was an illegal enterprise, and its implementation cannot therefore be explained by the high respect for authority and discipline that German officials were trained to observe. On the contrary, the bureaucrats' legalistic inertia caused them to oppose this innovation of the state going on a rampage against the weakest elements of the population, for whose welfare it was responsible. The euthanasia doctors, Karl Brandt and his team, who made ample use of the authorization they had been given by Hitler and, for the most part, knew their patients only from their files, were all of the type that is ready to take risks and is not bothered by legal niceties. They trusted their intuition; they were career-minded and flexible, venal, and unscrupulous.

It is estimated that up to 1939, some 200,000 to 350,000 persons were sterilized; of these, beginning in 1939, many fell victim to the Euthanasia Program. Some of them escaped that fate, either because it was felt that their sterilization had rendered them harmless or that they could still be useful as manpower, or because their families had made special efforts to bring them home before it was too late. On the other hand, many of the victims of the program who were gassed, shot to death, or killed by lethal injections had not been previously sterilized; these included children and patients found in hospitals and various other institutions in territories occupied at a later stage.

The first large-scale euthanasia action seems to have taken place in Pomerania and western Prussia shortly after the Polish campaign. During 1940, four euthanasia institutions went into operation: Grafeneck, in January; Brandenburg, in February; Hartheim, in May; and Sonnenstein, in June. In the first half of the year, 8,765 persons were gassed in these four institutions, three-quarters of them in May and June, a time when world attention was focused on the Battle of France. By the end of 1940, a total of 26,459 patients had been put to death, and in the first eight months of 1941, an additional 35,049 were "disinfected." These were the figures given by the accounting section of T4's head office.

Growing criticism of the Euthanasia Program—such as a sermon given by Bishop Clemens GALEN in Münster on August 3,

EUTHANASIA PROGRAM

1941—caused Hitler to bring it to an official end. In practice, however, the operation was continued up to the end of the war, under a more effective camouflage. By September 1, 1941, the date of its official termination, 70,273 people had been "disinfected," according to T4 figures. Another figure given by T4 was the number of beds that had been made available for other purposes up to the end of 1941: 93,521.

This has led Ernst Klee (1985) to the conclusion that by then, as many as 33 percent of all the beds that had been occupied by the mentally ill in the prewar period had been made available. A large number of mentally ill persons were also killed in the occupied areas in the east: in Riga, Jelgava (Mitau), and Dvinsk (Dünaburg), 1,800 to 2,200; in Aglona, 544; in Poltava, 545; in Minsk and Mogilev, 836; in Dnepropetrovsk, 1,500; in Markayevo, 240; in Kiev, 360; and so on.

Following the transfer of the Euthanasia Program staff to AKTION REINHARD, its functions were taken over, temporarily, by different institutions. In one place, Meserlitz-

Oberwald, 18,000 patients are said to have been killed between 1942 and 1945, mostly by lethal injections; among the victims, according to evidence given shortly before the end of the war, were sick German soldiers. Available data do not permit a precise figure to be given for the total extent of the Euthanasia Program. Its victims included the inmates of homes for the aged, homosexuals, the residents of welfare institutions, foreign workers, and concentration camp prisoners. As early as August 1942, Bishop Ludwig Sebastian of Speyer, in notes prepared for a conference of bishops held in Fulda that month, stated: "Far more than 100,000 people have been the victims of euthanasia. Men over seventy are no longer to receive medicine. Who is worth being kept alive at all? Only a Nazi." In the NUREMBERG TRIAL, the number of euthanasia victims was estimated at 275,000. It may be assumed that in the strict sense, 200,000 persons were murdered in the Euthanasia Program.

Mention should also be made of the role played by the Catholic and Evangelical churches in the period that led up to the Euthanasia Program and during its operation. Before embarking upon the program, Hitler held consultations on the reaction that he could expect from the two churches. With a few exceptions, his expectations of lack of opposition were borne out by the facts.

[*See also* Anthropology and National Socialism; Medical Experiments; Physicians, Nazi.]

BIBLIOGRAPHY

Klee, E. *"Euthanasie" im NS-Staat: Die Vernichtung "Lebensunwerten Lebens."* Frankfurt, 1985.

Lifton, R. J. *The Nazi Doctors: Medical Killing and the Psychology of Genocide.* New York, 1986.

Mielke, F. *Medizin ohne Menschlichkeit: Dokumente des Nürnberger Ärzteprozesses.* Frankfurt, 1960.

Nowak, K. *"Euthanasie" und Sterilisierung im Dritten Reich: Die Konfrontation der evangelischen und katholischen Kirche mit dem Gesetz zur "Verhütung erbkranken Nachwuchses" und der "Euthanasie"-Aktion.* Göttingen, 1978.

Wuttke-Groneberg, W. *Medizin im Nationalsozialismus: Ein Arbeitsbuch.* Rottenburg, 1982.

HANS-HEINRICH WILHELM

EVERT, ANGHELOS (1894–1970), head of the Athens police during 1943. Inspired by Metropolitan Damaskinos's public denunciation of the persecution of Jews, Evert ordered that new and false credentials be issued by the police to all Jews requesting them. Hundreds of such credentials were thus made available to needy Jews, some of them personally issued by Evert (such as those of Haim Efraim Cohen, an attorney, to whom Evert personally handed a new identity card with the name Pavlos Georgiou Panopoulos). Thanks to this courageous decision by Evert (which, owing to his personal involvement, placed him in jeopardy of arrest and severe punishment by the Germans, in the event of disclosure), countless Jews were able to ride out the German occupation undetected, under new identities. For this deed, Anghelos Evert was recognized by YAD VASHEM as a "RIGHTEOUS AMONG THE NATIONS" in 1969.

MORDECAI PALDIEL

EVIAN CONFERENCE, conference on the problem of Jewish REFUGEES that was held in Evian, France, on the shore of Lake Geneva, in July of 1938. From 1933 through 1937, about 130,000 Jews fled Germany. For the most part, this outflow was orderly; refugees were still able to take some property with them, and places for resettlement were generally available.

The extreme persecution that came in the wake of Germany's annexation of Austria in March 1938 rapidly erased all order from the refugee exodus. Within eleven days of the annexation, President Franklin D. ROOSEVELT proposed an international conference, (1) to facilitate the emigration of refugees from Germany and Austria; and (2) to establish a new international organization to work for an overall solution to the refugee problem. A primary motivation for the UNITED STATES DEPARTMENT OF STATE, which had first suggested the conference, was to blunt pressures in the United States for more liberal immigration legislation. Roosevelt made it clear from the start that no country would be expected to change its present policies significantly. The United States, he pointed out, contemplated no increase in its immigration quotas; but the German and Austrian quotas —until then far undersubscribed—would soon be opened for full use.

From July 6 to 15, 1938, delegates from thirty-two countries (the United States, Great Britain, France, six smaller European democracies, Canada, the Latin American nations, Australia, and New Zealand) met at the French resort town of Evian. In the opening public speech of the conference, Myron C. Taylor, the American delegate, stated that the United States' contribution was to make the German and Austrian quota of 27,370 per year fully available. As the sessions proceeded, delegate after delegate excused his country from accepting additional refugees.

The British representative declared that the overseas British territories were already overcrowded, were not suited to European settlement, or were unable to accept many refugees because of political conditions. Some areas, such as parts of East Africa, might offer possibilities, but only for limited numbers. He excluded Palestine from the

Evian discussion entirely. England itself, being fully populated and in the throes of the current unemployment problem, was not available for immigration. The delegate from France stated that his country would do what it could, but it had already reached "the extreme point of saturation as regards admission of refugees." The Belgian emissary reported that the same situation prevailed in his nation. The Netherlands could receive more immigrants only as refugees presently there moved on to lands of final settlement.

Australia could not encourage refugee immigration because, "as we have no real racial problem, we are not desirous of importing one." New Zealand's representative maintained that on account of economic problems, only a limited number could be accepted into his land. He went on to characterize the Evian Conference as a "modern 'wailing wall.'" Because of the depression,

Canada had almost no room for immigrants. For the Latin American countries, unemployment was the main factor in the need to keep immigration at a low rate. The tiny Dominican Republic, one of the last countries to report, alone offered encouragement, volunteering to contribute large but unspecified areas for agricultural colonization.

An American news correspondent accurately reflected the tenor of the conference: "Myron C. Taylor . . . opened proceedings: 'The time has come when governments . . . must act and act promptly.' Most governments represented acted promptly by slamming their doors against Jewish refugees."

Before adjourning, the Evian Conference established the INTERGOVERNMENTAL COMMITTEE ON REFUGEES (ICR) and commissioned it to negotiate on two fronts. One task was to "approach the governments of the countries of refuge with a view to developing opportu-

The Evian Conference was held in July 1938. James McDonald (seated, second from right) was one of the American delegates.

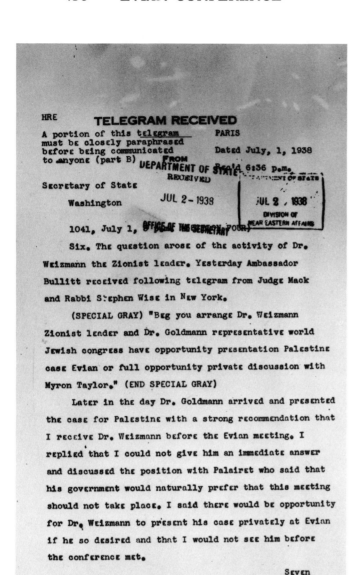

HRE **TELEGRAM RECEIVED**

A portion of this telegram PARIS
must be closely paraphrased
before being communicated Dated July, 1, 1938
to anyone (part B) FROM
DEPARTMENT OF 6:36 p.m.
RECEIVED
Secretary of State
Washington JUL 2- 1938 JUL 2, 1938
DIVISION OF
NEAR EASTERN AFFAIRS
1041, July 1,

Six. The question arose of the activity of Dr.
Weizmann the Zionist leader. Yesterday Ambassador
Bullitt received following telegram from Judge Mack
and Rabbi Stephen Wise in New York.

(SPECIAL GRAY) "Beg you arrange Dr. Weizmann
Zionist leader and Dr. Goldmann representative world
Jewish congress have opportunity presentation Palestine
case Evian or full opportunity private discussion with
Myron Taylor." (END SPECIAL GRAY)

Later in the day Dr. Goldmann arrived and presented
the case for Palestine with a strong recommendation that
I receive Dr. Weizmann before the Evian meeting. I
replied that I could not give him an immediate answer
and discussed the position with Palairet who said that
his government would naturally prefer that this meeting
should not take place. I said there would be opportunity
for Dr. Weizmann to present his case privately at Evian
if he so desired and that I would not see him before
the conference met.

Seven

Part of a telegram sent by Myron Taylor, the American representative at the Evian Conference, to Secretary of State Cordell Hull and Under Secretary Sumner Welles on July 1, 1938. Sir Michael Palairet was the second British delegate at this conference on the emigration and resettlement of refugees from Germany and Austria. [U.S. National Archives and Records Service]

nities for permanent settlement." The other step aimed at persuading Germany to cooperate in establishing "conditions of orderly emigration," which particularly meant to permit removal from the Reich of a reasonable amount of refugee property.

The ICR, however, received little authority and almost no funds or support from its member nations, and it had virtually no success in opening countries to refugees. The coming of war in September 1939 cut short its efforts to arrange with Germany for refugees to bring some property out with them, and the committee soon slipped into inactivity.

Many months before the demise of the ICR, it was evident that the Evian Conference had accomplished virtually nothing. Even as the conference closed, most observers agreed that it had failed in its main task, of finding places where the refugees could go. An immediate consequence of the conference was that it crushed the hopes of hundreds of thousands of European Jews, people who had been looking to the nations at Evian to save them from an increasingly impossible situation.

The Evian Conference stands in historical perspective as a critical turning point. At the conference the Western democracies made it clear that they were willing to do next to nothing for the Jews of Europe. Soon afterward, KRISTALLNACHT, which took place in the autumn of 1938, signaled to the world that Jews could no longer live where the Nazis ruled. At Evian, the world had shown that it would not make room for those Jews. Thus 1938 became the crucial year in the coming of the Holocaust. By its end, the world knew the Jews had to leave. Germany was still pressing the Jews to leave, and the Jews themselves were now anxious to do so. But the world's doors, closed at Evian, remained shut throughout World War II.

In the midst of the Holocaust, the United States and Great Britain held another conference to consider helping the Jews of Europe. The delegates to the BERMUDA CONFERENCE of April 1943 knew clearly that the Jews were being systematically exterminated. They too decided to do next to nothing.

BIBLIOGRAPHY

Abella, I., and H. Troper. *None Is Too Many: Canada and the Jews of Europe, 1933–1948.* New York, 1983.

Feingold, H. L. *The Politics of Rescue: The Roosevelt Administration and the Holocaust, 1938–1945.* New Brunswick, N.J., 1970.

Katz, S. Z. "Public Opinion in Western Europe

and the Evian Conference of July 1938." *Yad Vashem Studies* 9 (1973): 105–132.

Marrus, M. R. The *Unwanted*. New York, 1985.

Stein, J. B. "Great Britain and the Evian Conference of 1938." *Wiener Library Bulletin* 29/1 (1976): 40–52.

Wyman, D. S. *Paper Walls: America and the Refugee Crisis*. Amherst, Mass., 1978.

DAVID S. WYMAN

EVREISKI ANTIFASHISTSKI KOMITET.
See Jewish Antifascist Committee.

EXCHANGE: JEWS AND GERMANS. During much of World War II, an agreement between the Nazis and the Allies permitted small numbers of Jews to be exchanged for Germans living in Palestine or other countries of the British Empire. The Jews involved either were of Palestinian nationality, possessed immigration visas ("certificates") to Palestine, or had a valid claim thereto. The origin of the exchange lay in the fact that when the war broke out, some two thousand Germans were living in Palestine (descendants of Knights Templar who had settled in Palestine in the nineteenth century), while there were British nationals in Germany and German-occupied Poland whom the British government sought to repatriate to Britain. These British subjects included Jews from Palestine who were stranded in Poland at the outbreak of the war.

This led to lengthy negotiations for the exchange of their respective nationals between the two warring countries. In the initial stage the negotiations were conducted by way of the United States embassy in Berlin. In June 1941, when the United States recalled its ambassador in Berlin, Switzerland became the go-between. As time went on, the Germans were eager to increase the number of Germans who would be exchanged and were prepared to exchange them for Jews who were not Palestinian nationals and only had immigration visas in their possession.

Developments in the exchange issue can be divided into three phases:

1. The first phase, which lasted from the beginning of the war up to the second half of 1941, saw efforts being made from several quarters for an exchange to be arranged. In Palestine, pressure was brought on the Jewish Agency to intervene with the British authorities on behalf of relatives of Palestinian Jews who had been stranded in Germany or Poland. In the British Parliament, members frequently put questions to the government concerning the fate of Palestinian nationals stranded in Poland. At the same time, the families of German nationals in Palestine applied to their government for action to be taken to bring their relatives to Germany. Both governments were highly suspicious of each other, and as a result negotiations on the subject did not begin. The German attitude changed in July 1940, when the Spanish consul in Jerusalem (who represented German interests in Palestine) informed the German government that seven hundred German nationals, men, women, and children, had been notified that they were going to be transferred from Palestine to another destination. Subsequently, these Germans were deported to camps in Australia. This caused the German government to step up the pace of the negotiations, and coincided with increased pressure in Britain on the Foreign Office to effect an exchange.

2. The second phase lasted from mid-1941 to February 1943, and in that period three groups of exchangees arrived in Palestine. The first group, consisting of 46 persons (29 women, 16 children, and 1 man), arrived in December 1941, having been exchanged for 69 Germans. The second group arrived in Palestine in November 1942 and was made up of 139 British subjects, of whom 69 were Palestinians. They were exchanged for 305 Germans. This group of Palestinian residents had been staying in Poland at the time of the major *Aktionen* in the Polish ghettos and their reports deeply influenced the YISHUV and its rescue efforts. Another group, numbering 15 persons, arrived in February 1943. Both the Germans and the British made sure that only persons who answered the conditions of the agreement would be exchanged. With respect to Palestinians, those whom the British regarded as meeting the conditions were (a) holders of British passports; (b) women who had acquired Palestinian nationality in Poland by marriage prior to August

1939, and their children; (c) women and children who had gone abroad from Palestine before the war broke out; or (d) wives and children of residents of Palestine who were not Palestinian nationals.

The punctilious British observance of these conditions, in addition to the fact that many of the potential exchangees were no longer alive or could not be traced in the ghettos and camps, meant that in this period the number of Germans exchanged was twice as high as that of Palestinian Jews. There were also various obstacles to be overcome, created by the mutual suspicion of the two governments and requiring very precise timetables and details of the exchange method, by means of intermediaries.

3. In the third phase, which lasted from February 1943 to April 1945, positions on the exchange issue underwent a change; there was a trend to widen the range of categories that would qualify for exchange, both among German official circles and Jews in Nazi-occupied countries, and among Jewish organizations and institutions in Palestine and neutral countries. The deep impact of the exchange that had taken place in November 1942 persuaded Jewish Agency officials in Palestine and Switzerland that this method offered a crumb of hope. As Eliyahu Dobkin, head of the Immigration Department of the Jewish Agency, stated at a meeting held on October 8, 1943: "There was a time when we deluded ourselves that the Allied powers would be ready to propose an exchange plan to the Germans—hundreds of thousands of Jews, for German nationals in the democratic countries."

At this time also, the Jewish Agency's Palestine Office in Geneva distributed hundreds of letters stating that the bearer of the letter was a candidate for exchange. These letters had the effect of preventing, or at least postponing, the deportation of Jews to extermination camps, especially from the Netherlands and Belgium. For their part, Jews in the Netherlands and Belgium applied to Geneva for written confirmation that they had been granted immigration "certificates" as a means of saving themselves.

For several months in 1943, leading officials in the German government entertained the idea that preparations should be set in motion for a large-scale exchange. Top officials in the German Foreign Ministry believed that it would be possible to repatriate a large number of Germans from Palestine and various other countries in the British Empire and South America, in exchange for Jews in German-occupied countries. The German foreign minister, Joachim von RIBBEN-TROP, proposed that thirty thousand Jews be assembled for this purpose to serve as candidates for such an exchange. In a letter dated May 14, 1943, Eberhard von THADDEN, head of the German Foreign Ministry section dealing with Jewish affairs, wrote: "Since the British have more Germans in their hands than we have British, in this special case Jews could also be used for exchange." Heinrich HIMMLER agreed, but reduced the proposed number to ten thousand, and a special camp was put up at BERGEN-BELSEN to take in the candidates for exchange. In July 1943, several Jews who had been staying at the HOTEL POLSKI in Warsaw were sent to Bergen-Belsen and assured that they were candidates for exchange. Most of them were cheated and sent to the AUSCHWITZ extermination camp; a few did get to Bergen-Belsen and were saved. At the end of 1943 and the beginning of 1944, some four thousand Jews from the WESTERBORK concentration camp in the Netherlands were sent to Bergen-Belsen. In August 1943, twelve hundred children from the BIAŁYSTOK ghetto were sent to THERESIENSTADT for a temporary stay; they, too, were candidates for exchange, but in the end they were sent to Auschwitz and killed there. The negotiations with the British were conducted by Switzerland, as the power representing Britain's interest in contacts with Germany. The plan did not materialize. The Germans labored under two illusions: (1) that there were many Germans who wished to return to Germany, whereas in fact this was true of only a few; and (2) that the British were willing to go to great lengths in order to rescue Jews.

As 1943 drew to an end, the Germans no longer expected a large-scale exchange to take place. Negotiations with the British were kept up, but the purpose was to maintain a channel of communication. In January 1944, conditions were ripe for another exchange. In that month the United States established its

WAR REFUGEE BOARD, and a genuine effort was launched to rescue Jews from the Nazis' clutches. In March 1944 Ira HIRSCHMANN, as representative of the board, established himself in Istanbul and began negotiations from there, through the International RED CROSS; another board representative, Roswell Mc-Clelland, went to operate in Geneva with the same objective. In April 1944 a representative of Switzerland went to Berlin for negotiations on an exchange. These negotiations dragged on, and only on June 26, 1944, did an exchange take place, the fourth of its kind. A total of 283 Jews were exchanged, 222 from Bergen-Belsen and 61 from the VITTEL concentration camp in France. None of the Jews was a Palestinian national. All were taken to Vienna and from there went to Palestine, by way of Turkey. In exchange, 150 Germans were returned, 74 of them from South Africa. The deal took into account the larger number of Germans that had been permitted to leave in the previous exchange transactions.

Another exchange was made in March 1945, this time with Sweden acting as the intermediary. It affected 99 Jews from Bergen-Belsen and 38 from the RAVENSBRÜCK concentration camp. Ostensibly, the group was made up of Jews who were Turkish nationals, but this was not true of the majority. They boarded a ship in Sweden and went to Turkey, and from there to Palestine. When the war ended, some 600 to 700 Jews in Bergen-Belsen were in possession of immigration certificates and were candidates for exchange. It is not known how many of these starved to death in the final days of the war.

The number of Jews who were exchanged, in the five groups, is shown below.

December 1941	46
November 1942	69
February 1943	15
June 1944	283
March 1945	137
Total	550

The saving of 550 Jews was in itself important, but the exchange operation had an effect that was over and above these results, in three respects:

1. The rescue of persons who held Palestinian nationality or immigration visas to Palestine.

2. The saving of hundreds of Jews because they were in possession of a paper certifying that they would be granted immigration visas to Palestine and were therefore not sent to extermination camps. Some of these were sent to Bergen-Belsen; others stayed where they were. Many held out to the end of the war and were thus rescued.

3. The information supplied by the exchanges. This was particularly important in the case of those exchanged in November 1942, who had left Poland after the large *Aktionen* of the summer and fall of 1942. Theirs was the first testimony of the dimensions of the Nazi extermination operations, and it aroused in the YISHUV an awareness of the urgency of rescue efforts.

BIBLIOGRAPHY

Adler, H. G. *Der verwaltete Mensch.* Tübingen, 1974.

Barlas, C. *Rescue during the Holocaust.* Tel Aviv, 1975. (In Hebrew.)

Eck, N. "Jews in Exchange for Germans." *Studies in Holocaust and Resistance* 2 (1973): 23–49. (In Hebrew.)

From Bergen-Belsen to Freedom: The Story of the Exchange of Jewish Inmates of Bergen-Belsen with German Templars from Palestine. Jerusalem, 1986.

Kolb, E. *Bergen-Belsen: Geschichte des "Aufenthaltslagers," 1943–1945.* Hannover, 1962.

Wasserstein, B. *Britain and the Jews of Europe, 1939–1945.* Oxford, 1979. See pages 222–235.

RUTH ZARIZ

EXHUMATION OPERATION. *See* Aktion 1005.

EXODUS 1947, an "illegal immigration" ship that became the symbol of the struggle for the right of free Jewish immigration into Palestine.

Zionist policy, as it came to be formulated in the fall of 1945, regarded the Holocaust survivors and the DISPLACED PERSONS in Europe as the major force in the political struggle for the establishment of a Jewish state and for the continuation of ALIYA BET ("illegal" immigration)—the major arena of the struggle at the time. In November 1946 the Mosad le-Aliya Bet, the main Aliya Bet agency, acquired an American ship, the *President Garfield*. Originally an excursion ship for cruises in rivers and coastal waters, the *President Garfield* during the war had been converted to serve navy requirements. It had room for 4,000 passengers and was the largest ship ever used by the Mosad up until then. By organizing this voyage, the Mosad people sought to relieve the pressure by the Jewish displaced persons in Germany to leave the camps, and also to launch an "illegal immigration" operation, unprecedented in size, that would be covered by the media and draw the attention of the members of the United Nations Special Committee on Palestine (UNSCOP), then visiting Palestine on a fact-finding mission.

In early July 1947, within seven days, 4,500 Jewish refugees, equipped with a Colombian collective-transit visa, were moved from camps in Germany to the south of France. There they boarded the *President Garfield*, lying at anchor in the old port of Sète, near Marseilles. With discreet help from cabinet members of the French Socialist government and the French security agencies who supported the Jewish and Zionist cause (help that caused a sharp confrontation in the cabinet with the ministers who supported the British position), this logistically complicated operation was launched, with far-reaching political implications.

On July 11, at dawn, the ship departed for the shores of Palestine. Once it was on the high seas, the ship changed its name to *Exodus 1947*. The 4,500 "illegal" immigrants aboard the ship, made up of organized groups and individual refugees, maintained impressive internal discipline throughout the voyage, despite the overcrowding and shortages from which they suffered. During the voyage the ship was under the surveillance of the British fleet, and even before it had entered Palestine's territorial waters, British destroyers closed in on *Exodus 1947* and forced it to proceed to the Haifa port. There, the British used force to remove the passengers from the ship; the refugees offered strong resistance, and in the ensuing clash three Jews were killed and many were wounded.

On July 20 the *Exodus 1947* refugees were put on board three British deportation vessels, which were to take them back to their port of departure in France. This was an innovation in British policy; since August 1946, "illegal" immigrants who had been apprehended had been deported to Cyprus. On this occasion, the British decided to take the Jewish refugees back to the country that had enabled them to leave the Continent, hoping thereby to prevent that country from giving further aid to the Zionist struggle.

Emil Sandström, the Swedish judge who was chairman of UNSCOP, with two other members of the committee, was present in the Haifa port when British soldiers were dragging the resisting Jewish refugees on board the deportation ships. One of the two other members, in an on-the-spot opinion, said that the scene they were witnessing was the most convincing evidence that had yet been brought before the committee of the need for a Jewish national home. The report presented to the United Nations by the committee in September 1947, recommending that the British Mandate be terminated and a Jewish state be established in a part of Palestine, did indeed reflect the impact of the *Exodus* affair and of the post-Holocaust situation of the displaced Jews of Europe.

For an entire month, the three British deportation vessels lay at anchor off Port-de-Bouc, a French port in the Mediterranean. The thousands of Jewish refugees aboard the ship suffered from incredibly overcrowded conditions, poor sanitary arrangements, and the scorching summer heat. The French authorities refused to accede to the British demand that they force the refugees to land in France, but they offered asylum to any refugee who wanted to stay in France. The Mosad people on board and the leaders of the organized and well-disciplined groups among the passengers arranged for all of the thousands of Holocaust survivors to go on a hunger strike and thereby rivet world attention to their plight. Finally the British, at the proposal of Foreign Secretary Ernest Bevin, decided that the refugees would be taken back to the camps in Germany—a decision that raised the anger even of United States President Harry S. Truman and Secretary of State George Marshall, who, while trying to help the Jewish refugees, had until then stayed out of the *Exodus* affair.

Among the Zionist leaders a sharp debate developed as to how the affair should be resolved. When it first became known that *Exodus* refugees might be sent back to Germany, Chaim WEIZMANN and others felt that it would be preferable for the refugees to disembark in France. David BEN-GURION, however, was adamantly opposed, and insisted that the Zionist Executive adopt a unanimous stand rejecting all proposals that might wreck or weaken the strategy on which the Zionist struggle was based.

On September 8, 1947, British troops in the port of Hamburg, Germany, forcibly removed the refugees from the ship. Each refugee was dragged off the ship by a team of steel-helmeted soldiers, in full view of the hundreds of newspapermen from all over the world who were covering the event. The refugees, for the most part, stayed in the camps in Germany for over a year, and reached Israel only after the state was established, the last arriving in 1949. The *Exodus 1947* episode was the climax of the drama of the "illegal immigration" to Palestine, and even while it was being enacted, it turned into a test of strength between the British and the Jews of Palestine.

BIBLIOGRAPHY

Bauer, Y. *Flight and Rescue: Bricha.* New York, 1970.

Druz, J. *The Exodus Incident in a New Light.* Tel Aviv, 1971. (In Hebrew.)

Gruber, R. *Destination Palestine: The Story of the Haganah Ship Exodus 1947.* New York, 1948.

Holly, D. C. *Exodus 1947.* Boston, 1969.

Schaary, D. *The Cyprus Detention Camps for "Illegal" Immigrants to Palestine, 1946–1949.* Jerusalem, 1981. (In Hebrew.)

IDITH ZERTAL

EXPROPRIATION. *See* Arisierung; Einsatzstab Rosenberg; Haupttreuhandstelle Ost.

EXTERMINATION CAMPS (Ger., *Vernichtungslager*), Nazi camps in occupied Poland in which a huge number of Jews were killed, as part of the "FINAL SOLUTION of the Jewish question in Europe." These camps had a single goal: the blanket murder of the Jews, irrespective of age or sex. In contrast to the procedure at other camps, no *Selektionen* took place (with some exceptions in AUSCHWITZ-Birkenau); everyone brought to an extermination camp, including persons fit for work, was murdered. For this reason, such camps have sometimes been called "death factories."

The systematic mass murder of Jews began when the Germans invaded the Soviet Union, on June 22, 1941. In the first phase, carried out primarily by the SS EINSATZGRUPPEN, hundreds of thousands of Jews were shot to death. This method of killing, however, proved too slow for the Germans, and the considerable manpower required made it difficult to keep the project secret. Thus, senior SS officers devised a different murder technique, that of gassing. Experience in the lethal use of gas had been gained in the institutions involved in the mass murder of the EUTHANASIA PROGRAM.

An experiment in murdering human beings with poison gas was made on September 3, 1941, in the main camp of Auschwitz. A group of 600 Soviet prisoners of war was put in a hermetically sealed cell into which crystals of ZYKLON B gas were thrown; all the prisoners were soon dead of asphyxiation. Following this successful experiment, and others, in Auschwitz and elsewhere, the SS authorities in charge of the "Final Solution" planned to construct extermination camps that would use gas for the murder operations.

Thus, instead of killing the Jews where they lived throughout Europe, the Germans decided to bring them to extermination camps, all in occupied Poland: Auschwitz-Birkenau (Auschwitz II), CHEŁMNO, BEŁŻEC, SOBIBÓR, and TREBLINKA. Auschwitz-Birkenau was also a concentration camp; here, in some cases, *Selektionen* were made among the incoming transports, with some of the arrivals "selected" for work or for onward dispatch to other camps. Some scholars classify the MAJDANEK concentration camp as an extermination camp because there was a period when transports arriving there were handled as they were in Auschwitz, and murdered by gassing. The first extermination camp, at Chełmno, in the Łódź district, was put into

EXTERMINATION CAMPS

- Zbąszyń
- 6
- Chełmno ⊠
- Łódź •
- Treblinka ⊠
- Warsaw •
- Sobibór ⊠
- Radom •
- Lublin •
- Majdanek ⊠ ■
- 4
- ⊠ ■ Gross-Rosen
- Kielce •
- 9
- 5
- Bełżec ⊠
- 3
- Oświęcim ⊠ ■
- (Auschwitz-Birkenau)
- Kraków •
- ■ Płaszów • Tarnów

Administrative Divisions of Poland
under German Occupation, 1939–1945

1 Pomerania
2 Brandenburg
3 Saxony
4 Lower Silesia
5 Upper Silesia
6 Warthegau
7 Danzig (West Prussia)
8 East Prussia
9 Generalgouvernement
10 Białystok Region

■ Camp

⊠ Extermination Center

© Polish National Publishing House (Państwowe Wydawnictwo Naukowe) Warsaw, 1979

operation on December 8, 1941. In that camp the victims were killed in GAS VANS; the operation functioned uninterruptedly until April 1943, was then closed for over a year, and reopened for a short while in the summer of 1944. Some 320,000 people are estimated to have been murdered there.

Auschwitz-Birkenau began operating as an extermination camp in March 1942. At its height, it had four gas chambers using Zyklon B, as well as crematoria. Until it was closed in November 1944, up to 1.5 million Jews were murdered there, as were tens of thousands of GYPSIES and Soviet prisoners of war.

Bełżec, Sobibór, and Treblinka were established in the framework of AKTION REINHARD, the murder operation aimed at the Jews of the GENERALGOUVERNEMENT, in Poland. These extermination camps used carbon monoxide gas generated by a gasoline or diesel engine. Bełżec was in operation from March to December 1942, and some 600,000 Jews were murdered there; Sobibór, from April 1942 to October 1943, with 250,000 murdered; and

Treblinka, from July 1942 to August 1943, with 870,000 victims.

The existence of the extermination camps and their operations were classified as top secret in the Third Reich, with the SS coordinating an elaborate system of diversion and deception around them. The camps were concealed, first of all, from the prospective victims, but also from the local population and from German authorities not directly involved in the "Final Solution." From the outside the sites had the appearance of labor or concentration camps, and the gas chambers looked as though they contained showers and disinfection rooms. The Jews who were to be sent to the camps were told that they were going to labor camps somewhere in the east; when they arrived at their destination, they were informed that they had come to a transit camp or labor camp, and that they were to take a shower while their clothes were disinfected. As a further means of hiding the truth, the women and children were separated from the men. The actual murder operation lasted fifteen to thirty minutes. The bodies of the victims were removed from the gas chambers by crews of Jewish prisoners and cremated.

There were audacious attempts by Jews to escape from the extermination camps. Most of these ended in failure, but a few succeeded, and the survivors revealed the truth about the camps to the outside world. Uprisings took place in Treblinka on August 2, 1943, and in Sobibór on October 14 of that year; in each instance, hundreds of prisoners fled the camps. On October 7, 1944, Jews of the Auschwitz-Birkenau SONDERKOMMANDO, who worked in the gas chambers and crematoria, revolted. The majority of those who escaped during these outbreaks were captured and killed.

The extermination camps were under the jurisdiction and administration of the SS. Auschwitz-Birkenau was attached to the WIRTSCHAFTS-VERWALTUNGSHAUPTAMT (Economic-Administrative Main Office; WVHA), which controlled most of the concentration camps in the Third Reich. The other extermination camps were administered by the SS chiefs in their respective districts: Bełżec, Sobibór, and Treblinka came under the SS and Police Leader (*SS- und Polizeiführer*; SSPF) of the Lublin district, and Chełmno

under the SSPF of the WARTHEGAU. Command, administration, and guard duties within the camps were in the hands of the SS (in Bełżec, Sobibór, and Treblinka, the guard unit was made up of Ukrainian volunteers, most of them Soviet prisoners of war). Manual labor in the camps, which included the removal of corpses from the gas chambers and their interment or cremation, was carried out by Jews selected from among the arrivals to the camps.

A total of some 3.5 million Jews were murdered in the extermination camps, as well as tens of thousands of Gypsies and Soviet prisoners of war.

[*See also* Genocide.]

BIBLIOGRAPHY

Arad, Y. *Belzec, Sobibor, Treblinka: Operation Reinhard Death Camps.* Bloomington, 1987.

Arad, Y. *Treblinka: Hell and Revolt.* Tel Aviv, 1983. (In Hebrew.)

Broad, P. *KZ Auschwitz: Reminiscences of Perry Broad, SS-Man in the Auschwitz Concentration Camp.* Oświęcim, Poland, 1965.

Feig, K. *Hitler's Death Camps.* New York, 1981.

Gutman, Y., and A. Saf, eds. *The Nazi Concentration Camps: Structure and Aims; The Image of the Prisoner; The Jews in the Camps.* Proceedings of the Fourth Yad Vashem International Historical Conference. Jerusalem, 1984.

Kraus, O., and E. Kulka. *The Mills of Death: Auschwitz.* Jerusalem, 1961. (In Hebrew.)

YITZHAK ARAD

EXTRADITION OF WAR CRIMINALS. In the Moscow Declaration of November 1, 1943, the three principal powers in the anti-Nazi alliance—the United States, the USSR, and Great Britain—solemnly committed themselves to bring to trial those major war criminals whose crimes were not confined to any particular geographical location. Such trials were to be conducted within a framework that the three powers would agree upon. It was under this commitment that the Nuremberg and Tokyo International Military Tribunals were set up (*see* NUREMBERG TRIAL).

The declarations issued by the three major powers and their allies stated that each member of the alliance would try the war criminals who had committed crimes on that member's territory or against its nationals. It was further agreed, especially in the 1945 Potsdam Agreement, that war criminals would also be tried by tribunals that the major powers would establish in Germany, in their respective zones of occupation.

Like arrangements made to facilitate the extradition of Nazi war criminals in cases where a country had a particular interest in holding the trial, such declarations established the principle of universality of punishment applied to war criminals. This was the same principle applying to piracy on the high seas and other grave crimes and obliging every country that holds a person wanted for such crimes either to try or to extradite that person.

It follows from this that in the case of the trial and punishment of Nazi war criminals the rule that extradition depends on the existence of an extradition agreement between the two countries concerned does not apply. In practice, the principle of the universality of punishment of war criminals was recognized and enforced only before the cold war; specifically, until March 31, 1948, when the UNITED NATIONS WAR CRIMES COMMISSION ceased operating.

For political motives (especially their desire to exploit the information possessed by some Nazi war criminals for intelligence purposes or their expertise for military research projects), the Western powers stopped complying with the rules established by the United Nations War Crimes Commission. Under these rules, every person whose name appeared in the United Nations Commission's lists of war criminals had to be put on trial or extradited. The Soviet Union similarly ceased prosecuting Nazi war criminals, and failed to respond to Western requests for their extradition.

The result was that a large number of Nazi criminals escaped without being tried or extradited. They included Dr. Josef MENGELE, Klaus Barbie (*see* BARBIE TRIAL), and Alois BRUNNER. The Polish War Crimes Commission, which was attached to the United States military headquarters in the American zone of occupation in Germany, discovered Mengele in a prisoner-of-war camp and requested his extradition to Poland. Holocaust-survivor

organizations in Germany, as well as other Jewish and non-Jewish bodies, urged speedy compliance with the request made by Col. Marian Mushkat, the head of the Polish War Crimes Commission, for Mengele's extradition. Their efforts, however, were in vain; the Nazi criminal disappeared, and, as was subsequently discovered, was even helped to escape to South America.

At about the same time, a French commission located Klaus Barbie in an American camp for prisoners of war. Its request to extradite Barbie to France was denied, and it was only years later that he was found to be living in Bolivia. After extended negotiations with the Bolivian government, Barbie was extradited to France in February 1983.

Alois Brunner has been in Damascus since 1954, and arrest warrants have been issued by France, Austria, and the Federal Republic of Germany. A request to the Syrian authorities for extradition, made by West Germany in 1984, has so far brought no response.

[*See also* Wiesenthal, Simon.]

BIBLIOGRAPHY

Mushkat, M. "The Mengele File." *International Problems* 45 (1985): 25–31. (In Hebrew.)

Robinson, J. *And the Crooked Shall Be Made Straight*. Philadelphia, 1965. See chapter 2.

Ruzie, D. "The Klaus Barbie Case: War Crimes versus Crimes against Humanity." *Patterns of Prejudice* 20/3 (July 1986): 27–33.

MARIAN MUSHKAT

EYNIKEYT (Unity), Yiddish-language newspaper of the JEWISH ANTIFASCIST COMMITTEE that appeared from 1942 to 1948. The committee, which was organized by the Soviet government, was made up of Jewish representative figures and intellectuals in the USSR; its purpose was to gain world Jewry's support for the Soviet Union and Soviet policy. *Eynikeyt* first came out in Kuibyshev, where government offices had been relocated when the German siege of Moscow began, in October 1941, and it was later published in Moscow. Originally, it came out once every ten days. The first editor was Shakhno Epshtein, the committee's secretary; after his death, in 1945, he was replaced by G. Zhits. *Eynikeyt* was directed primarily at Yiddish-reading Jews in the United States and other countries, and it was also read by Jews in the Soviet Union, at home and at the war front. At its height, it was printed in ten thousand copies, and as of July 1943 it was appearing weekly. Both during and after the war, *Eynikeyt* published news reports and articles on Jewish subjects, such as the Nazi killings of Jews, Jews and their distinguished service in the Red Army and the partisan movement, and attempts at revolt in the ghettos—all topics that were barely mentioned in the regular Soviet press.

There is evidence that *Eynikeyt* created a great deal of interest among Soviet Jews; in a single year, five thousand letters to the editor were received. The paper had correspondents in the centers of Jewish population in the Soviet Union, as well as on the various fronts. It took special interest in the western areas of the country when these were liberated, seeking to gather information on the extermination of Jews and on Jewish survivors. In December 1943, the Soviet writer and journalist Vasily Grossman published in *Eynikeyt* an article titled "The Ukraine without Jews."

After the war, *Eynikeyt* reported on attempts at Jewish resettlement in Palestine and on the revival of Jewish culture in the Soviet Union. It appeared three times a week. The Jewish Antifascist Committee made efforts to turn it into a daily and increase its distribution, but these were unsuccessful—in the war years because of the shortage of paper, and after the war as a result of government policy against manifestations of Jewish culture. As of the autumn of 1946, *Eynikeyt* became increasingly critical of Jewish nationalist expressions and Jewish issues. In November 1948, when the Jewish Antifascist Committee was disbanded, *Eynikeyt* ceased publication.

BIBLIOGRAPHY

Redlich, S. *Propaganda and Nationalism in Wartime Russia: The Jewish Antifascist Committee in the USSR, 1941–1948.* Boulder, 1982.

SHIMON REDLICH

F

FAMILY CAMPS IN THE FORESTS, groups of Jews—men, women, and children, and families of various age groups—who took refuge in forests in the Holocaust period, struggling to save their lives. Such camps existed in the forests of eastern Poland, western Belorussia, and the western Ukraine. In size the camps ranged from those consisting of a few families only, to camps in which many hundreds of Jews gathered. As a rule, each camp had a group of armed men who defended the camp and obtained food for its inhabitants. The emergence of family camps coincided with the rise of the Jewish partisan movement (*see* PARTISANS), and indeed the two phenomena were interconnected; in most places in the forests with a concentration of Jewish partisans, a family camp existed. Sometimes partisan units were combined with family camps. The main difference between the two was that whereas the family camp's primary purpose was to save lives, with fighting the enemy secondary, for the partisans the priorities were reversed.

Family camps could exist only in areas with large forests, which in eastern Europe meant mainly Belorussia, Polesye, and northern Volhynia. For this reason most of the camps, and the largest, were situated in the Naliboki Forest of western Belorussia—for example, the camp commanded by Tuvia BIELSKI, with twelve hundred people, and Shalom ZORIN's camp, with eight hundred. A few family camps, with dozens of families each, also existed in Eastern Galicia and the Lublin district. The great majority of the

family-camp population were Jews from towns and villages located in the vicinity who were no strangers to the forest or to the conditions prevailing in it. But Jews from MINSK, VILNA, BARANOVICHI, Sarny, LIDA, and similar places were also to be found in the camps.

Some individual Jewish families appeared in the forests as early as the latter part of

FAMILY CAMPS IN THE FOREST

© Martin Gilbert 1982

467

1941, but most of the family camps were made up of refugees from the Nazi extermination drive that swept western Belorussia and the western Ukraine in the spring and winter of 1942. The flight of Jews into the forest camps kept up until the spring of 1943. Among those who took this route of escape were the survivors of uprisings in various ghettos, such as those of LACHVA, TUCHIN, and NESVIZH, who made their own way to the camps after the fighting was over and the ghetto had been set on fire.

Daily Life. The routine of life in the family camps was determined by the security problem; the need for mobility (that is, for moving quickly to another location when this was necessitated by information received in the camp or when military operations were being carried out by Germans or their collaborators); the search for food; and the difficulties posed by the climate and the general harsh conditions prevailing in the forest. The acquisition of food required military action by armed groups of men belonging to the camp who broke into the villages near the forest and seized foodstuffs by force; in some cases, fights broke out and shots were exchanged with the police and local security men, leading to casualties and loss of life.

For security reasons the camps were situated deep in the forests and in swampy areas. In summer, the people lived in lean-tos made of tree branches; in winter they built wooden huts, embedding them deep in the ground. Whenever there were indications that the existence and location of a camp had been discovered, it would be moved elsewhere. In most cases the local population was hostile to the Jews in the family camps, their age-old antisemitism being reinforced by Nazi propaganda and by the raids made by Jews from the camps on the farmers' food supplies. On occasion, local peasants who had discovered the location of a family camp informed the German military and police of their find and led them to the scene, and as a result many of the camp inhabitants were murdered. But in some places the family camps were given help by the local population. Most of the forests in which the Jewish family camps were situated also contained Soviet partisans, who had to contend with the same enemies as the Jews and also had to get their food from the villages in the area. This created a mixed

Jews in the Tuvia Bielski family camp in the Naliboki Forest (May 1944).

relationship of interdependence and competition between the camps and the partisans, in which the partisans were the predominant factor. As a result, the attitude of the Soviet partisans influenced the fate of the Jews in the family camps and the number of Jews whose lives were saved.

Whenever encouraging reports were received about the family camps and the rescue opportunities they offered, Jews from ghettos still in existence tried to make their way there. In contrast, reports of a hostile attitude displayed by the local population or the partisans, and of the murder of Jews in the forests, had a deterrent effect on people who had been considering the risk of breaking out of the ghetto. Until the end of 1942, Soviet partisans in western Belorussia and the western Ukraine were still in the initial stage of organization. The existing units were relatively small and in some cases had no regular contact with the headquarters of partisan movements operating in the east and in areas closer to the front line. Discipline in such units was poor. These circumstances provided a fertile ground for the emergence of criminal elements in the forests that, under the guise of being partisans, engaged in pillage and murder. Jews in the family camps suffered greatly from attacks by this kind of gang, which robbed them of their clothes, boots, and other belongings, and also murdered them. The situation of the family-camp Jews improved in 1943, during the course of which the Soviet partisan movement was organized and gained in strength. In some places the family camps were incorporated into partisan brigades and had tasks assigned to them—maintenance jobs, tailoring and shoe repairs, arms repairs, and the baking of bread for the fighting units. The large Bielski and Zorin camps were turned into maintenance units serving the partisan brigades deployed in their area.

Persecution. The family camps in the Lublin, Białystok, and Grodno districts were in the most difficult situation. The partisans active in these areas belonged to the Polish ARMIA KRAJOWA (Home Army) or NARODOWE SIŁY ZBROJNE (National Armed Forces). As anti-Soviet groups, they viewed the Jews in the forests as a pro-Soviet element and persecuted them; many Jews fell victim to these Polish partisans. In the western Ukraine, the situation of the Jews was still worse; this was the area in which groups of Ukrainian nationalists (BANDERA men, "Bulbowcy," and others) operated and murdered Jews in the forest camps or on their way there.

Apart from these enemies, the Jews had other dangers to face. Many died from starvation and disease. But the worst threat was the antipartisan raids staged by the Germans. From 1942 to 1944, such German raids took place in nearly every forest in which there were Jewish family camps. When such a raid occurred, thousands of German troops and collaborators would surround the forest to make sure that nobody could escape while other forces were combing the interior. The family camps suffered the most from these raids; their mobility was restricted, they had women and children to take care of, and they had no advance notice that would have enabled them to flee the area before the enemy forces closed in. The only way they could save themselves was by hiding in swampy areas deep in the forest, or in underground bunkers, prepared in advance and well camouflaged.

No exact data or credible estimates are available of the number of Jews who took refuge in the family camps and the number of those who survived. The most that can be said is that the number of Jews who were saved in the family camps did not exceed ten thousand.

BIBLIOGRAPHY

Arad, Y. "Jewish Family Camps in the Forests—An Original Means of Rescue." In *Rescue Attempts during the Holocaust.* Proceedings of the Second Yad Vashem International Historical Conference, edited by Y. Gutman and E. Zuroff, pp. 333–353. Jerusalem, 1977.

Barkai, M., ed. *The Fighting Ghettos.* Philadelphia, 1962.

Bornstein, S. *The Doctor Atlas Brigade: The Story of a Jewish Partisan.* Tel Aviv, 1965. (In Hebrew.)

The Jewish Partisans. Vol. 1. Merhavia, Israel, 1958. (In Hebrew.)

YITZHAK ARAD

FAR EAST. *See under* East Asia.

FAREYNEGTE PARTIZANER ORGANIZA-TSYE (United Partisan Organization; FPO), Jewish anti-German underground organization in the VILNA ghetto. In July 1940, when Lithuania—including Vilna—was occupied by the Soviet Union, the existing Zionist youth organizations had to go underground. When the city was taken by the Germans on June 24, 1941, the Zionist organizations preserved their underground framework. In the first few months of the German occupation, their efforts concentrated mainly on saving their members from the extermination *Aktionen* that were then being conducted in Vilna by the EINSATZGRUPPEN. At that time there was discussion in the Zionist underground groups about whether they should continue their underground activity in the Vilna ghetto, where most of the Jews had been murdered, or move to ghettos in Belorussia or the GENERALGOUVERNEMENT, where at the end of 1941 the Jews were still living in relative quiet. All the movements, except for He-Haluts ha-Tsa'ir–Dror, headed by Mordechai TENENBAUM (Tamaroff), were in favor of remaining.

On New Year's Eve, December 31, 1941, 150 members of the Haluts (Pioneer) youth movements in the ghetto attended a meeting, where for the first time Abba KOVNER's appeal "Not to Go like Sheep to the Slaughter" was read. Kovner declared that all the Jews who were taken from Vilna were murdered at PONARY, and called upon the Jewish youth to organize for armed struggle against the Germans. On January 21, 1942, representatives of the Zionist youth movements—among them Kovner of Ha-Shomer ha-Tsa'ir, Nissan Reznik of Ha-No'ar ha-Tsiyyoni, Josef GLAZMAN of Betar, and Yitzhak WITTENBERG of the Communists—held a meeting at which they decided to establish a united resistance movement, to be called the Fareynegte Partizaner Organizatsye. He-Haluts ha-Tsa'ir–Dror was absent, as was its leader Tenenbaum, who had left Vilna for the Warsaw and Białystok ghettos. Wittenberg was elected the commander of the FPO, with Kovner, Glazman, and Reznik serving on his staff.

The organization's aim was to prepare for armed resistance in the event of the ghetto's being in danger of liquidation, and also to spread the idea of resistance to other ghettos. The BUND, which had not taken part in the founding meeting, joined the FPO in the spring of 1942. Members of He-Haluts ha-Tsa'ir–Dror who had stayed in the ghetto established their own underground group, under the leadership of Yechiel Scheinbaum, calling themselves "Yechiel's Combat Group." The FPO divided itself into underground cells, with five to a cell, based on their places of residence in the ghetto; three such cells made up a platoon and six to eight platoons formed a battalion. The FPO had two battalions, each composed of one hundred to one hundred and twenty fighters. In addition, there were units that were subordinate to headquarters. The FPO headquarters included representatives of all the parties and YOUTH MOVEMENTS that had united to join in underground activities.

The FPO sent emissaries to the Grodno, Białystok, and Warsaw ghettos in order to establish contact with them, propagate the idea of resistance and rebellion, and inform them of the mass extermination of the Jews in Vilna and the rest of Lithuania. Attempts were also made to establish ties with the Polish underground army (ARMIA KRAJOWA) in Vilna, but these efforts failed. There was contact with a small non-Jewish Communist group that was active in Vilna, and the ghetto underground lent its aid to this group. An attempt was also made to send women emissaries through the front lines to the Soviet Union, to tell the world of the mass extermination of the Jews and to appeal for help. These emissaries were stopped by Germans near the front lines, but they managed to escape and make their way back to Vilna.

The FPO's most pressing problem was to obtain arms. Only a few possible sources existed. Weapons could be purchased from the local population, and members of the underground working in the German captured-weapons depot at Borbiszki were able to smuggle out some weapons and give them to the FPO. Primitive hand grenades and Molotov cocktails were manufactured in the ghetto itself. The weapons that the underground managed to acquire consisted primarily of pistols, plus a small number of rifles, hand grenades, and submachine guns; they

Jewish partisans from the Fareynegte Partizaner Organizatsye who left the Vilna ghetto and escaped to the Rudninkai Forest return to Vilna after the liberation in July 1944.

were kept in a cache in the ghetto. At its height, the FPO had some three hundred organized members, and for each a weapon of some sort was available. The FPO carried out acts of sabotage outside the ghetto—such as mining the railway used by trains heading for the front lines, or sabotaging equipment and arms in German plants in which underground members were employed.

The chairman of the Vilna JUDENRAT (Jewish Council), Jacob GENS, knew of the underground's existence and maintained contact with its leaders. In the spring of 1943, when the small ghettos and labor camps in the Vilna area were liquidated, the FPO intensified the smuggling of arms into the ghetto and contacted the partisans active in the forests of western Belorussia. Several groups of young people who were not FPO members headed for the forests, and partisan emissaries came to the ghetto. The Judenrat, warned of these activities by the German authorities, regarded them as endangering the continued existence of the ghetto, and this led to friction between it and the FPO. At the same time, the Communist underground became more active in the city of Vilna, and its ties

with the FPO grew stronger; the FPO commander, Wittenberg, was also a member of the Vilna Communist underground committee.

Acting on information that was passed on to them, the Germans arrested the members of the Vilna Communist underground committee and demanded from Gens that Wittenberg be handed over to them; otherwise the ghetto and its entire population would be liquidated. On July 15, 1943, Gens invited the FPO command to his house and arrested Wittenberg on the spot. As German security police were leading Wittenberg to the ghetto gate, they were attacked by FPO members, and Wittenberg was set free. The FPO mobilized its members and took up positions in several of the ghetto houses. On the following day there was a confrontation between the FPO and the ghetto police, in which many of the ghetto inhabitants sided with the latter and demanded that Wittenberg be handed over, in order to save the ghetto from the Germans. To avoid a bloody battle among the Jews, Wittenberg gave himself up to the Germans, and that same night he committed suicide. Abba Kovner was elected to take his place as the FPO commander. For the FPO the affair served as a warning, and it decided to establish a partisan base in the forest that would be available as a place of refuge for FPO members should the need arise.

On July 24, 1943, a group of FPO men, headed by Glazman, left the ghetto for the Naroch Forest. On September 1, when the Germans launched the deportation *Aktion* to Estonia, which was a step in the ghetto's liquidation, the FPO mobilized its members, took up positions in one section of the ghetto, and called on the Jews not to report for deportation and to rebel. The ghetto inhabitants did not respond to the call, believing that this time they were being sent away for work elsewhere and that they were not destined for extermination. On the evening of that day there was an armed clash between underground members and the German forces combing the ghetto; in the clash, Yechiel Scheinbaum, who was cooperating with the FPO at the time, was killed. When darkness fell, the Germans left the ghetto and did not return to it for the duration of the *Aktion*, which lasted until September 4. Gens, the Judenrat chairman, had promised to provide the Germans with the required quota for Estonia. In the wake of the *Aktion*, the FPO gave up the idea of an uprising, since the ghetto inhabitants had not heeded its call, and began moving its members out, to the Naroch and Rudninkai forests.

On the day the ghetto was liquidated, September 23, 1943, the last group of FPO members, numbering eighty to one hundred persons and headed by Abba Kovner, left the ghetto by way of the city sewers and made their way to the Rudninkai Forest. Most of the five hundred to seven hundred FPO members escaped to the forests and joined the PARTISANS, forming themselves into Jewish battalions as part of the Soviet partisan movement. Altogether, about six hundred to seven hundred young people left the Vilna ghetto for the forests and joined the partisans. Some of the Jewish units, however, were disbanded and their members absorbed, and others were joined by non-Jewish partisans, in line with Soviet partisan headquarters policy, which opposed the existence of separate Jewish units. Partisans from the Vilna ghetto fought in the forests until the Soviet army reached them, and they took part in the liberation of Vilna, on July 13, 1944.

BIBLIOGRAPHY

Arad, Y. *Ghetto in Flames: The Struggle and Destruction of the Jews of Vilna in the Holocaust.* Jerusalem, 1980.
Dworzecki, M. *Jerusalem of Lithuania in Revolt and Holocaust.* Tel Aviv, 1951. (In Hebrew.)
Korchak, R. *Flames in Ash.* Merhavia, Israel, 1946. (In Hebrew.)

YITZHAK ARAD

FASCISM, an intellectual, cultural, and political phenomenon in twentieth-century Europe. Fascism, in form and ideology, ruled ITALY in the period from 1922 to 1945, but in its broad sense the term came to be applied to similar regimes and ideologies in other countries.

Fascism has its roots primarily in the twentieth century. Its emergence was an expression of the accelerated modernization processes that the European continent experienced in the final few years of the nineteenth century and of the social changes and the intellectual revolution that occurred in the Western world at that juncture. Fascism, as an ideology and a mass movement, was not a regrettable accident that Europe encountered in the preceding generation; it was an organic part of Europe's culture, its social fabric, and its intellectual and political patterns of development.

The form in which fascism crystallized in the quarter of a century preceding World War I, and developed further in the interwar period, represents a synthesis of organic nationalism and anti-Marxist socialism, a revolutionary ideology whose principal elements are the repudiation of liberalism and Marxism, as well as democracy. In its essence, fascist ideology is the negation of materialism, and it considers liberalism, Marxism, and democracy to be nothing but different aspects of that "materialist" malady. On the basis of that repudiation of materialism, fascism pretends to have produced a total spiritual revolution. Fascist activism, which prides itself on its elitism, calls for absolute political rule, unfettered by the principles of democracy. The state is the expression of national unity and represents society with all its classes. Planning, a directed economy, and corporatism are the main elements of fascism, the concrete expressions of the victory of politics over economics, and, in the final analysis, represent the transfer to central control of society and the economy to the state. As an ideology of outright disassociation and rebellion, fascism rejects the political culture rooted in the eighteenth century and the French Revolution; it seeks to create a new community-based and anti-individualist civilization which, in the opinion of its followers, is the only kind of civilization that can assure the continued existence of human society. All sectors and classes of the population will find their place in this society, which is the natural framework of a harmonious and organic community, a nation that has been purified and strengthened and revitalized, and in which the individual is no more than a cell in the collective entity.

As an ideology that rejects rationalism, individualism, and the materialist and utilitarian concepts of society and state, fascism refuses to regard social organization as an artificial construction, the work of human beings who maintain frameworks of cooperation for the sole purpose of serving the interests of the individual. It totally negates the theory of "natural rights" and the individualist and mechanist views of society. In the fascist view, man is not a creature that takes precedence over society, a creature with rights of its own as a rational and moral being, or as a being created in the image of God; on the contrary, man is a social being, an integral part of an organic entity, which owes its very existence to the social entity. This is why fascism opposed the ideologies of liberalism and Marxism, which were prevalent in Western society around 1900. Liberalism and Marxism have a common root: they are both comprehensive systems based on nineteenth-century rationalism, which regards man as taking precedence over society. In both the liberal and Marxist views, society's sole purpose is to serve the needs of man, although the two systems differ over

the methods by which this purpose is to be achieved. For the fascist ideologists, both those from the beginning of the twentieth century and those of the 1930s, liberalism and Marxism are ideologies of social warfare. Both systems destroy the organic unity of the nation and undermine the foundations of tribal solidarity, without which no historical-cultural and biological entity is capable of waging the struggle for survival. Fascism's proclaimed purpose is to restore society's solidarity and unity.

Notwithstanding its origin as a repudiation of liberalism and Marxism, fascism arose out of a profound awareness of the social problem. The nation will not become a unit so long as the proletariat is not absorbed into it as an integral part, so long as the incessant struggle among economic, social, and political forces continues and no way is found to harness them all to a joint effort for the general good. Ever since the last decade of the nineteenth century, fascism has claimed that it represents a new type of social radicalism and socialism, a national socialism that is non-Marxist, anti-Marxist, and, in many respects, post-Marxist.

Fascism, however, is not only a political movement; it is also a cultural phenomenon, with its roots in the technological and intellectual revolution of the end of the nineteenth and the beginning of the twentieth century. Accelerated economic growth and technological progress brought in their wake tremendous changes in the pace and way of life and the standard of living. Antirational values and a cult of the emotions, the inner drives, and spontaneity became the fashion of the times. The rational and "mechanist" view of the world, a trend prominent in western European thought since the seventeenth century, was replaced by the "organic" view. The emphasis was now on a variety of historical values and idealistic directions, a trend that tended to undermine the adherence to rationalism and individualism. There was a growing belief in the individual's subordination to society and to the judgment of history. Thus, in the eyes of intellectuals of the 1890 generation such as Gustave Le Bon, Maurice Barrès, Georges Sorel, and Georges Vacher de Lapouge, society was not simply the arithmetical sum of individuals, driven by the liberal society's intellectual individualism and the "utilitarianism and materialism" by which it was ruled. The more profound fascist intellectuals of the interwar period considered these attitudes, which came to the fore as early as the first decade of the twentieth century, to have been the roots of fascism, with Giovanni Gentile, the leading philosopher of Italian Fascism, defining fascism as a revolt against positivism.

This new world view led to glorification of the nation, and to the emergence of nationalism as a political system based on an array of filter devices and defense mechanisms whose purpose was to safeguard the integrity of the "tribe." An ideological movement came into being that shook up not only the entire set of values bequeathed by the eighteenth century and the French Revolution, but also the Christian concept of morality. As Vacher de Lapouge put it, "A morality that believes in natural selection puts the obligation to the race in the highest place—the place in which Christianity puts obedience to God."

Here it is important to stress one element that is significant for the understanding of later developments. The reaction against rationalism in the form of democracy and Marxism was not just the result of literary neoromanticism or a new fashion in art; it was science that led the great attack on democracy and Marxism. This is the real meaning of the intellectual revolution of the end of the nineteenth and the beginning of the twentieth century. The new life sciences and social sciences—Darwinian biology (in its popular interpretation); history as taught by Heinrich von Treitschke, Ernest Renan, and Hippolyte Taine; social psychology according to Le Bon; and the Italian school of political sociology (Wilfredo Pareto, Gaetano Mosca, Robert Michels)—all rose up against the basic assumptions of liberalism and democracy. On the basis of the new social sciences (especially social anthropology and psychology), which adopted many aspects of Social Darwinism, a new theory of political behavior came into being. Thus it was that the new branches of science contributed to the rise of an intellectual climate which undermined the very foundations of democracy and in large measure facilitated the emergence and spread of fascism.

It is the rational explanation of the irrational, as contained in the elitist theory, that provides the link between the social sciences' rules and fascism's practice. This explanation, as put forth by the Italian school of political sociology, played a role in the rise of revolutionary syndicalism, but it also contributed to the rise of nationalism as a political ideology, and in many ways represents the point at which the two movements meet.

It thus happened, at the beginning of the twentieth century, that the new social sciences—primarily psychology and anthropology, which also fed sociology, political science, and the new studies of history—provided the conceptual framework for the antiliberal reaction. These sciences also enabled contributions from theorists of the 1850 generation—Charles Darwin, Joseph-Arthur de Gobineau, and Richard Wagner—to fuse with contributions of the 1890 generation. The ancient romantic element, the old trends of historicity, the theory of the origin of the nation in antiquity, the search for the vital forces that are "the soul of the people" —all of these were now endowed with the sanction of science. The idea that emotions and the subconscious were more important in politics than reason became increasingly accepted, leading as a logical conclusion to the growing disdain for democracy and for its institutions and agencies.

Biological and psychological determinism, which represent the core of the writings of Le Bon, Vacher de Lapouge, Edouard-Adolf Drumont, and even Hippolyte Taine, and which filled the pages of countless publications in every field of intellectual endeavor, in the end became the source from which the theory of racism was nourished. This is the background against which the new nationalism arose and was consolidated at the end of the nineteenth century, a nationalism that did not change up until World War II. Tribal nationalism, based on biological determinism and Social Darwinism—the nationalism of blood and soil—was not a German invention, nor was it confined to Germany. It flourished in France at the turn of the century, and in many respects it was France that served as the real ideological laboratory of fascism in those years. In Italy the growth of fascist ideology lagged behind that of France by fifteen to twenty years, and it was only at the end of the first decade of the new century that the gap was closed.

It was Barrès, one of France's outstanding writers at the beginning of the twentieth century, more than any other European thinker, who reflected the European cultural predicament on the eve of World War I. Barrès was among the first of the philosophers to use the term "national socialism," even before the end of the nineteenth century. This term for a new brand of socialism assumes that the continued existence of the nation depends upon reconciliation between the proletariat and society as a whole. This solution, which Barrès proposed in France, was raised in Italy by Enrico Corradini in the early years of the twentieth century. Corradini's idea was to base intersocial relations in Italy on a kind of family compact among the various sectors. He assigned two goals to national socialism: to make peace between the proletariat and the nation, and to make the Italians conscious of the fact that Italy, in both material and moral terms, was a "proletarian nation." The term was coined by Corradini, and it meant that the whole nation had to prepare for the struggle for existence—the natural state for the ongoing struggle among the nations.

The other basic element of fascism is the revision of Marxism. The challenge to the Hegelian, rational content of Marxism is identified with Georges Sorel and the Italian revolutionary syndicalists. "Sorelianism" did in fact blaze a new path of revolution. Contrary to Leninism, which has as its aim a revolution by and for the proletariat—albeit sponsored by an elite vanguard—Sorelianism lays the foundations of a revolution for and on behalf of society as a whole, including all its sectors and classes. Contrary to the French and Bolshevik revolutions, which, in different degrees of extremism, changed the social order, the new Sorelian revolution was to be a political, national, cultural, psychological, and moral revolution. Such a revolution becomes feasible when psychology takes the place of the rationalist and Hegelian elements of Marxism. This new socialism—vitalist and voluntarist in nature—represents a philosophy of action, based on intuition and the cult of energy, violence, and the myth of violence. Violence, in Sorel's view, is a permanent value and the wellspring of morality. Sorelian socialism sought to destroy Western culture—that materialist, individualist, and humanist culture; he rejected Cartesian rationalism, the theory of "natural rights," Immanuel Kant, and Jean-Jacques Rousseau.

That was the basis on which the fascist synthesis was created, a synthesis of tribal nationalism and a new kind of socialism that was revolutionary, antibourgeois, and anti-Marxist in character. This socialism replaced class as the subject of the revolution, and despised democracy, parliaments, political parties, and pressure groups. It regarded the rules of the game as practiced in a democracy as the source of corruption, decadence, and moral decay. Such a synthesis, which emerged in France and Italy, was unrelated to the events that took place in Europe beginning in the summer of 1914. It was around 1910 that the theoreticians of revolutionary syndicalism met the theoreticians of integral nationalism, a meeting that found its expression in publications such as *La Lupa* in Italy and *Cahiers du Cercle Proudhon* in France. In France the development had taken place earlier, but Italy caught up in the immediate prewar period. The disciples of Sorel and Charles Maurras in France, and the followers of Corradini and the revolutionary syndicalists (Arturo Labriola, Robert Michels, Sergio Panunzio, Paolo Orano, and Angelo Oliviero Olivetti), developed the socialist-nationalist synthesis into a genuine political force. During the war itself, revolutionary syndicalism turned into national syndicalism and fascism.

At this time the nonconformists of the Left were joined by one of their old followers, Benito MUSSOLINI. Mussolini had ties to revolutionary syndicalism as early as 1902, when he was a contributor to *Avanguardia Socialista*, Arturo Labriola's publication. Although Mussolini was not a revolutionary syndicalist in the precise sense of the term, intellectually and emotionally he did belong to that movement. Between 1909 and 1914 he and his revolutionary syndicalist mentors parted ways, in political terms, but the differences between them were tactical and temporary rather than substantive and basic. From the beginning of his political career up to the consolidation of the Fascist movement, Mussolini adhered to the basic principles of revolutionary syndicalism and took an active part in the process that led it to national syndicalism and from there to Fascism. As indicated, in taking this course Mussolini was preceded by the revolutionary syndicalists, and it was they who made the breakthrough to the Fascist synthesis. Mussolini followed them when he joined the camp that supported Italy's entry into the war in the fall of 1914, putting an end to their differences (in 1911, he had opposed the war with the Ottoman empire over Libya). In Mussolini's eyes World War I was conclusive proof that the revolutionary syndicalists were right. It demonstrated the sweeping power of nationalism and provided the opportunity to put into practice a heroic, vitalist socialism, the foe of bourgeois values. Once Mussolini and his erstwhile intellectual mentors were reunited, the emerging ideology of Fascism had found its leader, and the war provided the cadres and created the social and psychological conditions for its practical application.

The basic principles of that ideology, which had been established prior to August 1914, reemerged in the 1920s and 1930s, having in the meantime been steeled in the crucible of World War I. It was not the war, however, which produced fascism; it was the modernization of Europe that brought it about. But for that generation, the war provided the laboratory tests that proved the theses propounded by Le Bon, Michels, Pareto, and Sorel: the masses are conservative, they long for authority, and they behave irrationally; democracy is a luxury suitable for an era of peace and prosperity, and its restrictions can easily be dispensed with, even in countries that have a tradition of political freedom. Most importantly, the war revealed two facts of overriding significance: (1) it provided the definitive answer to the great question of modern history and proved that in industrialized countries nationalism—a sweeping force and the focus of solidarity—has absolute superiority over class; and (2) it revealed the immense power of the modern state.

World War I opened up new vistas for the functions of the state, for the controls that it could exercise, and for its driving power. It proved that the state was able to control the economy, the means of production, and labor relations, and that it was capable of dictating the basic elements of economic planning and mobilizing all sections of society for a concentrated national effort. The war also revealed the great extent to which people were prepared to accept state authority, to forego their freedoms, to accept what was in effect a dictatorship, and as far as the majority of the population was concerned, even to sacrifice their lives, on a scale that could not have been imagined. In other words, total war demonstrated that the national state was able to control the individual in every domain of his life, and that totalitarianism—whose initial ideological features had been outlined by theorists of the 1890 and 1910 generations—could really exist. Italy's revolutionary syndicalists were not the only ones to learn the lesson, but they were the first to have the opportunity to translate that lesson into terms of political victory and the seizure of power—an opportunity given to them by the social and political circumstances prevailing in their country at that time.

Fascism was a phenomenon that was to be found throughout Europe, although it differed from place to place, depending on the different cultural, social, and political circumstances. However, even the vast differences between the industrial centers of northern and central Europe and the peripheral areas of southern and eastern Europe could not obscure the common denominator of fascism in all these countries. The basic principles of fascism in Italy, France, Britain, Belgium, Spain, and Romania were identical. In France the term "fascist" applied to Georges Valois, who in 1925 founded the first fascist movement outside Italy; Marcel Déat and Gustave Hervé, who had come from socialism; Jacques Doriot, an erstwhile Communist; Bertrand Jouvenel, a former liberal; and the former right-wing nationalists Pierre Drieu La Rochelle and Robert Brasillach. In Italy it was true of the Hegelian philosopher Giovanni Gentile, the famous jurist Alfredo Rocco, the nationalist ideologue Corradini, and the revolutionary syndicalists Panunzio, Olivetti, Michels, Agostino Lanzillo, Paolo Mantica, Micele Bianchi, Edmondo Rossoni, Umberto Pasella, and Ottavio Dinale. In Britain it applied to Oswald MOSLEY; in Spain to José Antonio Primo de Rivera; in Belgium to Léon Degrelle; and in Romania to Corneliu Zelea Codreanu. All of these men entered upon the same struggle against the same divisive elements, on behalf of the same organic unity of the nation.

Fascism came up with two instruments of its own in order to maintain "the unity of the nation"—corporatism and the totalitarian state. Corporatism is fascism's original contribution to the emergence of a "third way," a way that is neither liberalism nor Marxism, and it symbolizes the fascists' belief in the power of politics to dominate market forces and class interests. The corporatist system is designed to enable the authoritarian state to plan the economy and settle labor relations and the differences between social classes. Once political and personal rights and freedoms are abolished, the workers' right to organize is also canceled. Corporatism puts an end to the legitimacy of special interests and subordinates the social and economic system to the state; it represents the real basis on which the totalitarian state rests.

As a historical phenomenon, fascism exists on three levels—as an ideology, a movement, and a form of government. Before fascism came to power anywhere (which it eventually did only in Italy, and for a short while during World War II in Romania), the corporate state served as the model of a solution that would enable all sectors of society to be mobilized by the state, in the service of the nation. But as soon as this ideology was applied, the result, in concrete terms, was that the class interests of the proletariat were set aside for the sake of the interests of the bourgeoisie, these latter being regarded as identical with the national interest. This had not been the goal of revolutionary-syndicalist ideology, the original backbone of fascism, but this was the result, in practice, of subordinating social relations in the authoritarian regime by means of the corporatist system.

The authoritarian state seeks to control every sphere of life—politics, the economy, society, and culture. It does away with all institutions or organizations that express a pluralism of ideas and beliefs—parliaments, political parties, a free press, and a choice of educational opportunities. It demands not only discipline but also identification and unconditional readiness for sacrifice.

Indeed, totalitarianism is the cornerstone of the fascist revolution's ideology. For Gentile, Mussolini, and Primo de Rivera the totalitarian state signifies the beginning of a new era, an era in which the commonwealth has absolute priority over the individual. The individual exists only to perform his duty and is only a means to an end—the state's achievement of the goals it sets itself. This means the end of liberal culture. It follows that the fascist revolution is a total revolution, a moral and spiritual revolution, which creates a new order for all sectors of society.

Mussolini, in his definitive work on fascism, *The Fascist Doctrine* (on which he collaborated with Gentile), leaves no doubt that the state embraces all spheres of human activity, organizes them, and determines what their content should be; there is no aspect of society's life that is not political, and there is therefore none that may be excluded from the state's grip.

In this sense, fascist ideology was truly revolutionary. It was unwavering in its resolve to dissociate itself from the established order, and it provided a complete alternative answer, in the political as well as the moral and aesthetic spheres. Fascism's idealism and appeal to the emotions provided the instruments for a total revolution, the sole revolution that was devoid of any elements of a class war. This revolution of the spirit, the will, and the instincts has a unity of purpose: to create a new man, inextricably tied to the nation and promoting the values of violence, heroism, and sacrifice. Such a cult of unity, altruism, and youth had a tremendous appeal in those days all over Europe, among young people who had only contempt for the bourgeois world of their parents. This was the great secret of the attraction—overt or covert—that fascism exerted for large sections of the young generation in the interwar period. In fact, the influence of fascist ideology went far beyond the hard core of its founders and devoted followers. Much wider circles, to one degree or another, were drawn to its promise of a violent rebellion of spiritual forces and basic instincts, of primitive and unrestrained reaction against the routine and conventional essence of bourgeois civilization. Even more widespread was the contempt for the clash of interests, the compromises, the give-and-take of liberal democracy. For many, dictatorship was a more natural form of government than one based on a social compact.

Although the fascist revolution was put into power in one country only, its impact was felt all over Europe. Like any other ideology, fascism ran into a constant struggle with reality. It soon turned out that it was extremely difficult to overcome social and economic interests and the influence of the traditional centers of power—the monarchy, the church, and high finance. Like every other movement, fascism was also forced into various compromises, which saved Italy from becoming an entirely totalitarian state. Nevertheless, in the case of Italian Fascism, the correlation between ideology and practice was very high. No one can claim that Stalinist terror was the fulfillment of Marxism, or that the social reforms introduced by Léon Blum were the realization of socialism, but fascism's practice was a direct projection of its ideology. The development of Italy into a totalitarian state, although never fully implemented, was based on the inner logic of the fascist ideology, and there was nothing improvised about it. The abolition of parliamentary and democratic institutions, along with fascist violence, political murder, and the physical or political liquidation of the opposition, were all expressions of the fascist system's essential character. The mobilization of the masses—the marches, the mass rallies, the militias, and the uniformed youth movements—was an effective translation into practice of the theories of the nature of man as they had been taught by some of Europe's greatest scientists. Thus a new political culture was born, in which the state took precedence over the individual and could demand of the individual whatever sacrifice it wanted. Such a political culture rejects the power of reason to conduct the life of society and transfers the emphasis to the sphere of the emotions and instincts.

This political culture spread all over Europe, and in the depressed conditions that prevailed in the 1920s and the 1930s it gathered destructive force, on an unprecedented scale. No society was invulnerable to it, and the inroads it made were not a function of social class, educational level, age, religion, or origin. Everywhere, in all sectors of society and in all religious groupings, people were to be found who were ready to accept fascism as a legitimate and original third way, with a stature equal to that of Marxism and liberalism.

ANTISEMITISM was not an integral and essential element of fascist ideology. This was the great difference between fascism and Nazism. Nazi ideology was based on the doctrine of biological determinism, in which antisemitism was a central, indispensable pillar. In fascism, on the other hand, antisemitism differed from place to place and from one trend to another. In principle, fascism was receptive to antisemitism or to creating its own version, based on its own component of integral nationalism. Organic nationalism, the nationalism of blood and soil, was by far the most fertile ground for antisemitism. In fascism, the extent of the antisemitic dimension was determined by the pervasiveness of the racist element within the nationalist ideology, but even there the versions differed greatly. Italian Fascism, in its early period, was generally free of antisemitism, which developed in its later stages, gradually and often as a result of external events. The 1938 Italian racist legislation resulted from the growth of extremist nationalist trends in Italian Fascism and the eradication of the original element of revolutionary syndicalism, as well as from Italy's rapprochement with Nazi Germany.

In France there were fascist groups (for example, ACTION FRANÇAISE) whose ideology differed only slightly from that of Nazism, and others that were practically untouched by antisemitism. As World War II approached, however, the antisemitic dimension in French fascism increased in strength, and by October 1940 the Vichy government, which was not formally a fascist government, introduced racist laws closely resembling the NUREMBERG LAWS. British fascism was extremely antisemitic, as was fascism in Belgium, Romania, and Hungary. Spanish fascism, in contrast, was free of antisemitism. In Italy, despite the official anti-Jewish policy that prevailed following the introduction of the racist legislation, and despite manifestations of antisemitism in the Fascist party, the persecution and hatred of Jews never came close to that in central and eastern Europe.

[*See also* Great Britain: Fascism in Great Britain; Racism; Spain: Spanish Fascism and the Jews.]

BIBLIOGRAPHY

Gregor, A. J. *Young Mussolini and the Intellectual Origins of Fascism.* Berkeley, 1979.

Hamilton, A. *The Appeal of Fascism: A Study of Intellectuals and Fascism, 1919–1945.* New York, 1971.

Laqueur, W., ed. *Fascism: A Reader's Guide; Analyses, Interpretations, Bibliography.* London, 1979.

Larsen, S. U., et al., eds. *Who Were the Fascists? Social Roots of European Fascism.* Oslo, 1980.

Mosse, G. L. *Masses and Man.* New York, 1980.

Mussolini, B. *Fascism: Doctrine and Institutions.* New York, 1968.

Nolte, E. *Three Faces of Fascism: Action Française, Italian Fascism, National Socialism.* New York, 1969.

Payne, S. G. *Fascism: Comparison and Definition.* Madison, Wis., 1980.

Turner, H. A., Jr., ed. *Reappraisals of Fascism.* New York, 1975.

Weber, E. *Varieties of Fascism.* New York, 1966.

ZEEV STERNHELL

FÉDÉRATION DES SOCIÉTÉS JUIVES DE FRANCE (Federation of French Jewish Organizations; FSJF),

umbrella organization of *Landsmannschaften* (fraternal lodges made up of Jewish immigrants in FRANCE from eastern and central Europe on the basis of common geographical origin—the same town, city, or region), established in 1913. In the late 1930s the FSJF was chaired by Marc JARBLUM, a Socialist Zionist leader. At the time it consisted of over two hundred societies and, for the first time in its history, lent its support to the Zionist movement. The very existence of the FSJF, and its comparative strength, reflected the problems affecting the relations between Jewish immigrants in France and the native-born Jews. The umbrella organization of the latter was the CONSISTOIRE CENTRAL DES ISRAÉLITES DE FRANCE (Central Consistory of French Jews), for which being Jewish was based exclusively on religious affiliation, and which did not take kindly to the existence of *Landsmannschaften*. For this reason, the immigrant activists did not find a place for themselves in the long-established Jewish organizations.

Under the Nazi occupation, several FSJF leaders in Paris established a clandestine committee, code-named AMELOT, which set up and ran welfare institutions for needy Jews. The Amelot committee continued to function as an underground organization even when the Gestapo ordered the closing down of all existing Jewish bodies and their replacement by a single central institution, the UNION GÉNÉRALE DES ISRAÉLITES DE FRANCE (General Council of French Jews; UGIF).

The leaders of the FSJF, however, had fled to Vichy-controlled southern France, together with more than half of the Jewish population that had been living in the German-occupied sector. Despite pressure from French authorities and Jewish leaders, Jarblum refused to accept membership in the UGIF, and instead created an underground FSJF committee in many places where Jews lived. These local committees undertook the care of tens of thousands of Jews, and provided them with forged "Aryan" identity papers. Funds that the American Jewish JOINT DISTRIBUTION COMMITTEE (known as the Joint) had previously given to the UGIF were now channeled to the FSJF. At the end of 1942, after the German occupation of Vichy France, the FSJF established an absorption center in the Italian-occupied zone of France, where the Italian authorities protected the Jews from persecution by the Nazis and Vichy officials.

On February 9, 1943, the Gestapo, under the command of Klaus BARBIE, raided the FSJF offices in Lyons, seized eighty-six Jews whom they found there, and deported them to extermination camps. Jarblum himself was not caught, and in the wake of the Gestapo raid he was smuggled into Switzerland. The FSJF, now led by Reuben Grinberg and Leo Glaser, kept up its work. From Geneva, Jarblum passed on instructions to the FSJF, as well as substantial amounts of money that he obtained from the Joint, the WORLD JEWISH CONGRESS, and the Jewish Agency. The FSJF also financed Jewish youth organizations that were smuggling children across the border into Switzerland, and the movement of young fighters to Palestine by way of Spain. In addition, it formed partisan units in several cities and in the Maquis.

The FSJF played the leading role in the establishment of the Comité Général de Défense (Jewish Defense Committee) in August 1943, in which all Jewish underground organizations—including the Jewish Communists—took part; FSJF leader Glaser was appointed its secretary-general.

Many FSJF activists were caught and murdered. This was also Leo Glaser's fate after he was arrested in Lyons, in June 1944.

BIBLIOGRAPHY

L'Activité des organisations juives en France sous l'occupation. Paris, 1947.

Adler, J. The Jews of Paris and the Final Solution: Communal Response and International Conflicts, 1940–1944. Oxford, 1988.

Klarsfeld, S. Vichy-Auschwitz: Le rôle de Vichy dans la solution finale de la question juive en France, 1942. Paris, 1983.

Lazare, L. La résistance juive en France. Paris, 1987.

LUCIEN LAZARE

SS-Oberführer Hermann Fegelein, Hitler's brother-in-law. [National Archives]

FEGELEIN, HERMANN (1906–1945), senior SS officer; confidant of Adolf HITLER. Fegelein was born in Ansbach. He served in the Rossbach Freikorps, in the Reichswehr cavalry, and then in the Bavarian police. After the Nazi rise to power he became director of the SS riding academy in Munich. In occupied Poland, Fegelein first had the assignment of setting up SS cavalry units, which were then formed into a cavalry brigade, under his command. When the Germans invaded the USSR, the brigade was sent to the east and, in July and August 1941, it "purged" the Pripet Marshes of whatever remnants of Red Army units it found there; in the course of this operation its men murdered some twenty thousand Jews.

From May to December 1942, Fegelein was inspector of cavalry in the REICHSSICHERHEITSHAUPTAMT (Reich Security Main Office; RSHA); in December 1942 he was promoted to SS-Oberführer and put in command of a task force (Kampfgruppe Fegelein) that operated on the central front. In September 1943 Fegelein was wounded and posted to the rear, and in January he was appointed Heinrich HIMMLER's and the SS's liaison officer in Hitler's headquarters. He married Gretel Braun, the sister of Eva Braun, Hitler's companion, and joined Hitler's inner circle. In June 1944 he was raised to the rank of SS-Gruppenführer in the Waffen-SS.

In the final days of the Reich, Fegelein was in Hitler's bunker. Wanting to escape from Berlin, he left the bunker without telling anyone, returned to his home, and changed into civilian clothes. At this point Hitler found out about Himmler's negotiations with Folke BERNADOTTE, the representative of the Swedish Red Cross, which in Hitler's eyes amounted to treason. Hitler therefore accused Fegelein too of having committed treason, and also of desertion, and on April 27 ordered his arrest. Fegelein was stripped of his rank and, on April 28, was executed. Eva

Braun, who was to marry Hitler the following day, did not intercede to save her brother-in-law's life.

BIBLIOGRAPHY

Trevor-Roper, H. R. *The Last Days of Hitler.* New York, 1947.

SHMUEL SPECTOR

FEINER, LEON (1888–1945), BUND activist and member of the Jewish underground in Poland. Feiner was born in Kraków and studied law at the Jagiellonian University there. As a longtime member of socialist movements and a Bund activist in independent Poland, he frequently defended leftist political activists in court. Feiner came from an assimilated background and was well versed in Polish culture, but his loyalty to the Bund, as well as the increasingly anti-Jewish policy that Poland was pursuing, brought him closer to the Jewish masses and made him want to share their fate. In the second half

Leon Feiner.

of the 1930s he was imprisoned in Bereza-Kartuska, a Polish concentration camp in which a large number of opposition figures, of various shades of political opinion, were held.

When the war broke out, Feiner fled to the Soviet-occupied part of Poland, only to be put in prison. Following the German conquest of the area in 1941, he escaped and made his way back to Warsaw, where he lived under an assumed identity on the Polish ("Aryan") side of the city and was an underground representative of the Bund and of the Jews in the ghetto. When the Bund joined the ŻYDOWSKA ORGANIZACJA BOJOWA (Jewish Fighting Organization; ŻOB), Feiner was appointed Bund representative on the "Aryan" side, and together with Abraham BERMAN (who represented the Żydowski Komitet Narodowy, or the Jewish National Committee), formed the coordinating committee for contacts with the Polish underground. In the fall of 1942 Jan KARSKI, a member of the Polish underground who was sent to London in its behalf, took a message from Feiner addressed to Samuel ZYGELBOJM, for transmission to all the Jews in the free world. Feiner asked Zygelbojm to tell the Jews "to lay siege to all important offices and agencies of the British and the Americans, and not to move from there until these Allied powers give guarantees that they will embark upon the rescue of the Jews. They [the demonstrators] should abstain from food and water, waste away before the eyes of the apathetic world, and starve to death. By doing so they may perhaps shock the conscience of the world." It was Feiner who drafted and forwarded to their destinations most of the Bund's reports and messages to London and the United States.

In the last few months of 1942, Feiner helped establish a Polish organization for giving aid to Jews and trying to rescue them, a project that had been initiated by various Polish circles—Catholics, liberal intellectuals, and representatives of political parties (mostly of the Center and the Left). From January 1943 to July 1944 Feiner was deputy chairman of ŻEGOTA, the Polish Council for Aid to Jews, and was its chairman from November to December 1944, until the liberation of Warsaw in January 1945.

After the liberation, Feiner, who was suffering from a malignant disease, was transferred to Lublin, the temporary seat of Poland's new regime. A month later he died.

BIBLIOGRAPHY

Neustadt, M., ed. *Destruction and Rising: The Epic of the Jews in Warsaw.* Tel Aviv, 1946. (In Hebrew.)

ISRAEL GUTMAN

FERRAMONTI DI TARSIA, internment camp (officially designated "concentration camp") for Jews near Cosenza in Calabria (southern Italy); the largest of the fifteen internment camps established on Benito MUSSOLINI's orders between June and September 1940.

Construction of the camp was started on June 4, 1940, six days before Italy's entry into the war; arrests of Jews, both foreign and Italian, commenced on June 15, and arrestees began arriving at Ferramonti on June 20. Between June 1940 and August 1943 there were 3,823 Jewish internees at Ferramonti; 3,682 were foreigners and 141 were Italians (Jews of Italian nationality were not interned unless guilty or suspected of anti-Fascist activities). The commandant of the camp, a commissioner of public security, was assisted by an official of the Ministry of the Interior, ten policy agents, and seventy-five Fascist militiamen commanded by a *centurione* (captain).

Living conditions at the camp, acceptable at first, became increasingly difficult as the situation of the Jews deteriorated. Even so, Ferramonti was never a "concentration camp" in the German sense of the term. The internees were not maltreated, and they were allowed to receive food parcels, to visit sick relatives, and to engage in cultural activities; nor were there periodic "selections" to swell the columns on their way to the gas chambers in Poland. Four weddings and twenty-one births took place at the camp. Relations between the internees and the camp authorities were tolerable throughout the camp's existence; there were no mutinies or revolts, and very few breaches of discipline. On September 4, 1943, six weeks after Mussolini's downfall, the BADOGLIO government released the internees.

BIBLIOGRAPHY

Zuccotti, S. *The Italians and the Holocaust: Persecution, Rescue, and Survival.* New York, 1987.

MEIR MICHAELIS

Moshe Sharett (Shertok), head of the political department of the Jewish Agency and later prime minister of Israel, visiting former inmates at the Ferramonti di Tarsia camp in Italy (April 1944). Sharett is standing at the center. [Eliyahu Ben-Hur]

FIGHTERS FOR THE FREEDOM OF IS-RAEL. *See* Loḥamei Ḥerut Israel.

FIGHTING ORGANIZATION OF PIONEER JEWISH YOUTH. *See* He-Haluts ha-Lohem.

FILDERMAN, WILHELM (1882–1963), Romanian Jewish leader. Filderman was born in Bucharest. He studied law in Paris, earning a doctorate. In 1912 he was one of the few Jews granted Romanian nationality; this enabled him to earn his livelihood by practicing law. In the interwar period Filderman was a member of the Romanian parliament, and he served as chairman of most of the important Jewish organizations in the country, among them the Federatia Uniunilor de Comunitati Evreesti (Federation of Jewish Communities), the Uniunea Comunitatilor Evreesti din Regat (Union of Jewish Communities in the Regat [the Old Kingdom; Romania in its pre–World War I borders]), the UNIUNEA EVREILOR ROMÂNI (Union of Romanian Jews), the JOINT DISTRIBUTION COMMITTEE's office in ROMANIA, and the Consiliul Evreesc (Jewish Council).

In the years following World War I, Filderman was active on behalf of the granting of Romanian nationality to the Jews of the Regat and in assisting the Jewish refugees from the Ukraine. He also aided in the preservation of Jewish rights in the face of the prevailing antisemitism in Romanian political and economic life, which also had its effect on Jewish religious life and education. Filderman persisted in this struggle even during the IRON GUARD's regime of terror (September 6, 1940, to January 24, 1941) and during Ion ANTONESCU's dictatorship, notwithstanding the fact that Antonescu dissolved the existing Jewish organizations and in their place set up the CENTRALA EVREILOR (Jewish Center). These activities finally led to Filderman's expulsion to TRANSNISTRIA in May 1943; the immediate cause was his opposition to the collective ransom of 4 billion lei (about $40 million) that Antonescu imposed on Romanian Jewry. Even in Transnistria, however, Filderman maintained his activities, and in August of that year he was permitted to return from exile.

Throughout the war years Filderman maintained contact with senior officials, cabinet ministers, and Premier Ion Antonescu and his close associate, Mihai ANTONESCU (who also held senior cabinet posts). The Romanian leaders were forced to accept Filderman as the authentic representative of the Jews (most of the leaders of the Jewish Center were Jewish converts to Christianity or collaborators who did not represent the Jews and had been appointed to their posts on the recommendation of the German legation). Filderman also earned the respect of Romanian opposition leaders, who cooperated with him; they included such renowned figures as Iuliu Maniu, head of the Peasants' Party (Partidul Na-

tional Taranesc), and Dinu Bratianu, head of the National-Liberal Party (Partidul National-Liberal). During the spring and summer of 1942 Filderman formed a clandestine Jewish leadership, the Jewish Council, composed of representatives of the Zionist Organization and other Jewish bodies. The Jewish Council sought to save the Jews of Romania from deportation to Poland and to alleviate the daily life of the Jewish population, then suffering from the effects of countless antisemitic laws and regulations.

In the fall of 1941, when he was still chairman of the Federation of Jewish Communities, Filderman failed in his efforts to prevent the deportation to Transnistria of the Jews of BESSARABIA and BUKOVINA. He played a decisive role, however, in foiling the plans to deport the entire Jewish population of Romania to the EXTERMINATION CAMPS in Poland in the fall of 1942, and in preventing the expulsion of Jews from neighboring countries who had taken refuge in Romania. In August and September of 1941, as a result of Filderman's intercession with Ion Antonescu, the decree on wearing the yellow badge (see BADGE, JEWISH) was abolished in the Regat. For two years, from the end of 1941 to the end of 1943, Filderman persisted in a struggle for the right to send aid to the Jews who had been deported to Transnistria, and he followed up by campaigning for their repatriation to Romania, meeting with partial success.

After the fall of the dictatorial regime in August 1944, Filderman continued his public activities. In the following three years, from 1944 to 1947, he fought for the restoration of Jewish rights and Jewish property, and against the drafting of Jews into the ranks of the antisemitic Romanian army. In pursuing his aims, Filderman exploited every available legal loophole, and he also lobbied in the senior echelons of the regime. He saved the Romanian Jews from deportation to the extermination camps by making this a national Romanian issue and by persuading the leaders of the regime that compliance with the German demand for deportation would be a violation of Romanian sovereignty.

After the war, the Jewish Communists campaigned against Filderman, as part of their efforts to gain control of the Jewish organizations in Romania. Filderman was forced to resign from all his positions of leadership, and in early 1948 he fled to France, where he remained for the rest of his life.

BIBLIOGRAPHY

Ancel, J., comp. *Yad Vashem Central Archives: The Dr. W. Filderman Archives.* Jerusalem, 1974.
Safran, A. *Resisting the Storm: Memoirs, Romania, 1940–1947.* Jerusalem, 1987.

JEAN ANCEL

FILMS, NAZI ANTISEMITIC. Film played an integral role in the dissemination of Nazi ideology. Anti-Jewish characters and themes recur throughout the cinema of the Third Reich, although only a minimal number of these films focus on antisemitic themes.

In the fall of 1938, the Propaganda Ministry sent a request to German film companies to begin the production of explicitly antisemitic films. Major themes to be developed were the world Jewish conspiracy, *völkisch* ideology, and pseudo-anthropological theories based on blood and physiognomy. It was felt that if these ideas were portrayed effectively in film and other media, they could help prepare the German people for a "solution" to the Jewish problem.

The first two anti-Jewish films, *Robert und Bertram* (Robert and Bertram; director, Hans Heinz Zerlett) and *Leinen aus Irland* (Linen from Ireland; Heinz Helbig), appeared in 1939 and used comedy to caricature the subhuman Jew. Both films rely on negative physical stereotypes, and both expose the Jew's tendency to infiltrate Aryan society, as well as the Jewish male's desire for the pure, blonde, Aryan female. In the end, no matter how cunning he is, the Jew is always foiled.

The major cinematic attack on the Jews occurred in the late summer and the fall of 1940. Two feature films, *Die Rothschilds* (The Rothschilds; Erich Waschneck) and *Jud Süss* (Jew Süss; Veit Harlan), and one so-called documentary, *Der ewige Jude* (The Eternal Jew; Fritz Rippler), were to be shown successively over a short period of time.

Die Rothschilds was both antisemitic and anti-British, using the historic backdrop of the Napoleonic wars to portray the financial control and cunning of the Rothschild banking family. The Rothschilds are depicted as having made their fortune from the blood of the Germans, with England appearing as a decaying society dominated by Jews. The final scene shows a flaming Star of David superimposed over a map of England. The film was unsuccessful and was withdrawn from circulation shortly after its premiere in the summer of 1940. It was shown later as *Die Rothschilds Aktien von Waterloo* (The Rothschilds' Stock since Waterloo).

Jud Süss appeared in September 1940. It focuses on the rootlessness of the Jew and his ability to penetrate Aryan society. Apart from the assimilated Süss, the Jewish characters are dirty, hook-nosed, or without scruples. One actor plays three Jewish characters, thereby depicting the eternal nature of the Jew. It is said that 120 Jews from the Lublin ghetto were used as extras in the film.

The story is set in eighteenth-century Württemberg. Süss Oppenheimer wields enormous power as financial adviser to the reigning duke, convincing him to allow Jews to enter Stuttgart. Süss rapes the blonde Aryan Dorothea while having her Aryan husband tortured. Tainted for life, Dorothea drowns herself. The duke dies; now powerless, Süss is arrested, tried, and publicly hanged. The Jews are exiled from the city with the hope, as the film notes, that this lesson "will never be forgotten."

Jud Süss was extremely successful. Heinrich HIMMLER ordered all members of the SS and police to see it. It was also viewed by concentration camp guards. Witnesses saw a HITLERJUGEND (Hitler Youth) group in Vienna trample a Jewish man to death after seeing the film. It was shown in small towns in Poland prior to deportations of the Jews in order to prevent help being given to them by the local population. The director, Veit Harlan, was tried for crimes against humanity at Nuremberg, but the case was dismissed because of the difficulty in obtaining evidence.

The most vile of the three films, *Der ewige Jude*, premiered in November 1940. It embodies the full gamut of Nazi antisemitic ideology in the style of Julius STREICHER's *Der STÜRMER*. In a "documentary" manner, it depicts the "filthy" ghettos of the Jews; the uncreative Jewish parasite; Jewish control of world finance, politics, and the arts; and the Jew as a homeless, rootless cosmopolite who infiltrates Aryan society. The final sequence depicts a Jewish ritual slaughter scene in a particularly cruel manner. "Authenticity" is provided by the use of maps and statistics to verify statements. The central aim of the film is to create the image of a wandering pest who must be exterminated. *Der ewige Jude* was not successful, the German public having had their fill with *Jud Süss.* Clearly, though, the appearance of these three films in 1940 was not coincidental but rather part of an overall plan connected with the destruction of European Jewry.

[*See also* Antisemitism; Propaganda, Nazi.]

BIBLIOGRAPHY

Hull, D. S. *Film in the Third Reich: A Study of the German Cinema, 1933–1945.* Berkeley, 1969.
Leiser, E. *Nazi Cinema.* New York, 1975.
Taylor, R. *Film Propaganda: Soviet Russia and Nazi Germany.* London, 1979.
Welch, D. *Propaganda and the German Cinema, 1933–1945.* Oxford, 1983.

JUDITH E. DONESON

FILMS ON THE HOLOCAUST. Both fiction and nonfiction films have helped to shape attitudes and stereotypes concerning the Holocaust. As a medium capable of educating as well as entertaining, film often establishes how this tragedy represents itself as history in the minds of people. Despite the diversity of subjects and themes (and without regard to aesthetic quality), it is possible to discern several general areas that provide insight into the scope and content of films on the Holocaust.

Among the earlier fiction films, many come from countries that suffered heavily under Nazi domination, especially in eastern Europe. Examples include two films from Poland, *Border Street* (1948; Aleksander Ford), about the Warsaw ghetto, and *The Last Stop* (1948; Wanda Jakubowska), filmed at AUSCHWITZ; and one film from Czechoslovakia, *Distant Journey* (1949; Alfred Radok), about a Jewish family deported to the THERESIENSTADT ghetto.

In the 1950s, Andrzej Wajda began his trilogy on the war and the postwar period in Poland. *Generation* (1954) portrays life in occupied Warsaw in 1942, and *Kanal* (1956) tells of Poles escaping from the Nazis via the city's sewers. These were followed by *Ashes and Diamonds* (1958). The persecution of the Jews plays a minor role in the trilogy. Wajda's 1961 film *Samson* depicts a Jew's inability to function in Warsaw during the war. *The Passenger* (1962; Andrzej Munk) relates the meeting of a woman once imprisoned in Auschwitz with her former guard, as she recalls her experiences in flashbacks.

A number of Czech films appeared in the 1960s: *Sweet Light in a Dark Room* (1960; Jiri Weiss), about a Czech boy hiding a Jewish girl from the Nazis; *Diamonds of the Night* (1964; Jan Nemec), depicting two boys who escape from a transport as they are chased by hunters in the woods; *The Shop on Main Street* (1965; Jan Kadar and Elmar Klos), which relates the crisis of conscience of a Slovak Christian in the face of the deportation of the town's Jews; and *And the Fifth Horseman Is Fear* (1968; Zbynek Brynych), a tale of frightened Jews and Czech informers.

A look at a cross-section of films from the late 1940s through the 1980s helps to illustrate how the Holocaust often plays a secondary role to the central story of the film. *Distant Journey* and *The Last Stop* are two examples. Others include *Judgment at Nuremberg* (United States, 1961; Stanley Kramer), a dramatization of the trial of German judges at Nuremberg; *Ship of Fools* (United States, 1965; Stanley Kramer), which tells in hindsight of a ship's passengers returning to Germany in 1932; *Landscape after Battle* (Poland, 1970; Andrzej Wajda), which focuses on attempts to return to normalcy in a DISPLACED PERSONS camp after the war; *Cabaret* (United States, 1972; Bob Fosse), set in Weimar in 1932, on the eve of Nazi rule; *Seven Beauties* (Italy, 1975; Lina Wertmüller), which tells of an Italian soldier who is without scruples in his attempt to survive a concentration camp; *Julia* (United States, 1977; Fred Zinnemann), based on the friendship of two women and set against the backdrop of the Nazi period; and *The Tin Drum* (West Germany, 1979; Volker Schlöndorff), the story of a young man in Danzig during the war who refuses to

The Diary of Anne Frank (United States, 1959; George Stevens). [Israel Film Archive, Jerusalem]

grow up in order to avoid entering the absurd world created by adults.

Though fewer in number, films that focus on Jewish characters provide insight into the problems confronted by European Jewry during the war. Representative of these are *The Diary of Anne Frank* (United States, 1959; George Stevens), demonstrating how Anne's diary became one of the first universal symbols of the Holocaust; *Kapo* (Italy, 1960; Gillo Pontecorvo), about a Jewish KAPO in a concentration camp; *The Two of Us* (France, 1966; Claude Berri), which portrays a breakdown of Jewish stereotypes; *The Garden of the Finzi-Continis* (Italy, 1970; Vittorio De Sica), the story of the deportation of the Jews of Ferrara; *Voyage of the Damned* (United States and Great Britain, 1976; Stuart Rosenberg), about the ship ST. LOUIS, with its Jewish refugees who sought a safe haven in Cuba and the United States, only to be refused and

sent back to Europe; and *Jacob the Liar* (East Germany, 1978; Frank Beyer), the story of a Jew in a ghetto who keeps hope alive among his fellow Jews by telling them that the Germans are losing the war. Included here are post-Holocaust films about the adjustment of survivors, such as *The Pawnbroker* (United States, 1965; Sidney Lumet) and *Madame Rosa* (France, 1977; Moshe Mizrahi).

The French film *The Sorrow and the Pity* (1970; Marcel Ophuls) demonstrates how film can participate in the historical discourse. This documentary, four and a half hours in length, touched a nerve in France as it destroyed the popular myth of the French as a nation of resisters and aggravated the wound made by the many French who collaborated with the Nazis. The controversy was pursued in a series of French fiction films, including *Lacombe, Lucien* (1974; Louis Malle), the story of collaboration as a tale of the banality of evil; *Black Thursday* (1974; Michel Mitrani), about the July 1942 roundup of Jews in Paris by the French police; *Mr. Klein* (1976; Joseph Losey), concerning the case of a man willing to capitalize on the plight of Jews fleeing from the Nazis, until he himself is mistaken for a Jew; and *The Last Metro* (1980; François Truffaut), a more gentle answer to the films that preceded it, which tells of a theatrical troupe that continues performing during the occupation, guided by its Jewish director, who is hidden in the cellar below the stage.

Turning to nonfiction films, it must be recognized that archival film footage on the Holocaust is either Nazi anti-Jewish propaganda film or footage shot by the liberating armies. This imposes obvious limitations on any interpretation of the Holocaust through archival film. Some films that utilize archival footage are *Night and Fog* (France, 1955; Alain Resnais), which depicts the world of the concentration camp; *Warsaw Ghetto* (Great Britain, 1968; BBC/TV); *Genocide* (Great Britain, 1973; Michael Darlow), from the Thames Television series *The World at War*; and *The Liberation of Auschwitz* (West Germany, 1986; Irmgard von zur Muehlen).

Topics portrayed in nonfiction film are broad and varied, from studies of the rise of fascism to the Allies' refusal to bomb Auschwitz. Among these are *The Illegals* (United States, 1947; Meyer Levin), showing the illegal immigration of refugees into Palestine; *Genocide* (United States, 1981; Arnold Schwartzman), which won an Oscar for the best documentary film; and *Who Shall Live and Who Shall Die?* (United States, 1981; Laurence Jarvik), which explores American guilt for not having done more to save the Jews of Europe. Marcel Ophuls's lengthy documentary *Hotel Terminus* (1988) traces the life of Klaus Barbie, the "butcher of Lyons" (*see* BARBIE TRIAL).

A docudrama nine and a half hours long that was made for American television, *Holocaust* (United States, 1978; Marvin Chomsky for NBC/TV), became the catalyst for an unprecedented public response to the period of the "FINAL SOLUTION." Telecast throughout Europe and the United States, and considered by many critics to be a soap opera and a

The Garden of the Finzi-Continis (Italy, 1970; Vittorio de Sica). [Israel Film Archive, Jerusalem]

trivialization of the Holocaust, this American miniseries elicited national discussions of the Holocaust in West Germany, France, and Switzerland, as well as in the United States. It also paved the way for other television dramas and films, making the subject acceptable for public consumption. One of these was the epic *War and Remembrance* (United States, 1988–1989; Dan Curtis for ABC/TV), which made an impressive attempt to portray the horror of Auschwitz.

After *Holocaust,* a number of interesting fiction films appeared on the "Final Solution." Examples are *The Boat Is Full* (Switzerland, West Germany, and Austria, 1980; Markus Imhoof), a story of Jewish refugees denied asylum in Switzerland; *Charlotte* (the Netherlands and West Germany, 1981; Franz Weisz), the story of Charlotte Salomon, a young Jewish artist deported and killed in Auschwitz; *The Revolt of Job* (Hungary, 1981; Imre Gyongossy and Barna Kabay), which tells of a Jewish couple who adopt a gentile boy and teach him the ways of Judaism; *Sophie's Choice* (United States, 1982; Alan Pakula), the story of a Polish survivor of Auschwitz and her ill-fated choices; *Angry Harvest* (West Germany, 1985; Agnieszka Holland), the portrait of a lonely Polish man who falls in love with the Jewish woman he is hiding during the war; and *Elysium* (Hungary, 1986; Erika Szanto), the tale of a young Jewish boy arrested in the streets of Budapest and taken to a camp where medical experiments are performed on children.

Shoah (France, 1985; Claude Lanzmann). [Israel Film Archive, Jerusalem]

Claude Lanzmann's *Shoah* (France, 1985) was eleven years in the making. It does not use a single frame of archival footage. Rather, through interviews with the perpetrators, survivors, and bystanders involved in the Holocaust, the film mercilessly explores, in more than nine and a half hours of film, the process that led to the death of six million European Jews. *Shoah* is a film that forces the viewer to confront and to attempt to understand, at some level, what was the Holocaust.

BIBLIOGRAPHY

Avisar, I. *Screening the Holocaust: Cinema's Images of the Unimaginable.* Bloomington, 1988.

Bettelheim, B. *Surviving and Other Essays.* New York, 1979. See pages 274–314.

Diamond, S. A. " 'Holocaust' Film's Impact on Americans." *Patterns of Prejudice* 12/4 (July–August 1978): 1–9.

Doneson, J. E. *The Holocaust in American Film.* Philadelphia, 1987.

Doneson, J. E. "The Jew as a Female Figure in Holocaust Film." *Shoah: A Review of Holocaust Studies and Commemorations* 1 (1978): 11–13.

Friedman, R. M. "Exorcising the Past: Jewish Figures in Contemporary Films." *Journal of Contemporary History* 19/3 (July 1984): 511–527.

Insdorf, A. L. *Indelible Shadows: Film and the Holocaust.* New York, 1983.

Langer, L. "The Americanization of the Holocaust on Stage and Screen." In *From Hester Street to Hollywood: The Jewish American Stage and Screen,* edited by S. B. Cohen. Bloomington, 1983. See pages 213–230.

Liehm, A. J. *Closely Watched Films: The Czechoslovak Film Experience.* White Plains, N.Y., 1974.

Stoil, J. M. *Cinema beyond the Danube: The Camera and Politics.* Metuchen, N.J., 1974.

JUDITH E. DONESON

"FINAL SOLUTION" (Ger., *Endlösung*), the Nazis' comprehensive program to solve their "Jewish question" by murdering every Jew in Europe. Initiated by Adolf HITLER in the summer of 1941 in the euphoria of his greatest successes and his seemingly imminent victory over the Soviet Union, the "Final Solution" was the culmination of a long evolution of Nazi Jewish policy—from Hitler's earliest articulation of a solution to the "Jewish question" in 1919, through the Nazi attempts to coerce Jewish emigration in the 1930s, to the schemes for mass expulsion after the outbreak of war, and, finally, the leap to mass murder with the EINSATZGRUPPEN assault on Russian Jewry in 1941. The emergence of the "Final Solution" as both concept and program was a complex phenomenon conditioned by Hitler's ideology and manner of governing, by the nature of the Nazi regime, and by the changing circumstances in which the Nazis found themselves.

In the very earliest document of Hitler's political career, a letter written on September 16, 1919, in reply to a query from Adolf Gemlich (a former agent of Hitler's superior, Capt. Karl Mayr), he articulated the view that the "Jewish question" would be solved not through emotional antisemitism and pogroms but only through an "antisemitism of reason" that would lead to a systematic legal struggle to deprive the Jews of their privileges and classify them as foreigners. "The final goal, however, must steadfastly remain the removal [*Entfernung*] of the Jews altogether." The "Jewish question" remained central for Hitler in the 1920s. For Nazis, he declared, the "Jewish question" was the "pivotal question" (*Kernfrage*), and the party was therefore determined to solve it "with well-known German thoroughness to the final consequence." For the most part the "final consequence" was expressed in terms such as "removal" (*Ausweisung*), "expulsion" (*Austreibung*), and "exclusion" (*Ausschaltung*). Occasionally, however, his language became more ominous, particularly when he made the analogy between the tuberculosis bacillus, which had to be destroyed (*vernichtet*), and the Jew—the "racial tuberculosis" (*Rassentuberkulose*) of peoples who had to be removed if the German *Volk* were to recover its health. On one occasion in 1922, he fantasized about publicly hanging every Jew in Germany and leaving the bodies dangling until they stank.

Such statements indicate the depth of Hitler's obsession with the Jews as the source of all of Germany's historical misfortunes and current problems, indeed as the "greatest evil"; his determination to seek an uncompromising and comprehensive solution to this "Jewish question" by getting rid of the

Jews one way or another; and his violent and murderous predisposition. They do not, however, constitute a grand design, blueprint, or decision for the "Final Solution" of 1941 to 1945: the comprehensive and systematic mass murder of all European Jewry.

In the early 1930s, between the Nazis' electoral breakthrough and Hitler's assumption of power, there was little or no preparation in the party for its subsequent Jewish policy. In the years immediately following the attainment of power, various Nazi factions pursued different and often conflicting policies, with Hitler generally favoring the approach of systematic legislative discrimination—the "antisemitism of reason" of the Gemlich letter—over the public violence of pogroms and "wild actions." Lacking at this time, however, was any articulation of what had been so common in Hitler's statements during the early 1920s, namely, the determination of the final goal of Nazi Jewish policy. Few Nazis seemed to be looking ahead to where the persecution of the Jews might lead. In the SS, however, as early as 1934 a report for Heinrich HIMMLER on the "Jewish question" emphasized the need to work toward a total emigration of German Jewry.

While emigration became the centerpiece of SS Jewish policy thereafter, this remained a "voluntary solution" until the ANSCHLUSS with Austria in March 1938. The Jewish expert of Reinhard HEYDRICH's SD (Sicherheitsdienst; Security Service), Adolf EICHMANN, was then sent to Vienna, where he organized assembly-line procedures for expediting and coercing Jewish emigration.

The year 1938 was a turning point for Nazi Jewish policy in other ways as well. Expulsion began to characterize Nazi Jewish policy throughout Germany, as Soviet Jews were ordered out of the country in the spring, followed by Polish Jews in the fall. Hermann GÖRING began the systematic ARISIERUNG ("Aryanization") of Jewish property, which threatened to pauperize the Jews of Germany within months and make emigration even more difficult. Joseph GOEBBELS made his bid for power over Nazi Jewish policy by instigating the KRISTALLNACHT pogrom of November 9 and 10, 1938.

In the wake of Kristallnacht, the Nazis finally moved to coordinate the disparate and often conflicting Jewish policies pursued by the regime until then. Göring announced Hitler's instructions to the Nazi leaders gathered before him on November 12, 1938:

> The Jewish question is to be summed up and coordinated once and for all and solved one way or another. . . . If the German Reich should in the near future become involved in conflict abroad then it is obvious that we in Germany will first of all make sure of settling accounts with the Jews. Apart from that, the Führer is now at last to make a major move abroad, starting with the powers that have brought up the Jewish question, in order to get around to the Madagascar solution. He explained this to me in detail on November 9. There is no longer any other way.

In the following months Hitler approved the negotiations between Hjalmar SCHACHT and George Rublee for the resettlement of German Jewry, and Göring established the Reichszentrale für Jüdische Auswanderung (Reich Central Office for Jewish Emigration) on the model of Eichmann's Vienna experiment. The office was placed under Heydrich's control, with the charge that the "emigration of the Jews from Germany [was] to be furthered by all possible means."

Hitler himself spoke before the Reichstag on January 30, 1939, reiterating the two themes of Jewish emigration and of the dire consequences of war that Göring had summarized earlier. He chided those states that criticized Germany's treatment of its Jews for their own reluctance to accept Jews: "The world has sufficient space for settlements." If, however, war broke out first, "then the result will not be the Bolshevization of the earth, and thus the victory of Jewry, but the annihilation of the Jewish race in Europe."

Should Hitler's threats at this time be seen as a literal statement of his clear intention to kill the Jews upon the outbreak of war? They may have had other motives: on the one hand, a desire to exercise diplomatic blackmail against governments presumed to be under Jewish influence to accept Germany's impoverished Jewish refugees and not thwart its imminent destruction of Czechoslovakia; on the other, a wish to impart to Hitler's followers the notion that a policy more radical than emigration would be needed after the outbreak of war to solve the "Jewish question." Several facts support the latter interpretation. First, less than two weeks before the Reichstag speech, Hitler made the same threat to the Czech ambassador, František Chvalkovsky—an unlikely person in whom to confide premeditated mass murder, but an entirely appropriate target for diplomatic pressure. Second, when war did break out in September 1939, Hitler did not immediately initiate the systematic mass murder of the Jews under German control. Instead, with his clear approval, Nazi Jewish policy became radicalized in a different way; solving the "Jewish question" still meant removing the Jews one way or another.

The conquest and partition of Poland brought an additional two million Jews into the German sphere, including more than one-half million in the "incorporated territories" annexed directly to the Reich. In addition, however, some seven million Poles resided in the incorporated territories. If the "Jewish question" was one major obsession in Hitler's world view, the conquest of *Lebensraum* ("living space") in eastern Europe was the other. Poland thus presented a major challenge to the Nazis, not only in the new magnitude of the "Jewish question" its conquest entailed but also in the extent of territory inhabited by Poles that was to be transformed into German "living space." According to a plan approved by Hitler in late September 1939, the Poles and Jews of the incorporated territories were to be expelled into the GENERALGOUVERNEMENT, and the very concept of Polish nationhood was to be eradicated through the "liquidation," including physical destruction, of the Polish intelligentsia, deemed the bearers of Polish nationalism. The incorporated territories were to be repopulated with ethnic Germans (VOLKSDEUTSCHE) evacuated from the Baltic states and eastern Poland, areas that had been surrendered to the Soviets as the price of the Nazi-Soviet non-aggression pact of August 1939 (*see* NAZI-SOVIET PACT). As for the Jews, they were to be expelled not just from the incorporated territories but from all of the Third Reich into a reservation on the outer edge of the German empire, at that time the Lublin region on the demarcation line with Soviet-occupied eastern Poland.

The Nazis set in motion a massive demographic upheaval, but the overall plan could not be realized. Very quickly, Jewish deportations from within prewar German boundaries were prohibited. Deportations of Jews from the incorporated territories were scaled down, while precedence was given to deporting Poles, whose farms, businesses, and homes could be turned over to incoming *Volksdeutsche*. By the spring of 1940, Hitler let it be known that the Lublin Reservation was no longer the target of a solution to the "Jewish question" (*see* NISKO AND LUBLIN PLAN). There was not enough territory in Poland to spare for the Jews.

Himmler was receptive to this hint, and in late May 1940 he presented Hitler with a memorandum on the treatment of the populations of eastern Europe that included the notion of expelling all the Jews to some colonial territory in Africa. Other eastern Europeans not suitable for "Germanization" were to be turned into slave laborers. Concerning this systematic eradication of the ethnic composition of eastern Europe, Himmler concluded: "However cruel and tragic each individual case may be, this method is still the mildest and best, if one rejects the Bolshevik method of physical extermination of a people out of inner conviction as un-German and impossible." Hitler judged Himmler's proposals "very good and correct." Within weeks, this notion of expelling the Jews overseas was concretized in the form of the MADAGASCAR PLAN, which Hitler discussed approvingly with Mussolini in late June. Until the German defeat in the Battle of Britain in September 1940 rendered its imminent realization impossible, the Madagascar Plan was briefly the centerpiece and preoccupation of Nazi Jewish policy.

However ephemeral and unrealized the Lublin Reservation project and the Madagascar Plan proved to be, they represented an important stage in the evolution of Nazi Jewish policy. Shortly before the war a Foreign Office circular had noted, in reference to the large Jewish populations in Poland, Hungary, and Romania: "Even for Germany the Jewish question will not be solved when the last Jew has left German soil." With direct control over much of Europe and a growing list of unequal alliances with states not directly occupied, the Nazis considered the "Jewish question" no longer a German but rather a European issue; German domination of the Continent imposed the obligation to solve this problem in a fundamental way. The removal of the Jews altogether, once Hitler's prescription for Germany, was now the unquestioned premise of the Nazis' commitment throughout Europe. Clearly, with notions such as the Lublin and Madagascar programs, the Nazis had already accustomed themselves to the idea of an unprecedented loss of life and population decimation among the Jews.

This changing mentality among the Nazis was reflected in their increasing references to a "final solution to the Jewish question." In June 1940, Heydrich referred to the Madagascar Plan as a "territorial final solution." Beginning in September 1940, Eichmann's staff routinely referred to "the doubtless imminent final solution to the Jewish question" (*die zweifellos kommende Endlösung der Judenfrage*) when refusing to permit Jewish emigration from any country in Europe other than Germany, so that the latter would be the first *judenrein* ("cleansed of Jews") nation in Europe. By 1940, therefore, even before mass murder became the goal of Nazi Jewish policy, the Nazis were already committed to a way of thinking about the "Jewish question" that precluded any solution that was less than both "final" and transEuropean.

At the same time, large-scale, systematic mass murder as a method of problem-solving was becoming commonplace. It was already established that the denationalization of Poland was to be achieved through the systematic liquidation of the Polish intelligentsia. Simultaneously, Hitler initiated the killing of mentally and hereditarily ill Germans, deemed "unworthy of life." This was euphemistically referred to as the EUTHANASIA PROGRAM, although it had nothing to do with any voluntary request of the victim to be released from his suffering. In its personnel, technology (including the use of carbon monoxide in gas chambers), and bureaucratic mode of operation, this murder program in particular foreshadowed the mass murder of the Jews that was soon to follow.

Hitler's decision to invade the Soviet Union

and the ensuing preparations for it in the spring of 1941 were especially significant in the accelerating movement toward the mass murder of European Jewry. The invasion of the Soviet Union promised to aggravate the conditions of the vicious circle in which the Germans had entrapped themselves, for each new military success increased the number of Jews under their control whom they were committed to get rid of through a "final solution" of one kind or another. The campaign against Russia, as Hitler made clear to his generals, was to be not a conventional war, but a war of destruction against National Socialism's racial and ideological enemies. Not only was *Lebensraum* to be conquered, but Bolshevism and its Jewish progenitor were to be eradicated. With the formation of the Einsatzgruppen, systematic mass murder as a method of solving the Nazis' self-imposed "Jewish question" began.

Even then, however, the evolution to the "Final Solution" was not yet complete. The Einsatzgruppen were targeted against Jews in the newly occupied territories only, and moved into their tasks gradually as their commanders tested the limits of their men and of army cooperation, as well as the usefulness of local collaboration. Only in late July or early August 1941 did all the mobile killing units begin the systematic mass murder of all Jews in the Russian territories, including women and children.

At this point, Hitler stood at the pinnacle of his success. The German army had torn through Soviet defenses, encircled huge numbers of Soviet troops, destroyed most of the air force, and rampaged through two-thirds of the distance to Moscow. Victory seemed imminent, and Hitler faced the intoxicating prospect of having all of Europe at his feet. In the euphoria of the conquest of Poland, he had approved plans for a massive demographic reorganization on Polish territory, including the expulsion of Jews to the Lublin Reservation. With victory over France, he had approved the Madagascar Plan. Now, with the seeming victory over Russia, the last inhibitions fell away. Precisely when and how instructions were given is not known, but Göring, Himmler, and Heydrich now knew what Hitler expected of them. On July 31, 1941, Heydrich visited Göring and had

him sign an authorization to prepare and submit "an overall plan of the organizational, functional, and material measures to be taken in preparing for the implementation of the aspired final solution of the Jewish question."

If the notion of the "Final Solution" was now clear to the leading Nazis, the means of its implementation were not. The Einsatzgruppen had encountered numerous problems, most importantly the lack of secrecy, the psychological burden on the killers, and the logistic inadequacy of the killing methods in relation to the number of intended victims. If unsatisfactory for the Soviet Union, the firing-squad method was even less suitable for murdering the rest of European Jewry. The Nazis chose to become pioneers of mass murder in an uncharted land. The past offered no suitable landmarks, but in the fall of 1941 new killing techniques were improvised. The perverse organizational genius of the Nazis was now revealed, as they merged elements of their past programs in order to create something entirely new.

The physical setting of the concentration camp, the killing methods of euthanasia, and the deportation techniques of the population-resettlement programs were combined to create a system of EXTERMINATION CAMPS. In relative secrecy, a small number of camp personnel using assembly-line techniques could kill millions of victims, brought trainload by trainload, day after day, to these factories of death. A bureaucratic apparatus, detached from direct contact with the killing process but long inured to the notion that the Jews had to be removed one way or another, could perform on a business-as-usual basis all the diverse functions necessary to uproot and ship to their death millions of people. The German population in general, accepting the notion of the Jew as an enemy against whom it was legitimate for the state to take preventive measures, looked on with indifference.

In the fall of 1941, steps were taken to turn the conception of a "final solution to the Jewish question" into reality. The deportation of the German Jews was sanctioned by Hitler in late September and began in mid-October. The first gassing experiment was conducted in AUSCHWITZ in early September, and con-

struction of two extermination camps at BEŁ-
ŻEC and CHEŁMNO began in late October or
early November. The first mass murder of
German Jews took place in KOVNO and RIGA
in late November and early December, and
the first extermination camp, at Chełmno,
began full-time operations also in early December. The last step in turning the idea of
the "Final Solution" into reality was the
WANNSEE CONFERENCE of January 20, 1942. At
this conference, Reinhard Heydrich and his
Jewish expert, Adolf Eichmann, met with the
state secretaries of the ministerial bureaucracy. Most of those attending were already
aware that Jews were being killed, but the
full scope of the mass murder program was
only now revealed. Eleven million Jews, from
Ireland to the Urals and from Scandinavia to
Spain, were the intended victims—in short,
every Jew in Europe. Heydrich requested the
support of the state secretaries, and was
pleasantly surprised by their enthusiasm for
the project.

Though initially conceived as a program to
be carried out following Germany's expected
victory over the Soviet Union, the "Final Solution" henceforth endured through Germany's changing fortunes of war. In 1942,
with victory postponed, the Nazis made a
virtue of necessity, proclaiming that the "Final Solution" had to be effected during the
war to avoid an outcry from abroad. In 1944,
with their fortunes in decline, they rushed to
finish their gruesome task—to achieve a victory in their racial war that imminent military defeat could not undo. Nazi Jewish policy was shaped by a number of factors and
evolved toward the "Final Solution" in fits
and starts over many years, but this in no
way detracts from the fact that in the end it
was the most important legacy, indeed the
epitome, of National Socialism.

[See also Deportations; Genocide.]

BIBLIOGRAPHY

Adam, U. D. *Judenpolitik im Dritten Reich.* Düssel-
dorf, 1972.
Browning, C. R. *Fateful Months: Essays on the
Emergence of the Final Solution.* New York,
1985.
Browning, C. R. "Nazi Resettlement Policy and
the Search for a Solution to the Jewish Ques-
tion, 1939–1941." *German Studies Review* 9/3
(1986): 497–519.
Hilberg, R. *The Destruction of the European Jews.*
New York, 1985.
Jäckel, E., ed. *Hitler: Sämtliche Aufzeichnungen,
1905–1924.* Stuttgart, 1980.
Jäckel, E. *Hitler's Weltanschauung: A Blueprint for
Power.* Middletown, Conn., 1972.
Mayer, A. J. *Why Did the Heavens Not Darken? The
"Final Solution" in History.* New York, 1989.
Schleunes, K. A. *The Twisted Road to Auschwitz:
Nazi Policy toward German Jews, 1933–1939.*
London, 1972.

CHRISTOPHER R. BROWNING

FINLAND. In 1939, about two thousand Jews
lived in Finland, including some three hundred refugees from Germany, Austria, and
Czechoslovakia. The local community was
composed mostly of Jews who had come
from Russia during the nineteenth century,
and had been made equal citizens of independent Finland in 1917. Jews lived in Helsinki,
Turku, and Viipuri (Vyborg).

Before and during World War II, antisemitism in Finland was virtually nonexistent and the Finnish government resisted the
spread of Nazi ideology. As Finnish citizens,
Jews fought the Red Army in the Winter War
toward the end of 1939. During the one hundred days of fighting, the Jewish casualty
rate was proportionately higher than that of
the rest of the population; fifteen Jewish soldiers were killed and many wounded. Following the German invasion of the country in
1941, Finland was involved in the war
against the Soviet Union, and at least three
hundred Jews fought in Finnish uniforms.
Many Jewish women were active in the civil-
defense corps, and eight Jewish soldiers lost
their lives. Speaking of these events in 1944
at the Helsinki synagogue, the marshal of
Finland, Carl Gustaf Emil Mannerheim, extolled the Jewish contribution to the national
defense.

Although at the WANNSEE CONFERENCE the
Jews of Finland were included in the plans
for the "FINAL SOLUTION," Finnish Jewry
came through the war unscathed. The Nazis
did not press the Finns very strongly regarding the "Jewish question," because they

feared alienating them and losing the much-needed Finnish military presence on the eastern front. When Heinrich HIMMLER raised the issue during a visit to Finland in the summer of 1942, he was rebuffed by Prime Minister Johann Wilhelm Rangell. Rangell later wrote:

> Himmler asked: "How is the situation with the Jews in Finland?" I said to him that in Finland there are roughly a couple of thousand Jews, decent families and individuals whose sons are fighting in our army like the rest of the Finns and who are respected citizens as all the rest. I concluded my statement with the words, *"Wir haben keine Judenfrage"* (We have no Jewish question), and I said it with such a clarity that the discussion of the matter ended then and there. The Jewish question was not discussed with Himmler any other time.

Later the same year, however, in correspondence with the Gestapo chief, Heinrich MÜLLER, the head of the Finnish State Police (Valpo), Arno Anthoni, agreed to deport eight Jewish refugees whose names had appeared on the Valpo's extradition lists. The total

number of prisoners handed over to the German authorities in TALLINN on November 6, 1942, was twenty-seven. Nineteen were non-Jewish citizens of the Soviet Union and the republic of Estonia. Five were Jewish prisoners, one of whom was accompanied voluntarily by his wife and minor son, and another by his son. One of the eight Jews survived the ordeal.

In his trial after the war, Anthoni explained the action as simply a police measure. The Valpo's extradition lists contained the names of more central European Jewish refugees, but this deportation remained the only one.

The story of the Jewish-refugee extradition was blown up by Swedish and Finnish newspapers in early December 1942 into a major scandal. The resignation of Karl August Fagerholm, minister of social affairs and a leading Social Democratic politician, was also connected with this issue. Eventually, in the spring of 1944, the Swedish government accepted a Valpo recommendation that it receive about one hundred and sixty of the Jewish refugees still remaining in Finland. The rest of the Jewish refugees in Finland survived the war, along with all the Finnish nationals of the Jewish faith.

BIBLIOGRAPHY

Mikola, K. J. "Finland's Wars during World War II." In *Finland's War Years: A List of Books and Articles concerning the Winter War and the Continuation War, Excluding Literature in Finnish and Russian*, edited by K. Nyman, pp. iii–xxxii. Mikkeli, Finland, 1973.

Rautkallio, H. *Finland and the Holocaust: The Rescue of Finland's Jews.* New York, 1987.

HANNU RAUTKALLIO

FINLAND

© Martin Gilbert 1982

FISCHER, LUDWIG (1905–1947), governor of the Warsaw district in occupied Poland. Born in Kaiserslautern, in the Rhine district of Germany, Fischer became a member of the Nazi party in 1926 and joined the SA (Sturmabteilung; Storm Troopers) in 1929, rising to the rank of *Gruppenführer*. In 1937 he was elected to the Reichstag. He was appointed governor of the Warsaw district in October 1939, and remained in that post until the

German withdrawal from Warsaw in January 1945. In April and May of 1943 he was also acting governor of the Lublin district. Fischer was responsible for the establishment of the Warsaw ghetto in November 1940, as well as of other ghettos in the Warsaw district. He was heavily involved personally in organizing terror operations against Jews and Poles in his district and in the liquidation of the ghettos during 1942 and 1943. Fischer was arrested in West Germany after the war and in 1946 was extradited to Poland, where he was tried for his crimes, sentenced to death, and hanged.

BIBLIOGRAPHY

Gutman, Y. *The Jews of Warsaw, 1939–1943.* Bloomington, 1982.
Raporty Ludwiga Fischera gubernatora dystryktu warszawskiego. Warsaw, 1987.

SHMUEL KRAKOWSKI

FLEISCHMANN, GISI (1897–1944), Zionist activist in SLOVAKIA; leader of the Women's International Zionist Organization and of the PRACOVNÁ SKUPINA (Working Group).

When the ÚSTREDŇA ŽIDOV (Jewish Center) was established in Slovakia in 1940 on order of the authorities, Fleischmann was appointed head of its Aliya (immigration to Palestine) section. This section became the cover for the continuation of Zionist activities among the youth and of the *hakhshara* (agricultural training) network; it also provided vocational training.

Among Gisi Fleischmann's early achievements was the aid she helped organize for 326 Jews from Prague. These men had been interned in a camp in Sosnowiec, Poland, and had made their way to Slovakia early in 1940. Fleischmann managed to convince the Slovak government to allow the men to remain in Slovakia temporarily while she searched for a more permanent haven for them. They were housed in a camp at VYHNE. With the help of Richard Lichtheim (the Jewish Agency representative in Geneva) and Henry Montor (of the United Palestine Appeal in New York), she found safer places for them. Eventually, al-

Gisi Fleischmann.

most all of the men reached Palestine or other free countries before the deportations from Slovakia began in the spring of 1942.

Early that spring, a group of Slovak Jewish leaders had come to the conclusion that in order to help rescue the Jewish population in Slovakia and other occupied countries, underground methods would have to be employed. Fleischmann was one of the early founders of this "Working Group," as it came to be called. After the deportation of Slovakia's Jews began, in March 1942, the Working Group tried to stop it by bribing Adolf EICHMANN's representative in Slovakia, Dieter WISLICENY. In order to raise the required funds, the group entered into an exchange of letters with Nathan Schwalb of the American Jewish JOINT DISTRIBUTION COMMITTEE's office in Geneva. When the first wave of deportations ceased (there were to be none from October 1942 to the fall of 1944), the Working Group was greatly encouraged and came up with an even bolder proposal, the EUROPA PLAN. This called for the cessation of deportations from all parts of German-occupied Europe in exchange for foreign currency or goods that would be transmitted to the Germans by Jews in free countries. The proposal was submitted to Wisliceny. Fleischmann played a major role in formulating the plan, in bringing it to fruition, and in establishing contacts for this purpose with individuals and organizations abroad. Not taking the proper precautions, she was arrested by the Gestapo and held in prison for four months, rejecting all efforts made in this period to enable her to leave Slovakia. On her release she resumed her previous work.

After the SS entry in force into Slovakia in the summer of 1944 and the suppression of the SLOVAK NATIONAL UPRISING in October of that year, Fleischmann sought to obtain an appointment with Alois BRUNNER, another representative of Eichmann. She also tried to persuade Kurt BECHER to discontinue the deportations; both these efforts were unsuccessful. Fleischmann turned down an offer to be hidden from the Germans in a Bratislava bunker.

On September 28 of that year, most members of the Working Group, including Fleischmann, were arrested during an SS raid. They were all taken to the SERED labor camp except for Fleischmann and one other member of the group, who were permitted to stay behind in Bratislava to take care of the needs of the detainees and to close down the Jewish Center's affairs.

At the beginning of October 1944, Fleischmann was deported to AUSCHWITZ in one of the last transports of the war, with a special instruction to the Auschwitz authorities labeling her as "RU" (*Rückkehr unerwünscht*, "return undesirable"). She was gassed on arrival in the camp.

BIBLIOGRAPHY

Campion, J. *In the Lion's Mouth: Gisi Fleischmann and the Jewish Fight for Survival*. Lanham, Md., 1987.
Fuchs, A. *The Unheeded Cry*. New York, 1984.
Neumann, Y. O. *Gisi Fleischmann: The Story of a Heroic Woman*. Tel Aviv, 1970.

GIDEON GREIF

FLIGHT. *See* Beriḥa.

FLIGHT OF NAZI CRIMINALS. *See* Extradition of War Criminals.

FMZ. *See* Front of the Wilderness Generation.

FOMENKO, WITOLD (1905–1961), a "RIGHTEOUS AMONG THE NATIONS." Born in Warsaw into a Ukrainian family, Fomenko was still a child when he moved with his family to Chełm, where he grew up in a Jewish neighborhood, learning to speak and write Yiddish. In 1924 the family moved to LUTSK, where Fomenko played in a military band and gave music lessons. Many of his students were Jewish, and through them he came to know the Stoliner Rebbe, Rabbi Yohanan Perlov, and composed tunes for Perlov's Hasidic songs. In the mid-1930s, Fomenko had to give up his musical activities on doctors' orders, and with the help of Jewish friends he learned to be a barber.

In 1941, following the occupation of Lutsk and the establishment of a ghetto in the city, Fomenko began providing help to the Jews, bringing into the ghetto food, medicines, firewood, and other supplies, mainly for the soup kitchen where the needy received their meals. Fomenko paid for these purchases with his own income from the large barbershop he had opened, which had Jews among its employees. Whenever he visited the ghetto he tried to raise the morale of the Jews by telling them jokes and good news, and by singing anti-Nazi songs he had composed.

On the eve of the liquidation of the Lutsk ghetto, Fomenko began helping Jews to leave the ghetto and providing them with false "Aryan" documents that he had acquired or had had his Christian friends prepare for him. Following the arrest of a Jewish woman who had one of these documents in her possession and was tortured by her captors, Fomenko and his father were arrested, but the military commander of the city, who was a customer of Fomenko's, intervened on their behalf and they were released. Fomenko kept up his aid and rescue efforts even after the ghetto's liquidation, for those Jews who were being held in a labor camp in the city. When that camp was also liquidated, in December 1942, Fomenko concentrated on finding hiding places for Jews with Christian families in Lutsk, in most cases paying the families for their trouble. He also provided refuge for many Jews in his own house and among the members of his family in the city. Not all the Jews whom Fomenko helped survived the war—only thirty-six of them were still alive on the day the city was liberated.

After the war, Fomenko married one of the Jewish women he had saved, and with her made his home in Israel. He was awarded the Righteous among the Nations medal of YAD VASHEM, and planted a tree on Righteous among the Nations Avenue on Remembrance Hill in Jerusalem.

BIBLIOGRAPHY

Sharon, N., ed. *Sefer Lutsk*. Tel Aviv, 1961. (In Hebrew.)
Spector, S. *The Holocaust of Volhynian Jews, 1941–1944*. Jerusalem, 1986. (In Hebrew.)

SHMUEL SPECTOR

FORCED LABOR. [*This entry consists of two articles. The first,* Fremdarbeiter, *deals with the Nazi policy of using within the Reich forced labor from occupied countries. The second,* Jews in Occupied Poland, *surveys the use of Jewish slave labor in the ghettos and labor camps in Poland. For different aspects of the Nazis' exploitation of labor, see* Deutsche Ausrüstungswerke; HASAG; I.G. Farben; Munkaszolgálat; Organisation Schmelt; Organisation Todt; Ostindustrie GmbH.]

Fremdarbeiter

Laborers from Germany's satellites or occupied territories brought to work in the Reich were called *Fremdarbeiter* (foreign workers). The idea of using foreign workers for forced labor in the Third Reich was conceived in Berlin even before the September 1939 attack on Poland. It was first put into practice in Austria, after the ANSCHLUSS, in March 1938. Some 100,000 Austrian civilians, including 10,000 engineers, were taken to work in Germany, and by August 31, 1939, 70,000 workers from the Protectorate of BOHEMIA AND MORAVIA had gone the same route.

The German victories in the first phase of World War II and the ensuing occupation of many lands gave the Germans large reservoirs of manpower for their exploitation. Accordingly, the central German authorities in charge of employment policy worked out a detailed program for the drafting of these human resources. The plan provided for extremely harsh methods of recruitment to be applied in Poland and the occupied Soviet areas, whereas in the other countries under German occupation or in the satellite countries, far more lenient methods were to be used.

The first contingents of *Fremdarbeiter* were meant to replace the millions of Germans who had been taken out of the work force to be drafted into the army, and to spare the Germans the need to impose emergency labor drafts on their own population. When the BLITZKRIEG failed to achieve its purpose and the war dragged on with no end in sight, the German authorities needed the foreign workers to enable them to intensify recruitment for the armed forces and provide for the growing needs of the armaments industry.

Initially, the Germans tried to persuade people in the occupied countries to volunteer for work in Germany. To those who were ready to do so—mostly among the unemployed and those refugees who were in dire economic straits—the Germans promised all sorts of material benefits. At no time, however, did the number of volunteers fill the quota of workers required by the German economy.

Starting immediately after the outbreak of the war, the Germans used prisoners of war (POWs) on jobs in support of the German economy, contrary to international law on the subject. As early as the autumn of 1939, 340,000 Polish POWs were put to work on the land.

In the spring of 1940 the Germans decided to introduce in the GENERALGOUVERNEMENT various compulsory measures, such as conscriptions for work, seizures of persons who

Ukrainian women and girls waiting to be sent as forced laborers to Germany (1942).

did not possess papers exempting them from such conscription, and withholding of food rations from persons refusing to work. In August 1942 a decree was enacted imposing FORCED LABOR (*Zwangsverpflichtung*) in all occupied countries and POW camps. In western European countries, the local authorities on occasion cooperated with the Germans in their recruitment drives, in exchange for the release of POWs by the Germans or for a change in the status of POWs to that of foreign workers in Germany.

By 1942, the German drive for the recruitment of foreign workers had become a sophisticated and brutal manhunt, which also met with growing opposition and was an important element in the rise of organized resistance movements in Nazi-occupied Europe. Although millions of persons were conscripted for work in Germany between 1942 and 1944, the gap between the quotas set by the Germans and the actual number of workers who were brought to Germany grew apace. Reports on the poor working conditions in Germany and the treatment of foreign laborers, together with the growing signs of an impending German defeat, made it increasingly difficult for the Germans to obtain the help of local collaborators and overcome the general opposition of the local populations to working in Germany. The German retreat in the east and the shrinking area under their control also had the natural

effect of reducing the reservoir of manpower available to them.

The great majority of foreign laborers were brought from Poland and the Soviet Union. In early 1941 there were 800,000 Polish foreign workers in Germany, representing 55 percent of the total foreign labor force in Germany at the time. From June 1941, when Germany invaded the USSR, German-occupied areas of the Soviet Union became the major source of foreign laborers. In September 1944 the total number of foreign workers in Germany was 5.5 million, to which must be added another 2 million POWs. Of the total number of 7.5 million foreign workers, 38 percent belonged to Soviet peoples, and 20 percent were Poles. The rest of the foreign laborers were drafted in France, Czechoslovakia, the Netherlands, Belgium, and Norway. Among the satellite countries and Germany's allies, Italy was the only one to provide foreign workers in significant numbers. The percentage of foreign workers employed by the German economy never came up to German expectations, but it grew all the time. In May 1940 foreign laborers were only 0.8 percent of the total work force; by May 1941 that percentage had risen to 8.4, and in September 1944, foreign laborers represented 20.8 percent of the total work force in Germany. By late 1944 the number of foreign laborers had risen to 8 million, and together with the POWs, it amounted to approximately 9 million. One out of five workers in Germany was a foreigner, and one out of every four tanks and every four aircraft manufactured in Germany was produced by foreign workers.

There were differences of opinion in the top Nazi echelons in charge of the work force and the economy concerning the policy to be followed in exploiting the manpower available and the foreign laborers. Albert SPEER, who in February 1942 was appointed *Reichsminister für Bewaffnung und Munition* (Minister of Armaments and War Production), was an efficient administrator who sought to put the emphasis on raising war production, both in Germany and in the occupied countries. Fritz SAUCKEL, on the other hand, who in March 1942 became *Generalbevollmächtigter für den Arbeitseinsatz* (Chief Plenipotentiary for the Labor Effort), made it his goal to accelerate the conscription of foreign laborers. Sauckel prided himself on the large number of workers he had brought to Germany from other countries, enabling Germany to avoid taking drastic measures to recruit workers among the German population, even if this did not always coincide with efficiency and the requirements of production.

The people responsible for the work force and production were well aware that the conditions under which the foreign laborers were living, the wages they were paid, and the treatment they were given had a direct bearing on the results of the recruiting drives of foreign laborers and on their productivity. In most instances, however, the supervision of the laborers was in the hands of the police—the Sicherheitspolizei (Security Police) and the Ausländische Arbeiter (Foreign Workers) section of the GESTAPO—and they were guided by racist principles, partisan considerations, and xenophobia. The situation of the laborers from eastern Europe, in terms of their living conditions and the attitude toward them, differed sharply from that of the laborers from western Europe. Poles and Russians were regarded as inferior—in racist terms, they were *Untermenschen*, or "subhumans"—and as a rule, they were put on hard physical labor and were subjected to harsh control, humiliation, and severe penalties. They had to wear an identifying sign on their clothes, *P* for Poles and *Ost* (east) for the

Ukrainian women and girls waiting to be sent to Germany as forced laborers (1942). They are being photographed and registered before their departure.

Russians. They were not permitted to leave their lodgings after working hours; to use public transportation; to attend cultural events, places of entertainment, or restaurants attended by Germans; or even to participate in church services together with Germans. The pay they received for their work was especially low. Germans were warned not to have any social contact with Poles or Russians and, above all, to abide by racial purity, that is, to shun sexual intercourse with them. Germans who did have sexual intercourse with foreign workers were charged with *Rassenschande* (race defilement), which carried the sentence of death.

The conditions for foreign workers from the west were much better, but they, too, complained of being treated like slaves. The employers, and especially the farmers who had foreigners working for them, did, however, often disregard the strict rules on the treatment of foreign laborers laid down by the Nazi party, since these laborers were indispensable to them. Moreover, the defeats suffered by the Nazis on the war fronts created a need for an increased work force and led them to consider improving the treatment of foreign laborers, as well as some changes in policy toward other sources of potential labor. Eventually, some changes were implemented.

The racist policy and the policy of mass killings applied to laborers caused much damage to the Reich's total war effort. Racist considerations precluded the sending of Jews to Germany as foreign workers. The few Jews who did infiltrate the ranks of workers coming to Germany from various countries made every effort to avoid identification as Jews. At a time when Germany was suffering from a severe shortage of manpower, millions of Russian POWs were dying of starvation, illtreatment, and deliberate murder; and masses of Jews who were working as forced laborers in the occupied countries or as prisoners in concentration camps were taken away from their places of work and deported to the extermination camps.

BIBLIOGRAPHY

Billstein, A. *Fremdarbeiter in unserer Stadt, 1939–1945.* Frankfurt, 1980.

Evrard, J. *La déportation des travailleurs français dans le IIIe Reich.* Paris, 1972.

Ferencz, B. *Less than Slaves: Jewish Forced Labor and the Quest for Compensation.* Cambridge, Mass., 1979.

Homze, E. L. *Foreign Labor in Nazi Germany.* Princeton, 1967.

Luczak, C. *Polscy robotnicy przymusowi w Trzeciej Rzeszy podczas II Wojny Światowej.* Poznań, 1974.

Luczak, C., ed. *Położenie polskich robotników przymusowych w Rzeszy, 1939–1945.* Poznań, 1975.

Pfahlmann, H. *Fremdarbeiter und Kriegsgefangene in der deutschen Kriegswirtschaft, 1939–1945.* Darmstadt, 1968.

CZESŁAW LUCZAK

Jews in Occupied Poland

The forced labor for which the Jews of occupied POLAND were drafted took various oppressive forms and lasted from the beginning of World War II until its end. As soon as the German army entered Poland in September 1939, individual Jews and groups of Jews were forced to clear roadblocks and debris and to pave roads. Units of the Wehrmacht played an active role in forcibly recruiting Jews for such work, seizing them at random on the streets or dragging them out of their homes, and maltreating them while they were at work. Often the only purpose for subjecting Jews to forced labor was to degrade them, by compelling them to carry out hard physical tasks that had no practical purpose at all, while subjecting them to beatings and to harassments such as cutting off their beards; or by making them do physical exercise.

On October 26, 1939, compulsory labor was introduced in the GENERALGOUVERNEMENT by law, applying to Jewish males aged fourteen to sixty; implementation was put into the hands of the SS command. Subsequently the law was extended to apply also to women, and to children aged twelve to fourteen. In the period from October to December 1939 compulsory labor was also introduced by locally issued decrees for Jews living in those parts of Poland incorporated into the Reich.

On January 13, 1940, orders were issued by Generalgouverneur Hans FRANK for the implementation of the October 26, 1939, law. The decrees provided for compulsory service, in the form of labor, by all Jews, men and women alike, from the ages of fourteen to sixty, whether or not they had employment of their own. The compulsory service was scheduled to extend over two years, but it could be prolonged "in case the desired reeducational goal had not been achieved in that period." To facilitate the imposition of the law, the Germans ordered all Jews aged fourteen to sixty to register; this process was to be enforced by the Judenräte (Jewish Councils; *see* JUDENRAT) under the supervision of the mayors. The Jews registered were divided into six categories, based on their professional or trade qualifications. In addition, in measures unrelated to the registration, Jews were forced into temporary labor assignments, such as removing snow, loading goods the Nazis had confiscated from Jews, and building walls around areas earmarked as ghettos.

As time went on, special labor camps were put up for Jews, who were summoned by name to report to them. In these labor camps the Jews were quartered in barracks and had to work under very harsh conditions. In the Lublin district, twenty-nine such camps were in operation by July 1940. In August of that year twenty thousand Jews in the nineteen to thirty-five age group were ordered to report to labor camps. Many chose to disregard the call-up, despite the heavy risks involved, because of the intolerable conditions of life and work in the camps, where the inmates were also exposed to such torments as pursuit by vicious dogs, humiliation, and beatings. Frequently the men on forced labor had no living quarters assigned to them, did not receive minimal food rations, and had to sleep under the open sky; those working on land amelioration projects sometimes had to stand in water during their work. Many people perished in the camps; others were completely exhausted when they returned and were permanently disabled. One vivid illustration of conditions in the camps is the fact that out of six thousand men from the WARSAW ghetto sent to the labor camps, one thousand were no longer fit for work within two weeks. In certain ghettos (for example, that of ŁÓDŹ) the entire population was on forced labor and the ghettos, in effect, became labor camps.

In addition, Jews in large numbers also worked in German factories in Poland and in ghetto "shops" (workshops), especially during the last stage of the ghettos' existence. At the end of 1940 over 700,000 people were on forced labor in Poland. That number dropped to 500,000 in 1942 and a little over 100,000 in mid-1943; the reasons for the decrease were the high mortality rate in the ghettos and the destruction by the Nazis of the Jewish population. Conditions of work in places other than labor camps differed from one to the other; all had in common a ten- to twelve-hour workday and the total absence of social benefits and vacations.

From the beginning, the forced-labor operation was administered by the SS. In the areas that were incorporated into the Reich, the SS remained in charge of forced labor up until the total annihilation of the Jewish population, but in the Generalgouvernement responsibility for the project was taken over by the Ministry of Labor, in July 1940. Two years later, on June 25, 1942, the forced-labor administration was again changed, and this time the Sicherheitspolizei (Security Police; Sipo) took over. In practice, the remuneration paid to persons on forced labor was tiny

Jewish men and boys rounded up in Warsaw for forced labor.

Jewish forced labor in Będzin, Poland.

or nonexistent. The rule concerning Jews was that their pay had to be lower than that of other nationalities. Even when minimum wages were paid, substantial deductions were made for various purposes, as determined by the Germans. In Białystok, for example, the deductions amounted to 50 percent of the total, and for the work on the Frankfurt-Posen highway, as much as 80 percent was deducted from the pay.

The following figures, relating to Warsaw, illustrate the extent to which forced labor was not remunerated: out of 2 million workdays by persons on forced labor in the period from October 21, 1939, to November 15, 1940, nearly three-quarters (1.44 million) were not paid at all. Where wages were paid, they were so low that the recipients could not buy any extra food on the black market—which meant that they starved like all the others. It follows that the German policy on forced labor by Jews, and on the wages for such labor, contributed directly to the physical destruction of the Jews.

When the great majority of the Jews had been killed, those remaining in the ghettos were forced to keep on working—in the "shops"; in sorting out for the Germans the possessions of the murdered Jews; and in various institutions and factories serving the needs of the Reich. Factories employing Jews had to pay substantial sums to the Sipo. The Jews in turn had to pay bribes in order to obtain employment—which they sought to do by any means, in the belief that this would save them from deportation to the extermination camps.

In mid-1942 and in April and May of 1943, some of the Jews in the Generalgouvernement ghettos were taken to labor camps at TRAWNIKI and PONIATOWA, where they were put to work in various workshops. In November 1943 the Germans murdered forty thousand Jews in these camps (see "ERNTEFEST"). In Łódź, forced labor was kept up longer than anywhere else, until the ghetto was liquidated in August 1944.

BIBLIOGRAPHY

Ferencz, B. *Less than Slaves: Jewish Forced Labor and the Quest for Compensation.* Cambridge, Mass., 1979.

ZBIGNIEW LANDAU

FOREIGN ORGANIZATION OF THE NSDAP. *See* Auslandsorganisation der NSDAP.

FORSTER, ALBERT (1902–1948), German politician and Nazi official. Forster was born in Fürth, Bavaria, and became a tradesman. In 1923 he joined the Nazi party, and in 1930 was elected to the Reichstag; that same year he also became *Gauleiter* of DANZIG, then a free city. When Adolf Hitler came to power, Forster was charged with the Nazification of Danzig and was one of the persons responsible for the actions taken against the Poles and Jews in the city. When the Germans occupied Poland in September 1939, Forster was appointed *Chef der Zivilverwaltung* (head of the civil administration) of the Pommern (Pol., Pomorze) district. He later became the Reich governor (*Reichstatthalter*) of Danzig and *Gauleiter* of Danzig and West Prussia.

Forster was responsible for the extermination of entire populations; mass deportations; deportations for forced labor; the forced "Germanization" of Poles; and the destruction of Polish cultural treasures. When the war ended he was captured by the Allies and in 1946 was extradited to Poland. There he was tried by the Supreme National Tribunal, sentenced to death, and hanged, on April 28, 1948.

BIBLIOGRAPHY

Jastrzebski, W., and J. Sziling. *Okupacja hitlerowska na Pomorzu Gdańskim w latach 1939–1945.* Gdańsk, 1979.

STEFAN BIERNACKI

FORT ONTARIO, so-called free port for REFUGEES in the United States proposed by the United States WAR REFUGEE BOARD (WRB). The idea, modeled on the pattern of customs-free ports, was to bring imperiled refugees from Europe to shelters in the United States, where they would be held without legal status until the war's end, at which time they would be returned to their countries of origin.

The idea of a free port, originally proposed and supported by both the BERGSON GROUP and the WORLD JEWISH CONGRESS, was offi-

Albert Forster, *Gauleiter* of Danzig, reviews a parade of the Danzig SS-Heimwehr (Home Guard) in August 1939.

Eleanor Roosevelt with the director of the Fort Ontario Refugee Center, visiting the shelter at Oswego, New York (September 20, 1944). [Franklin D. Roosevelt Library]

cially put forward by John Pehle, director of the WRB, in February 1944. Many important individuals in both the State Department and the War Department opposed the idea. A bill introduced in Congress to establish free ports died in committee.

In the midst of his 1944 re-election campaign, President Franklin D. ROOSEVELT announced his plan to create a free port at Fort Ontario in Oswego, New York. His announcement did not presage any major change in the president's refugee policy. The creation of the free port was only a token act; Roosevelt made it clear that it would serve only 1,000 refugees, who would be returned to Europe at the termination of hostilities. The president also instructed his assistants to make sure that the group would contain others besides Jews. In fact, refugees brought to Oswego came not from Nazi-occupied zones but from liberated

areas, and did not therefore face imminent death.

The refugees, once settled in the shelter, were not permitted to work in town or to leave the camp, and a great deal of tension arose among them. At the end of the war there was an attempt, supported by Congress and important elements of the administration, to have the refugees sent back to Europe. Other elements, however, prevailed, and the refugees interned at Fort Ontario were permitted to remain in the United States.

BIBLIOGRAPHY

Gruber, R. *Haven: The Unknown Story of 1,000 World War II Refugees.* New York, 1983.
Lowenstein, S. *Token Refuge: The Story of the Jewish Refugee Shelter at Oswego, 1944–1946.* Bloomington, 1986.
Strum, H. "Fort Ontario Refugee Shelter, 1944–1946." *American Jewish History* 73/4 (June 1984): 398–421.

ARIEL HURWITZ

FOUR-YEAR PLAN (*Vierjahresplan*), Nazi economic program. The memorandum for the establishment of the Four-Year Plan was written by Adolf HITLER himself in August 1936 and kept secret because of possible opposition from economic circles. It was seen as a watershed in the German economy, marking Hitler's first intervention in German economic policy, and for the first time stating his war aims and a self-imposed timetable of intensified rearmament.

In the memorandum, Hitler set a twofold task: to make the German army operational and the German economy fit for war within four years. To achieve this goal, the plan aimed at creating a self-sufficient and independent German economy and particularly at protecting German agriculture against war conditions, making it able to withstand a blockade to the maximum. Hitler sought the goal of self-sufficiency through the pursuit of an expansionist policy and through stress on making Germany less dependent on outside raw materials.

For this purpose, the Göring Reich Works (Reichswerke Hermann Göring) were founded and refineries and aluminum works established. The plan also promoted the development of a synthetic-materials industry in order to replace raw materials and control the allocation of labor. Hermann GÖRING, in spite of his ignorance of economic affairs, was nominated as commissioner for the implementation of the plan, receiving extraordinary general powers in the economic sphere. During the war, these powers were extended to the economic structure of the occupied countries so as to extract everything possible from them in a policy of ruthless plundering. Göring also directed the deportation of millions of people from the occupied territories for FORCED LABOR.

The increased self-sufficiency of Germany had a direct effect on the potential for speeding up the Reich's antisemitic policy. In order to begin Germany's economic mobilization, Hitler had the thought of issuing a law making the whole of Jewry liable for all the damage allegedly inflicted by individual Jews upon the German economy.

BIBLIOGRAPHY

Barkai, A. *Das Wirtschaftssystem des Nationalsozialismus: Der historische und ideologische Hintergrund 1933–1936*. Cologne, 1977.

Eicholtz, D. *Geschichte der deutschen Kriegswirtschaft 1939–1945*. Berlin, 1985.

Petzina, D. *Autarkiepolitik im Dritten Reich: Der nationalsozialistische Vierjahresplan*. Stuttgart, 1968.

Speer, A. *Inside the Third Reich: Memoirs*. London, 1970.

Treue, W. "Hitlers Denkschrift zum Vierjahresplan 1936." *Viertel-jahreshefte für Zeitgeschichte* 3/2 (April 1955): 184–210.

DAVID BANKIER

FPO. *See* Fareynigte Partizaner Organizatsye.

FRANCE. [*This entry consists of four articles. The first is a general survey of French history during the Vichy regime and the Nazi occupation. The second*, The Jews and the Holocaust, *reviews the Nazi efforts to carry out the "Final Solution" in France with the assistance of French collaborators, and the third*, Jewish Responses to Persecution, *is an inquiry into the Jewish reactions in France to these efforts. The fourth article*, After the Holocaust, *surveys the recovery of French Jewry after the end of the war. See also* Action Française; Fédération des Sociétés Juives de France; French Police; Youth Movements: France.]

General Survey

From the 1870s until 1940, France was governed as a republic, which had been instituted by the National Assembly. Designated as the Third Republic, it never had a constitution, and instead was governed by constitutional laws. After the fall of France to the German army in June 1940, and the signing of the armistice with Germany, the National Assembly voted in July to suspend the constitutional laws of the Third Republic. Marshal Philippe PÉTAIN was granted full powers as head of state by the National Assembly, and a new regime was set up at the spa town of Vichy, in the south of France.

The French defeat had immediate consequences for the nature of French society. Desirous of ending the war as rapidly as possible and returning to a normal way of life, the new French government entered into hurried negotiations with Germany to obtain an armistice. By the end of June 1940, the armistice was already taking effect. France was divided into two areas: the occupied zone, under German rule and occupation, and the unoccupied zone, under the new Vichy regime. The occupied zone, which included PARIS, encompassed the entire Atlantic and Channel coasts and contained the more fertile regions in western, northern, and eastern France. The armistice and the official division of France left millions of Frenchmen in a quandary as to whether their hurried exodus to the south at the beginning of the German invasion had been a necessary precaution. French officials, and above all Pétain, urged them to return to their homes and allow France to emerge from the ravages of war and begin the process of reconstruction. Hundreds of thousands of Frenchmen heeded the call and returned to the occupied north before the borders between the zones were more firmly instituted in late September 1940.

FRANCE

Beyond the geographic rearrangement of France, a major upheaval in France's social and political orientation was engendered by the lightning defeat. Following the dissolution of the Third Republic and its liberal principles, the Vichy regime embarked on a policy of returning the country to the hallowed ideals of prerevolutionary France. The regime, which was generated by internal disenchantment with republican ideals and by the turbulent xenophobic atmosphere of the

1930s, replaced the principles of *liberté* (liberty), *égalité* (equality), *fraternité* (fraternity) with *travail* (work), *famille* (family), and *patrie* (homeland). Riding on the nationalist appeal to bring France back to the French, a common refrain of those years, Vichy methodically went about curbing the influence of foreigners in the country and harassing the rights of Jews and various refugee groups. Vichy read French public opinion well. Following the trauma of defeat, the deflated

French temperament eagerly awaited a national renewal. Pétain's nomination as the head of the new French state was a source of renewed pride and hope. His call for a "new order"—a collective submission to authoritarianism and to the exalted sources of authority (*travail, famille, patrie*)—was resoundingly welcomed by almost all elements of French society.

Opposition to Pétain during his first year in office came from a very small segment of French society, while sincere enthusiasm for his attempts to save France from reliving the hardships of World War I emanated from diverse corners of the French political and cultural spectrum. For example, the Catholic church in France, which had been in constant conflict with the Third Republic, could not remain unresponsive to Pétain's efforts to bring France back to what the church regarded as pure Christian principles. The marshal was seen as the redeemer of France and the church, and loyalty to him and his policies was the order of the day.

This adulation went further and penetrated into political circles of opposing ideologies. Thus, when the Pétainist mystique was at its height and a sense of *attentisme* ("wait and see") prevailed, open resistance of the kind advocated by Charles de GAULLE attracted few. This, notwithstanding Vichy's concerted efforts and strategy to court Nazi Germany and procure a more tenable arrangement with the German authorities. Minister of State Pierre LAVAL, who had been most active in this direction, worked diligently behind the scenes to bring Pétain and Hitler together. Their eventual meeting at Montoire from October 22 to 24, 1940, provided sufficient evidence that Vichy's "national revolution" included a policy of collaboration. France, under the "new order," was to become part of the New Europe under Hitler's tutelage. Laval's negotiations with the Germans eventually backfired and he was removed from office at the end of 1940, to be replaced by Adm. Jean-François DARLAN, commander in chief of the French navy. Darlan too was convinced that France's best interests were served by an accord with Germany. In May 1941 he met with Hitler at Berchtesgaden and granted the Germans military facilities in North Africa and Syria, in return for which the French received virtually no German concessions in the area that counted the most—in the terms of the armistice.

French society began to show increasing signs of displeasure and opposition to the Vichy regime from the summer of 1941, in part owing to the German invasion of the Soviet Union. Communist and socialist elements in France, which had been reticent to engage in resistance activity against Vichy, declaring themselves to be in favor of "neither Pétain nor de Gaulle," were now provoked to increased action. This was still far from a total break with Pétain, but it was nonetheless a significant step forward.

The growing internal fissure in French society failed to convince Vichy to change its goal of rapprochement with Nazi Germany —indeed, almost the contrary could be claimed. In April 1942, Laval succeeded in maneuvering himself back into power, replacing Darlan, and he openly declared his support for a Nazi victory to withstand Bolshevik world domination. Although the Nazi leadership paid little attention to these statements, Vichy proceeded, hoping to strengthen its bond with Germany. As part of this new drive, Laval agreed to send more French laborers to Germany and to enact intensified anti-Jewish legislation in the occupied zone. French officials were instructed to grant the German occupying forces all the assistance necessary in their plans for mass roundups of Jews in the summer of 1942. Laval's concerns at this juncture necessitated harmony with the country that demanded French forced labor and that was building a New Europe, free of communism. However, Vichy's image emerged tainted from the collaboration. More and more Frenchmen raised their voices in protest against their government, among them leading figures in the Catholic and Protestant churches. Resistance activity of various orientations, spurred on by increasing German repression and French concessions, grew considerably.

The rather peaceful occupation of the Vichy zone by the German and Italian forces in early November 1942 put an end to the euphemistically named "free zone." Italy began a liberal and humane occupation of eight southern departments east of the Rhône that lasted until September 1943. It was the German occupation and Vichy's acquiescence that heightened the internal decay in the country. The hope of improved living conditions through a policy of collaboration had proved to have no solid foundation. The French population felt itself increasingly taxed by the armistice agreement as occupation costs rose to approximately 500 million francs a day. The financial exploitation of France included a constant siphoning-off of French foodstuffs and raw materials, but more critical and alienating was the growing number of French workers in Germany, which by 1943 had reached some 700,000. All this did not convince Laval to reappraise his gamble on a German victory.

In September 1943, Germany hastened to fill the vacuum left after the fall of Benito MUSSOLINI and the Italian armistice agreement with the Allies by occupying the Italian zone in southern France. On the horizon, however, loomed the growing strength of the Résistance, which in the same month liberated Corsica. From that point on, Maquis fighters (the name came from Corsican Résistance units that fought in wild terrain) became an ever-present nemesis to Vichy and the German occupation. They were not alone. De Gaulle's Free French organized militarily and politically for a takeover of France, and when the time came they were able to fill a void in the French administration. The Allied landing in Normandy on June 6, 1944, signaled the end of the occupation. The liberation of France came two months later, and as de Gaulle marched triumphantly into Paris, Pétain, Laval, and other Vichy officials fled ignominiously to Germany. They would later be returned to Paris and tried for treason.

BIBLIOGRAPHY

Kedward, H. R., and R. Austin, eds. *Vichy France and the Resistance.* New York, 1985.
Whitcomb, P. W., trans. *France during the German Occupation, 1940–1944.* 3 vols. Stanford, 1959.

RICHARD COHEN

The Jews and the Holocaust

Evidence of a Jewish presence in France exists from the first century A.D. From 465,

A trial of members of the French Résistance by a German military court in Paris between April 7 and 14, 1942. The defendant in the photograph is a Jewish woman, Simone Schloss.

the Jewish population in a number of French towns increased considerably. France became a center of Jewish learning from the eleventh century. However, one hundred thousand Jews were expelled from the country in 1306. This mass expulsion was followed by a decree of Charles VI in 1394 stipulating that Jews would no longer be tolerated in the kingdom of France, and by subsequent expulsions from other French provinces.

On the eve of the French Revolution, the Jewish community in France numbered forty thousand. The largest concentration was in Alsace-Lorraine, where Ashkenazic Jews had established themselves. Some three thousand Portuguese Jews had settled in the south, and they were the first to receive full emancipation, on January 28, 1790. The Ashkenazic Jews were granted full civil rights on September 27, 1791.

Jewish integration into French society proceeded more or less smoothly, notwithstanding occasional antisemitic occurrences; the most serious among them was the Dreyfus affair at the end of the nineteenth century. Throughout that century, in a spirit of modernization and urbanization, Jews migrated in large numbers to Paris, making it the center of Jewish life in France. Jews developed a deep-seated attachment to France and French culture, attested by the large migration from Alsace-Lorraine after its annexation to Germany in 1870. Moreover, France continued even after the Dreyfus affair to appear as the land of liberty and equality in the eyes of world Jewry. In the interwar period, immigrants from eastern Europe flocked by the tens of thousands to Paris, while thousands of Jewish refugees from Germany sought refuge in the city in the 1930s. On the eve of World War II Paris contained two-thirds of French Jewry, and this group had become a vibrant institutional and cultural community.

In the 1930s the Third Republic began to reassess its open-door policy of the preceding decade. Increasing voices called for a hold on Jewish immigration and an abrogation of Jewish emancipation. Yet, though stringent restrictions against refugees were gradually introduced and internment camps were set up for them, Jewish emancipation remained in force until the fall of France and the establishment of the Vichy regime.

RICHARD COHEN

In the summer of 1940, about 350,000 Jews lived in France, more than half of whom were not French citizens. Among these were tens of thousands of Jewish REFUGEES from Belgium, the Netherlands, and Luxembourg, some of whom had fled the Reich several years earlier. Persecution of these Jews began almost immediately, both in the German-occupied zone and in the zone left under French control.

The unusual context of the Holocaust in France is the considerable degree of autonomy accorded the French during the Nazi occupation. In this respect France differed substantially from fully occupied countries like Belgium, the Netherlands, and Denmark, or puppet states like Norway. Notably, throughout the entire period of the deportations of Jews, France had a French government, based in Vichy; a head of state (Marshal Pétain); an administration at least nominally responsible for the whole of the country; and a powerful police force. Even after the Nazis moved across the demarcation line, in November 1942, the French government remained formally in charge of the nation and retained a substantial degree of authority.

The Germans needed and received a great deal of assistance from the French to carry out their plans. After the war, defenders of Vichy claimed that the work of this government limited the damage, preventing even higher numbers of deportees from France. German documents lend a superficial plausibility to this notion, for it is plain that the Nazis in charge of the "FINAL SOLUTION" had hoped to do better in France, envisioning a completed task by the end of 1943. The SS in charge of the deportations failed to meet their own quotas, and Vichy claimed the credit for this failure. However, close examination of the German record, as well as research on the role of Vichy and its agencies, tells a different story.

The deportations of 1942 to 1944 (see below) did not begin in a political vacuum. The dispatch of the Jews "to the east" was, rather, the culmination of two years of aggressive legislation and persecution, including the passage of laws defining who was to be considered Jewish, isolating Jews in French society, taking away their livelihood, interning many, and registering them with the police. In the German-controlled zone the SS in France, under Obersturmführer Helmut KNOCHEN, set the apparatus of persecution in place. Matters concerning Jews were assigned to SS-Hauptsturmführer Theodor DANNECKER, who reported directly to the office of Adolf EICHMANN in Berlin.

Remarkably, however, the Vichy government too moved against the Jews, taking the initiative to issue the comprehensive STATUT DES JUIFS (Jewish Law) in October 1940, and to establish a central agency for coordinating anti-Jewish legislation and activity in March 1941, the COMMISSARIAT GÉNÉRAL AUX QUESTIONS JUIVES (General Office for Jewish Affairs; CGQJ). In November 1941, moreover, Vichy established the UNION GÉNÉRALE DES ISRAÉLITES DE FRANCE (General Union of Jews of France; UGIF), a Jewish agency operating under Vichy authority that was intended to control Jewish activities and communal affairs. During the two years following France's defeat, the French government deliberately incorporated antisemitic activity into its *révolution nationale*—the officially declared policy of turning France in an authoritarian, nationalist, and corporatist direction.

The French government considered it extremely important that its laws should apply throughout the entire country, in the occupied as well as the unoccupied zone; through the enforcement of such measures, Vichy assumed it was strengthening French sovereignty and hastening the day when full French sovereignty would be restored. Vichy's leadership believed that the Germans would be grateful to the French for pursuing their own anti-Jewish policy, and would respond by yielding greater control over this and other spheres of national policy. In addition, the French were anxious to see that the property confiscated from the Jews did not fall into the hands of the Germans. Vichy inaugurated an extensive program of "Aryanization" in July 1941, with the important objective of maintaining formerly Jewish property in France. In practice, "Aryaniza-

tion" simply meant the confiscation of Jewish possessions by the state. It developed into a vast property transfer, involving some forty-two thousand Jewish businesses, buildings, and other properties. For their part, the Nazi occupation authorities engaged in a subtle form of entrapment. Nudging Vichy ever deeper into measures against the Jews, and withholding serious pressure on the French for about a year, the occupation relieved itself of much of the trouble of antisemitic persecution while drawing the French into areas where even some Vichyites showed signs of discomfort.

All Jews suffered grievously from the first two years of persecution, except for a tiny handful of well-established French Jews who received exemptions from the Vichy government. In legal terms, the way was cleared for persecution without limits, using the powerful judicial and administrative apparatus of the French state. The confiscation of Jewish property and the elimination of Jews from professions and the government service transformed thousands into penniless refugees in France. Foreign Jews were particularly vulnerable, and were especially victimized by both the Germans and Vichy. Thousands were forced into labor camps or interned, often in conditions that approached the Nazi concentration camps of the 1930s. The first victims of the Holocaust in France died in these camps, their number eventually totaling about three thousand.

Following the WANNSEE CONFERENCE of January 1942, the Nazis began to prepare for the deportation of Jews from France and other western European countries. They proceeded slowly and methodically, for the task was enormous and the German personnel that could be spared for the operation were relatively few. In particular, the Nazis did their best to ensure the cooperation of the French government and administration.

The spring and summer of 1942 were turning points. At the end of April, Pierre Laval, who was committed to intensifying collaboration with Germany, became head of the French government under Marshal Pétain. In May the legalistic and anti-German Xavier VALLAT was replaced at the head of the CGQJ by the racist collaborator Louis DARQUIER DE PELLEPOIX. Darquier had no scruples about

The concentration camp at Le Vernet in the south of France, about 31 miles (50 km) south of Toulouse. [JDC Archives, New York]

extending full support to the Nazis in their murderous enterprise. Simultaneously, the Wehrmacht yielded authority over repressive activity in France to the SS, now headed there by Höherer SS- und Polizeiführer (Higher SS and Police Leader) Carl Albrecht OBERG. The French police under René Bousquet worked out an arrangement with the SS whereby the former were given an important degree of autonomy, in exchange for agreeing to work against the enemies of the Reich. In their own zone the Germans cleared the way for deportations by imposing the wearing of a yellow star by all Jews (June 7), rounding up large numbers, and controlling the movements of the rest.

On June 11, a decisive meeting took place in Berlin at which arrangements were made for regular deportations of Jews from France, Belgium, and the Netherlands. Demands for cooperation now rained down on Vichy. After deliberations, Laval and the French cabinet agreed to help. Throughout the summer and fall of 1942, roundups of Jews took place in both the occupied and unoccupied zones.

Most of the work was done by the French police. On July 16 and 17, in one of the most cruel and spectacular operations, they rounded up 12,884 Jews in Paris, some 7,000 of whom—families with small children—were crowded for days in the Vélodrome d'Hiver sports arena with no food, water, or sanitary facilities. Elsewhere, parents were torn from their children, with the victims unceremoniously packed into cattle cars and shipped to the transit camp at DRANCY, just outside Paris. In all, 42,500 Jews were sent eastward in 1942, perhaps one-third of them from the unoccupied zone.

The cover-up of the Germans, which Laval agreed to repeat, was that the Jews were being sent to work camps "in the east." Officially, Vichy would only report that the victims had gone "to an unknown destination." In fact, the end of the line was AUSCHWITZ, where most of the deportees were immediately killed.

The deportations of the summer and fall of 1942 stirred the first serious opposition to Vichy among certain segments of French opinion. The roundups of Jews could scarcely be concealed, and the cruelty of the separation of families was heavily criticized. A split developed in the Catholic church, hitherto solidly behind Pétain and the *révolution nationale*. Highly placed clergymen now made their first open protest against the anti-Jewish activity of the regime. For Vichy, the deportations signaled the failure of its strategy on the Jewish issue. Far from winning greater independence, the French were now being heavily importuned by the Germans. After November 1942, with Nazi troops in the formerly unoccupied zone, this worsening situation was obvious to all.

Difficulties arose as the deportations gradually included French Jews as well as outsiders. Having agreed to the deportation of foreign Jews from both zones, the Vichy authorities found themselves drawn into satisfying the Nazis' deportation quotas, which were fixed by the available railway transport from Drancy to Auschwitz and not by technicalities such as nationality. As early as January 1943, when massive deportations from both zones resumed, the Germans reported that the French police were no longer as reliable as they once had been in assembling and dispatching the Jews. Even Laval dragged his feet—refusing, in August 1943, to agree to strip French Jews of their citizenship so as to facilitate their deportation.

Yet despite occasional protests and difficulties, the deportations continued, the last convoys leaving France in the summer of 1944. Laval, Pétain, and the government would not change course. To the end, Vichy enforced the extensive apparatus of anti-Jewish laws that legitimized the deportations in the eyes of some, and it certainly facilitated the process of deportation. Some Jews managed to escape for a time, by fleeing to the Italian-occupied zone of France. There the Italian Fascist troops provided a remarkable sanctuary—not only against German demands for deportations, but against the application of Vichy antisemitic laws as well. This protective screen was shattered in September 1943 when the Italians surrendered to the British and Americans. Other Jews escaped to SPAIN or to SWITZERLAND, although passage across either frontier was not normally permitted by the host countries and

was fraught with danger from the German and Vichy police.

Thousands of Jews were assisted by a small but sympathetic element in the French population, often at great risk to those providing rescue or aid. Such Frenchmen were to be found among all groups but particularly among Protestants, many of whom by tradition also felt themselves to be a beleaguered minority in France. Help and sanctuary came from a variety of other sources: the Quakers, the American Jewish JOINT DISTRIBUTION COMMITTEE (known as the Joint), the YMCA, the Catholic Témoignage Chrétien, and Jewish resistance networks. An outstanding example was the Protestant village of LE CHAMBON-SUR-LIGNON, which became a kind of underground railway, smuggling several thousand Jews to safety.

In all, over 77,000 Jews from France were either killed in concentration camps in Poland or died while in detention. Approximately 70,000 went to Auschwitz, and the rest to other camps—MAJDANEK and SOBIBÓR, and a few dozen to BUCHENWALD in August 1944. Of all these Jews, about one-third were citizens of long standing; 8,700 were sixty years of age or over, 6,000 were under thirteen, and 2,000 were under the age of six.

The "Final Solution" in France was a Nazi project from beginning to end. Few Frenchmen advocated massacre, and only a small number of extreme collaborationists in Paris ever carried antisemitism to the murderous conclusions of Hitler and his associates. However, it seems highly unlikely that the Germans would have been capable of deporting large numbers of Jews from France without the help provided by the French authorities. Two years of persecution by the French government and administration helped snap the bonds that bound Jews to French society, leaving many helpless once the Nazis' machinery of destruction turned to France.

It is true that the final toll—about one-fifth of the country's Jews were killed—seems less, proportionately, than in many other countries, but the circumstances the Nazis faced in France must be taken into account and the considerable difficulties they had to overcome noted. Unlike Belgium or the Netherlands, where Jews were concentrated in a few urban areas and were therefore easy to capture, those in France were scattered about a large country in thousands of localities. Many were living in the countryside, where only the local authorities could keep track of them and round them up. (This had been the case since the collapse of the French armies in 1940 and the scattering of the French population to the south and east. The Germans themselves had contributed to the dispersion, by not allowing Jews back into the occupied zone after the armistice.) Unlike Poland, where there was always a heavy German police presence, there were few men to spare for France—only three battalions for the occupied zone, for example, or about three thousand men.

There is no evidence, on the other hand, that Vichy authorities attempted in a concerted way to limit the deportations. No models for alternative strategies occurred to Vichy leaders, and they seem to have considered the entire question of Jewish persecution as of secondary importance. Like everyone else, the Vichy leadership was slow to fathom the "Final Solution," despite the Nazis' repeated declarations that all the Jews would be deported, and despite the periodic hints of the slaughter in Poland. Most of the officials at Vichy seem to have shared in the widespread anti-Jewish mood of 1940, and many agreed with the legalistic antisemitic strategy of Vallat. Others were indifferent, kept their views to themselves, and carried out the anti-Jewish legislation in their sphere of authority. Recent research, therefore, rejects the theory of a consciously plotted strategy to save as many Jews as possible.

MICHAEL R. MARRUS

BIBLIOGRAPHY

Billig, J. *Le Commissariat général aux questions juives (1941–1944)*. 3 vols. Paris, 1955–1960.

Hyman, P. *From Dreyfus to Vichy: The Remaking of French Jewry, 1906–1939*. New York, 1979.

Klarsfeld, S. *Le mémorial de la déportation des Juifs de France*. Paris, 1978.

Klarsfeld, S. *Vichy-Auschwitz: Le rôle de Vichy dans la solution finale de la question juive en France, 1942*. 2 vols. Paris, 1983, 1985.

Marrus, M. R., and R. O. Paxton. *Vichy France and the Jews*. New York, 1981.

Paxton, R. O. *Vichy France: Old Guard and New Order, 1940–1944*. New York, 1982.

Rutkowski, A., ed. *La lutte des Juifs en France à l'époque de l'occupation (1940–1944)*. Paris, 1975.

Szajkowski, Z. *Analytical Franco-Jewish Gazetteer, 1939–1945*. New York, 1966.

Tint, A. "The Jews of France in the Last Half Century." *Jewish Journal of Sociology* 1/1 (April 1959): 127–131.

Weinberg, D. *Community on Trial: The Jews of Paris in the 1930s*. Chicago, 1977.

Wellers, G., A. Kaspi, and S. Klarsfeld, eds. *La France et la question juive, 1940–1944*. Paris, 1981.

Jewish Responses to Persecution

When the Germans struck at France in May 1940, the Jewish community sensed an immediate blow to its security. Together with millions of Frenchmen, it took part in a massive exodus to the unoccupied southern zone. More than 100,000 Jews took to the roads in those panic-stricken days, among them Jewish leaders and rabbis, stripping occupied France of experienced leadership and rabbinical guidance. After the armistice was signed on June 22 and the French leadership called on Frenchmen to return to the north, as many as 30,000 Jews are reported to have returned there, trusting the new agreement, and raising the Jewish population in the Seine region to almost 150,000. During the initial months of turmoil and indecision after the armistice, some 30,000 Jews were successful in crossing the southern French border in the hope of finding refuge abroad.

The process of reorganizing the community slowly began to unfold in the fall of 1940 amid contradictory assessments as to the possibility of Jewish life under Nazi occupation and Vichy rule. Jews in France were not alone in this quandary. French people of opposing political and social views tended to favor a quick return to normal life rather than venture into a period of constant struggle with the authorities. Indeed, a certain resignation set in, as well as a desire to see France return to a more nationalist outlook. Jews in France shared some similar sentiments, yet their situation was confounded by the Nazi threat. Inevitably within this crucible, the tensions that had prevailed in the Jewish community during the 1930s between leaders of the native Jews and the eastern

European immigrants surged to the surface and prevented a united stand, both in the northern occupied region and in the southern unoccupied zone.

In the north, prior to the Vichy STATUT DES JUIFS, immigrant Jewish leaders had established in Paris a special clandestine committee, known as AMELOT, to coordinate relief activity in the community. Its attempt to involve native French Jews in the enterprise failed to materialize owing to their trepidation at cooperating with immigrant Jews at a time when French nationalism and xenophobia were at their height. Without the support of the more established community, Amelot's efforts were necessarily limited. As for the native Jews, a sense of organizational disarray was apparent in the summer of 1940, although the return of Rabbi Julien Weill, the Chief Rabbi of Paris, to the city in August improved the situation somewhat.

Dannecker entered into this vacuum of communal leadership. He met with various Jewish leaders, native and immigrant, and after several months of pressure and threats, and of intercommunal disagreement, succeeded in cajoling them into joining together to form an umbrella organization in January 1941, to be known as the Comité de Coordination des Oeuvres Israélites de Bienfaisance (Coordinating Committee of Jewish Welfare Societies). Uppermost in the minds of the leadership when it succumbed to this unprecedented decision were concern and awareness of the growing pauperization of the community as a result of the extensive economic problems. Members of the CONSISTOIRE CENTRAL DES ISRAÉLITES DE FRANCE (Central Consistory of French Jews)—the official Jewish community—were now openly participating with members of the immigrant community to improve and coordinate relief activity; only the Jewish Communists aligned in Solidarité (see UNION DES JUIFS POUR LA RÉSISTANCE ET L'ENTR'AIDE) were excluded from this organization. Although the body was established "voluntarily," it probably would not have come into existence without German pressure. However, the unification that Dannecker sought was not forthcoming, and his continuous, devious efforts to consolidate the Coordinating Committee were counterproductive, making the already

reticent immigrant leaders even more hesitant to remain part of the committee. The sense that working in the committee involved cooperation with the Germans on one level or another became a growing problem, leading eventually to several resignations. The committee was gradually stripped of its immigrant participation, thereby exacerbating relations within the community.

The Coordinating Committee underwent a major realignment, co-opting respected native leaders (among them André BAUR, Juliette Stern, Marcel Stora, and Fernand Musnik), but it remained stigmatized in the eyes of the immigrant community, especially after the mass internments in Paris in May 1941. Thus, as the "Aryanization" of Jewish property took on serious proportions from the summer of 1941, as the newly established transit camp at Drancy began to intern thousands of Jews in squalid conditions, and as pockets of poverty deepened in the Jewish community, the organizing of relief and aid of different kinds remained divided among the Coordinating Committee, Amelot and its subsidiary bodies, and Solidarité. The Joint Distribution Committee provided considerable funds to the Coordinating Committee and to Amelot. Throughout the first half of the year, Dannecker expressed his overall dissatisfaction with this situation and continued his efforts for a more influential and cohesive committee.

The attitude toward participation in the Coordinating Committee reflected the divisions within the Jewish community. Although no significant resistance activity emerged during the first year and a half of the occupation, it was apparent that far more elements within the immigrant community and its organizations had gravitated to illegal activity and clandestine behavior, fearing the slightest association with the Germans. This was especially true for Solidarité. On the other hand, the Consistory and the Coordinating Committee, representing the more established sectors of the native community, continued to bide for time, adhered to the legalistic approach, and counted on the French authorities for support. These polar attitudes widened when Dannecker tried to establish a compulsory Jewish organization in the fall of 1941.

In the south of France, where the massive migration had increased the Jewish population to approximately 150,000, the needs were no less urgent than in the north, though without the oppressive Nazi occupation. Jews had flocked to the major cities—Lyons, Marseilles, Toulouse—and to hundreds of smaller cities. Former leaders of the community resettled in Lyons and Marseilles and gradually began to map out plans for relief. Here, too, the conflict and lack of trust that had characterized immigrant-native relations in the 1930s were revived, and certain aggressive positions of native leaders were reasserted. The Joint's diligent European director, Joseph SCHWARTZ, was instrumental in cutting through some of the mutual suspicion, and encouraged the Chief Rabbi of France, Isaïe Schwartz, to initiate an umbrella organization to solve the divisiveness and make efforts to ward off persecution.

At the end of October 1940, two weeks after the publication of the *Statut des Juifs*, which equally affected the Jews of the unoccupied zone, leaders of the major relief organizations met in Marseilles to establish the Commission Centrale des Organisations Juives d'Assistance (Central Commission of Jewish Relief Organizations; CCOJA). The CCOJA was to unite all the major relief organizations and to guarantee contacts with governmental and public authorities, to establish a communal fund, and to coordinate the various bodies within the community. Although it continued to function until the beginning of 1942, the CCOJA proved to be ineffectual. Once again, the division between immigrant organized relief (concentrated in the Fédération des Sociétés Juives) and native relief (centered in the Comité d'Assistance aux Réfugiés d'Allemagne, or Committee to Aid German Refugees) could not be easily circumvented; the different agencies maintained a mutual distrust and thus feared indirect funding from the Joint. Moreover, the individualistic mentality of French Jewry, nourished by generations of emancipation, was hesitant to succumb to the CCOJA's call for a new communal orientation.

In southern France, expressions of rebellion and outright opposition to the Vichy government among the general population were few and far between in 1941, even among the

radical Left. This was true of the Jewish community as well. A sense of "wait and see" dominated their outlook and behavior. Notwithstanding the flood of antisemitic legislation initiated by the Vichy regime, trust in the leadership of France was still a basic postulate for the widest sections of the community, native and immigrant, and individual and community activity centered on coping with the daily difficulties. Nazi Germany was considered responsible for the anti-Jewish legislation, yet its awesome presence in northern France remained a distant reality. However, as the war progressed and the Nazi designs against the Jews became more extreme, opposition within the community grew. A case in point was the German-Vichy attempt to establish a compulsory umbrella organization for French Jewry in the fall of 1941.

Dannecker's original plan, following the strategy of the SD (Sicherheitsdienst; Security Service) in the Nazi-occupied territories from the beginning of the war, was seized upon by Vichy. In its reluctance to allow the SD control over the "Jewish question," Vichy proposed extending such an organization to the unoccupied zone as well. After months of negotiations between the French authorities and leaders of the Jewish organizations, the UGIF was established in late November 1941 and was to replace both the Coordinating Committee and the CCOJA.

Internal Jewish deliberations in the north pitted members of the Coordinating Committee against the immigrant leaders, who condemned the UGIF participants as collaborators with the Nazis and refused to join. In the south, native Jewry was split between members of the Central Consistory, who saw the racial definition of the organization as an affront to the French-Jewish symbiosis, and members of native relief organizations, who considered participation a necessity to safeguard the relief activity. Immigrant leaders, in particular Marc JARBLUM, were vociferous in their opposition and called for a rejection of the German-Vichy design. Nonetheless, the UGIF began to function in both zones, committed to preserving the welfare and relief activity, but severely compromised by the widespread opposition within the community.

The deportations that began in March 1942 jolted the community and sent thousands of Jews into a frenzy, looking frantically for refuge from the Nazis and the French police. Jews began to seek hiding places in thousands of French villages and rural communities, aided by the local population, while thousands more attempted to cross over the border to Switzerland. More than twenty-seven thousand Jews were caught and deported in the German *Aktionen* of that summer. Countless families were separated, and many were left homeless. Vichy's responsibility for this was considerable. It had allowed the German authorities to deport Jews from French internment camps in the unoccupied zone, clearly exposing its dependency and releasing significant public protests. The nature and extent of these events impelled more and more Jews to question their acceptance of a legalistic existence and accelerated the resistance tendencies in organizations in both north and south.

Buoyed by French protests and humanitarian actions, Jewish relief groups assumed a more active role in directing the population to seek alternative ways of existence and to cease all official contacts. This was especially so in the occupied zone, where the immigrant groups energetically advocated a bolder response to the authorities and some began to engage in forms of sabotage against German officers and institutions. As Jewish organizations turned to illegal activity—removing Jewish children to Christian homes and monasteries, forging identification papers and documents, aiding Jews in hiding and in crossing the border to Spain and Switzerland, and the like—tension mounted between these organizations and the centers of the UGIF in the north and south. The UGIF continued to uphold a legalistic orientation, although in the south, participant organizations had begun to operate on a basis that was partly legal and partly illegal. For some, like the OEUVRE DE SECOURS AUX ENFANTS (OSE), this pattern continued until the fall of 1943, when a direct Gestapo raid on a children's home showed the bankruptcy of the dualistic orientation.

French Jewry's predicament deteriorated still further in the wake of the German occupation of the south in November 1942. One of the first victims of this new situation was the Jewish community in Marseilles. Some two thousand foreign and native Jews were seized in a large-scale roundup at the end of January 1943, followed by minor roundups in Lyons and other southern cities. These events brought home to the Jewish organizations in the south the implications of the German occupation and, in contrast, the apparent benevolence of the Italian occupation of eight southern regions.

From November 1942, Jewish organizations of every persuasion in France went all out to capitalize on the protection from antisemitic legislation that the Italian authorities granted the Jews. As many as thirty thousand Jews had found their way into the Italian zone by September 1943, when they were confronted by the crude reality of a German takeover and an aggressive attempt to seize as many Jews as possible. Thousands were rounded up by the German net, but thousands avoided arrest by immediately going into hiding.

The lot of the Jews who remained under German occupation, in the north and south, was uneven during this period. For example, Parisian Jews enjoyed a certain relief after the traumatic days of July 1942. They did not experience another major roundup, but their numbers dwindled markedly as a result of constant dispersion outside the city into small villages and hamlets, and widespread hiding within its limits. By the summer of 1944, only fifteen thousand Jews lived openly in the capital, thousands of whom continued to receive relief in one form or another from Jewish organizations. Alongside material aid to the needy, care for orphaned children, and assistance to the thousands of internees in Drancy, armed resistance emerged in Paris from within a number of organizations, especially the units of Solidarité and the ARMÉE JUIVE, an armed unit composed of members of several youth movements.

In the German-occupied south, where Gestapo efforts to increase the lagging deportation count were supported by the French militia, Jews were often on the run, foreseeing the impending danger. A sign of the times could be detected in the community realignments: Jewish organizations were slowly mending their differences and joining forces.

The beginning of 1943 witnessed a rapprochement between the UGIF and the Central Consistory, while toward the end of the year a dramatic alliance took place between the Consistory and representatives of all the functioning organizations outside the orbit of the UGIF.

In 1944 the CONSEIL REPRÉSENTATIF DES JUIFS DE FRANCE (Representative Council of French Jewry; CRIF), an umbrella organization, was founded to coordinate resistance activity among the Jewish groups. This was a remarkable step on the part of Jewish leaders to set aside their distinct ideological differences and agree to consolidate measures for the community and to contribute to the overall French Résistance movement. The movement in this direction reflected an increasing consensus of opinion in the Jewish community, buttressed by the activities of the Armée Juive, which arranged border crossings to Spain and later took part in military operations against the German occupation in the north and south. Hundreds of Jews from these ranks lost their lives in military encounters with the Germans.

A divided community at the outset of the war, beset with political and social differences, French Jewry emerged severely depleted at liberation, but somewhat reoriented. It had lost some seventy-eight thousand Jews and harbored thousands of broken families in its midst, but it had also shown an ability to confront the catastrophe with diverse forms of aid and assistance. Facing the combined opposition of the Gestapo and the French authorities, the community resorted to traditional forms of relief throughout most of the war. In its struggle for existence, French Jewry had to reappraise its trust and confidence in the French authorities before it was able to overcome internal differences and open up new avenues of opposition and self-help. This emerged only in the latter part of the war, when the designs of its enemies had been extensively realized. The trend toward organizational unity would serve the community in good stead in the very difficult period of reconstruction that followed liberation.

Jews in France, individually and collectively, were continuously seeking new havens of rescue. As the demographic distribution of the community during the war attests, Jewish internal migration was extraordinary, and Jews were recorded in more than six thousand localities within France, a fact of considerable importance when assessing the overall number of victims and the assistance of local French people. Not always, as in the case of the Italian buffer zone, were their perceptive changes of location capable of foreseeing political developments, but this was part of the tragedy that they could not control.

BIBLIOGRAPHY

L'activité des organisations juives en France sous l'occupation. Paris, 1947.
Adler, J. *The Jews of Paris and the Final Solution: Communal Response and Internal Conflicts, 1940–1944.* New York, 1987.
Cohen, R. I. *The Burden of Conscience: French Jewish Leadership during the Holocaust.* Bloomington, 1987.
Kedward, H. R. *Resistance in Vichy France: A Study of Ideas and Motivation in the Southern Zone, 1940–1942.* Oxford, 1978.
Latour, A. *The Jewish Resistance in France (1940–1944).* New York, 1981.
Lazare, L. *La résistance juive en France.* Paris, 1988.
Marrus, M. R. "Jewish Leadership and the Holocaust: The Case of France." In *Living with Antisemitism: Modern Jewish Responses,* edited by J. Reinharz, pp. 380–396. Hanover, N.H., 1987.

RICHARD COHEN

After the Holocaust

Like many other Jewish communities in post-Holocaust Europe, French Jewry confronted the massive task of reconstruction with despair and trepidation. Parisian Jewry was weakened seriously by the loss of approximately fifty thousand members. Throughout France, Jews agonized over the disappearance of hundreds of small communities and the reduction of many large settlements to a mere handful of Jewish families.

However, in comparison with other European Jewish communities, the situation of French Jewry after liberation seemed far from hopeless. French Jews were in the unique position of having experienced the

Holocaust yet having survived in large enough numbers to reassert themselves after the war. The continuous influx of Jewish survivors fleeing DISPLACED PERSONS' camps and emerging from hiding—more than thirty-five thousand in the first three years after the war—meant that France would soon contain the most populous Jewish community on the Continent.

Of the many pressing problems facing the newly reconstituted community in the early days after the end of the war, three consumed most of its energy and interest: the restoration of spoliated property; the care and feeding of refugees; and the plight of orphaned and "adopted" children. The attempts at solution were checkered. Despite intense efforts by community leaders to petition government officials for restitution, French Jewry had only limited success in reclaiming the businesses, furniture, and apartments of deportees. More successful were the activities of the Comité Juif d'Action Social et de Reconstruction (Jewish Committee for Social Action and Reconstruction), which was able to feed and house nearly three-quarters of the forty thousand Holocaust survivors who sought refuge in France. Thanks to the efforts of organizations such as the Oeuvre de Protection des Enfants Juifs and the OEUVRE DE SECOURS AUX ENFANTS, nearly one hundred institutions were created to care for orphaned children and to reintegrate them into the community. While the French Jewish community was able to provide foster parents for orphans, however, it had little success in recovering Jewish children adopted by non-Jews during the war.

Postwar reconstruction involved more than simply responding to immediate needs. If French Jewry was to successfully confront the challenges raised by post-Holocaust Europe, it would have to accomplish two major tasks: to set about restructuring the Jewish community to ensure its survival and growth; and to seriously reevaluate deeply rooted beliefs concerning French-Jewish relations in light of the Vichy experience.

Despite elements of goodwill and repeated calls for unity, native and immigrant leaders quickly lapsed into prewar patterns of organizational behavior. However, the failure to create a unified communal structure did not preclude coordinated activity on specific issues. Pressured by the Joint Distribution Committee to coordinate its fragmented relief effort, in October 1949 the community formed the Fonds Social Juif Unifié (United Jewish Social Fund; FSJU), which soon emerged as the central agency for the collection of funds and the distribution of services among French Jewry. In leading French Jewish philanthropy from traditional reliance on individual acts of beneficence to a commitment to professional community service, the FSJU helped to forge communal solidarity and Jewish pride.

The CRIF served as the political arm of French Jewry and was an active participant in public debates on a number of important postwar issues of interest to the French Jewish community in the 1940s and 1950s. These included German rearmament, the prosecution of German war criminals, reparations for Holocaust victims, monitoring the activities of antisemitic organizations, and the passage of anti-racist legislation. Though CRIF's effectiveness in the political arena depended in large part on the policies of the French government, it clearly strengthened the community by developing what one observer called a *judaïsme musculaire*, that is, a willingness to assertively defend Jewish interests.

The success of the massive reconstruction effort waged by organizations such as the FSJU and CRIF attests to the significant transformations that French Jewry underwent in the late 1940s and early 1950s. Yet the community structure rested on weak ideological foundations, attitudes, and assumptions about Jews and France that had been shaped by prewar experiences and by contradictory responses to the events of World War II. Despite their public demands for the banning of anti-Jewish groups and demonstrations and their expressions of outrage at government leniency with regard to collaborators, most native Jews chose to define French wartime attitudes toward Jews in terms of the resistance of a minority to Nazism rather than in the collaboration or at least passive acceptance of the majority. Even immigrants who suffered the greatest losses in the Holocaust quickly fell prey to the national mythology surrounding the French Revolution and the Résistance that dominated French political discourse in the immediate postwar period.

Nowhere was the fragility of French Jewish consciousness more clearly revealed than in the community's response to the creation of the state of Israel. Aside from the obvious issue of financial support, there was little in communal discussions concerning the Jewish state that pointed to a distinctive French Jewish contribution to the new nation. Nor was there any interest in the question of how Israel could help to ensure the future of Jews in France. Most committed French Jews undoubtedly shared the sentiments of the journalist Bernard Kessler, who wrote in 1946: "Without a Jewish homeland in Palestine, Judaism will disappear sooner or later, either through persecution or through assimilation and conversion."

What was missing in this intense and important discussion, as well as in the response to postwar antisemitism, was a strong defense of a Jewish presence in France. Despite its impressive successes in creating new institutions and in rehabilitating the tens of thousands of broken men and women who returned from the Nazi extermination camps and emerged from hiding, French Jewry in the 1940s and early 1950s lacked confidence in its future. Though far from moribund, the French Jewish community seemed to be marking time, waiting, as it had done in the past, for a fresh infusion of immigrants, which in fact took place from the mid-1950s, with the influx of Jews from North Africa.

BIBLIOGRAPHY

Blumenkranz, B., ed. *Histoire des Juifs en France.* Toulouse, 1972.

Rabi (Rabinovitch, W.). *Anatomie du judaïsme français.* Paris, 1962.

Roland, C. *Du ghetto à l'occident: Deux générations yiddiches en France.* Paris, 1962.

Weinberg, D. "The French Jewish Community after World War II: The Struggle for Survival and Self-Definition." *Forum* 45 (Summer 1982): 45–54.

DAVID WEINBERG

FRANK, ANNE. [*This entry is divided into three parts. The first tells about Anne Frank's family and recounts the story of her life; the second describes her diary. The third part is about the Anne Frank House in Amsterdam.*]

Family. Otto Heinrich Frank (1889–1980) was born in Frankfurt, Germany. He grew up in an assimilated, liberal Jewish environment, attended high school, and trained for a while at Macy's department store in New York. During World War I he was a reserve officer in the German army. After the war Frank started his own business, with mixed success. In 1925 he married Edith Holländer, the daughter of factory owners in Aachen. The couple had two daughters, Margot Betti (born February 16, 1926) and Annelies Marie (born June 12, 1929), called Anne.

Soon after the Nazis came to power in January 1933 and the first anti-Jewish measures were announced, the Frank family decided to leave Germany. Otto Frank went to Amsterdam. He knew the city well from frequent visits and had several good friends there. After finding an apartment he brought over the rest of his family. He set up a company, Opekta, that made and distributed pectin for use in homemade jams and jellies. In 1938, together with Hermann van Pels, Frank started a second company, Pectacon, which specialized in the preparation of spices for sausage making. Van Pels, his wife Auguste, and their son Peter had recently fled to Amsterdam from Osnabrück in Germany.

Anne and Margot quickly adapted themselves to their new life. They learned Dutch and attended the local Montessori school. The Franks joined the liberal Jewish congregation of Amsterdam.

This relatively carefree existence came to an end on May 10, 1940, when the Germans invaded and occupied the Netherlands. The invasion was soon followed by anti-Jewish measures. That October a law was passed requiring all Jewish-owned businesses to be registered. With the help of non-Jewish friends and colleagues both Opekta and Pectacon were "Aryanized" on paper, and the businesses continued. Another law stipulated that Jewish children could attend only Jewish schools, and Anne and Margot switched to the Jewish Lyceum.

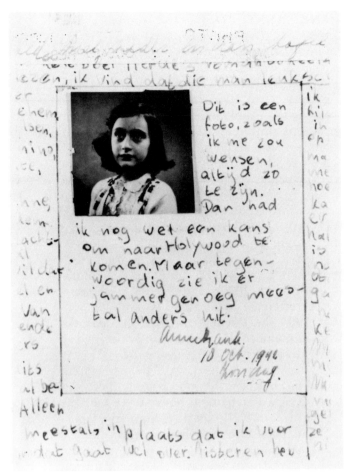

Photo and excerpt from Anne Frank's diary. [© 1988, Copyright by Cosmopress, Geneva & Anne Frank-Fonds.]

Meanwhile, Otto Frank, who had no illusions about the Nazis, had begun preparations to go into hiding, if this proved necessary. Little by little, the family's possessions were brought to the vacant annex to Frank's office at Prinsengracht 263. Four employees were informed of his plans and agreed to help: Victor Kugler, Johannes Kleiman, Elli Voskuijl, and Miep Gies (born Hermine Santrouschitz). Miep had worked with Otto Frank for years and had become his right hand. Born in Vienna, she had been one of the many thousands of Austrian children who after World War I were taken into Dutch foster homes to improve their health. Miep had stayed on, and in 1941 she married Jan Gies.

The Franks' hiding plans went into high gear on July 5, 1942, when Margot received a registered letter from the ZENTRALSTELLE FÜR JÜDISCHE AUSWANDERUNG (Central Office for Jewish Emigration), a Nazi bureau. Margot, then sixteen years old, was ordered to register for what the letter called "labor expansion measures." After consultation with the van Pels family, the Franks decided to go into hiding immediately. The next day they moved into the annex, followed a week later by the van Pels family and their fifteen-year-old son, Peter. On November 16, 1942, they were joined by an eighth *onderduiker* (lit., "one who dives under"), the dentist Fritz Pfeffer, who had fled from Berlin in 1938. These eight people were to spend two years living in a few cramped rooms made in an attic. As food and clothing became scarce and could be bought only with coupons, which Jews in hiding could not obtain, the four helpers in the office managed somehow to buy enough supplies to feed and clothe eight additional people, often at great risk to their own lives.

On August 4, 1944, the SD (Sicherheitsdienst; Security Service) in Amsterdam received an anonymous phone call—it has never been established from whom—with information about Jews in hiding at Prinsengracht 263. A police van immediately drove to the Prinsengracht, and the eight Jews were found and arrested. A policeman named Silberbauer demanded money and jewelry; to hide these he emptied an attaché case full of papers, which he threw on the floor. Among the papers was Anne Frank's diary. Also arrested were Kleiman and Kugler, two of the employees who had assisted the families. After the police left, Miep Gies and Elli Voskuijl went back to the annex to pick up many personal items, such as photographs, books, and other papers. A few days later all the furniture and clothing were hauled away from the annex, a customary procedure after an arrest. During the arrests Miep Gies had realized that Silberbauer, like her, came from Vienna. This may have been why he did not arrest her, although he made it clear that he suspected her as well of having helped the Jews. The next day Miep sought him out to see if there was a way the prisoners could be set free, but Silberbauer indicated there was nothing he could do. Kugler and Kleiman were taken to the concentration camp in Amersfoort, in the Netherlands. Kleiman suffered a hemorrhage of the stomach, and through the intervention of the Red Cross was sent home in September 1944. Kugler was able to escape during a transport in March 1945 and remained in hiding until the liberation of the Netherlands in May.

The Jewish prisoners arrived at the WESTERBORK transit camp on August 8, 1944. From there a full trainload of prisoners left for the extermination camps every week. On September 3 the last transport to leave Westerbork for AUSCHWITZ departed. According to the meticulously kept transport lists, there were 1,011 people on board, among them the Franks, the van Pels family, and Pfeffer. On arrival at Auschwitz-Birkenau, 549 of them were immediately gassed. Hermann van Pels was one of these. Edith Frank, her daughters Margot and Anne, and Auguste van Pels were interned in the Frauenblock. Pfeffer was the next to die. He is listed in the death book of the NEUENGAMME camp on December 20, 1944. Edith Frank perished at Auschwitz-Birkenau on January 6, 1945. It has not been established where and when Auguste van Pels died, but it is assumed that it was at the end of March or early April, somewhere in Germany or Czechoslovakia. Peter van Pels was one of the many thousands of prisoners who, because of the advancing Russian army, were put on DEATH MARCHES. He died shortly before the liberation in May 1945 in the MAUTHAUSEN camp in Austria.

Anne and Margot were sent to BERGEN-BELSEN at the end of October 1944. This camp filled up with thousands of prisoners from other camps that were being vacated as the Russians advanced. Housing, food, and medicine became totally inadequate, and many prisoners weakened from hunger and the cold. A typhus epidemic took many victims. Margot died of typhus around the beginning of March; Anne, who believed that both her parents had perished, died a few days later. Two sisters from Amsterdam who had been with the Frank sisters in both Westerbork and Auschwitz later stated that they had carried Anne's body from the sick barrack. She was buried in one of the mass graves at Bergen-Belsen. Otto Frank was the only survivor of the eight in hiding. The Soviet army liberated Auschwitz on January 27, 1945, and Frank returned to Amsterdam the following June. After Anne's death had been confirmed, Miep Gies returned to him the papers she had kept.

Diary. On June 12, 1942, her thirteenth birthday, Anne received from her father a red-checked diary. That same day, Anne wrote on the first page:

I hope I shall be able to confide in you completely, as I have never been able to do in anyone before, and I hope that you will be a great support and comfort to me.

In letters to her imaginary friend, Anne painted a picture of herself and of her personal development in the context of the problems and fears of eight Jews trying to hide from deportation. The frightening news about the developments on the outside reached those in hiding through the radio and through their helpers. On October 9, 1943, Anne wrote:

Dear Kitty, I've only got dismal and depressing news for you today. Our many Jewish friends are being taken away by the dozen. These people are treated by the Gestapo without a shred of decency, being loaded into cattle trucks and sent to Westerbork, the big Jewish camp in Drente. Westerbork sounds terrible: only one washing cubicle for a hundred people and not nearly enough lavatories. . . . It is impossible to escape; most of the people in the camp are branded as inmates by their shaven heads and many also by their Jewish appearance.

If it is as bad as this in Holland whatever will it be like in the distant and barbarous regions they are sent to? We assume that most of them are murdered. The British radio speaks of their being gassed.

Perhaps this is the quickest way to die. I feel terribly upset.

When Pfeffer arrived at the annex, Anne noted:

Pfeffer has told us a lot about the outside world, which we have missed for so long now. He had very sad news. Countless friends and acquaintances have gone to a terrible fate. Evening after evening the green and gray army lorries trundle past. The Germans ring at every front door to inquire if there are any Jews living in the house. If there are, then the whole family has to go at once. If they don't find any, they go on to the next house. No one has a chance of evading them unless one goes into hiding. Often they go around with lists, and only ring when they know they can get a good haul. Sometimes they let them off for cash—so much per head. It seems like the slave hunts of old times. But it's certainly no joke; it's much too tragic for that. In the evenings when it's dark, I often see rows of good, innocent people accompanied by crying children, walking on and on, in the charge of a couple of these chaps, bullied and knocked about until they almost drop. No one is spared—old people, babies, expectant mothers, the sick—each and all join in the march to death.

Still, the *onderduikers* tried to lead a normal life. For Anne as well as Margot and Peter, this meant doing homework with the help of their old schoolbooks and new books borrowed from the library by Miep and Elli.

Fear of discovery created enormous pressure on those in hiding. During the day they could not move around or use the bathroom because not everyone in the office below was aware of their presence. The close quarters and constant tensions were often too much for Anne. On October 29, 1943, she wrote:

> I wander from one room to another, downstairs and up again, feeling like a song-bird whose wings have been brutally clipped and who is beating itself in utter darkness against the bars of its cage. "Go outside, laugh, and take a breath of fresh air," a voice cries within me, but I don't even feel a response any more; I go and lie on the divan and sleep, to make the time move quickly, and the stillness and the terrible fear, because there is no way of killing them.

Anne described the difficulties with her mother, her special relationship with her father, her sexual development, and her efforts to improve her character. She fell in love with Peter but later wrote about her disappointment in him.

Anne's diary is also a monument to the helpers who for two years struggled to obtain food and clothing and provided spiritual support:

> Our helpers are a very good example. They have pulled us through up till now and we hope they will bring us safely to dry land. Otherwise, they will have to share the same fate as the many others who are being searched for. Never have we heard one word of the burden which we certainly must be to them, never has one of them complained of all the trouble we give. They all come upstairs every day, talk to the men about business and politics, to the women about food and wartime difficulties, and about newspapers and books with the children. They put on the brightest possible faces, bring flowers and presents for birthdays and bank holidays, are always ready to help and do all they can. That is something we must never forget; although others may show heroism in the war or against the Germans, our helpers display heroism in their cheerfulness and affection.

On March 28, 1944, Anne heard over the British radio about a plan to gather diaries and letters about the war. "Of course, they all made a rush at my diary immediately," she wrote the following day. "Just imagine how interesting it would be if I were to publish a romance of the 'Secret Annex.' The title alone would be enough to make people think it was a detective story." On May 11 she wrote:

> Now, about something else: you've known for a long time that my greatest wish is to become a journalist some day and later a famous writer. Whether these leanings towards greatness (of insanity?) will ever materialize remains to be seen, but I certainly have the subjects in my mind. In any case, I want to publish a book entitled *Het Achterhuis* [The Annex] after the war. Whether I shall succeed or not, I cannot say, but my diary will be a great help.

Anne prepared a list of pseudonyms for possible publication: Van Pels became Van Daan, Pfeffer became Dussel, and so on.

Anne observed herself and her environment, made plans for the future, commented and criticized, and did not spare herself in that regard. In the high-pressure situation of the annex, she changed from a shy young girl to a young woman. Superficial comments about girlfriends and admirers made place for philosophical statements about herself and the world around her. One of the last entries in the diary is from July 15, 1944:

> That's the difficulty in these times: ideals, dreams, and cherished hopes rise within us, only to meet the horrible truth and be shattered. It's really a wonder that I haven't dropped all my ideals because they seem so absurd and impossible to carry out. Yet, I keep them, because in spite of everything I still believe that people are really good at heart. I simply can't build up my hopes on a foundation consisting of confusion, misery, and death. I see the world gradu-

ally being turned into a wilderness, I hear the ever-approaching thunder, which will destroy us too, I can feel the sufferings of millions, and yet, if I look up into the heavens, I think that it will all come right, that this cruelty too will end, and that peace and tranquillity will return again. In the meantime, I must uphold my ideals, for perhaps the time will come when I shall be able to carry them out. Yours, Anne.

Apart from the diary, Miep had also saved a book of stories ("Stories and Adventures from the Annex") and the "Book of Beautiful Phrases." In this Anne had copied quotations that had pleased her.

Friends of Otto Frank's to whom he had shown some of the passages from Anne's diary persuaded him to find a publisher. After the historian Jan Romein published an article in which he related his emotions on reading parts of the diary, the publisher Contact approached Otto Frank, and *The Annex* appeared in June 1947 as edited by Frank, who had deleted several passages that he deemed either offensive or too personal. Several pieces from the "Story Book" were added to the diary.

The book went through many reprints. In 1950 it appeared in Germany and France, and in 1952 in England and the United States. For the American edition, Eleanor Roosevelt wrote in the preface: "This is a remarkable book. Written by a young girl—and the young are not afraid of telling the truth—it is one of the wisest and most moving commentaries on war and its impact on human beings that I have ever read."

The diary has been published in more than fifty editions; the total number of copies printed amounts to almost twenty million. Dramatic presentations have also reached a large public. The stage version by Albert Hackett and Frances Goodrich premiered on Broadway on October 5, 1955, and received the Pulitzer prize for the best play of the year. The film version followed in 1959.

Numerous other artists, including sculptors, painters, composers, and choreographers, have been inspired by Anne Frank. Many schools have been named after her. Anne's wish—"I want to live on, even after my death"—has become a reality. Throughout the world she has become a symbol of the millions of victims of the Holocaust. For many people, Anne's diary is the first confrontation with the Nazi persecution of the Jews. The influence of the diary is such that those who try to deny the Nazis' crimes also denounce the diary as a fraud. To counter such efforts, the RIJKSINSTITUUT FOR OORLOGSDOCUMENTATIE (Netherlands State Institute for War Documentation) in Amsterdam published in 1986 an annotated edition of both versions of Anne's diary, the earlier edition with passages deleted, and the later

The home of the Frank family in Amsterdam (Prinsengracht 263), where Anne and her family lived hidden in the attic for two years. The house is now a museum. [Anne Frank Stichting]

complete version. The English translation appeared in 1989.

After Otto Frank's death in 1980, Anne's papers went to the Rijksinstituut. The diary is on loan to the Anne Frank House, and is on display there. The copyright is owned by the independent Anne Frank Foundation in Basel.

The Anne Frank House. After the publication of *The Annex* many visitors found their way to the house at Prinsengracht 263, which was still being used as an office. In 1957 there were plans to raze the house to make room for a new building, but the public outcry prevented this action. The owner of the building then donated the house to the newly established Anne Frank Foundation on condition that the building be open to visitors.

The museum opened its doors in 1960. Besides the maintenance of the Annex, it has as its second goal the struggle against antisemitism and racism. It was Otto Frank's wish that the museum not become a memorial to Anne but instead contribute to an understanding of prejudice and discrimination. The Anne Frank Foundation maintains a documentation center on antisemitism and racist groups in Western Europe and the United States. It produces teaching aids and organizes traveling exhibits in various languages. The foundation has an office in New York City.

The number of visitors to the Anne Frank House continues to increase each year. In 1988 there were a total of 550,000 from around the world. The impact of Anne's diary has not diminished and continues to confront readers with the cruel truth: "Six million Jews were not murdered. One Jew was murdered, six million times over" (Abel Herzberg, survivor of Bergen-Belsen).

BIBLIOGRAPHY

Anne Frank Foundation. *Anne Frank in the World, 1929–1945*. Amsterdam, 1985.
The Diary of Anne Frank. Dramatized by F. Goodrich and A. Hackett. New York, 1956.
Frank, Anne. *The Diary of Anne Frank: The Critical Edition.* New York, 1989.
Frank, Anne. *The Diary of a Young Girl.* New York, 1952.
Frank, Anne. *Tales from the Secret Annexe.* New York, 1956.
Gies, M., with A. Gold. *Anne Frank Remembered: The Story of Miep Gies, Who Helped to Hide the Frank Family.* New York, 1985.
Schnabel, E. *Anne Frank: A Portrait in Courage.* New York, 1959.

JOKE KNIESMEYER
Translated from Dutch by
Elly Dickason

FRANK, HANS (1900–1946), jurist and Nazi official; governor-general of POLAND from 1939 to 1945. When Hitler's Germany conquered Poland in September 1939, the eastern third of the country was occupied by the Soviet Union (in accordance with the secret terms of the NAZI-SOVIET PACT), the western third was annexed to the Third Reich, and the central region became a German-occupied territory known as the GENERAL-GOUVERNEMENT. Appointed governor-general was the legal expert of the Nazi party and Hitler's personal lawyer, Hans Frank, who henceforth played a major, albeit vacillating, role in implementing the racial policies that the Nazis pursued so relentlessly in eastern Europe.

Hans Frank graduated from a Munich *Gymnasium* in 1918. The young Frank displayed his commitment to militant nationalist and right-wing politics by joining the Epp Freikorps (a paramilitary group commanded by Ritter von Epp) in 1919 while he was pursuing the study of law at the universities of Kiel and Munich. In 1923 he passed his first-level exams, joined the SA (Sturmabteilung; Storm Troopers) and Nazi party, and took part in Hitler's ill-fated Beer-Hall Putsch in Munich. He fled briefly to Austria, then returned to Germany to finish his doctorate at the University of Kiel in 1924.

In 1926, Frank left the Nazi party in protest against Hitler's renunciation of German claims over the South Tyrol, only to rejoin a year later. His career in the party then flourished as he undertook the legal defense of various party members, most prominently in Hitler's many libel cases and in the 1930 Leipzig trial of three Nazi army officers. He also handled the very delicate matter of researching Hitler's family tree for possible Jewish ancestors.

After Hitler took power, Frank's usefulness rapidly diminished. He was given numerous honorific but powerless positions that helped to make plausible the charade of Hitler's "legal revolution." In 1933, he was appointed minister of justice for the state of Bavaria, and in 1934, minister without portfolio. From 1934 to 1941 he was president of the Academy for German Law, with the self-assigned task of reformulating German law on the basis of National Socialist principles. A middle-class intellectual who was never admitted to the inner circle of Nazi leaders, Frank remained oblivious to Hitler's open aversion to law, lawyers, and any procedures that threatened to curtail his own freedom of action. He came to prominence when Hitler appointed him head of the Generalgouvernement in October 1939.

Frank's ambitions in the Generalgouvernement, both to build up a strong power base for himself and to retain Hitler's favor, encountered almost constant frustration. Hitler's practice of presiding over a chaotic system of "institutional Darwinism"—leaving his various vassals to engage in a constant internal struggle for power and jurisdiction and keeping for himself the role of indispensable arbiter and pacesetter—was incompatible with Frank's mania for "unity of administration." While Frank managed to curtail the influence of the military and to reach an agreement for close cooperation with Hermann GÖRING concerning the economic exploitation of the Generalgouvernement, his efforts to control the activities of Heinrich HIMMLER's SS and police were totally futile.

As a result, Frank was torn between two opposing tactics. In his desire to build up his own domain, he inclined toward a pragmatic policy of economic stabilization, less arbitrary and oppressive treatment of the Poles, and their closer integration into the Third Reich. However, in response to contrary hints periodically emanating from Hitler, or in order to outbid his rival Himmler, Frank often veered suddenly to support policies of radical brutality and destructiveness, usually accompanied by bombastic pronouncements delivered with great rhetorical flourish. Thus, Frank vacillated between opposing and supporting the influx of Poles and Jews expelled from the "incorporated territories," between

Hans Frank in his prison cell in Nuremberg during his trial before the International Military Tribunal. [United States Army]

approving the self-sufficiency and rational exploitation of ghetto economies and encouraging the starvation and then mass murder of the Jews, between a genocidal repression of Polish culture and national consciousness and recruitment of Polish collaboration through assuring the Poles a place in the New Order.

Ultimately, Frank's loyalty to Hitler and his own ambition could not be reconciled. He saw himself as the head of the model "crusader kingdom" of Germany's *Drang nach Osten* (drive to the east), while Hitler saw the Generalgouvernement as the racial dumping ground, the slave-labor reservoir, and finally the slaughter yard of the Third Reich. Since Himmler's views more closely approximated those of Hitler, Frank's defeat was inevitable. On March 5, 1942, the hapless Frank was summoned before a tribunal consisting of Himmler, Hans Heinrich LAMMERS, and Martin BORMANN, and stripped of all jurisdiction over racial and police matters. These were now to be the exclusive domain of Himmler's *Höherer SS- und Polizeiführer* (Higher SS and Police Leader), Friedrich Wilhelm KRÜGER.

Perhaps feeling himself free to play the fool, or hoping to force Hitler to relieve him from his humiliating position, Frank delivered a series of lectures at four German universities in the summer of 1942, denouncing the emasculation of German justice by the police state. He also sent Hitler a long memorandum criticizing SS policies in Poland. "You should not slaughter the cow you want to milk," he concluded. Hitler relieved Frank of all his party positions and forbade him to speak publicly within the Reich, but refused to accept his numerous letters of resignation. Thus Frank remained as governor-general until he fled before the Russian advance; he took with him the many volumes of his official diary that have since become a major source for historians of the Third Reich and an important document for the Nuremberg Military Tribunals. Frank was tried among the major war criminals in the NUREMBERG TRIAL, and hanged at Nuremberg.

BIBLIOGRAPHY

Fest, J. *The Face of the Third Reich*. New York, 1970.
Piotrowski, S. *Hans Frank's Diary*. Warsaw, 1961.
Präg, W., and W. Jacobmeyer, eds. *Das Diensttagebuch des deutschen Generalgouverneurs in Polen, 1939–1945*. Stuttgart, 1975.
Rich, N. *Hitler's War Aims: The Establishment of the New Order*. New York, 1974.
Wulf, J. *Das Dritte Reich und seine Vollstrecker: Die Liquidation von 500,000 Juden im Getto Warschau*. Munich, 1978.

CHRISTOPHER R. BROWNING

FRANK, KARL HERMANN (1898–1946), Sudeten German leader and later virtual ruler of the Protectorate of BOHEMIA AND MORAVIA. Frank served in the Austrian army in the latter part of World War I and then became a bookseller in his native Karlsbad, but failed in business. In 1933 he entered Sudeten German politics as propaganda chief under Konrad Henlein. He became a Sudeten German delegate in the Czech parliament in 1935, and in 1938, after the MUNICH CONFERENCE, deputy *Gauleiter* in the Sudetenland. In March 1939, following the German annexation of the remainder of Czechoslovakia, Frank served as state secretary to the Protectorate under Konstantin von NEURATH, with the rank of SS-*Gruppenführer*. In 1942 Frank

Karl Hermann Frank at his public hanging in Prague (1946).

manifested his vengefulness when the Czechoslovak village and inhabitants of LIDICE were destroyed after the assassination of Reinhard HEYDRICH. When Frank became virtual ruler of Czechoslovakia in 1943 as minister of state, he maintained the same policy of terror, particularly against Czech Jewry. At the end of the war he fled to the West, but the Americans extradited him to Czechoslovakia, where a Czech court sentenced him to death. He was executed by public hanging.

BIBLIOGRAPHY

Frank, E. *Karl Hermann Frank: Staatsminister im Protektorat*. Heusenstamm, West Germany, 1971.

LIONEL KOCHAN

FRANK, WALTER (1905–1945), Nazi historian. Frank was born in Fürth, and even as a young man developed a marked antisemitic outlook. This was reinforced during his student years at the University of Munich, where he came under the influence of Professor Alexander Von Müller, the pro-Nazi president of the Bavarian Academy of Sciences. Frank graduated in 1927 with a dissertation on the antisemite Adolf Stoecker and the Christian Social movement (published in 1928). His later historical writings were imbued with the same nationalist spirit; in *Nationalismus und Demokratie im Frankreich der Dritten Republik, 1871–1918* (published in 1933), he claimed to unmask the noxious role of the "international Jew" in French political life.

Frank first met Hitler in 1923, and after 1933 he advanced rapidly as professor and president of the Reichsinstitut für Geschichte des Neuen Deutschlands (Reich Institute for the History of the New Germany). He saw himself as the destined leader of German historiography, with the task of forming the soul of the nation in a Nazi spirit. In 1936 a special Research Department for the Jewish Question (Forschungsabteilung Judenfrage) was created within the institute and directed by Frank. Its publications included the notorious nine-volume *Forschungen zur Judenfrage* (Research into the Jewish Question; 1937–1944). Conflict developed, however, between Frank's institute and a rival institute under Nazi party auspices, the Institut des NSDAP zur Erforschung der Judenfrage. Frank's influence declined, especially after 1941, when Rudolf HESS, his patron, fled to England. Frank committed suicide in May 1945 at Gross-Brunsrode, near Brunswick.

BIBLIOGRAPHY

Heiber, H. *Walter Frank und sein Reichsinstitut für Geschichte des neuen Deutschlands.* Stuttgart, 1966.

LIONEL KOCHAN

FRANKFURT AM MAIN, German city, now part of the state of Hesse in the Federal Republic of GERMANY. Founded in Charlemagne's time, Frankfurt was for many years the site of the election and coronation of the German emperors, and in the fourteenth century it became an imperial free city, a status it retained until its annexation by Prussia in 1866. Jews first settled there in 1074, and over the course of time its Jewish community became one of the most important in Europe. In the nineteenth century, Frankfurt was a cultural center of the Jewish Enlightenment (Haskalah), as well as of Neo-Orthodoxy. It also played an important role in commerce, industry, and banking (the Rothschild Bank had its center in Frankfurt until the early twentieth century). Two of the outstanding personalities based in Frankfurt in the twentieth century were the philosophers Franz Rosenzweig and Martin Buber. In 1817 the city had a Jewish population of 3,300 (10 percent of the total); in 1930 it numbered 30,000 (5.5 percent); and in June 1933, 26,158. Frankfurt was one of the largest Jewish centers in Germany, second only to Berlin. In early 1933 it even had a Jewish mayor, Ludwig Landmann.

Following the Nazi rise to power on January 30, 1933, Frankfurt Jews were subject to physical assaults. The Nazis in the city did not wait for the official launching of the anti-Jewish BOYCOTT on April 1, 1933, to take boycott action against Jewish stores, and they persisted in such action after April 1, extending it also to German-owned stores with Jewish employees. Trade went down sharply in the Jewish stores, and many went bankrupt or were transferred to Nazi ownership. In the period from March to October 1933, 536 Jewish business enterprises in Frankfurt were closed. The new Nazi mayor dismissed all Jews employed by the city even before the enactment of the national law to that effect. (When the law was passed, the mayor had to reinstate employees who had seen active service in World War I, since the new law specifically exempted them from dismissal.) Following the example set by the city government, all public institutions gradually dismissed the Jews on their staffs—the hospitals, law courts, schools, university, and institutions of culture and the arts. When the NUREMBERG LAWS went into effect in 1935, Jews who had been frontline soldiers lost their exemption and were also discharged. Most privately owned commercial establishments also dismissed their Jewish employees.

As a result of the deterioration of economic conditions among the Jews, the two Jewish communities—the general and the "secessionist" Orthodox community—faced financial collapse. Their members, however, were willing to pay high community taxes and make substantial contributions in the form of cash or property, and thereby enabled the communities and welfare organizations to continue functioning. In fact, in response to the growing needs, a large welfare network was established. In 1935, forty-five hundred Jews were in need of help, almost 20 percent of the Jewish population. In addition to financial assistance or help in kind (mainly clothing and food), a vocational training program was set up, for the retraining of hundreds of youngsters of both sexes in productive occupations, trades, and agriculture.

Frankfurt's Jews—like Jews elsewhere in Germany—responded to their exclusion from society and cultural life by setting up their own cultural activities. In 1933 Martin Buber reactivated the Jüdisches Lehrhaus (Jewish Academy), which Franz Rosenzweig had established in the 1920s, with a varied program of lectures. A Jewish symphony orchestra was formed, as were other musical groups and theatrical troupes, and the Jews had a rich schedule of performances and exhibitions from which to choose, ranging from music to photography. A sports program was also organized, with thousands of youngsters participating. These activities were confined to special sports complexes; in 1935 a special swimming pool was allocated as the only one to which Jews were admitted (the community paid an annual fee for its use).

In 1937 Jacob Hoffmann, the leader of the Mizraḥi movement in Germany and the Orthodox rabbi serving the main community, was expelled to Hungary. Among the Polish Jews expelled from Germany on October 26, 1938, 2,000 were from Frankfurt. On October 31 they were allowed to return to the city, but were denied access to their homes, which in the interval had been sealed by the police. The community provided accommodation for them in school buildings and private houses, and the Jewish welfare agencies took care of them until they were able to return to their own homes. During the KRISTALLNACHT pogroms on November 9–10, 1938, five of the city's large synagogues and most of the small prayer houses were burned down. Gangs of rioters roamed the streets, ransacking and

destroying Jewish stores, and also causing loss of life. In the following days, thousands of Jews were arrested in their homes, on the streets, and in the railway stations. For several days they were detained in a large public hall, and were then taken to BUCHENWALD (2,161 Jews) and DACHAU. Nazi propaganda stressed the point that the family of German diplomat Ernst vom Rath (whose assassination was the pretext for the pogroms) came from Frankfurt, and that the assassin, Herschel GRYNSZPAN, had been a student at the Frankfurt Yeshiva (rabbinical academy). The yeshiva building was destroyed by the Nazis.

In the wake of the pogrom and the ensuing riots and arrests, the Jews started fleeing from the city. In November 1938, 618 Jews left Frankfurt; in May 1939, 13,751 Jews (identified by religion) were left, half of the 1933 total; in addition, there were another 440 "members of the Jewish race," by Nazi definition, and 2,687 persons of "mixed blood." By the end of September 1941, the total number of "members of the Jewish race" had gone down to 10,592.

The Frankfurt municipality purchased properties from the Jewish community—belonging to both the main and the "secessionist" communities, which had merged in the wake of *Kristallnacht*—at a price much lower than their real value. The large synagogues, except for one, were torn down. The old Jewish cemetery was leveled, and from the other Jewish cemeteries all pieces of metal were removed, including the lettering on the tombstones, "for use in the war effort." The municipality had an official who was in charge of Jewish welfare, but in February 1940 a Gestapo officer in charge of "Jewish welfare" was appointed, representing both the Gestapo and the municipality; such a post existed only in Frankfurt. This officer, Ernst Holland, handled all affairs relating to Jews in the city, and supervised all the Jewish property and the operations of the Jewish institutions still in existence. His mandate was to reduce Jewish activities and save the costs involved, and to transfer Jewish property and financial assets to "Aryans." This involved, in part, evacuating Jews from their apartments and forcing them to move in with others or to find accommodation in the Jewish community buildings; in this way, the officer was able to transfer hundreds of Jewish apartments into German hands. On March 4, 1941, the Jews were put on forced labor, and this too was under the Gestapo officer's supervision. Between *Kristallnacht*—November 1938—and 1943, 715 Jews committed suicide in Frankfurt.

On October 19, 1941, the first transport of Jews left Frankfurt for Łódź, with 1,125 Jews on board the train. On November 11, 1,052 Jews were deported to Minsk, and on November 22, 902 Jews were sent to Riga. In another three transports (May 8 and 24, and June 11, 1942), 2,886 Jews were deported to eastern Europe; in three more transports (August 18, and September 1 and 15, 1942), 2,952 Jews were sent to THERESIENSTADT. On September 24 another 234 Jews were deported to the east. In 1943, 120 more Jews were deported, in six groups, to various destinations. On January 8, 1944, 56 Jews were sent to Theresienstadt. In June 1943 the post of officer in charge of Jewish welfare was abolished, since there was no longer any need for it.

After the war a new Jewish community was established in Frankfurt; it is now the second largest in Germany. The one remaining large synagogue in the Westend quarter is again being used for religious services. The Jewish community takes care of the cemeteries, but on several occasions Jewish cemeteries have been desecrated.

BIBLIOGRAPHY

Heuberger, R., and H. Krohn. *Hinaus aus dem Ghetto . . . Juden in Frankfurt am Main 1800–1950.* Frankfurt, 1988.
Kommission zur Erforschung der Geschichte der frankfurter Juden. *Dokumente zur Geschichte der frankfurter Juden, 1933–1945.* Frankfurt, 1963.
Schembs, H.-O. *Bibliographie zur Geschichte der frankfurter Juden, 1781–1945.* Frankfurt, 1978.
Wipperman, W. *Das Leben in Frankfurt zur NS-Zeit.* Vol. 1 of *Die Nationalsozialistische Judenverfolgung.* Frankfurt, 1986.

JACOB BORUT

FRANKFURTER, DAVID (1909–1982), medical student. Born in Daruvar, Croatia, Frankfurter was the son of the local rabbi, Dr. Moshe Frankfurter. In 1929 David Frankfurter began to study medicine, first at Leipzig and

David Frankfurter.

later at Frankfurt; he witnessed the Nazi rise to power and their persecution of the Jews in the first years of their rule. In 1934 he moved to Bern, Switzerland, to continue his studies, while maintaining his interest in the events taking place in Nazi Germany. The NUREMBERG LAWS, enacted in September 1935, strengthened his conviction that he had to make a move against the Nazis that would arouse the world's attention. In November of that year he began to follow the activities of Wilhelm GUSTLOFF, the National Socialist leader of Switzerland; on the evening of February 4, 1936, he shot and killed Gustloff at Davos, the famous resort town, and then surrendered to the police.

Frankfurter's trial before a court at Chur, in the Graubünden canton, began on December 9, 1936. His action was received with great admiration by wide circles of the Swiss population, but Switzerland, apprehensive about its Nazi neighbor, did all it could to restrict the trial to its criminal aspect. The prosecution and the court both rejected the modest effort made by the defense to raise the issue of a young Jew's reaction to the Nazis and their antisemitic policy. Frankfurter was convicted and sentenced to eighteen years in prison.

On February 27, 1945, as Germany was on the verge of collapse in the war, Frankfurter applied for a pardon, which was granted on June 1. He was released, but was expelled from Switzerland and went to Palestine, where he settled in Tel Aviv.

It was only in September 1969 that Switzerland rescinded Frankfurter's banishment from the country, after friends had interceded on his behalf. His memoir of the events appeared in English (published in *Commentary*) in February 1950 and in Hebrew (*First of the Nazi Fighters*) in 1984.

BIBLIOGRAPHY

Frankfurter, D. "I Killed a Nazi Gauleiter: Memoir of a Jewish Assassin." *Commentary* 9/2 (1950): 133–141.

SHMUEL SPECTOR

FRANZ, KURT (b. 1914), SS officer; deputy commandant of the TREBLINKA extermination camp. Franz enlisted in the army in 1935, and on completion of his army service he volunteered for the SS, serving initially in the BUCHENWALD concentration camp. Late in 1939 he was transferred to the EUTHANASIA PROGRAM. In April 1942, after AKTION REINHARD had begun, he was sent to the BEŁŻEC extermination camp, with the rank of SS-*Oberscharführer*. In late August or early September of that year he was transferred to Treblinka as deputy to the camp commandant, Franz STANGL.

At Treblinka, Franz dominated daily life at the camp. He was the cruelest and most terrifying of the SS officers there; his handsome appearance earned him the nickname Lalka ("doll" in Polish) among the prisoners. He regularly toured the camp, reviewed the prisoner parades, and abused, struck, and shot prisoners at every opportunity and for the slightest infraction. Franz's work at Treblinka was rated "excellent," and as a result

he was promoted to the rank of *Untersturmführer*, in June 1943. After the revolt at Treblinka that August, and with the cessation of the extermination activities there, Stangl left and Franz remained to dismantle the camp and obliterate the traces of the slaughter there. In late November 1943 the last Jews engaged in the demolition of the camp were killed.

After the war, Franz stood trial in his native Düsseldorf, together with nine other SS officers who had served at Treblinka. At this First Treblinka Trial (there were three trials, all conducted in Germany), held from October 12, 1964, to August 24, 1965, Franz was sentenced to life imprisonment.

BIBLIOGRAPHY

Arad, Y. *Belzec, Sobibor, Treblinka: Operation Reinhard Death Camps.* Bloomington, 1987.
Arad, Y. *Treblinka: Hell and Revolt.* Tel Aviv, 1983. (In Hebrew.)

YITZHAK ARAD

FREEMASONS, secret fraternal order. The Masonic movement, founded in England in 1717, admitted Jews to its lodges as early as 1732, first in England and later in the Netherlands, France, Germany, and other countries. The attitudes of European Freemasons toward Jews tended to be ambivalent. Until the 1870s the lodges opened their doors to Jews, but with the rise of political antisemitism in the 1880s, Freemasonry began to reject them. This was the main reason for the creation of Jewish fraternal lodges such as B'NAI B'RITH, whose German branch was founded in Berlin in 1885. The anti-Jewish views held in German Masonic lodges are borne out by the small number of Jews in their membership: in the Weimar period, for example, Jews constituted only 4 percent of the eighty thousand Masons registered in Germany.

The slogan "Jews and Freemasons" as a battle cry of right-wing organizations originated in Germany in the late 1840s, spreading from there to France, and later to the rest of the world. The belief that the Masonic lodges were a cover for a Jewish conspiracy to destroy Christianity and national traditional society was especially strong in Catholic circles. When an anti-Masonic world congress was convened in Trent, Italy, in September 1894, it was supported not only by notorious French antisemites such as Edouard Drumont, but also by Pope Leo XIII. In France, monarchist reactionaries propagated the idea that the Republic was a creation of Jews and Masons. The notorious antisemite Charles Maurras developed the doctrine of the four confederate states—Jews, Protestants, Freemasons, and aliens—who were responsible for undermining Christian society in a sinister plot to control the world. The legend of Ahasver, "the wandering Jew," was also associated in France with a conspiracy of Freemasons and Jews.

These ideas were repeated in the post–World War I antisemitic literature. Thus, the PROTOCOLS OF THE ELDERS OF ZION linked Jewish and Masonic conspiracies, arguing that the Freemasons were in the service of the "Elders of Zion." In Germany, pan-Germans and racists such as Dietrich Eckardt, Alfred ROSENBERG, Erich LUDENDORFF, and his wife, Mathilda Ludendorff, were the main figures spreading the anti-Masonic and antisemitic slogans, using the periodical *Auf gut Deutsch* (In Good German) as one of their vehicles. In Nazi Germany an anti-Masonic museum was established. All members of German lodges who had not left them until after January 30, 1933 (the date of the Nazi seizure of power), were not accepted in the Nazi party, and some were sent to concentration camps. The lodges were forced to dissolve themselves in September 1935, and their property was confiscated.

Since Freemasonry was considered an ideological foe of Nazism, a special section of the SD (Sicherheitsdienst; Security Service), II/111, dealt with it. Later, section VII B 1 of the REICHSSICHERHEITSHAUPTAMT (Reich Security Main Office; RSHA) performed the same function. In the SD analysis, Freemasonry was not only a part of the "Jewish problem" but also an autonomous ideology with political power, ruling the press and public opinion and motivating wars and revolutions. The SD believed that the Jews used Freemasonry, with its international links, as a means for achieving world domination. The Freemasons were able to operate openly on behalf of the Jews, who preferred to remain inconspicuous. In fact, Freemasonry's principles of racial equality and human progress served Jewish interests, since they paved the way for Jewish emancipation. Freemasonry's humanitarian goals of spreading toleration and humanist principles were interpreted as aiming to establish a world Jewish republic. Both the French Revolution, which had emancipated European Jewry, and World War I were perceived as combined Judeo-Masonic actions to destroy Russia and Germany, in order to install Jewish domination.

BIBLIOGRAPHY

Katz, J. *Jews and Freemasons in Europe.* Cambridge, Mass., 1970.

DAVID BANKIER

FREMDARBEITER. *See* Forced Labor: Fremdarbeiter.

FRENCH JEWISH ORGANIZATIONS, FEDERATION OF. *See* Fédération des Sociétés Juives de France.

FRENCH JEWISH SCOUTS. *See* Eclaireurs Israélites de France.

FRENCH JEWS, GENERAL COUNCIL OF. *See* Union Général des Israélites de France.

FRENCH POLICE (Police et Gendarmerie Françaises). The entire French police force, including the section serving in the German-occupied zone of FRANCE, functioned under the authority of the Vichy government in the region of the country that until November 1942 did not come under German occupation. Some one hundred thousand policemen served in the Vichy government police force, thirty thousand of them in Paris. They included men in the *gendarmerie* responsible for the provincial regions, as well as the special branches such as intelligence and the squads for suppressing Résistance activists.

In the fall of 1941 a special police section was set up to deal with Jewish affairs on behalf of the Ministry of the Interior, but it came under the supervision of the COMMISSARIAT GÉNÉRAL AUX QUESTIONS JUIVES (General Office for Jewish Affairs) in France, and its functions were officially restricted to intelligence and investigation.

In contrast to this large French police force, the German force numbered at most some three thousand police, whose performance was hampered by inability to speak French and unfamiliarity with the terrain in which they were stationed. Consequently, the Germans assigned to the French police the tasks of maintaining public order, preventing subversive activities, suppressing crime, and implementing the German anti-Jewish policy.

On July 16 and 17, 1942, thirteen thousand Jews were arrested in Paris, among whom were four thousand children, as well as old people and the handicapped and ill. They were concentrated mainly in the Vélodrome d'Hiver, a closed structure in which even minimal amenities had not been prepared, and lacking in toilet facilities. For this operation nine thousand French policemen were brought in, and they carried out the arrests.

More than ten thousand Jews whose names appeared on the lists of those to be arrested succeeded in leaving their homes in time, some because of warnings passed on by police officials out of humanitarian considerations. From the end of July 1942 agreements were signed between Carl Albrecht OBERG, *Höherer SS- und Polizeiführer* (Higher SS and Police Leader) in France, and René Bousquet, chief of the Vichy police, defining the authority of the French police and the amount of weapons and equipment they were allowed. The leaders of the Vichy government considered these agreements proof that despite the German occupation they had succeeded in maintaining the sovereignty of France and freedom of action regarding its citizens.

Until the summer of 1943, a policy of cooperation was maintained throughout France in keeping with the Oberg-Bousquet agreement with no particular difficulty. The police force carried out the registration of the Jews and the expropriation of their property and businesses, conducted mass arrests and *Aktionen*, and made sure that the Jews wore the yellow Jewish BADGE and that their identity cards were stamped with the word *Juif* ("Jew"). The police force was also responsible for the construction, operation, and guarding of concentration camps. In addition, they provided armed guards to escort the trains transporting Jews to the German border. Negligence, corruption, and neglect of sanitary and medical services were common in the concentration and transit camps under the responsibility of the French police. The special police section in Paris was active in the liquidation of the underground Communist partisan units, which included a large number of Jews.

In the summer of 1943, after recruitment notices were sent out to thousands of young Frenchmen for forced labor in Germany, groups of partisans became organized throughout the country and inflicted losses not only on the occupation forces but also on the French police. The French police services gradually stopped arresting Jews, and the French administration in the DRANCY concentration camp was replaced by the Gestapo under Alois BRUNNER.

In 1944, Joseph Darnand, head of the French fascist militia established during the previous year, was appointed chief of police in place of Bousquet, who had been dismissed. From then on the operations against the Jews were carried out by the brutal militia forces, which executed their tasks industriously and pitilessly against the Jews of France.

BIBLIOGRAPHY

Klarsfeld, S. *Vichy-Auschwitz: Le rôle de Vichy dans la solution finale de la question juive en France, 1942.* 2 vols. Paris, 1983, 1985.

Marrus, M. R., and R. O. Paxton. *Vichy France and the Jews.* New York, 1981.

Paxton, R. O. *Vichy France: Old Guard and New Order, 1940–1944.* New York, 1982.

LUCIEN LAZARE

FREUDIGER, FÜLÖP (1900–1976), Hungarian Jewish leader. Born in BUDAPEST to a well-to-do family ennobled by Emperor Franz Josef, Freudiger succeeded his father, Abraham, as the head of the Orthodox Jewish community of Budapest in 1939. As a founder and leading figure of the Orthodox RELIEF AND RESCUE COMMITTEE OF BUDAPEST in 1943 and 1944, he helped many of the illegal foreign Jewish refugees in HUNGARY. After the German occupation of the country on March 19, 1944, he was appointed to the Central Jewish Council (Központi Zsidó Tanács), the JUDENRAT of Budapest—a position he retained after the council's reorganization on April 22.

Through the intermediacy of Rabbi Michael Dov WEISSMANDEL of Bratislava, Freudiger established close contact with Dieter WISLICENY of the Eichmann Sonderkommando almost immediately after the occupation. He also received from Weissmandel a copy of the AUSCHWITZ PROTOCOLS (a report by two Auschwitz escapees), and disseminated information about the mass killings taking place at Auschwitz to Jewish and non-Jewish leaders in Hungary. By bribing Wisliceny, Freudiger succeeded in rescuing eighty prominent Orthodox Jews from various ghettos in Hungary. Partly with Wisliceny's aid, he and his family escaped to Romania, on August 9, 1944. Freudiger eventually settled in Israel, where his role in the Central Jewish Council and his escape were subjects of controversy. He served as a prosecution witness in the EICHMANN TRIAL in 1961.

BIBLIOGRAPHY

Diamant, S., and G. Link. "Report on Hungary, March 19–August 9, 1944." *Hungarian Jewish Studies* 3 (1973): 75–146.

RANDOLPH L. BRAHAM

FRICK, WILHELM (1877–1946), Nazi leader. Frick was one of Hitler's earliest followers. He studied law, earning the degree of D.Juris, and then joined the Munich Police Commission. He was dismissed from that post for taking part in Hitler's attempted coup in 1923 and sentenced to fifteen months' internment, but did not serve the full term, being released on his election to the Reichstag. In 1928, Frick became party whip of the Nazi Reichstag faction. He was the first Nazi to become a minister in a German provincial government (Thüringen), and through the conduct of his office presented a general out-

line of Nazi policy, earning a wide reputation by his purges of public officials, his incitements to antisemitism, and his Nazi-oriented policy in cultural affairs.

From January 30, 1933, Frick, as Reich minister of the interior, was responsible for the enactment of most of the racial laws, and he extolled them in his public appearances. After the creation of Heinrich HIMMLER's police department in his ministry, Frick gradually lost his control of the ministry's affairs; this eventually led to his replacement by Himmler in August 1943. Frick was then appointed *Reichsprotektor* (governor) of BOHEMIA AND MORAVIA, an appointment he held until the end of the war. The International Military Tribunal found Frick guilty of crimes against peace and humanity and of war crimes, and he was one of the major war criminals hanged on October 16, 1946.

BIBLIOGRAPHY

Bracher, K. D. *The German Dictatorship: The Origins, Structure, and Effects of National Socialism.* London, 1971.

UWE ADAM

Wilhelm Frick in his prison cell in Nuremberg, where he was held during his trial before the International Military Tribunal. [United States Army]

FRONT OF THE WILDERNESS GENERATION (Hazit Dor Bnei Midbar; HDBM), Zionist youth movement in the ŁÓDŹ ghetto, founded on August 14, 1940, by Aharon Jacobson. The official name of the group was Front Młodożydowski (Jewish Youth Front; FMZ), but Hazit Dor Bnei Midbar was the name by which they knew themselves. The latter was a biblical reference (to Isaiah and Jeremiah) alluding to the sufferings of the Israelites during the Exodus; this was the members' way of linking their suffering to the continuum of Jewish history. The nucleus of the group was made up of Zionist graduates of the Jewish vocational school in Łódź.

The HDBM's declared objective was to unify all the ghetto's Zionist youth movements in order to centralize mutual aid, education, and defense in face of the negative influences of the ghetto, which had been established on February 8, 1940. Members were not required to give up their political outlooks, but were told that their realization had to be postponed until after the war.

The movement had about four hundred members and was headed initially by a five-member command. In 1942, young people who had been deported from the surrounding towns joined the HDBM, and its command became a leadership composed of the Zionist youth movements members of Ha-Shomer ha-Tsa'ir, Gordonia, Ha-No'ar ha-Tsiyyoni, Ha-Tehiyya, and Betar. On September 22, 1943, the HDBM merged with Ha-No'ar ha-Tsiyyoni and the movement's name was changed to Hazit ha-No'ar ha-Tsiyyoni (Zionist Youth Front). After the merger a core of oppositionists to German policy, headed by Dov Lemberg, was organized in the HDBM.

The movement functioned until the last days of the ghetto. One of its leaders, Raphael Zelwer, attempted to assemble in AUSCHWITZ-Birkenau the survivors of the HDBM who had been deported there, organizing meetings until the remaining members were dispersed among other camps, where most of them perished.

BIBLIOGRAPHY

Bauminger, A. "Chazit Dor Bnei Midbar." *Yad Vashem Bulletin* 1 (April 1957): 29–31.

ARIEH BEN-MENAHEM

FSJF. *See* Fédération des Sociétés Juives de France.

FÜHRERPRINZIP ("leadership principle"), Nazi term referring to the creation of authority from above downward and of responsibility from below upward. A special characteristic of NATIONAL SOCIALISM was a religious veneration of the leader, a cult of the Führer. This was based on pseudo-Germanic ideas of order, authority, and hero worship, placing the leader and his followers in a military relationship of dominance and obedience. After Hitler became the leader of the National Socialist party in July 1921, its organizational structure became thoroughly authoritarian and defined by this principle. The function of the leadership principle combined the political-charismatic idea, racial criteria, and the bureaucratic-authoritarian concepts of the totalitarian order. The structure of all Nazi organizations, economic enterprises, and social institutions was also adapted to the leadership principle. The principle went on to be implemented outside Germany through the Nazi war policy, with its programs of racial persecution, territorial expansion, and exploitation of "inferior" races. The manifestation of the leadership principle in the organization of political and social life was intended to create a perfect monolithic state governing the extension of power to the lower echelons. Paradoxically, however, in order to achieve the supervisory functions of the totalitarian regime, the machinery of both party and state had to be expanded. This expansion hindered the full implementation of the *Führerprinzip*.

BIBLIOGRAPHY

Bracher, K. D. *The German Dictatorship: The Origins, Structure, and Effects of National Socialism.* London, 1971.
Wörtz, U. *Programmatik und Führerprinzip.* Nuremberg, 1966.

DAVID BANKIER

FUNK, WALTHER (1890–1960), Nazi economist and politician. Funk was born in East

Center: Walther Funk, finance minister of the Third Reich. At his right, in top hat, is State Secretary Fritz Reinhardt; at his left is Reich Minister Albert Speer. [National Archives]

Prussia and studied law and economics at the universities of Berlin and Leipzig. From 1922 to 1930 he was editor in chief of the *Berliner Börsenzeitung* (Berlin Stock Exchange Journal). An early member of the Nazi party, he joined in 1924 and became one of its leading figures. In 1931, Adolf HITLER appointed Funk to be his personal adviser on economic affairs. Funk was the party's liaison with the top figures in German industry, among them Emil Kirdorf, Fritz Thyssen, Albert Voegler, and Friedrich Flick.

Owing to Funk's initiative and influence, leading companies in the Reich, such as the chemical conglomerate I.G. FARBEN, made large contributions to the Nazi party treasury. It was also Funk who impressed upon Hitler the importance for the Nazi cause of German heavy industry and private enterprise.

Funk rose rapidly, as evidenced by the many offices he held. From 1933 to 1937 he was in charge of the German press and *Staatssekretär* (state secretary) of Joseph GOEBBELS's Propaganda Ministry, as well as a member of the board of the Reich Broadcasting System and vice-chairman of the Reich Chamber of Culture. In 1937 he was appointed minister of economics (succeeding Hjalmar SCHACHT in that post), and in 1939 he became president of the state bank, the Reichsbank. In the final years of the war, however, it was Albert SPEER who was the main influence in the Reich economy, despite Funk's wide range of activities in the field—a situation that illustrates the fragmentation of the assignments held by the top men in the Nazi hierarchy and the rivalry that prevailed among them.

In the NUREMBERG TRIAL Funk was found guilty of war crimes, crimes against peace, and crimes against humanity. He had taken part in the confiscation of murdered Jews' valuables and financial assets and their transfer to the SS. He was sentenced to life imprisonment, but was released in 1957 because of ill health.

BIBLIOGRAPHY

Neumann, F. *Behemoth: The Structure and Practice of National Socialism, 1933–1944.* New York, 1966.

Petzina, D. *Autarkiepolitik im Dritten Reich: Der nationalsozialistische Vierjahresplan.* Stuttgart, 1968.

Speer, A. *Inside the Third Reich.* New York, 1970.

ZVI BACHARACH

G

GALEN, CLEMENS AUGUST GRAF VON (1878–1946), Catholic bishop in Münster; one of the most prominent Catholic opponents of Adolf Hitler. In 1933 Galen became an archbishop, and at the end of World War II he was raised to the rank of cardinal.

When the Nazis came to power, Galen pledged his loyalty to the new regime, hoping that the Nazis would retrieve for Germany the honor lost in its World War I defeat. Before long, however, his support of the Nazis turned to opposition, on account of the anti-Catholic propaganda that they were conducting and the pagan concepts that he discovered in Alfred ROSENBERG's book *Der Mythus des 20. Jahrhunderts* (The Myth of the Twentieth Century; 1930). Galen launched a sharp attack against that book by the Nazi party's chief ideologue because of its racist views.

The single most significant act in the record of Galen's campaign against Nazism was his courageous denunciation of the EUTHANASIA PROGRAM; in a sermon he gave on August 3, 1941, he declared that euthanasia was simply murder. There is a widely held belief that Galen's public statements on the subject caused Hitler to put an end to the project (although the killing of the chronically ill was not completely abandoned). Some scholars believe that public opinion in Germany, at a time when the Third Reich's military success was at its height, had an effect on Hitler's decisions. The fact is, however, that no such public protest was made, by the churches or by any other German institutions, against Nazi policy on the Jews and the "FINAL SOLUTION." In the eyes of the Nazi leadership the archbishop's statements on euthanasia were tantamount to an act of treason; his life was saved only because Hitler did not want to clash openly with the Catholic church. Following the July 20, 1944, attempt on Hitler's life, Galen was imprisoned in the SACHSENHAUSEN camp. He was held there until the war came to an end.

BIBLIOGRAPHY

Lewy, G. *The Catholic Church and Nazi Germany.* New York, 1964.

ZVI BACHARACH

GAMZON, ROBERT (1905–1961), French partisan commander. Gamzon, who was born in Paris, founded the Jewish scout movement in FRANCE (ECLAIREURS ISRAÉLITES DE FRANCE), guiding it to become a pluralist organization attracting young Jews from different countries and backgrounds and with various shades of political opinion. In 1939 and 1940 Gamzon, who was an electronic-sound engineer, served as communications officer in the French Fourth Army headquarters. Following the French surrender in June 1940, Gamzon reestablished the Jewish scout movement's institutions in the cities of unoccupied France into which Jewish refugees were pouring, as well as in Algeria. He took the initiative in establishing children's homes, welfare centers, workshops, and agricultural training farms in the villages (the last so as to provide an

Robert Gamzon.

educational network for the Jewish youth). He also arranged courses in Jewish culture and tradition for youth instructors. In January 1942 Gamzon was appointed to the executive board of the UNION GÉNÉRALE DES IS-RAÉLITES DE FRANCE (UGIF) in southern France and was active in the organization up to the end of 1943. In order to help Jews escape the Gestapo manhunts, Gamzon formed a clandestine rescue network in the summer of 1942 code-named "The Sixth" (La Sixième), which produced forged identity papers, found asylum for children and teenagers in non-Jewish private homes and institutions, and smuggled Jews of all ages across the borders into Spain and Switzerland. In May 1943 Gamzon, in his capacity as a member of the UGIF board, went to Paris, where he helped coordinate clandestine operations.

In December 1943, Gamzon (who by now had the code name "Lieutenant Lagnès") formed a Jewish partisan unit in the Tarn district of southwest France, which graduates of the village workshops and the Jewish scout movement came to join. By entering the command of the ARMÉE JUIVE, Gamzon helped unify all the Jewish armed organizations in France; he then took over command of the partisan unit he had set up in Tarn. This became, by June 1944, a trained and disciplined military unit of 120 men, affiliated with the Forces Françaises de l'Intérieur; the unit bore the name of Marc Haguenau, who had been the leader of "The Sixth" and had committed suicide when he fell into Gestapo hands. Following the orders of the underground district military commander, Gamzon received the parachute drops for Allied saboteurs and large quantities of light and medium arms for use in ambushing German patrols. On August 19, 1944, the Jewish scout unit seized a powerful German armored train, and on August 21 it liberated two cities, Castres and Mazamet.

In 1949 Gamzon settled in Israel together with a group of fifty graduates of the Jewish scout movement in France, who followed his lead.

BIBLIOGRAPHY

Latour, A. *Jewish Resistance in France (1940–1944)*. New York, 1981.

Lazare, L. *La résistance juive en France*. Paris, 1987.

Michel, A. *Les Eclaireurs israélites de France pendant la seconde guerre mondiale*. Paris, 1982.

Pougatch, I. *Un bâtisseur: Robert Gamzon, dit "Castor soucieux," 1905–1961*. Paris, 1972.

LUCIEN LAZARE

GANZENMÜLLER, ALBERT (1905–d. after 1973), Nazi official; state secretary of the Reich Transportation Ministry from 1942 to 1945, a period during which the German railway system carried some three million Jews to extermination camps. Born in Passau, Ganzenmüller completed his studies in engineering and began work for the German RAILWAYS in 1928. He rose rapidly and entered the railway section of the Reich transportation ministry in 1937. Unlike many of his colleagues, Ganzenmüller was anything but an apolitical technocrat. He had been involved in paramilitary activities in Bavaria as a teenager in the early 1920s and joined the Nazi party and SA (Sturmabteilung; Storm Troopers) in 1931.

Following the German invasion of the Soviet Union in June 1941, Ganzenmüller volunteered for service in the east and was put in charge of restoring the system of the Main Railway Directorate East in Poltava in the bitter winter of 1941–1942. He was then appointed state secretary of the transportation ministry, at the age of thirty-seven.

While almost no internal documents of the German railways have surfaced that explicitly delineate its role in deporting Jews to the extermination camps, one fragment of correspondence of July or August 1942 between Ganzenmüller and Heinrich HIMMLER's adjutant, Karl WOLFF, has survived. It concerns the "special joy" of the SS over the state secretary's efforts in providing trains to deport five thousand of "the chosen people" from WARSAW daily to TREBLINKA and twice weekly to BEŁŻEC. Such documents provide only the slightest glimpse into the vital role of the German railways in carrying out the "FINAL SOLUTION."

After the war Ganzenmüller escaped to Argentina; he returned to Germany in 1955. An initial indictment against him was dismissed for lack of evidence in 1970. In 1973 he was finally brought to trial, in Düsseldorf, but he suffered a heart attack shortly after the proceedings began. The trial was never resumed.

BIBLIOGRAPHY

Hilberg, R. *Sonderzüge nach Auschwitz*. Mainz, 1981.

CHRISTOPHER R. BROWNING

GARDA DE FIER. *See* Iron Guard.

GAS CHAMBERS, method used by the Nazis for "efficient" mass murder. Both mobile and stationary gas chambers were put into use. The first recorded instance of mass murder by gas took place in December 1939, when an SS SONDERKOMMANDO used carbon monoxide to kill Polish mental patients. The following month, January 1940, Viktor BRACK, head of the EUTHANASIA PROGRAM, also decided on the use of pure carbon monoxide, having already tested it successfully. In the program's institutions, the facilities in which the gassing was performed were disguised as shower rooms, the steel tanks containing the gas being attached to the outer wall of the gas chambers.

After the inauguration of the "FINAL SOLUTION" in the summer of 1941, gas chambers were introduced as a method for the mass murder of Jews. The method was launched in December 1941 at CHEŁMNO, by SS-Sonderkommando Lange, using mobile vans that had been constructed and equipped for this specific purpose—a project that the REICHS-SICHERHEITSHAUPTAMT (Reich Security Main Office; RSHA) had been working on since September of that year.

Unlike the method used for the euthanasia murders, the exhaust gas from the trucks was piped into the closed van. Depending on the size of the truck, forty to sixty persons could be gassed at a time. A total of twenty such mobile gas chambers were constructed, and most of them were used by the four EINSATZGRUPPEN deployed on Soviet soil.

The first stationary gas chambers that were to help facilitate the "Final Solution of the Jewish question" were put up at BEŁŻEC, in February 1942. Following several trial gassings with carbon monoxide cylinders and exhaust gas, the latter was chosen as the better alternative, since it was cheaper and did not require special supplies. The next month, regular killings commenced at Bełżec, by means of three gas chambers in a single wooden barrack. SOBIBÓR was next, in May, but here the installation was a brick building, with concrete foundations, that contained the gas chambers. The third and last of the AKTION REINHARD extermination camps in the GENERALGOUVERNEMENT was TREBLINKA, whose three gas chambers could be sealed hermetically (which was not the case in the other two extermination camps).

In the summer and fall of 1942 the capacity of the three extermination camps was greatly increased, both by enlarging the existing gas chambers and by adding new ones. Thus, in the ten gas chambers of Treblinka, twenty-five hundred persons could be put to death in a single gassing round, lasting an hour. The victims were forced to enter with their arms raised so that as many people as possible could be squeezed into the chambers. Babies and small children were thrown on top of the human mass. The tighter the chambers were packed, and the warmer the temperature inside the chamber, the faster the victims suffocated. All the gas chambers in the extermination camps were disguised as shower rooms; in Treblinka the Nazis went even further. By planting flower beds and creating what on the surface appeared to be a pleasant environment, they attempted to practice complete deception.

Each of the Aktion Reinhard killing centers operated in approximately the same way. When a transport arrived at the well-camouflaged station, a few of the victims were selected to form a Sonderkommando. A handful of victims with special talents were selected for work in the repair shops that serviced the camp SS staff and their Ukrainian helpers. The vast majority went through an assembly-line procedure, moving along the various camp stations, at which they surrendered any valuables left in their possession, undressed, and had their hair shorn. This procession culminated in the gas chambers, with the men of the transport being murdered first to prevent resistance. Once

the victims were dead, the members of the Sonderkommando removed their bodies from the gas chambers and were responsible for their burial (and, later on, their cremation). After a time, the men of the Sonderkommando were killed as well, and were replaced by new victims from later transports.

In their search for a more efficient means of extermination, the Nazis experimented with other forms of poison gas, and also with electrocution. When the latter proved impractical, gassing experiments with ZYKLON B were made at the main camp of AUSCHWITZ, using Soviet prisoners of war, in preparation for the mass murder of Jews in the adjoining Birkenau camp. Zyklon B proved far superior to the diesel exhaust gas that had been used in the Generalgouvernement extermination camps, and Auschwitz camp commandant Rudolf HÖSS decided in its favor. A crystalline form of hydrogen cyanide, Zyklon B turned to gas immediately upon contact with oxygen, giving off deadly fumes that killed everyone in the gas chamber. Depending on weather conditions, primarily temperature and humidity, the murder operation in the

The large gas chamber at the Majdanek concentration camp. Together with other buildings, it is preserved as a Polish national memorial. [Geoffrey Wigoder]

Auschwitz-Birkenau gas chambers took from twenty to thirty minutes. According to Höss, "In all the years, I knew of not a single case where anyone came out of the chambers alive."

The existing gassing facilities at Auschwitz could not possibly meet the Nazis' requirements, and they were repeatedly enlarged. After an inspection of the Auschwitz-Birkenau facilities in the summer of 1942 by Reichsführer-SS Heinrich HIMMLER, the decision was taken to construct updated and more efficient crematoria, which were connected to the gas chambers in Birkenau. The J. A. Topf und Söhne company of Erfurt, Germany, was contracted to rebuild the facilities, a project that was completed in the spring of 1943. These units came into operation between March 22 and June 28 of that year. The use of the new combined gas chambers and crematoria considerably speeded up the murder process in Auschwitz, which soon became the Third Reich's main killing center.

In Lublin-MAJDANEK, mass murder by gassing was introduced in September 1942 with the use of carbon monoxide cylinders, which were replaced by Zyklon B in the spring of 1943. Although not primarily operated as mass extermination sites, some of the other major concentration camps also had gas chambers. One each was in operation in MAUTHAUSEN (beginning in the fall of 1941), NEUENGAMME (September 1942), SACHSENHAUSEN (mid-March 1943), STUTTHOF (June 1944), and RAVENSBRÜCK (January 1945). All of them used Zyklon B.

BIBLIOGRAPHY

Cohen, E. *Human Behavior in the Concentration Camp.* New York, 1953.
Gutman, Y., and A. Saf, eds. *The Nazi Concentration Camps: Structure and Aims; The Image of the Prisoner; The Jews in the Camps.* Proceedings of the Fourth Yad Vashem International Historical Conference. Jerusalem, 1984.
Kogon, E., et al., eds. *Nationalsozialistische Massentötungen durch Giftgas: Ein Dokumentation.* Frankfurt, 1983.

UWE ADAM

GAS VANS. Poison gas was used by the Nazis to murder many hundreds of thousands of people. Various methods were employed, one of them being gas vans. The first time that the Nazis used gas was in the EUTHANASIA PROGRAM, in which the victims were retarded persons, the mentally or chronically ill, and habitual criminals. They were put into hermetically sealed chambers, into which carbon monoxide gas was released from metal containers. The first experiment utilizing a gas van was made in 1940, at Kochanówka, near Łódź: mentally ill children were locked inside a sealed van and put to death by the same method.

In the early stages of the war with the Soviet Union, the EINSATZGRUPPEN (mobile killing squads) killed many thousands of people by shooting. But before long the men in these units complained about the "mental anguish" they suffered from having to kill women, children, and ill people. Their superiors at the REICHSSICHERHEITSHAUPTAMT (Reich Security Main Office; RSHA) in Berlin then began to look for an alternative method of murder, one that would reduce the mental stress to which the executioners were exposed.

The first to find such a method was Arthur NEBE, the commander of Einsatzgruppe B. His men had been killing mental patients by shooting and with explosives, but these procedures had not proved satisfactory. Consequently, he tried out a technique of killing them by channeling exhaust gas from a truck into a sealed chamber, and was able to report to Berlin on the success of the experiment. Nebe had been in charge of the Reichskriminalpolizeiamt (Reich Criminal Police Office) and of the RSHA's Kriminal Technische Institut (Police Forensic Institute), and he put the institute's chemists to work on more experimentation based on this method. The results led to a decision by the RSHA to introduce the exhaust-gas method for the killing of people.

Walter RAUFF, who was in charge of Section II D (Technical Affairs) of the RSHA, was instructed to implement the decision. The Gaubschatt firm in Berlin installed hermetically sealed vans on the chassis of large trucks, and the SD (Sicherheitsdienst; Security Service) workshop provided the specialized apparatus needed. As the workshop foreman, Harry Wentritt, described it at a postwar trial,

A flexible exhaust pipe was installed at the truck's exhaust, with a diameter of 58 to 60 millimeters [2.26 to 2.34 inches], and a hole of the same size was drilled in the van floor; a metal pipe was soldered into the hole from the outside to which the flexible exhaust pipe was fixed. When the various parts were connected, the truck engine was started and the exhaust fumes were channeled into the van, through the pipe leading from the exhaust to the hole in the van floor.

When the first gas vans were ready, in September 1941, they were tried out in the SACHSENHAUSEN camp, the victims being Soviet prisoners of war. The second test was attended by two chemists of the Criminal Identification Institute, Dr. Walter Hees and Dr. Theodor Friedrich Leidig. Leidig gave the following description at a postwar trial in West Germany: "The van was opened; some bodies fell out, others were removed by prisoners. As our chemists had predicted, the bodies had the pinkish tinge typical of victims of carbon monoxide poisoning." Following the successful tryouts, more trucks were fitted with the new apparatus, and by June 23, 1942, twenty such vehicles were in operation, with ten others in various stages of preparation. Some of the trucks, made by the Saurer firm, were larger in size, with a capacity of fifty to sixty people, while others, made by the Diamond Reo firm, had a smaller capacity of twenty-five to thirty people.

The first gas vans were apparently put into use as early as November 1941. According to evidence given by Einsatzgruppen men, a gas van was used in the November 1941 *Aktion* in POLTAVA, in the Ukraine, and one in December 1941 in KHARKOV; also in December 1941, three vans were put into operation in the CHEŁMNO extermination camp. A memorandum submitted to Rauff by Willy Just of the SD, on June 5, 1942, attests to the effectiveness of the vans: "Since December 1941 . . . 97,000 persons have been processed [*bearbeitet*] with the help of three vans, without a single disruption." Some 320,000 persons were killed by this method in the Chełmno camp, most of them Jews.

GAS VANS

© Martin Gilbert 1982

Fifteen gas vans were in operation in German-occupied Soviet territory, where the Einsatzgruppen put them at the disposal of their sub-units, the Einsatzkommandos. The commander of the SS and police for REICHS-KOMMISSARIAT OSTLAND in Riga had one or two gas vans for use in Latvia and Estonia and in the area between these states and the eastern war front.

Four vans were operated in Belorussia, by the commander of the SD and SICHERHEITS-POLIZEI (Security Police; Sipo) in MINSK and by Einsatzkommandos 6, 7, 8, and 9. From evidence given by the drivers and the SS men who operated the vans it is possible to reconstruct how the killing was carried out and to learn about the victims. As a rule, the gas vans served to empty prisons that had filled up with Jewish prisoners—men, women, and children—most of whom had been caught while trying to hide or escape from *Aktionen*. In Borisov and Minsk the vans were used to kill the workers, most of them Jewish, who were employed by AKTION 1005 units to disinter and burn the corpses of Jews murdered in large-scale operations. Heinze Schlechte, the driver of a gas van that operated in Mogilev, estimated that in his van alone, five thousand to six thousand persons had been killed by the fall of 1942.

In Minsk, the gas vans were used to kill the Jews transported from the Reich and the Protectorate of Bohemia and Moravia, and in October 1943 they were used in the liquidation of the Minsk ghetto. One of the transports, carrying a thousand Jews from THERE-SIENSTADT, arrived in Minsk while the ghetto was being liquidated; it was diverted to Baranovichi, and two gas vans were dispatched in its wake to kill the Jews in the transport. A local Jewish resident, Dr. Zalman Loewenbuch, who was working in the Baranovichi railway station at the time, gave evidence of what he saw (quoted in the Baranovichi *Memorbuch*): "The trucks had huge doors which sealed hermetically. . . . In Russian the sealed vans were called *dushegubki*—killers of souls."

Einsatzgruppe C, in the Ukraine, had five or six vans at its disposal, two used by Sonderkommando 4a, two by Einsatzkommando 6, one by the SD and Sipo commander in Kiev, and, apparently, one by Sonderkommando 4b.

As noted above, two vans were used in Poltava and Kharkov in November and December 1941. Anton Lauer, the commander of a Sonderkommando 4a sub-unit operating in the area, testified at a postwar trial:

> They [the trucks] entered the [Poltava] prison courtyard, and the Jews—men, women, and children—had to enter, straight from the prison cells. I was familiar with the inside of the vans; [it was lined] with aluminum sheets and had a wooden grating on the floor. The exhaust fumes were pumped in . . . the driver started the engine . . . then the doors were shut and the trucks left for a field outside Poltava, where the trucks came to a halt. . . . I saw that, too. . . . When the doors opened, a thick cloud of vapor was emitted, followed by a heap of contorted human bodies. . . . It was a frightful sight.

In late December 1941 and early January 1942, Sonderkommando 4a liquidated the remaining Jews of Kharkov by shooting and gassing them. Some Jews had gone into hiding, and when they were discovered they were taken to the Kharkov prison and then killed in gas vans together with the prisoners. A similar method of killing prisoners was used in Kiev, as recounted by former SS-Oberscharführer Wilhelm Findeisen, the driver of a gas van for Sonderkommando 4a, at a postwar trial: "The truck was loaded in the [Sicherheitsdienst] compound, and forty people were put in—men, women, and children. I had to tell them that they were being taken to work."

In the southern Ukraine, the Crimea, and Ciscaucasia (the Krasnodar and Stavropol territories), three or four gas vans were used by Einsatzgruppe D and its sub-units. By means of the vans, the Simferopol and Kerch prisons were emptied of Jews, the Jews of Sevastopol and Feodosiya were liquidated, the chronically ill and sick Jewish children in the large hospitals of the Kislovodsk and Mineralnye Vody spas were murdered, and the Jews of Piatigorsk and Cherkessk were put to death.

After several months of use in the Soviet Union, the gas vans were found to have technical deficiencies, and problems developed in their operation. In May 1942, Unter-sturmführer Dr. August Becker of the RSHA was sent on an inspection tour, in the course of which he visited all the Einsatzgruppen units. On his return to Berlin, he submitted a written report to the RSHA in which he singled out two major problems: (1) the mental stress on the SS men who had to unload the vans themselves, since they could not entrust prisoners with the task, lest they flee; and (2) the frequent breakdowns, caused by the poor condition of the Soviet roads. Becker's report was used as an exhibit (PS-500) by the prosecution in the postwar Nuremberg Trials.

Information on the use of gas vans in other places is scanty. One such place was SAJMIŠTE, a concentration camp in Yugoslavia. In March 1942 there were 7,000 prisoners in the camp, mostly Jewish women and children. At the request of the military governor and the SD in Serbia, an Einsatzkommando accompanied by a gas van and two drivers was assigned to the camp, and within a short while all the prisoners were killed. The only exceptions were non-Jewish women married to Jews, and their children. One of these women, a Swiss national named Hedwig Schönfein, gave evidence on these events before a postwar Yugoslav tribunal. When the murder of the Sajmište prisoners was completed, the SS commander, Obersturmbannführer Dr. Emanuel Schäfer, sent the following telegram to Berlin: "The drivers, SS-Scharführers Götz and Mayer, have completed their special assignment [Sonderauftrag], and they and the above-mentioned vehicles are therefore free to go back." Gas vans are also known to have been used in LUBLIN, where they were employed from time to time to kill Polish and Jewish inmates of the prison in the Lublin fortress. The vans then went to the MAJDANEK camp, where the corpses were burned in the camp crematorium.

After the war, Otto OHLENDORF, the commander of Einsatzgruppe D, testified at the SUBSEQUENT NUREMBERG PROCEEDINGS (Trial 9, The Einsatzgruppen Case, July 3, 1947– April 10, 1948) that Heinrich HIMMLER had given the order to kill Jewish women and children by gassing, and it was for this purpose that the vans were supplied. As it turned out, the gas vans did not meet the expectations that the Nazi leaders had had for them— to be an effective instrument for the trouble-free killing of masses of people. For that purpose, stationary gas chambers using hydrogen cyanide gas (ZYKLON B) proved speed-

ier and more efficient. Still, the total number of victims of the gas vans was approximately 700,000, half of them in the occupied areas of the Soviet Union and the other half in the Chełmno extermination camp.

BIBLIOGRAPHY

Browning, C. R. *Fateful Months: Essays on the Emergence of the Final Solution.* New York, 1985.

Krakowski, S. "In Kulmhof: Stationerte Gaswagen." In *Nationalsozialistische Massentötungen durch Giftgas,* edited by E. Kogon et al., pp. 110–145. Frankfurt, 1983.

Spector, S. "Tötungen in Gaswagen hinter der Front." In *Nationalsozialistische Massentötungen durch Giftgas,* edited by E. Kogon et al., pp. 81–109. Frankfurt, 1983.

SHMUEL SPECTOR

GAULLE, CHARLES DE (1890–1970), French army officer, statesman, and political leader. An expert on intensive armored warfare, which he had anticipated, de Gaulle was one of the few French commanders to gain success against the German attack in the west in May 1940. On June 6, 1940, he was appointed deputy minister of war. Ten days later, de Gaulle was among the first who refused to go along with the surrender to Germany by French prime minister Philippe PÉTAIN. Arriving in London, de Gaulle announced the formation of a Free France Committee and called on French soldiers and civilians, wherever they might be, to join him. He sought to engage French forces in battles for the liberation of French colonies, even when this meant fighting against the French army that had remained loyal to the Vichy regime. This was the case in SYRIA AND LEBANON in June 1941, when the Free French fought alongside the British. On this occasion de Gaulle visited Palestine, from June 13 to 23. In the November 1942 battle for the liberation of North Africa, however, the Allied forces did not inform de Gaulle of their plans, preferring to entrust the civilian administration of Algeria to François DARLAN and the Vichy officials who surrendered to them. The anti-Jewish legislation that the Pétain government had introduced in Algeria remained in force until it was rescinded by de Gaulle in

October 1943, when he overcame his rivals and placed Algeria under Free French control.

In 1943 and 1944 the participation of French forces in the fighting grew increasingly prominent during the campaigns in Italy and France. When Paris was liberated in late August 1944, de Gaulle became premier of the Provisional French government. He abolished all the racial laws and took steps to ensure that the Jews' rights and property were restored. After the war, his efforts to institute a new constitution that would have provided for a presidential form of government failed, and he resigned from the government in 1946.

In May 1958, under the impact of the war in Algeria, de Gaulle returned as premier. This time he won a majority for the creation of a presidential form of government in France. He was elected president under the new constitution, retaining the post until 1969, when he resigned. Before World War II, de Gaulle wrote a book on the art of war; after the war he wrote three volumes of wartime memoirs, *The Call to Honor* (1955), *Unity* (1959), and *Salvation* (1960).

BIBLIOGRAPHY

Abitbol, M. *The Jews of North Africa during the Second World War.* Jerusalem, 1986. (In Hebrew.)

Aron, R. *De Gaulle before Paris: The Liberation of France, June–August, 1944.* London, 1962.

Aron, R. *De Gaulle Triumphant: The Liberation of France, August 1944–May 1945.* London, 1964.

Lacouture, J. *Le rebelle.* Vol. 1 of *Charles de Gaulle.* Paris, 1984.

LUCIEN LAZARE

Gen. Charles de Gaulle, second from right; Prime Minister Winston Churchill; Gen. Władysław Sikorski, second from left, prime minister of the Polish government-in-exile and commander in chief of the Polish armed forces. The photograph was taken somewhere in Great Britain.

GDAŃSK. *See* Danzig.

GEBIRTIG, MORDECAI (pen name of Mordecai Bertig, 1877–1942), Yiddish folk poet. Born in KRAKÓW to a poor family, Gebirtig attended a Jewish school only up to the age of ten. He became a carpenter and plied this trade for the rest of his life, even when he had gained great fame. At an early age he took an interest in theater, poetry, literature, and music, becoming acquainted with Yiddish literature as an amateur actor and through the Jewish workers' movement. In World War I Gebirtig worked as a medical orderly in a Kraków military hospital, where he heard the songs of the many peoples of the Habsburg Empire serving in its army— Czechs, Hungarians, Romanians, Ukrainians, Serbs, and Croatians. Gebirtig could not read music, and the tunes for his poems were composed by others; he wrote the lyrics after first learning the tune.

Gebirtig wrote of the simple Jewish folk, and his talent lay in his ability to give expression to the sentiments felt by the Jewish masses of eastern Europe. His poems, set to music, were performed in theaters, concert halls, and on the radio, and were sung at public meetings, by street singers, and by ordinary Jews. During World War II they were sung in the Kraków and other ghettos and in the concentration camps. In his lifetime Gebirtig wrote about one hundred poems.

Of the poems he wrote during the Holocaust period, fifteen to twenty are known; most of them were published in Kraków in 1946 in a special volume, *S'Brent (1939– 1942)*, with a foreword by Joseph Wolf. Wolf, who was a member of the Kraków ghetto underground from 1941 to 1943 and was close to Gebirtig, relates that Gebirtig was very pleased to hear from him that "S'Brent" (a poem Gebirtig had written in 1938, under the impact of the pogrom that took place that year in Przytyk) was highly popular with the young people in the ghetto, inspiring them to take up arms against the Nazis and serving as a slogan for their appeals to the Jewish population at large. Other settings for his poems were sung in the Kraków ghetto and also in the Warsaw ghetto theater, as revealed by an exchange of letters between Gebirtig and Diana Blumenfeld, an actress in the Warsaw ghetto. Just as his poems before 1939 had reflected the life of his people, those he wrote during the Nazi regime are a direct expression of pain, despair, hope, anger, and the desire for revenge.

Gebirtig's writings during the war cover three different periods, corresponding to his fate and that of the Jews of Kraków. First was the period from September 5, 1939, to October 24, 1940, which he spent in occupied Kraków. An outstanding example from this period is "S'Tut Vey," a song of rage and anger, in which he indicts the Poles who, despite the bitter fate they shared with the Jews at the hands of the joint Nazi enemy, could not help gloating over the sufferings of the Jews. Other poems from that period express both pain and hope. In the second period, from October 24, 1940 (when he had to flee from Kraków and took refuge in Lagiewniki, a nearby village), until the spring of 1942, Gebirtig wrote poems of revenge, such as "A Tog fun Nekome" (A Day of Revenge), as well as poems of hope and yearning. The third period covers the time Gebirtig spent in the Kraków ghetto, from April 1942 to June 4, 1942, the day he was killed. In that period his songs became somber, dominated by gloom and fear. He was then sixty-five years old, and in these last months of his life his spirits were raised by a report that the fighters of the underground had made "S'Brent" their anthem. In January 1943 or later, after Gebirtig's death, Gusta Dawidson DRAENGER, then in the MONTELUPICH PRISON, translated "S'Brent" into Polish. It became a folk ballad, sung in the ghettos and forests of occupied Poland and, after the war, by Holocaust survivors.

The 1946 Kraków edition of Gebirtig's writings, which contains nearly all his known work from the Holocaust period, cannot be regarded as definitive. The poem "Minuten fun Yiush" (Moments of Despair), which Gebirtig wrote a year after the war had started, was excluded, probably because it expressed the poet's momentary weakening of faith and his heretical thoughts about God.

In 1967, *Ha-Ayara Bo'eret* (The Town Is Burning) was published in Israel, containing a selection of Gebirtig's poems in Yiddish together with Hebrew translations. The book also contains photocopies of Gebirtig's manuscripts of poems from the Holocaust period, as well as an account of the manuscripts' history and how they were saved.

BIBLIOGRAPHY

Bauminger, A. *The Fighters of the Cracow Ghetto.* Jerusalem, 1986.

Kalisch, S. *Yes, We Sang: Songs of the Ghettos and Concentration Camps.* New York, 1985.

Niger, S. "Yiddish Poets of the Third Destruction." *Reconstructionist* 13/10 (June 27, 1947): 13–18.

Rubin, R. "Yiddish Folksongs of World War II: A Record of Suffering and Struggle." *Jewish Quarterly* 11/2 (Summer 1963): 12–17.

YEHIEL SZEINTUCH

GEHEIME STAATSPOLIZEI. *See* Gestapo.

GENDARMERIE, HUNGARIAN, police force, formally known as the Magyar Kiralyi Csendorseg (Royal Hungarian Gendarmerie), employed primarily for the maintenance of law and order in the Hungarian countryside. The gendarmerie was established under a law of February 14, 1881; during World War II it became a major force in protecting the regime against its opponents and implementing anti-Jewish policies. In the summer of 1941, units of the gendarmerie were involved in the roundup and deportation of nearly 18,000 Jews who were not Hungarian citizens. Most of these Jews were subsequently slaughtered near KAMENETS-PODOLSKI. In January and February 1942, gendarmerie units were also involved in the massacre of over 3,300 Serbs and Jews in and around Novi Sad (Hung., Újvidék). After the German occupation of HUNGARY on March 19, 1944, the gendarmerie became the major instrument of state power in the ghettoization and deportation of approximately 440,000 Jews.

The gendarmerie was under the overall command of the *Magyar Kiralyi Csendorseg Felugyeloje* (Superintendent of the Royal Hungarian Gendarmerie), a position that was held in 1944 by Lt. Gen. Gábor Faragho. The three thousand to five thousand gendarmes employed in the anti-Jewish operations served under Lt. Col. László FERENCZY. Ferenczy was nominally the liaison officer in charge of coordinating the operations of the

GENDARMERIE

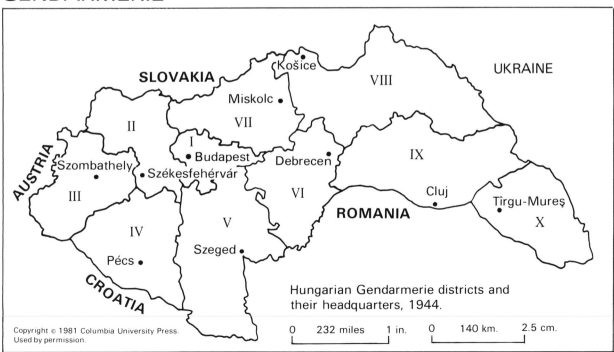

Hungarian Gendarmerie districts and their headquarters, 1944.

0   232 miles   1 in.   0   140 km.   2.5 cm.

The Hungarian Gendarmerie round up the Jews of Bezdan and move them into the ghetto (1944). Bezdan is located 60 miles (96.5 km) northwest of Novi Sad in Yugoslavia, near the present Hungarian-Yugoslav border. During the war Bezdan was in the territory annexed by Hungary.

gendarmerie with the German SD (Sicher-heitsdienst; Security Service) and with Adolf EICHMANN's Sonderkommando.

The gendarmerie operated on a territorial basis. There were ten district commands, each headed by a colonel, who played a crucial role in planning and implementing the anti-Jewish policy in the territory under his jurisdiction. The district commanders were actively involved in the conferences organized by the leaders in charge of the "de-Judaizing" process, including Ferenczy, László ENDRE, the representatives of the county and local administration, and the special advisers of the Eichmann Sonderkommando. For purposes of the anti-Jewish drive, Hungary was divided into six operational zones, each zone encompassing one or two Gendarmerie districts.

The ghettoization process began on April 16, 1944, in Zone I, which encompassed Gendarmerie District VIII, covering the areas of the TRANSCARPATHIAN UKRAINE and northeastern Hungary. This was followed by Zone II, encompassing Gendarmerie districts IX and X—the area of northern TRANSYLVANIA. These territories, closest to the eastern front, were inhabited largely by unassimilated Orthodox Jews. The gendarmes played a determining role in all aspects of the ghettoization, concentration, entrainment, and deportation of the Jews. During each of these phases, special investigative units of the gendarmerie were involved in expropriating the property of the Jews. These units were particularly active in the larger ghettos, usually established in the county seats, which also served as entrainment centers.

In each of these entrainment centers, the investigative units set up a *penzverde* ("mint"), a place where Jews were tortured into confessing where they had hidden their alleged valuables. The gendarmes' barbarous behavior during the interrogations as well as during the ghettoization and entrainment of the Jews has been highlighted in countless accounts by survivors. It shocked many decent Hungarians and even some of the Germans involved in the anti-Jewish drive. To ensure the effectiveness of the gendarmes, the "de-Judaizing" command saw to it that the anti-Jewish operations in a particular county were carried out by a gendarmerie unit from another part of the country, in order to prevent possible corruption or leniency based on personal contacts with the local Jews.

The gendarmerie served the pro-Nazi regimes of both Döme SZTÓJAY and Ferenc SZÁLASI until Hungary was liberated by Soviet troops on April 4, 1945. Shortly after the end of the war, the Provisional National Government of Hungary dissolved the gendarmerie by a decree of June 9, 1945, citing its prewar and wartime abuses.

BIBLIOGRAPHY

Braham, R. L. *The Politics of Genocide: The Holocaust in Hungary.* New York, 1981.

Hollos, E. *Rendorseg, csendorseg, VKF 2.* Budapest, 1971.

RANDOLPH L. BRAHAM

GENERALGOUVERNEMENT (General Government), administrative unit established by the Germans on October 26, 1939, comprised of those parts of POLAND that had not been incorporated into the Reich, an area with a total population of twelve million. The full official designation was Generalgouvernement für die Besetzten Polnischen Gebiete (General Government for the Occupied Areas of Poland), and it was only in July 1940 that the shortened name came into use. The Germans had used this name previously, when they occupied Poland in World War I and set up an administration there, also called the Generalgouvernement.

The Generalgouvernement area was divided into four districts, KRAKÓW, WARSAW, RADOM, and LUBLIN, which in turn were split into subdistricts. The administrative center was Kraków. In the summer of 1941, following the German attack on the Soviet Union, Galicia became the fifth district, adding between three million and four million to the population. Only a few Polish institutions were permitted by the Nazis to function, among them the bank that issued the country's currency; the POLNISCHE POLIZEI, or Polish Police, known as Granatowa (Blue), from their dark blue uniforms; and the Central Relief Committee, all of them operating under the strict supervision of the occupation authorities. Heading the Generalgouvernement was the governor-general, Hans FRANK. As of May 1940, Frank operated through the Gene-

ralgouvernement administration, headed by Josef Bühler. The SS and police were headed first by SS-Obergruppenführer Friedrich KRÜGER, and then by Wilhelm KOPPE.

The occupation authorities believed that the task of the Polish population of the Generalgouvernement was to obey the Germans and work for them. At first the Poles were regarded as a reservoir of manpower, to be exploited for the needs of the Reich. Later, the Germans considered a number of projects, such as the establishment of colonies, "Germanization," expulsion of the population of ZAMOŚĆ, and identification of those Poles who were *deutschstämmig* (of German origin).

The obedience of the Polish population was attained by extreme terrorization. For every

GENERALGOUVERNEMENT, January 1940

© Martin Gilbert 1982

German killed by the underground, fifty to one hundred Poles were executed. Of exceptional cruelty were two terror actions that the Germans carried out. The first was Sonderaktion Krakau (Special Action Kraków) in November 1939, in which 183 staff members of schools and colleges in Kraków were arrested while attending a meeting with the German police. They were deported to SACHSENHAUSEN, from which many never returned. The other action took place in LVOV, where 38 Polish professors were executed shortly after the Wehrmacht entered the city.

The Germans destroyed Polish cultural and scientific institutions, and a large-scale program of plundering artistic and archeological treasures was instituted. In the economic sphere, the Poles were left only with small industries and work on the land. Heavy food quotas were levied on the villages, and trade in foodstuffs was prohibited, so as to restrict the urban population to the starvation diet provided by the food rations. As a result, the Poles engaged in widespread food smuggling.

The Ukrainians in the Generalgouvernement were intended by the Germans to provide a counterweight to the Poles. In contrast to the treatment that the Germans meted out to the population of the REICHSKOMMIS-SARIAT UKRAINE (Reich Commissariat for the Ukraine), which was exceedingly harsh, the Ukrainians in the Generalgouvernement received concessions and their living conditions even improved, in comparison with the prewar situation.

The Jewish population of the Generalgouvernement, numbering 1.8 million, were the victims of discriminatory decrees. Their property was confiscated, and they were drafted for forced labor. From early 1940, the Jews were imprisoned in ghettos, where they suffered from severe shortages and were isolated from the rest of the world. In the spring of 1942 the Germans began deporting the Jews from the ghettos to extermination camps in the Lublin district, and by 1944 all the ghettos in the Generalgouvernement were liquidated. By early August 1944 a part of the Generalgouvernement—the area between the Vistula and Bug rivers—was liberated by Soviet forces and the Polish National Liberation Council had been formed, with its center in Lublin. The rest of the Generalgouvernement was set free in January 1945, in the course of the Soviet army's winter offensive.

[*See also* Aktion Reinhard.]

BIBLIOGRAPHY

Gross, J. T. *Polish Society under German Occupation: The Generalgouvernement, 1939–1944.* Princeton, 1979.
Madajczyk, C. *Polityka III Rzeszy w okupowanej Polsce.* Warsaw, 1970.
Piotrowski, S. *Hans Frank's Diary.* Warsaw, 1961.

CZESŁAW MADAJCZYK

GENERALPLAN OST (General Plan East), the plans of the Nazis for the territories of eastern Europe. The term is mentioned in mid-1940 in documents of the Stabshauptamt (General Staff Main Office) of the REICHS-KOMMISSARIAT FÜR DIE FESTIGUNG DES DEUT-SCHEN VOLKSTUMS (Reich Commissariat for the Strengthening of German Nationhood). Shortly after his appointment as head of the planning section in the Stabshauptamt, as well as of the Zentralbodenamt (Central Lands Office), SS-Oberführer Professor Konrad Meyer-Hetling, in July 1941, submitted initial proposals for the settlement and regional planning of Polish territories that had been incorporated into the Reich. Describing these proposals as "preliminary suggestions for *Generalplan Ost,*" he addressed them to Heinrich HIMMLER, who headed the Reich Commissariat for the Strengthening of German Nationhood. The final version of the plan was presented by Meyer-Hetling in an exhibition called "Planning and Construction in the East," and in a book of that title, published in Berlin in 1942.

The earliest mention of the Reich's plans for its eastward expansion was made by Reinhard HEYDRICH, in a speech in Prague in October 1941, on the occasion of his appointment as Reich Protector of BOHEMIA AND MORAVIA. The term *Generalplan Ost* as such does not appear in the speech, but its contents forecast the permanent takeover by Germany, in stages, of eastern Europe. Guidelines in this vein were also contained in a memorandum drawn up by Erhard Wetzel, the official in charge of racial policy in the political section of the Reichsministerium für die Besetzten Ostgebiete (Reich Ministry for the Occupied Eastern Territories). In February 1942, Wetzel identified Section III B of the REICHSSICHERHEITSHAUPTAMT (Reich Security Main Office; RSHA) as the source of *Generalplan Ost*. Wetzel had known since November 1941 that the RSHA, which also played a role in the "strengthening of German nationhood," was working on an overall plan for the territories in the east, according to which thirty-one million people were to be settled there. Adolf Hitler envisaged that within ten years, four million Germans would be settled in the east, with the number of such settlers (Germans and "Germanized") rising to ten million at a minimum within twenty years.

Wetzel's memorandum—presented as an "expert opinion"—was highly critical of the RSHA's plans and questioned the expertise of the plan's RSHA author. In his opinion, the figure given by the RSHA for the current population of the territories was too low, the estimate of the human reservoir available for settlement in the east was too optimistic, the racial makeup envisaged was not arrived at scientifically, and the proposal that western Siberia be earmarked for the resettlement of Poles, "who cannot be liquidated like Jews," Ukrainians, and others was against the interests of the Reich. Despite these reservations, however, Wetzel's memorandum supported the aim of *Generalplan Ost*, which was to transform central-eastern Europe into a German colony.

It seems clear that *Generalplan Ost* was formulated in late 1941 and early 1942, that it was considered as reflecting the views of Himmler, and that it was to be implemented after the war over a period of thirty years. The "settlement of the east" was to be carried out by ten million Germans moving there from German territories and from non-German countries in Europe that had a German population. The territories designated for settlement were the occupied areas of PO-LAND, the Baltic states, BELORUSSIA, the districts of ZHITOMIR and KAMENETS-PODOLSKI, a part of the VINNITSA district of the UKRAINE, the Leningrad district, the Crimea, and parts of the Dnieper basin.

The contemporary population of the areas that were to be resettled by Germans was estimated at 45 million, and the number of Jews among them at 5 million to 6 million. Of the 45 million, 31 million were classified as "racially undesirable" and were to be expelled to western Siberia, and a small number were to be put to work in the administration of the vast expanses of Russia.

According to *Generalplan Ost* as drawn up by the RSHA, 80 percent to 85 percent of the population of Poland, 64 percent of the population of the western Ukraine, and 75 percent of the population of Belorussia were to be expelled and resettled. The rest of the local population was to stay in place; most of them were to be Germanized, or, as Himmler put it, they would "either be absorbed or killed." The RSHA version of *Generalplan Ost* was an elaboration of Hitler's ideas of expelling and resettling elsewhere the population of Polish territories that were incorporated into the Reich.

The Stabshauptamt began active preparations for *Generalplan Ost* in late January of 1942, on Himmler's orders. With Meyer-Hetling in charge, the Stabshauptamt worked out a plan that laid down the legal and economic principles on which the future "reconstruction" of the east was to be based, and included the settlement of the Crimean peninsula. The project was to be completed within twenty-five years after the end of the war. The Polish areas that had been annexed to the Reich were to be completely Germanized; in the rest of Poland and in large parts of the Soviet Union, *Reichsmarken* (points of settlement) and *Siedlungsstutzpunkte* (settlement bridgeheads) were to be established.

In compliance with racist doctrine, priority would be given to agricultural settlement, and the urban population was to be kept at a minimum, especially in the north, where agricultural settlement was to consist of 90 percent to 95 percent of the population. Meyer-Hetling estimated that the costs of the project would amount to 45.7 billion reichsmarks. The funds would be provided by various sources—special tax levies on the conquered countries, credits, and the Reich state budget.

Himmler lost no time in reacting to the plan when it was presented to him. He demanded that the length of time allowed for its implementation be cut down to twenty years, and that Germanization also include the GENERALGOUVERNEMENT, LATVIA, and ESTONIA (for which the original version provided for "settlement points" and "bridgeheads"), in addition to the Polish territories that had been annexed. In September 1942 Himmler made reference in a statement to the establishment of settlement (i.e., colonization) bases as far afield as the Don and the Volga.

In late 1942 Meyer-Hetling followed up by presenting to Himmler an overall detailed plan, including a financial estimate. Again Himmler gave the subject his immediate attention, this time demanding that the area to be colonized in eastern Europe include the Generalgouvernement, the Baltic states, Belorussia, the Crimea (including KHERSON), and the Leningrad district. On Himmler's orders, Meyer-Hetling hastily revised and completed the plan, which now became the *Generalsiedlungsplan*, the master plan for the colonization of the east. In its new version, the area earmarked for settlement by Germans was larger than in the RSHA's version of *Generalplan Ost*.

In early 1943, Section III B of the RSHA arranged for a meeting at which consultations were held on the implementation of Meyer-Hetling's plan and further details that were to be incorporated into it. The area in which the plan was to be realized now comprised 270,000 square miles (700,000 sq km), of which 135,000 square miles (350,000 sq km) was cultivated land; in 1938 the entire area of the Reich was 225,000 square miles (583,000 sq km). Among the subjects that came up at the meeting was the transfer of the existing population in the area earmarked for German settlement: 6 million to 7 million people were to be moved from the Polish area incorporated into the Reich; 10 million from the Generalgouvernement; 3 million from the Baltic states; 6 million to 7 million from the western Ukraine; and 5 million to 6 million from Belorussia.

The Jews were singled out for "total removal" (i.e., extermination). In the first decade of the plan's operation, the "racially undesirable" population was to be removed, presumably to be followed, in the second de-

cade, by the "politically undesirables." The Protectorate of Bohemia and Moravia was not included in the immediate plans of resettlement. After the battle of STALINGRAD, Himmler rapidly lost interest in having a definitive version of the plan drawn up. Also, following his proclamation of total war, Hitler ordered a halt on the planning of all postwar projects.

The work on *Generalplan Ost* and the *Generalsiedlungsplan* coincided with the period when massacres in eastern Europe were at their height, with millions of Soviet prisoners of war and millions of Jews being murdered. In 1941 and 1942 the loss of life in Poland and in the occupied areas of the Soviet Union ran to several million people. In addition, in that period a million Poles and two million Ukrainians were sent to the Reich on FORCED LABOR, and another two million Poles were subjected to forced Germanization in the areas that had become part of the Reich; in other occupied areas similar plans were in preparation. At this time the German authorities also embarked upon the settlement of Germans in several of the areas designated for that purpose in *Generalplan Ost*, encountering some resistance in that operation or running into difficulties arising out of the military situation. About thirty thousand German repatriates from Lithuania who had been waiting to be resettled in the Polish areas annexed to the Reich were directed to the southwestern part of Lithuania.

Between November 1942 and August 1943, Poles living in the southeastern part of the Lublin district (the so-called ZAMOŚĆ region) were expelled from their homes and replaced by Germans. This area was being prepared for complete or partial settlement by Germans, and was part of the territories that under *Generalplan Ost* were to be totally Germanized, resettled, or used for the establishment of colonization bases.

Germany was able to carry out, almost in full, the "Final Solution"—the murder of the Jews, whom the Nazis regarded as their main racial enemy. This operation cost the lives of millions of people. *Generalplan Ost* demonstrates that there were other plans based on racism that while not calling for extermination, provided for the expulsion of many populations, especially Slavs. These racist-motivated plans were only begun, and were to be fully executed after the Germans had won the war.

BIBLIOGRAPHY

Koehl, R. L. *RKFDV: German Resettlement and Population Policy, 1939–1945: A History of the Reich Commission for the Strengthening of Germandom.* Cambridge, Mass., 1957.

Madajczyk, C. "Generalplan Ost." *Polish Western Affairs* 3/2 (1962): 1–54.

CZESŁAW MADAJCZYK

GENOCIDE (from Greek *genos*, "race," and Latin *caedes*, "killing"), liquidation of a people. The term "genocide" was first introduced by Raphael LEMKIN, a Jewish jurist, who used it at a 1933 conference of jurists in Madrid and further defined and analyzed it in books that he wrote during World War II. On December 9, 1948, the United Nations General Assembly adopted a convention for "the prevention of genocide and the punishment of the organizers thereof."

The term, now widely used in legislation, international conventions, legal judgments, and scientific and general literature, is generally applied to the murder of human beings by reason of their belonging to a specific racial, ethnic, or religious group, unrelated to any individual crime on the part of such persons, the intention of the murderer or murderers being to cause grievous harm and destroy the specific group per se.

Lemkin pointed out that the crime of genocide need not mean the immediate and total destruction of the group; it may also consist of a series of planned actions designed to destroy basic components of the group's existence, such as its national consciousness, its language and culture, its economic infrastructures, and the freedom of the individual.

The United Nations Genocide Convention specifically mentions the following actions, which, when carried out against a national, ethnic, racial, or religious group in order to destroy that group, in full or in part, come under the rubric of genocide:

1. Killing persons belonging to the group

2. Causing grievous bodily or spiritual harm to members of the group
3. Deliberately enforcing upon the group living conditions which could lead to its complete or partial extermination
4. Enforcing measures designed to prevent births among the group
5. Forcibly removing children from the group and transferring them to another group

As indicated by this list of crimes, a close link exists between them and many of the crimes that the International Military Tribunal (IMT) at Nuremberg was empowered to deal with and that were defined as "CRIMES AGAINST HUMANITY." These crimes included murder, cruel treatment, and persecution on racial and ethnic grounds that were not directed against individuals or groups of individuals as such, but rather had the purpose of destroying the very existence of the group or groups to which the victims belonged. The IMT did not seek to determine the guilt of the accused brought before it for the crime of genocide, since that crime was not listed in the London Agreement under which the IMT was established, but the charge of genocide was included in the SUBSEQUENT NUREMBERG PROCEEDINGS and in several of the trials of Nazi criminals held in Poland. Among these were the trial of Amon GOETH, the liquidator of the Kraków and Tarnów ghettos and a commandant of the PŁASZÓW camp; and the case of Rudolf HÖSS, the commandant of AUSCHWITZ-Birkenau. In its verdict against Arthur GREISER, announced on July 9, 1946, a Polish court defined several of the crimes committed by the defendant against the Polish people as "genocide." These included:

1. Placing Poles in a special unlawful category with regard to rights of possession, employment, education, and the use of their native tongue, and applying a special criminal code to them
2. Religious persecution, having the characteristics of genocide, of the local population, by mass murder and the imprisonment of Polish clergy (including bishops) in concentration camps; reduction of the availability of religious facilities to a bare minimum; and destruction of churches, cemeteries, and church- owned buildings

3. Genocide-like actions against cultural and educational treasures and institutions
4. Humiliating the Polish people by treating them as second-rate citizens, and differentiating between the Germans as the "master race" and the Poles as the "servant race"

That court also found, on the basis of the evidence submitted to it, that the defendant had ordered or cooperated in actions designed to cause criminal harm to the lives, well-being, and property of thousands of Polish residents of the occupied area and had made it his objective to carry out a total genocide-like attack on the rights of small- and medium-sized ethnic populations, on their national identity and culture, and on their very existence.

The government of Israel joined the Convention on the Prevention and Punishment of Genocide, and on the basis of that convention enacted, in 1950, the Genocide Prevention and Punishment Law 5710-1950; the definition of genocide in that law follows that of the United Nations Genocide Convention. Israeli legislation also used that definition in another law, the Nazis and Nazi Collaborators (Punishment) Law 5710-1950. That law, first used against a Nazi criminal in the EICHMANN TRIAL, contains the definitions of crimes against humanity and war crimes as laid down in the London Agreement on the establishment of the International Military Tribunal, and it also contains the definition of "Crimes against the Jewish People." The latter is defined as applying to any one of the following actions, carried out with the intent of exterminating the Jewish people, totally or partially:

1. Killing Jews
2. Causing grievous bodily or mental harm to Jews
3. Placing Jews in living conditions calculated to bring about their physical destruction
4. Imposing measures intended to prevent births among Jews
5. Forcibly transferring Jewish children to another national or religious group
6. Destroying or desecrating Jewish religious or cultural assets or values

7. Inciting to hatred of Jews

Like the Polish definition in the Greiser case, and in other cases, the Israeli law mentions the concept of cultural genocide, but in the main it refers to the special form of crimes against humanity as contained in the NUREMBERG LAWS, and particularly to the specific form in which genocide was in fact carried out, especially against the Jewish people. The crime against the Jewish people was a crime against that people only, since it was committed against Jews only, and is *sui generis*. Nevertheless, in formal legal, as well as in social, terms, and in its political and moral aspects, the crimes against the Jewish people were also crimes against the principles of humanity and an offense against the whole of mankind, by seeking to remove from its midst one of its component parts.

The experts on the subject all agree that genocide is a component of the Holocaust, but it has been contended that the Nazi crime against the Jewish people was unique and extended far beyond genocide, by virtue of the planning that it entailed, the task forces allocated to it, the killing installations set up for it, and the way the Jews were rounded up and brought to extermination sites by force and by stealth; and above all, because of the stigma and charge of collective guilt with which the Jews as a whole were branded—of being a gang of conspirators and pests whose physical destruction must be carried out for the sake of society's rehabilitation and the future of mankind.

On November 4, 1988, President Ronald Reagan signed legislation that enabled the United States to become the ninety-eighth nation to ratify the United Nations Genocide Convention.

[*See also* "Final Solution"; Racism.]

BIBLIOGRAPHY

Bauer, Y. "Whose Holocaust?" In *Confronting History and Holocaust: Collected Essays, 1972–1982*, edited by J. N. Porter, pp. 35–45. Washington, D.C., 1983.

Harf, B. *Genocide and Human Rights: International Legal and Political Issues*. Denver, 1984.

Lemkin, R. *Axis Rule in Occupied Europe: Laws of Occupation, Analysis of Government, Proposals for Redress*. Washington, D.C., 1944.

Robinson, N. *The Genocide Convention.* New York, 1949.

MARIAN MUSHKAT

GENS, JACOB (1905–1943), head of the JU-DENRAT (Jewish Council) in the VILNA ghetto. Gens was born in Illovieciai, a village in the Šiauliai district of LITHUANIA. In 1919, when Lithuania was fighting for its independence, he volunteered for the Lithuanian army. Sent to an officers' training course, he graduated as a second lieutenant, and was sent to the front to join the fight against Poles. He served in the army until 1924. (In the late 1930s, as an officer in the reserves, he was sent to a staff officers' course and promoted to captain.) In 1924 Gens enrolled in Kovno University, earning his living as a teacher of Lithuanian and of physical education in the Jewish schools of Ukmerge and Jurbarkas. Three years later, he became an accountant in the Ministry of Justice in Kovno. He completed his university studies in law and economics in 1935.

In July 1940, when Lithuania became a Soviet republic, Gens was dismissed from his post. A Zionist who was close to the Revisionists, Gens feared that he was in danger of being arrested in a campaign that was being waged against anti-Soviet elements, and he moved to Vilna, where he was not known. A Lithuanian friend who headed the municipal health department there helped him obtain work as an accountant in the department.

When the Germans occupied Vilna in late June 1941, his Lithuanian friend appointed Gens director of the Jewish hospital. At the beginning of September, when a ghetto was set up in Vilna, Anatol Fried, chairman of the Judenrat, who had become acquainted with Gens as a patient in the Jewish hospital, appointed Gens commander of the ghetto police. Gens set up the police force, organized it, and made it into an orderly and disciplined body. The Jewish police were assigned a role in the *Aktionen* that were conducted in the ghetto from September to December 1941, in which tens of thousands of Jews were killed. According to most of the evidence available, Gens, within the framework of his job, did his best to help the Jews. He became the predominant personality in the ghetto and its de facto governor. His direct contact with the German authorities, bypassing the Judenrat, added to his prestige among the Jews in the ghetto. Gens involved himself in affairs that had nothing to do with the police: employment, cultural activities, and other aspects of ghetto life.

In July 1942 the Germans dismissed the Judenrat and appointed Gens head of the ghetto administration and sole representative of the ghetto (*Ghettovorsteher*), thereby making official his de facto position. Gens promoted the idea of "work for life," meaning that the survival of the ghetto Jews depended on their work and productivity. He believed that efforts had to be made to gain time and keep the ghetto in existence until Germany was defeated in the war, and that this could be achieved by working for the

Jacob Gens.

Germans. He constantly sought to increase the number of Jews in such positions. In the last few months of the ghetto's existence, 14,000 out of the total ghetto population of 20,000 were employed inside or outside the ghetto. On one occasion, Gens was ordered by the Germans to send the Vilna ghetto police to the Oshmiany ghetto, to carry out a *Selektion* there and to hand over 1,500 children and women who were not employed. Instead, Gens delivered to the Germans 406 persons who were chronically ill or old. He justified this action to the Jews by claiming that if the Germans and the Lithuanians had done the selecting, they would have taken the children and the women, whom he wanted to keep alive for the sake of the future of the Jewish people.

Gens's attitude toward the ghetto underground was ambivalent. On the one hand, he maintained contact with the underground leaders and declared that when the day of the ghetto's liquidation arrived, he would join them in an uprising; but on the other hand, when the underground's activities endangered the continued existence of the ghetto, he opposed it, and he complied with a German demand to hand over to them the underground commander, Yitzhak WITTENBERG.

Once the process of liquidating the ghetto had been set in motion, in August and September 1943, Gens knew that his life was in danger. His Lithuanian wife and his daughter were both in Vilna, where they lived outside the ghetto. He had several offers from his Lithuanian relatives and friends to leave the ghetto and take refuge with them, but he refused, believing that in his role he was engaged in a mission on behalf of the Jewish people. On September 14, 1943, nine days before the final liquidation of the ghetto, Gens was summoned to the Gestapo. The previous day, he had been warned that the Germans were planning to kill him, and had been urged to flee. He replied that his escape would mean disaster for the Jews who remained in the ghetto.

Gens reported to the Gestapo on September 14, and at 6:00 p.m. he was shot to death in the Gestapo courtyard. News of his death reached the ghetto at once, and the Jews who were still alive mourned his passing. Gens's belief that if the ghetto were productive its Jews would be saved proved baseless; but under the terrible conditions prevailing at the time, he did his best, as he understood it, to save as many as possible.

BIBLIOGRAPHY

Arad, Y. *Ghetto in Flames: The Struggle and Destruction of the Jews of Vilna in the Holocaust.* Jerusalem, 1980.
Dworzecki, M. *Jerusalem of Lithuania in Revolt and Holocaust.* Tel Aviv, 1951. (In Hebrew.)
Friedman, P. *Roads to Extinction: Essays on the Holocaust.* Philadelphia, 1980. See chapter 14.
Korchak, R. *Flames in Ash.* Merhavia, Israel, 1946. (In Hebrew.)

YITZHAK ARAD

GEPNER, ABRAHAM (1872–1943), businessman and public figure; member of the WARSAW ghetto JUDENRAT (Jewish Council). Gepner was born in Warsaw, into a poor family; his father died when Abraham was still a boy, and his studies had to be cut short. Owing to his drive and diligence, he rose from errand boy to become the owner of a trading firm and a number of factories in the metals industry in Poland, with far-flung international ties.

Gepner was a fervent Polish patriot and in his youth was inclined to join the assimilationists. In 1912, when the Polish nationalists declared an economic boycott of the Jews, Gepner abandoned assimilation and became active in the Jewish community. For many years he played a leading role in the Association of Jewish Businessmen in Poland, serving as its chairman from 1935 to 1939. He was a member of the Warsaw city council, and became known for his generous support of orphanages and vocational training institutions and for his efforts to raise productivity. Gepner was known for his austere private life; he set himself the rule of tithing, contributing a tenth of all his income to charity and welfare.

When World War II broke out, Gepner was sixty-seven years old. He and Samuel ZYGELBOJM were the two Jews among the twelve hostages whom the Germans seized in Warsaw when they captured the city in October 1939. Gepner was a member of the Judenrat

Abraham Gepner.

from its inception and was close to Adam CZERNIAKÓW, the Judenrat chairman. From the beginning, Gepner assisted in organizing Jewish self-help, and when the ghetto was set up in November 1940, he was appointed head of the supply department (Zakład Zaopatrywania). This department had the task of supplying food and other essential items to the ghetto—under the prevailing conditions, a most delicate and responsible task. Gepner was not able to prevent hunger and mass deaths from starvation, but he had the ghetto population's confidence, and his organization was efficient (in relative terms); as a result, the supply organization was the target of far less criticism than the other Judenrat departments.

In the ghetto, too, Gepner was involved in aid and welfare; his main concern was children, and especially orphans. Early in the ghetto's existence, Gepner established contact with the Jewish political underground, lent support to the clandestine pioneer movements, and kept track of the latter's activities. He was in favor of youth movements and aided them even after the ŻYDOWSKA ORGANIZACJA BOJOWA (Jewish Fighting Organization; ŻOB) was established and preparations were under way for the ghetto uprising.

When the revolt broke out, on April 19,

1943, Gepner at first refused to take refuge in a bunker, but he gave in to his friends' appeals and together with his family went into the bunker of 30 Franciszkanska Street, where the staff of the supply department had gathered in the last days of the ghetto's life. On May 3 the Germans dragged Gepner, together with many others, out of the bunker and killed him. A letter he wrote on January 1, 1943, contains the following passage: "I have no regrets about staying in the ghetto, nor about any of the decisions that I made. Recently I reached the age of seventy, and remaining in the ghetto, together with my brothers and sisters, I regard as the most important step I took in my life. If I have succeeded in drying a single tear—that is my reward. I have a daughter living in the United States. Tell her that I served my people faithfully."

BIBLIOGRAPHY

Ringelblum, E. *Notes from the Warsaw Ghetto.* New York, 1974.

ISRAEL GUTMAN

GERMAN ARMAMENT WORKS. *See* Deutsche Ausrüstungswerke.

GERMAN VANGUARD, GERMAN JEWISH ADHERENTS. *See* Deutscher Vortrupp, Gefolgschaft Deutscher Juden.

GERMANY. The first few Jews to arrive in Germany came there in the wake of the Roman legions and settled in the cities along the Rhine. The earliest documents attesting to a sizable Jewish population are imperial edicts, dating back to A.D. 321 and 331, concerning the city Colonia Agrippensis (Cologne). There is no clear evidence, however, of an uninterrupted presence of a Jewish population in Germany after the Roman empire came to an end, and it is only from the tenth century, when Jewish merchants from Italy and France settled in Germany, that a continuous history of Jews in Germany is certain.

By the late Middle Ages the Jewish population of Germany was consolidated. The German Jewish community became one of the centers of spiritual creativity among European Jewry, and the cradle of Ashkenazic Jewry and the Yiddish language. In the economic sphere the Jews gained prominence in commerce (including trade with Near Eastern countries) and later primarily as moneylenders. This period, however, witnessed widespread persecution of Jews and, on occasion, the destruction, in various parts of Germany, of entire Jewish communities. The persecution of Jews, in most cases, was set against a background of religious and social ferment and political upheaval. The worst persecutions took place during the Crusades (especially the first Crusade, in 1096) and during the period of the Black Death (1348–1349). From the fifteenth century, and especially during the Reformation, the status of the Jews and of the role they played deteriorated, and they were expelled from most of the large German cities. Some of those expelled remained in Germany, taking up residence in hundreds of small communities, while others migrated to the newly emerging centers of Jewish population in the countries of eastern Europe. In the Age of Absolutism the situation of Jews improved, one of the reasons being the status and activities of the "court Jews" (*Hofjuden*), who were instrumental in enabling Jews to resettle in the large cities.

The economic rise of an elite Jewish group and the penetration into late eighteenth-century Jewish society of the ideas of the Enlightenment marked the beginning of the process of the social and political emancipation of the Jews, the struggle for which was waged throughout the nineteenth century and reached its goal, in formal terms, when Germany was unified in 1871. The drawn-out struggle for emancipation, and the new ideological trends that had emerged among German Jewry since the Haskalah (the Jewish Enlightenment movement) in the eighteenth century, had a very significant impact on Jewish communities in other parts of Europe and overseas. Among the important transformations that took place in German Jewry in the nineteenth century and that affected Judaism as a whole were the rise of the *Wissenschaft des Judentums* (the modern scholarly study of Judaism and Jewish history); the growth of new religious movements in Judaism—Reform, Conservative, and Neo-Orthodox; the rapid urbanization of the Jews; and their integration into modern society and economic life. In the nineteenth century the Jews of Germany made important contributions to cultural life, to social and political philosophy, to the economy, and even to political life. Among outstanding Jews were the poet Heinrich Heine; the fathers of socialism, Ferdinand Lasalle and Karl Marx; the bankers of the Rothschild and Bleichröder families; and the leaders of the National Liberal party, Eduard Lasker and Ludwig Bamberger.

The emancipation of the Jews, however, and their integration into the various spheres of German life, met with resistance from a sizable part of German society. By the 1870s this opposition led to politically organized ANTISEMITISM—which in its modern form also had RACISM as a basic ingredient. In the following two decades antisemitic political parties ran in elections and scored successes. The influence of these parties waned toward the end of the nineteenth century, but antisemitism continued to flourish in economic, social, and academic organizations. It also penetrated the major political parties in various ways and became a factor in the struggle between the national conservative and democratic socialist camps over the future political character of German society.

The rise of modern antisemitism, in addition to other factors, led to the establishment of political organizations among German Jewry in Imperial Germany. The most important organization established in this period (in 1893) for the defense of the Jews' civil rights was the CENTRALVEREIN DEUTSCHER STAATS-BÜRGER JÜDISCHEN GLAUBENS (Central Union of German Citizens of Jewish Faith). It had been preceded by the non-Jewish Verein zur Abwehr des Antisemitismus (Association for Combating Antisemitism), founded in 1890. Also in the 1890s, during the Jewish national renaissance movement, the German Zionist Organization was formed. Before long, its leaders, including David Wolffsohn, Otto Warburg, Arthur Ruppin, and Max Bodenheimer, assumed leading posts in the World Zionist Organization. From the death of Theodor Herzl up to the end of World War I, the organizational center of the Zionist movement was located in Germany.

During World War I, antisemitism was again on the rise. Its most humiliating manifestation was the German High Command's decision in 1916, in response to the demand of certain sectors of public opinion, to take a special census of Jewish soldiers to determine whether the number of Jews serving in the armed forces, and especially the number in combat units, was in proportion to their percentage of the general population. The results of that census were not published.

Weimar Republic. 1918–1933. A new era in the history of German Jewry began when Imperial Germany collapsed and was replaced by the democratic regime of the Weimar Republic. The outstanding feature of this period was the polarization between the unprecedented integration of the Jews in every sphere of life, and the growth of political antisemitism among various organizations and political parties, especially in the immediate postwar years.

Important achievements by Jews were recorded in the theater (Max Reinhardt), in music (Arnold Schönberg), in the visual arts (Max Liebermann), in philosophy (Herman Cohen), and in science (Albert EINSTEIN). Among the Nobel prize winners in Germany up to 1938, 24 percent were Jews (nine Jews out of a total of thirty-eight). It was in political and public life, however, that the Jewish role was most prominent. Jews played an important role in the first cabinet formed after the 1918 revolution (Hugo Haase and Otto Landsberg), the Weimar Constitution was drafted by a Jew (Hugo Preuss), and Jews were conspicuously present in the abortive attempts to create radical revolutionary regimes, especially in Bavaria. The revolutionary government in Munich was headed by a Jewish intellectual, Kurt Eisner, and after his assassination, two other Jewish leaders, Gustav Landauer and Eugen Levine, assumed positions of major influence in the "Räterepublik" ("Soviet" Republic). Rosa Luxemburg, who was also assassinated, was a leader of the revolutionary Spartakusbund, which was one of the predecessors of the German Communist party.

In the following years as well, Jews held

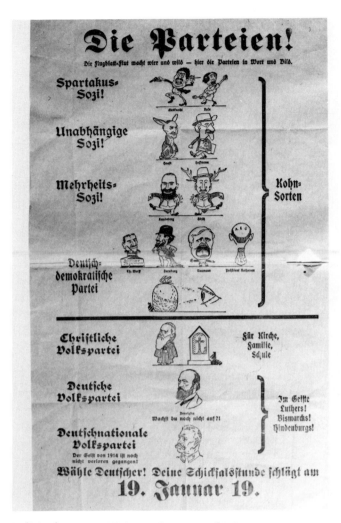

Political poster, Weimar Germany. [A Living Memorial to the Holocaust—Museum of Jewish Heritage, New York]

major political posts, primarily in the leadership of the democratic and socialist parties. The most prominent Jewish political figure was Walther RATHENAU, who served first as minister for economic affairs and then as foreign minister. Rathenau's murder by right-wing radicals in June 1922 was one of the dramatic high points of the antisemitic incitement that charged the Jews with responsibility for Germany's defeat in the war (the DOLCHSTOSSLEGENDE, or "stab-in-the-back" myth) and for the economic and social crises that struck the newly born republic after the war, reaching their climax in the terrible inflation of 1922 and 1923. The presence of Jews from eastern Europe (*Ostjuden*), who had immigrated to Germany before, during, and after the war, was also a favorite subject of antisemitic incitement.

Among the antisemitic movements and political parties, the most radical was the relatively small National Socialist party, which had been founded in Bavaria in 1919. Its platform included conspicuous paragraphs calling for the abolition of civil rights for Jews and far-reaching measures for eliminating Jews from various spheres of life. The propaganda speeches and publications of the party's leaders, especially those of Adolf HITLER, presented a radical antisemitic ideology that did not stop short of demands for the "total elimination of the Jews" and called for the *Ausrottung* ("extermination") of the Jews *mit Stumpf und Stiel* ("root and branch"). Despite the party's nationalist character, the antisemitism it advocated went beyond the confines of national categories, its ideology demanding a radical solution of the "Jewish question" in order to save all of human society. The National Socialist racial doctrine, which was based on the inequality of races and a Social Darwinist struggle for survival among them, regarded the Jews as a biological source of ideologies (including Marxism, democracy, and even Christianity) that defy the "natural order." As a result of the stabilization of the German economy and of the republic in 1924, the strength of the antisemitic parties went into a temporary decline and the number of their members in the Reichstag dropped from forty to fourteen.

According to the 1925 census, the Jewish population of Germany was 564,379, representing 0.9 percent of the total population. The great majority (377,000, or 66.8 percent) lived in six large cities, which also had the largest Jewish communities: BERLIN (with 180,000 Jews, a third of the entire Jewish population in the country), FRANKFURT, HAMBURG, Breslau, Leipzig, and Cologne. Approximately 90,000 Jews (16 percent) lived in the smaller cities, and 97,000 (17.2 percent) in over a thousand towns and villages with a population of less than 10,000. For the most part the Jews belonged to the middle class and were self-employed, in various branches of business and in the professions. The Jews' intensive participation in the life of German society accelerated the process of assimilation, which was manifested in the growing number of mixed marriages, secessions from the organized Jewish community, and conversions to Christianity. Thus, in 1927, 54 percent of all marriages of Jews were contracted with non-Jews, and in that year one thousand Jews are estimated to have opted out of Judaism, about half of them by conversion to another faith.

On the other hand, in the Weimar era the activities of the Jewish political, religious, and social organizations were maintained and even expanded. New organizations were added to the Centralverein, the Zionist Federation, the Orthodox and Liberal organizations, and the HILFSVEREIN DER DEUTSCHEN JUDEN (German Jews' Aid Society), which all had their beginnings before Weimar. The major new organizations were the REICHSBUND JÜDISCHER FRONTSOLDATEN (Reich Union of Jewish Frontline Soldiers); left- and right-wing Zionist parties such as the Jüdische Volkspartei, or Jewish People's Party; youth and sports organizations; student groups; and so forth. The Jewish communities retained the officially recognized legal status they had attained under the Kaiser; the innovations in the Weimar era were the establishment of Landesverbände Jüdischer Gemeinden (State Unions of Jewish Communities) and attempts to organize all of German Jewry into a nationwide body.

Religious and general Jewish studies taught in the rabbinical seminaries in Berlin and Breslau (founded in the nineteenth century) were broadened and intensified under the impact of the encounter with east European Jews and their culture. In fact, the influx of Jewish scholars and intellectuals from eastern Europe, coupled with the revival of Jewish consciousness among the established Jewish population, turned Germany in that period into a great center of modern Jewish scholarship and culture. As a result of efforts of Jewish thinkers and educators—men like Franz Rosenzweig and Martin Buber—large groups among the general Jewish population began to take an interest in Jewish learning, leading to the establishment of *jüdische Lehrhäuser* (institutes of Jewish learning) for adult Jewish education. A wide range of Jewish periodicals and Jewish publishing houses played an important role in Jewish life; two of the significant publishing projects undertaken were the five-volume *Jüdisches Lexikon* and the *Encyclopaedia Judaica* (of which ten volumes had appeared when its publication came to a halt in 1934).

The final years of the Weimar Republic, during which Germany was hard hit by the global economic crisis, were marked by the rise of the National Socialist party. Just before the crisis broke out, in 1928, the Nazis won only 3 percent of the vote; however, in the first elections that took place during the crisis, in September 1930, their share jumped to 18 percent, and in July 1932 to 37 percent of the vote. With 230 members in the Reichstag, the Nazis became the largest party—and retained that position in the next elections, in November 1932, despite a drop to 33 percent of the vote and 196 Reichstag members.

During those years, antisemitism came to have a profound effect on Jewish life. It was one of the central elements in the Nazi party's violent struggle for power, and its effect on the Jews was not confined to physical violence (desecrations of synagogues and Jewish cemeteries, and even attacks on individual Jews). Nazi political propaganda succeeded in making the "Jewish question" into a major issue in the Nazi struggle against the democratic regime. As a result, not only was the position of the Jews in German society impaired, but the Jews themselves underwent a crisis of Jewish consciousness and began to reexamine their Jewish identity.

From 1933 to 1938. In January 1933, on the eve of Hitler's rise to power, the Jewish population of Germany (including the Saar district, which two years later was reincorporated into Germany) numbered 522,000 Jews by religion; under the racist criteria established by the Nazis, which were to form the basis of their persecution of the Jews and to find formal expression in racist legislation, the number of Jews by race was 566,000.

On January 30, President Paul von HINDEN-BURG appointed Hitler Reich chancellor. This appointment was the outcome of a continuous economic and parliamentary crisis in which the democratic system of government became an authoritarian regime, on the basis of the emergency powers granted to the president by the constitution. As soon as Hit-

ler was appointed, the National Socialist party and its paramilitary organizations— primarily the SA (Sturmabteilung; Storm Troopers) and the SS—launched a drive to seize, by violent means where necessary, all government and public institutions and to transform Germany into a totalitarian state. In the ensuing terrorist actions (as early as February and March 1933) against opponents of National Socialism, especially members of the Left political parties, liberals, and intellectuals, the Jews were a major target. Many Jews were subjected to public humiliation and were arrested; others were forced to quit their posts, especially at the universities and the law courts. Before 1933, the Nazis had called for the plundering of Jewish property and for a boycott of Jewish businesses and services; this was now adopted as the official policy of the ruling party. A climax was reached with the Anti-Jewish BOYCOTT of April 1, 1933, the first occasion on which the new regime openly took discriminatory action against a part of the country's citizens. It caused a deep shock to Germany's Jews and evoked a sharply hostile reaction from world public opinion.

The boycott was brought to a halt after a day had passed, but from April 7, anti-Jewish laws were enacted that in effect abolished the principle of equal rights for Jews, rights that had been established by the German constitution in 1871. The legal basis for these measures was the *Ermächtigungsgesetz* (Enabling Law), passed on March 24, 1933, which gave the government dictatorial powers first for a four-year period and subsequently for the life span of the Third Reich. The regime used this emergency law to abolish the democratic freedoms that had been in force under the republic and brought about the dissolution of Germany's independent political parties and organizations. The process of totalitarian *Gleichschaltung* ("coordination," that is, Nazification) led to the reorganization of all spheres of public and official life, including control of the media and all forms of publication, and a thorough and far-reaching purge of the civil and public service. In the March 5 elections, which nominally were still democratic and were held before the Enabling Law was passed, the Nazis received only 44 percent of the vote, as against the more than

90 percent support they achieved in the November 1933 referendum and later.

Anti-Jewish policy was put into effect on two parallel levels: by means of laws, decrees, and administrative terror; and by "spontaneous" acts of terror and incitement of the population to hostility against the Jews. The early anti-Jewish laws included the Law for the Restoration of the Professional Civil Service. The racist basis of that law was expressed by the ARIERPARAGRAPH ("Aryan Paragraph"), which became the foundation for all anti-Jewish legislation passed before the enactment of the NUREMBERG LAWS in the fall of 1935. Other laws passed at that stage restricted the practice of law and medicine by Jews; a special law mandated that the number of Jews in an educational institution must not exceed that proportional to their percentage of the population; and Jews were excluded from cultural life and journalism. The only exception to these laws applied to Jews who had served as frontline soldiers in World War I.

The main purpose of the legislation was to give formal expression to the ideology and policy of discrimination against and persecution of the Jews, but it was also meant to serve as a means of restraining "spontaneous" terror and stabilizing the status of the Jews in the National Socialist state. In particular, it was the conservative elements in the government coalition who in the second half of 1933 advocated such "stabilization," out of concern for the country's international standing and the adverse effect that unrestrained Nazi action against the Jews could have on efforts to restore the country's economy. Among the officials who warned of the impact that a foreign economic boycott might have on Germany was Hjalmar SCHACHT, head of the Reichsbank, and Foreign Minister Konstantin von NEURATH. Hitler spoke in a similar vein in July 1933, when he called for a curb on the revolutionary zeal and the need to direct it into channels designed to consolidate the foundations of the new regime.

The methods employed in the regime's terror campaign against its opponents consisted mostly of arrest and imprisonment in concentration camps. The percentage of Jews among the detainees was quite high, and they were singled out for particularly cruel and humiliating treatment, which in many instances resulted in death. Shocked by such terrorization and the overall onslaught on their position in the country, many Jews reacted with headlong flight, a wave of emigration that encompassed thousands of people. According to the census taken in June 1933, the Jewish population in Germany was 502,799 (by religion) or 540,000 (by race); these figures show that since January of that year about 26,000 Jews "by race" had left the country. By the end of 1933, 63,000 Jews had emigrated, according to retrospective statistics compiled in 1941 by the Reichsvereinigung der Juden in Deutschland (Reich Association of Jews in Germany).

Support of the German people for the regime's policy against the Jews was not uniform, and while there was broad recognition of the need to find a "solution" to the "Jewish question," there were also reservations about the violent methods being applied, as well as individual cases of solidarity with the Jews. However, few public protests were made by the leadership of institutions that were still relatively independent, such as the Protestant and Catholic churches; the objections raised to the persecution of the Jews referred primarily to the thousands of Christians of Jewish origin who were affected by the racist legislation.

Among the Jews, the reaction to what was happening was different on the individual and the organizational level. Although the Jews' social and political status had suffered a tremendous blow, their existing organizational network was scarcely touched—indeed, new organizations came into being. In this respect the situation of the Jews was in stark contrast to the prevailing trend of totalitarian *Gleichschaltung*, the purpose of which was to destroy the existing social and political fabric of German society and construct a homogeneous national society in its place. It was the exclusionary racist principle on which the policy toward the Jews was based—their separation and isolation from the general society—that made possible the continuing existence of the Jews' own institutions. Moreover, "alien" and "decadent" ideas and principles such as political pluralism and democracy, which were now beyond the pale among the general population, were still the rule in Jewish public life. This was, however, the freedom of the outcast, of a community that now seemed doomed to disappearance (at this stage of the Nazi regime) through emigration.

The mass emigration and the large number of suicides were manifestations of the crisis experienced by German Jewry as it saw the fundamental premises on which its existence had been based collapsing. At the same time, the organizational structure of German Jewry adapted itself to the changing conditions, and even intensified its varied internal activities. Prior to 1933 the Jewish communities had been entities recognized by public law—a status they retained under the Nazis, in that early stage—but no nationwide organization of communities of similar status had come into being. In 1932 a beginning was made with the formation of a loose national federation of existing Landesverbände (State Unions) of communities, which in the Third Reich made its first public appearance with a memorandum it published in May 1933. It was only in September of that year, however, that a truly representative and comprehensive national organization was established, which, in addition to the Landesverbände, included the major political bodies and the large communities. This was the REICHSVERTRETUNG DER DEUTSCHEN JUDEN (Reich Representation of German Jews), under the leadership of Rabbi Leo BAECK and Otto HIRSCH. Its major operational instrument was the Zentralausschuss, which had been formed even before the Reichsvertretung was formally constituted.

The Reichsvertretung, an umbrella organization, set itself the purpose of representing the Jews of Germany vis-à-vis both the authorities and Jews in other countries, assuming the leadership of the Jewish population and coordinating the wide range of new activities through which the Jews had attempted to cope with the changed situation. Prominent among these activities was the creation of an expanded network of educational institutions for youth and adults, especially through the work of the MITTELSTELLE FÜR JÜDISCHE ERWACHSENENBILDUNG (Jewish Center for Adult Education), founded and administered by Martin Buber. Other areas covered by the Reichsvertretung were vocational training and retraining, expanded welfare operations, economic assistance, aid in find-

ing employment for Jews who had lost their jobs, and preparing for emigration. In the political sphere, it submitted memorandums to the authorities and published statements in the Jewish press in which it demanded safeguards for Jewish life, even under the existing circumstances. On several occasions, as when the Nazi newspaper Der STÜRMER (The Attacker) came out with a special issue on the blood libel—the accusation that Jews kill gentiles to obtain their blood for Jewish rituals—the Reichsvertretung did not hesitate to react with public protests.

The Jewish press at this time greatly increased in size and circulation. In 1934 the combined monthly circulation of national and community newspapers was 1,180,000. In the area of cultural activities, a special organization was founded in July 1933, the KULTURBUND DEUTSCHER JUDEN (Cultural Society of German Jews), which set itself the tasks of finding employment for the many Jewish artists and intellectuals who had been dismissed from their posts, and of serving as the cultural center for the Jewish population. Before long, the Kulturbund became one of German Jewry's largest and most proficient organizations.

The emergence of umbrella organizations did not remove from the Jewish scene the competition among different political and religious orientations for influence among the Jews and for representation in the community institutions. The main polarization was between the mainstream of German Jewry and the Zionist movement. The former was represented by the Centralverein and the Reichsbund der Deutschen Frontsoldaten, and its main purpose was to struggle for Jewish existence and the preservation of Jewish rights in Germany. The primary goal of the latter was gradually to prepare the Jews for a

Overleaf: In the autumn of 1935 a Dutch motorcyclist traveled from Bentheim (on the Dutch frontier) to Berlin by way of Hannover. During the trip he took photographs of the antisemitic signs he saw. (The Nazis had been in power less than three years.) Among the legends on the signs are: "Jews are not wanted in this place"; "The residents of this place want nothing to do with Jews"; "Jews enter this place at their own risk"; "The Jew is our misfortune. Let him keep away"; "Hyenas are scum and so are Jews"; "Jews get out!"

new life in the national home in Palestine. By this time the Zionist movement had made substantial gains in Germany, especially among the young people. The He-Haluts pioneering movement had a strong base, and Recha Freier had established the YOUTH ALIYA organization.

All public activities by Jews were under the watchful eye of the authorities, mainly the Gestapo and the SD (Sicherheitsdienst; Secret Service), whose policy was to put restraints on any that were designed to encourage German Jews to stay in the Reich (mainly by the Centralverein and the Reichsbund der Deutschen Frontsoldaten). On the other hand the Zionist movement was able to carry on with relative freedom of action and with little interference. Notwithstanding National Socialism's sharp opposition to the Zionist movement's political aim of establishing a Jewish state, the Nazi regime at this time encouraged the work of the Zionists, believing that it promoted the emigration of Jews from Germany.

As far as official antisemitic policy was concerned, 1934 was a relatively uneventful year, and some of the Jewish emigrés living in difficult circumstances as temporary refugees in neighboring countries even decided to return to Germany. The restriction of Jewish rights now took the form of decrees and regulations issued by local authorities and professional organizations that applied in practice the principles enunciated in the 1933 anti-Jewish legislation.

The clash between the regime's tendency toward stabilization and consolidation as an authoritarian and totalitarian state and the still-existing revolutionary radicalism in the party ranks prompted Hitler, in June 1934, to stage a purge in which the top echelon of the SA, as well as other opposition leaders, were executed. One outcome of this confrontation was the strengthening of the conservative elements in the government, mainly among the army officers and the officials dealing with economic affairs; another was the rise of new centers of power, primarily the SS. The ongoing process of centralization resulted in the seizure of control over all police forces in the Reich by Heinrich HIMMLER, chief of the SS and the Gestapo. The effect of this development on the situation of the Jews was the establishment of special sections in the Gestapo and SD to deal with the "Jewish question."

In the wake of the sweeping victory in the Saar plebiscite in January 1935, which restored that district to the Reich, a new drive of violence against the Jews was launched. This time it took the form of a series of locally initiated actions (*Einzelaktionen*), accompanied by a high-powered campaign of incitement against the Jews in the press and in mass rallies, a campaign orchestrated by Joseph GOEBBELS and Julius STREICHER. A special feature of it was the denunciation and public humiliation of persons accused of having committed *Rassenschande* ("race defilement"), that is, sexual intercourse between Jews and "Aryans." The various German states passed anti-Jewish legislation of their own, for example, forbidding Jews to display the German flag and outlawing marriages between Jews and Aryans. It was in the smaller population centers that the Jews suffered most in this campaign, and as a result more and more Jews left their homes in the provinces and took up residence in the large cities.

The terror campaign reached its height in the summer of 1935 and was one of the factors leading to the enactment of the NUREMBERG LAWS in September of that year. These laws were designed to serve two purposes: to restore "law and order," and to meet the demands of radical party circles for implementation of the original antisemitic planks in the Nazi platform. The Nuremberg Laws were *Verfassungsgesetze* (constitutional laws), one of them the Reich Citizenship Law and the other the Law for the Protection of German Blood and German Honor, and they contained a new definition of the term "Jew," based on race. This was the definition on which all subsequent anti-Jewish legislation was based until 1943, when a final decree was enacted under which Jews were denied protection of the courts.

Secret government and party reports on the mood of the German population revealed that the reaction to the Nuremberg Laws was mixed. In wide circles it was believed that Hitler's statement describing the laws as a possible formal framework for the continued existence of the Jews in Germany meant that the laws were a solution of sorts, providing for racial and cultural segregation of the Jews from the German people and for their social isolation. Other circles, especially those with religious leanings and among the liberal bourgeoisie, expressed strong reservations and even criticism. Yet a third group, consisting mainly of radical Nazi party members, found the Nuremberg Laws too moderate, called for a more far-reaching solution of the "Jewish question," and, on their own initiative, continued anti-Jewish violence on the local level. The church leadership took no public stand on the Nuremberg Laws, despite the fact that the laws also affected thousands of converts, an issue that had confronted the churches from the moment the first anti-Jewish legislation was enacted in April 1933.

The SD's Section for Jewish Affairs was also reorganized in 1935, with Herbert Hagen as section chief and Adolf EICHMANN as his deputy. Henceforth, the section was to make persistent efforts to have exclusive charge of Jewish affairs in the Reich and beyond its borders.

The Jewish population and its leaders tried to cope with the deteriorating situation by intensifying and broadening their own activities in the social and economic spheres. In some Jewish quarters it was believed that under the situation created by the Nuremberg Laws the Jews would experience a kind of "group emancipation." The resulting status would safeguard certain civil rights of German Jews as a group, replacing the nineteenth-century Emancipation, which had endowed the individual Jew with equal civil and political rights. On the political level, the Reichsvertretung reacted by lodging protests and issuing a statement for publication by the Jewish press. Other Jewish reactions included a manifesto of August 1935 remonstrating against the rising tide of terror, and a special prayer written by Leo Baeck on the eve of the Day of Atonement. Both these protests led to punitive action by the Gestapo. In its memorandum reacting to the Nuremberg Laws, the Reichsvertretung gave expression to the sense of humiliation and insult aroused among the Jews by the laws, but it also saw in them a possible basis for some kind of continued autonomous Jewish existence in Germany.

In 1936, when the Olympic games were held in Berlin, there was a relative relaxation in public anti-Jewish activity. It seemed that the continued economic activities of the Jews and the consolidation of their newly established organizational and social structures had created a pattern of life that could be maintained even under a racist totalitarian regime. At that very time, however, a new antisemitic policy that was to have far-reaching consequences was being formulated for translation into practice during the following years. Hitler's secret memorandum on the FOUR-YEAR PLAN, which he wrote in August 1936, contained an ideological and political section in which he called for an all-out war against Judaism as a driving motive in Germany's future foreign policy and its preparations for the war against the Soviet Union that was sure to come within four years. The last part of this document contained the principles of the draconian punitive measures against the Jews that were to be the guidelines of future policy. In late 1936 and early 1937 the practical details of this radical policy were spelled out in documents drafted by the SD's Jewish section, for future application. The interim goals for the "solution of the Jewish question" were to include an intensified drive to eliminate Jews from the economy, and increased pressure for their emigration by such means as the "people's fury," that is, officially organized terror. The implementation of this policy on an informal basis was launched in the second half of 1937, mainly by the "Aryanization" (ARISIERUNG) of Jewish business enterprises. In this operation the SD contested the policies of other official agencies, especially the moderate pragmatic policy advocated by the Ministry for Economic Affairs; the struggle intensified when the minister, Hjalmar Schacht, was dismissed from his post in the fall of that year.

The year 1937 was a time of crisis inside the Third Reich, with signs of opposition to the regime manifested in various sectors of German society. One expression of the crisis was the sharpening conflict (Kirchenkampf) between the churches and the regime. Its most prominent manifestation was the German-language encyclical issued by Pope Pius XI, Mit brennender Sorge (With Burning

GERMANY—February 1938

Concern), which was distributed all over Germany. The encyclical denounced Nazi neo-paganism and the cult of racism, but it did not explicitly condemn the persecution of the Jews. The reactions of the regime varied, and included the staging of numerous show trials of clerics, who were imprisoned in concentration camps. According to secret official reports, by the end of the year the disapproval of and outright opposition to the regime were fast becoming a threat to its stability. These attitudes were especially prominent in conservative circles, with the churches and the army in the lead, but they were also evident among the workers. This was the background of the "crisis of the generals," which erupted in early 1938, and of the drastic changes introduced by Hitler in the top echelons of the army and the ministries of war and foreign affairs. Werner von BLOMBERG and Konstantin von Neurath fell from power, and Joachim von RIBBENTROP was appointed foreign minister, in preparation for a radicalized policy in both internal and foreign affairs.

This policy soon resulted in the annexation of Austria in March 1938, the Czech crisis and subsequent annexation of the Sudetenland in September of that year, the creation of the Protectorate of Bohemia and Moravia out of the occupied western part of Czechoslovakia in March 1939, and, finally, the invasion of Poland in September 1939, which

marked the beginning of World War II. Of special significance was the declaration that Hitler made on January 30, 1939, which he was to repeat during the war on various public occasions and in closed meetings with party and army leaders: "If international-finance Jewry in Europe and elsewhere once again succeeds in dragging the nations into a world war, its outcome will not be the Bolshevization of the globe . . . but the annihilation of the Jewish race in Europe."

The year 1938 witnessed a significant stage in the further radicalization of the Third Reich's anti-Jewish policy, which was applied in the newly acquired territories. The radical policy took the form of a series of new laws and decrees, mass arrests of Jews, and a variety of "spontaneous" and official terror actions, the latter culminating in the pogrom of November 9–10. The first important step in this process was a law put into effect on March 28, 1938, that abolished the legally recognized status of the Jewish communities, a status they had been accorded in the nineteenth century. This was followed, on April 26, by a decree ordering the registration of Jewish property, and on June 15, by the arrest of 1,500 Jews and their imprisonment in concentration camps (the "June Operation"). Other anti-Jewish laws passed at this time forbade Jews to practice medicine (June 25), ordered male Jews to assume the name Israel, and female Jews, the name Sarah (August 17), forbade Jews to practice law (September 27), and stipulated that the passports of Jews be marked with a capital *J*, standing for *Jude* (October 5). In this period, and especially during the Czech crisis, there was a sharp rise in the number of "unofficial" terror actions taking place. They included the destruction of Jewish property, the expulsion of Jews, mainly from smaller population centers, and the desecration and destruction of synagogues, among them the main synagogue at Munich (June 9) and at Nuremberg (August 10).

On October 28, 1938, fifteen thousand to seventeen thousand Jews of Polish nationality were expelled from Germany. The Polish government refused to admit them into Poland, and for a considerable period of time they were trapped in the no-man's-land between the two countries. Their bitter fate caught the attention of public opinion all over the world (*see* ZBĄSZYŃ). On November 7, Herschel GRYNSZPAN, a Jewish youth whose parents were among the expelled Jews, shot Ernst vom Rath, a German diplomat in Paris. The Nazis used this act as the pretext for an organized pogrom against the Jews, which took place on November 9–10 in every part of Germany and in the areas it had annexed that year (Austria and the Sudetenland). In this pogrom, which came to be called KRISTALLNACHT, or "Night of Broken Glass" (so named from the shattering of the show windows of Jewish enterprises), hundreds of synagogues and thousands of Jewish businesses were burned down, destroyed, or damaged. Some thirty thousand Jews were put into concentration camps, and almost one hundred Jews were murdered.

The pogrom was followed by a collective fine of 1 billion marks imposed on the Jews and by a new series of harsh laws and regulations. Among these were a law providing for elimination of the Jews from the German economy (November 12); a regulation on the final expulsion of Jewish pupils from public schools, also on November 12; restrictions on the freedom of movement by Jews in public places (November 28); and a regulation ordering all Jewish newspapers and periodicals to be shut down (there were sixty-five newspapers and periodicals and forty-two organizational bulletins with a total monthly circulation of 956,000). All Jewish organizations were dissolved, leaving only the Reichsvertretung, the Kulturbund, and, temporarily, the Palestine Office of the Zionist organization. The only paper permitted to be published was the *Jüdisches Nachrichtenblatt*, the semi-official newspaper of the Reichsvertretung.

Classified reports by the Reich security services revealed that the reaction of the German public to the *Kristallnacht* pogrom, like that to the Nuremberg Laws, was not uniform. The disapproval voiced was on a much larger scale, but it focused primarily on the damage caused to German property and the German economy, and only in small degree on the moral aspect of the terror directed against the Jews and the destruction of their property. Once again the church leadership refrained from taking a public stand. A few individual clerics denounced the riots for their barbarity, which, they said, "contradicted the spirit of the Gospels." The underground German Communist party devoted an entire issue of its newspaper *Die Rote Fahne* (The Red Flag) to condemning the pogrom.

From 1938 to 1945. Before the end of November 1938 the Reichsvertretung resumed its activities, which centered mainly on intensifying the emigration of Jews from Germany and obtaining the release of those who had been imprisoned in concentration camps. It also proceeded to implement its earlier decisions to revise its organizational structure and its position within Jewish society and the National Socialist state, a process begun when the legal status of the Jewish communities was abolished in March 1938. By July that year all the Landesverbände of Jewish communities and the major Jewish organizations had decided to merge and to establish a new central organization, a nationwide Jewish community with a democratic constitution that would seek official recognition by the authorities. The name proposed for the new body was the Reichsverband der Juden in Deutschland (Reich Federation of Jews in Germany). Based on this initiative, which did not materialize in the wake of the November pogrom and its immediate repercussions, the Jewish leadership announced in February 1939 the formation of the Reichsvereinigung der Juden in Deutschland (Reich Association of Jews in Germany). The Reichsvereinigung regarded its main concerns as emigration, Jewish edu-

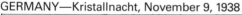

GERMANY—Kristallnacht, November 9, 1938

© Martin Gilbert 1982

cation, and welfare. This development took place at a time when the authorities as well had an interest in the existence of a more authoritative, centralist Jewish organization. On July 4, 1939, a law was passed granting recognition to the Reichsvereinigung. This law, however, required that all Jews by race, as defined in the Nuremberg Laws, had to belong to the new organization. The Reichsvereinigung was put under the supervision of the Ministry of the Interior, which in practice meant that it was under the control of the SS.

In 1938 and 1939, emigration of Jews ("by race") from Germany reached new heights—49,000 in 1938 and 68,000 in 1939—despite the many difficulties that stood in the way, such as new restrictive entry regulations in the target countries, restrictions on immigration to Palestine, and the failure of the EVIAN CONFERENCE. Long before November 1938, the Reichsvertretung

had recognized the importance of the role it had to play in emigration, and early that year it had set up a coordinating office for this purpose. The Reichsvereinigung kept up its efforts on behalf of Jewish emigration even after the war broke out, routing the emigrants through neutral Spain and Portugal to the Western Hemisphere, through the Soviet Union to East Asia, and through Italy and the Balkan states to Palestine by means of Aliya Bet ("illegal" immigration). These efforts came to an end in October 1941, when all Jewish emigration was prohibited.

As the agency with the sole responsibility for Jewish education, the Reichsvereinigung created a network which ensured that Jewish schooling was available wherever Jews lived in Germany and also supervised the training of teachers. The Kulturbund continued its activities and, indeed, added to them by taking over some of the functions of the Mittelstelle, those for adult education.

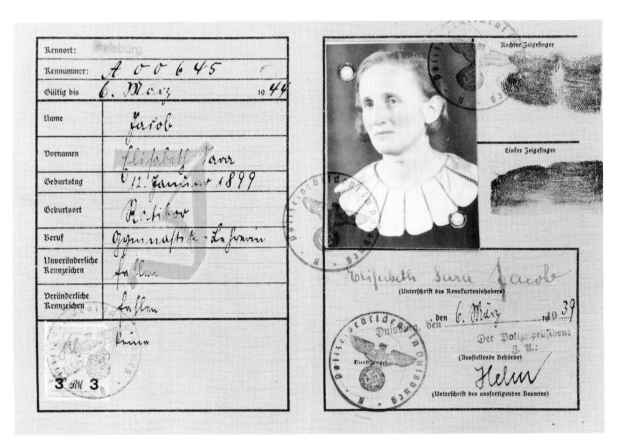

Jewish identity card in the German Reich. Note the large "J" printed on the left side. The card was issued to Elisabeth Sara Jacob, a gym teacher of Duisburg, on March 6, 1939.

With regard to social welfare, the Reichs-vereinigung was confronted with enormous problems, owing to the fact that practically all German Jews had been deprived of their livelihood, that the average age of the Jews remaining in Germany was quite high, and that financing had to be found for the emigration of the growing number of would-be emigrants who had no means of their own. To deal with these problems the Reichs-vereinigung gave its support to existing fund-raising institutions for mutual help, but its main source of funds was the revenue it obtained from a progressive tax imposed on Jews who still had property in their possession, including Jews who were about to emigrate. The Reichsvereinigung also continued to receive financial assistance from American Jewish welfare agencies, until America's entry into the war in December 1941.

As a growing number of countries became involved in the war, the Germans expanded their policy of Jewish persecution as it had evolved in Germany since 1933, applying it in the countries that occupied or that were under their influence. The form of this policy differed from one country to another, but its ultimate aim was the same everywhere—the "FINAL SOLUTION" of the "Jewish question." In Germany proper the outbreak of the war set off a new round of anti-Jewish decrees and regulations affecting nearly every sphere of the Jews' life. Among the first was a decree that prohibited Jews from leaving their homes after dark and placed certain sections of cities out of bounds to them. Another that reduced their allocation of rationed foods and restricted their purchases to certain shops and certain times of day. Other decrees, by the dozen, ordered the Jews to hand over their jewelry, radios, cameras, electrical appliances, and any other valuables in their possession. In September 1941 all Jews aged six and above were ordered to wear the *Judenstern* (the Jewish star; *see* BADGE, JEWISH), and Jews were no longer permitted to use public transportation. In contrast to the situation in most other countries of Europe, no ghettos were created in Germany, and the isolating of the Jews was achieved by imposing residential restrictions that forced them out of their homes and concentrated them in *Judenhäuser* ("Jewish buildings"). Jews who

were declared "fit for work" were put on forced labor, and the practice of arresting individual Jews and sending them to concentration camps was continued. The persecution of the Jews by means of decrees and regulations was formally ended, in July 1943, by another decree that removed them from the protection of the law and placed them under the exclusive jurisdiction of the security services and the police.

The first deportations of Jews from Germany took place in February 1940, and affected Jews from Stettin (now Szczecin) and Schneidemühl (Piła) and their environs (*see* NISKO AND LUBLIN PLAN). These deportations were discontinued in the spring of that year, but in the summer, after the victory over France, the idea came up of deporting the Jews to Madagascar (*see* MADAGASCAR PLAN). In October 1940, in a single night, all the Jews of Baden, the Palatinate, and the Saar district—a total of 7,500 persons—were deported to France, most of them to the GURS camp, and from there to extermination camps in the east. In October 1941 the deportation of masses of Jews on a systematic basis was launched, a process that led to the liquidation of German Jewry. The majority of these transports had as their destination the Łódź and Warsaw ghettos in Poland, and the ghettos of Riga, Kovno, and Minsk in the German-occupied parts of the Soviet Union.

By then the mass murder of Jews by the EINSATZGRUPPEN was in full swing in the German-occupied Soviet territory; the first phase of the total annihilation of the Jews of Europe had begun. Some of the transports from Germany to these territories were liquidated upon their arrival in the ghettos (as in Riga and Minsk) during the course of local *Aktionen;* the other deportees, if they did not perish from epidemics and starvation, were deliberately killed. In 1942 and 1943, these German Jews were deported by the tens of thousands directly to the extermination camps, mainly to AUSCHWITZ. Some forty-two thousand Jews from Germany, mostly elderly people and those with "privileged status," were sent to the THERESIENSTADT ghetto; the majority either perished there or were deported to the extermination camps. Even before the systematic mass annihilation started, several hundred Jews were murdered

GERMANY — November 1942

between 1939 and 1941 inside Germany, within the EUTHANASIA PROGRAM.

The link of ideology and political policy with the destruction of the Jews in Europe in relation to the impending war was propounded by Hitler in public speeches (as of January 1939), in secret operational directives that he issued during the war, and in his last testament, dictated in April 1945. Most scholars believe that there was a close connection between the radicalization of the war that was inaugurated by the invasion of the Soviet Union and the beginning of the mass murder of the Jews, and that the *rassenideologische Vernichtungskrieg* (the racist and ideologically motivated war of extermination) deliberately coincided with the campaign against "Jewish Bolshevism" and its "biological sources," the millions of Jews in eastern Europe.

But despite its unique character, the Nazi extermination of the Jews should be seen as part of a larger concept, the racial revolution planned by the Nazis, which was to restructure the face of Europe by exterminating and subjugating entire sectors of the population and by uprooting millions of people from

their homes, mainly in eastern Europe (*see* GENERALPLAN OST). During the war, in addition to the Jews, the Nazis also murdered GYPSIES, the chronically and mentally ill in Germany itself, Soviet prisoners of war, and intellectual and political elites in Poland and in the Soviet Union.

In practical terms, the policy toward the Jews in all its phases, both before the "Final Solution" and during its course, was shaped by the Third Reich's bureaucracy and police, and especially by the section for Jewish affairs, headed by Eichmann, in the REICHSSICHERHEITSHAUPTAMT (Reich Security Main Office; RSHA). Also taking part in the mass murder of the Jews or witnessing it were the tens of thousands who served in the Einsatzgruppen and millions of soldiers in the German occupation army; these were also the main sources that channeled information on the fate of the Jews to the German population.

The attitude of the German population to the "solution of the Jewish question" during the war years does not appear to have been different from that during the years preceding the war, but because of the far harsher treatment meted out to the Jews once the war began, the German people's reaction takes on a different meaning. The growing isolation of the Jews during the war, prior to their deportation, is reflected mainly in the absence of concern on the part of the German population to what was happening to the Jews. But even at that stage, particularly before the start of the mass deportations, there was pressure by various groups for a more extreme anti-Jewish policy in Germany, along the lines of the policy that had been introduced in Poland by this time. There were appeals for further restrictions to be imposed on the Jews in day-to-day life, for the introduction of the Jewish badge, and even for the expulsion and liquidation of the Jews. On the other hand, secret reports on public opinion in Germany at that time noted that there were reservations about the treatment of the Jews, especially with respect to the introduction of the yellow badge and the first deportations to the east, the more so after information had been received concerning the fate of the deportees and the mass murder of Jews in eastern Europe. These reservations were expressed primarily in the educated circles of the middle class, among religious Germans, and in the lower ranks of the clergy. As before, the church leadership did not protest. Only in 1943, when it seemed that a similar fate was in store for the thousands of German Jews who had hitherto been safe because they were living with their Christian spouses, and also for their (mostly Christian) descendants, was a public protest issued.

A stronger reaction to reports on the extermination of German Jewish deportees and of Jews from other countries was expressed after the defeat at Stalingrad and the massive air raids on German cities in 1943. On the whole, however, it appears that the majority of the German people maintained a passive attitude toward the fate of the Jews, and this was also true of the "conservative resistance" circles, led by army chiefs. The political plans drawn up by the participants in the 1944 plot against Hitler contain little reference to the Jews, and the leading figures in the conspiracy did not believe that there was room for the resettlement of Jews in Germany, or anywhere in Europe, for that matter. At the same time, there is evidence that thousands of Germans risked their lives and the lives of their families to extend help to Jews, thus saving some of the Jews who had gone into hiding.

Despite the progressive radicalization of the Nazi policy on the Jews, the Reichsvereinigung continued to function throughout the war years according to the policy that had crystallized when it was reorganized in 1938 and 1939. The new situation, and especially the onset of the mass deportations in 1940, created problems and posed unprecedented challenges to the Reichsvereinigung. The welfare needs, which in the past had been confined to a minority, now came to involve the great majority of the Jewish population in Germany. In addition to the regular subsidies that it made, the Reichsvereinigung had to provide emergency housing for the thousands of Jews who had been evicted from their homes, and particularly for the patients and inmates of medical institutions and old-age homes that had to be evacuated and turned over to the authorities. The Reichsvereinigung provided educational facilities to all German Jews, even after emigration and, later on, mass deportation, had

thinned out the ranks of both students and teachers. Only in the summer of 1942 was the Jewish school system closed down, on orders issued by the Gestapo when the wave of deportations was at its height. The Reichsvereinigung also continued to run its training and retraining institutions, and to help support the agricultural training farms (*hakhsharot*) of the Zionist movements, which in the eyes of their participants were "the remaining islands of self-contained Jewish life" in Germany. These establishments, too, were gradually closed down in 1942 and 1943, during the mass deportations.

The Reichsvereinigung did not abandon its independent role as the responsible Jewish leadership, as demonstrated forcefully by its reaction to the first mass deportations from Germany in 1940 and to the Madagascar Plan broached that year. When Eichmann presented to the Reichsvereinigung leaders the plan for the expulsion to Madagascar of the European Jews, their response was that the only possible place for the mass settlement of Jews was Palestine. After the deportation of all the Jews of Baden and the Palatinate in October 1940, the Reichsvereinigung undertook a number of protest actions to which the Nazi authorities retaliated sharply, in part by arresting and murdering one of the organization's leading officers, Julius Seligsohn. From then on, until the liquidation of German Jewry, the leadership's activities in relation to the authorities were conducted in an atmosphere of growing terror, with some of the leaders arrested and deported to concentration camps. One of the first victims was Otto Hirsch, who perished in the MAUTHAUSEN camp in June 1941. In those years, a major concern of the Reichsvereinigung leadership vis-à-vis the authorities was to assert its rights of ownership of Jewish public property. Such property was gradually being sold, and the proceeds were one of the most important sources for the financing of the Reichsvereinigung's operations on behalf of the Jews remaining alive in Germany in the wake of the deportations.

Beginning in the fall of 1941, the procedure for the mass deportations usually consisted of rounding up Jews and taking them to special assembly points in the large cities. The RSHA planned the deportations, and the lists of the candidates for deportation were compiled by the Gestapo offices in the various districts and large cities. In some places the local Jewish community was ordered to distribute the deportation orders to its members. Contrary to an assumption prevailing among survivors for many years after the war and consequently found in research literature, the Reichsvereinigung did not participate directly in the deportations; this has been revealed in documents in its archives, which came to light only relatively recently. Many of the Reichsvereinigung leaders and staff were among the victims imprisoned and deported in June 1942 in retaliation for an attack on an anti-Soviet exhibition in Berlin by the underground Jewish Communist BAUM GRUPPE. During the retaliatory operation, hundreds of Jews from Berlin and elsewhere were executed.

At the end of January 1943, when the mass deportations were drawing to an end, two of the remaining leaders of the Reichsvereinigung, Leo Baeck and Paul EPPSTEIN, were transferred to the Theresienstadt ghetto. In February of that year a drive was made to round up the Jews who were still left in Berlin, working in war-essential industrial plants. Some of these Jews, who were married to gentile women, were saved when their wives staged public demonstrations in their behalf. Several months later, in July, after the deportations had come to an end, the liquidation of German Jewry was officially declared to have been completed; the offices of the Reichsvereinigung and the Berlin Jewish community were closed down and the remainder of the staff was deported. The semiofficial Jewish newspaper was also closed down. During the time it was published, it had served primarily as a source of information on emigration opportunities and on the ways and means of organizing emigration. When emigration was forbidden, the paper's main role was to inform the German Jews about decrees and orders issued by the authorities concerning Jewish affairs.

After the disbandment of the Reichsvereinigung in July 1943, the affairs of the approximately fifteen thousand Jews who were left in Germany (most of them because they were married to non-Jews) were put in the hands of an organization known as the Rest-Reichsvereinigung (Residue Reich Associa-

tion). It had little authority and played a very modest role, but it remained in existence until the end of the war.

Conclusion. Of the 566,000 Jews (by race) who lived in Germany when Hitler came to power, some 200,000 fell victim to the Nazi extermination policy and some 300,000 were saved, mostly by emigrating from the country. (These and subsequent figures refer to Jews by "race" and are rounded off in thousands.) During the existence of the Third Reich, the surplus of deaths over births among the Jewish population of Germany (which had a rate of aging that was high even before 1933, and that rose further as a result of emigration) was 66,000.

The actual number of Jewish emigrants from Germany between 1933 and 1945 was 346,000. This figure includes 98,000 who emigrated to European countries conquered later by the Nazis; of these, an estimated 70,000 were deported during the Nazi occupation, together with Jews from the local population. Some 5,000 of these deportees survived the war. Approximately 137,000 Jews were deported directly from Germany, of whom about 9,000 survived. The figure of 200,000 German Jews who fell victim to Nazi extermination also includes several thousand Jews who were murdered in the Euthanasia Program or who committed suicide (most of the suicides occurred at the time of the deportations). In addition to the 20,000 Jews surviving the war in Germany (15,000 in the open, mostly MISCHLINGE, and 3,000 to 5,000 who had gone undergound), another 5,000 survived in the Theresienstadt ghetto and 4,000 in other concentration camps.

In the early stage of the war no Jews were sent to Germany on forced labor, but this policy changed in the final stages, during which tens of thousands of Jews were taken out of concentration camps and brought to Germany. They worked there under subhuman conditions, mostly in the armament industry and in the removal of debris in the German cities caused by the Allied air raids. The majority of these Jews soon lost whatever physical strength they had left and were sent back to the extermination camps, to be killed there; only a small number were left in Germany and liberated when the war ended.

During the last few months of the war, tens

of thousands of Jews were taken out of concentration camps in the east, where the war front was drawing near, and put on DEATH MARCHES to Germany. Those who survived the marches were put in concentration camps in Germany, Austria, and the Protectorate of Bohemia and Moravia. Many of them died there, after the camps were liberated, from exhaustion and the epidemics that broke out. In some of the concentration camps, such as DACHAU and BUCHENWALD, Jewish underground resistance groups were organized in the final months of the war, and shortly after liberation they formed the core of the She'erith ha Peletah, or "surviving remnant," the seventy thousand to eighty thousand Holocaust survivors on German soil.

"The Third Reich has put an end to a thousand years of Jewish history in Germany." These prophetic words, uttered by Rabbi Leo Baeck as early as 1933, proved true to an unfathomably tragic extent.

[See also Education on the Holocaust: West Germany; Literature on the Holocaust: Germany; Reparations and Restitution; Trials of War Criminals: Germany and Postwar Dispensation of Justice in Germany; Youth Movements: Germany and Austria.]

BIBLIOGRAPHY

Adam, U. Judenpolitik im Dritten Reich. Düsseldorf, 1972.

Bracher, K. D. The German Dictatorship: The Origins, Structure, and Effects of National Socialism. New York, 1970.

Craig, G. Germany: Eighteen Sixty-Six to Nineteen Forty-Five. New York, 1980.

Genschel, H. Die Verdrängung der Juden aus der Wirtschaft im Dritten Reich. Göttingen, 1966.

Jäckel, E. Hitler's Weltanschauung: A Blueprint for Power. Middletown, Conn., 1972.

Jäckel, E., and J. Rohwer, eds. Der Mord an den Juden im Zweiten Weltkrieg. Stuttgart, 1985.

Krausnick, H., et al. The Anatomy of the SS State. New York, 1968.

Kulka, O. D. "Public Opinion in Nazi Germany and the Jewish Question," Jerusalem Quarterly 25 (Fall 1982): 121–144; 26 (Winter 1982): 34–45.

Kulka, O. D., and Mendes-Flohr, eds. Judaism and Christianity under the Impact of National Socialism. Jerusalem, 1987.

Mosse, G. L. Germans and Jews. New York, 1970.

Mosse, W., and A. Paucker, eds. Entscheidungsjahr 1932. Tübingen, 1965.

Niewyk, D. The Jews in Weimar Germany. Baton Rouge, La., 1980.

Paucker, A., ed. Die Juden im Nationalsozialistischen Deutschland, 1933–1943. Tübingen, 1986. (In German and English.)

Schleunes, K. The Twisted Road to Auschwitz. Urbana, Ill., 1970.

Strauss, H. "Jewish Emigration from Germany." Leo Baeck Institute Year Book 25 (1980): 313–358; 26 (1981): 343–409.

Walk, J. Das Sonderrecht für die Juden im NS-Staat. Karlsruhe, 1984.

OTTO DOV KULKA
and ESRIEL HILDESHEIMER

GERSTEIN, KURT (1905–1945), SS officer and head of the Waffen-SS Institute of Hygiene in Berlin who vainly tried to make known the reality of the "FINAL SOLUTION." Gerstein was born in Münster and qualified as a mining engineer. He joined the Nazi party in 1933 but combined party membership with adherence to the Confessing Church (Bekennende Kirche), for which he was dismissed from state service in 1936. After a period of imprisonment in a concentration camp, he was expelled from the party in 1938. Gerstein then took up the study of medicine. After the death of his sister-in-law under the EUTHANASIA PROGRAM, he resolved to learn more of the truth about the killing of mental patients in "euthanasia institutes." He volunteered for the Waffen-SS, and in 1941 was assigned to its hygiene institute as a contaminations expert.

Early in 1942, Gerstein was appointed to head the Technical Disinfection Department within the Health Technology section. In this capacity he worked with ZYKLON B (hydrogen cyanide). In August 1942, on an inspection visit to the extermination camps of TREBLINKA, SOBIBÓR, and particularly BEŁŻEC, Gerstein saw Zyklon B in operation. His sole desire, as he said, was to ascertain the facts of the machinery of destruction "and then shout them to the whole world."

Gerstein's first contact was with Baron Göran von Otter, a Swedish diplomat, whom Gerstein met by chance on the Warsaw-Berlin express train while returning from

Bełżec. Gerstein was also in contact with Bishop Otto DIBELIUS of the Confessing Church; Archbishop Cesare Orsenigo, the papal nuncio in Berlin; and members of the Dutch underground. His efforts to make known the facts of the mass murder had little success, although his reports have been shown to be accurate in all essential respects. After the war Gerstein was arrested by the French as a suspected war criminal and member of the SS. He committed suicide in his prison cell, apparently out of despair at his failure to have halted the mass murder, but it has also been suggested that he was killed by SS fellow prisoners.

BIBLIOGRAPHY

Franz, H. *Kurt Gerstein: Aussenseiter des Widerstandes der Kirche gegen Hitler.* Zurich, 1964.
Friedländer, S. *Kurt Gerstein: The Ambiguity of Good.* New York, 1969.
Hochhuth, R. *The Deputy.* New York, 1964.
Joffroy, P. *A Spy for God: The Ordeal of Kurt Gerstein.* New York, 1971.

LIONEL KOCHAN

GESTAPO (acronym of Geheime Staatspolizei; Secret State Police), the Prussian, and later the Third Reich's, secret state police and the Nazis' main tool of oppression and destruction.

The Prussian Gestapo (1933–1944). The Gestapo originated in the political department of the police headquarters in Berlin during the Weimar Republic. At that time, the department served the government of Prussia as a domestic intelligence agency. Later in the 1920s, the Prussian political police became a semi-official federal bureau of investigation, although a much less powerful one than the American FBI. When Adolf Hitler became the chancellor of Germany, Hermann GÖRING was made the interior minister of Prussia, thereby taking over the Prussian political police. Göring appointed Rudolf Diels its first executive director in his bid to consolidate Nazi power in Prussia.

Diels, a Prussian civil servant and fellow traveler with the Nazis, served as the necessary tool for transforming an intelligence or-

ganization serving a democratic state of law into a separate and executive police-intelligence apparatus of a totalitarian dictatorship. He helped purge "politically unreliable elements" and Jewish officials. He also established a semi-independent headquarters, the Gestapa (Geheimes Staatspolizeiamt), comprised of low-level but experienced Prussian bureaucrats. When Göring was made prime minister of Prussia on April 11, 1933, the Gestapa was separated entirely from the overall police structure.

The First Gestapo Law, of April 26, 1933, officially gave Diels the authority of an independent state political-police commissioner, although his field branches (*Staatspolizeistellen*) at first remained under the control of the Prussian provincial governors. The emergency regulations of February 28, 1933, gave the Gestapa complete freedom to impose "protective custody" (*Schutzhaft*) upon anyone it wanted, to prevent undesirable political activities, and to wiretap political suspects and follow all their activities. The torture and execution of prisoners without regular legal proceedings remained illegal, but it nevertheless often took place in makeshift SA (Sturmabteilung; Storm Troopers) and SS bunkers and concentration camps already in existence. Diels tried to gain control over the concentration camps. However, he eventually had to come to terms with the SA and the growing power of the SS, and to be satisfied with playing a major role in the camp system without controlling it. During 1933, SA and SS intrigues drove Diels to flee abroad for a time, but he reassumed his position in November of that year, accepting an honorary SS officer's rank.

The Second Gestapo Law, of November 30, 1933, made Göring head of the political police and Diels directly responsible to him. The secret police now became officially known as the Gestapo. It was free of legal or administrative lawsuits against its actions, and it assumed direct control over its field branches. Specially trained, ruthless bureaucrats produced regular intelligence reports on political and ideological "enemies of the Reich." In 1934, a Jewish Section was established in the Gestapa. Diels eventually managed to gain nominal control of the Prussian concentration camps; his efforts to gain such control, along with his efforts to centralize the political police, ultimately served the Nazis, who were the real masters of Germany.

The Gestapo under Himmler and Heydrich. Under Heinrich HIMMLER and Reinhard HEYDRICH, the Gestapo played an important role in the amalgamation of the SS and the police. First, Himmler established SS control over the political police and concentration camps in Bavaria in early 1933. Later he imposed the Bavarian model on all the German states, including Prussia, where as Göring's deputy he took over the Gestapo on April 20, 1934. He made Heydrich its director, and a group of low-ranking Bavarian political-police officials were made SS officers in allegiance to Himmler. Later in the year, Himmler was made the chief of all the political police in Germany.

Although throughout Germany the concentration camps came under the control of the SS, the Gestapo had the power to send its victims to them. Moreover, through a "political section" in the camps' headquarters, it could order that prisoners be released, tortured, or executed. Similar treatment awaited its victims in its own basements. To circumvent the criminal code that forbade torture and murder, the Gestapo adopted methods, tested in the DACHAU concentration camp, of fabricating natural causes of death or serving the inmates' families notice that the prisoners had been "shot while trying to escape."

In June 1936 Himmler officially became the chief of all the German police, his title being *Reichsführer-SS und Chef der Deutschen Polizei* (Reich Leader of the SS and Chief of the German Police). Now that he controlled both the concentration camps and the police, the amalgamation of the SS and police could be completed. Himmler set about reorganizing the police system. This whole process, which had Hitler's consent, helped him gain complete independence from the state and the Reich bureaucracy. Himmler set up two main branches of the police force, the ORDNUNGSPOLIZEI (Order Police; Orpo) and the Sicherheitspolizei (Security Police; Sipo). The Orpo was the "regular" police and included the Schutzpolizei (Protection Police—the uniformed officers), the Gendarmerie (rural police), the Feuerschutzpolizei (firefighting police), and various technical and auxiliary services. Sipo was composed of the Gestapo and the KRIMINALPOLIZEI (Criminal Police). The Gestapo and the field units (now renamed Staatspolizeileitstellen; state regional headquarters) took over all the German political-police agencies. After Himmler's takeover, the Gestapo grew enormously with the recruitment of personnel lacking the traditional qualifications for public service.

From the time of Himmler's takeover until September 1939, when the REICHSSICHERHEITSHAUPTAMT (Reich Security Main Office; RSHA) was established, the structure of the Gestapo stayed the same. Division I was responsible for organization and finance, including legal matters. Its director between 1935 and 1939 was Dr. Werner BEST, the SS lawyer and SD (Sicherheitsdienst; Security Service) executive who perfected the legal side of the Gestapo's circumvention of the criminal code and its other activities. Division II, under Heydrich's direct control, was the main body of the Gestapo. Under Heinrich MÜLLER, Section II 1 was charged with fighting the "enemies" of the regime, to which belonged the Communists, Social Democrats, the outlawed trade unions, monarchists, and anti-Nazi ultraconservatives. Special sections dealt with Austrian matters, Jews, other religious groups, FREEMASONS, and immigrants. The Gestapo intensified the regime's policies of segregation and emigration until 1938, in competition with the SD's radical and aggressive treatment of the "Jewish question." Division III was the counterintelligence unit (Abwehrpolizei), under an SD agent, Günther Palten, who had already penetrated the Gestapo in Diels's time. Between November 1937 and October 1938, special Gestapo-SD units were trained to terrorize and Nazify foreign countries. Following Adolf EICHMANN's initiative in driving many Jews from Austria later in 1938, Müller, with Eichmann as executive, assumed the overall control of the forced emigration of the Jews from all Nazi-controlled territories. After KRISTALLNACHT (November 9–10, 1938), the Gestapo became the main instrument of the regime's anti-Jewish policies.

The Gestapo during World War II (1939–1945). In 1939 the Gestapo, as part of the Sipo, was fused with the SD to form the RSHA. Thus, young, ruthless, and fanatical SD agents such as Eichmann became Gestapo officers; the academics, lawyers, and old-style Prussian civil servants, who had completed their transitional role, either were pushed aside or integrated themselves into the spirit and practices of the SS-infested civil service. With the creation of the RSHA, the Gestapo was expanded, with the border police now coming under its auspices. As with the rest of the RSHA and the SS, the Gestapo, with the onset of the war, took part in the enslavement of "inferior races," "pacifying" and subduing the occupied territories in the west, persecuting the Jews, and, finally, carrying out a major role in the "FINAL SOLUTION." It also continued its activities in the Reich itself. Throughout this period, the head of the Gestapo (Amt IV of the RSHA) was Müller, and the head of the Jewish section (IV B 4) was Eichmann.

The Gestapo's main tool remained the "protective custody" procedure, which was simplified and which allowed the Staatspolizeileitstellen freedom of action against "enemies of the Reich." These activities were carried out according to general or specific directives issued by Heydrich; by his successor, Ernst KALTENBRUNNER; by Müller; or by RSHA section chiefs such as Eichmann. The Gestapo did not even take the trouble to place Jews and GYPSIES in the category of "enemies of the Reich" but rather rounded them up, stole their propoerty, deprived them of their citizenship, and finally deported them. Such acts could be committed with impunity because the Gestapo was allowed to function outside the rule of law, acting instead in accordance with an "overall political mission." Its position above the law and its special mission were spelled out in an RSHA decree of April 15, 1940: "The powers required by the Gestapo for the execution of all measures necessary to their task stem not from specific laws and ordinances, but from the overall mission allotted to the German police in general and the Gestapo in particular in connection with the reconstruction of the National Socialist State" (Buchheim, in Krausnick, pp. 189–190).

In the occupied territories, each headquarters of the Befehlshaber der Sicherheitspolizei und des Sicherheitsdienstes (Commanders of the Sipo and SD; BdS) had a Gestapo representative (Amt IV of the BdS). They hood-winked the Judenräte and took their members hostage, perfected a special jargon of deceit (SPRACHREGELUNG), and supervised the phasing out of the ghettos. They also maintained pressure on satellite countries to deport their Jews. Eichmann's Jewish section and his field representatives generally arranged the deportation to concentration and extermination camps. In particular, Eichmann maintained direct control over the special camp in THERESIENSTADT, and a special Sonderkommando under his command deported most of Hungarian Jewry to AUSCHWITZ in 1944.

Persecuting defenseless Jews and maintaining control through terror in Germany itself and in the occupied territories, the Gestapo relentlessly served Hitler and the goal of remaking the world in the Nazi image. Millions of Germans accepted the Gestapo in its initial phase, collaborated with it later, and supplied the military-organizational framework that made Gestapo atrocities possible.

BIBLIOGRAPHY

Aronson, S. *The Beginnings of the Gestapo System: The Bavarian Model in 1933.* Jerusalem, 1970.

Delarue, J. *The Gestapo: A History of Horror.* New York, 1964.

Krausnick, H., et al. *The Anatomy of the SS State.* New York, 1968.

SHLOMO ARONSON

GETTER, MATYLDA (d. 1968), mother superior of the Warsaw branch of the Order of the Franciscan Sisters of the Family of Mary, a Polish religious order that carried on educational work, mainly among orphans, and cared for the sick in hospitals. In 1942, Sister Matylda decided to accept all the Jewish children fleeing from the WARSAW ghetto who were brought to her and to shelter them in the order's many locations, but especially in its branch at Pludy, some 7.5 miles (12 km) outside Warsaw, on the right bank of the Vistula River.

It is estimated that Sister Matylda was instrumental in rescuing several hundred Jewish children from certain death. Her principal aim was not to gain new souls for the church, but to rescue human lives. She was accused by some of unnecessarily endangering the lives of the many non-Jewish orphans in the order's homes by harboring Jewish children in their midst. Her reply was that by virtue of the Jewish children's presence, God would not allow any harm to befall the other children. Special precautions were taken to remove the too obviously Jewish-looking children for temporary shelter elsewhere when Sister Matylda was alerted to possible Gestapo raids on the orphanages. When time proved too short for this, children with a more Jewish appearance would have their heads or faces partially bandaged, to look as though they had been injured. Sister Matylda was at the time an elderly person and ill with cancer. After the war, the children were released to their parents or relatives.

Sister Matylda Getter was posthumously recognized by YAD VASHEM as a "RIGHTEOUS AMONG THE NATIONS."

BIBLIOGRAPHY

Bartoszewski, W., and Z. Lewin. *Righteous among Nations: How Poles Helped the Jews, 1939–1945.* London, 1969.

MORDECAI PALDIEL

GHETTO. [*This entry gives a general survey of the Jewish ghettos in Nazi-occupied Europe. For detailed descriptions of the life and fate of the ghettos, see under individual cities and towns; some of the major ghettos were those of* Białystok; Kovno; Łódź; Minsk; Riga; Vilna; *and* Warsaw. *For information on Nazi-sponsored Jewish organizations in the ghettos, see* Judenrat *and* Jüdischer Ordnungsdienst. *On Jewish attempts to document their plight, see* Łódź Ghetto, Chronicles of the; *and* Oneg Shabbat. *Resistance in the ghettos is detailed in* Fareynegte Partisaner Organizatsye; Resistance; Jewish; Warsaw Ghetto Uprising; Żydowska Organizacja Bojowa; *and* Żydowski Związek Wojskowy.]

The word "ghetto" originally referred to a city quarter or street in which only Jews lived, confined and separated from the other parts of the city. The term had its origin in Venice, where in 1516 the Jews were forced into a closed quarter call the Geto Nuovo (New Foundry). Other Italian cities—with the exception of Leghorn (Livorno)—also put their Jews into ghettos, and the practice was adopted by towns in southern France that belonged to the pope; by several large cities in Germany; in Bohemia and Moravia; and in some Polish cities. The purpose of ghettoizing the Jews was to restrict contacts between them and Christians and to confine the Jews to certain economic activities. Inside the ghettos, the Jews lived their lives in accordance with their traditional customs. From the end of the eighteenth century, the forcible restriction of Jews to ghettos was gradually abandoned; the last ghetto to exist in Europe was the one in Rome, which came to an end in 1870, when papal rule of the city was terminated.

Separate city quarters, on a voluntary or compulsory basis, for both Jews and Christians existed in many Muslim countries until the twentieth century. For the most part, the Jews lived in separate quarters of their own free will and were not barred from residing in other parts of the city. In more recent times the term "ghetto" came to be applied to urban areas inhabited by blacks in the United States and South Africa and to quarters inhabited by any minority that was oppressed and living in slum conditions.

None of these forms of ghetto can be compared to the ghettos established by the Germans in the countries they occupied in World War II. These were not designed to serve as a separate area for Jewish habitation; they were merely a transitional phase in a process that was to lead to the "FINAL SOLUTION" of the Jewish question. The Nazi-instituted ghettos were, in fact, camps where the Jews were held under duress, with their internal life and organization imposed on them and enforced, through violent means, from the outside, by the Nazi regime. The ghettos were introduced after the outbreak of the war in the towns and cities of eastern Europe—in Poland, the Baltic states, and the occupied parts of the Soviet Union. The ghetto established in Amsterdam, which was not a closed ghetto; the houses in BUDAPEST marked as "Jewish" in the final stage of the war; and the THERESIENSTADT camp, near Prague, differed in their form and structure from the

A sign in the Kovno ghetto (1941). The Yiddish text reads: "JEWS! Contribute for the poor and the naked. Give used winter clothes and shoes that you no longer need. Do not begrudge, and give with an open hand." [Centre Commémoratif de l'Holocauste à Montréal; J. Glasrot Collection]

ghettos in eastern Europe, and are not included in this survey.

Nazi-instituted Ghettos during the War. There is no record of any general order having been issued for the establishment of ghettos, and it may be assumed that they were the result of local initiative. True, Reinhard HEYDRICH's directive of September 21, 1939, on the policy to be adopted toward the Jews in the occupied territories, stated that "the concentration of the Jews in the cities may require, for reasons of general police security, that orders be issued prohibiting Jews from entering certain parts of the cities; also, while taking into consideration the needs of the economy, Jews will not be permitted to leave the ghetto after a certain time in the evening, and so on." The directive, however, did not contain a specific order for the establishment of ghettos, and Heydrich apparently used the term to refer to the Jewish quarters existing at the time in Polish cities. At any rate, when Hans FRANK became responsible for the GENERALGOUVERNEMENT, he did not issue a general order providing for the creation of ghettos, as he did with regard to Judenräte (Jewish councils; *see* JUDENRAT), the Jewish BADGE, and the forced-labor system.

As a result, the ghettos in the various parts of occupied Poland were not set up at one and the same time, nor was there uniformity in the method of separating the ghettos from the outside world, or in the internal regimes of the ghettos. The first ghetto in Poland, in PIOTRKÓW TRYBUNALSKI, was started as early as October 1939, while the ghetto in ŁÓDŹ, Poland's second largest city (situated in the WARTHEGAU, the part of Poland that was annexed to the Reich), was closed on April 30, 1940, at which time it had a population of 164,000. The WARSAW ghetto, the largest in occupied Europe (Warsaw having contained Europe's largest Jewish community), was fenced in during November 1940; its population reached its maximum in March 1941, when it numbered 445,000. In LUBLIN and KRAKÓW the ghettos were established in March 1941, followed in April by RADOM, KIELCE, and CZĘSTOCHOWA, the remaining large cities of the Generalgouvernement. In Silesia, an area that was annexed to the Reich, Jews were locked into ghettos only at the end of 1942 and the beginning of 1943, at the time when its Jewish communities were about to be annihilated. The SOSNOWIEC ghetto was established in October 1942. When the German invasion of the Soviet Union was in full swing, in the latter part of 1941, ghettos were set up in the areas captured from the Soviet Union—in VILNA, in KOVNO, in the Baltic states, and in Belorussian towns. At the end of August 1941, the military administration in the Ukraine ordered that ghettos be established "in places with a relatively large Jewish population, primarily in the cities." In those towns and cities of eastern Europe in which the Jews constituted a majority of the population, the establishment of ghettos ran into difficulties and took time. In the Soviet areas the establishment of the ghettos was preceded by massacres, carried out by the EINSATZGRUPPEN; in some places, such as Vilna, the congregation of the Jews in a ghetto was planned as part of an operation, in which the next steps were to seize masses of Jews and to take them to sites that had been designated for their murder. In areas that had been part of the Soviet Union before World War II, the mass murder and annihilation of Jews were carried out as soon as the German army and the Einsatzgruppen reached the scene, and only a few ghettos were set up; the largest was in MINSK, the capital of Belorussia, which had a maximum population of 100,000.

Euphemisms, Brick Walls, and Barbed Wire. The Germans did not use the term "ghetto" in every instance in which they locked Jews into a separate quarter. In Piotrków Trybunalski they did use the term in the order for the establishment of such a quarter, as they did in Łódź, where it was officially called the Litzmannstadt ghetto (the Germans used the name Litzmannstadt for Łódź). In Warsaw, Kraków, and other places they referred to the ghetto as the *Jüdischer Wohnbezirk* (Jewish residential quarter), carefully avoiding the use of any other term.

The methods by which the ghettos were locked in and guarded took various forms. The Łódź ghetto was enclosed by a barbed-wire and wooden fence and, in some places, a brick wall, with guards posted on both the inside and the outside of the dividing line. The Warsaw ghetto was surrounded by an 11-mile (18-km) wall, with guards posted at the gates and patrolling the length of the wall; the Kraków ghetto was also behind a wall. The Łódź ghetto was hermetically closed, non-Jews being able to enter only by special permission and Jews unable to leave at all; there was hardly any smuggling in the ghetto, in either direction. In the Warsaw ghetto, on the other hand, smuggling went on throughout its existence, by way of the wall or checkpoints, and there was also infiltration by individuals into the ghetto. In medium-sized cities and towns, there were ghettos that Jews were permitted to leave at certain hours of the day only, to make food purchases, while in other places it was possible to move in and out without special difficulties. Piotrków Trybunalski, for example, did not have a fence and was not under guard, and hundreds of Poles were able to go back and forth, while the Jews had no difficulties in leaving. This situation, however, began to change at the end of 1941, and by the spring of 1942 the ghetto was locked in. When the deportations and the "Final Solution" were launched, most of the ghettos were put under lock and key. Under a decree issued in October 1941 by Hans Frank, chief of the Generalgouvernement, any Jew found outside the ghetto without permission was to be put to death; on the basis of this order, Jews from Warsaw—including women and children—were executed at the end of 1941. Nevertheless, the smuggling did not stop for as long as the ghettos remained in existence, despite the cost in human lives.

A ghetto and its administration required the provision of services and institutions in which Jews had had no previous experience. In their cynical propaganda, the Nazis often described the ghetto as a form of self-government, a sort of autonomy, that they had granted to the Jews. In addition to the Judenräte, which were created before the ghettos were established and without connection with them, the ghetto framework, as well as specific orders issued by the authorities, forced the Jews to organize a police force and postal services, to distribute food rations, and to provide work, housing, and health facilities—the kind of municipal and other services that had not previously been within the range of functions carried out by Jewish community organizations.

Reasons and Excuses. The German authorities justified the introduction of ghettos on various grounds: they were to prevent the spread of contagious diseases by the Jews, to combat Jewish profiteering and political rumormongering, and the like. Some of these claims were unfounded and partly invented as excuses for their actions. A number of scholars maintain that the ghettos were designed to serve as an indirect instrument of destruction, as a means of physically destroying the Jews by denying them the basic necessities of life, rather than by the use of lethal weapons. The situation in the two large ghettos—Łódź and Warsaw—seems to support this thesis. In 1941 and 1942, 112,463 persons died in the two ghettos of starvation and disease, which means that 20 percent of the population perished in the space of two years, while the birthrate was practically nil. Joseph GOEBBELS spoke of the ghettos as *Todeskisten* ("death crates"), and Hans Frank, in August 1942, stated: "Clearly, we are sentencing 1.2 million Jews [i.e., the Jewish population of the Generalgouvernement] to death by starvation; and if they do not die from hunger, we will have to adopt other anti-Jewish measures." When Frank made this statement he was already well aware of the "Final Solution" and its implications; previously he had said it would be worthwhile to exploit skilled Jewish laborers, who would be working practically for free. Senior Nazi officials in the Generalgouvernement had on several occasions suggested that Jewish food rations be increased to raise productivity. In the medium-sized cities the Jews in the ghettos suffered from severe shortages, from the hard labor forced on them, and from the overall intolerable conditions, but in many cases there was no death from starvation. It is correct to say that although the Nazis had no qualms about masses of Jews dying from hunger and shortages of other basic necessities, especially if they were not part of the needed labor force, no conclusive evidence exists that the ghettos were created for the purpose of the physical destruction of the Jews, or that in the course of time the Nazis sought to transform the ghettos into places where the total liquidation of the Jewish people would be carried out.

The "Final Solution" Implemented. The ghettos established in the cities housed not only the local Jewish population and those classified as Jews according to the racial laws, but also refugees from other towns and villages, near and far. Thus, by the time the Warsaw ghetto was enclosed, in November 1940, ninety thousand refugees had been added to the city's Jewish population. In addition to Polish Jewish refugees, Jews from Germany, Austria, and the Protectorate of Bohemia and Moravia were also brought to the ghettos; at the end of 1941, twenty thousand Jews from these countries were deported to the Łódź ghetto, and thousands to the Riga, Minsk, and Warsaw ghettos. The Łódź ghetto, at one stage, also took in Gypsies, who were housed in a special section. Some places had more than one ghetto, or the ghetto consisted of several separate parts. In most cases, two ghettos existed—one with a working population, the other for Jews whose annihilation was imminent. Such differentiation was instituted at an early stage, when the Einsatzgruppen were being deployed, as in Vilna. The procedure was also followed in the final stage of the liquidation of the ghettos; in Warsaw, for example, from the great deportation of the summer of 1942 until the final annihilation of the Jews in the city during the spring of 1943, there were three separate ghettos, or separate divisions of the ghetto. In Minsk, Jews brought in from western Europe were confined to a ghetto of their own.

The liquidation of the ghettos coincided with the beginning of the "Final Solution," in the spring of 1942. The last ghetto to be liquidated was that of Łódź, in the summer of 1944. On July 19, 1942, Heinrich HIMMLER issued an order for the physical destruction of the Jews of the Generalgouvernement by the end of the year: "After December 31, 1942, no person of Jewish origin must be found in the Generalgouvernement, with the sole exception of those in the concentration camps [*Sammellager*] in Warsaw, Kraków, Częstochowa, Radom, and Lublin." Another Himmler order, dated June 21, 1943, provided that "all Jews who may still be found in ghettos in the Ostland must be confined in concentration camps." Most of the Jews taken out of the ghettos were murdered in the extermination camps, and only a small percentage were put into concentration and forced-labor camps in the latter stages of the war. Himmler's orders also specified that "the presence of the remaining Jews in labor camps is also to be regarded as temporary; they will stay there only as long as there is a need for the work they do and they are physically able to perform it."

All the Jews of the occupied countries in eastern Europe were enclosed in ghettos, but when the territories in which ghettos had been established were liberated, in the Soviet Union, Poland, and Lithuania, not a single ghetto was left standing, in whole or in part.

BIBLIOGRAPHY

Blumenthal, N. *Conduct and Actions of a Judenrat: Documents from the Bialystok Ghetto.* Jerusalem, 1962. (In Hebrew and English.)

Blumenthal, N. *Documents from the Lublin Ghetto: Judenrat without Direction.* Jerusalem, 1967. (In Hebrew and English.)

Dobroszycki, L., ed. *The Chronicle of the Lodz Ghetto, 1941–1944.* New Haven, 1984.

Trunk, I. *Ghetto Lodz.* New York, 1962. (In Yiddish.)

Trunk, I. *Judenrat: The Jewish Councils in Eastern Europe under Nazi Occupation.* New York, 1972.

ISRAEL GUTMAN

GHETTO FIGHTERS' MUSEUM. *See* Museums and Memorial Institutes: Bet Loḥamei ha-Getta'ot.

GHETTO POLICE. *See* Jüdischer Ordnungsdienst.

GHETTOS, NUTRITION IN. The Polish ghettos received food supplies in two ways—from official and from unofficial sources. Official supplies were distributed on the basis of ration cards issued by the occupation authorities, a method that was introduced even before the Jews were confined to separate city quarters. Already at that early stage, the food rations allocated to the Jews were far short of those supplied to the rest of the population. (This entry will deal solely with the ghettos in Poland.)

When the ghettos were established, their supply departments were authorized to purchase food in specific quantities, according to allocations determined by the German authorities. In the GENERALGOUVERNEMENT these allocations were very meager and did not meet the minimum requirements. In the second half of 1941, the daily food ration received by Jews on the basis of their ration cards consisted of an average of 184 calories; in comparison, a person employed on light work requires 2,400 calories a day. In other words, the Jews received 7.5 percent of the normal quota of food. The Germans received the full ration, while the Poles were given 26 percent of their basic requirements.

The quantity and quality of the food rations for the Jews in the Generalgouvernement led to their physical extermination. Generalgouverneur Hans FRANK, in a speech on August 24, 1942, made the following statement: "In passing, may I say that we are sentencing 1.2 million Jews to death by hunger. It is obvious that if the Jews do not die from hunger, the execution of anti-Jewish orders will have to be speeded up."

In most of the ghettos of western Poland, in the areas that had been incorporated into the Third Reich, except for Łódź and a few other ghettos, the standard of nutrition was a little better than in the Generalgouvernement. At first, the daily food ration for the Jews contained 1,500 calories, with those who were employed on hard labor receiving 1,800 calories. This level of nutrition was planned for the people employed in the armaments industry and other branches of the economy that were of importance to the Reich, and was to be maintained until the time came for the liquidation of the Jewish population. In practice, however, the food ration in many of the ghettos in the incorporated areas was reduced to 513 calories per day, and 638 for those employed on hard labor.

Items supplied on the basis of ration cards were sold at a much lower price than they were on the free (black) market. The items supplied on the basis of ration cards were few in number: bread, 2.47 to 8.82 ounces (70–250 g) in the Generalgouvernement; a few potatoes; sugar, 8.82 ounces (250 g) per person per month; and sometimes also such items as jam, cabbage, and beets. Since the food supplied on the ration cards was far from enough, people of means tried to buy more food. This was easier to do in the ghettos of the Generalgouvernement than in the areas that had been annexed to the Reich. In the ghettos of the annexed areas there was no free, unfettered market where goods smuggled in by local peasants could be bought; the food that did reach the ghettos, in small quantities, had to be smuggled in at the risk of life. Such goods were more expensive in the ghetto than in the free market outside; in the Warsaw ghetto, bread cost 32 percent more and potatoes 25 percent to 73 percent more than in "Aryan" Warsaw.

Most of the Jews were impoverished, having been robbed of their possessions by the Germans and having lost their sources of livelihood when they were confined to walled-in ghettos, where there were no openings for work (this applied to 60 percent of the Jewish population). This meant that in the Generalgouvernement ghettos, only the relatively wealthy could afford to buy food on the black market; but even those who had not lost their source of income, or had accumulated savings, had to scale down their food purchases because of the high prices and the uncertain future they were facing.

For example, in December 1941, Warsaw Judenrat employees—who were regarded as having a privileged status—consumed an average of 1,665 calories per day; the various types of teamsters, 1,544; shopkeepers, 1,429; self-employed artisans, 1,407; unemployed professionals, 1,395; house superintendents, 1,350; employees of "shops" (ghetto workshops), 1,229; refugees in bunkers, 805; beggars, 785 calories.

In general, the Jews paid for their food purchases with the proceeds of the sale of their possessions on the "Aryan" side. As a result, the price of clothes and household goods declined the most. People who did not have any savings went hungry, or starved to death, despite the additional nourishment available in the soup kitchens; the latter, at a fairly low price, provided a calorie-poor soup (the nutritional value of one portion of soup in the Warsaw ghetto at the end of 1941 was 110 calories). At the height of their operation, the soup kitchens in Warsaw supplied 128,000 soup portions per day. In the first eighteen months of the ghetto's existence, 15 percent to 20 percent of its population starved to death. In other ghettos the situation was much the same, as shown by the statistics of the huge rise of the mortality rate and of diseases caused by hunger. Particularly hard hit was the Łódź ghetto, where a special currency was introduced in the Jewish quarter and Jews were not allowed to have regular money in their possession. In this way, the Jews in the ghetto were completely isolated economically, without means of smuggling, and were unable to purchase food to any appreciable extent. This caused the mortality rate in the Łódź ghetto to soar, from 0.96 percent in the prewar period to 3.92 percent in 1940, 7.57 percent in 1941, and 15.98 percent in 1942.

Some of the ghetto population, who were employed on jobs in German-operated factories and were housed in barracks (mainly in the period when the ghettos were being liquidated, beginning in mid-1942), had part of their food requirements provided to them by the management of these factories, the rations they received depending on the type of work they were doing. The official rations were close to starvation level and the workers were forced to obtain their own food, which became increasingly difficult during the liquidation of the ghettos, when unofficial supplies were drastically reduced.

The lack of food in the ghettos was sometimes exploited by the Germans to persuade the Jews to report for deportation of their own free will. In one period, Jews in Warsaw who volunteered for deportation were given 6.6 pounds (3 kg) of bread and 2.2 pounds (1 kg) of jam.

BIBLIOGRAPHY

Dobroszycki, L., ed. *The Chronicle of the Lodz Ghetto, 1941–1944.* New Haven, 1984.
Gutman, Y. *The Jews of Warsaw, 1939–1943: Ghetto, Underground, Revolt.* Bloomington, 1982.
Trunk, I. *Judenrat: The Jewish Councils in Eastern Europe under Nazi Occupation.* New York, 1972.

ZBIGNIEW LANDAU

GILDENMAN, MOSHE ("Uncle Misha"; d. 1958), partisan commander. A resident of the town of Korets in eastern Volhynia, Gildenman was an engineer by profession. After the Nazis' first *Aktion* in Korets on May 21, 1942, in which his wife and daughter died, Gildenman, together with his son, Simha, organized a rebel unit. On September 23 of that year, on the eve of the final liquidation of the Jews of

Moshe Gildenman.

Korets, Gildenman, Simha, and ten young men left for the forests, armed with two revolvers and a butcher knife. After wandering northward for about two weeks, they took in the survivors of an armed group of Jews in the Klesov area, together with whom they made their base in the wooded and swampy terrain north of the Sarny-Rokitno railway track. All of the unit members armed themselves with weapons taken in battles, attacked German farms and Ukrainian police centers, and took revenge on collaborators.

In late January 1943, the unit joined Gen. Aleksandr Saburov's partisan group. The resulting company that Gildenman formed was initially entirely Jewish, but as it grew the Jews became a minority. The company operated independently in the northern area of the Zhitomir district until its liberation in October 1943. Early that month, Gildenman rescued beleaguered units of the Thirteenth Soviet Army; he went on to volunteer for the Soviet army and served as a captain in the engineer corps until the end of the war. He subsequently described the exploits of his unit in articles and in books (*On the Road to Victory: Types of Jewish Partisans*, 1946; and *The Destruction of Korets*, 1949; both in Yiddish). In the early 1950s, Gildenman emigrated to Israel; he died in Rehovot.

BIBLIOGRAPHY

Suhl, Y. *They Fought Back*. New York, 1967. See pages 261–273.
Suhl, Y. *Uncle Misha's Partisans*. New York, 1973.

SHMUEL SPECTOR

GITTERMAN, YITZHAK (1889–1943), director of the American Jewish JOINT DISTRIBUTION COMMITTEE (the Joint) in POLAND, an organizer of Jewish welfare in occupied Poland, and an active member of the underground and the ŻYDOWSKA ORGANIZACJA BOJOWA (Jewish Fighting Organization; ŻOB). Born in Horonstopol, a town in the Ukraine, Gitterman at an early age aided in organizing support to refugees and victims of persecution. In World War I war refugees from towns in Galicia and Lithuania benefited from his assistance, which also included facilitating their emigration from war-torn Europe. In 1921 he was appointed head of the Joint in Warsaw and took part in the postwar rehabilitation of the Jewish population and the establishment of welfare institutions. He was deeply involved in the relief efforts designed to alleviate the grave problems caused by the economic crisis of 1926 and its disastrous effect on the position of the Jews. Gitterman created a network of institutions that provided interest-free loans, the Centralna Kasa Bezprocentowa covering every city and town in Poland. This became an important instrument in Polish Jewry's defense against economic discrimination and boycott. There were places where no organized Jewish community existed, but the loan institution was there, representing every public institution whose services were required by a Jewish community. In the 1930s Gitterman was able to slow down somewhat the rapid pauperization process of Polish Jewry through vocational retraining and the introduction of new occupations.

When World War II broke out, Gitterman made his way to Vilna, which had a large concentration of refugees, and set up aid operations. He was on his way to Sweden to appeal for help when the boat on which he was sailing was seized by the Germans on the high seas. Gitterman was interned in a prisoner-of-war camp and returned to Warsaw in April 1940. He lost no time in taking over responsibility for the major functions of the Jewish Self-Help Society (Żydowska Samopomoc Społeczna) and the Jewish Mutual Aid Society (Żydowskie Towarzystwo Opieki Społecznej). When the Joint's financial resources were exhausted, Gitterman and his associates in the Joint leadership turned to the Jews of Poland themselves with an appeal for financial contributions.

As soon as the Jewish underground was set up, it benefited from Gitterman's support. The Self-Help Society, in which Gitterman played a prominent role, also had an underground council, made up of the leaders of the political underground in the Warsaw ghetto. Gitterman took a direct part in underground activities, together with Emanuel RINGELBLUM (a close friend), in the clandestine cultural programs and in social work for the underground organizations and YOUTH MOVE-

MENTS. He was a member of the ONEG SHAB-BAT and Idische Kultur Organizacje (Yiddish Culture Organization) executive boards.

When the first reports came in of the mass murder of Jews in eastern Europe, Gitterman lent his support to the emerging ŻOB, and provided funds to the Białystok ghetto fighters for the acquisition of arms. When the ŻOB was established in Warsaw in October 1942, Gitterman joined its coordinating committee's financial subcommittee, whose main task was to obtain funds for the purchase of arms.

Gitterman was killed on January 18, 1943, the first day of the second *Aktion* in the Warsaw ghetto.

BIBLIOGRAPHY

Bauer, Y. *American Jewry and the Holocaust: The American Jewish Joint Distribution Committee, 1939–1945.* Detroit, 1982.
Ringelblum, E. "Yitzhak Gitterman." In vol. 2 of *Dziennik Warszawskiego Getta: Natatki i szkice (1942–1943)*, pp. 122–141. Warsaw, 1961.

ISRAEL GUTMAN

GLASBERG, ALEXANDRE (1902–1981), French priest, born a Jew in Zhitomir, in the Ukraine. Glasberg wandered about central Europe, converted, and became a priest in France. In 1940, after the German conquest of France, he established a charitable organization, Amitié Chrétienne (Christian Friendship), to help the victims of the anti-Jewish measures. Under the patronage of Cardinal Pierre-Marie Gerlier, the head of the Catholic church in France, Glasberg's organization set up shelter institutions that took in hundreds of Jewish prisoners who had been released from internment camps run by the French authorities.

When the mass arrests and deportations of Jews began in the summer of 1942, Glasberg turned his rescue efforts into clandestine operations. He cooperated closely with the Jewish rescue organizations, taking special care to ensure that no attempt was made to influence the religious convictions of the persons who were in the care of his institutions. In December 1942, when the Gestapo discovered his activities, Glasberg joined the French parti-

sans, under an assumed name. After the war he played an important role in the operations of the Mosad Aliya (the organization that dealt with the "illegal" immigration of Jews into Palestine) in France and Iran.

BIBLIOGRAPHY

Lazare, L. *La résistance juive en France.* Paris, 1987.
Marrus, M. R., and R. O. Paxton. *Vichy France and the Jews.* New York, 1981.
Wellers, Z. G., A. Kaspi, and S. Klarsfeld, eds. *La France et la question juive, 1940–1944.* Paris, 1981.

LUCIEN LAZARE

GLAZER, GESJA (d. 1944), underground fighter in LITHUANIA. Before World War II Glazer was a member of the Communist party in KOVNO, and she spent years in jail and concentration camps on account of her party activities. When the Germans invaded the Soviet Union on June 22, 1941, Glazer fled to the Soviet interior. From Moscow she was

Gesja Glazer.

dispatched to Lithuania (dropped by parachute), where she became active in setting up an underground and partisan movement to fight the German invaders. On one occasion she entered the Kovno ghetto and, in the name of the Communist party, handed a pistol to the committee of the Antifascist Organization, in appreciation of its operations; she suggested that she would be prepared to lead fighting units of the Jewish underground into the Augustów forest and establish partisan bases there. According to her plan, the bases were to take in the entire membership of the ghetto underground.

After a week Glazer departed for the forest, remaining in touch with the ghetto underground until February 1944. She then left to take part in the VILNA underground operations. When she saw the German police closing in on her, Gesja Glazer committed suicide.

ISRAEL GUTMAN

Josef Glazman.

GLAZMAN, JOSEF (1913–1943), Jewish underground and partisan leader. Born in the town of Alytus, in southern LITHUANIA, Glazman was given a nationalist and traditional upbringing and was active in the Betar Zionist youth movement. In 1937 he was appointed Betar leader for Lithuania, retaining the post until July 1940, when the Soviets dissolved all Jewish political movements in the country. In the first phase of Soviet rule in Lithuania, from July 1940 to the end of June 1941, Glazman was one of the underground leaders of the Revisionist party. When the Germans occupied Lithuania, Glazman was in VILNA, where he was apprehended and sent on forced labor in nearby Reise. In early November of 1941 Glazman returned to the Vilna ghetto, where he organized an underground group made up of Betar members. In order to aid his underground activities he joined the Jewish ghetto police, and at the end of November 1941 he was appointed its deputy chief.

Glazman was one of the founders of the FAREYNEGTE PARTIZANER ORGANIZATSYE (United Partisan Organization; FPO) of the Vilna ghetto and participated in its founding meeting on January 21, 1942. He became the FPO's deputy commander and was also in charge of its intelligence section and commander of one of its two battalions. His official post as deputy chief of the ghetto police was of great help to the underground's operations. Glazman also took an active part in the ghetto's educational and cultural activities. In June 1942, when the ghetto administration was reorganized, Glazman left the police and was appointed head of the ghetto housing department within the JUDENRAT (Jewish Council).

Glazman's relations with Jacob GENS (chief of the ghetto police and, as of July 1942, ghetto head) were strained because of Glazman's underground activities and their differences over policy. At the end of October 1942, Glazman was arrested on Gens's orders and dismissed from his post. He was released in mid-December 1942 after spending several weeks in jail; at the end of June 1943 he was again arrested and sent to the Reise labor camp, on Gens's orders. His arrest was accompanied by a clash between FPO members and the ghetto police.

A few weeks later, Glazman was returned to the ghetto. In the wake of the WITTENBERG affair (July 15, 1943), Glazman left the ghetto, leading the first group of FPO members into the forest in order to establish a partisan base there. On the way they fell into a German ambush and in the ensuing fight the group lost a third of its men. At the end of July, Glazman and his men reached the Naroch Forest, where he formed the Nekama (Revenge) Jewish partisan unit of the partisan brigade commanded by Fyodor Markov. At the end of September the Soviet command decided to dissolve the Jewish unit. As a result of this decision the unit also lost most of its arms. Glazman and a group of his comrades went over to the Lithuanian partisan command.

At this time the Germans launched a determined drive against the partisans in the Naroch and Kozhany forests. Glazman and a group of thirty-five Jewish partisans tried to break through to the Rudninkai Forest in the south in order to join up with FPO members who had gone there from the Vilna ghetto. On October 7, 1943, Glazman and his men were encircled by a superior German force. In the fierce struggle that followed he and his comrades were killed; only one member of the group, a young girl, was saved.

BIBLIOGRAPHY

Arad, Y. *Ghetto in Flames: The Struggle and Destruction of the Jews in Vilna in the Holocaust.* New York, 1978.

Lazar, C., ed. *Josef Glassman.* Publications of the Museum of the Combatants and Partisans, 4/10. Tel Aviv, 1983.

Tushmet, L. *Pavement to Hell.* New York, 1972.

YITZHAK ARAD

GLIK, HIRSH (Hirshke; 1922–1944), poet and partisan in Lithuania. Born in Vilna, Glik began working at the age of fifteen. He joined the Ha-Shomer ha-Tsa'ir Zionist youth movement, and in 1935, when he was only thirteen, he began to write Hebrew poems. Later he wrote mostly in Yiddish; in the period preceding the war he was the most outstanding member of the Yungwald (Young People) group of young writers (named after the literary journal of that name). In 1940 he published poems in *Vilner Emes* (Vilna Truth) and in the Kovno *Naye Bleter* (New Bulletin).

When Vilna was occupied by the Germans at the end of June 1941, Glik and his father were among the Jews who were seized at random and taken to labor camps, to work in the peat deposits at Biała-Waka and Rzesza. Even there Glik continued to write prodigiously, and the Vilna Writers' and Artists' Association awarded him a prize for a play he wrote that dealt with the life of the Jews working in the peat bogs.

In early 1943, when the Biała-Waka camp was liquidated, Glik was moved to the Vilna ghetto. He joined the FAREYNEGTE PARTIZANER ORGANIZATSYE (United Partisan Organization; FPO), and continued his writing. At this time he wrote *Di Balada fun Broynem Teater* (The Ballad of the Brown Theater), a macabre work that describes the terrible suffering of the Jews in the Lukishko prison before they were sent to their death at PONARY. On September 1, 1943, the FPO unit to which he belonged was captured and Glik was deported to Estonia, where he was imprisoned first in the Narva camp and then in the Goldfilz camp. In the summer of 1944 Glik broke out from the camp together with eight other FPO men, but all were killed by the Germans while trying to make their escape.

Even in the camps Glik did not cease writing, and he recited his poems to his comrades. Among the poems he wrote there were "In Gehenem bay Leningrad" (In Hell near Leningrad) and "Der Fay fun Mototsikl," (The Five from Mototsikl), a sarcastic verse composition about the Narva camp commandant, as well as poems about Vilna and hiding places in the ghetto. None of these works survived.

Glik's poems are very musical, and during the Holocaust years he composed poems that were to be sung. Most of these were designed to raise morale among the Jews, to glorify the deeds of the partisans, and to strengthen the Jews' faith and hope in the future. He gained fame with his "Song of the Partisans," which began: "Zog nisht keynmol az du geyst dem letztn Veg" (Never say that you are on your last journey). Glik based the song on a tune by two Soviet Jewish composers, the brothers Dimitri and Daniel Pokras. It became the partisan anthem as soon as it was written, and was sung in many places under Nazi rule. After the war it was translated into numerous languages and became popular among Jews all over the world.

BIBLIOGRAPHY

Dworzecki, M. *Hirsch Glik: The Author of the Jewish Partisan Hymn.* Paris, 1966. (In Yiddish.)

Dworzecki, M. *Jewish Camps in Estonia, 1942–1944.* Jerusalem, 1970. (In Hebrew.)

Meisel, N. "Hirsch Glik: His Life and Works." In *Hirsch Glik: Songs and Poems*, pp. 11–40. New York, 1953. (In Yiddish.)

YEHIEL SZEINTUCH

GLOBKE, HANS (1898–1973), civil servant in the Reich Ministry of the Interior and coauthor of an official commentary on the NUREMBERG LAWS of 1935. Globke was born in Düsseldorf and studied law in Bonn and Cologne before joining the civil service in 1929, as ministerial councillor in the Prussian Ministry of the Interior. Before 1933 he belonged to the Catholic Center party, and he never joined the Nazi party.

Globke used his legal training in helping to draft the emergency legislation that gave Adolf Hitler dictatorial powers. He also worked on the legislation that dissolved the Prussian State Council and coordinated all Prussian parliamentary bodies (the Prussian Enabling Act of June 1, 1933). He achieved notoriety through a commentary that he wrote, together with Wilhelm STUCKART, on the racial legislation in the Nuremberg Laws and through his participation in drafting the Reich Citizenship Law (1935) and the Law for the Protection of German Blood and German Honor (1935). These laws excluded "persons of alien blood" and opponents of the regime from citizenship and the exercise of civil rights. They also aimed at the "biological separation" of Jews from "Aryans." Globke prepared later legislative instruments whereby all German Jews were required to adopt the middle name Israel or Sarah, and the Jewish-owned property of concentration camp victims devolved to the state (1944). During the war Globke worked with Heinrich HIMMLER in applying these Nuremberg racial laws in occupied Europe.

After the war, Globke was arrested but later released because he had been only a Nazi "fellow traveler." He became a Reichstag deputy for the Christian Democratic party and, in 1953, state secretary in the Chancellery of the Federal Republic and head of its personnel division. His association with the Nazis made him a target for widespread criticism, especially from East Germany. Although he offered to resign several times, he was always defended by Chancellor Konrad Adenauer, who accepted Globke's claim that he had in fact sought to alleviate the legal measures demanded by Hitler. Globke retired to Switzerland in 1963; he died in Bad Godesberg on February 13, 1973.

BIBLIOGRAPHY

Zaborowski, J. *Dr. Hans Globke, the Good Clerk.* Poznań, 1962.

LIONEL KOCHAN

GLOBOCNIK, ODILO (1904–1945), senior SS commander; a principal participant in the extermination of Polish Jewry. Born in Trieste to an Austrian-Croat family of minor officials, Globocnik was a contractor by profession. He joined the Nazi party in Austria in 1931 and the SS in 1934. His illegal activity on behalf of the party led to a number of short spells of imprisonment. Before the ANSCHLUSS (the annexation of Austria to Germany in 1938), Globocnik was already active in the formation of Nazi factory cells in the provinces, and in 1936 he was appointed provincial party leader in Carinthia. He earned rapid promotion in 1938, in March to SS-*Standartenführer*, and in May to state secretary and *Gauleiter* of VIENNA. He lost this position in January 1939 on account of illegal currency dealings, but was pardoned by Heinrich HIMMLER, and in November 1939 was appointed district SS- *und Polizeiführer* (SS and Police Leader) for the Lublin district of Poland and promoted to SS-*Brigadeführer und Generalmajor*.

In 1941 Himmler entrusted Globocnik with the planning and establishment of police- and SS-fortified strongpoints in Poland, and, in 1942, with the implementation of AKTION REINHARD. For this purpose Globocnik was

Odilo Globocnik.

put in charge of special SS troops subordinate only to Himmler. He used the camps of BEŁŻEC, SOBIBÓR, TREBLINKA, and MAJDANEK to carry out a fourfold task: the exploitation of the Jewish work force, the extermination of Jews, the acquisition of the real estate of the murdered Jews, and the seizure of their valuables and movable property. More than two million Jews were killed during Aktion Reinhard, and property to the value of 178 million reichsmarks was seized for the benefit of the Reich.

In August 1943, as a result of differences with other party and SS leaders, Globocnik, was transferred to Trieste. He was taken captive by British troops at the end of the war and committed suicide in May 1945.

BIBLIOGRAPHY

Arad, Y. *Belzec, Sobibor, Treblinka: The Operation Reinhard Death Camps.* Bloomington, 1987.
Hilberg, R. *The Destruction of the European Jews.* New York, 1985.

LIONEL KOCHAN

GŁÓWNA KOMISJA BADANIA ZBRODNI HITLEROWSKICH W POLSCE. *See* Documentation Centers: Main Commission for Investigation of Nazi Crimes in Poland.

GLÜCKS, RICHARD (1889–1945), SS officer. A native of Düsseldorf, Glücks served as an officer in World War I and then became a merchant. He joined the Nazi party only after its rise to power. In 1936 he became chief aide to Theodor EICKE, the *Inspekteur der Konzentrationslager* (Inspector of Concentration Camps), rising to the rank of SS-*Brigadeführer*. Shortly after the war broke out, Glücks was appointed as Eicke's successor and promoted to SS-*Gruppenführer*.

Under Glücks there was a sharp rise in the number of concentration camps and their imprisoned population. At the time he took charge, the camps' main function was to serve the war effort by utilizing masses of forced laborers, mostly from the German-occupied territories. A large number of non-Jews were among the concentration camp inmates, in addition to the Jews. All were put on hard labor, and a great many inmates perished in the camps, from starvation, disease, and illtreatment.

Glücks was responsible for the establishment of the AUSCHWITZ camp, which was to become a major instrument for the implementation of the Final Solution. He was also responsible for the construction of the GAS CHAMBERS that helped serve this goal, and he had a part in the MEDICAL EXPERIMENTS that were being performed in the concentration camps.

In 1942, Glücks was put in charge of one of the units of the SS WIRTSCHAFTS-VERWALTUNGSHAUPTAMT (Economic-Administrative Main Office; WVHA), which was headed by Oswald POHL. At the end of the war, Glücks had the rank of SS-*Obergruppenführer*. He died in Flensburg in May 1945, apparently by committing suicide.

BIBLIOGRAPHY

Hilberg, R. *The Destruction of the European Jews.* New York, 1985.

Reitlinger, G. *The Final Solution: The Attempt to Exterminate the Jews of Europe, 1939–1945.* London, 1953.

DAVID HADAR

Joseph Goebbels.

GOEBBELS, JOSEPH (1897–1945), Nazi leader. Goebbels was born in Rheydt, in the Rhine district, into a poor and pious Catholic family. Born with a clubfoot, he did not serve in the army in World War I; instead, he studied at the University of Heidelberg and earned a doctorate in literature and philosophy. After failing in his attempts to become a writer, Goebbels found ample room for his talents as a propagandist and speaker for the Nazi party, which he joined in 1924. At first he worked together with Gregor Strasser, a rival of Adolf HITLER, but before long he became one of Hitler's most ardent admirers and in 1926 was appointed *Gauleiter* of Berlin, his assignment being to win over the capital for the party. In 1928 he was elected to the Reichstag. Two years later he was also appointed the party's chief of propaganda, and it was he who ran the Nazis' stormy election campaigns from 1930 to 1933.

On March 13, 1933, soon after Hitler's accession to power, Goebbels was appointed minister of propaganda and public information. He imposed Nazification upon the country's artistic and cultural life, working through the branches of the ministry that he headed. He controlled the media (although he had to contend with some rivals in that regard), and it was at his prompting that "un-German" books were burned on May 10, 1933. Goebbels was also one of the creators of the "Führer" myth, an important element in the Nazis' successful bid for the support of the masses.

By the time the Nazi regime was firmly established, Goebbels's position was weakened and he also lost some of his standing in Hitler's eyes. Once the political forces that had opposed the Nazis were destroyed, Goebbels no longer had an "enemy" to fight (except for the Jewish "enemy"), and Hitler was angered by the frequent crises in Goebbels's marital life, fearing that they might cause damage to the party's image.

When the war broke out, Goebbels assumed a key role in psychological warfare (although in that field, too, he had rivals), and when the situation on the fronts took a turn for the worse, he again played a central part in the leadership. His ties with Hitler resumed their closeness, although the feelers that he put out to bring the war to a "political end" were disregarded, as, for a long while, was his demand for the "totalization" of the war. It was only in July 1944 that he was appointed to the coveted task of having responsibility for the total mobilization of the population for the war effort.

When Hitler put an end to his life in the besieged capital, Goebbels refused to accept the post of Reich chancellor, to which he was appointed in Hitler's will. On May 1, 1945, on the morrow of Hitler's suicide, Goebbels and his wife, Magda, followed Hitler's example and also committed suicide in the Führer bunker, after first ordering the killing of their six children, aged four to twelve.

Joseph Goebbels, minister of propaganda, speaking before a crowd on April 1, 1933, the day of the economic boycott against the Jews of Germany.

Goebbels was the father of modern propaganda in a totalitarian state (a term that he coined), in which he made use of every available means. The propaganda he spread was remarkably replete with defamations, libels, and lies; he was convinced that people would believe the lies if only they were repeated often enough, and the bigger the lie, the better chance it had of being believed. Goebbels's propaganda always incited hate against some enemy. He was a radical and fanatic antisemite, but his hatred of Jews was also based on utilitarian considerations of exploiting antisemitism for the furthering of his propaganda aims.

Goebbels was relentless in depicting "the Jew" as an abominable creature and the principal enemy of the German people. It was Goebbels who conceived the idea of the KRISTALLNACHT pogroms in November 1938, and it was he who gave the event its flippant designation. Following these pogroms, he drastically reduced organized Jewish activities and freedom of movement in the sphere that he controlled. Once the war had broken out, the ministry he headed launched a concerted effort designed to aggravate living conditions for the Jews of Berlin. The first deportations of Berlin Jews to the Łódź ghetto, in October 1941, were carried out to fulfill an express promise that Goebbels had given to Hitler, to make Berlin *judenrein* ("cleansed of Jews") as soon as possible. In pursuit of this aim, Goebbels always kept in touch with Hitler and with the REICHSSICHERHEITSHAUPTAMT (Reich Security Main Office; RSHA). His diary contains specific mention of the destruction of the Jews; in an entry that he made in May 1943, when the extermination operation in Poland was at its height, Goebbels stated: "The nations that were the first to reveal the true face of the Jew will be the ones that will take the Jew's place in ruling the world."

[*See also* Propaganda, Nazi.]

BIBLIOGRAPHY

Bramsted, E. K. *Goebbels and National Socialist Propaganda, 1924–1945.* Lansing, Mich., 1965.

Frölich, E., ed. *Die Tagebücher von Joseph Goebbels: Sämtliche Fragmente. Teil 1: Aufzeichnungen, 1924–1941.* 4 vols. Munich, 1988.

Heimer, H. *Joseph Goebbels.* Berlin, 1962.

Lochner, L. P., ed. *The Goebbels Diaries, 1942–1943.* Garden City, N.Y., 1948.

Reimann, V. *Goebbels.* Garden City, N. Y., 1976.

Trevor-Roper, H., ed. *Final Entries, 1945: The Diary of Joseph Goebbels.* New York, 1978.

YEHOYAKIM COCHAVI

Amon Goeth.

GOETH, AMON LEOPOLD (1908–1946), SS officer. Born in Vienna, Goeth joined the National Socialist party in 1932. In 1940 he joined the SS, where he rose to the rank of SS-*Hauptsturmführer*. Goeth was assigned to the headquarters of the SS Command and to the Lublin police. Subsequently he was transferred to KRAKÓW, where he was in charge of liquidating the ghettos and labor camps at Szebnie, Bochnia, TARNÓW, and Kraków, among other places. From February 1943 to September 1944 Goeth commanded the concentration camp at PŁASZÓW, near Kraków. After the war he was extradited to Poland at the request of the Polish authorities and tried before the Polish Supreme Court, on a charge of committing mass murder during the liquidation of the ghettos at the Szebnie camp and at Płaszów. He was sentenced to death, and executed in Kraków.

BIBLIOGRAPHY

Proces ludobojcy Amona Leopolda Goetha przed Najwyższym Trybunalem Narodowym. Warsaw, 1947.

STEFAN BIERNACKI

GOGA, OCTAVIAN (1881–1938), Romanian national poet and one of the leaders of the antisemitic movement in ROMANIA. Goga developed his antisemitic philosophy under the impact of the nationalist conflict between the Romanians and the Hungarians in Transylvania, and the role (in the view of the Romanian nationalists) that the Jewish minority played in this struggle. He was convinced that the Jews in Transylvania were "irrevocably" pro-Hungarian; that they were the leaders of the anti-Romanian cultural conflict in the region, demonstrating loyalty to the Hungarian language and culture; and that, consequently, they were a corrupt, dangerous, and alien entity in the united Romanian state.

At the beginning of the 1930s, Goga formed the Partidul Agarar (Agrarian Party), which derived its main strength from farmers in Transylvania, but the party did not gain significant support. This political activity enabled Goga to express his hatred for the Jews as well as for the Hungarians. It brought him close to the thinking of "classic" Romanian antisemites such as Alexandru CUZA, and to support of the Nazis. Through the intervention of representatives of the National Socialist party, and in particular of Alfred ROSENBERG, Goga and Cuza established the Partidul National Crestin (Christian National Party) in 1935. It became the second most important antisemitic organization after the Totul Pentru (IRON GUARD).

The Nazis viewed the new party, and Goga himself, as constituting an upcoming force worth cultivating. The ceremony marking the amalgamation of the Liga Apararii Nationale Crestin (League of National Christian Defense) and Goga's tiny Agrarian Party was held in the cathedral of IAŞI, and Goga and Cuza undertook to implement a virulent antisemitic platform. Despite his loyalty to King Carol II and his support of the parliamentary system, when it came to antisemitism, Goga completely lost control of himself;

the national poet became the leader of an antisemitic movement dependent on Nazi Germany to support its efforts to achieve power. Its gang of hooligans, based on the Nazi model, spread havoc, attacking Jews and political rivals no less than did the Iron Guard. In his speeches and at mass demonstrations Goga always made reference to the "Jewish problem," describing the Jews as lepers who had spread throughout Romania.

At the end of 1937 Goga was appointed prime minister of Romania, and he devoted himself to implementing his antisemitic policies. His was the first Romanian government with a manifest antisemitic platform like that of the Nazis. During the forty days that he headed the government he did everything within his power to implement his principles, closing down the democratic newspapers, promulgating laws and regulations dismissing Jews from government posts, annulling work permits, and so forth. His most serious act was the passing, on January 22, 1938, of the Law for the Reexamination of Citizenship of the Jews, according to which the civil rights of one-third of Romania's Jewish citizens were annulled. Goga stated that "a new page in the history of Romania has been opened and it cannot be turned back." The following month, he was forced to resign by virtue of pressure brought to bear by France and Britain. He claimed that his resignation was a "victory of the Jews." After his death, Goga's wife, Veturia Goga, continued to play a leading role in the antisemitic movement, especially during the government of Ion ANTONESCU, through her influence on the Romanian dictator.

BIBLIOGRAPHY

Seicaru, P. *Poezia si politica: Octavian Goga.* Madrid, 1956.

Vago, B. *The Shadow of the Swastika: The Rise of Fascism and Anti-Semitism in the Danube Basin, 1936–1939.* London, 1975.

JEAN ANCEL

GOLDMANN, NAHUM (1895–1982), Jewish and Zionist leader. Goldmann was born in Lithuania and taken to Germany when he was five years old. He studied at German universities, obtaining doctorates in humanities and law. At the outbreak of World War I, he joined the staff of the German Foreign Ministry's Jewish section. With his friend, the philosopher Jacob Klatzkin, Goldmann formed Eshkol Publishing House for the publication of the *Encyclopaedia Judaica.* The encyclopedia's completion was prevented by Hitler's rise to power, and only ten volumes in German and two in Hebrew were issued. In the 1960s, Goldmann initiated the publication of the English-language *Encyclopaedia Judaica,* which appeared in 1971.

Forced to leave Germany when Hitler came to power in 1933, Goldmann settled in Switzerland and, at the end of that year, was elected chairman of the Committee of Jewish Delegations, which had come into existence after World War I to present the Jewish case at the Paris Peace Conference. In the summer of 1932 the leaders of the Committee of Jewish Delegations and of the AMERICAN JEWISH CONGRESS, aware of the significance of the Nazi menace, had called the first preparatory conference for the WORLD JEWISH CONGRESS (WJC). At that conference, warnings concerning the Nazi danger had been voiced by the WJC's future leaders Stephen S. WISE and Nahum Goldmann. The new organization, founded after several more preparatory conferences, in August 1936 called for the mobilization of the Jewish people and of democratic forces against the Nazi onslaught; the struggle for equal political and economic rights everywhere, particularly for the Jewish minorities in central and eastern Europe; and support for the Jewish national home in Palestine. The WJC was established as a worldwide Jewish representative body, democratically organized and based on the concept of the unity of the Jewish people.

Goldmann was elected chairman of the WJC's Administrative Committee and until 1939 was its representative at the League of Nations; from 1934, he also represented the Jewish Agency for Palestine at the league. In this capacity he led the WJC's efforts with governments and the League of Nations to obtain prolongation of the Minority Rights Agreement covering Upper Silesia (*see* BERNHEIM PETITION) and thereby prevent the application of Nazi discriminatory measures in that region. When the government of Octavian GOGA introduced anti-Jewish measures in ROMANIA in 1937, the WJC petitioned the League of Nations, whose condemnation of Romania led to Goga's resignation early in 1938. Before and after the ANSCHLUSS, the WJC repeatedly appealed to the League of Nations for protection of the Jews of Austria.

Goldmann represented both the WJC and the Jewish Agency at the ill-fated EVIAN CONFERENCE, held in 1938, of which he later wrote: "The Evian Conference is an irrefutable indictment of the civilized world in its attitude to the Nazi persecution of the Jews." To facilitate the immigration to Palestine of Jews from Nazi Germany, Goldmann, who proclaimed a Jewish anti-Nazi boycott (*see* BOYCOTTS, ANTI-NAZI), was instrumental in concluding the HAAVARA AGREEMENT between the Jewish Agency and Nazi Germany.

Goldmann moved to the United States in June 1940, and throughout the war worked for both the WJC and the Jewish Agency. With Stephen S. Wise, he tried to mobilize American Jewry and public opinion to help the Jews in Nazi-occupied Europe, keeping in close contact with WJC offices in Geneva and London, and through these offices monitoring the havoc wrought by the Nazis. When in August 1942 Dr. Gerhart Riegner (*see* RIEGNER CABLE), the WJC representative in Geneva, cabled news of the "FINAL SOLUTION," Goldmann and Wise broke the media silence on the mass annihilation of Jews and bombarded President Franklin D. ROOSEVELT and the administration with pleas for help. This activity led to a December 1942 collective Allied condemnation of the Nazi extermination policy toward Jews and a stern warning of retribution.

An Advisory Council on European Jewish Affairs, under Goldmann's chairmanship, was set up in New York with representative committees from eighteen European countries. Tens of thousands of individual parcels were sent to concentration camps, and tons of food and medicines to Jewish communities in occupied Europe. A far-reaching rescue program was submitted to the 1943 refugee conference in Bermuda (*see* BERMUDA CONFERENCE); a memorandum on Jewish aspects of relief and rehabilitation was submitted to the first session of the UNITED NATIONS

Nahum Goldmann (right) with Louis Lipsky, American Zionist leader, at the inaugural assembly of the World Jewish Congress in Geneva (1936). [World Jewish Congress]

RELIEF AND REHABILITATION ADMINISTRATION (UNRRA) in 1943; and in December 1943 a license was obtained from the United States Treasury to transmit funds to Europe for the rescue and assistance of persecuted Jews, a step leading to the eventual establishment of the WAR REFUGEE BOARD.

At the 1944 WJC War Emergency Conference in Atlantic City, Goldmann presented the first comprehensive program for the postwar rehabilitation of the Jewish people, including calls for REPARATIONS AND RESTITUTION from Germany to Jews, use of heirless Jewish property for Jewish rehabilitation, and punishment of Nazi persecutors of Jews. With the end of war in Europe, Goldmann was in the forefront of the struggle for the admittance into Palestine of the survivors, and for the reconstruction of destroyed Jewish communities. As chairman of the Conference on Jewish Material Claims against Germany, which he created, he led the negotiations for restitution and indemnification to Israel and to individual victims of Nazi persecution.

Looking back on the years of the Holocaust, Goldmann said that the greatest tragedy of all was that both the Jews and the democratic world failed to realize the magnitude and the depth of evil that Nazism embodied. He acknowledged the failure of his generation to stand up to the challenge.

After the war, Goldmann was co-chairman

of the executive of the World Zionist Organization (1948–1956), its president (1956–1968), and president of the WJC (1953–1977). He published his recollections in *The Autobiography of Nahum Goldmann: Sixty Years of Jewish Life* (New York, 1969), *Mein Leben als deutscher Jude* (My Life as a German Jew; Munich, 1980), and *Mein Leben: U.S.A.—Europa—Israel* (Munich, 1981).

BIBLIOGRAPHY

Dränger, J. *Nahum Goldmann: Ein Leben für Israel.* 2 vols. Frankfurt, 1959.
Garai, G., ed. *Forty Years in Action: A Record of the World Jewish Congress, 1930–1976.* Geneva, 1976.
Kubowitzki, A. L. *Unity in Dispersion: A History of the World Jewish Congress.* N.p., 1948.

ELIZABETH E. EPPLER

GOMEL, city in BELORUSSIA. In the nineteenth century Gomel had a Jewish population of over twenty thousand (56 percent of the city's population). On the eve of World War II, fifty thousand Jews were living in the city, a third of the total population. The Germans occupied Gomel on August 19, 1941. In the two months that passed between the Germans' invasion of the Soviet Union and their capture of the city, many Jews succeeded in fleeing from Gomel into the Soviet interior. Once the city was in German hands, the military governor, Schwach, ordered the Jews to wear the yellow badge (*see* BADGE, JEWISH). Ten Jews were put to death on the pretext that they were "Bolsheviks and terrorists."

A ghetto was established in Gomel, divided into four parts. In addition, three camps were set up for Jews: the Monastyrsk camp, with eight hundred Jews; Novo-Lubiensk, with five hundred Jews; and Novaya Belitsa, with two hundred. The inmates of these camps did not receive any food rations. At a later stage a fourth camp was set up in Povski Bazarchik, for Jews from foreign countries; its inmates were employed in clearing mine fields near the front line.

According to a December 1941 report by an Einsatzgruppe (*see* EINSATZGRUPPEN), 2,365 Jews were executed for having given aid to

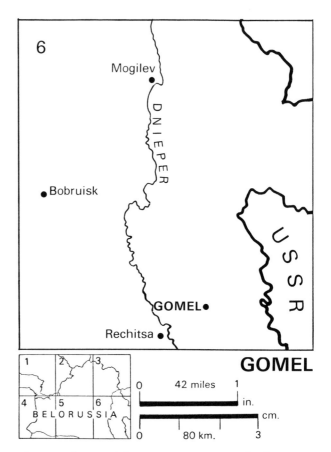

GOMEL

the partisans. They were apparently buried in military trenches near Leshtsinets on the way to Rechitsa. That same month, another 4,000 Jews from Gomel were put to death, in antitank ditches 5.6 miles (9 km) from Gomel, on the way to Chernigov. The women and children were gassed. These murders were most likely the work of Einsatzkommando 7b, commanded by Günther Rausch.

Gomel was liberated by the Soviets on November 26, 1943.

BIBLIOGRAPHY

Kahanovitch, Y. "Homel." In vol. 2 of *Jewish Mother-Cities,* edited by Y. L. Hacohen Fishman, pp. 187–269. Jerusalem, 1948. (In Hebrew.)

SHALOM CHOLAWSKI

GORDONIA. *See* Youth Movements.

GÖRING, HERMANN (1893–1946), Nazi leader. Göring was born in Rosenheim, Bavaria, the son of a wealthy family. In World War I he distinguished himself as a fighter pilot and commander of a renowned fighter squadron. He joined the Nazi party in 1922, was appointed commander of the SA (Sturmabteilung; Storm Troopers), and in November 1923 took part in the abortive Nazi putsch in Munich, in which he was wounded. In 1928, Göring was elected to the Reichstag on the Nazi ticket; he was elected Reichstag speaker in 1932. When Adolf HITLER came to power, Göring was appointed minister without portfolio, and then commissioner of aviation and Prussian minister of the interior. In April 1933 he became prime minister of Prussia and was one of the men responsible for the creation of the Gestapo. In the minds of many people, Göring was regarded as being behind the plot to burn down the Reichstag, in February 1933. In June 1934 he played a major role, together with Heinrich HIMMLER, in the liquidation of the SA leader Ernst RÖHM and his cohorts. Göring was appointed commander of the German air force (the Luftwaffe) in January 1935; this was followed by his promotion to *Reichsmarschall*. In 1936 he was put in charge of the FOUR-YEAR PLAN

and given dictatorial powers in the economic sphere. From August 1939 Göring chaired the ministerial Reich Defense Council (Reichsverteidigungsrat), and on September 1, 1939, when war broke out, Hitler appointed him to be his successor.

As the person in charge of the country's economy, Göring was responsible for the confiscation of Jewish property in 1937. Following the KRISTALLNACHT pogroms, Hitler put him in charge of the "Jewish question," and Göring lost no time in accelerating the plundering of the Jews, imposing on them a collective fine of a billion reichsmarks. On January 24, 1939, he issued orders for the establishment of the ZENTRALSTELLE FÜR JÜDISCHE AUSWANDERUNG (Central Office for Jewish Emigration), on the model of Eichmann's operations in this sphere in Vienna. When Poland was occupied, Göring became involved in the expulsion of Jews from the western parts of Poland that were annexed to the Reich, and he set up the HAUPTTREUHANDSTELLE OST (Main Trusteeship Office East), to take charge of and administer confiscated Jewish property. On July 31, 1941, Göring ordered Reinhard HEYDRICH to "carry out all necessary preparations with regard to

Berlin. Generalfeldmarschall Hermann Göring reviews a parade of his regiment on Luftwaffe Day in March 1939. To his left is Generaloberst Wilhelm Keitel.

the Jewish question in the German sphere of influence in Europe." In the opinion of many scholars, this order was the first important document that set the "FINAL SOLUTION" in motion, and it establishes Göring's share in the responsibility for the extermination of the Jews of Europe.

As a result of the failures of the Luftwaffe in the Battle of Britain (1940–1941), its weak performance on the Soviet front, and its inability to defend Germany's skies, relations between Hitler and Göring soured. In the last few days of the Nazi regime, Göring lost whatever standing he had left, and was dismissed from all his posts and from the party; Hitler appointed Adm. Karl Dönitz in his place.

Göring was arrested by the Allies and was one of the defendants in the trial of major war criminals by the International Military Tribunal (the NUREMBERG TRIAL). He was sentenced to death, but on October 15, 1946, the eve of his scheduled execution, he poisoned himself in his prison cell.

BIBLIOGRAPHY

Bewly, C. *Hermann Goering and the Third Reich: A Biography Based on Family and Official Reports.* Toronto, 1962.

Fest, J. C. *The Face of the Third Reich: Portraits of the Nazi Leadership.* New York, 1970.

Irving, D. *Göring.* New York, 1989.

Manvell, R., and H. Fraenkel. *Goering: A Biography.* New York, 1962.

Mosley, L. *The Reich Marshal.* New York, 1975.

YEHOYAKIM COCHAVI

GORODENKA (Pol., Horodenka), town in Eastern Galicia. In the interwar period, Gorodenka was part of independent Poland; in September 1939 it was occupied by the Red Army, and like the rest of eastern Poland, was annexed by the Soviet Union, becoming part of the Ukrainian SSR. On the eve of World War II, Gorodenka had a Jewish population of four thousand. When the war broke out in September 1939, a large number of Jews from the German-occupied areas of western Poland took refuge there. Following the German invasion of the Soviet Union on June 22, 1941, a few dozen of the town's Jews escaped into the Soviet interior.

On July 2, 1941, units of the Hungarian army, which was allied with the Germans, entered Gorodenka. The local Ukrainian inhabitants began to attack the Jews, but the Hungarian troops tried to restrain them. The Ukrainian militia seized Jews in the streets for forced labor and abused them. In September of that year Gorodenka was put under direct German control, and the situation of the Jewish community became even worse. More Jews were seized for forced labor, fines were imposed, Jewish-owned apartments with all their contents were confiscated, and freedom of movement by Jews, inside and outside the town, was restricted.

In November a JUDENRAT (Jewish Council) was set up. Although forced to follow German orders, the Judenrat members did what they could to improve conditions in the community, establishing soup kitchens and intervening with the German authorities in an attempt to postpone anti-Jewish measures.

On December 4 and 5, Gorodenka's Jews were ordered to report to the Jewish school, ostensibly for vaccination, but actually to be sent to their death. A few skilled craftsmen were released; the rest of the twenty-five hundred who gathered were taken to a forest situated between the villages of Siemakowce

and Michalcze, 8 miles (13 km) from Gorodenka, and murdered there.

At the beginning of 1942 many Jews from small places in the vicinity were moved to the Gorodenka ghetto. The resulting overcrowding by far exceeded its capacity; many people died of starvation and disease. On April 13, another *Aktion* took place, and fourteen hundred persons were taken to the BEŁŻEC extermination camp; sixty Jews were murdered in the Gorodenka Jewish cemetery. In May and June several dozen Jews from Gorodenka were sent to the KOLOMYIA ghetto.

In July 1942 the liquidation of the ghetto began, with the murder of the remnants of the community in the town and of those Jews who had taken refuge in the nearby forests; some of the Gorodenka ghetto inhabitants were transferred to other ghettos in the area. Others fled to Tluste, hoping to find at least temporary asylum there, but most of these were murdered, together with the local Jews. After the liquidation of the Gorodenka ghetto some of the surviving Jews were taken to the JANÓWSKA camp in Lvov, and the rest to Bełżec.

Several dozen Gorodenka Jews escaped to the forests, and some of them joined the Soviet partisans. Many of those who reached the forest were killed by Ukrainian nationalists of the UKRAINSKA POVSTANSKA ARMYIA (Ukrainian Insurgent Army). Gorodenka was liberated by the Red Army on March 27, 1944. The few Jewish survivors eventually made their way to the West.

BIBLIOGRAPHY

Meltzer, S., ed. *Sefer Horodenka*. Tel Aviv, 1963. (In Hebrew and Yiddish.)

AHARON WEISS

GRÄBE, HERMANN FRIEDRICH (1900–1986), a "RIGHTEOUS AMONG THE NATIONS." Born in Solingen, Germany, Gräbe was a member of the Nazi party for a few months, but he later spoke out against the Nazi regime and served a short prison term. A construction worker, he was employed as a foreman at the Jung Company in Solingen. In October 1941 he was entrusted with setting up a branch of Jung in Zdolbunov, Volhynia,

Hermann Gräbe, seated at left, receiving a medal and certificate as a "Righteous among the Nations" from Aryeh Kubovy, chairman of Yad Vashem in Jerusalem (September 20, 1965).

for the construction and repair of buildings used by the railway directorate in the REICHSKOMMISSARIAT UKRAINE. Thousands of Jews were employed by Gräbe, and he insisted that his subordinates treat the workers properly. An intervention on his part with the Zdolbunov district commissar resulted in the cancellation of fines that had been imposed on the Jews; he also saved his Jewish employees from the *Aktionen* in Rovno in November 1941 and July 1942, not hesitating to intervene with the SD (Sicherheitsdienst; Security Service) commander in Rovno for this purpose.

Several dozen Jewish men and women were employed by Gräbe in the company's head office. In the summer of 1942, when they were seen to be in danger, they were given "Aryan" papers and sent to POLTAVA to work in what was purported to be a company branch; in actuality, it had been established by Gräbe without the authorization or knowledge of his employers, and it was maintained out of his own funds. In October of that year, alerted by his Jewish secretary, Gräbe went to Dubno, where he witnessed the murder of the city's Jews.

Gräbe saved the lives of dozens of Jews. At the NUREMBERG TRIAL, where he gave evidence on the crimes committed by the Nazis in Volhynia, his description of the slaughter of the Dubno Jews made a deep impression. This created widespread animosity against him in Germany, and with the help of Jewish organizations he emigrated with his family to the United States, settling in California. In 1966, Gräbe was invited to Israel to be presented with the "Righteous among the Nations" Award. There he planted a tree on the "Avenue of the Righteous" at Yad Vashem in Jerusalem.

BIBLIOGRAPHY

Spector, S. *The Holocaust of Volhynian Jews, 1941–1944.* Jerusalem, 1986. (In Hebrew.)

SHMUEL SPECTOR

GRAND MUFTI OF JERUSALEM. See Husseini, Hajj Amin al-.

GRAWITZ, ERNST ROBERT (1899–1945), Nazi official; head of the SS health services. The chief SS physician, in 1936 Grawitz was made head (*Reichsarzt*) of the SS health services, with the rank of SS-*Obergruppenführer*, and head of the German Red Cross. When implementation of the "FINAL SOLUTION" was officially approved in 1941, it was Grawitz who advised Heinrich HIMMLER on the use of GAS CHAMBERS.

As chief SS physician, Grawitz was among those responsible for carrying out different kinds of MEDICAL EXPERIMENTS on prisoners in the concentration camps, and by virtue of his rank in the SS he was administratively responsible for all these experiments. He was associated with almost every kind: survival experiments (testing how long a person can survive in severely adverse environmental conditions), healing experiments (involving infection with contagious and epidemic diseases, war wounds, and wounds from chemi-

cal warfare), and sterilization of women.

Grawitz committed suicide at the end of the war.

BIBLIOGRAPHY

Lifton, R. J. *The Nazi Doctors: Medical Killing and the Psychology of Genocide.* New York, 1986.

ZVI BACHARACH

GREAT BRITAIN. [*This entry consists of four articles:*

> General Survey
> Appeasement of Nazi Germany
> Fascism in Great Britain
> Jewish Refugees

The first is an overview of British and Anglo-Jewish history during the 1930s, and the second deals with British efforts to avert hostilities by the policy of appeasing Germany. The shifting fortunes of the British fascist movement are reviewed in the third article. British immigration policy toward Jewish refugees from continental Europe is the subject of the fourth article, which also discusses the efforts of British Jewry to aid the refugees.]

General Survey

At the outset of World War II, Britain's strategic interests were seriously overextended. With involvements stretching from East Asia through India, the Middle East, the Mediterranean, and to the North Sea, Britain was unable to defend the empire on its own. Since the beginning of the century, British politicians had been aware of the fundamental weakness underlying Britain's position. The huge manpower and material losses of World War I were still keenly felt, and until 1936 there was little public support for a serious rearmament program. Not surprisingly, British foreign policy attempted to appease potential enemies and win friends among neutral countries by making concessions to their demands. After the complete German takeover of Czechoslovakia, however (contrary to the agreement reached at the MUNICH CONFERENCE), Prime Minister Neville Chamberlain reversed his government's foreign policy based on appeasement and resolved to offer a mutual defense pact to Poland in order to deter German aggression against that state.

Militarily, Britain was too weak to present any meaningful threat to Germany. Rearmament had started late, and the British army was totally unprepared for war. When it broke out in September 1939, there were only two fully trained divisions in the United Kingdom. Other British troops were dispersed in the colonies, including almost seventeen thousand in Palestine. Despite the initial weakness of the army, Britain (together with its ally, France) declared war on Germany on September 3, 1939, two days after Germany invaded Poland.

The months that followed the declaration of war were popularly called the "phony war." Once Poland had fallen, there were no further German advances until May 1940. Britain was able to use this period to dramatically improve its fighting ability. Although the United States was technically neutral, President Franklin D. ROOSEVELT promised that American supplies would be available to Britain. The dominions—Canada, South Africa, Australia, New Zealand—and India also declared war on Germany. However, they were too far away from the main theater of action in Europe to make any significant contribution at this stage. When the fighting spread to North and East Africa and to Asia, the British dominions played a more active role.

Britain's most significant ally was France. Anglo-French strategy was based on a combined use of their navies to prevent German control of the seas—a vital consideration, since none of the belligerents was self-sufficient in natural resources.

In May 1940, the Germans moved against Belgium, Luxembourg, and the Netherlands and invaded France. Soon afterward, Italy joined the Axis and declared war on Britain. Despite German peace feelers and the fact that Britain was the only country in Europe still fighting Hitler, the British refused all negotiations. The successful evacuation of 200,000 British troops from France at Dunkerque, at the beginning of June 1940, enabled Britain to prepare for an expected

German invasion of the British Isles. During this period of crisis the government of Neville Chamberlain was replaced by a national coalition led by Winston CHURCHILL. Churchill announced that Britain would continue fighting until the defeat of Germany.

The threat of an imminent German invasion lessened when, between August and October 1940, the Luftwaffe failed to defeat the Royal Air Force in the prolonged Battle of Britain. Nevertheless, the overall strategic situation had seriously deteriorated. The fall of France deprived Britain of the support of the French navy and of the substantial number of French troops in France, the Middle East, and North Africa. The entry of Italy into the war meant that the British could no longer safely transport soldiers or supplies to India via the Middle East. Italian forces in Libya attacked the large British bases in Egypt, but British forces managed to defeat the Italian thrust. As a result, German forces under Gen. Erwin Rommel were sent to North Africa to reinforce the Axis position.

British isolation during this period was alleviated by the growing willingness of the United States to support the British war effort. In March 1941, Roosevelt succeeded in having Congress pass the Lend-Lease Act, which allowed the administration to supply Britain with weapons under a leasing arrangement. The act recognized the importance for American security of an eventual British victory against Hitler. The growing political alliance between the two powers was given expression in the Atlantic Charter of August 14, 1941.

Throughout the late 1930s, Britain had attempted to strengthen its position in the Middle East by seeking the support of the independent Arab states. Although there were a number of differences between Britain and the Arab leaders, Britain decided that the conflict in Palestine was the most significant cause of Anglo-Arab disagreement. The 1939 British WHITE PAPER on Palestine, limiting Jewish immigration and the sale of land to Jews, and undertaking to establish a future independent Palestinian state with a large Arab majority, was in part an attempt to win Arab support in the inevitable war against Germany. Appeasement, however, failed in the Middle East, just as it had failed in Europe. The British had to threaten the use of force in Egypt to induce the government there to break off diplomatic relations with Italy after that power declared war against Britain. The Transjordan Frontier Force, which had been created by the British, proved unreliable in the Iraq campaign. A pro-Axis government rose to power in Iraq in April 1941, leading to the British occupation of that country shortly afterward. Syria and Lebanon were taken over by British and Free French troops in July 1941. These were holding operations, designed to prevent the emergence of a strategic threat to Britain's position in Egypt from the east. The main theater in the Middle East remained the battle of the Western Desert.

When the German air force lost the Battle of Britain, Hitler abandoned his plan for the invasion of the British Isles and turned his attention to the Soviet Union. On June 22, 1941, German troops invaded Russia on a broad front from the Baltic to Romania. Despite Churchill's strong anti-Communist beliefs, he immediately offered Joseph STALIN assistance in supplies and weapons. Hitler's decision to strike out eastward transformed the nature of World War II, and considerably relieved the pressure on Britain and on British positions in the Middle East. The Japanese attack on Pearl Harbor on December 7, 1941, and the official declaration of a state of war between the United States and Japan (followed soon after by the German declaration of war against the United States), meant that the war had become truly global. Britain was no longer fighting alone, or only in the Middle East.

By the beginning of 1942 a grand alliance, led by Churchill, Roosevelt, and Stalin, had been formed. A number of basic principles guided the joint Allied effort against the Axis. The war against Germany was given priority over the war in the Pacific, despite the rapid advance of Japanese forces during 1942. Given the disproportionately large number of troops fighting on the Russian front, Britain and America undertook to open a second European front against the Germans as soon as possible.

The three remaining principles of Allied policy toward Germany eventually had major implications for Allied policy on the relief and rescue of European Jewry. First, the blockade of occupied Europe was recognized as an essential weapon against the German war effort. It was central to British wartime strategy, and the British government refused all efforts to circumvent it. This included British opposition to the sending of relief supplies to the civilian populations under German control (although there were some exceptions). The second principle was that there would be no negotiations with Hitler. This was designed to reassure Stalin that Britain and America would not join with the Germans in a joint effort to destroy the Soviet Union. Although there were contacts with the Germans by means of neutral states and the International RED CROSS on various humanitarian issues, the principle of "no negotiations" prevented any serious consideration of German proposals for the ransom of Jews. The third principle was that the Allies would fight until the unconditional surrender of Germany and the Axis. This ensured that there would be no negotiations for a compromise peace and that the war would come to an end earlier.

The tide of war turned in late 1942. The halting of the German advance into Russia at Stalingrad in October, and the defeat of Rommel at El Alamein in November, marked the beginning of the eventual defeat of Nazi Germany.

World War II was a total war, both in its global spread and in the full mobilization of resources that it required. Its impact on domestic society, particularly in Britain, was far-reaching. As large numbers of men were enlisted in the army, women entered the work force in unprecedented numbers.

The important role played by organized labor in the war effort, and the central role of the Labour party in the coalition government, led to a new awareness of the importance of social-welfare policies. Britain had been a hierarchical society preoccupied with questions of class and status, dominated by Conservative politicians and badly affected by the mass unemployment of the Great Depression. War made the government and the civil service sensitive to public opinion and to demands for social reform. The first proposals for reform were published in the 1942 Beveridge Report, which formed the basis for

British social-welfare planning in the post-war period.

The desire for change was reflected in the results of the elections, held immediately after the end of the war in Europe. Despite the immense popularity of Churchill as a war leader, his Conservative party lost the elections in July 1945 to the Labour party.

World War II also transformed Britain's dependent empire. The occupation of colonies in East Africa by Italian forces and in Asia by the Japanese went far to destroy the mystique of European supremacy and British power. As was true for other European colonial powers, Britain was not able to reestablish her authority in a number of colonies even after the Japanese had been defeated. In other parts of the empire, most notably India, political concessions were granted to nationalist forces in order to secure their continued support during the period of Britain's great vulnerability. The revolution in the relations between Britain and its empire brought about by World War II led to the effective dissolution of the empire by the mid-1950s. Although the war ended victoriously, with British troops occupying large parts of central Europe, the human and material destruction suffered in Britain was immense. Added to the impact of World War I, from which Britain had barely recovered when World War II began, and to the loss of empire, the war marked the end of Britain's role as a great power.

[*See also* Yishuv.]

BIBLIOGRAPHY

Agar, H. *The Darkest Year: Britain Alone, June 1940–June 1941.* New York, 1973.
Collier, B. *The Defense of the United Kingdom.* London, 1957.
Longmate, N. *How We Lived Then: A History of Every-Day Life during the Second World War.* London, 1971.
Wasserstein, B. *Britain and the Jews of Europe, 1939–1945.* London, 1979.
Wheatly, R. *Operation Sea Lion: German Plans for the Invasion of England, 1939–1942.* Oxford, 1958.
Zweig, R. W. *Britain and Palestine during the Second World War.* Suffolk, England, 1986.

RONALD W. ZWEIG

Appeasement of Nazi Germany

Great Britain's policy toward Germany in the period between the two world wars, and particularly in the second half of the 1930s, may accurately be characterized as one of appeasement. "Appeasement" was originally a positive term, describing a desire and an effort to establish peace between antagonistic countries. After World War II, however, the term acquired a negative sense, being linked with capitulation and faintheartedness in the face of aggression. This negative meaning was a result of the association with British policy, particularly during Neville Chamberlain's term of office as prime minister from 1937 to 1940. The agreement signed by Chamberlain at the MUNICH CONFERENCE in September 1938 was considered *a posteriori* the lowest point of appeasement. It surrendered Czechoslovakia, a friendly and free country, to Adolf Hitler, whether out of cowardice or foolish blindness concerning Hitler's true aims.

Britain's appeasement policy was adopted many years before the Nazis' rise to power and their policy of aggression. It was a direct result of the peace agreements at the end of World War I, and in particular of the Treaty of Versailles with Germany. Even at the Versailles Conference, the harsh terms dictated to the Germans aroused misgivings among the British and Americans. Penetrating discussions centered on the question of whether to aim for a peace treaty in a spirit of appeasement or to insist on harsh terms. The latter option was accepted, a fact that produced a sense of guilt toward Germany among many of the politicians involved. In Britain and the United States, sympathy developed for Germany because of the injustices that were felt to exist in the peace treaty.

Appeasement toward Germany was also sustained by the traditional interest of Britain, as a nation dependent on international trade, in maintaining peace through commerce and the renewal of commercial ties in Europe, especially with Germany. During the Weimar Republic, however, the British did not succeed in overcoming the objections of the French, who, justifiably concerned with their security, were far more hostile to Germany and wished to restrict its capacity for economic and military recovery. Appeasement, which produced a willingness to change the conditions of the peace treaty, was supported in Britain by all the political parties. It had a following among the intellectual Left of the Labor party, which tended to discuss foreign relations in terms of political morality, and stressed among the wrongs done to Germany the inclusion of the Sudeten Germans in the new Czechoslovak republic against their wish and against their right to self-determination.

British politicians tended to see the Nazi rise to power as a result of the mistaken policy toward Germany, and their negative attitude to Nazi rule did not change their appeasement policy. Rather, as the danger of German strength grew, Britain increasingly sought to attain relief in the international arena through accords with Germany. Various initiatives were proposed in the British government for the economic appeasement of Germany: the granting of colonies in Africa, trade agreements, and even military agreements. Germany, however, adopted a policy of presenting *faits accomplis* that modified the terms of the peace treaty, such as the abolition of military restrictions and the entry of its army into the demilitarized Rhine region. It thereby denied Britain political compensation, in the form of international peace, for its steps.

Up to 1937 Britain practiced a policy of passive appeasement, accepting *a posteriori* unilateral actions taken by Hitler. Chamberlain, who became prime minister in May 1937, initiated a policy of active appeasement, advocating negotiations with the Germans on the modifications desirable for Germany and necessary for the removal of the threat and insecurity aroused by Germany in Europe. Chamberlain informed the Germans of his desire for change, while stressing as a basic condition that no international modification be made violently. However, when Hitler annexed Austria in March 1938 in violation of the peace treaty, the West limited itself to a protest. When it became clear that Hitler's next target was Czechoslovakia, Chamberlain took a series of steps aimed at preventing a German attack on it. Such an attack was liable to lead to war with France

and the Soviet Union, Czechoslovakia's allies, and it also entailed the danger of an unavoidable British involvement.

Chamberlain attempted to prevent war through cooperation with Germany, in order to stabilize international relations with that country. The means of attaining cooperation was to compel Czechoslovakia to make far-reaching concessions to the Sudeten Germans, thus preventing any need for German action. The British and French demands on Czechoslovakia aggravated the relations between the Czechs and the Germans, and by mid-September 1938 a real danger of war seemed to be hovering over Europe. Chamberlain went to meet with Hitler in Germany. Prior to the talks, the British government had decided to accord autonomy to the Germans within Czechoslovakia, but at their meeting, Hitler and Chamberlain immediately agreed on the annexation of areas of Czechoslovakia to Germany. The Munich agreement was signed after two weeks of talks.

At that time, the attempt to appease Germany by putting pressure on an independent state was not seen in Britain as a base or treacherous act, but as a bold step to save Europe from war. The granting of self-determination to the Sudeten Germans "returning to their homeland," Germany, was seen as a just act. During the negotiations, however, when Hitler introduced new demands, other than those already agreed on, doubts intensified in various circles in Britain concerning the morality and even the utility of this act of appeasement. After the signing of the agreement, Alfred Duff Cooper, the First Lord of the Admiralty, resigned from the government, and Winston CHURCHILL, a longtime critic of appeasement, harshly criticized in Parliament the stupidity and danger of the Munich agreement. Both in Parliament and in the press, the agreement was attacked as a shameful capitulation that would encourage Hitler to further acts of aggression. Nevertheless, the government continued the appeasement policy, hoping to achieve international peace by encouraging Germany to take agreed-upon economic control over southeastern Europe.

When Hitler violated his pledges and occupied the rest of Czechoslovakia in March 1939, all were convinced that the policy of appeasement was a complete failure, and both morally and politically indefensible. Chamberlain was obliged to surrender to internal pressures and change his policy. He gave guarantees of support to Poland and Romania, which were expected to be Hitler's next victims. Nonetheless, he did not abandon hope of salvaging peace by maintaining contact with leading figures in Germany. Even after the German invasion of Poland, when an ultimatum had to be presented demanding that Germany retreat from Polish territory, and even when he was forced to declare war on Germany, Chamberlain did so with a heavy heart and without being entirely convinced of the need to fight. Thus, appeasement was accepted over a long period of time by the great majority of the British, and was embodied first and foremost in the personality and policy of Chamberlain.

Two arguments are presented for diminishing the personal culpability of Chamberlain. One stresses that Britain, as a world power with responsibilities outside the European continent, refused to accept commitments in a region where it had no interests. This was especially so since Britain's overseas empire opposed an involvement in Europe, which was liable to lead again into an expensive and, from the empire's viewpoint, superfluous war. Britain had no land army, and militarily, the British Empire's commitments throughout the world were a decisive consideration against war, which was seen as being beyond its military capacity, especially in view of the expiration of the treaty with Japan and the danger to the British Empire in the Far East. According to this argument, appeasement stemmed from Britain's interests in the Far East, the Mediterranean (particularly in Palestine), the North Sea, and the Atlantic Ocean. At a time of economic crisis, unemployment, and pacifism, when industry was just beginning to recover from the depression, the government refused to finance a comprehensive transformation of industry to the production of war materials, or to gamble on United States support. A strong psychological factor against war was the exaggerated military estimates of the German air force's capacity for destruction.

A second explanation of appeasement is connected with the mood then prevailing: the

general changes in Britain's political culture as the empire began to decline and society experienced the rise of new social forces, some socialist, some pacifist, and some enthusiastically supporting the League of Nations as an alternative to any international struggle. The reaction against the aggressive jingoism of the pre–World War I period, and against the belief that Britain had the right to rule the world, aroused doubts and self-criticism, a retreat from excessive rigidity in the international arena, and tolerance even toward despotic regimes. The intellectuals of that period, especially of the Left, wished to rid themselves of narrow British approaches and to understand the desires of other peoples, especially of the Germans.

BIBLIOGRAPHY

Bruegel, J. W. *Czechoslovakia before Munich: The German Minority Problem and British Appeasement.* Cambridge, 1973.

Fuchser, L. W. *Neville Chamberlain and Appeasement.* New York, 1982.

Gilbert, M. *The Roots of Appeasement.* New York, 1966.

Mommsen, W. J., and L. Kettenacker, eds. *The Fascist Challenge and the Policy of Appeasement.* London, 1983.

HEDVA BEN-ISRAEL

Fascism in Great Britain

The first organization in Britain to possess a distinctively fascist title appeared in the 1920s and reflected the changing economic and social conditions that followed World War I. The British Fascisti was formed in 1923 and the Imperial Fascist League was established in 1928. The former, associated particularly with R. Lintorn Orman, had only a brief existence, but the latter, associated predominantly with Arnold S. Leese, continued its existence until Leese's death.

In the 1930s a number of small and short-lived organizations came and went, but with the formation of the British Union of Fascists (BUF) by Sir Oswald MOSLEY in 1932, FASCISM in Britain took an important step forward. Mosley viewed the BUF as a political vehicle through which his restless and impatient ambitions could be satisfied. However, developments in National Socialist Germany lost the BUF some support, as did its involvement in political violence. In these circumstances, the BUF became increasingly embroiled in the local politics of London's East End, and this development brought into the open the BUF's antisemitic ideology. It resulted also in violent clashes with antifascists, a conflict symbolized by the "Battle of Cable Street" in October 1936, in which the BUF and antifascist groups fought each other. Such developments in the East London campaign also helped to sideline the BUF. With the government's ban on the wearing of uniforms in public under the Public Order Act of 1936, the development of the BUF (whose hallmark was the wearing of a black shirt) was further hindered. Moreover, the recovery of the economy in the course of the 1930s did not assist the BUF's cause. Even so, Mosley's movement remained active until World War II, and Mosley continued to attract large crowds at public meetings.

The outbreak of World War II soon resulted in the restriction of fascist activity, although it never disappeared entirely. In early 1940 leading members of the BUF, including Mosley and key members of his organization such as Neil Francis Hawkins and Alexander Raven Thomson, were interned under Regulation 18B(1A), which permitted the government to detain persons who had had associations with enemy powers. Arnold Leese was among the other fascist internees.

By the end of the war, fascism in Britain had become equated with the excesses of National Socialist Germany. For some individuals, however, this situation brought no change in their political stance. Arnold Leese, supported by a legacy from H. H. Beamish, a racial nationalist who had founded the antisemitic group The Britons in 1919, retracted nothing and remained a committed fascist until his death in 1948. Through his postwar activity, evidenced in his newsletter, *Gothic Ripples*, Leese assumed an important role in securing the continuity of the fascist tradition in Britain. Mosley, by contrast, attempted to distance himself from the prewar days when he revived his activity in the Union Movement. But no success followed from this adjustment, and following his defeat in North Kensington in the 1959 general election, Mosley retreated from any direct personal involvement in British politics.

By the time of Mosley's death in 1980, however, important developments had taken place in the world of British fascism and the related political province of racial nationalism. When Arnold Leese died, the mantle of National Socialism in Britain fell upon Colin Jordan, who, like Leese, continued to proclaim Adolf Hitler's message. That political stance was a quick route to political obloquy and oblivion. Indeed, none of the fascist groups of the early 1960s managed to achieve any political clout. However, in 1967 various organizations that had attempted to perpetuate the fascist tradition united with racial nationalist organizations to form the National Front (NF).

The NF openly eschewed the designation of being a fascist group. But in view of its nationalism, its political authoritarianism, its opposition to Jews (the NF played its part in the spread of Revisionist ideology of the Holocaust), its opposition to black and Asian immigration (which it viewed as a Jewish plot to undermine Britain), and its involvement in violent street politics, not all commentators were persuaded that the NF had effectively discarded the fascist tradition. The political heyday of the NF, under the leadership of John Tyndall, occurred in the late 1960s and 1970s, but after its failure to achieve any political impact in the 1979 general election, the front split into opposing factions. Ten years later, the leaders of the organization, which continued to call itself the National Front, were still reorientating its political direction.

BIBLIOGRAPHY

Benewick, R. *The Fascist Movement in Britain.* London, 1971.
Lebzelter, G. *Political Anti-Semitism in England, 1918–1939.* New York, 1978.
Lewis, D. S. *Illusions of Grandeur: Mosley, Fascism, and British Society, 1931–1981.* Manchester, 1987.
Lunn, K., and R. C. Thurlow, eds. *British Fascism.* London, 1980.
Skidelsky, R. *Oswald Mosley.* London, 1975.
Taylor, S. *The National Front in English Politics.* London, 1982.

Thurlow, R. *Fascism in Britain: A History, 1918–1985.* Oxford, 1987.

COLIN HOLMES

Jewish Refugees

Between 1933 and 1945, Britain was an important country of refuge for Jews fleeing Nazi-controlled Europe. For many, Britain, with its liberal tradition of granting asylum to REFUGEES, was the preferred country of immigration. Others sought temporary refuge there while awaiting transshipment overseas. A third category looked to Britain as the entry point for the large number of territories in Britain's dependent empire. In relation to its population and its size, Britain gave shelter to a significant number of Jews during the Holocaust.

British immigration policy, like that of all other countries of refuge for Jews from Nazi-controlled Europe, evolved in response to events. The first wave of refugees arrived in Britain during the months following Hitler's rise to power in January 1933. Church groups, in particular the Quaker Society of Friends, were active on their behalf, and Parliamentary opinion was sympathetic to these first victims of Nazism. But the official attitude toward Jewish refugees was dictated by the determined adherence of the British government to its policy of nonintervention in Germany's internal matters. The humanitarian approach to the refugees, advocated by circles and organizations outside the government, was seen as harming Britain's political and economic interests. After the ANSCHLUSS in March 1938 the government's position toward refugees changed significantly, and Great Britain became a haven for a considerable number of refugees. At that time, the government announced that all refugees who were en route to other destinations, and all children whose maintenance could be guaranteed, would be permitted to enter Great Britain.

Immigration and the coordination of the means necessary for assisting refugees reached their pinnacle in the last year before the outbreak of World War II. Among the non-Jewish public there was a great deal of support for Jews who had escaped from the Third Reich. However, despite the prevailing generosity, many refugees discovered streaks of antagonism. Several trade unions assumed a threatening posture and even took action against the refugees. The fear of aliens was also spurred by a number of newspapers. The Jewish press stood at the forefront of efforts to mollify the fears and prejudices against the refugees.

Because Britain was not an immediate neighbor of Germany, the number of refugees arriving there shortly after the Nazi seizure of power was small; in December 1933 there were only three thousand, and in April 1934 only two thousand. Despite these low figures, the refugees who wished to enter Great Britain met with many difficulties, primarily because of the immigration laws of 1919 (the Aliens Law), whose statutes remained in effect until 1938. The authorities made no distinction between refugees and other immigrants, demanding financial guarantees on their behalf and pledges that they would remain in Great Britain only temporarily, either to arrange further transit or to receive some sort of preparatory training that would help them along their way. After the Anschluss, the limitations became stricter, with visas now required for all who wished to enter Great Britain.

However, the waves of refugees caused by the Anschluss in March 1938, the German occupation of the Sudetenland that October, and *Kristallnacht* in November all brought British immigration policy under renewed pressure. In part because of the activities of pro-refugee groups and members of Parliament, and in part because of the acute political embarrassment caused by the British campaign against Jewish immigration into Palestine, Britain responded by further liberalizing the regulations governing the entry of refugees. This was contrary to the practice of most other countries of refuge in the immediate prewar months. But with the outbreak of war in September 1939, all immigration into Britain and the British Empire from enemy or enemy-controlled territory was banned.

Jewish refugees continued to reach Britain after 1939, but in radically reduced numbers. Following the fall of France, Norway, Denmark, Belgium, the Netherlands, and other

Jewish refugee children arrive in Great Britain (1938).

countries, entry was permitted only from neutral countries. The difficulties of transport during wartime made even that limited inflow almost impossible. A number of Polish Jews arrived in units of the Polish army stationed in the United Kingdom. Later, as the tide of war turned, the restrictions on entry were partly lifted. According to estimates made by Jewish organizations after the war, a further ten thousand Jews were permitted entry between 1939 and 1945.

From an early stage, Jewish organizations in Great Britain addressed themselves to the refugee problem. In March 1933, Otto Schiff established the Jewish Refugees Committee (for a time called the German Jewish Aid Committee), which was the most important voluntary organization to deal with refugee aid. In April, Schiff and the chairmen of the BOARD OF DEPUTIES OF BRITISH JEWS and of the Anglo-Jewish Association (Neville Laski and Leonard Montefiore) met with the Home Secretary. They pledged that no refugee would become a public charge and that the Jewish community would ensure support of the refugees until they either had been inte-

grated into British life or had emigrated to another country. Despite the enormous growth in the number of refugees, sufficient money was allocated for their upkeep by the Central British Fund and the COUNCIL FOR GERMAN JEWRY until the end of 1939, that is, as long as the pledge remained in force.

The Jewish Refugee Committee looked after the needs of the refugees—their maintenance, education and training, and further emigration. Its work was conducted through subcommittees for reception, accommodation, agricultural training, vocational training, education, emigration, assistance to academics and professional workers, information, and press. Special organizations were established to deal with aid to emigré students and academics who had lost their positions or had been prevented from continuing their studies for reasons of religion or race.

Eventually, more than 10,000 unaccompanied refugee children, most of them Jewish, reached Great Britain from central Europe. The 431 children who had come to Great Britain up to November 1938 were assisted by the existing Jewish refugee organizations and the Children's Inter-Aid Committee. In the wake of *Kristallnacht*, 9,354 refugee children, of whom 70 percent were Jewish, arrived between December 1938 and September 1939. Five main organizations assisted the young refugees: B'NAI B'RITH, the Women's Appeal Committee (which worked with YOUTH ALIYA in Great Britain), the Chief Rabbi's Religious Emergency Council (headed by Rabbi Solomon SCHONFELD), the Children's Inter-Aid Committee, and the Movement for the Care of Children from Germany. In March 1939 these last two groups merged and were incorporated into the Refugee Children's Movement (RCM), chaired by Lord Gorell. Apart from the main RCM body, local committees of the organization found and inspected homes, supervised the children, and arranged for their general, vocational, and religious education. The children were chosen by the children's emigration departments of the central Jewish organizations in Germany, Austria, and Czechoslovakia. An additional 500 children were brought to Great Britain as members of Youth Aliya groups, and 1,350 arrived as agricultural trainees.

The children were divided into two categories: those guaranteed by private sponsors, and those guaranteed by the RCM. In February 1939, the government insisted that sponsors post a fifty-pound bond for each child to cover his reemigration. The bonds were later paid for by the Lord Baldwin Fund, which was created to offer financial assistance to Jewish refugees from Germany. Once in Britain, the children were housed in reception camps and later taken to foster homes or hostels. After heated discussion, it was decided by the leaders of the Jewish organizations assisting the children to accept offers of hospitality in non-Jewish homes. The representatives of the Chief Rabbi's Religious Emergency Council, however, continued to warn against growing missionary attempts aimed at the children.

Unlike the RCM, which promoted the integration and assimilation of the children, the London office of Youth Aliya, under the leadership of Eva Michaelis Stern, strove to keep the children together. It therefore created a number of agricultural training centers where children lived collectively, studied, and worked. Many of the RCM children eventually requested to join these centers in search of companionship and values lacking in their foster placement surroundings.

Because of difficulties in distinguishing between Jews and non-Jews and between permanent residents and transmigrants in official statistics, it is not possible to ascertain the exact number of German Jewish refugees in Britain. It has been estimated that until the outbreak of the war more than 80,000 Jewish refugees reached Great Britain and some 55,000 remained there. In addition to the 10,000 children, there were some 14,000 women who entered the country as domestic help. In a special camp, Kitchener, in Richborough, Kent, some 5,000 people who needed immediate shelter were housed during an eighteen-month period from the end of January 1939. These 5,000 refugees had been released from concentration camps, or their internment had been deferred by the Nazis, who were willing to let them alone on condition that they leave Germany immediately. The Home Office gave them a group entrance visa and waived the normal regulations for passports and individual permits.

The government's decision, after *Kristallnacht*, to simplify the entrance procedures for refugees, and the subsequent large growth in their numbers, placed a great responsibility on the Jewish organizations and caused them difficulties of a magnitude for which they were not prepared. The major problem was financial. The organizations were still pledged to support the refugees, and this became such a great burden that they were forced to implement very strict criteria for the selection of those who would be allowed to enter, and had to turn away thousands of applicants. From early 1939 pressure was brought to bear on the government to share in the financing of the refugees, but it refused, resting on the principle, established at the EVIAN CONFERENCE, that all aid to refugees must come from private sources. However, owing primarily to the fear that the relief organizations might collapse, the government changed its policy. The change was gradual, and only after the outbreak of the war were the Jewish organizations released from their pledge.

British Jewry did all it could in the last year before the war to effect the release and rescue of as many Jews as possible from the Nazis. In addition to their generous contributions to the various funds, their aid to children, and their help in setting up the agricultural training centers, British Jews gave personal bonds that enabled thousands of refugees to make their entrance into Great Britain and guaranteed their support once they arrived. They also provided work as domestics for thousands of women and teenage girls, providing for them and, when necessary, for their children. Many volunteers worked in the relief organizations, whose proportions reached those of a government office.

With the outbreak of war, refugee children were evacuated, along with British schoolchildren and other vulnerable persons, to the Midlands and Wales. The treatment of refugees at this time became worse. Following the outbreak of hostilities, all Germans and Austrians in Great Britain, including Jewish refugees, were defined as "enemy aliens." All enemy aliens were examined before special tribunals, and some were interned. The tribunals were not always astute bodies, and Jews and pro-Nazi Germans were occasionally interned together. The fear of foreigners, the developments in the European war, and especially the anxiety (which increased after the fall of the Netherlands) about the activities of a supposed fifth column caused mass hysteria and open hostility toward the refugees. The government, with the full support of the public and the press, decided on the mass internment of aliens from Germany and Austria in the early summer of 1940. Within several weeks about thirty thousand were interned in camps, most of them Jewish refugees who unhesitatingly supported the Allies, and some of them older children. Later in the summer of 1940 the government took an additional step that had great ramifications: it deported aliens from Great Britain. Some eight thousand aliens were sent to CANADA and AUSTRALIA, and for this purpose ships badly needed for the war effort were used.

Only after the scandals and disasters resulting from the deportations (such as the sinking of the ship *Arandora Star* carrying deportees, with great loss of life) had taken place was severe criticism raised in public, and the injustice being done to the deportees—already victims of Nazism—and the folly of the policy became evident. Shortly thereafter, the government changed its policy, canceling the deportations and returning some of the deportees to Great Britain. Within a year almost all of the internees were released and were integrated into British society. Thousands of them joined the British army in the war against the Nazis.

BIBLIOGRAPHY

Bentwich, N. *They Found Refuge: An Account of British Jewry's Work for the Victims of Nazi Oppression.* London, 1956.

Berghahn, M. *German-Jewish Refugees in England.* London, 1984.

Gilbert, M. "British Government Policy towards Jewish Refugees: November 1938–September 1939." *Yad Vashem Studies* 13 (1979): 127–167.

Sherman, A. J. *Island Refugee: Britain and Refugees from the Third Reich, 1933–1939.* London, 1973.

Stevens, A. *The Dispossessed: German Refugees in Britain.* London, 1975.

Wasserstein, B. *Britain and the Jews of Europe, 1939–1945.* Oxford, 1979.

JUDITH TYDOR-BAUMEL, NANA SAGI,
and RONALD W. ZWEIG

GREECE. A kingdom prior to 1924, Greece became a republic that year. In November 1935, following years of political turmoil after the end of World War I, an overwhelming majority in Greece voted in a plebiscite to restore the monarchy, and King George II returned to Greece from exile. At the 1936 elections, neither the Liberal party nor the Populists and their royalist allies received a majority. In the midst of the political stalemate, the king appointed Gen. Ioannis Metaxas as prime minister, although in the past the general had been involved in one of numerous military coups. Metaxas temporarily instituted a dictatorship in Greece. His regime manifested hostility toward liberalism, communism, and parliamentary government, and it evinced profascist tendencies. This ideological attachment to fascism was paralleled by an increase in trade with Germany. Despite Metaxas's admiration for the domestic policies of Nazi Germany and Fascist Italy, he did not disturb Greece's relationship with Great Britain, for he was wary of its sea power. Although he failed to make an alliance with Britain, a few days after the Italian occupation of Albania, in April 1939, Britain and France offered Greece a guarantee of its territorial integrity in the event that it chose to resist aggression.

At the outbreak of World War II in September 1939, Metaxas tried to maintain a position of neutrality. When Italy provoked Greece in August 1940 by torpedoing the cruiser *Elli*, anchored off the island of Tinos, Greece did not retaliate. Metaxas, however, refused to agree to Italy's humiliating ultimatum of October 28, 1940, that Greece give up its sovereignty, and Italy invaded Greece. The Italian force crossing the Albanian border met fierce opposition by the Greek army, led by its chief of staff, Gen. Alexander Papagos. Within a few days, the Italians occupied major towns in northern Epirus. The Greeks fought valiantly and drove the Italians back into Albania. The war reached a stalemate in the snowbound mountains of Albania and the Greeks were prevented from capturing Valona, the principal port in the south, which would have enabled the Greek forces to receive supplies by sea.

Metaxas died in January 1941, but the war continued. On April 6, Hitler intervened to secure his southern flank for the upcoming invasion of the Soviet Union, and his forces now also invaded Greece, by way of Yugoslavia and Bulgaria. The Greek army, aided by a small British force, was outflanked and unable to stop the German attack. As a result, Prime Minister Alexandros Koryzis committed suicide on April 18 and the Greek army and the king fled to Crete as the Germans closed in on Athens. Most of the British troops (forty-two thousand out of fifty-eight thousand) were evacuated from Greece. The intention of making Crete into a stronghold never materialized, and following the massive airborne German attack of May 20, 1941, and intense fighting, the island fell to the Germans. Many British soldiers became prisoners of war, including a large number of Palestinian Jewish soldiers abandoned in the Peloponnese. The remaining British and Greek fighting forces withdrew to Egypt. The Greek government-in-exile and King George set up their headquarters in London and, after disturbances in the Greek armed forces in the Middle East, moved to Cairo in March 1943.

Greece was divided into three zones of occupation. The Italians occupied Epirus, the Ionian islands, central and southern Greece from the Platona line southward, and ATHENS, with its strategic position. The Germans held central Macedonia and a strip of land at the eastern edge of Greek Thrace (which included Orestiás, Dhidhimótikon, and Souflion). The Bulgarians occupied Thrace. Gen. George Tsolakoglu was made prime minister in a puppet government subordinate to the

GREECE

© Martin Gilbert 1982

Germans. He was succeeded by the civilians Constantine Logothetopoulos and Ioannis Rallis.

The Greek Communist party chairman, Nikos Zakhariadis, was imprisoned in DACHAU for the duration of the war, but the experienced and organized party from the Metaxas era succeeded in forming the resistance Ethnikon Apeletherotikon Metopon (National Liberation Front; EAM) in September 1941. Its military arm, the Ellenikos Laikos Apelethorotikos Stratos (Popular Greek Liberation Army; ELAS), was formed at the end of December 1941. The first guerrilla units arrived in the mountains early in the summer of 1942. The most important of the units was led by Athanasios Klaras, known as Aris Velouchiotis.

The main non-Communist resistance movement was the Ellenikos Dimokratikos Ethnikos Stratos (National Republican Greek League; EDES), led by the republican general Napoleon Zervas. EDES began its partisan activities early in the summer of 1942. Another republican resistance organization, Ethniki kai Koinoniki Apeletherosis (National and Social Liberation; EKKA), led by Col. Dimitrios Psarros, became militarily active in the spring of 1943.

That September, the Italian regime fell in Greece and the Germans took full control over the previous Italian zone. Some fifteen thousand Italian troops stationed in Greece transferred their allegiance to the Allies through British liaison officers who were attached to the Greek resistance movement.

In anticipation of the German defeat, British and American units infiltrated into Greece throughout 1944 to harass the retreating Germans and also to ensure an Allied presence after the liberation. The Germans evacuated Greece in September 1944, with the exception of RHODES, Crete, and some other islands, where the Germans surrendered only in May 1945. Following its liberation, Greece entered a long period of political turmoil. This erupted into a civil war that continued until October 1949, when the Communist forces conceded defeat to the monarchists.

Greek Jewry in the Holocaust. The major stages in the destruction of Greek Jewry include the deportation from Bulgarian-occupied Thrace and Macedonia in March 1943; the deportations from German-occupied SALONIKA and its environs from March to May 1943; and the deportations from the former Italian zone after Italy's surrender (September 1943), in March, April, and the summer of 1944. All the deportations took place after the Italians had recognized that the war was lost. This attitude, plus their antipathy to German brutality, caused Italian military and diplomatic personnel to aid as many Jews as possible to escape, either to the Italian-occupied zone or out of the occupied Balkans.

In April 1941 the Jewish archives and libraries in Salonika and Athens were confiscated by EINSATZSTAB ROSENBERG. During the spring and summer of 1941 Germany stripped Greece of its edible and cash crops and sequestered its natural resources. In the resulting famine of 1941 and 1942, which severely affected the Greek population, the Jews suffered especially. On July 11, 1942, nine thousand Salonikan Jewish males aged eighteen to forty-five were humiliated and later assigned to ORGANISATION TODT labor battalions within Greece; many died and others suffered from disease and exhaustion. The Jewish community sought to ransom the young Jewish laborers, but the communal leaders did not succeed in raising the needed sums. To compensate for the remainder, the famous Jewish cemetery of Salonika was expropriated, turned over to the municipal authorities, and destroyed.

The first Greek Jews to be deported were those of Macedonia and Thrace, which had been annexed by BULGARIA. In mid-February 1943, the Bulgarian minister of internal affairs, Petur Gabrovski, agreed to the deportation to the Reich of 20,000 Jews, including those of Macedonia and Thrace. The deportation was organized by Yaroslav Kalitsin, chief of the administrative section of the Komisarstvo za Evreiskite Vuprosi (Commissariat for Jewish Questions) in Bulgaria. He established three concentration points, at Radomir, Dupnitsa, and Gorna Dzhumaya. At 4:00 a.m. on March 4, 1943, the Jews of Thrace were arrested, interned for several days in tobacco warehouses, and sent by train to Bulgaria. Only some 200 Jews escaped the roundup, either by fleeing to the

Italian zone or by having been drafted into labor battalions. The remaining 4,100 were sent by train and barge to Vienna and then by train directly to TREBLINKA, where they were gassed on arrival.

The local population in the Bulgarian zone was completely cowed by savage German reprisals for acts of sabotage and dissent (beheading, mutilation, firing squads, and so on). Bulgaria was determined to repopulate the new territories with Bulgarian peasants, and it encouraged Greek migration to the German zone. Even so, some Jews who escaped the roundup were hidden or escorted to the partisans in the mountains. Many acts of kindness by non-Jews toward the deportees are recorded, along with acts of theft.

In the German-occupied zone, Dieter WISLICENY and Alois BRUNNER, representing the office of Adolf EICHMANN, orchestrated the deportations through the JUDENRAT (Jewish Council) headed by Chief Rabbi Zvi KORETZ,

who was appointed its president in December 1942. During February 1943 the NUREMBERG LAWS were implemented through Dr. Maximilian Merton, adviser to the German military administration, and the Jews were mainly isolated in three ghettos: the Hagia Paraskevi district, the so-called 151 quarter, and the Baron de Hirsch transit camp, all in or near Salonika. From the last they were transported by train to AUSCHWITZ during March and April. Some 48,000 Jews were deported; 37,000 were gassed on arrival and 11,000 were selected for the labor camp. Between April 30 and May 8, 1943, the Jews of Dhidhimótikon, Orestiás, Florina, Veroia, and Souflion were arrested by the Germans. They were brought to Salonika, and shipped to Auschwitz on May 9. Most were gassed on arrival as part of the seventeenth Salonikan transport. The last transport from Salonika, which included the Judenrat (74 individuals), went to BERGEN-BELSEN in August 1943. The

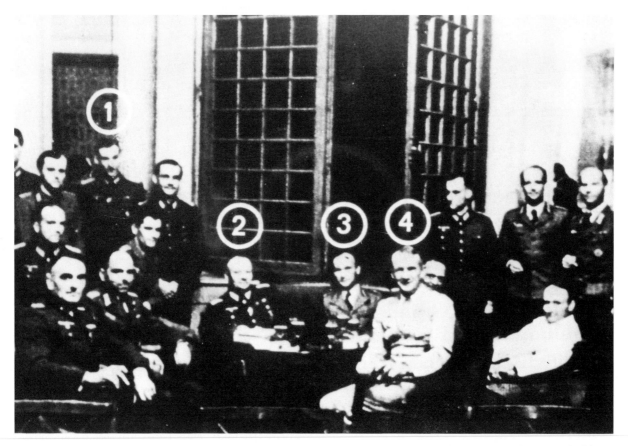

Oberleutnant Kurt Waldheim (1) relaxing in 1943 at the Hotel Grande Bretagne in Athens with fifteen other German officers. [World Jewish Congress]

Wehrmacht supplied all the trains, at the command of Gen. Alexander Löhr of Army Group E.

The Greek leaders made numerous protests to the Greek government and the Italian and German occupiers. About one hundred and fifty Salonikan lawyers, after approaching Simonides, the Greek governor of Macedonia, appealed to the government in Athens to at least shift the goal of the deportations from Poland to a Greek island. The response was that the Germans would not allow it. Salonikan Jewish refugees in Athens, aided by Athenian Jews, tried to pressure the government. They were joined by the intellectual and religious leadership, especially Archbishop Damaskinos and the heads of the institutions of higher learning, who argued eloquently on behalf of the Jews. However, Dr. Constantine Logothetopoulos, who headed the government in 1943, wanted to settle the Greek Orthodox refugees of Bulgarian-occupied Thrace in the vacant Jewish quarters of Salonika. His halfhearted attempt to stop the deportations through a letter to the German plenipotentiary in Athens, Günther Altenberg, on March 23, 1943, arrived too late. On March 29, Athenian nongovernment leaders made an appeal, unprecedented in occupied Europe, to Prato, the political secretary of the Italian embassy, to halt the deportations of loyal Greek citizens. This too failed, because Salonika was in the German zone. The government of Ioannis Rallis protested to the Gestapo over the deportations, contributing to an atmosphere in which the Greek Jews were assisted by the population. In particular, Professor Nikolaos Louvaris, the minister of education and later of communications, expended considerable effort to save the Jews.

The officials in the Italian consulate in Salonika—consul Guelfo Zamboni, vice-consul Cavalliere Rosenberg, Stabila, Emilio Neri, Doefini, Merci, Mark Mosseri, and Valerie Torres—assisted Jews to escape to the Italian zone. All their efforts helped many hundreds of the three thousand Salonikan Jews to escape to Athens. More than three hundred held false Italian documents issued by the consulate.

The surrender of Italy brought under German control the remainder of Greek Jewry, which had hitherto enjoyed the protection of Gen. Carlo Geloso, the Italian police commander in Athens and administrator of southern Greece, and his successor, General Vecchiarelli. Under the direction of Wisliceny, with the assistance of SS general Jürgen STROOP, 800 Athenian Jews were arrested and deported to Auschwitz, along with Jews from smaller mainland towns who were arrested on March 24 and 25, 1944: Arta (352), Préveza (272), Patras (12 families), Chalcis (90), Volos (130), Larissa (225), Trikkala (50), Ioannina (1,860), and Kastoria (763). Most were gassed on arrival.

The Jews of CORFU were arrested on June 6, 1944; nearly 1,800 out of 2,000 were sent to Auschwitz, of whom 200 were selected for forced labor and the remainder gassed. On July 20, 1,700 Jews of Rhodes were sent by way of Piraeus to Auschwitz, where 700 were selected for forced labor and the rest killed. The 260 Jews of Canea were arrested on May 21, 1944, and the boat carrying them sank mysteriously; there were no survivors.

According to extant Auschwitz figures, at least 54,533 Greek Jews were transported there. Of these (for whom figures are available), 41,776 were sent immediately to the gas chambers and 12,757 (8,025 men and 4,732 women) were selected for forced labor, the orchestra, MEDICAL EXPERIMENTS (sterilization and experiments involving twins), and the SONDERKOMMANDO. Periodically, Greek Jews were assigned to the Auschwitz crematoria in 1943 and 1944. One group of 400, selected in the summer of 1944 to expedite the destruction of Hungarian Jews, refused the assignment, knowing that the punishment was death. The incident is reported by a number of Auschwitz survivors. Also in the summer of 1944, Albert Errera of Larissa, part of an ash-emptying detail, wounded his guards and escaped across the Vistula. Recaptured, he was tortured to death. One hundred and thirty-five Greek Jews, former officers in the Greek army, participated in (and perhaps instigated) the revolt that broke out on October 6–7, 1944 (or on September 9, according to some sources). Greek survivors claim responsibility for blowing up Crematorium III; nearly all those involved died singing the Greek national anthem.

By August 2, 1944, there were 292 Greek

A Jewish couple from Salonika wearing the Jewish badge.

men in Auschwitz I (the main camp), 929 men in Auschwitz II (Birkenau), and 517 men in Auschwitz III (Buna-Monowitz), in addition to 731 women. Most of the Salonika women and men selected for forced labor died subsequently from the cold, hunger, typhus, dysentery, and the cruelty of guards. Many committed suicide when they learned the fate of their families. The above-mentioned 400 (or 435) Jewish prisoners, who were from Salonika, were gassed after refusing to serve in the Sonderkommando; and at least 135 Greeks died in the Sonderkommando revolt. Many of those who survived into 1945 left with the DEATH MARCHES of January 17 to MAUTHAUSEN, Bergen-Belsen, STUTTHOF, and other places. By the end of the war, the survivors numbered only in the hundreds. Fewer than 2,000 of the more than 54,000 deported returned to Greece.

In August 1943 about 300 Salonikan Jews were part of a contingent comprised of non-Polish-speaking Jews, sent to WARSAW to re-cycle the ruins of the ghetto. That October a second group of Salonikan Jews was sent to the Warsaw ghetto. Many died from starvation and disease. Shaul Senor, a Salonikan Jew from Palestine (later hanged for attempted escape), is credited with saving many sick prisoners. At the end of July most of the Greek Jews were transferred to Dachau. During the Warsaw Polish uprising of August and September 1944, the surviving Greeks participated in the fighting or hid in the bunkers. Many were killed by the Germans, and a few by antisemitic Poles who took part in the revolt. The Greeks split up to improve their chances of survival. Later, some re-formed as a unit and fought under a Greek flag. Only about 27 Greeks survived that revolt.

Greek Jews were active in the resistance in Greece both before and after the formation of organized fighting partisan units. The Greek resistance went through several stages. Soldiers who were demobilized after the war with Italy or the surrender of Greece to Germany formed militant bands in the mountains. They were organized and supplied by the British Middle East Command late in 1942, especially those in Epiros, who were republican or royalist (EDES, EKKA). Others fled to areas in central Greece (the Pindus and Olympic ranges) controlled by nationalist democratic forces with a strong Communist leadership (EAM/ELAS). Active military resistance against the Germans did not begin until well into 1943.

A number of Jewish communities survived in their entirety or in part. All the Jews of Agrinion (40) dispersed into the countryside, and the planned deportation of Zante (275) never took place. Most of the Jews of Thessaly and central Greece—Volos (750), Katerínē (35), Larissa (500), Trikkala (450), Kardhitsa (100 to 150), Chalcis (270), Athens (2,000), and Patras (200)—hid with neighbors, fled to the mountains, or escaped to Palestine by way of Turkey.

The Greek population in the Italian-occupied zone rallied to the support of the Jews, whom they publicly acknowledged as Greek citizens. The successive Greek governments protested, though ineffectively, against the deportations from the German zone in 1943. Leading intellectuals in Salonika and

Athens submitted protest letters; the Germans closed the University of Athens in retaliation for protests. The Greek Orthodox church, led by the metropolitan of Athens, Archbishop Damaskinos, resisted, by making formal protests; by issuing encyclicals to the clergy, calling upon them to protect Jewish refugees; by hiding Jewish children (over two hundred and fifty); and by issuing false baptismal certificates. More than six hundred Greek clergy were arrested and many deported as a result. The Athens police supplied forged papers. The foreign consulates of Spain, Turkey, and Italy protected any Jew who could remotely claim their citizenship. Those so saved numbered many thousands. The Greek underground hid Jews, smuggled them to unoccupied Greece, or transported them to Turkey. Their efforts also aided many of the Palestinian Jewish soldiers, trapped in Greece after the collapse of the British Expeditionary Force in 1941, to escape from the Germans.

STEVEN B. BOWMAN

The Postwar Period. In 1941 the population of the Greek Jewish communities (including that of Rhodes, which was annexed to Greece after World War II) was 77,178, with 56,000 living in Salonika. About 96 percent of Salonika's Jews died in the Holocaust; 1,000 returned after the war and another 1,000 emigrated to Palestine, France, or the United States. Today in Salonika a small Jewish community maintains a cultural center, a historical library, two synagogues, a cemetery, an old-age home, and an elementary school.

Most Jews in Greece now live in Athens. Although soon after the war 4,930 Jews lived there, as of the end of the 1980s there were slightly under 3,000. They maintain a synagogue, a Jewish museum, an elementary school, and a cemetery.

The majority of the Jews of Thessaly (Larissa, Trikkala, and Volos) survived the war in the mountains. After the war, there was a significant emigration to Israel and Athens from this area. These communities, as well as smaller communities such as those of Rhodes, Chalcis, Corfu, and Ioannina, are too small to support Jewish education, cultural activities, or many opportunities for prayer. Generally, the young people have left these places for Athens or the United States, and the older generation in these small urban communities throughout Greece is dying out.

No survivors returned from the Thracian deportation. A group of forty Jews who survived because they were sent on forced labor to Bulgaria emigrated to Israel after the war. Jewish life in communities like those of Serrai, Dráma, Xánthi, Komotinē, and Alexandroupolis ceased to exist after the Holocaust. The community of Zákinthos survived, with the exception of some thirty victims of starvation, but after the war most of the community settled in Israel.

After the war, the Kentriokon Israelitikon Symvoulion (Board of Jewish Communities in Greece), along with the American Jewish JOINT DISTRIBUTION COMMITTEE, helped rebuild synagogues, schools, clubs, and old-age homes throughout Greece. The Holocaust survivors returned to Greece penniless, and through the help of these organizations, were able to rehabilitate themselves.

The Greek government entrusted the Organization for the Assistance and Rehabilitation of Greek Jews with the task of recompensing the Jews and reallocating their lost property. Although the Greek Jewish survivors in Greece received reparations from West Germany, some seven hundred Greek Holocaust survivors in Israel received no compensation for the Nazi pillaging of their families' property.

YITZCHAK KEREM

BIBLIOGRAPHY

Avni, H. "Spanish Nationals in Greece and Their Fate during the Holocaust." *Yad Vashem Studies* 8 (1970): 31–68.

Ben, Y. *Greek Jewry in the Holocaust and the Resistance, 1941–1944.* Tel Aviv, 1985. (In Hebrew.)

Carpi, D. "Notes on the History of the Jews in Greece during the Holocaust Period: The Attitude of the Italians (1941–1943)." In *Festschrift in Honor of Dr. George S. Wise,* edited by H. Ben-Shahar et al., pp. 25–62. Tel Aviv, 1981.

Chary, F. B. *Bulgarian Jews and the Final Solution, 1940–1944.* Pittsburgh, 1972.

Molho, M., and J. Nehama. *The Destruction of Greek Jewry, 1941–1945.* Jerusalem, 1965. (In Hebrew.)

Molho, M., and J. Nehama. *In Memoriam: Hommage aux victimes juives des nazis en Grèce.* Salonika, 1973.

Novitch, M. *Le passage des barbares: Contribution à l'histoire de la déportation et de la résistance des Juifs grecs.* Nice, 1962.

GREISER, ARTHUR (1897–1946), prominent figure in the Nazi party and the Third Reich administration. Greiser was born in the town of Środa, in the Poznań (Ger., Posen) province; his father was a government official. In World War I Greiser served as an air force officer. After the war he spent some time in the Freikorps and then tried his hand at business, without much success. In 1924 Greiser was one of the founders of Stahlhelm (Steel Helmet), a nationalist association of former servicemen, in DANZIG. In 1928 he joined the Nazi party, and then the SA (Sturmabteilung; Storm Troopers); after a while, he switched to the SS. Greiser held various Nazi party posts in Danzig, was elected to the city senate, and was appointed its president in 1934, replacing Hermann RAUSCHNING. (Between the two world wars Danzig had the status of a free city, under international trusteeship.)

During the Polish campaign in September 1939, Greiser was appointed head of the civilian administration of Poznań. In October and November he became *Gauleiter* and *Reichsstatthalter* (governor) of the WARTHEGAU, the large Polish territory (which included the city of Łódź) that was incorporated into the Reich. Unlike the other governors of the Polish territorial units, Greiser was able to gain the support of persons with influence in the Reich Chancellery in Berlin and to maintain good relations with Heinrich HIMMLER. In 1942 he was appointed an SS-*Gruppenführer.* Greiser was determined to uproot the Polish population from the area under his administration, in order to speed up its "Germanization." His fanatic anti-Polish policy expressed itself in various forms, such as

At a festive gathering, Wilhelm Frick, Reich minister of the interior (seated to the left of the empty chair), inducts Gauleiter Arthur Greiser as *Reichsstatthalter* (governor) of the Warthegau. Greiser delivers his address in the old throne room of the Poznań castle (November 1939).

confiscating Polish property, restricting educational and cultural activities, "Germanizing" Polish orphans, and persecuting the Catholic church and the Polish clergy. His most severe action, however, was the expulsion of Poles and Jews from the territory. In the period from 1939 to 1945, some 630,000 Poles and Jews were removed or expelled from the Warthegau, and 537,000 VOLKS-DEUTSCHE (ethnic Germans) were brought in from areas in the Baltic states, southeastern Poland, Romania, and the Soviet Union.

In 1945 Greiser was captured by the Americans in the Alps and extradited to Poland. During the trial of Hans BIEBOW in 1946, the former German commissar of the Łódź ghetto testified that Greiser had rejected appeals to improve the food rations of the Jews in the ghetto, and that his radical anti-Jewish attitude had served as a model to his subordinates. Greiser had praised the men of the German unit that from December 1941 operated the CHEŁMNO extermination camp in the area under his administration, the first of its kind in occupied Poland. Upon the conclusion of a *Sonderbehandlung* ("special treatment," that is, extermination) operation in which one hundred thousand Jews from the Warthegau had been killed, Greiser wrote a letter to Himmler proposing that the same treatment be meted out to Poles afflicted with tuberculosis, because they were endangering the health of the German population.

Greiser was tried in June and July 1946 by a Polish national tribunal and was sentenced to death. He was hanged in front of the house in Poznań that had served as his residence when he was governor of the Warthegau.

BIBLIOGRAPHY

Broszat, M. *Nationalsozialistische Polenpolitik, 1939–1945*. Stuttgart, 1961.
Proces Artura (Greisera): Przed Najwyższym Trybunalem Narodowym. Warsaw, 1946.

ISRAEL GUTMAN

GREYSHIRTS, South African national socialist movement founded in October 1933 by Louis Weichardt. Its original name was the South African Christian National Socialist Movement, which changed in May 1934 to the South African National Party. "Greyshirt" referred to the upper part of the uniforms worn by the militant sector, or advance guard, of the movement, which was responsible for maintaining order at political meetings and protecting the leader.

Although centered in Cape Town, the Greyshirt organization had cells throughout the country. The movement published a fortnightly bilingual newspaper, *Die Waarheid* (The Truth), from February 23, 1934, to July 29, 1938. Its monthly organ, *Die Blanke Front* (The White Front), appeared from July 1947 to May 1948.

Weichardt, an Afrikaner antisemite who had joined up to fight for Germany in World War I, fashioned the movement's racist, antisemitic, and fascist philosophy. Parliamentary politics and liberalism were attributed to "British-Jewish" contamination. The movement was eventually absorbed into the Reunited National Party, which defeated the Jan Smuts government in 1948. Weichardt subsequently became a senator.

[*See also* South Africa.]

BIBLIOGRAPHY

Roberts, M., and A. E. G. Trollip. *The South African Opposition, 1939–1945*. London, 1947.
Shimoni, G. *Jews and Zionism: The South African Experience (1910–1967)*. Cape Town, 1980.

MILTON SHAIN

GROBELNY, JULIAN (1893–1944), Polska Partia Socjalistyczna (Polish Socialist Party) activist. From 1919 to 1921 Grobelny strove for the annexation of Silesia to Poland. Subsequently employed in Łódź, he was active in the organization of social assistance. In 1940 he joined Wolność, Równość, Niepodległość (Freedom, Equality, Independence), the right-wing faction of the Polish Socialist party, and was a member of the party's regional labor committee in the Warsaw suburbs (he was known by the code name "Trojan").

Under Grobelny's chairmanship, from January 1943, ŻEGOTA, the Polish Council for Aid to Jews, greatly expanded its activity and in-

Julian Grobelny.

creased its budget. Grobelny was of great assistance to the large group of people in the organization's care, and he was particularly sensitive to the distress of the children.

Arrested in March 1944 and imprisoned, Grobelny developed tuberculosis and was admitted to the prison hospital. After about a month he was smuggled out by the Polish underground and went into hiding in MIŃSK MAZOWIECKI. After the liberation he became mayor of that town.

BIBLIOGRAPHY

Prekerowa, T. *Konspiracyjna Rada Pomocy Żydom w Warszawie, 1942–1945.* Warsaw, 1982.

TERESA PREKEROWA

GRODNO, city in the western part of BELO-RUSSIA. In the interwar period Grodno was part of Poland; in September 1939 it was occupied by the Red Army and annexed to the Soviet Union. Grodno had one of the oldest and largest Lithuanian Jewish communities, which took pride in its numerous social and cultural institutions and was a center of Zionism. One the eve of World War II, Grodno had a Jewish population of twenty-five thousand.

On the first day of their invasion of the Soviet Union, June 22, 1941, the Germans reached Grodno. As soon as they entered the city, they put all Jews aged sixteen to sixty on forced labor. In July of that year, eighty Jews belonging to the intelligentsia were put to death. Some time after the occupation, the Germans administratively transferred Grodno from Belorussia to the district of Białystok, and annexed it, in March 1942, to East Prussia.

On November 1, 1941, the Germans ordered the establishment of two ghettos, ghetto "A" for skilled workers and ghetto "B" for "nonproductive" Jews. The ghettos were the scene of educational, cultural, communal, and youth movement activities, with the participation of community leaders, educators, and members of Zionist youth movements.

Because of its location, between Vilna and Białystok, Grodno became a center for the Jewish underground. It was one of the first places to hear reports of the large-scale massacres at PONARY. At the beginning of 1942 an underground movement was founded in the Grodno ghetto, based on non-Zionist and Zionist youth movements (Ha-Shomer ha-Tsa'ir, Dror, Betar), the BUND, and the Communists. The pioneering Zionist movements wanted to fight inside the ghetto, whereas the Communists urged escaping from the ghetto into the forests. Mordechai TENENBAUM (Tamaroff) twice went to Grodno seeking to set up an underground that would encompass the whole gamut of movements, from the Revisionist Zionists to the Communists. Such cooperation was in fact achieved, and some of the underground activists were transferred to the Białystok ghetto.

On November 22, 1942, 2,400 Jews from Grodno were taken to AUSCHWITZ. While this *Aktion* was underway, Zerah Silberberg, one of the Ha-Shomer ha-Tsa'ir activists in the Białystok underground, went to Grodno to train the underground commanders and try to establish a common front of Zionist and non-Zionist youth movements.

A further 2,000 Jews were deported from Grodno at the end of November 1942; their destination was Kielbasin, a transit camp for onward deportation to extermination camps. A second transport of Jews from Grodno to Kielbasin followed in early December. The underground had a plan to assassinate the

GRODNO

German commander of ghetto "B," Streblow, but failed to carry it out. Five members of Dror and Ha-Shomer ha-Tsa'ir were sent to the forests; four found their death there and the one survivor returned to the ghetto, declaring that Jews without arms in their possession could not survive in the forest. The determination to stay in the ghetto and fight there gained in strength among the underground members, but some groups of Jews continued to escape into the forests. Several women members of the underground who had set up a workshop for forging documents were moved to Białystok on orders of the underground, to serve as liaison officers; they included Bronka Winicki (Klibanski), Hasya Belicka (Borenstein), Zila Schachnes, and Liza Czapnik. Two underground members, Motl Kuperman and Nahum Kravyets, set an ambush one night for Streblow, but they were shot before they could draw their guns. Another assassination attempt, by Shayke

Matus, whose target was the commander of ghetto "A" and Streblow's superior, Kurt Wiese, also failed.

In an *Aktion* that came to an end on January 22, 1943, 10,500 Jews were deported to Auschwitz. Many of the deportees jumped off the trains, and some of these made their way to the Białystok ghetto. The last group of Jews to be deported from Grodno, numbering some 500 persons, was taken to Białystok. The flight to the forests, mostly on an individual basis, continued in the winter of 1943, the destination being the nearby forests of Nacha and Augustów. These escapees were not accepted by the non-Jewish partisan units, and hunger and cold forced some of them to return to the Grodno ghetto. A number of young people from Grodno who had gone to Białystok left that ghetto for the forest in August 1943 and operated in the Knyszyn and Jasinowka areas under the name "White Furs," mainly taking revenge on local peasants who had collaborated with the Germans. The group finally managed to join a Soviet partisan unit, and fought with it up to the liberation.

Grodno was liberated by the Red Army on July 14, 1944. Approximately two hundred Jews were still alive, including partisans and persons who had survived locally or who came back to Grodno from other places in the Soviet Union.

BIBLIOGRAPHY

Rabin, D., ed. "Grodno." In vol. 9 of *Encyclopedia of the Jewish Diaspora: Memorial Books of Countries and Communities.* Jerusalem, 1973. (In Hebrew.)

SHALOM CHOLAWSKI

GROJANOWSKI REPORT, report on the murder of Jews in the CHEŁMNO extermination camp, composed in the Warsaw ghetto in the winter of 1942 by ONEG SHABBAT (the Ringelblum Archive). The report is based on the testimony given by Jacob Grojanowski, the first person to escape from the Chełmno camp.

Grojanowski was taken to Chełmno from Izbica, his place of residence, on January 6, 1942, together with a group of twenty-eight other Jews. In the extermination camp he was put to work burying the victims of the GAS VANS, together with Jews who had been brought to the camp from various other places in the area. The victims—men, women, and children—were Jews, with the exception of eight groups of GYPSIES, who were shipped to the camp in the course of Grojanowski's stay. Grojanowski managed to escape from the camp and make his way to the Warsaw ghetto, apparently in February 1942. His testimony contains an exact and detailed description of the extermination procedure followed in Chełmno—the deception practiced on the inmates up to the very last moment, their asphyxiation by exhaust gas in the special vans constructed for this purpose, the removal of the bodies from the vans by prisoners turned gravediggers, the clean-up of the van interiors following the murders, and the method of burying the corpses in pits. Grojanowski also describes the grim mental and emotional state of the men who were forced to handle the bodies, the sadism displayed by the murderers, and his own escape from the camp. On the basis of this testimony, Oneg Shabbat prepared a report on the Chełmno murders, in Polish and German. The Polish version was meant for the DELEGATURA (the representation, in Poland, of the POLISH GOVERNMENT-IN-EXILE), which passed it on to London, where it was received in March or April 1942. The German version was intended for distribution among the German people, in the hope that the information it contained would have some effect.

BIBLIOGRAPHY

Shaul, E., trans. "The Testimony of a Forced Grave-Digger: Jacob Grojanowski, Izbica-Kolo-Chelmno." *Yalkut Moreshet* 35 (April 1983): 101–122. (In Hebrew.)

ELISHEVA SHAUL

GROSMAN, HAIKA (b. 1919), underground activist and partisan. Born in BIAŁYSTOK, Grosman became a member of the Zionist youth movement Ha-Shomer ha-Tsa'ir at an early age. At the outbreak of World War II

Haika Grosman.

she moved to VILNA and helped to concentrate members of the pioneering Zionist youth movements in that city. Following the German invasion of the Soviet Union (June 22, 1941), Grosman returned to Białystok, where she became one of the organizers of the underground there. Posing as a Polish woman, she went on many underground missions to various cities and ghettos, including the Warsaw ghetto. She belonged to the "Antifascist Białystok" cell and, together with five other young women who posed as Poles—Marila Ruziecka, Liza Czapnik, Hasya Belicka (Borenstein), Ana Rud, and Bronka Winicki (Klibanski)—gave assistance to the Jewish underground and to the partisans who were then organizing themselves in the forests around Białystok. She participated in the Białystok ghetto revolt in August 1943 and was a member of a Jewish partisan unit that operated in the area.

After liberation, Grosman served as the Ha-Shomer ha-Tsa'ir representative in the institutions set up by the remnants of the Jewish population in Poland. She settled in Israel in 1948, joining Kibbutz Evron in western Gali-

lee. Grosman became politically active in Israel and was a member of the Knesset (the Israeli parliament) from 1969 to 1981, and again from 1984. She is the author of *People of the Underground* (published in English as *The Underground Army*, 1988), which contains memoirs and chapters on the struggle of the Białystok Jews.

BIBLIOGRAPHY

Grossman, C. *The Underground Army: Fighters of the Bialystock Ghetto*. New York, 1988.
Syrkin, M. *Blessed Is the Match*. Philadelphia, 1976. See chapter 7.

ISRAEL GUTMAN

GROSSMAN, MENDEL (1917–1945), photographer in the ŁÓDŹ ghetto. Grossman commemorated the horrors of the Łódź ghetto in more than ten thousand pictures taken throughout the ghetto's existence. Since Jews were forbidden to photograph in the ghetto, he risked his life carrying out the task. He used his position in the ghetto's statistics department, where he received photographic materials and was permitted to keep a cam-

Mendel Grossman, the photographer of the Łódź ghetto, in his laboratory.

era. Upon the liquidation of the ghetto he was sent to the Königs Wusterhausen labor camp, where he secretly continued photographing, but not developing and printing. When the war front advanced and came closer, and the prisoners of the camp were taken out on the liquidation march, Grossman collapsed and died with his camera on him. The negatives of his photographs, hidden by him in the ghetto, were found and sent to Israel, but most of them were lost during the War of Independence. Those photographs that were saved were used in the book *With a Camera in the Ghetto* (New York, 1977).

BIBLIOGRAPHY

Ben-Menahem, A. "Mendel Grossman: The Photographer of the Lodz Ghetto." *Dappim: Studies of the Holocaust and the Jewish Resistance* 1 (1969): 279–288. (In Hebrew.)

ARIEH BEN-MENAHEM

GROSS-ROSEN, concentration camp established in the summer of 1940 as a satellite camp of SACHSENHAUSEN, in the vicinity of the granite quarry of Gross-Rosen, in Lower Silesia. On May 1, 1941, Gross-Rosen became an independent concentration camp; it remained in operation until mid-February 1945. Its commandants were, successively, SS-Obersturmbannführer Arthur Rödl, SS-Hauptsturmführer Wilhelm Gideon, and SS-Sturmbannführer Johannes Hassebroock. At first, the camp prisoners were put to work in the quarry, owned by the SS-Deutsche Erd- und Steinwerke GmbH (SS German Earth and Stone Works), and in the construction of the camp, which was speeded up in the summer of 1943. This was followed by the building of a large number of subcamps. The number of prisoners grew steadily, from 1,487 in 1941 to 6,780 in 1942, 15,400 in 1943, 90,314 in 1944 (not allowing for the fact that many prisoners were counted twice), and 97,414 on the eve of the camp's liquidation.

In its final stage Gross-Rosen had a prison population of 78,000 (52,000 men and 26,000 women), representing 11 percent of all the prisoners then in Nazi concentration camps.

A total of 125,000 prisoners of different nationalities passed through Gross-Rosen; the number of victims who perished in the camp and in the evacuation transports is estimated at 40,000.

Jews represented the largest group among the victims in Gross-Rosen, and their proportion in the camp population was considerable, especially in late 1943 and early 1944. Beginning in late 1943, 57,000 Jews were brought there, including 26,000 women. The assignment of Jews to the camp, and their use as manpower for the German war economy, resulted from a reorganization of the SS methods for exploiting Jews and from the evacuation of the PŁASZÓW camp and of AUSCHWITZ-Birkenau. The Jews, among them a high proportion of women, were distributed among satellite camps outside the main camp.

The first Jewish prisoners to arrive in Gross-Rosen were sent there from DACHAU (48 Jews, on June 18, 1941) and Sachsenhausen (32 on August 13, 1941, 21 on September 18 of that year, and 94 on September 20). In 1942 small groups of Jews, totaling 100 persons, arrived, from the RADOM district, from the prison in TARNÓW, and from Sachsenhausen and BUCHENWALD. They were housed in Block 4, which was run by German convicts: G. Prill, A. Radtke, and P. Alt. Prill and Radtke were particularly brutal sadists and murderers.

The living and working conditions of the Jewish prisoners were extraordinarily harsh and inhumane. In addition to the backbreaking work in the quarry and the construction of the camp, they were exploited for special work assignments during what were supposed to be their hours for rest. The Jewish prisoners were not permitted to establish contact with one another, each prisoner being restricted to his own block. They were also denied medical attention. Before long their state of health had deteriorated and they were completely exhausted. The mortality rate was high, and by the end of 1941, 84 had died. Others became *Muselmänner* (*see* MUSELMANN), and in December 1941, 119 of these were victims of a EUTHANASIA PROGRAM *Selektion*. The high mortality rate continued in 1942. Prisoners classified as "disabled" were sent to Dachau. The last 37 Jewish prisoners were transferred to Auschwitz on October 16 of that year, in the course of an operation designed to remove Jews from all camps situated in the Reich. For a period of twelve months, Gross-Rosen was *judenfrei* ("free of Jews").

In October 1943 the influx of Jewish prisoners into Gross-Rosen was renewed, this time in larger groups and transports. The first such group consisted of 600 prisoners moved from the Markstadt labor camp to Fünfteichen, a new Gross-Rosen satellite camp, where they were put to work in Krupp factories. Another group of 600 Jewish prisoners was put at the disposal of I.G. FARBEN, to work in the factories at Dyhernfurth, where poison gas was to be produced. More groups came in March 1944, inaugurating an uninterrupted flow of Jewish prisoners that continued until January 1945. Additional Gross-Rosen satellite camps were put up to accommodate them.

Most of the Jewish prisoners were from Poland and Hungary, but others were from Belgium, France, Greece, Yugoslavia, Slovakia, and Italy. The Jewish prisoners of Gross-Rosen were distributed among over fifty satellite camps, designated as *Arbeitslager* (labor camps). Most were situated in Lower Silesia, and the rest in the Sudetenland and Luzyce. Some of these satellite camps were put up when Gross-Rosen took over a number of *Zwangsarbeitslager* (forced-labor camps) from Heinrich HIMMLER's special plenipotentiary for recruiting foreign labor in Upper Silesia, ORGANISATION SCHMELT. A total of twenty-eight such forced-labor camps were appropriated by Gross-Rosen, twenty-three in Lower Silesia and five in the Sudetenland. Of these, twenty were kept in operation as Gross-Rosen satellite camps, and the prisoners from the remaining eight camps were transferred to existing satellite camps. The following satellite camps were established in this way: Bunzlau I (for men); Dyhernfurth II (for men); Gräben (for women); Gräflich-Röhrsdorf (women); Grünberg (women); Hirschberg (men); Kittlitztbren (men); Langenbielau (women and men); Merzdorf (women); Neusalz (women); Peterswaldau (women); Waldenburg (men); Wolfsberg (men); Zillerthal-Erdmannsdorf; and five camps in the Sudetenland: Bernsdorf, Gabersdorf, Ober Altstadt, Parschnitz, and Schatzlar (all for women).

A second group of completely new satellite camps for Jews was put up when more transports came in at the demand of the armaments inspector for the Silesia military district (Wehrkreis VIII) and of the ORGANISATION TODT, and, later, upon the partial evacuation of the Płaszów and Auschwitz camps. Conspicuous among these camps were the twelve in the Sudetic Mountains that comprised the *Arbeitslager Riese* (Giant Labor Camp) complex, all for men: Dörnhau, Erlenbusch, Falkenberg, Fürstenstein, Kaltwasser, Lärche and Märzbachtal, Oberwüstegiersdorf, Säuferwasser, Schotterwerk, Tannhausen, and Wolfsberg. Established from April to June 1944, these camps were a manpower reserve for the construction of Hitler's subterranean home. They held 13,000 Jews, most of them from Hungary. The hard labor involved in building subterranean passages, roads, and so forth, together with the poor living conditions and total lack of hygiene, soon caused a large number of prisoners to become *Muselmänner*. A *Selektion* was made and 857 prisoners from these camps were sent to Auschwitz, on September 29 and October 19, 1944. The mortality rate in the *Arbeitslager Riese* complex was exceptionally high; extant records reveal that at least 3,068 prisoners died there.

Other satellite camps for Jewish prisoners were Bad Warmbrunn, Balkenhain, Friedland, Schertendorf, Grünberg, Brünnlitz, and Geppersdorf, whose inmates were employed in local armaments factories. The women, distributed over forty-two satellite camps, came mostly from Poland and Hungary. They arrived from Poland when Organisation Schmelt was disbanded (and fifteen satellite camps were transferred) and, in late 1944, when Płaszów, Auschwitz-Birkenau, and the Łódź ghetto were evacuated (the last via Auschwitz). They also came from Hungary in transports that first passed through Auschwitz-Birkenau. The women's camps (*Frauenarbeitslager*) taken over from Schmelt contained 6,000 to 7,000 women. The prisoners in thirteen of these camps were employed in textile factories; in one camp, in the aircraft industry; and in another, in an armaments factory. The regime in the women's camps was less harsh; out of 5,000 prisoners, only 58 died. The other satellite camps for women were put up at the following times:

the Grafenort satellite camp in March 1944; Christianstadt in June; Breslau-Hundsfeld, Guben, and Weisswasser, in July; Freiburg and Mittelsteine, in August; Görlitz, Liebau, Wiesau, and Ober Hohenelbe, in September; Birnbaumel, Hochweiler, Kurzbach, Sackisch, Schlesiersee, Halbstadt Kratzau (I and II), and Zittau, in October; and Brünnlitz and Saint Georgenthal, in November. More women's satellite camps were established in 1945: Langenbielau, Wüstegiersdorf, Gablonz, and Morchenstern. Tens of thousands of women were concentrated in these camps and put to work in armaments factories (the prisoners from eight camps); in the aircraft industry (five camps); in the radio industry (four camps); in the Organisation Todt, constructing trenches (four camps); in textile factories (two camps); and so on.

Before 1944 there were no large transfers of Jewish prisoners from Gross-Rosen to other concentration camps, and available records show only the transfer of some 200 *Muselmänner* to Auschwitz and of 400 prisoners to Buchenwald. There were, however, frequent internal transfers from one satellite camp to another to meet current requirements of the war economy, and, at a later stage, as part of the gradual liquidation of Gross-Rosen.

In the first phase of the evacuation—the last ten days of January 1945—the satellite camps on the eastern bank of the Oder were liquidated. The men's satellite camps located there (including Fünfteichen and Dyhernfurth, with their Jewish prisoners) were moved to the main camp. The prisoners in the women's camps, for the most part, were transferred to concentration camps deep inside the Reich. The prisoners were evacuated by foot, in what came to be known as DEATH MARCHES, in the cold of winter and without food. Many prisoners perished on those marches, but no accurate estimate can be made of their number. The ultimate fate of some columns of prisoners remains unknown.

The main camp, Gross-Rosen itself, was evacuated in early February 1945, and the remaining satellite camps thereafter. Although the prisoners in the main camp were evacuated by rail, the condition of the cars that were used (they normally carried coal) and the lack of food caused the death of many after a few days in transit. The prison-

ers of the satellite camps were evacuated on foot; those of the Bunzlau camp, for example, were on the march from February 12 to March 26, 1945, with 260 perishing en route.

During the evacuation of Gross-Rosen and the satellite camps, 3,500 Jews were moved to BERGEN-BELSEN (mostly women prisoners from the Birnbaumel, Christianstadt, Hochweiler, and Kurzbach camps); 5,565 were moved to Buchenwald; 489 to Dachau; 4,930 to Flossenbürg; 2,249 to MAUTHAUSEN (mostly from the *Arbeitslager Riese* network); and 1,103 to Mittelbau. The NEUENGAMME camp also took in a small number of women prisoners from Weisswasser.

Including the transfers made in 1944, a minimum of 19,500 Jewish prisoners were moved from Gross-Rosen to concentration camps in the Reich, that is, 35 percent of the total number of Jewish prisoners in Gross-Rosen. The fate of the other 37,500 has not been established so far; some of them, no doubt, were included in the evacuation. The number of Jewish prisoners in the Gross-Rosen camp complex who did not survive is unknown, except in the case of *Arbeitslager Riese*. About half of the Jewish prisoners in the satellite camps are known to have been left behind. The surviving prisoners in these camps were liberated by Soviet troops on May 8 and 9, 1945. Of the women's satellite camps, twenty were liberated; in thirteen of them, 9,000 women survived. In Langenbielau, 1,400 surviving Jews were recorded upon liberation; in Brünnlitz, 800 had survived; and in Waldenburg, 600.

Even from these incomplete data it is clear that a large proportion of the prisoners lived to see the Nazi regime's downfall. When the satellite camps were liberated, Jewish committees were formed in them that took the prisoners under their care, especially the many who were sick. They obtained food and clothing and assisted in the prisoners' repatriation to their countries of origin.

A large number of the former Gross-Rosen prisoners gathered in Dzierżoniów (Reichenbach), and on June 17, 1945, representatives of the Jewish committees of six Lower Silesian towns convened there and formed a district committee of Polish Jews. The purpose was to coordinate activities in behalf of the surviving Jewish population under the new social and political conditions.

BIBLIOGRAPHY

Gutman, Y., and A. Saf, eds. *The Nazi Concentration Camps*. Jerusalem, 1980.

Moldawa, M. *Gross-Rosen: Obóz koncentracyjny na Śląsku*. Warsaw, 1967.

ALFRED KONIECZNY

GROSSWARDEIN. *See* Oradea.

GRUENBAUM, ITZHAK (1879–1970), Polish Jewish and Zionist leader. Gruenbaum was born in Warsaw, studied law, and was a Zionist from an early age. He edited newspapers and periodicals in Polish, Yiddish, and Hebrew, was prominent in the radical wing of the General Zionist party, and fought for the secularization of Jewish life and the promotion of the Hebrew language. From 1919 to 1932 he was a member of the Sejm (the

Itzhak Gruenbaum. [Israel Government Press Office]

Polish parliament), where he fought for equal rights for Jews as citizens and as a national minority, and was one of the sponsors and organizers of the parliamentary National Minorities Bloc.

In 1932 Gruenbaum moved to Paris, and a year later, after being elected a member of the Zionist Executive, he settled in Palestine. From 1933 to 1935 he headed the Jewish Agency's Immigration Department, and from 1935 to 1948, its Labor Department. That year he became a member of Palestinian Jewry's quasi government in the months preceding the establishment of the state. In the period of the provisional government (1948–1949), he was minister of the interior.

When World War II broke out in 1939, Gruenbaum took the initiative in establishing a Committee of Four in the Jewish Agency Executive, for assisting Polish Jewry, and became the committee's head. In January 1943, when the Jewish Agency's Joint Rescue Committee was created, he was elected its chairman. During the two years of the Rescue Committee's activities (1943–1944) Gruenbaum was the butt of harsh criticism, and there were calls for his resignation. This criticism was based on several grounds. First, Gruenbaum for a long time would not believe the reports that were coming in—with increasing frequency in 1942 —of the systematic murder of the Jews and the existence of extermination camps. As a result, by the end of that year, when he delayed making public the RIEGNER CABLE (which, on the basis of information received from a reliable German source, confirmed the systematic extermination of the Jews), he was accused of deliberately hushing up these reports. Second, by early 1943 Gruenbaum despaired of the chances of any large-scale rescue efforts succeeding, and concluded that Palestine Jewry's main task was to prepare a haven of refuge in Palestine for those Jews who would survive; therefore, the needs in Palestine took priority over those of the Jews in the Diaspora. He was of the opinion that no public mourning over what was happening in Europe should take place in Palestine, and that the Zionist National Funds should not allocate money for rescue efforts.

Gruenbaum aired his views in no uncertain terms, in a manner that many found objectionable. A third complaint was that Gruenbaum was not devoting all his attention to rescue work because of the many posts he held, as head of a Jewish Agency department and a member of numerous committees. Gruenbaum's critics failed to realize that despite his opinions and his refusal to resign from his many other posts, he was exerting himself in behalf of rescue. He did this mainly by raising funds from sources other than the national funds, and by means of the far-flung correspondence he conducted with statesmen and institutions the world over, to solicit their support for the saving of Jews—even though he had little hope on that score. He initiated various ideas and proposals that he tried to implement, and advocated "rescue for rescue's sake," to any place in the world, and not necessarily in order to bring Jews to Palestine.

Gruenbaum's chairmanship of the Rescue Committee eventually became the great tragedy of his life. Subsumed in that tragedy were the severe censure to which he was exposed, the Rescue Committee's weak status and lack of authority, his strained relations with David BEN-GURION, his ongoing dispute with the religious political parties over his efforts for the separation of religion and state, the knowledge that his son Eliezer was a prisoner in Birkenau (and later in BUCHEN-WALD), and, above all, the destruction of Polish Jewry, which he had not been able to prevent.

After the war Gruenbaum's son was charged with having been a KAPO, but was cleared of the charge. He settled in Israel and fell in Israel's War of Independence, in 1948. During Palestinian Jewry's struggle with the British, Gruenbaum was arrested and interned for a time in Latrun, together with other Zionist leaders. When the state of Israel was declared, on May 14, 1948, Gruenbaum did not affix his signature to the Independence scroll, since he refused to leave besieged Jerusalem to attend the ceremony (which took place in Tel Aviv). As minister of the interior, Gruenbaum organized the elections to the constituent assembly (the First Knesset), but he himself was not elected. Thereafter he kept up his writing and Zionist activities, in which he stated his views, now strongly leftist.

BIBLIOGRAPHY

Porat, D. "Al-Domi: Palestinian Intellectuals and the Holocaust." *Studies in Zionism* 5/1 (Spring 1984): 92–124.

Prister, R. *Without Compromise: Yitzhak Gruenbaum, Zionist Leader and Polish Patriot.* Tel Aviv, 1987. (In Hebrew.)

DINA PORAT

GRÜNINGER, PAUL (1891–1972), local police commandant of the Saint Gall canton in Switzerland, on the Austrian frontier, who was responsible for assisting thousands of Jewish refugees.

After Austria's annexation by Germany in March 1938, the stream of Jewish refugees seeking to leave the Reich increased, and many sought to gain access to Switzerland. But at this critical juncture, the Swiss government closed its borders to Jewish refugees. Grüninger was instructed on August 18, 1938, to refuse entry to refugees fleeing Germany for racial reasons. Confronted by an unending wave of Jewish refugees at his border post, he defied his government's instructions and allowed all the Jews crossing the border at his

Paul Grüninger (left) in police uniform (February 15, 1934).

checkpoint entry into the country. As a cover-up, he predated official seals in the refugees' passports to indicate that their holders had entered the country prior to the August 1938 government ruling. Thus, from August through December 1938, when he was summarily suspended, Grüninger allowed some thirty-six hundred persons (according to the state prosecutor) illegal entry into Switzerland.

Alerted by the German legation in Bern, the Swiss government in January 1939 opened an inquiry into Grüninger's activities, and charges were filed against him. Found guilty of insubordination, he was sentenced in 1941 to a stiff fine and the forfeiture of all retirement and severance payments. Grüninger was later denied access to other suitable positions in the government and the private sector, and he was never fully rehabilitated by the Swiss government. In 1971, he received recognition from YAD VASHEM as a "RIGHTEOUS AMONG THE NATIONS."

BIBLIOGRAPHY

Häsler, A. A. *The Lifeboat Is Full: Switzerland and the Refugees, 1933–1945.* New York, 1969.

MORDECAI PALDIEL

GRYNSZPAN, HERSCHEL (1921–1943?), refugee assassin of a German diplomat in Paris. Born in Hannover of Polish nationality, Grynszpan fled to Paris in 1936. On November 7, 1938, having learned of the deportation of his parents from Germany to ZBĄSZYŃ, on the Polish frontier, he shot the third secretary of the German embassy in Paris, Ernst vom Rath, as a protest, and promptly surrendered to the police. When the diplomat died two days later, the Nazis launched the KRISTALL-NACHT riots throughout the Reich.

In 1940, the Vichy government turned Grynszpan over to the Germans. Two years later, the Nazi authorities planned a great show trial, orchestrated by Joseph GOEBBELS, hoping to demonstrate Grynszpan's link with a Jewish conspiracy to plunge Europe into war. Grynszpan himself seems to have sabotaged this scheme by reviving a story he had fabricated about a homosexual liaison between the

Herschel Grynszpan being taken from police headquarters in Paris.

diplomat and his assassin. His manner of death has never been clarified, but he almost certainly did not survive the war.

BIBLIOGRAPHY

Heiber, H. "Der Fall Grünspan." *Vierteljahrshefte für Zeitgeschichte* 5 (1975): 134–172.

Marrus, M. R. "The Strange Story of Herschel Grynszpan." *The American Scholar* 57 (1987–1988): 69–79.

Roizen, R. "Herschel Grynszpan: The Fate of a Forgotten Assassin." *Holocaust and Genocide Studies* 1/2 (1986): 217–228.

MICHAEL R. MARRUS

GUNSKIRCHEN, assembly camp for the Jewish prisoners from the MAUTHAUSEN concentration camp that went into operation in March 1945. It was situated in the vicinity of the town of the same name, which was close to Wels, a city in Upper Austria. In April 1945 the camp comprised seven unfinished huts and

Under the supervision of the Seventy-first Infantry Division of the United States Third Army, German soldiers, prisoners of war, remove dead victims from the Gunskirchen concentration camp. [United States Army]

two huts used as auxiliary structures. Administratively, the camp was separate from the Mauthausen camp network, and was utilized as an assembly point for Jewish prisoners only. The camp commandant was an SS-Obersturmführer Werner.

In the second half of April, some seventeen thousand to twenty thousand prisoners were brought from the tent camp that had been set up at Mauthausen, and from other camps. All of them were packed into the Gunskirchen camp. The prisoners already there had ceased to work; their weakness was such that they were close to death. There was one toilet for all the prisoners, and drinking water was distributed from a tank holding 396.4 gallons (1,500 l), brought to the camp once a day on a fire truck. The prisoners fought for a sip of water and even sold their daily bread ration in exchange for it. About twenty-five hundred people were compressed into each hut; as a result, the weak were crushed to death at night. Epidemics of typhus and dysentery

were rife. The doctors among the prisoners were unable to offer assistance, for there were no medical facilities whatever, and the mortality rate in the camp increased daily. The food rations were even smaller than those in the tent camp at Mauthausen, and many prisoners were saved only by small supplements of food from the Red Cross packages that were distributed once or twice. A truck arrived daily in the camp to transport the day's corpses to a grave dug in the nearby forest. As the mortality rate increased, burial pits were dug in the camp's limited area.

On May 4, 1945, all the SS officers disappeared from the camp. The prisoners overran the food stores next to the kitchen and seized everything they could lay their hands on. On the following day, May 5, a United States Army Medical Corps unit arrived at the camp. It was littered with corpses, and those prisoners still alive were filthy, lice-infested skeletons. The American unit transferred the sick and the dying to a temporary hospital in nearby Wels. At the time of the liberation there were 5,419 survivors; an unknown number of prisoners had departed on the eve of the liberation. Seven communal graves were discovered in the camp, containing the remains of 1,227 victims.

BIBLIOGRAPHY

Adler, S. *In the Valley of Death: A Year in the Life of a Youth in a Concentration Camp.* Jerusalem, 1979. (In Hebrew.)
Eckstein, B. *Mauthausen: Concentration and Annihilation Camp.* Jerusalem, 1984. (In Hebrew.)

BENYAMIN ECKSTEIN

GURS, the first detention camp to be established in FRANCE, and one of the largest. The Gurs camp was situated in a locality of the same name, 50 miles (80 km) from the Spanish border and 10 miles (16 km) from the town of Oloron-Sainte-Marie, on the plateau overlooking the lower Pyrenees.

The Gurs camp was set up in April 1939, coinciding with the collapse of the Spanish republic, and the first prisoners to be detained in it were Spanish republican soldiers who had fled to France in the wake of Franco's victory; among them were Jewish volunteers of the International Brigade. In early 1940 some four thousand German and Austrian nationals—most of them Jews—were interned in Gurs, as well as leaders of the French Communist party who had denounced the war against Germany, in line with the NAZI-SOVIET PACT. Between October 22 and 25, 1940, four months after France had surrendered, the German authorities—in violation of the armistice with France—deported to Gurs the entire Jewish population of Baden and the Palatinate, as well as Jews from some locations in Württemberg. Some seventy-five hundred Jews were included in Aktion Bürckel, so named after Josef Bürckel, the *Gauleiter* of Alsace-Lorraine.

All the non-Jewish German nationals and pro-Nazis had been released from Gurs in mid-July 1940, shortly after the French defeat. The French Communists were set free at the end of October 1940; of the Jews, some two thousand were released in stages between November 1940 and August 1942, with the help of HICEM, and emigrated overseas.

Conditions in the camp were very harsh: the sanitary arrangements were primitive, there was a shortage of water, and all the detainees suffered constantly from hunger. In the winter of 1940–1941, 800 detainees died in epidemics of diseases such as typhoid fever

A view of the Gurs concentration camp.

and dysentery that broke out in the camp. A total of 1,187 detainees were buried in the Gurs cemetery; 20 of these were non-Jewish Spaniards and all the rest Jews.

Despite the harsh conditions in the camp, many cultural activities were conducted there, in various fields and on a very high level—concerts, theater performances, lectures, and exhibitions. There were also courses of instruction in Hebrew, French, and English, Jewish history, the Bible, and the Talmud, and thousands of prisoners attended religious ceremonies and prayer services on the holy days.

Six thousand Jewish prisoners were deported from Gurs to AUSCHWITZ-Birkenau and SOBIBÓR by way of the DRANCY camp, the first transport leaving Gurs on August 6, 1942, and the last in the fall of 1943; by December 29, 1943, no more than forty-eight Jews were left. The camp was liberated in the summer of 1944. The French poet Louis Aragon said of the Gurs camp: "Gurs is a strange sound, like a moan stuck in the throat."

BIBLIOGRAPHY

Krehbiel-Darmstaedter, M. *Briefe aus Gurs und Limonest, 1940–1943.* Heidelberg, 1970.

Marrus, M. R., and R. O. Paxton. *Vichy France and the Jews.* New York, 1981.

Rutkowski, A. "Le camp d'internement de Gurs." *Le Monde Juif* 100 (1980): 128–146; 101 (1981): 13–32.

Schramm, H. *Menschen in Gurs: Erinnerungen an ein französischen Internierlager (1940–1941).* Worms, 1977.

ADAM RUTKOWSKI

GUSEN, camp established in Germany as the first branch of the MAUTHAUSEN camp. Gusen was 2.8 miles (4.5 km) to the west of the main camp, near St. Georgen, and was put into operation on March 9, 1940. In its first two years, the Gusen camp maintained its own register of prisoners, but later they were listed and numbered together with the Mauthausen prisoners. From May 1940 to the end of that year, 5,000 prisoners were brought to Gusen, where they were put to work in local quarries and brickyards. During that period 1,507 prisoners died in the camp, their deaths recorded in the camp's separate register. In addition, 240 Polish officers and students were shot to death in Gusen, on orders of the Gestapo in Poland and in accordance

A general view of the Gusen concentration camp, which was liberated on May 5, 1945, by the United States Army. [United States Army]

with a list it submitted to the camp administration (which was commanded by SS-Hauptsturmführer Karl Chmielewski). The camp contained thirty wooden barracks and two stone buildings. At first, six of the barracks were used as a hospital; four more were designated as hospital barracks in the winter of 1943–1944. In 1943, railway lines were laid to the quarries and to the Messerschmitt and Steyr plants operating in the camp, which employed many of the prisoners in the manufacture of aircraft parts and machine guns.

A second camp, designated as Gusen II, was opened on March 9, 1944, with 10,000 prisoners, followed by a third, Gusen III, in December 1944, with 262 prisoners. Gusen II prisoners were engaged in the construction of underground passages leading to the armament plants' workshops; one of the passages —which was 4 miles (7 km) long, 26 feet (8 m) wide, and 23 feet (7 m) high—was completed, enabling Steyr to manufacture ball bearings there. No other passage had been completed by the end of the war.

Living conditions for the prisoners in the camps were extremely harsh. Driven by the camp staff, which was made up primarily of ex-convicts, the prisoners had to maintain a fast pace in their work, and those who were unable to keep it up were killed. In the period from October 1941 to May 1942, 2,151 Soviet prisoners were listed in the camp's register of death, in addition to prisoners of other nationalities.

Barrack No. 30 was an assembly point for prisoners who had been selected for killing by phenol injections. This was also where debilitated prisoners were beaten to death by the *Blockälteste* (barrack elder). From time to time groups of prisoners were taken to nearby Hartheim castle, to be killed in the gas chambers that had been set up there.

A total of 67,677 persons were imprisoned in the Gusen camps, nearly half of whom —31,535—were listed as having died there. The figure does not include at least 2,500 persons, mostly Jews, who died in the camps without having their deaths recorded, and the 2,630 Gusen prisoners who were taken to Hartheim to be gassed there.

The Gusen camps were liberated on May 5, 1945, by American troops, but the condition of some two thousand of the prisoners was so poor that they died at about the time the camps were set free. Chmielewski, who had been camp commandant up to 1942, was tried by a court in Ansbach after the war and sentenced to life imprisonment.

BIBLIOGRAPHY

Eckstein, B. *Mauthausen: Concentration and Annihilation Camp.* Jerusalem, 1984. (In Hebrew.)
Le Chêne, E. *Mauthausen: The History of a Death Camp.* London, 1971.
Marsalek, H., and K. Hacker. *Kurzgeschichte der Konzentrationslager Mauthausen und seiner drei grössten Nebenlager Gusen, Ebensee, und Melk.* Vienna, n.d.

BENYAMIN ECKSTEIN

GUSTLOFF, WILHELM (1895–1936), German leader of the Nazis in Switzerland. Gustloff was born in Schwerin. In 1917 he moved to Davos, Switzerland, for reasons of health. He joined the Nazi party in 1929 and in 1932 was appointed head of the party's AUSLANDSORGANISATION (Foreign Organization) in Switzerland.

Gustloff made special efforts to have the PROTOCOLS OF THE ELDERS OF ZION, an antisemitic forgery, widely distributed, causing Jewish circles in Switzerland to sue for libel the book's distributor, the Swiss Nazi party. Gustloff himself remained in the background, since as a foreigner he was in danger of being expelled from the country. His share, however, in the unrestrained anti-Jewish agitation being stirred up at the time was public knowledge. This caused David FRANKFURTER, a Jewish student, to ambush Gustloff at his home in Davos and shoot him to death, on February 4, 1936.

The Nazi regime made him a martyr, and at his funeral in Schwerin, Adolf Hitler himself eulogized Gustloff. Nazi propaganda claimed that the assassination was a conspiracy planned by "international Jewry," although in fact Frankfurter had acted on his own initiative. Because of the Olympic games, however, which were about to be held in Berlin, in August 1936, Nazi reaction to the assassination was restrained.

BIBLIOGRAPHY

Diewerge, W. *Der Fall Gustloff.* Munich, 1936.

Diewerge, W. *Ein Jude hat geschossen.* Munich, 1937.

Frankfurter, D. "I Killed a Nazi Gauleiter: Memoir of a Jewish Assassin." *Commentary* 9/2 (February 1950): 133–141.

DAVID HADAR

GWARDIA LUDOWA (People's Guard), underground army organization in occupied PO-LAND. Created in January 1942 by the Polska Partia Robotnicza (Polish Workers' Party; PPR), the Gwardia Ludowa was active in the GENERALGOUVERNEMENT and the areas of Poland annexed to the Reich. It was directed by a supreme command and had a staff that was divided into sections.

The organization's area of activity was broken down by districts and regions. In the spring of 1942 the first Gwardia Ludowa partisan units were formed according to the instructions of the heads of the PPR, and they commenced sabotage activities immediately. Various estimates for late 1943 put the organization's membership at fifteen thousand to twenty thousand; its scores of units directed and conducted military and sabotage actions.

In 1942 and 1943, Gwardia Ludowa units carried out about seventeen hundred military actions, according to the organization's records. In January 1944, the Gwardia Ludowa became the Armia Ludowa (People's Army), by order of the Krajowa Rada Narodowa (Polish National Council), an organization founded on January 1, 1944, by Communists and Communist sympathizers. Gen. Michał Zymierski, known as "Rola," was appointed commander of the Armia Ludowa, which retained the same organizational structure as that of the Gwardia Ludowa.

By the summer of 1944 the Armia Ludowa had about thirty-four thousand members. From January 1944 to January 1945, according to the estimates of its General Staff, Armia Ludowa forces carried out more than fifteen hundred military actions of different kinds, about half of them against German transport and communications.

Several units of Jewish partisans, which had initially operated independently, joined the ranks of the Gwardia Ludowa and the Armia Ludowa. The best known was Yehiel

A group of partisan fighters from Yehiel Grynszpan's unit attached to the Armia Ludowa.

Grynszpan's unit in the Parczew Forest (*see* PARTISANS). Originally an independent unit, it became a family camp (*see* FAMILY CAMPS IN THE FORESTS) and subsequently received aid from the Armia Ludowa.

The Gwardia Ludowa provided the ŻYDOWSKA ORGANIZACJA BOJOWA (Jewish Fighting Organization; ŻOB) in the WARSAW ghetto with a small quantity of arms, and during the WARSAW GHETTO UPRISING its units attempted several unsuccessful military holding actions outside the ghetto walls. In July 1944 the Armia Ludowa merged with the Polish army formed in the Soviet Union, which fought under the command of Gen. Zygmunt Berling together with the Soviet army. In this way the Polish army of the new Polish government was created.

[*See also* Armia Krajowa.]

BIBLIOGRAPHY

Ciechanowski, J. M. *The Warsaw Rising of 1944.* Cambridge, 1974.

Historia Polskiego Ruchu Robotniczego: 1939–1944. Vol. 4. Warsaw, 1984.

Korbonski, S. *The Polish Underground State: A Guide to the Underground, 1939–1945.* New York, 1969.

Wieczorek, M. *Armia Ludowa: Powstanie i organizacja 1944–1945.* 2 vols. Warsaw, 1979, 1984.

EUGENIUSZ DURACZYNSKI

GYPSIES, a people living in Europe from the fifteenth century, bound by a common language and culture, and—until the twentieth century—by a nomadic way of life. The Gypsies, also called Rom, were among the groups singled out by the Nazi regime for persecution.

While there are differences of opinion regarding their early history, it seems fairly clear that the Gypsies originated in India and were in Iran by the fourteenth century. By 1438, they had reached Hungary, and had entered Serbia and other Balkan countries. They then spread into Poland and Russia, and by the sixteenth century had reached Sweden and England. In Spain they settled in fairly large numbers at the same time. While some Gypsies became Muslims (in Bosnia, the Crimea, and elsewhere) or Orthodox (in Serbia), most European Gypsies became Roman Catholics, but kept many of their pre-Christian beliefs alongside their new religion. Split into many dialects, their language is only now becoming a written language, though Romany publications appeared in the Soviet Union in the early years of the Communist regime.

Prejudice and animosity toward Gypsies were and are widespread. Their professions were dictated by their wandering way of life; they were usually not allowed to obtain land in their adopted countries. Generally, they bought and sold horses and other animals, engaged in petty trade, and practiced arts such as silverwork, goldwork, and music. Fortune-telling, for which they gained a wide reputation, was usually a sideline. Gypsies were frequently accused of stealing and dishonesty, largely because of their living habits and language. Aggression was diverted toward them in a process of transference, to a certain extent similar to that applied to the Jews. On occasion, this animosity turned into murderous policies. Thus, the Prussian king, Frederick William I, decreed in 1725 that all Gypsies over eighteen were subject to killing. At the same time, their music and their poetry were the inspiration of famous artists, for example Franz Liszt. Although for different historical reasons, in many ways they shared with the Jews the doubtful honor of being the quintessential strangers in an overwhelmingly sedentary, Christian Europe.

With the advent of modern industrial society, the Gypsies were out of place in the eyes of the authorities. In 1899 Bavaria established a special office for Gypsy affairs; it was the center for anti-Gypsy policies in Germany until the Nazi period. In February 1929, the Munich office became a Central Bureau, with close ties to a similar office in Vienna. In 1929, regulations came into effect that enabled the police to coerce Gypsies, who had no permanent occupation, to work at forced labor. Similar regulations were operative in a number of other European countries.

The Gypsies occupied a special place in Nazi racist theories. According to a report submitted to Heinrich HIMMLER in 1941, there were some twenty-eight thousand Gypsies in Germany, and an additional eleven thousand in Austria. Most of these Gypsies belonged to the Sinti and Lalleri tribes. The basic attitude of the Nazi regime was extremely hostile; old prejudices and animosities were added to an ideal of a "pure" Nordic society that emphasized peasant life and sedentary habits. This stood in clear contradiction to the Gypsies' way of life. In the eyes of the regime, the Gypsies were "asocials" who did not fit into the new society that was to be built. While one could not very well doubt the Aryan parentage of the closely knit Gypsy families, they were also clearly "people of different blood" (*Andersblütige*).

With the advent of the NUREMBERG LAWS in September 1935, the interpreters of the decrees explicitly included the Gypsies, along with the Jews, in their regulations. In 1936, groups of Gypsies were delivered to the DACHAU camp as "asocials." At this time a racist ideologue, Dr. Robert Ritter, was empowered to set up a Research Office for the Science of Inheritance (Erbwissenschaftliche Forschungsstelle). In 1937 it became the Research Office for Race Hygiene and Population Biology (Rassenhygienische und Bevölkerungsbiologische Forschungsstelle). Dr. Ritter was to examine the Gypsy population from the Nazi point of view and propose solutions as to what to do with them.

According to Dr. Ritter and his co-workers, an examination of some twenty thousand Rom showed that over 90 percent were to be considered MISCHLINGE (of mixed blood). This solved the problem of having to deal with an Aryan minority; the Nazis simply denied that the Gypsies were Aryans. Ritter's proposals were to prevent Gypsies from mixing with people of "German blood," to separate "pure" Gypsies from *Mischlinge* Gypsies, and to perform sterilizations on the latter, while putting them in forced-labor camps. Both "pure" and *Mischlinge* Gypsies were considered "asocial"—work-shy individuals and aliens. Here the Nazis maintained an important element of continuity with traditional European discriminatory thought. According to Himmler's decree of December 14, 1937, "preventive" arrests could be made of persons who, while not guilty of any criminal act, "endangered the communality by their asocial behavior." Administrative regulations implementing this decree, which were issued on April 4, 1938, specified that it was directed against "beggars, vagabonds (Gypsies), prostitutes . . . without a permanent residence."

It soon became clear to the Nazis that this provision was too broad and could not be implemented at the time. Therefore, further regulation of March 1, 1939, classified Himmler's underlying ideas and his practical policies. As a basis for dealing with what he labeled "the Gypsy plague," he called for a separation between Gypsies and Germans, and between "pure" and *Mischlinge* Gypsies. The way of life of both latter categories would be regulated by the police.

Contrary to this provision, but in line with the general radicalization of Nazi racial policies, the fate of the German Gypsies became tied up with that of the Poles and Jews after the Nazi conquest of Poland. In September 1939, Reinhard HEYDRICH issued instructions projecting the removal of thirty thousand Gypsies from all of Germany to the GENERALGOUVERNEMENT, together with the removal of Poles and Jews from the newly occupied western Polish territories. This order may have been designed to remove all *Mischlinge* Gypsies from Germany. However, plans went amiss—with respect to the Gypsies as well as to the Jews and the Poles. In the end, in April 1940, the Nazi governor of the Generalgouvernement, Hans FRANK, received twenty-five hundred Gypsies, who were removed from the western territories to the Generalgouvernement. These Gypsies were mostly released in Poland.

Attitudes toward the Gypsies became more brutal as time went on. In the fall of 1941, 5,007 Austrian Gypsies of the Lalleri tribe were deported to the ŁÓDŹ ghetto. They were included among the victims of the mass murders committed against the Jews in the CHEŁMNO extermination camp in early 1942. No survivors are known. Three thousand more Austrian Gypsies were put into concentration camps at the same time.

In the meantime 18,922 (or roughly two-thirds) of the 28,607 German Gypsies had been classified by Ritter: 1,079 were defined as "pure," 6,992 as "more Gypsy than German," 2,976 as "half-breeds," 2,992 as "more German than Gypsy," 2,652 were "Germans who behaved as Gypsies," and 2,231 were still being investigated. From the Nazi point of view, and in light of the radicalization of Nazi racial policies, the "problem" was one of thoroughgoing clarification, which meant —in Nazi logic—murder on the one hand, control on the other. "Pure" Gypsies could not, by this logic, be excluded from society —that is, murdered. And so, on October 13, 1942, Himmler issued a clarification "relating to Gypsy chiefs," concerning pure "Sinti Gypsies for whom in the future a certain freedom of movement is to be permitted." *Mischlinge,* "who are good *Mischlinge* in the Gypsy sense, are to be reintroduced into racially pure Sinti Gypsy clans." The same would apply to the surviving Austrian Lalleri. For these "pure" or relatively "pure" Gypsies, there would be appointed nine chiefs *(Obmänner),* who would supervise the "certain freedom of movement" to be allowed their charges. According to a document of January 11, 1943, 13,000 Sinti and 1,017 Lalleri were to be considered under this lifesaving provision. As to the others, Himmler issued a clear order on December 16, 1942, indicating that they were to be sent to AUSCHWITZ, except for those who were "socially adapted," "former Wehrmacht soldiers," or "war industry workers in important positions." For these exempted categories, sterilization was proposed.

In reality, the distinctions were not that clear. The first large transport of Gypsies arrived in Auschwitz on February 26, 1943, and a Gypsy family camp was established in Birkenau. The number of Gypsies in the Auschwitz "Gypsy camp" is believed to have been about 20,000. Living, or rather existing, in the most indescribable conditions, a great many of them died from starvation, epidemics, and "medical experiments," such as Josef MENGELE's experiments with twins. On August 2, 1944, 2,897 Gypsies were gassed as part of the destruction of the Gypsy family camp. Practically all the women and children were killed, this being a time when the Hungarian Jewish transports had ceased arriving in large numbers and the gas chambers were available. Some of the men were sent to slave-labor camps or other concentration camps to do vital war work. Others were recruited into the Wehrmacht to clear away mines or perform other life-endangering

functions, from which only a fraction returned.

It is unlikely that German statistics on Gypsies and "Germans wandering about in the Gypsy manner" were very accurate, nor need the documents regulating exceptions be taken literally. Auschwitz survivors have related stories of Gypsies—good Nazis and loyal Germans, some of officer rank—who were weeded out of German army units and sent to Auschwitz. Others, apparently, were not touched; it depended on the zeal of the local commander or the civilian party boss, and on his interpretation of the instructions. Nor were the Gypsies shipped to Auschwitz all German citizens. The order of December 16, 1942, mentioned above referred to "Gypsy *Mischlinge,* Rom Gypsies, and members of clans of Balkan origins who are not of German blood." Clearly, the Nazis got mixed up in the intricacies of their own language. What was meant, it seems, were non-Sinti Gypsies; members of the clans known as Rom were "of Balkan origins."

The total number of German and Austrian Gypsies deported to Auschwitz was 13,000. If one excludes the category of "Germans who behaved as Gypsies," Ritter's German Sinti "Gypsies" numbered 25,955. This number, combined with the roughly 11,000 Austrian Lalleri, made for a total of about 37,000. Of this total, 2,500 were deported to Poland in 1939 and 1940 and mostly killed later; 3,000 were interned in Austrian camps, and presumably mostly killed; 5,000 were sent to Łódź and gassed at Chełmno; and 13,000 were deported to Auschwitz and mostly killed there. This breakdown, totaling 23,500, leaves 13,500 unaccounted for. These probably are the 14,017 Sintis and Lalleri defined by Himmler as pure or nearly pure Gypsies who would be spared.

Before the dismemberment of Czechoslovakia, about thirteen thousand Gypsies lived in the territories that would constitute the Protectorate of BOHEMIA AND MORAVIA. About half escaped to SLOVAKIA before the Nazis began to deport Gypsies. Some four thousand were sent to Auschwitz between July 1943 and May 1944, and only a few hundred Czech Gypsies survived the war.

Information as to the fate of the Gypsies in

the rest of Europe is sketchy. According to one source, more than two hundred thousand were killed all over Europe (Zulch, 1979). This, however, may be an underestimate. In Yugoslavia, Gypsies were murdered together with Jews by the USTAŠA regime; possibly as many as ninety thousand were killed.

In the occupied areas of Europe, the Nazis generally interned Gypsies and later transported them to Germany or Poland for use as workers or to be killed. Apparently BULGARIA, DENMARK, FINLAND, and GREECE were the only countries where the Gypsies escaped this treatment. In the NETHERLANDS, Gypsies, like the Jews, were interned in WESTERBORK and from there sent to Auschwitz. Gypsies from LUXEMBOURG and BELGIUM were also sent to the notorious extermination camp.

Before the Nazi occupation, French authorities had already restricted the movement of Gypsies. After the defeat of FRANCE in June 1940, Gypsies from Alsace and Lorraine were interned in a camp at Schirmeck, where they were kept separate from "asocials" and "criminals." Shortly before Christmas 1941, they were deported. In unoccupied France, thirty thousand Gypsies were interned under the supervision of Xavier VALLAT and the Ministry for Jewish Affairs. Later, most were sent to camps in Germany, including BUCHENWALD, Dachau, and RAVENSBRÜCK, where between sixteen thousand and eighteen thousand perished. In Algeria as well, Gypsies were interned; seven hundred were restricted to the Maison Carrée area near Algiers.

Gypsies in ITALY, like the Jews, had a mixed experience. Often persecuted, many were also saved by the Italians. Before the war the authorities rounded up Gypsies and put them on islands off the mainland. Later, Gypsies in the Three Venices area were sent to Germany on forced labor or to extermination camps. Others, however, who managed to escape the Ustaša massacres in Croatia, were sheltered by the authorities. In the fall of 1943, when the Germans took over territories that the Italians had held in Yugoslavia and Albania, they interned the Gypsies and sent some to Buchenwald, MAUTHAUSEN, and other camps.

Although the Hungarians planned to intern Gypsies in labor camps as early as February 1941, the policy was never fully implemented. After the ARROW CROSS PARTY coup in October 1944, persecution of Gypsies began in earnest in HUNGARY. Germans and Hungarian collaborators rounded up Gypsies, deporting some together with Hungarian Jews. Reputedly, some thirty-one thousand Gypsies were deported within a few months and only three thousand returned. The sources for these figures, however, are not clear.

The large Romanian Gypsy population was not exposed to an outright extermination policy. According to a postwar Romanian People's Court, however, tens of thousands met their death through the expulsion. In 1941 and 1942, about twenty-five thousand Gypsies from the Bucharest area were sent to TRANSNISTRIA, and others were sent to the Ukraine.

Slovak Gypsies were treated somewhat better than those in the Protectorate. On January 18, 1940, along with young Jewish men, they were drafted into labor brigades. Orders issued in 1941 to expel them from their quarters in most towns and villages were carried out unevenly. Slovak fascists, however, murdered hundreds of Gypsies in pogromlike rampages.

Most Gypsies in Poland faced deportation to concentration and extermination camps. Beginning in September 1944, the majority of those remaining in the ghettos were killed. About twenty-five thousand persons, some two-thirds of the Polish Gypsies, died during the Nazi occupation.

In the Baltic States and the SOVIET UNION, Gypsies were murdered by the EINSATZGRUPPEN, who mentioned the killings in their reports. A report by the secret army field police (Geheime Feldpolizei), dispatched on August 25, 1942, stressed the need to "ruthlessly exterminate" bands of wandering Gypsies. Apparently, Gypsies were murdered along with Jews at BABI YAR near Kiev. In May 1943, Alfred ROSENBERG, the minister for the Eastern Occupied Territories, proposed that the Gypsies be concentrated in special camps and settlements. They were not, however, to be "treated as Jews." Himmler, in his order of November 15, 1943, said: "(1) Sedentary Gypsies and part Gypsies are to be treated as citizens of the country. (2) Nomadic Gypsies and part Gypsies are to be placed on the same level as Jews and placed in concentration camps. In cases of doubt, the police commanders will decide who is a Gypsy." The distinction between sedentary Gypsies and nomadic Gypsies was applied only in the Baltic states and the occupied areas of the Soviet Union. Some sedentary Gypsies in the latter were drafted into labor brigades or sent to concentration camps.

The Nazis' killing of wandering groups of Gypsies stood in contradiction to the notion that the "pure" Gypsies were the wandering ones, and should therefore be spared. Moreover, there is no evidence that the Germans tried to ferret out sedentary Gypsies, or even conducted special campaigns to find and register wandering Gypsies with the aim of murdering them.

What emerges is a seemingly confused picture. In the Reich, the Nazis murdered those whom they saw as *Mischlinge* while they mostly spared the "pure" Gypsies. In the rest of Europe they did not have a very clear policy, except that wherever they found wandering clans of Gypsies, they murdered them —as "asocials," as Otto OHLENDORF, commander of SS-Einsatzgruppe D, said at his trial. The fate of the Gypsies was in line with Nazi thought on the whole: Gypsies were not Jews, and therefore there was no need to kill all of them. Those Gypsies who were of "pure blood" or who were not considered dangerous on a racial level could continue to exist, under strict supervision. The *Mischlinge* were, as a matter of course, doomed to death. The difference between the fate of the Gypsies and that of the Jews is clear. The Jews were slated for total annihilation, whereas the Gypsies were sentenced to selective mass murder on a vast scale. Even today the Gypsies are still a persecuted minority, and research about their history in the Nazi period remains sketchy.

BIBLIOGRAPHY

Kenrick, D., and G. Puxon. *The Destiny of Europe's Gypsies.* London, 1972.

Porter, J. N., ed. *Genocide and Human Rights: A Global Anthology.* Washington, D.C., 1981. See pages 151–192.

Yoors, J. *Die Zigeuner.* Stuttgart, 1970.

Zulch, T., ed. *In Auschwitz vergast; bis heute verfolgt.* Hamburg, 1979.

YEHUDA BAUER

H

HAAVARA AGREEMENT, an agreement between the German economic authorities on the one hand and the Zionistische Vereinigung für Deutschland (German Zionist Federation; ZVfD) and Anglo-Palestine Bank on the other; the Hebrew word *haavara* means "transfer." The pact was signed in early August 1933 after three months of negotiations. It made possible the export of Jewish capital from Germany to Palestine in the form of goods, by either immigrants or investors, and also assisted Jewish emigration from Germany.

While the Jewish response to the Nazi persecution of German Jewry was principally aimed at the preservation of Jewish rights, as symbolized by the anti-Nazi BOYCOTTS, the Zionist interest focused primarily on the prospects of utilizing the crisis to attract immigration to Palestine. The main obstacle in the way of emigration from Germany was the German legislation banning the export of foreign currency. These laws had been enacted by pre-Nazi governments during the world economic crisis in order to stop the flight of capital, but some loopholes had been left that were soon grasped by German Zionist leaders, both in Germany and Palestine.

In May 1933 Chaim Arlosoroff, head of the Jewish Agency's Political Department, visited Germany. He concluded that massive immigration from Germany depended on the establishment of an internationally guaranteed liquidation bank that would dispose in an orderly manner of Jewish assets in Germany and transfer their equivalent to Palestine through the export of German products. Thus Germany would be compensated for the loss of foreign currency by the increase in its production and international trade. At the same time, a Jewish businessman from Palestine, Sam Cohen, made a private agreement with the German Ministry of Economics that allowed prospective immigrants to transfer their capital in the form of certain goods through Cohen's company, up to the limit of 3 million reichsmarks.

After the murder of Arlosoroff in Tel Aviv in June 1933, Cohen made a new pact with the German authorities that expanded the previous one. This time the ZVfD opposed the move and put pressure on both Cohen and the German officials to bring in the Anglo-Palestine Bank as trustee of the transferers. Under the combined pressure, the Transfer Agreement was concluded. It served as a basis for all subsequent understandings concerning "capitalist" immigration to Palestine, though various changes were introduced throughout the 1930s.

The pact provided for two separate categories of transferers: (1) immigrants who wished to transfer money in excess of 1,000 pounds sterling; (2) investors who wanted to invest money in Palestine but for the time being remained in Germany. This second category also permitted the transfer of contributions to the Zionist national funds, tuition money for students, and pensions. Two companies were established for the implementation of the accord: PALTREU (Palästina Treuhandstelle zur Beratung Deutscher Juden) in Berlin and Haavara in Tel Aviv. The first was a partnership of the Anglo-

Palestine Bank (represented by the Zionist movement's Palestine Office in Berlin) and the German Jewish banks of Max WARBURG and Oskar Wassermann; it received the deposits in reichsmarks and purchased the German products for export. The second was a subsidiary company of the Anglo-Palestine Bank that disposed of the imported goods in Palestine and reimbursed the immigrants accordingly, or acted as a trustee for investors who remained in Germany.

Zionist interest in the Transfer Agreement emanated from the aspiration to attract affluent immigrants to Palestine. The German motivation was threefold: (1) the desire to get rid of Jews; (2) economic interests, such as the promotion of production and creation of new jobs; (3) propaganda considerations aimed at undermining the anti-Nazi boycott in a particularly symbolic place, namely Palestine.

The agreement was sharply criticized by sectors of Jewish public opinion, notably in the Diaspora, as a breach of Jewish solidarity and a violation of the boycott. The official Zionist attitude claimed for a time that the agreement was a private arrangement between the German Zionists and the German government. This changed only in the summer of 1935, under the pressure of the Zionist labor movement, when Haavara alone emerged as a practical way to ensure immigration from Germany.

Until 1935 the agreement concerned only immigrants whose property exceeded 1,000 pounds. This sum was required by the British authorities in order to obtain a "capitalist" certificate (*Vorzeigegeld*), for immigration to Palestine. It was allocated in foreign currency by the German authorities, and in 1935 the *Vorzeigegeld* became an additional liability for the Haavara and depended on Haavara's capability to distribute German products. The Palestine market was small, and in order to overcome the problem of disposal, Haavara had to expand its activities to neighboring Arab countries.

Attempts were made to reach similar settlements with several countries of central and eastern Europe. The most successful was the arrangement with the Czech government, which made possible the importation to Palestine of a half-million pounds and the immi-

gration of several thousand Jews on the eve of World War II.

The Haavara agreement functioned until a few months after the outbreak of the war, when it had to be stopped because of the economic blockade on Germany. In less than seven years it brought to Palestine about 8 million pounds sterling directly, and 6 million indirectly. Several thousand immigrants used its services, and many times more than this number benefited from the general increase in the country's absorptive capacity, thanks to the influx of German Jewish capital.

BIBLIOGRAPHY

Feilchenfeld, W., D. Michaelis, and L. Pinner. *Haavara-Transfer nach Palästina und Einwanderung deutscher Juden, 1933–1939.* Tübingen, 1972.
Gelber, Y. "Zionist Policy and the Transfer Agreement, 1933–1935." *Yalkut Moreshet* 17 (January 1974): 97–152; 18 (November 1974): 23–100. (In Hebrew.)
Krojanker, G. *The Transfer: A Vital Question of the Zionist Movement.* Tel Aviv, 1936.

YOAV GELBER

HA-BONIM. *See* Youth Movements.

HADASSAH WOMEN'S ZIONIST ORGANIZATION. *See* American Zionist Emergency Council.

HAGUE, THE (Du., 's Gravenhage), city in the NETHERLANDS; administrative center of the government. The Hague had its beginnings in the thirteenth century; Jews have been living there since the seventeenth century. In 1940 it had a population of a half million, with 18,000 Jews, representing 3.6 percent of the total. There were three Jewish communities: the large Ashkenazic community, with 17,379 members; the Portuguese community, with 200 members; and the relatively new Liberal community, to which seventy-five families belonged. The Ashkenazic community included a large number of eastern European Jews, concentrated, for the most part, in the coastal town of Scheveningen (which is part of The Hague). The Ashkenazic community and its religious societies had about ten synagogues. Dozens of Jewish organizations were active, including charitable and social-service institutions, leisure and sports clubs, and local branches of national bodies such as the Zionist Organization and Agudat Israel (the ultra-Orthodox Jewish movement). The Hague also had a Jewish home for the aged.

When the Germans occupied the Netherlands in May 1940, thirty Jews in The Hague committed suicide, among them a member of parliament and a member of the city council. The Germans established the main offices of their administration in The Hague; this meant that, unlike in the rest of the Netherlands, Jewish affairs were not exclusively in the hands of the Gestapo office in Amsterdam, but were also dealt with by SS-Sturmbannführer Franz Fischer, representing Section IV B 4 (Evacuations and Jews) of the REICHSSICHERHEITSHAUPTAMT (Reich Security Main Office; RSHA) in Berlin, headed by Adolf EICHMANN. The Jews of The Hague were subject to all the laws, regulations, and decrees that the German administration issued against the Jews of the Netherlands, but because of the city's status, its Jews were singled out for special treatment. Thus, about two thousand Jewish residents of The Hague who did not have Dutch nationality were forced to leave the city as early as September 1940 and look for accommodation elsewhere in the country.

In the early days of the occupation, The Hague was the scene of several anti-Jewish demonstrations organized by the NATIONAAL SOCIALISTISCHE BEWEGING (National Socialist Movement; NSB). On February 2, 1941, German Nazis tried to burn down the Great Synagogue, but the local fire department put out the flames. Following the February strike of Dutch workers protesting the deportation of Jews, the German administration tightened its control and did not permit antisemitic elements to riot.

Late in 1940 a Joodse Coördinatiecommissie (Jewish Coordinating Committee) was formed in order to determine the Jewish reaction to the anti-Jewish legislation. Chairing the committee was Lodewijk Ernst VISSER, the former president of the supreme court (he had been removed from his post), who lived in The Hague. Among the eight members of the committee were two other residents of The Hague—Jozef Emanuel Stokvis, a socialist member of parliament, and August David Belinfante, a lawyer—both of whom headed the committee's branch in The Hague. The Coordinating Committee first had its main office in Amsterdam, but when it ran into difficulties with the JOODSE RAAD (the Jewish Council, established on German demand), Visser decided to move the committee to The Hague (April 1941), with Henri Edersheim, an attorney, as director. Visser, who was also the chairman of the city's Jewish community board, called on the Jews to hold their heads high in response to the attacks on them, for, as he put it, "we are Dutch, but Dutch who for generations have maintained their unique identity." Accordingly, he decided that the synagogues would be kept open, despite the arson attempt that was made on the main synagogue.

In October 1941 the Coordinating Committee was closed down, and a local branch office of the Amsterdam Joodse Raad was set up in The Hague. Edersheim, who headed the office, went out of his way to collaborate with the Germans, establishing a close relationship with Franz Fischer, and putting Joodse Raad employees at Fischer's disposal to bring the Gestapo card index up to date, since it had proved unreliable during deportation operations.

On August 18, 1942, deportations of Jews from The Hague began, with 4,000 Jews summoned to travel by rail to the WESTERBORK camp. Only 1,200 responded to the summons. In The Hague no Jews were apprehended in the streets; the arrests were made in their homes, according to a list of addresses. The first such wave of arrests took place on August 22, and it mainly affected Scheveningen. Not all of the deportees were ordered to go straight to Westerbork; some were directed to move to Amsterdam. When the VUGHT camp was set up and the Jews were ordered out of all the Dutch cities (except Amsterdam), large numbers were commanded to report to the new camp, in April 1943.

Large-scale deportations were resumed in January 1943, when 1,000 Jews were sent to Westerbork. On February 18, forty-three Jewish boardinghouses were raided, and all their residents—together with other Jews, 780 in all—were taken to Westerbork. The Dutch police cooperated with the Germans at all times, and had a special section staffed by detectives who searched for Jews in hiding. Section IV B 4 also had a mixed German-Dutch team that searched for Jews, and it managed to seize 2,000 persons—Jews and Dutchmen who had helped them. This team was in touch with a Jew named Weinreb, who had begun by assuring Jews that, for a fee, he could arrange for them to make their way to freedom, and had later become an informant for the Germans.

A total of fifteen thousand Jews from The Hague were deported to the Nazi camps, and only a handful came back. Two thousand Jews stayed in The Hague and survived there, mainly by going into hiding. Jewish partners of mixed marriages were not deported, but they were put on forced labor.

Following the surrender of the German forces in the Netherlands, on May 5, 1945, The Hague was liberated and the Jewish community set about restoring its institutions; the first synagogue was reopened on May 17, 1945. In 1977 the Ashkenazic community consisted of twelve hundred persons; only a few were left from the Portuguese community. The Liberal community, on the other hand, had a membership of 125 families in the 1970s, and acquired the old Portuguese synagogue for its use.

BIBLIOGRAPHY

Houwaert, D. *Kehillo Kedousjo Den Haag*. The Hague, 1986.
Michman, J., et al., eds. *The Netherlands*. In *Pinkas Hakehillot; Encyclopaedia of Jewish Communities*. Jerusalem, 1986. See pages 238–260. (In Hebrew.)
Presser, J. *The Destruction of the Dutch Jews*. New York, 1969.

JOZEPH MICHMAN

HAHN, LUDWIG (b. 1908), SS officer. A native of the province of Schleswig-Holstein in northern Germany, Hahn studied law at the universities of Jena and Göttingen and

Ludwig Hahn.

earned a law degree. He joined the Nazi party in February 1930 and in April 1933 enrolled in the SS. In June 1935 he joined the SD (Sicherheitsdienst; Security Service), and held various senior posts in the Staatspolizei (State Police) in Hannover and Weimar. He became an SS officer in 1936, rose rapidly in rank, and by the end of 1938 was a *Sturmbannführer* (major).

In September 1939 Hahn was the commander of an Einsatzkommando operating in Poland. In January 1940 he was appointed Sicherheitspolizei (Security Police; Sipo) and SD commander in Kraków, and in August of that year was posted to Bratislava as special representative of the *Reichsführer-SS* (Heinrich HIMMLER) and as senior police officer at the German legation in the Slovak capital.

Appointed Sipo and SD commander in WARSAW on August 1, 1941, Hahn was in charge of the deportation of Warsaw's Jews to TREBLINKA. He took part in suppressing the WARSAW GHETTO UPRISING and was responsible for the murder of thousands of Poles, mainly in the PAWIAK PRISON in Warsaw.

Hahn was posted to the western front in December 1944 and was appointed commander of the Einsatzgruppe active in the Moselle region of France. From there he was transferred to the Weichsel (Vistula) Army Group, commanded by Himmler, and then to the senior SS commander's staff in Dresden. In March 1945 he became senior Sipo and SD commander in Westphalia.

After the war, Hahn went into hiding under an assumed name. In 1949, when he was no longer in danger of being extradited to Poland, he resumed his own name and worked as an insurance agent. He was arrested in July 1961 but was released. Arrested again in December 1965, he was again released two years later, for reasons of health. Hahn was finally put on trial in June 1975, and on July 4 of that year was sentenced to life imprisonment.

BIBLIOGRAPHY

Gutman, I. *The Jews of Warsaw, 1939–1943: Ghetto, Underground, Revolt.* Bloomington, 1982.

SHMUEL SPECTOR

HALUTS YOUTH MOVEMENTS. *See* Youth Movements.

HAMBURG, GERMANY's second largest city and its largest port. Hamburg was founded in the ninth century and became a free city in the fourteenth century; it was a center of Germany's economic life, commerce, shipping, culture, and the arts. In 1871 it became a member state in the German Empire.

Spanish and Portuguese Jews first settled in Hamburg at the end of the sixteenth century, and Ashkenazic Jews in the early seventeenth century, in Altona and then in Wandsbek (both close to Hamburg); as time went on they also moved into Hamburg itself. In 1671 the three congregations united to form a single community. Hamburg was one of the first Haskalah (Jewish Enlightenment) centers and a pioneer of Reform Judaism. Ortho-dox Jewry in Hamburg was more moderate than elsewhere in Germany. In the latter half of the nineteenth century and the first three decades of the twentieth, the general atmosphere in Hamburg was favorable for its Jews, who were well integrated into the city's life and society.

The June 1933 census recorded Hamburg's Jewish population at 16,885 (1.5 percent of the total). It was the fourth largest Jewish community in Germany, with more than one hundred societies, institutions, charitable funds, and cultural, youth, and sports bodies. Of special significance were the three religious organizations in Hamburg—the Orthodox Synagogenverband (Union of Synagogues), the Reform Tempelverband, and the Conservative Neue-Dammtor Synagoge—all three cooperating within the framework of the community organizations. Jewish coexistence was also expressed by the joint participation of both the acculturated CENTRAL-VEREIN DEUTSCHER STAATSBÜRGER JÜDISCHEN GLAUBENS (Central Union of German Citizens of Jewish Faith) and the Zionists. In economic terms the Jews were prosperous and were entrenched in banking (an example was the Warburg Bank), commerce (department stores and international trading companies), shipping (for example, the company of Albert Ballin), and the academic profession. Until 1933 there were no serious antisemitic incidents in Hamburg, except for some instances of desecration of synagogues and cemeteries. Assimilation was widespread and the percentage of mixed marriages among Jews was very high (close to 40 percent, in 1933).

After the Nazi rise to power, when it became known that in Morocco the Jews had imposed a boycott on German goods, the Hamburg authorities asked the Jewish Community Board to intervene, which the board agreed to do without delay. On the day of the boycott, April 1, 1933 (*see* BOYCOTT, ANTI-JEWISH), the local Nazi paper came out with large headlines about the impending operation. According to many eyewitness accounts, however, in some parts of the city the population did not cooperate with the Nazis, and in some instances non-Jews demonstrated their solidarity with the Jews. People found it ridiculous that SA (Sturmabteilung; Storm

Troopers) patrols were posted at the entrance to shops owned by observant Jews, since these shops were closed in any case because of the Sabbath. A few weeks later, Jews were being dismissed from government posts, the judiciary, health institutions, and the university.

The new situation led to large-scale emigration by Hamburg Jews (five thousand in the period from 1933 to 1937), but it also called for the reorganization of communal institutions. The two schools maintained by the community—the Talmud Torah and the girls' school on Karolinen Street—took in hundreds of new students who had been forced to leave the public schools. New consulting and welfare organizations were set up, as well as cultural and sports clubs, some on a local basis, and others as branches of countrywide organizations. According to a list submitted to the state police by the chairman of the Jewish community, Dr. Max Plaut, in 1935 Hamburg had approximately one hundred Jewish institutions, including thirty-four social and cultural societies, thirteen branches of national organizations (one was the Zionist movement, which had eighteen local chapters), and eighteen synagogues, with a total of forty-three hundred seats.

The change in the social environment and the mass dismissals brought new faces into active community affairs. Among these, an outstanding figure was Dr. Leo Lipmann, who for many years had held a senior post in the Hamburg state finance department as a *Staatsrat*, or state councillor. In 1935 he was elected as one of the two chairmen of the community board and handled many of the community's financial affairs, especially in the final few years, when the community was dissolved and its property had to be sold. In April 1936, Dr. Joseph Carlebach, the rabbi of Altona, was appointed Chief Rabbi of Hamburg. The new chief rabbi, who was intimately involved in community affairs and in the 1920s had been principal of the Talmud Torah, became Hamburg Jewry's spiritual leader, in fact as well as in title. Max WARBURG, the banker, came to play an increasingly large role in the affairs of the community, as well as in national Jewish affairs. He was one of the leading members of the Reichsvertretung der Juden in Deutschland (Reich Representation of Jews in Germany) and chairman of the HILFSVEREIN DER DEUTSCHEN JUDEN (Relief Organization of German Jews). When the date for the election of a new community assembly drew near, in 1937, the various constituents came to an agreement on the composition of the assembly, without going through elections. The new assembly consisted of seven Liberals, five Orthodox, five Zionists, and four representatives of the Economic party; after a year it was disbanded by the authorities. In early 1938 the Jewish community lost its legal status and was renamed the Jüdischer Religionsverband Hamburg E.V. (Hamburg Jewish Religious Organization).

In the KRISTALLNACHT pogrom of November 1938, most of the Hamburg synagogues were vandalized. The central synagogue, on Bornplatz, was sold to the state and was torn down in 1939. The Tempel on Ober Street was also sold (it now serves as the North German Broadcasting Station). The Neue-Dammtor Synagoge was repaired, only to be completely destroyed by air attacks during World War II.

The disbanding of the various organizations, and the handing over of their assets to the community, had begun even earlier. The Jewish calendar published by the community orphan asylum on the eve of Rosh Hashanah (the Jewish New Year) 5698 (1938) mentions some fifty institutions. In the wake of *Kristallnacht*, the authorities ordered that the Jewish organizations be dissolved more rapidly; this process was further speeded up after the outbreak of the war. In April 1939 the two schools run by the community were merged. The unified school had a total attendance of 1,337 pupils and continued to receive financial aid from the state, in the amount of 180,000 reichsmarks. It existed until the second half of 1942. In November of that year the Hamburg Jewish community was attached to the northwestern district office of the Reichsvereinigung der Juden in Deutschland (Reich Association of Jews in Germany; the successor to the Reichsvertretung), which also included the Bremen and Hannover Jewish communities. Dr. Max Plaut was put in charge of the district office of the Reichsvereinigung.

That year deportations were already in full swing, and the community was dwindling. In the period from 1941 to 1945, seventeen transports of Jews left Hamburg for ŁÓDŹ, MINSK, RIGA, AUSCHWITZ, and THERESIENSTADT. Among the deportees were some of the community's leading figures: Rabbi Carlebach, who would not leave his flock, having chosen not to emigrate when this was still possible (he was killed in Riga in December 1941); Dr. Nathan, the community's legal adviser; Dr. Jonas, principal of the girls' school; Max Mendel, a member of the Hamburg Senate; and many more. More than three hundred members of the community committed suicide, eighty of them when the deportations were at their height, in the second half of 1941. In that year the city's Jewish population dropped from eight thousand to four thousand. By early 1943 only eighteen hundred Jews remained in Hamburg, most of them partners of mixed marriages; more Jews were to be deported before the war came to an end. In June 1943 the Jewish community was officially liquidated and its officers, too, were deported (Dr. Lipmann and his wife committed suicide before the deportation). The total number of victims is estimated at seventy-eight hundred. Hamburg's Jewish community was revived after the war and within two years grew to twelve hundred, but few of these Jews had lived there before the war. In 1960 a new community synagogue was consecrated in Hamburg.

BIBLIOGRAPHY

Freimark, P., ed. *Juden in Preussen—Juden in Hamburg.* Hamburg, 1983.
Gilbert, M. *The Holocaust.* New York, 1985.
Randt, U. *Carolinenstrasse 35: Geschichte der Mädchenschule der Deutsch-Israelitischen Gemeinde in Hamburg, 1884–1942.* Hamburg, 1984.
Wolfsberg, Y. "Altona, Hamburg and Wandsbek." In vol. 2 of *Jewish Mother-Cities,* edited by Y. L. Fishman, pp. 5–57. Jerusalem, 1948. (In Hebrew.)

ELIEZER DOMKE

"HARVEST FESTIVAL." *See* "Erntefest."

HASAG (Hugo Schneider Aktiengesellschaft-Metalwarenfabrik, Leipzig), one of the privately owned German industrial companies manufacturing armaments that employed concentration camp prisoners. HASAG was the third largest after I.G. FARBEN and the Hermann Göring Werke.

HASAG was founded in Leipzig in 1863 as a small lamp factory and became the Hugo Schneider Aktiengesellschaft in 1899, when it was converted into a metal products factory. In 1930 the company had about one thousand employees and an annual turnover of 5 million marks.

In 1932, Paul Budin, a member of the Nazi party and a *Sturmbannführer* in the SS, was appointed general manager of HASAG. His deputies were Dr. Georg Mumme, Hans Führer, and Gustav Hessen; Dr. Ernst von Schön was chairman of the board, and the shareholders included Hugo Zinsser, Ernst von Wildeneg, and Richard Koch.

Beginning in 1933 the company developed contacts with the infantry ordnance branch of the Wehrmacht High Command, and it became a regular supplier of ammunition to the infantry and the air force. In 1934 HASAG was classified as a *Wehrmachtsbetrieb* (a company working for the armed forces). By 1939 its annual turnover was 22 million marks and it employed thirty-seven hundred workers.

HASAG's status was raised to that of *Rüstungsbetrieb* (armaments company) in 1939. When the German armaments industry was reorganized in 1940, Budin was appointed the chairman of Special Committee II, which had the task of supervising the production in the Reich of light ammunition for the infantry and the air force. When Albert SPEER was appointed minister of armaments in 1942, the committee's range of responsibilities was broadened and Budin's stature also grew as a result. In 1944 HASAG was charged with the mass production of infantry rocket launchers and received Hitler's thanks for its achievements. HASAG-Leipzig was also singled out as an "Exemplary National Socialist Enterprise."

In Germany. During the war HASAG had eight plants in Germany, with two categories of workers. The first was that of civilian workers, men and women from all over Eu-

TABLE 1. *Work Force in the HASAG Camps on January 31, 1945*

AUSSENKOMMANDO NUMBER	LOCATION	NUMBER OF JEWISH MEN	NUMBER OF JEWISH (AND OTHER) WOMEN	TOTAL
3	Altenburg	52	2,616	2,668
24	Colditz	300		300
42	Flössberg	396		396
65	Leipzig	221	5,067	5,288
74	Meuselwitz	290	1,376	1,666
95	Schlieben	2,339	242	2,581
107	Taucha	426	1,256	1,682
Total		4,024	10,557	14,581

rope, especially the Slavic countries. Some chose to work for HASAG, but the majority were forced laborers (*see* FORCED LABOR). By 1941 HASAG was employing a large number of Polish and Croatian voluntary workers, and in subsequent years it also employed French and Russian workers. Special open camps were established in the vicinity of the plants for the Slavic workers, but they were kept under strict police surveillance. The pay for these workers was very low.

The second category was that of concentration camp prisoners. Beginning in the summer of 1944, labor camps were established next to each HASAG plant, all of them as *Aussenkommandos* (satellite units) of the BUCHENWALD camp. According to incomplete data based on the Buchenwald card index, the composition and size of the work force in the HASAG labor camps on January 31, 1945, were as shown in Table 1. In addition, according to an entry of August 5, 1944, HASAG employed 2,000 prisoners at Aussenkommando 53, Herzberg am Elster, in the manufacture of explosives.

The employment by the HASAG industries of such a large number of female forced laborers was determined by a number of factors:

1. The mechanization and automation of the production of small- and medium-size munitions enabled women to replace men in the assembly line.
2. Women cost less than men. HASAG paid the SS less for women prisoners, both in Germany and the GENERALGOUVERNEMENT.

3. HASAG's experience with Jewish forced labor showed that, all other things being equal, women's adaptability and resilience were much greater than men's. The average mortality rate was higher for men than for women.

Between twenty thousand and twenty-two thousand prisoners of different nationalities passed through the HASAG labor camps in Germany from their establishment until their final liquidation in April 1945. With the advance of the Allied armies, some of the prisoners were transferred to other camps. Others, who were put on DEATH MARCHES, were dispersed in many small groups, and therefore no estimate can be made of the number of prisoners who died or were killed en route. Between 70 percent and 80 percent of the Jewish prisoners in the HASAG camps in Germany may be presumed to have survived.

In Poland. Following the German invasion of Poland in September 1939, HASAG began operating in the RADOM district in the central part of that country. In 1940, on the recommendation of the Armed Forces High Command, HASAG was put in charge of the administration of the ammunition factories in Skarżysko-Kamienna, the Granat grenade factory in KIELCE, and the Rakow foundry in CZĘSTOCHOWA. The three plants were also classified as *Wehrmachtsbetriebe*. Early in 1943 HASAG acquired the plants from the Generalgouvernement, for a payment of 16.5 million zlotys (1.5 million reichsmarks).

After the German invasion of the Soviet Union in June 1941, HASAG became the

TABLE 2. *Average Number of Prisoners and Total of Jewish Prisoners in the HASAG Camps*

CAMP	PLACE	DATE OF ESTABLISHMENT	DATE OF LIQUIDATION	AVERAGE NUMBER OF PRISONERS	TOTAL OF JEWISH PRISONERS
HASAG-Skarżysko-Kamienna	Skarżysko-Kamienna	August 1942	August 1, 1944	6,000–8,000	25,000–30,000
HASAG-Granat	Kielce	September 2, 1943	August 20, 1944	500	800
HASAG-Apparatexbau	Częstochowa	September 22, 1942	January 16, 1945	5,000	7,000
HASAG-Częstochowianka	Częstochowa	June 1943	January 16, 1945	2,000	
HASAG-WARTA	Częstochowa	June 1943	January 16, 1945	2,000	4,000
HASAG-Rakow	Częstochowa	June 1943	January 16, 1945	500	

main supplier of ammunition to the General-gouvernement. Figures show that on February 1, 1942, HASAG was the largest employer among the sixty-four *Wehrmachtsbetriebe* in the Generalgouvernement, with a work force of 13,850, mostly Poles. Of these, 10,267 worked at the Skarżysko-Kamienna factories, 1,379 at Granat, and 2,204 at the Częstochowa foundry.

In the spring of 1941, HASAG began transferring its Polish workers in the Generalgouvernement to its factories in Germany. In 1942, when absenteeism became rife among the Polish workers, HASAG set up two *Arbeitserziehungsanstalten* (labor training schools) in Skarżysko-Kamienna and Kielce. The prevailing shortage of workers led to an agreement between the Inspectorate of Armaments and SS-Obergruppenführer Friedrich Wilhelm Krüger, the *Höherer SS- und Polizeiführer* (Higher SS and Police Leader) of the Generalgouvernement, for the employment of Jews in the armaments industry. Under this agreement, signed on October 12, 1942, six forced-labor camps were established by HASAG in the vicinity of Radom. Jews from Poland, Austria, Czechoslovakia, Germany, and Hungary were imprisoned in them and put to work in armaments plants. The average number of prisoners in the HASAG labor camps and the total number of Jewish prisoners who passed through them are shown in Table 2. In late June 1943 the HASAG forced-labor camps held approximately 17,000 Jewish prisoners, 6,408 of them in Skarżysko-Kamienna.

For each Jewish prisoner in the labor camps HASAG paid four to five zlotys per day, less maintenance costs, into the account of Herbert Böttcher, the *SS- und Polizeiführer* for the Radom district. The prisoners' living conditions differed from one camp to another, depending on the attitude of the factory managers. In general, the policy of "Vernichtung durch Arbeit" (extermination through work) was applied, and in all the camps *Selektionen* were launched from time to time, culminating in the killing of all those who were no longer considered "fit for work."

From July 1944 until early 1945, HASAG transferred to Germany most of the equipment and raw materials it had in its factories in the Generalgouvernement, together with groups of Polish workers. After the final *Selektionen*, most of the remaining Jewish prisoners were also moved to HASAG factories in the Reich.

Paul Budin is assumed to have committed suicide, together with his wife, in April 1945, when he blew up the company's head office building in Leipzig. HASAG personnel were not put on trial at the SUBSEQUENT NUREMBERG PROCEEDINGS.

BIBLIOGRAPHY

Buchenwald—Mahnung und Verpflichtung: Dokumente und Berichte. Frankfurt, 1960.

Frey, H. *Die Hölle von Kamienna unter Benutzung des amtlichen Prozessmaterials.* Berlin, 1949.

Kaczanowski, L. *Hitlerowskie fabryki śmierci na Kielecczyznie.* Warsaw, 1984.

Rutkowski, A. "Martyrologia: Walkai zagłada ludności żydowskiej w dystrykcie radomskim podczas okupacji hitlerowskiej." *Biuletyn Żydowskiego Instytutu Historycznego* 15–16 (1955): 75–182.

FELICJA KARAY

HA-SHOMER HA-TSA'IR. *See* Youth Movements.

HASSELL, ULRICH VON (1881–1944), German diplomat and foreign-affairs adviser to the German anti-Nazi resistance. Hassell was born in Pomerania to an old, established north German family of public officials. He entered the Foreign Office in 1908, after studying law, and held a number of diplomatic posts abroad both before and after World War I; he was ambassador in Copenhagen (1926–1930), Belgrade (1930–1932), and Rome (from 1932 until his dismissal in 1938). In 1918 he joined the German National People's Party (Deutschnationale Volkspartei) and was initially sympathetic to the Nazis owing to his Prussian nationalist outlook. In 1933 he joined the Nazi party despite his contempt for its "vulgarity." He deplored Nazi adventurism abroad and foresaw disaster for Germany from the policy of Italian-German rapprochement and war against Britain and France.

Hassell was dismissed from his post when Joachim von RIBBENTROP became foreign minister in 1938. He now sought contacts elsewhere in Europe and associated himself with the German resistance of Ludwig Beck and Carl Friedrich Goerdeler. After the outbreak of war in 1939 he tried in vain to win the support of German generals such as Walther von Brauchitsch and Erwin Rommel for a negotiated peace. In the case of a successful coup d'état Hassell was to occupy the post of foreign minister in a Goerdeler cabinet. But in 1942 he was informed by a former colleague, Ernst von WEIZSÄCKER, that he had aroused the suspicion of the Gestapo. A few days after the failure of the July 1944 plot to assassinate Adolf Hitler, Hassell was arrested and sentenced to death; he was hanged in September 1944. After the war his diaries, *Vom anderen Deutschland: Aus den nachgelassenen Tagebüchern 1938–1944* (The Other Germany: From Posthumous Diaries, 1938–1944), which had been buried in the garden of his Bavarian home, were published. They are an invaluable source of information about the day-to-day activities of the German resistance.

BIBLIOGRAPHY

Deutsch, H. C. *The Conspiracy against Hitler in the Twilight War.* Minneapolis, 1968.
Hoffman, P. *The History of the German Resistance, 1933–1945.* Cambridge, Mass., 1978.

LIONEL KOCHAN

HAUPTTREUHANDSTELLE OST (Main Trusteeship Office East; HTO). The Haupttreuhandstelle Ost was established on October 19, 1939, by Hermann GÖRING in his capacity as the official responsible for the FOUR-YEAR PLAN. It dealt with the confiscation of Polish state property and the property of Polish citizens, including Jews, in the Reich and in the territories annexed to it. Shortly after the HTO's establishment, the confiscation of farms, forests, art treasures, and the property of Polish government offices and Polish political organizations was excluded from its purview.

The HTO, headed by Göring and managed by Max Winkler, had its head office in Berlin, with branches (*Treuhandstellen*) in Ciechanów, Katowice, and Poznań (the last with a sub-office in Łódź). District representatives (*Kreisvertrauensmänner*) of the HTO were appointed for the districts of Danzig–West Prussia, the Warthegau, and Ciechanów. They in turn had subdistrict representatives in Będzin, Bielsko-Biała, Chorzów, Cieszyn, Lubliniec, Sosnowiec, Żywiec, and, as of 1941, also in Białystok.

By 1942 the HTO had confiscated in the annexed territories over 200,000 factories, transport agencies, workshops, and commercial shops; over 290,000 plots of land; the contents of 500,000 apartments; and movable property and valuables worth several billion zlotys. The HTO also confiscated Polish state and private property in Germany, Austria, and other countries incorporated into the Reich, amounting to 270 million reichsmarks ($108 million).

The administration of the plundered property was handled partly by companies set up for this purpose, such as the Auffangsgesellschaft für Kriegsteilnehmer–Betriebe des Handels (Receiving Company for War Veterans–Commercial Shops). This company administered shops confiscated from their Polish or Jewish owners and staffed them with German war veterans. A similar role was played by the Grundstückgesellschaft (Real Estate Company), regarding residential houses and lots in the cities, and the Hotel und Gaststättengesellschaft (Hotels and Inns Company), regarding restaurants and hostelries. The confiscation of raw materials was handled jointly by the HTO, the Verwaltungs- und Verwertungsgesellschaft (Administration and Utilization Company), and the Treuhänder für Textilstoffe (Trusteeship Office for Textile Products), which operated in Łódź until the end of December 1939. Other companies functioning under the aegis of the HTO promoted German industry, labor, and trade in the annexed territories and also sought to integrate this economic activity into that of the rest of the Reich.

Agricultural land confiscated from Poles in the annexed areas was administered by the Ostdeutsche Landbewirtschaftungs—Ostland (East German Land Cultivation Authority—Ostland), later renamed Ostdeutsche Landbewirtschaftungs—Reichsland. In 1943 it administered 2,400 plots of land and 390,000 confiscated Polish farms. The same company also operated in France, on the basis of the experience and expertise it had acquired in Poland.

BIBLIOGRAPHY

Czubinski, A. "Poland's Place in Nazi Plans for a New Order in Europe in the Years 1934–1940." *Polish Western Affairs* 21 (1980): 19–46.

Luczak, C. *Polityka ekonomiczna Trzeciej Rzeszy w latach drugiej wojny światowej.* Poznań, 1982.

Madajczyk, C. *Polityka III Rzeszy w okupowanej Polsce.* Warsaw, 1970.

CZESŁAW LUCZAK

Gideon Hausner, Israeli attorney general and chief prosecutor at the Eichmann trial.

HAUSNER, GIDEON (b. 1915), Israeli jurist and public figure. Hausner was born in Lvov and settled in Palestine with his family when he was twelve years old. In Israel's War of Independence (1948–1949) he served as a military prosecutor and then as president of the military court in Jerusalem. He also taught at the Hebrew University Law School. From 1960 to 1963, Hausner was the legal adviser to the Israel government (the attorney general), and in that capacity he became the prosecutor in the EICHMANN TRIAL in Jerusalem. His opening speech was one of the highlights of the trial.

Hausner was active in the Progressive party and in the Independent Liberal party that succeeded it. He was a member of the Knesset (the Israeli parliament) from 1965 to 1981, and from 1972 to 1974 served in the cabinet as minister without portfolio. When he retired from political life he devoted himself to the commemoration of the Holocaust, becoming chairman of the World Council of YAD VASHEM and frequently lecturing on the

Holocaust in Israel and abroad. He is the author of *Justice in Jerusalem* (New York, 1966), a book on the Eichmann trial, which has been translated into several languages.

ISRAEL GUTMAN

HAUTVAL, ADELAIDE (b. 1906), French physician. Born into a Protestant family, Hautval studied medicine in Strasbourg and later worked in several psychiatric clinics in Strasbourg and Switzerland.

In April 1942, Hautval was arrested trying to cross without a permit from the occupied to the unoccupied zone in France in order to attend her mother's funeral. Awaiting trial in the Bourges prison, she vehemently protested to the Gestapo against the harsh treatment of Jewish prisoners incarcerated with her. In reprisal, she was transferred to the Romainville prison with other political detainees, and eventually sent as a doctor to AUSCHWITZ with a convoy of Jewish women, arriving there in January 1943. She reportedly bore a yellow badge attached to her overcoat, with the inscription "A friend of the Jews."

At Auschwitz, she helped hide a group of women afflicted with typhus on the top floor of her block and treated them as well as conditions allowed. She was later approached by SS-Hauptsturmführer Dr. Eduard Wirths, the garrison doctor (*Standortarzt*), and asked to practice gynecology. Aware of the sterilization experiments practiced in Block 10, Hautval accepted in order to gain a firsthand view of the Nazi procedure. She soon discovered that in this block Wirths was in charge of a team of doctors (Horst Schumann, Carl CLAUBERG, and Władysław Dering) who used women as guinea pigs, sterilizing them by means of X rays and ovariectomy (surgical removal of ovaries). These experiments were part of a large-scale plan: sterilization was intended to be applied (worldwide) to all half and quarter Jews who were left alive after the Nazi victory. Hautval expressed her complete opposition and refused to participate in these experiments (in which Dr. Josef MENGELE was also involved). She feared retribution, but was not punished.

After her confrontation with Wirths, Hautval continued practicing medicine in the nearby Birkenau camp (Auschwitz II) as best she could until August 1944, when she was transferred to the women's camp at RAVENSBRÜCK. She survived and was liberated in April 1945.

A libel trial (*Dering* v. *Uris*) was held in London in 1964, at which Dering claimed that the author Leon Uris had slandered him in his book *Exodus*. At the trial, Hautval refuted Dering's claim that it was futile to refuse to obey orders in Auschwitz, maintaining that one could bypass SS commands to remove women's ovaries and still manage to avoid punishment. The presiding judge, Justice Frederick Horace Lawton, in his summation to the jury called Hautval "perhaps one of the most impressive and courageous women who have ever given evidence in the courts of this country."

Hautval received recognition by YAD VASHEM as a "RIGHTEOUS AMONG THE NATIONS" in 1965.

BIBLIOGRAPHY

Hill, M., and L. N. Williams. *Auschwitz in England: A Record of a Libel Action*. London, 1965.

MORDECAI PALDIEL

Adelaide Hautval, who received the "Righteous among the Nations" award at Yad Vashem on April 17, 1965.

HAZIT DOR BNEI MIDBAR. *See* Front of the Wilderness Generation.

HDBM. *See* Front of the Wilderness Generation.

HEBREW LITERATURE ON THE HOLOCAUST. *See* Literature on the Holocaust: Hebrew Literature.

HE-HALUTS HA-LOHEM (Organizacja Bojowa Żydowskiej Młodzieży Chalucowej; Fighting Organization of Pioneer Jewish Youth in Kraków), Jewish underground organization. It was created in KRAKÓW in mid-August 1942, not in order to save lives but out of a desire "to die as Jews without the shame of dying as slaves." The initiative for its creation came from the pioneer youth movement Akiva, which was also the guiding force in its activity. Other members came from Dror, Ha-Shomer ha-Dati, Ha-Shomer ha-Tsa'ir, and the Pioneer Youth Organization (*see* YOUTH MOVEMENTS). He-Haluts ha-Lohem had about one hundred members.

The decision to form the organization was taken after the deportation of about six thousand of the Jews of Kraków in June 1942, after news had arrived of mass slaughter in parts of eastern Poland and the Soviet Union occupied by the Germans. At its head was a four-member command: Aharon LIEBESKIND, who was responsible for obtaining arms; Avraham Leibovich ("Laban"), a member of Dror, who was appointed treasurer; Shimshon DRAENGER, in charge of the "technical office" for forging official documents; and Manik Eisenstein, a member of the Pioneer Youth Organization.

He-Haluts ha-Lohem was in close contact with the ŻYDOWSKA ORGANIZACJA BOJOWA (Jewish Fighting Organization; ŻOB) in Warsaw, but it was autonomous in determining the timing and the place of the armed struggle. Its command had a unique conception of the system of opposition and fighting, the essence of which was transferral of the arena of action and struggle to the area outside the ghetto. The organization's fighters wished to hide their Jewish identity so that the responsibility for their actions would not be placed on the ghetto and thereby lead to the ghetto's liquidation. Only in January 1943 was their Jewish identity revealed, as a result of the "Cyganeria" action (see below).

There were several reasons for this method of struggle:

1. A sense of responsibility for the ghetto's fate was a consideration for precluding a link between the sabotage activities outside the ghetto and the ghetto residents.

2. The ghetto in Kraków was small. The GENERALGOUVERNEMENT ruler, Hans FRANK, did not want many Jews in Kraków, the capital and administrative center of the Generalgouvernement. From the June 1942 deportation until December 1942 the ghetto area was reduced twice, and it was finally divided into two ghettos, Ghetto A and Ghetto B. This prevented the creation of hiding places.

3. The Kraków ghetto population was small and unstable. After June 1942 many of the Jewish ghetto residents were not from Kraków, were strangers to the members of the local underground, and in some instances were considered unreliable.

4. The creation of a labor camp in PŁASZÓW, near the city, gave the Jews a sense of hope for survival. There was no feeling of "nothing to lose" and it was difficult to obtain support from the inhabitants of the ghetto, which was liable to be liquidated in the event of a revolt.

5. Since Kraków was the capital of the Generalgouvernement, there were many sabotage objectives, and it was possible to operate in the "Aryan" part of the city with a handful of men having a meager supply of weapons in their possession. The aim was to undermine the self-confidence of the authorities, to harm their position, and to injure as many Germans as possible.

Many preparations were made for the armed struggle. Forged documents were prepared by the "technical office" to ensure freedom of movement for members of the organization. Money was obtained for the purchase of arms by the sale of forged documents and by "expropriations" (forcible collection of money from rich Jews), and arms were acquired by attacks on German soldiers alone or in pairs, in the middle of the night on the city boulevards. Arms were purchased principally with the aid of the Polska Partia Robotnicza (Polish Workers' Party; PPR [Communists]). Efforts were made to find an ally to assist with the military and underground work and with arms, and the PPR was approached through Gola Mire, a member of the Polish Communist party. The number of members in He-Haluts ha-Lohem was increased by adding members from youth movements, principally Akiva and Dror, in cities close to Kraków. Through liaisons, He-Haluts ha-Lohem was organized into groups of five, each with a commander in contact with the principal command.

On September 20, 1942, the first group of five went out to the forests in the Rzeszów district. It had been promised aid by the PPR, which it was supposed to join so as to prepare the ground for the many who were to follow. The promised aid did not materialize, however, since the PPR had not yet begun activities in the forests, and contact with the PPR was terminated.

In October a group was sent to the forests in the Dębica area. Before it left, points were established in the small towns close to the forests, which were to serve as bases for those going there. This attempt too ended in failure and in battle losses. It was then concluded that the time had not yet arrived to leave for the forests, and that the organization should confine itself to opposition activities in Kraków itself and to organizing points of support in the directions of Warsaw and Lvov, where members could take refuge after carrying out their activities.

Until November 1942, operations within the ghetto consisted of attacks on German soldiers and Gestapo men, seizure of their weapons, and surveillance of informers in order to liquidate them. A second fighting organization, which operated in the ghetto and which was in touch with the PPR, carried out similar activities and also sabotaged German installations in the city and its surroundings.

During that period, the ghetto served as a base for operations outside the ghetto. After members of the command had been traced, the location was transferred to the "Aryan" part of the city, and members of the organization were dispersed outside the ghetto. In preparation for a large-scale operation, He-Haluts ha-Lohem renewed its contact with the PPR, and coordination was established with the command of the Jewish group. Most of the latter's members came from Ha-Shomer ha-Tsa'ir, and it operated in the framework of the PPR; a joint command was created for the two organizations in October and November of 1942. The date of the action was determined—December 22, 1942, just before Christmas, when the city would be flooded with German soldiers on holiday leave.

The targets of the action were cafés in the center of town where the German soldiers passed their time. Best known was the Cyganeria, which was attacked with homemade hand grenades. The Germans announced twenty dead and wounded. None of the attackers was injured, but about twenty He-Haluts ha-Lohem fighters, returning to their base in the deserted Jewish hospital, walked into a Gestapo ambush and were taken to the MONTELUPICH PRISON. Among those captured was command member "Laban"; Aharon Liebeskind was killed in combat in the headquarters apartment.

That action concluded the organization's operations in the city. Activity was renewed after the escape on April 29, 1943, of Shimshon DRAENGER and Gusta DRAENGER from the Montelupich prison, where they had been held since January 1943. On March 13 the remaining fighters, who had assembled in Bochnia after the Cyganeria action and who were to have gone out to the Wisnicz Forest, were arrested and brought to Montelupich.

The Draengers and Hillel Wodzisławski, a member of the command from Wisnicz, worked in the Wisnicz Forest to assemble the remaining fighters there. Their principal objectives were to offer defense and aid to save the survivors of the ghettos, and to take reprisals against farmers who handed over Jews. They also renewed publication of the underground journal *He-Haluts ha-Lohem*, which was the link among the forces scattered in the forest. It issued warnings to the Polish farmers, and described the history and problems of the ŻOB in Kraków. In November 1943, after the Draengers fell into German hands, the He-Haluts ha-Lohem organization ceased to exist.

Only fifteen members of He-Haluts ha-Lohem survived. Almost all of them emigrated to Israel.

BIBLIOGRAPHY

Dawidson, G. *Justina's Diary*. Tel Aviv, 1978. (In Hebrew.)

Hechalutz Halochem: Organ of the Chalutz Underground Movement in Occupied Cracow, August–October 1943. Naharia, Israel, 1984. (In Hebrew.)

Memorial Journal: In Honor of Jews from Cracow Who Perished, 1939–1945. New York, 1967.

Perlis, R. "The Hechalutz Fighting Resistance in Cracow." *Studies on the Holocaust Period* 2 (1981): 150–176. (In Hebrew.)

YAEL PELED (MARGOLIN)

HE-HALUTS YOUTH MOVEMENTS. *See* Youth Movements.

HELBRONNER, JACQUES (1873–1943), Jewish leader in Vichy FRANCE. The son of a distinguished lawyer, Helbronner was born in Paris. In 1927 he was appointed to the Conseil d'Etat (Council of State), in which he too became a noted lawyer. During the 1930s, Helbronner was an active member of the CONSISTOIRE CENTRAL DES ISRAÉLITES DE FRANCE (Central Consistory of French Jews), becoming its vice president. Deeply rooted in French society and culture, Helbronner was well qualified to represent the native French Jews, who maintained close contacts and associations with the French bureaucracy.

With the fall of Paris in June 1940, the Consistory joined other major Jewish organizations in the mass exodus to the unoccupied southern zone. Since the president of the Consistory had succeeded in leaving France, Helbronner quickly emerged as his successor, a choice no doubt reinforced by his close personal relations with the French chief of state, Marshal Philippe PÉTAIN. There is evidence that during the first year and a half of the occupation, Helbronner met privately with Pétain twenty-seven times and continued his adoration of the World War I hero, after whom he had named his own son. A sense of trust in the French leader and his principles helped shape the direction in which Helbronner guided the Consistory in the face of Vichy's anti-Jewish laws. Reasoned but impassioned pleas that invoked the spirit of the glorious French traditions and were directed to the "father of the homeland" (*père de la patrie*) characterized Helbronner's approach as president from the first official meeting of the Consistory after the armistice, in March 1941. In this same vein, Helbronner, who was seemingly the first Jewish leader in the south to learn of the intention to establish a compulsory Jewish organization (later to be called the UNION GÉNÉRALE DES ISRAÉLITES DE FRANCE, or UGIF), stood on principle and legal precedents and succeeded in negotiating a special status for the Consistory that kept it independent of the UGIF throughout the war. Simultaneously, he counseled Jewish leaders to refrain from joining the UGIF and pursued an active campaign against its supporters. Defying the racial and national definition of Jews propounded by Vichy, Helbronner continued to adhere to the Consistory's historical definition of Judaism as a religion alone.

Helbronner's leadership of the Consistory came under strong criticism from various sectors of the Jewish community in the wake of the mass deportations of Jews from the south of France in August 1942. Attacked for timidity and for disregarding the plight of foreign-born Jews in France, Helbronner persisted in upholding his elitist and legalistic orientation and remained at his post. Signs of a changing perspective appeared only after the German occupation of most of southern France in November 1942. Helbronner advanced the negotiations that had been taking place between members of the Consistory and the UGIF, and looked for ways to widen the scope of aid to the needy community. A telling blow, the roundup of native and foreign Jews in Marseilles in January 1943, impelled Helbronner to a clear act of reconciliation with the leaders of the UGIF and to cooperation with them. Throughout this trying period, Helbronner protested sharply to the French authorities against the deterioration of Jewish life in France and raised his voice against the arrests of the UGIF leaders in the summer of 1943. These protests seem to have contributed to his eventual arrest on October 19 of that year and to his deportation a month later, together with his wife, to AUSCHWITZ, where they were killed.

A man of sixty-eight when he assumed the presidency of the Consistory, Helbronner regarded himself as the spokesman of the Jews "of old vintage" (*de vieille souche*) and throughout the difficult years in Lyons he remained anchored in legalistic diplomacy. Encumbered by his trust and confidence in France and its head of state, Helbronner directed the Consistory on the path of least resistance, which began to change course with his deportation.

BIBLIOGRAPHY

Cohen, R. I. "French Jewry's Dilemma on the Orientation of Its Leadership (From Polemics to Conciliation: 1942–1944)." *Yad Vashem Studies* 14 (1981): 167–204.

Cohen, R. I. "Religion and Fatherland: The Central Consistory in France during the Second World War." In *Israel and the Nations: Essays Presented in Honor of Shmuel Ettinger*, edited by S. Almog et al., pp. 307–334. Jerusalem, 1987. (In Hebrew.)

Szajkowski, Z. *The Analytical Franco-Jewish Gazetteer, 1939–1945*. New York, 1966.

RICHARD COHEN

HELMRICH, EBERHARD, German who rescued Jews in Poland during the war. Helm-

Israeli consul general Michael Arnon, left, presents Eberhard Helmrich with the Yad Vashem Righteous among the Nations medal in New York (1968). [Paul Schumach, Metropolitan Photo Service Inc.]

rich had the rank of major. As head of a farm at the Hyrawka labor camp in DROGOBYCH (Pol., Drohobycz), Eastern Galicia, he had the task of supplying German army units with foodstuffs. Helmrich used this opportunity to employ Jewish men and women from the Drogobych ghetto, who constituted over half of the nearly three hundred workers on his farm—most with no previous farming experience. He protected them from deportation roundups, hiding some in his home and helping to release others already arrested, with the excuse that they were needed for the proper functioning of the farm.

Realizing that the Germans were planning the liquidation of all the Jews in his region, Helmrich devised a plan—together with his wife, Donata—by means of which he succeeded in spiriting about twelve Jewish girls out of Poland. Provided with false credentials that he himself helped manufacture, the girls were sent to Germany as Ukrainian and Polish housemaids with German families. Helmrich coordinated this underground operation with his wife over vast distances—between Drogobych and Berlin. Donata Helmrich looked after her charges, making sure that they were not placed as domestics near Ukrainian and Polish women, so that there would be no suspicion as to their origins.

When asked about their motivation, after the war, the Helmrichs answered: "We were fully aware of the risks and the clash of responsibilities, but we decided that it would be better for our children to have dead parents than cowards as parents. After that decision, it was comparatively easy. We figured that after we had saved two people, we'd be even with Hitler if we were caught, and with every person saved beyond that, we were ahead."

Eberhard and Donata Helmrich were recognized by YAD VASHEM as "RIGHTEOUS AMONG THE NATIONS."

BIBLIOGRAPHY

Boehm, E. H. *We Survived*. New Haven, 1949.

MORDECAI PALDIEL

HESS, RUDOLF (1894–1987), Nazi leader; a close aide of Adolf HITLER. In World War I,

Hess volunteered for service in the German army, serving first as an infantry officer and later as a pilot.

Hess was among the first to join the Nazi party, in 1920. He took part in the abortive November 1923 putsch, when Hitler tried to overthrow the Bavarian government, and was imprisoned in the Landsberg prison with Hitler, whom he helped to compose MEIN KAMPF. When the two were released in 1925, Hess became Hitler's personal aide and private secretary, a position he held until the Nazi rise to power, in January 1933. In April of that year, Hitler appointed Hess deputy leader of the Nazi party, and in December he was also named minister without portfolio; henceforth all the laws issued by the Nazi regime bore Hess's signature. A member of Hitler's inner circle, Hess was entrusted in 1938 with important missions relating to Germany's takeover of Austria and the Sudeten region of Czechoslovakia.

On the eve of World War II, Hess was a member of the Geheime Kabinetsrat (Secret Cabinet Council) and the Ministerrat für die Reichsverteidigung (Reich Ministerial Defense Council), two bodies with little influence. Hess's belief that he had been removed from the decision-making process, coupled with Hitler's intention to attack the Soviet Union, seem to have been among the factors that gave him the bold idea of flying to Britain. In May 1941 Hess took that step, in the hope that the impending invasion of Russia would persuade the British to make peace with Germany. No authoritative information has ever emerged as to whether Hess undertook his daring mission entirely on his own initiative, or whether he was inspired to do so by Hitler, directly or indirectly.

In the event, Hitler repudiated the attempt as soon as its failure was known. Hess was arrested when he landed in Britain and was held there until the end of the war. After the war he was one of the defendants at the main NUREMBERG TRIAL, together with the other leaders of the Nazi regime. In October 1946, Hess was acquitted of war crimes and crimes against humanity, but was found guilty of crimes against the peace; he was sentenced to life imprisonment. The Soviet judge in the trial had demanded that he be condemned to death.

From that time on Hess was held in the

Rudolf Hess in his prison cell in Nuremberg during his trial before the International Military Tribunal. [United States Army]

Spandau Prison in West Berlin, under the joint control of the United States, Great Britain, the Soviet Union, and France. At no time would the Soviets agree to his release, and for many years, until his death by suicide in August 1987, Hess was the sole inmate of the huge prison.

BIBLIOGRAPHY

Bird, E. K. *The Loneliest Man in the World.* London, 1974.
Douglas-Hamilton, J. *Motive for a Mission: The Story behind Hess's Flight to Britain.* London, 1971.
Hutton, J. B. *Hess: The Man and His Mission.* London, 1970.
Leasor, J. *Rudolf Hess: The Uninvited Envoy.* London, 1962.

DAVID HADAR

HEYDRICH, REINHARD (1904–1942), head of the Nazi SICHERHEITSPOLIZEI (Security Police; Sipo), the SD (Sicherheitsdienst; Security Service), and, later, the REICHSSICHER-

HEITSHAUPTAMT (Reich Security Main Office; RSHA); key person in planning and executing the anti-Jewish policies of the Third Reich.

Heydrich was born in Halle, a provincial Saxon town, to a family of musicians. His father was an opera singer and the director of a conservatory. In his youth Heydrich was exposed to his father's cult of Richard Wagner, his mother's stern discipline, and the worship of the authority of the state and its rulers. He was also exposed to a (false) suspicion that he was partly of Jewish origin.

Commissioned as an ensign and trained as a signal officer, Oberleutnant zur See Heydrich was discharged from the navy in April 1931. A naval court of honor found him guilty of misconduct toward a female friend, whom he mistreated and whose reputation he further blemished during the court proceedings.

Frustrated by the rules of civil society, Heydrich, who initially had regarded the Nazi party with contempt, was introduced by a family friend to Heinrich HIMMLER. Himmler made him an intelligence officer and entrusted him in 1931 with the organization of the SS espionage and surveillance apparatus, the SD. Freed from the restraints of navy discipline and the civil code of behavior, and benefiting from his threatening mien and "Aryan" look, Heydrich gave full rein to his ruthlessness, cynicism, and ambition, combining them with loyalty to his new masters. Inquiry into his alleged Jewish ancestry showed the rumor to be false, but his superiors capitalized on the suspicion, which guaranteed his loyalty. As SD chief, Heydrich was entrusted with the information-gathering, blackmail, and intrigue needed to establish Himmler's control over the secret state police (GESTAPO) during the first years of the Nazi regime. He was assisted by able administrators such as Carl Albrecht OBERG. At the same time, Heydrich became executive director of the Bavarian political police, the nucleus of the Gestapo system under Himmler. The SD, together with the Gestapo, of which he later became executive director, was instrumental in establishing the Nazi terror apparatus and executing the leaders of the SA (Sturmabteilung; Storm Troopers) on June 30, 1934.

Heydrich played a role in purging the army high command in 1938, and also helped plant the false information that led to STALIN's purge of the Red Army's high command. Reflecting Himmler's fanatical race ideology, the SD developed into a political network of espionage and warfare, both ideological and practical, while suggesting increasingly radical solutions to the "Jewish question," such as pogroms and forced emigration. In 1936 Heydrich was made chief of the Gestapo and the KRIMINALPOLIZEI (Kripo), retaining separate control over the SD.

As Gestapo chief, Heydrich had unlimited power to confine to concentration camps "enemies of the Reich," among them Jews. He encouraged competition between the SD and the Gestapo, which under his aegis vied with each other to execute Hitler's Jewish policies. They also competed with other party elements, under Joseph GOEBBELS's influence, and with the SA. SD functionaries such as Adolf EICHMANN were encouraged to implement "solutions" to the "Jewish question," such as the assembly-line deportation organized primarily for Jews in Austria and Czechoslovakia.

In KRISTALLNACHT, the Goebbels-instigated pogrom of November 9 and 10, 1938, the SA and the Nazi party took the lead. Heydrich, however, assisted by Heinrich MÜLLER and using prepared lists, saw to it that thousands of Jews were arrested by the Gestapo and SS. On January 24, 1939, Hermann GÖRING established the Reich's ZENTRALSTELLE FÜR

Reinhard Heydrich.

JÜDISCHE AUSWANDERUNG (Central Office for Jewish Emigration), appointing Heydrich's subordinate Müller as its executive director. This transferred the implementation of the Reich's Jewish policy to the SS; from then on, Heydrich was the chief executor of this policy.

When war broke out in 1939, Heydrich was in charge of the EINSATZGRUPPEN. In a special ordinance of September 21, 1939, he ordered them to carry out the ghettoization and concentration of Polish Jews and the establishment of Judenräte (Jewish councils). He then unified the Gestapo and SD within the framework of the newly established RSHA, giving ruthless SD functionaries such as Eichmann complete executive power in their anti-Jewish actions. Heydrich was instrumental in such schemes as the NISKO AND LUBLIN PLAN and the proposed mass deportations to Madagascar (see MADAGASCAR PLAN). In 1941, prior to Hitler's assault on the Soviet Union, Heydrich concluded, apparently on Hitler's order, an agreement with the army high command securing military assistance for the Einsatzgruppen in Russia. Heydrich ordered the latter to implement the "special tasks" of immediate annihilation of the Jews and Soviet officials in the Russian areas soon to be occupied.

On July 31 of that year, Göring, possibly on Heydrich's initiative, charged him with the "final solution of the Jewish question" in the entire German sphere of influence in Europe. To carry out this task, Heydrich required the cooperation of the Reich's ministerial agencies, and to this end he convened a meeting of top officials at Wannsee, a Berlin suburb (see WANNSEE CONFERENCE), on January 20, 1942, to confirm the program for the planned extermination. Heydrich enjoyed direct access to Hitler and steadily increasing power, but it is debated to what extent he initiated the rationale and the methods adopted for the "final solution."

Late in 1941, Heydrich was rewarded for his anti-Jewish terror and extermination campaign by being appointed acting governor of the Protectorate of BOHEMIA AND MORAVIA. Attacked by Czech resistance fighters in an ambush near Prague, Heydrich died of his wounds on June 4, 1942. In retaliation, five days later the Germans destroyed the Czech village of LIDICE and killed all its male inhabitants.

[See also Aktion Reinhard.]

BIBLIOGRAPHY

Aronson, S. *Reinhard Heydrich und die Frühgeschichte von Gestapo und SD.* Stuttgart, 1971.
Calic, E. *Reinhard Heydrich.* New York, 1985.
Deschener, G. *Reinhard Heydrich: A Biography.* New York, 1981.
MacDonald, C. *The Killing of SS Obergruppenführer Reinhard Heydrich.* New York, 1989.
Wykes, A. *Heydrich.* New York, 1973.

SHLOMO ARONSON

HICEM, organization founded in 1927 by amalgamating three Jewish migration agencies: the New York–based HIAS (Hebrew Sheltering and Immigrant Aid Society); the Paris-based ICA (Jewish Colonization Association), founded by Baron Maurice de Hirsch; and the Berlin-based Emigdirect, an association founded in 1921 to centralize the work of organizations and local committees involved with Jewish immigration. The name HICEM is an acronym of HIAS, ICA, and Emigdirect.

The agreement called for the merger of all local branches of the three organizations outside the United States, while allowing HIAS to continue to deal with all matters pertaining to Jewish immigration to the United States. With the outbreak of World War II in 1939, the Paris-based HICEM was faced with ever-increasing applications to help service the emigration of Jewish refugees. Emigdirect had withdrawn from the agreement in 1934, and ICA, registered as a British philanthropic agency, was—owing to English wartime regulations—prohibited from using its funds outside the Sterling area. Thus, the HICEM budget was financed for a limited period solely by HIAS.

The German invasion of France prompted the closing of HICEM's European headquarters in Paris on June 10, 1940, and, after various temporary relocations in the south of France, a permanent European headquarters was reestablished in Lisbon, Portugal, on June 26, under HICEM's European director,

Dr. James Bernstein, with Ilja Dijour as secretary.

Portugal, unlike Spain, had an incorporated and officially recognized Jewish communal organization, and HICEM operated under the transparent guise of the immigration section of the local community. Local Jews, notably Professor Moses B. Amzalak and Dr. Augusto d'Essaguy, greatly aided the work of HICEM by helping it maintain and develop a cordial relationship with the authorities. Moreover, Portugal had a friendly relationship with Britain and the Allies, in contrast to Spain's links with the Axis camp; in addition, Lisbon was a neutral port that served as the only European continental point of departure for North and South America. This made Lisbon the natural place for HICEM to relocate its European headquarters. The move was duplicated by other Jewish organizations, such as the American Jewish JOINT DISTRIBUTION COMMITTEE (known as the Joint), and non-Jewish organizations, such as the AMERICAN FRIENDS SERVICE COMMITTEE and the Unitarian Service Committee.

HICEM's main activities were geared toward helping the refugees with information, visa applications, and transportation. Financial matters were generally handled by the Joint, both for the refugees and, to a great extent, for the HICEM budget. The relationship between these two Jewish organizations was often abrasive, especially between the United States headquarters of HIAS-HICEM and the Joint. This infighting focused on problems of prestige, credit, and jurisdiction. The Joint, a philanthropic organization of German Jewish background, entered into the field of Jewish immigration with the Nazi rise to power and the ensuing Jewish emigration from Germany, Austria, and Czechoslovakia. HICEM, which basically reflected an eastern European Jewish background, strongly protested this incursion into what it regarded as its sphere of activities and made it clear that, although its background was eastern European, it felt capable of dealing with the emigration of German Jews.

Further points of friction centered on the two organizations' approaches to dealing with the strictly restrictive immigration laws of the United States. HICEM maintained a far less legalistic approach to such questions as payment by the individual refugee for his own passage and the procurement of affidavits, while the Joint was much less flexible about these and other questions regarding United States currency and immigration regulations.

Nonetheless, a working arrangement was reached that helped solve some of the more pressing problems, such as ethnic quotas and insufficient transportation and accommodation. As a result, some ninety thousand Jews were able to flee Europe by way of Lisbon during the Holocaust.

BIBLIOGRAPHY

Avni, H. *Spain, the Jews, and Franco.* Philadelphia, 1974.
Bauer, Y. *American Jewry and the Holocaust.* Detroit, 1981.

YITZCHAK MAIS

HIGH COMMISSION FOR REFUGEES FROM GERMANY. *See* McDonald, James Grover.

HILFSVEREIN DER DEUTSCHEN JUDEN (Relief Organization of German Jews), organization established by German Jews in 1901 to engage in social welfare and educational activities among needy Jews. It remained in operation until 1941, and during the Nazi period it assisted German Jews trying to emigrate. The Hilfsverein was founded by an elite group of Jews, active in economic and cultural life, in order "to promote the moral, spiritual, and economic progress of our coreligionists," especially in eastern Europe and the Near East. One of its basic objectives was to spread the German language and German culture.

After World War I the Hilfsverein concentrated its efforts on Jewish refugees from eastern Europe who were stranded in Germany while trying to emigrate overseas. The experience accumulated in this period, and the institutions created, were utilized in the wake of the Nazi rise to power, when Germany's Jews were seeking to emigrate. Pressure by German Jews for such assistance began as early as March 1933, on the eve of the Boycott of April 1 (*see* BOYCOTT, ANTI-JEWISH). The help that the Hilfsverein was able to give encompassed all aspects of emigration: up-to-date information, based on reports received from hundreds of contacts abroad; vocational counseling; technical arrangements; bureaucratic formalities; and financial advice. Where necessary, the society provided grants to tide the emigrants over during the transitional period. At that juncture, the leading figure in the organization was Max WARBURG, and its practical operations were headed by the secretary-general, Mark Wischnitzer. When the Hilfsverein began to assist Jewish emigration from Germany, a clear division of responsibility was made between it and the Jewish Agency; the latter, through the Palästina-Amt (Palestine Office), dealt exclusively with emigrants to Palestine, while the Hilfsverein dealt with Jews seeking to emigrate elsewhere.

The lull in the pressure to emigrate, which lasted from the end of 1933 until early 1935, gave the Hilfsverein a breathing space that enabled it to improve its organizational setup and prepare some long-range planning. In the second half of 1935, prospects for the emigration of Jews from Germany took a drastic turn for the worse. Emigration to Palestine was severely curtailed, and few openings were left for the absorption of Jews in European countries. It was just at this time that the demand for emigration grew rapidly, as a result of the NUREMBERG LAWS published in September 1935. The Hilfsverein reacted by opening more branch offices in German cities, exploring new possibilities, and generally adapting itself to the growing needs, in part by accelerating cooperation with Jewish relief agencies abroad and with local committees in the target countries. Together with the American Jewish JOINT DISTRIBUTION COMMITTEE, the Hilfsverein drew up a four-year emigration plan, based on the premise of 25,000 emigrants per year (or, according to another version, 40,000), not including emigration to Palestine. At this point the Hilfsverein also became active in group migration and resettlement, which it felt represented a unique contribution to Jewish survival.

The sharp growth of anti-Jewish persecution in 1937, further exacerbated in the wake of the KRISTALLNACHT pogrom of November 1938, turned the Hilfsverein's work into an emergency operation. Even so, the principle of planned and organized emigration was not abandoned. Representatives of the society participated in the EVIAN CONFERENCE in the summer of 1938, presenting to the conference leaders a memorandum with detailed proposals for organizing and increasing emigration. In practice, however, the possibilities for emigration fell desperately short of the needs. The Hilfsverein continued to function as an independent agency until 1939, when it became a section of the Reichsvereinigung der Juden in Deutschland (Reich Association of Jews in Germany). In 1941, when emigration was prohibited altogether, that section, too, went out of existence.

BIBLIOGRAPHY

Rinot, M. *The German Jewish Aid Society: Its Formation and Struggle.* Jerusalem, 1972. (In Hebrew.)
Zentralausschuss der Deutschen Juden für Hilfe und Aufbau. *Arbeitsbericht für Hilfe und Aufbau.* 7 vols. Berlin, 1933–1938.

YEHOYAKIM COCHAVI

HILFSWILLIGE ("volunteer helpers"; abbr., Hiwis), designation applied to Soviet prisoners of war and Soviet civilians in the Nazi-occupied areas of the Soviet Union who volunteered for auxiliary services in the rear-echelon units of the German army, or were drafted into such services.

Even in the early stages of the campaign against the Soviet Union, the German army commanders realized that because of the wide expanses of the area under their control and the shortage of German manpower, they would have to resort to local recruits. Soviet citizens therefore came to be employed as auxiliaries, functioning as drivers, mechanics, fitters, coachmen, kitchen workers, porters, and so on. They served either as individuals or as members of a group (up to company size) attached to German units, mainly supply units operating in the rear.

Based on this successful experience, the

Germans gradually expanded the range of jobs on which Hiwis were employed; their conditions of service were formalized, they were given German uniforms, and their food and pay were made almost equal with those of German soldiers.

At the beginning of the winter of 1941–1942, guard units made up of Hiwis were added to the existing service units. These units were armed, and assigned to guard military objects in the rear. They grew rapidly in number and size (to battalion strength), and became known as OSTBATAILLONE.

BIBLIOGRAPHY

Dallin, A. *German Rule in Russia, 1941–1945: A Study of Occupation Policies.* New York, 1957.

SHMUEL SPECTOR

HIMMLER, HEINRICH (1900–1945), Reich Leader (*Reichsführer*) of the SS, head of the GESTAPO and the Waffen-SS, minister of the interior from 1943 to 1945, and, next to Adolf Hitler, the most powerful man in Nazi Germany. Himmler was born in Munich into a middle-class Catholic family; his father was a schoolteacher with authoritarian views. Educated at a secondary school in Landshut, Himmler joined the army in 1917 as an officer cadet, but he never saw service at the front. Later he studied agriculture and economics at the Munich School of Technology. He worked briefly as a salesman and as a chicken farmer in the 1920s. During this period he developed a close contact with the embryonic Nazi party. Himmler took part in the Hitler Putsch of 1923 at the side of Ernst RÖHM, joined Röhm's terrorist organization, the Reichskriegsflagge (Reich War Flag), and held various positions in the *Gau* (region) of Bavaria.

In 1926 Himmler became assistant propaganda leader of the Nazi party. He joined the SS in 1925 and in 1929 became its head. This personal bodyguard of Hitler, which at that time numbered some two hundred men, became under Himmler's leadership a key element in the power structure of the Nazi state. Himmler was elected a Nazi Reichstag dep-

Heinrich Himmler (right) talking to Obergruppenführer Sepp Dietrich (left), the commander (1933–1943) of the Leibstandarte Adolf Hitler (Adolf Hitler Bodyguard Regiment), on September 13, 1940. [Bildarchiv Preussischer Kulturbesitz]

uty in 1930, and immediately after the Nazi seizure of power in January 1933 was appointed police president in Munich and head of the political police throughout Bavaria. This gave him the power base to extend SS membership, organize the SD (Sicherheitsdienst; Security Service) under Reinhard HEYDRICH, and secure their independence from Röhm's SA (Sturmabteilung; Storm Troopers).

In September 1933 Himmler was appointed commander of all the political police units throughout the Reich (except Prussia). The following year, Hermann GÖRING appointed him deputy head of the Gestapo in Prussia. Himmler was instrumental in crushing the abortive SA putsch of June 1934, which eliminated Röhm and the SA as potential rivals for power and opened the way to the emergence of the SS as an independent force. The next stage in Himmler's ascendancy came in 1936, when he won control of the entire police force throughout the Third Reich, with the title of *Reichsführer-SS* and Head of the German Police. He created a state within a state, using his power to terrorize all opponents of the regime as well as his personal enemies. Himmler established the first concentration camp at DACHAU in 1933, and the further organization and administration of the camps continued to be the work of the SS.

Himmler was inspired by a combination of fanatic racism and a belief in occult forces. His concern for "racial purity" led to the encouragement of special marriage laws that would further the systematic procreation of children of perfect "Aryan" couples, and also to the establishment of the Lebensborn (Fountain of Life) institutions at which girls would couple with SS men, both selected for their perfect Nordic qualities. Himmler aimed to create an aristocracy of the "master race," based on the traditional virtues of honor, obedience, and courage. By recruiting "Aryans" of different nationalities into the Waffen-SS, he would establish a pan-European order of knighthood, owing allegiance to Hitler alone. These fantasies went hand in hand with Himmler's efficiency, utter lack of scruples, and competence in administration. He suffered, however, from psychosomatic illnesses that took the form of intestinal cramps and severe headaches. Himmler was squeamish, and on one occasion he almost fainted at the spectacle of a hundred Jews, including women, being shot to death on the Russian front. This helped lead to the introduction of poison gas as "a more humane means" of execution.

The war gave Himmler the opportunity to implement the other side of his program, that is, the elimination of Jews and Slavs as "subhumans." This made Himmler one of the greatest mass murderers in history. In October 1939 he was appointed *Reichskommissar für die Festigung des deutschen Volkstums* (Reich Commissar for the Strengthening of German Nationhood) and was also given absolute authority in the newly annexed part of Poland. This entailed responsibility for the replacement of Poles and Jews by VOLKSDEUTSCHE (ethnic Germans) from the Baltic states. By the time of the invasion of the Soviet Union in 1941, Himmler controlled all the organs of police and intelligence power, and through the SS he dominated the concentration and extermination camps in Poland. His Waffen-SS with its thirty-five divisions almost constituted a rival army to the Wehrmacht. He also controlled the political administration in the occupied territories. When he was made minister of the interior in 1943, Himmler gained jurisdiction over the courts and the civil service as well. He used these powers to exploit Jews and Slavs as slave laborers, to gas millions of Jews, and to institute pseudo-MEDICAL EXPERIMENTS on "asocial individuals" (Jews, Gypsies, and criminals), to determine their resistance to extremes of cold and decompression.

The killing of the Jews represented for Himmler the fulfillment of a mission. The "Final Solution" was the means to achieve the racial supremacy of the "Aryan" and purify the world of contamination by subhumans. His four EINSATZGRUPPEN in the east were the agencies of extermination when the SS established the extermination camps of BEŁŻEC, SOBIBÓR, and TREBLINKA in the spring of 1942. After the July 1944 bomb plot on Hitler's life, Himmler received even further advancement, as commander in chief of the Reserve Army and commander of Army Group Vistula.

Toward the end of the war, aware of the inevitable German defeat, Himmler made a number of gestures, apparently hoping to ingratiate himself with the Allies. He sanctioned negotiations in Budapest that would have allowed the release of Hungarian Jews in return for trucks supplied by the Allies. In November 1944, he tried to conceal the evidence of mass murder in the extermination camps and permitted the transfer of several hundred camp prisoners to Sweden. He also tried to initiate peace negotiations with the Allies through Count Folke BERNADOTTE, head of the Swedish Red Cross. Himmler ordered a cessation of the mass murder of Jews at this time, and proposed surrendering to Gen. Dwight D. EISENHOWER in the west while continuing the struggle in the east. This proposal infuriated Hitler, who stripped Himmler of all his offices. Even Adm. Karl Dönitz, who succeeded Hitler in the last days of the war as head of the German government, spurned Himmler's services. After the German surrender, Himmler assumed a false identity and tried to escape, but he was captured by British troops. He committed suicide on May 23, 1945, before he could be brought to trial as one of the major war criminals.

BIBLIOGRAPHY

Frischauer, W. *Himmler: The Evil Genius of the Third Reich.* London, 1953.

Kersten, F. *The Kersten Memoirs, 1940–1945.* New York, 1957.

Krausnick, H., et al. *Anatomy of the SS State.* London, 1968.

Manvell, R., and H. Fraenkel. *Heinrich Himmler.* London, 1965.

Smith, B. F. *Heinrich Himmler: A Nazi in the Making, 1900–1926.* Stanford, 1971.

Smith, B. F., and A. F. Peterson. *Geheimreden 1933 bis 1945 und andere Ansprachen.* Frankfurt, 1974.

LIONEL KOCHAN

HINDENBURG, PAUL VON BENECKENDORFF UND VON (1847–1934), German army officer and statesman; president of Germany. Born in Posen (present-day Poznań), Hindenburg attended officers' school and served in the German army until 1911, retiring with the rank of general. At the outbreak of World War I, he was recalled to the army and appointed commander in chief of the

Reich President Paul von Hindenburg (left) with Reich Chancellor Adolf Hitler (1933).

eastern front, where his decisive victory over the Russians in the battle of Tannenberg earned him great fame. In 1916 he became chief of staff of the German army, with the rank of *Generalfeldmarschall* (General of the Army), his principal aide being Gen. Erich LUDENDORFF, who made the real decisions. Under the leadership of these two men the German high command put its stamp on all the internal political moves made by Imperial Germany in the final stages of the war, foiling all efforts to bring the war to an end by a compromise peace.

Nevertheless, Hindenburg remained a war hero in the eyes of many Germans, and this, in 1925, helped him to be elected the second president of the Weimar Republic, as the candidate of the right-wing parties. In the early part of his term of office, Hindenburg acted in strict compliance with the Weimar Constitution, which restricted presidential powers. From 1930, however, as a result of the economic crisis and the growing unemployment, democracy in Germany was shaken to the core and was no longer able to function properly.

Hindenburg's first term ended in 1932. Despite his age (he was eighty-five at the time), he decided to run again, this time as the candidate of the moderate left-wing and Center parties (except for the Communists), who all gave their support to the chancellor, Heinrich Brüning. But as soon as he was re-elected, Hindenburg abandoned his supporters, dismissing Chancellor Brüning in May 1932 and appointing Franz von PAPEN in his place; Papen, who had bolted the Center party, had only the support of the right-wing parties (excluding the Nazis).

In the July 1932 elections, the Nazis gained the largest number of votes. Hindenburg, however, was not prepared to entrust Adolf HITLER with forming a cabinet, and used his powers to dissolve the Reichstag. The new elections, held in November 1932, did not change the political constellation in the Reichstag to any appreciable extent; the Nazis suffered some losses but remained the largest political party. Again Hindenburg refused to appoint Hitler chancellor, nominating Gen. Kurt von Schleicher to the post in December. When Schleicher failed in his efforts to create a broad popular base of support for his cabinet, Hindenburg finally gave in to the urgings of his close confidants and appointed Hitler the new chancellor, but not before extracting the agreement that the new cabinet would retain the moderate conservative-national character of its predecessor by giving its non-Nazi members a decisive majority. However, as soon as Hitler was installed, on January 30, 1933, he took complete control of the regime. The staged Reichstag fire persuaded the old president, on February 28, to sign a decree "for the protection of the people and the state" that put an end to the regime of the Weimar Republic and abolished basic civil rights as they had been in force in Germany. Thereafter, Hindenburg no longer played any real role in the political life of the country. He died on August 2, 1934, at the age of eighty-seven.

Mention should be made of Hindenburg's intervention concerning the Law for the Restoration of the Professional Civil Service, which was the Nazis' first anti-Jewish legislative act, designed to eliminate Jews from the German civil service. On Hindenburg's request, the new law was not applied to persons who had been front-line soldiers in World War I. This restriction was abolished when the NUREMBERG LAWS went into effect in September 1935.

BIBLIOGRAPHY

Dorpalen, A. *Hindenburg and the Weimar Republic.* Princeton, 1964.
Görlitz, W. *Hindenburg: Ein Lebensbild.* Bonn, 1953.
Hubatsch, W. *Hindenburg und der Staat: Aus den Papieren des Generalfeldmarschalls und Reichspräsidenten von 1878 bis 1934.* Göttingen, 1966.
Wheeler-Bennett, J. W. *Hindenburg: The Wooden Titan.* London, 1936.

DAVID HADAR

HIRSCH, OTTO (1885–1941), chairman of the REICHSVERTRETUNG DER DEUTSCHEN JUDEN (Reich Representation of German Jews). Hirsch was born in Stuttgart, the capital of Württemberg, and studied law. He joined the civil service, first on the municipal and later on the provincial level.

In 1919 Hirsch represented Württemberg at the Weimar National Assembly and the Paris Peace Conference. Active in Jewish affairs, he became one of the leaders of the CENTRALVEREIN DEUTSCHER STAATSBÜRGER JÜDISCHEN GLAUBENS (Central Union of German Citizens of Jewish Faith), and was among those of its members advocating that the Centralverein promote Jewish settlement in Palestine. Hirsch was on the committee that prepared for the establishment of the Jewish Agency, a Zionist organization; he also belonged to the Committee of Friends of the Hebrew University and the Provincial Council of Württemberg Jews, whose chairman he became in 1930. A meeting with Martin Buber aroused his interest in adult education, and on Hirsch's initiative a Lehrhaus (Bet-Midrash, or Jewish house of study) was established in Stuttgart, with Buber as one of its lecturers. Hirsch headed the Lehrhaus board together with Jews of various shades of opinion.

In 1933 Hirsch was among the founders of the Reichsvertretung (as of 1939 the Reichsvereinigung der Juden in Deutschland) and became its chairman. He played a major role in the Reichsvertretung's activities: economic aid to Jews, vocational training and retraining, expansion of the Jewish network of schools, and Jewish emigration. He also had a part in the establishment and operation of the Center for Jewish Adult Education, headed by Buber. Hirsch was a courageous representative of the Reichsvertretung vis-à-vis the German authorities. He guided the organization through its internal problems, successfully mediating between opposing views and conflicting demands. An authority on organization and budgeting, he was the liaison between the Reichsvertretung and Jewish aid organizations abroad, especially the British COUNCIL FOR GERMAN JEWRY and the American JOINT DISTRIBUTION COMMITTEE, gaining their full confidence as a representative of German Jewry.

In the summer of 1935 Hirsch was arrested for the first time, in connection with a sermon that the Reichsvertretung had prepared to be read out in all the synagogues of Germany on the Day of Atonement. Refusing to go into hiding at the time of the KRISTALLNACHT pogroms in November 1938, Hirsch was arrested for a second time and held for two weeks in the SACHSENHAUSEN concentration camp. On resuming his post, he focused most of his efforts on emigration and rescue. His plan was to establish transit camps for refugees in Britain and other countries; he hoped that this would facilitate and speed up the release of the many thousands of Jews who had been arrested in Germany and that it would bolster the rescue efforts. He held numerous meetings in Britain and the United States in 1938 and 1939 with representatives of aid organizations and government officials, and was the Reichsvertretung delegate to the EVIAN CONFERENCE.

On February 16, 1941, Hirsch was again arrested, and a few months later was taken to the MAUTHAUSEN concentration camp, despite the fact that his wife had obtained an entry visa for him to the United States. He was tortured to death in the camp, and his family was later informed by the camp administration that he had died on June 19, 1941. After the war, a memorial to Otto Hirsch was erected in his native city of Stuttgart and in Shavei Zion, a settlement in northern Israel founded by Jews from Württemberg.

BIBLIOGRAPHY

Marx, L. "Otto Hirsch: Ein Lebensbild." *Bulletin des Leo Baeck Instituts* 6/24 (1963): 295–312.

YEHOYAKIM COCHAVI

HIRSCHLER, RENÉ (1905–1944), Chief Rabbi of Strasbourg on the eve of World War II, prominent in welfare activity in Vichy France. Born in Marseilles, Hirschler became an important figure for Jewish youth in Alsace in the 1930s as the editor of *Kadimah*, a French-language periodical that both supported Zionism and advocated increased Jewish involvement in community affairs. Hirschler was instrumental in organizing the welfare structure for the thousands of Jews from Alsace-Lorraine who fled to the south of France with the outbreak of war in September 1939 or were evacuated to that region in the summer of 1940. Acutely aware of the needs of the Jewish refugees in the south, he also encouraged Isaïe Schwartz, the Chief Rabbi of France, to unite the various Jewish welfare societies in an umbrella organization. Herschler emerged as the chief figure in the Commission Centrale des Organisations Juives d'Assistance (CCOJA), established on October 30–31, 1940, in Marseilles. He called upon the community leaders and their constituents to build a strong and effective organization in anticipation of the dire days ahead, but his call fell on deaf ears, and notwithstanding his efforts, the CCOJA remained an insignificant body.

In early 1942, Hirschler turned his energies to establishing the Aumônerie Générale Israélite (Jewish Chaplaincy), which diligently served the Jews in French internment camps in the south of France. He developed a wide network of rabbis and laymen who traveled throughout the camps, assigned residences, hospitals, and so on, and offered both religious support and general relief. Although often at odds with the CONSISTOIRE CENTRALE DES ISRAÉLITES DE FRANCE, his supporting agency, Hirschler was undaunted in pursuing his relief goals, even to the point of overriding the chief rabbi's directives. His wide-ranging activity and forceful interventions with the authorities eventually led to his arrest, on December 22, 1943. Together with his wife and close collaborator, Simone Hirschler, he was deported to AUSCHWITZ on February 3, 1944, and perished there.

BIBLIOGRAPHY

Cohen, R. I. *The Burden of Conscience: French Jewish Leadership during the Holocaust.* Bloomington, 1987.

Cohen, R. I. "The Jewish Community of France in the Face of Vichy-German Persecution, 1940–1944." In *The Jews in Modern France,* edited by F. Malino and B. Wasserstein, pp. 181–204. London, 1985.

RICHARD COHEN

HIRSCHMANN, IRA A. (1901–1989), American business executive; vice president of Bloomingdale's department store in New York City from 1936 to 1946. In 1935 Hirschmann served as board chairman of the University in Exile (of the New School for Social Research), which offered positions to exiled German scholars.

In the summer of 1943, Hirschmann was asked by the Emergency Committee to Save the Jewish People in Europe of the BERGSON GROUP to investigate rescue possibilities in Turkey. After delays, he reached Ankara in February 1944 as the special attaché of the WAR REFUGEE BOARD (WRB) to the United States embassy. Hirschmann and Ambassador Laurence Steinhardt exploited Balkan fears of postwar Allied retribution to obtain rescue of or improved conditions for thousands of Jews in Romania, Bulgaria, and Hungary. Hirschmann also helped Steinhardt overcome Turkish reluctance to allow refugees to land in Turkey. Nearly seven thousand Jews reached Turkey and Palestine under the WRB's aegis during the tenures of Hirschmann and his successor, Herbert Katzki.

Hirschmann contributed to a spectacular success in March 1944 when he helped per-

Ira Hirschmann (third from right), special inspector general for UNRRA, visiting the Bergen-Belsen displaced persons' camp in June 1946.

suade the Romanian ambassador to Turkey, Alexander Cretzianu, to prevail upon the Romanian government to transfer the remaining forty-eight thousand Jews in TRANSNISTRIA to the Romanian interior. In June, Hirschmann interviewed Joel BRAND in Cairo and recommended that the Allies continue negotiations in order to win time for the Hungarian Jews. Hirschmann contributed to additional successes that summer, including the provision of baptismal certificates by apostolic delegate Monsignor Angelo Roncalli (later Pope John XXIII) for Hungarian Jews in hiding, the Romanian government's agreement to allow Hungarian Jews to escape secretly to Romania and continue to Turkey, and the Bulgarian government's August 31 decision to abrogate its anti-Jewish laws.

In May 1946, Hirschmann was appointed special inspector general for the UNITED NATIONS RELIEF AND REHABILITATION ADMINISTRATION (UNRRA) to examine the conditions of Jewish DISPLACED PERSONS in Germany. He described his experiences in *Lifeline to a Promised Land* (1946) and *Caution to the Winds* (1962).

BIBLIOGRAPHY

Feingold, H. L. *The Politics of Rescue: The Roosevelt Administration and the Holocaust, 1938–1945.* New York, 1980. See pages 285–291.

Wyman, D. S. *The Abandonment of the Jews: America and the Holocaust, 1941–1945.* New York, 1984. See pages 215–220.

DAVID SILBERKLANG

HISTORIOGRAPHY OF THE HOLOCAUST.

The twelve years of the Nazi regime, from its rise in 1933 to its demise in 1945, represent the most tragic era in Jewish history. Of the total world Jewish population of eighteen million in 1939, one in three had been killed. Specifically, two of every three European Jews alive in 1939 were dead in 1945. Before the war, the Jew in the Greater German Reich suffered every indignity, losing his citizenship, his civil rights, and his property. As the Nazis occupied most of Europe, the danger to Jewry's very survival increased. The Jew was herded into ghettos and concentration camps, where he was beaten, starved, and overworked. With the "FINAL SOLUTION," the Nazis took the last right away from the Jew—his right to life. The survivors and the bystanders found themselves at a loss to explain this heinous crime perpetrated against an innocent people by an ostensibly civilized nation.

As with all epoch-making events, considerable attention has been focused on making the Holocaust comprehensible to scholars and laymen alike. Almost every methodology that could be used to analyze the destruction of European Jewry has been used, to one degree or another: those of history, political science, sociology, psychology, philosophy, and theology. Although not yet authoritative, Holocaust historiography has made considerable strides since the end of World War II. It is now both possible and desirable to summarize trends that have developed in the decades since 1945.

Research Trends. Overall, historians have approached the Holocaust in two ways: (1) a global approach, which tries to explain the Holocaust as a whole; and (2) a modular approach, which attempts to view the component parts of the Holocaust, preparing the ground for an eventual synthetic history. Historical studies may be divided into three periods: (1) an initial period, from the end of the war until the EICHMANN TRIAL; (2) a middle period, from the Eichmann trial to the mid-1970s, and, finally, (3) the period from the 1970s to the present. In each, different focuses and methodologies have been used.

In the initial period, writers concentrated primarily on collecting the facts in order to explain the Nazis' cold-blooded program of mass extermination and to chronicle its impact on the Jewish victims. Authors writing in this period made considerable use of documents from the Nuremberg war crimes trials, in addition to the few published sources then available, including the *Black Book*, published by the Jewish Black Book Committee in 1946. Significant contributions of this period included Léon Poliakov's *La bréviaire de la haine* (1951; published in English as *Harvest of Hate*, 1954) and Gerald Reitlinger's *The Final Solution* (1953). Both authors emphasize description of the events over evaluation, and may be seen as chroniclers trying to establish the facts. Both place heavy emphasis on the question of the number of victims. Poliakov, anticipating questions that attained crucial importance at a later date, dedicates separate chapters to Jewish resistance and to Nazi treatment of "inferior" peoples, that is, Slavs. Reitlinger's account covers neither issue systematically and suffers from an almost complete dependence on German documents, to the extent of repeating German evaluations of Jewish behavior *in extremis*.

The Eichmann trial renewed interest in the Holocaust, while also opening new sources for study. The period after the trial witnessed an increasing sophistication in Holocaust historiography. Some of the most important works on the Holocaust were published in the middle period (1960 to 1973), including Raul Hilberg's *The Destruction of the European Jews* (1961) and Nora Levin's *The Holocaust* (1973). Hilberg's book, now in a revised and definitive edition (1985), is a masterful reconstruction of the Nazi murder process as seen through the prism of the bureaucratic machinery created for the sole purpose of extermination.

In *The Destruction of the European Jews* Hilberg, like Reitlinger, made almost exclusive use of German documentation, despite the increasing number of Jewish documents, published and unpublished, that had become available during the late 1950s, especially in the evaluation of Jewish behavior. On this basis, Hilberg attempted to generalize about what he termed the Jewish "compliance reaction," whereby Jews are said to have almost completely cooperated in their own destruction. Similar conclusions by Hannah Arendt (*see* ARENDT CONTROVERSY) and Bruno Bettelheim stimulated considerable interest in the question of Jewish resistance (*see* RESISTANCE, JEWISH), the history of the Holocaust, and the nature of the Nazi regime. Numerous responses to the Hilberg-Arendt-Bettelheim thesis were published. One of the most immediate reactions to appear on the subject was Jacob Robinson's *And the Crooked Shall Be Made Straight* (1965), a detailed response to Arendt representing an almost line-by-line response to her assertions.

Although it languished in the late 1960s, interest in the Holocaust never completely ceased. Two unrelated events, the Yom Kippur War (October 1973) and the coincidental flourishing of collegiate-level Judaic studies in the United States beginning in 1970, led to further attempts at a synthetic account. Four such works have been published. Lucy S. Dawidowicz's *The War against the Jews* (1975), the most widely read, is essentially based on secondary sources. Dawidowicz was able to integrate a wealth of Jewish documentation for the first time. Nathan Eck's *The Holocaust of European Jewry* (1976) is similar to Dawidowicz, but is not as well known. Whereas Dawidowicz eschewed a global approach, preferring to concentrate on the key Jewish communities of Germany, Russia, and Poland, Eck attempted to provide a readable, chronologically organized, comprehensive account. However, significant historiographical issues, such as resistance, are lost in this approach, which also suffers from repetition. More recently, Yehuda Bauer has provided a concise college text in *A History of the Holocaust* (1982), while Martin Gilbert's *The Holocaust* (1985) has developed the use of Jewish documentation, in this case almost to the exclusion of German documents. Bauer and Gilbert also represent a concerted effort to view the Holocaust within the broader context of Jewish history.

Two interim surveys of Holocaust historiography have also been published. The first is Dawidowicz's *The Holocaust and the Historians* (1981), in which she initially seeks to explain why the history of the Holocaust has been virtually ignored by Anglo-American historians. Dawidowicz also studies the distortion of the Holocaust in Eastern Europe and, finally, tries to summarize the place of the Holocaust in Israel's historiography. More conscious of the interim nature of his conclusions is Michael R. Marrus, in *The Holocaust in History* (1987), an attempt to summarize the trends of Holocaust historiography in a thematic approach. Both of these summaries contribute to a clarification of the questions that have been studied since the end of World War II.

Methodological Issues. A number of issues have become the focus of intensive debate over the years. While some of these debates have been bitter and characterized by mutual accusations of falsification, others have been relatively mild. In general, passions have flared when issues relating to victims or survivors have been involved, although this has not always been the case. Basically, two types of disagreements have arisen, one concerning methodological problems and the other a variety of controversial questions raised by historians.

Undoubtedly, the most important methodological problem relates to the use of sources. Authors such as Hilberg have been accused of placing too heavy an emphasis on German or other non-Jewish sources, while ignoring or downplaying the significance of Jewish materials. Yet it must be remembered that although Jewish primary sources (existing chiefly in the form of diaries, testimonies, and postwar accounts of survivors) are great in number, they are considerably less extensive than the Nazi documentation. The historian's dilemma is that he has to document his assertions; his temptation is to study the subject from the perspective of his documentation. However, most of the individual victims left no records of their own, and such documents as did survive do not represent a systematic overview. The ONEG SHABBAT archive in the Warsaw ghetto, and the Białystok and Łódź ghetto archives, do contain systematic and almost full accounts of some aspects of ghetto life. In other major ghettos—those of Kraków, Lvov, Riga, and Vilna—and in most of the small ghettos, the Jewish records are more fragmentary.

One possible way to augment these written Jewish sources has been the use of oral histories or other ex post facto statements by survivors, who are interviewed with the intention of gleaning new or useful perspectives on historical questions. Oral history is, however, fraught with difficulties. Memory tends to fade over time, and it becomes increasingly difficult for the survivor to keep events in chronological order. The posing of leading questions by the interviewer, and the survivor's inability to verify assertions, for lack of other sources of information, also tend to lessen the usefulness of oral histories. Yet precisely because of this lack of verifying sources, oral histories have become an important element in Holocaust research; the

truism that researchers must use care is even more relevant in this case.

Great care must also be taken in the use of terms. Terms such as "ghetto" or "concentration camp" conjure up for the reader an image that may be misleading. Thus, when using the term "ghetto," readers almost automatically picture a hermetically sealed, overcrowded, and dirty part of a city into which Jews were forced to move from their former residences. While this picture is accurate for all of the large ghettos and most of the smaller ghettos in Poland, Russia, and the Baltic republics, there also existed a number of so-called open ghettos that were not sealed. In a few cases they encompassed the areas where Jews had lived before the occupation, and from which they were not forcibly relocated. Even greater care must be taken with terms originating with the Nazis, since they were purposely misleading. *Aussiedlung*, which literally means "resettlement" in German, was used by the Nazis as a camouflage for deportation to extermination sites; *Sonderbehandlung*, literally "special treatment," meant expeditious murder (*see* SPRACHREGELUNG).

Historiographic Controversies. At least six questions raised by historians have become centers of significant controversy: the decision to implement the "Final Solution"; the role of Jews in the murder process; resistance; rescue; Jewish-gentile relations; and the response of the free world. Each has become the vortex of bitter debate, with many accusations and counteraccusations of distortion being leveled by one or another side.

Regarding the question of the nature and development of the Nazi plan for extermination, two schools of thought exist, the intentionalist and the functionalist. Intentionalists emphasize the role of Hitler's virulent antisemitism and generally posit a straight line from the Nazi *Machtergreifung* (seizure of power) to Auschwitz. They therefore tend to concentrate on ideological factors and the totalitarian nature of the Third Reich to establish what may be seen as a top-down theory for the emergence of the "Final Solution." Stated briefly, intentionalists view the "Final Solution" as the culmination of a Nazi plan that can be dated at least to 1933, if not earlier. In contradistinction, functionalists argue that the "Final Solution" was more an example of bureaucracy run amok, with neither pre-planning nor an initial murderous intent. They emphasize the fluid political situation in Germany during the entire Nazi era and the dynamic nature of Nazi policy regarding Jews.

Both schools have strengths and weaknesses. Most notably, the intentionalists have great difficulty in explaining the often contradictory policies carried out by the Nazis before extermination began en masse in 1941, while the functionalists can explain neither the ideological background of Nazi antisemitism nor the fixation with the pursuit of a racial millennium that animated the Nazis to place a higher priority on killing Jews than on winning the war. It is difficult to say at this time in which direction the study of the question is heading, although it appears that an eclectic position, adopting some of the arguments by both groups, is presently emerging.

Similarly contentious, but for different reasons, is the question of the role, if any, that Jews played in their own destruction. Here, the writings of a number of historians and scholars, including Hilberg and Arendt, have been interpreted as a slight on the victims and survivors. More specifically, Arendt, in *Eichmann in Jerusalem*, pointed an accusing finger at the leaders and workers of the Judenräte (*see* JUDENRAT), claiming that they assisted the Nazis in their goals. According to her argument, Jews would not have suffered more than they actually did if they had been completely leaderless, while without Judenrat assistance in effecting deportations and slave labor, more Jews might have survived. Hilberg, in *The Destruction of the European Jews*, wrote about a Jewish "compliance" reaction based on two thousand years of being a persecuted minority.

These apparent accusations led to a two-phased response: an initial apologetic response, and a response through scholarship, which seeks an objective evaluation of the facts. In the apologetic phase, works were written as impassioned defenses of the martyrs, seeking to disprove the accusations by documenting the heroic Jewish response to Nazi persecution. In the second, and still continuing phase, an attempt has been made to both depict and evaluate the behavior of the Jewish leaders and masses *in extremis*. Perhaps the most significant contribution to the study of this question is Isaiah Trunk's *Judenrat* (1972), which showed the way for much of the recent scholarship on the Holocaust. The application of social- and political-history techniques to the subject of Jewish response is the logical outcome of the debate, and forms the basis for almost all of the studies on the Holocaust produced in the 1980s.

The problem of Jewish resistance is an inherent part of questions regarding Jewish response to Nazi persecution. Here too, accusations of Jewish passivity led to an initially apologetic response, followed by a later emphasis on objective scholarship. Apologists attempted to defend the honor of the victims who stood accused of going to their deaths like sheep. Exemplifying this type of literature is Karl Shabbetai's *As Sheep to the Slaughter?* (1963), a response to young Israelis' comments about the victims, and Ruben Ainsztein's massive *Jewish Resistance in Nazi-occupied Eastern Europe* (1974).

However, if the history of Jewish resistance is ever to be clearly understood, it must be seen in the context of the trans-European resistance movement. Every European country, including Germany, produced some form of an anti-Nazi resistance movement, just as all of them produced collaborators and quislings. The objective study of the resistance is actually still in its infancy; the mythologized view of the brave Maquis that was popular during and after the war is now giving way to a more sophisticated view, in which both resistance and collaboration are viewed as competing responses to the reality of defeat and occupation. Similarly, as the study of Jewish resistance matures, the issue is no longer viewed as "death with dignity" versus "cowardly fatalism." Conditions for successful resistance, now finally being studied, point to the fact that the Jewish uprisings in ghettos and in extermination and concentration camps, as well as the existence of Jewish partisan groups in both eastern and western Europe, was nothing short of a miracle.

In short, the accusations about Jewish complicity in the murder process, coupled with the question of Jewish resistance, has led to an outpouring of research, including numerous significant contributions to the understanding of the Holocaust. These include, to name only a few, Shmuel Krakowski's *The War of the Doomed* (1984), Dov Levin's *Fighting Back* (1984), Yisrael Gutman's *The Jews of Warsaw* (1982), Yitzhak Arad's *Ghetto in Flames* (1978), and Richard I. Cohen's *The Burden of Conscience* (1987).

Although the Nazis created their racial theory based on the assumption of a Jewish threat to the "Aryan" world, inherent in which was the all-powerful and rapidly multiplying Jew, the reality was considerably different. European Jews constituted slightly more than 1 percent of the total European population, and only in Poland did they comprise as much as 10 percent of the population. The question of how non-Jews in various countries reacted to the extermination of their Jewish neighbors is thus a crucial one, and is fraught with considerable difficulty. As a result, the issue has not been given the attention it deserves. Here too, earlier works tended to emphasize what may be characterized as an all-or-nothing approach, either by placing all European gentiles into a monolithic camp that did not make any exertions on behalf of the threatened victims, or by absolving the gentiles of all responsibility through the blanket conclusion that everything that could be done to help the victims was done. Between these two extremes, scholarly opinion—now being formed in monographic studies—seems to lean toward a more complex understanding that a majority of the European population neither helped nor hindered the "Final Solution."

A minority of collaborators, varying in size from country to country, did help murder Jews, while another minority, smaller yet, actively risked life and limb to save some Jews. Examples of works on these topics include Susan Zuccotti's *The Italians and the Holocaust* (1987) and Michael Marrus and Robert Paxton's *Vichy France and the Jews* (1981); the latter is not primarily concerned with the French population, but rather with the policies and views of the collaborationist Vichy regime.

Within the context of the popular response to the persecution of the Jews, the attitude of specific altruists, known collectively as *hasidei umot ha-olam* (righteous gentiles), has been reviewed, for example by Philip Friedman in *Their Brothers' Keepers* (1957) and, more recently, by Nechama Tec in *When Light Pierced the Darkness* (1986). With the exception of the Danish people, who acted collectively, the "righteous gentiles" acted alone or in small groups, with little or no public support (*see* "RIGHTEOUS AMONG THE NATIONS"). The non-Jewish response cannot, therefore, be seen as one of European civilization's finer hours. Yet it must be noted that in more than half of the countries of Europe, 50 percent or more of the Jewish population survived.

The possible implications of the demographic facts of Jewish victimization and survival prompted Helen Fein to attempt a sociological investigation of the Holocaust, in *Accounting for Genocide* (1979). Using a synthesis of available secondary sources as a basis, Fein was able to develop a workable statistical model that could be used to predict whether or not a random Jewish community could survive. Such variables as prewar antisemitism, the type of Nazi occupation, and the number of Jews, as well as the extent of their integration, meant the difference between a 90 percent victimization rate in Poland (over 3 million Jews killed out of a prewar population of approximately 3.5 million), a 30 percent rate in France (about 100,000 out of 350,000), and the very nearly zero rate in Denmark (although 700 Danish Jews were deported, almost all survived the war).

Two related questions have also received considerable attention. One is the question of the response of the CHRISTIAN CHURCHES—Catholic and Protestant—to the murder of the Jews. As a result of the debate over Rolf Hochhuth's *The Deputy* (1964), a play in which Pope Pius XII is accused of callously watching the slaughter without making any effort to help Jews, the issue of church responses has now become interlocked with the response of the various national groups, as it should in fact be. Although specific evaluations differ, the consensus seems to be that in countries where proportionally more Jews survived, many did so because of the timely intervention of local clergy, while in countries where proportionally fewer survived, there tended to be a lack of such interventions.

Also related to the broader issue of intergroup relations under the impact of Nazism is the claim that, to a degree, non-Jews in many countries did not help Jews since they too suffered under the barbaric heel of the Nazis. Such a view has been particularly adopted by apologists, generally, though not exclusively, by those dealing with the thorny issue of Polish-Jewish relations. One author, Richard Lucas, has entitled his book on life in Nazi-occupied Poland *The Forgotten Holocaust* (1986). The implication is that since Poles too suffered grievously, they were absolved from trying to help their neighbors. It is true, of course, that the Nazis did persecute almost everyone—Poles, homosexuals, Gypsies, Jehovah's Witnesses, Communists, pacifists—the list could go on ad infinitum. Only one group, however, was marked by the Nazis for *Ausmerzung,* or total eradication: the Jews. As such there can be no comparison in suffering. To date the only readily available objective study on Polish-Jewish relations is Emanuel Ringelblum's *Polish-Jewish Relations during the Second World War,* the English translation (1974) of a study done by the Warsaw ghetto archivist.

One further area of study has become popular in recent years, and also very controversial: the question of the response of the free world to the Holocaust. This question is in fact comprised of two interrelated issues: the response of the governments, neutral or anti-Nazi, of the countries not within the Nazi sphere of influence; and the response of the Jewish communities in those countries. Most particularly, the actions and inactions of the United States and of American Jewry have come under close scrutiny. Attention has also been focused on the attitudes of Great Britain and Anglo-Jewry, the Palestinian YISHUV, and Switzerland.

Here again two positions exist, of accusers who point a finger of guilt, or at least of moral responsibility, at the entire free world, including the Jewish communities; and of those who maintain that all that could be done was done to rescue European Jewry. Both positions are nuanced and should not be seen as monolithic; those who accuse governments often defend the actions of Jewish communities, and vice versa. Although the issue is highly emotional and controversial, a consensus seems to emerge from works on the subject such as Henry Feingold's *The Politics of Rescue* (1970), Bernard Wasserstein's *Britain and the Jews of Europe* (1979), Monty N. Penkower's *The Jews Were Expendable* (1983), David Wyman's *The Abandonment of the Jews* (1984), and Dina Porat's *An Entangled Leadership: The Yishuv and the Holocaust* (1986; in Hebrew). This is a view that while the various governments probably could have done more to save European Jewry, the existence of a number of domestic factors —ranging from antisemitism to simple bureaucratic inertia—meant that what aid was given was invariably too little, too late. On the other hand, the free-world Jewish communities probably could not have effected changes in governmental policy, although they could have been more vocal in publicizing the plight of European Jewry. Removing the polemics from much of the writing on the free-world Jewish response leads to one clear and unfortunate conclusion: that the Nazis caught European Jewry in a murderous stranglehold at a time when world Jewry was politically powerless and racked by internal dissensions, and when there was no other group ready or willing to take up the case for the victims.

Conclusions. Several decades have passed since the end of World War II, and the significance of the Holocaust as a historic event is only now becoming widely recognized. As the survivors pass on and take their experiences with them, the Holocaust becomes "merely" one more event recorded in history books. Increasingly, Holocaust research is being undertaken by scholars who are personally unacquainted with the events. To an extent, this means a greater degree of scholarly dispassion, but it also implies that greater care is needed to ensure that the moral lessons of the "Final Solution" not be lost on future generations. Although it is premature to attempt to draw any long-term conclusions, one thing is clear from a review of the questions asked by scholars since the end of the war: while some questions have already been answered, many more have yet to be asked.

[*See also* Holocaust, Denial of the.]

BIBLIOGRAPHY

Arendt, H. "Social Science Techniques and the Study of Concentration Camps." *Jewish Social Studies* 12/1 (1950): 49–64.

Dawidowicz, L. S. *The Holocaust and the Historians*. Cambridge, Mass., 1981.

Edelheit, A. J., and H. Edelheit. *Bibliography on Holocaust Literature*. Boulder, 1986.

Esh, Shaul. "Words and Their Meaning: 25 Examples of Nazi Idiom." *Yad Vashem Studies* 5 (1961): 133–168.

Friedman, Philip. *Roads to Extinction*. Philadelphia, 1980.

Gutman, Y., and G. Greif, eds. *The Historiography of the Holocaust Period*. Proceedings of the Fifth Yad Vashem Historical Conference. Jerusalem, 1988.

Marrus, M. R. *The Holocaust in History*. New York, 1989.

Yad Vashem–YIVO Joint Bibliographic Series. 15 vols. Jerusalem–New York, 1960–1978.

ABRAHAM J. EDELHEIT

HITLER, ADOLF (1889–1945), Führer (leader) of the Third German Reich. Born in Braunau, Austria, the son of a customs official from a smallholder family, Hitler spent his youth in the country of his birth. From 1900 to 1905 he attended the intermediate grades of the *Realschule* (secondary school), which concluded his formal education. Hitler's father died in 1903. In 1907 Hitler took the entrance test for the Vienna Academy of Art's School of Painting, and failed. His mother died that year, of breast cancer; the doctor who treated her was a Jew named Eduard Bloch. In 1908 Hitler made Vienna his home, living on the orphan's stipend that he received. Antisemitism was rife in Vienna at the time. In Hitler's own words, the Vienna period of his life was formative and decisive in shaping his views, and especially his concept of the Jews; but it is not certain whether by then he was already an antisemite.

In 1913 Hitler moved to Munich. When World War I broke out in 1914, he volunteered for the Bavarian army. He served as a dispatch runner in Belgium and France, was promoted to private first class (lance corporal), and was awarded medals for bravery, one of them the Iron Cross, First Class, in 1918. That October he was temporarily blinded in a British gas attack, and in the military hospital at Pasewalk he learned of Germany's collapse. It was then and there, by his own admission, that Hitler decided to enter politics, in order to fight the Jews.

On his return to Munich, Hitler stated, in his first political document (written on September 19, 1919), that the final goal of antisemitism must be "the total removal of the Jews." He served as a political spokesman and agent for the Bavarian army, and in 1919 joined a small antisemitic party that in 1920 took the name Nationalsozialistische Deutsche Arbeiterpartei (National Socialist Workers' Party, or NSDAP; *see* NAZI PARTY). The party's 1920 platform called for all the Jews of Germany to be deprived of their civil rights and for some of them to be expelled. Hitler gained attention as a public speaker, and in 1921 became the party chairman, with unlimited powers. In November 1923 he headed an attempt to bring the government down by an armed putsch, known as the Munich (Beer-Hall) Putsch, for which he was sentenced in 1924 to five years' imprisonment in a fortress.

During his imprisonment in Landsberg, Hitler dictated the first volume of his book MEIN KAMPF (My Struggle). He was released after only nine months. In 1925 he reestablished the National Socialist party and created the Schutzstaffel (Protection Squad; SS) to serve as the party's fighting force. Several of the German states prohibited his appearance as a public speaker.

The second volume of *Mein Kampf* was published in 1926, a year after the first. Another book, written in 1928 but not published in his lifetime, appeared in 1961 as *Hitler's Second Book*. It contains Hitler's grounds for his antisemitism, based on the race theory (*see* RACISM). In the book, Hitler now promoted his antisemitism as the central aspect of his personal and political career.

Hitler aimed to use constitutional means

to gain a parliamentary majority in order to destroy the constitution by due process. In 1928 the National Socialist party ran in the Reichstag elections for the first time, receiving only 2.8 percent of the votes. The party began its rise in 1929, and in the 1930 elections it won 18.3 percent of the total vote. In 1932 Hitler was granted German citizenship, which enabled him to run in the presidential elections. He lost, against Paul von HINDENBURG, but received 36.8 percent of the vote. In the Reichstag elections of July 1932, the National Socialist party received 37.3 percent, the highest it ever obtained in free elections, and it became the largest political party represented in the Reichstag. But in the elections held in November of that same year, the party received only 33.1 percent of the vote, and Hitler failed in his attempt to seize control of the government.

On January 30, 1933, Hitler was appointed chancellor of a minority government. The conservative opponents of the Weimar Republic hoped to use him as a means to gain mass support while controlling him and his radical movement, but it was he who took control of the state apparatus and later the state power to establish a regime of terror.

Although his party held only three out of the eleven ministries, Hitler managed to set up a dictatorship. Following the Reichstag fire of February 27, basic civil rights were suspended and, after elections held on March 5, parliamentary rule was abolished by the *Ermächtigungsgesetz* (Enabling Law). This law transferred all legislative power from the Reichstag to the cabinet, where the conservatives held a solid majority. Eventually, by outmaneuvering them, Hitler became all-powerful. Antisemitic riots took place in March, culminating in the boycott of April 1, 1933 (*see* BOYCOTT, ANTI-JEWISH), and in a law, passed on April 7, that inaugurated the Jews' elimination from public life in Germany. On July 14, after the dissolution of the trade unions and the other political parties, the NSDAP became the only recognized party in the land.

After Hindenburg's death, on August 2, 1934, Hitler also became head of state and commander in chief of the Wehrmacht, and assumed the title of *Führer und Reichskanzler* (Leader and Reich Chancellor). He

was now the dictator of Germany. The rearmament of the country was accelerated, as was the persecution of the Jews. The NUREMBERG LAWS were adopted on September 15, 1935, and many other decrees issued by Hitler or in his name led to the exclusion of the Jews from German society. By the end of 1937 about 150,000 Jews had left Germany, approximately one-third of the country's Jewish population.

After the ANSCHLUSS of Austria on March 13, 1938, nearly 200,000 Jews were added to the Reich. Although a quarter of them left the country within six months, at the end of 1938 Germany again had the same number of Jews that it had had in 1933. In October 1938, some 17,000 Jews of Polish nationality were expelled from Germany to Poland (*see* ZBĄSZYŃ). This was soon to be followed by the November KRISTALLNACHT pogrom.

Hitler's radical racial *Weltanschauung* was

Hitler at a *Reichsparteitag* in Nuremberg (1934).

combined with a Social Darwinism that saw the Jew as a source of danger to Germany and humanity, and as a central factor in the dynamic development of hostile ideological trends such as democracy, liberalism, and socialism. Even the Christian sources of ethnic political thinking in Western society were perceived by Hitler as manifestations of the infiltration of the Jewish spirit into western European civilization.

As early as the 1920s, in *Mein Kampf*, Hitler presented the Jews, or rather "international Jewry," as the world's foremost enemy:

> [The National Socialist movement] must open the eyes of the people concerning foreign nations and must over and over again recall who is the real enemy of our present world. In place of the insane hatred for Aryans . . . it must condemn to general wrath the evil enemy of humanity as the true creator of all suffering. . . . It must see to it that, at least in our country, the most deadly enemy is recognized and that the struggle against him, like an illuminating sign of a brighter epoch, also shows to the other nations the road of salvation of a struggling Aryan humanity.

On January 30, 1939, Hitler declared in the Reichstag that a new world war would lead to the destruction of the Jewish race in Europe. When the war began in Poland, on September 1 of the same year, the Germans embarked upon the destruction of Jews in that country, although for a while this was done in a haphazard rather than a methodical way. It was also at about this time that the systematic killing of the mentally ill with toxic gas was undertaken, on Hitler's orders (*see* EUTHANASIA PROGRAM).

In September 1939, Reinhard HEYDRICH told his assistants that Hitler had agreed to the expulsion of the Jews from Germany into the Polish territories annexed by the Reich. Hitler informed Alfred ROSENBERG that he wished to concentrate all the Jews from the territories under German rule in an area between the Vistula and Bug rivers. He told Hans FRANK on June 19, 1941 (three days before the attack on the Soviet Union), that the Jews would be dispatched from the GENERALGOUVERNEMENT, which would then serve only as a kind of Jewish transit camp.

The systematic killing of Jews (the "FINAL SOLUTION") began after the German invasion of the Soviet Union on June 22, 1941. According to Hitler's world view and his political strategy, the goal of the territorial expansion—to gain LEBENSRAUM ("living space") in the east—and the destruction of the Jewish people as the central ideological enemy were connected and were the focal point of the whole struggle.

The first massacres of Jews in the Soviet Union were carried out by the EINSATZGRUPPEN in June 1941; the killing was then extended to include the rest of the Jews of Europe. On several occasions Hitler reminded the public about his prophecy concerning the destruction of the Jews, and on April 2, 1945, he boasted that he had "exterminated the Jews of Germany and central Europe." His political testament of April 29, 1945, ended with a call for "merciless resistance to the universal poisoner of all nations—international Jewry." The following day he committed suicide in Berlin.

EBERHARD JÄCKEL

Decision Making and Jewish Policy. A fundamental tenet of Nazi ideology with regard to decision making was the so-called FÜHRERPRINZIP ("leadership principle"), which called for the exercise of absolute authority from above and absolute obedience from below. The iron discipline and maximum efficiency implied in this conception of decision making, the Nazis assumed, set them apart from the divisiveness and inefficiency of their supposedly chaotic predecessors, the democrats and liberals of the Weimar Republic. After 1933 many German institutions, including schools and universities, adopted the *Führerprinzip* to emphasize their allegiance to the new regime. Hitler was glorified by the principle because it made him the fount of all wisdom and the universal giver of orders. When historians and social scientists after the war were called upon to explain the functioning of the Nazi system, they found variations of the *Führerprinzip* a congenial component for their models of totalitarianism.

Scholars have subsequently discovered the decision-making process of the Third Reich to have been considerably more chaotic than the *Führerprinzip* would suggest. Hitler's work habits alone were too unsystematic to allow him to run a smoothly functioning decision-making apparatus. His interests, moreover, were not sufficiently broad for him to perform the role of a universal giver of orders. Only in matters of foreign policy, rearmament (and, after 1939, war), and the architectural reconstruction of Berlin was he able to concentrate his attention consistently and effectively.

Hitler's erratic work habits have long been known by scholars, but have not always been taken sufficiently into account in their analyses of the Nazi system. To be sure, Hitler was at times capable of working for weeks at a pace that left his aides exhausted, but these bouts of frenzied activity would be followed by weeks of lethargy. During these periods of lethargy, aides had difficulty prevailing on him to perform even the necessary routines of his office, let alone make important decisions. Albert SPEER's memoirs provide the most accessible evidence of Hitler's work habits, but they were already attested to by his private secretaries in interrogations conducted shortly after the war ended.

Hitler was not an effective delegator of responsibility. He did not generally assign subordinates to take responsibility for policy areas that, for whatever reason, he chose not to supervise himself. The result was often a competitive free-for-all among ambitious subordinates eager to demonstrate their competence to the Führer as well as to assure for themselves a position in the top ranks of the Nazi hierarchy. To secure these positions they had to be able to overcome rival claimants who sought the same powers and status. Those most successful in this fight for survival, such as Hermann GÖRING and Heinrich HIMMLER, wound up in charge of vast empires; those less able or less ambitious, like Alfred ROSENBERG or Wilhelm FRICK, had to be satisfied with occupying a less prestigious rung on the Nazi ladder.

Hitler's authority over these empire builders rested largely upon his unique personal qualities, the wellspring of his charismatic powers, and less upon his legal position at the top of a bureaucratic hierarchy. Although he rarely did so, Hitler could at any time intervene authoritatively in any of the innumerable disputes between his ambitious underlings. This was learned by Ernst RÖHM and the SA (Sturmabteilung; Storm Troopers) leadership during the June 1934 "Night of the Long Knives," in which Röhm and others were murdered on Hitler's orders. Hitler's powers, though not always exercised, have been called permanently potential: they could be exercised with unexpected and brutal swiftness. Indeed, the relationship of Hitler to his subordinates has been compared to the feudal relationship between lord and vassal.

Controversies about the Nazi decision-making process and Hitler's role in it have been particularly prevalent among scholars of the Holocaust. As it became clear to them during the 1960s that the *Führerprinzip*, at least as it was defined by the Nazis, did not reflect how most major decisions on Jewish policy in the Third Reich were actually made, an interpretive school arose. This school suggested that the rivalries between would-be claimants for control over Jewish policy were themselves an important radicalizing element in the persecutions of the Jews, propelling them from the ARIERPARAGRAPH ("Aryan clause") legislation (*see* ANTI-JEWISH LEGISLATION) of 1933 to the NUREMBERG LAWS of 1935, the "Aryanization" (ARISIERUNG) of Jewish-owned properties, and the DEPORTATIONS of 1938 and 1939.

Ultimately, in this view, it was the most radical claimants, Heinrich Himmler and the SS, who managed to outmaneuver their rivals and establish themselves, after the war broke out, as chief executors of a policy of mass murder. This interpretation suggests that the "Final Solution" and the AUSCHWITZ extermination camp that has become its symbol were the result of a radicalization process that, in the wake of the extraordinary Nazi military successes against the Soviet Union in the summer of 1941, was freed of all external constraints. Because they focus their analysis on how the Nazi system functioned in practice, these scholars have come to be called "functionalists." They see Hitler primarily as the legitimizer of the process of persecution, a process in which he only occasionally played a directing role, but one that he heartily endorsed and encouraged.

The "intentionalists," on the other hand, suggest that Nazi Jewish policy was from its beginning the product of long-term Nazi intentions. They point to utterances made by Hitler from the 1920s about the killing of Jews as evidence of his early intention to solve "the Jewish problem" by physical annihilation. Hitler and his minions, in their view, hid their ultimately murderous intentions until time and circumstances in 1941 were ripe for the "Final Solution" to be implemented. The escalation of the persecution of German Jewry during the years after 1933 was, accordingly, part of a clearly conceived design whose incremental unfoldings were realized only as circumstances allowed.

Neither the fundamentalists nor the intentionalists have managed to prevail in the debate, partly because the documentation that might allow either side to prove its argument is lacking, either because it was destroyed or because it never existed. Abundantly clear to both sides, however, is the fact that Hitler paid less attention to the details of Jewish policy than he did to foreign policy, rearmament, or war.

Although, as far as is known, Hitler never devoted one of his bouts of frenzied activity to the making of Jewish policy, it is instructive to observe his role at several critical turning points in the making of that policy. The notorious Nuremberg Laws of September 1935 and the infamous *Kristallnacht* pogrom of November 1938, both milestones in the escalating persecution of Jews, came about—at least in their timing—not as a result of long-range planning but by the accident of circumstance. In the case of the Nuremberg Laws, the underlying racist logic that Aryans and Jews should no longer be allowed to marry or have sexual relations was so much a part of Nazi ideology that civil servants in the Interior Ministry had long before prepared drafts of legislation to prevent such race mixing. However, Hitler's sudden decision at the 1935 Nuremberg party rally to present to his puppet Reichstag a law governing such mixing was the product of his need to fill an unexpected hiatus in the rally's agenda. The officials suddenly called upon to draft the concrete legislation were caught off guard, and had to improvise without the extensive files back at their offices in Berlin.

The circumstances leading to the *Kristallnacht* pogrom in November 1938, although different from those surrounding the creation of the Nuremberg Laws, demonstrate a similar inclination on Hitler's part to act impulsively. On November 7 a Jewish youth, seeking revenge for the deportation of his parents from Germany, shot and killed a German diplomat in Paris. This inspired Propaganda Minister Joseph GOEBBELS, eager to ingratiate himself with the Führer and to gain additional influence in Jewish policy, to propose to Hitler that the SA be set free all across Germany to wreak vengeance against the "Jewish crime in Paris." The result was a brutal night of murder, rioting, and looting. The decrees issued two days later served to complete the process of excluding Jews from German economic and cultural life. The Nazis announced those decrees as punishment, but in fact they had been ready for some time beforehand. Nevertheless, their sudden implementation was the result of Hitler's impulse. Thus was a significantly new stage in Nazi Jewish policy inaugurated.

Against this background it may be possible to understand more fully the decision in 1941 to implement the "Final Solution" by means of extermination camps established in eastern Europe. No single document with Hitler's signature calling for the mass murder of Jews has ever been found. This lack has sometimes been attributed to the chaotic way in which the Nazi system functioned, suggesting that the order could have been delivered orally, or even that by 1941 the system no longer required an order from Hitler to set the machinery of murder in action. Another possibility is that Hitler and the Nazi leaders deliberately tried to keep the order secret, either by delivering it orally or marking it "Destroy after reading." Alternatively, such a document might have been destroyed by an act or accident of war. There is no debate among scholars, however, about Hitler's responsibility for the decision to implement the "Final Solution," even if its execution was carried out largely by the elaborate SS machinery under the command of Himmler.

KARL A. SCHLEUNES

BIBLIOGRAPHY

Broszat, M. *Hitler and the Collapse of Weimar Germany*. Leamington, England, 1987.

Bullock, A. *Hitler: A Study in Tyranny.* London, 1974.

Fest, J. C. *Hitler.* London, 1974.

Flood, C. B. *Hitler: The Path to Power.* Boston, 1989.

Haffner, S. *The Meaning of Hitler.* New York, 1979.

Heiden, K. *Hitler: A Biography.* New York, 1975.

Jäckel, E. *Hitler's Weltanschauung: A Blueprint for Power.* Middletown, Conn., 1972.

Langer, W. C. *The Mind of Adolf Hitler.* London, 1972.

Maser, W. *Hitler: Legend, Myth, and Reality.* New York, 1973.

Schleunes, K. A. *The Twisted Road to Auschwitz.* Urbana, Ill., 1970.

Toland, J. *Adolf Hitler.* Garden City, N.Y., 1976.

Trevor-Roper, H. *The Last Days of Hitler.* London, 1971.

Waite, R. *The Psychopathic God: Adolf Hitler.* New York, 1977.

HITLERJUGEND (Hitler Youth; HJ), the National Socialist youth movement. The Hitlerjugend had its origins in the Jungsturm Adolf Hitler (Adolf Hitler Boys' Storm Troop), an SA (Sturmabteilung; Storm Troopers) offshoot founded in 1922. It changed its name to Hitlerjugend in 1926. Originally a boys' movement only, from 1928 it also admitted girls, into a separate organization that in 1930 became known as the Bund Deutscher Mädel (League of German Girls; BDM).

In 1931, Baldur von Schirach was appointed Reich Youth Leader (*Reichsjugendführer*) in the Nazi movement. Schirach's immediate goal was to bring the different youth organizations in the party under a single authority; these included, in addition to the BDM, the NS-Schülerbund (League of Nazi Students) and the Deutsches Jungvolk (German Young Folk), which inducted youngsters at the age of ten. Schirach achieved his goal when he was appointed *Jugendführer des Deutschen Reiches* (Youth Leader of the German Reich) in June 1933. By 1935, the HJ was a huge organization, comprising 60 percent of the country's youth.

The HJ admitted children at the age of ten; its membership was organized into two age brackets, from ten to fourteen and from fourteen to eighteen. The organizational chart devised by Schirach followed the military pat-

Hitler Youth at a *Parteitag* rally in Nuremberg (c. 1934).

tern, involving squads, platoons, and companies. The companies were within territorial formations based on the *Gau* (a term used for the territorial division of Germany for purposes of the NAZI PARTY), the *Untergau* (Lower *Gau*), and the *Obergau* (Upper *Gau*). They were all organized into the Gauverband (Association of *Gaue*) and subject to the authority of the Reichsjugendführung (Reich Youth Leadership). BDM affairs were handled by the *Reichsreferentin BDM* (Official in Charge of the BDM), who was given broad powers to execute her tasks.

The HJ and its organizational form were outgrowths of Hitler's ideology, in which the young generation represented the reserve manpower that would ensure the continued existence of the "Thousand-Year Reich." Accordingly, Nazi educational doctrine was based on Hitler's anti-intellectualism, and on a preference for body building at the expense of the mental and intellectual development of the individual. One of the guiding principles of Nazi education was to keep the young people in constant action and to constantly spur them to activism. This was the system to which a boy was subjected from the moment he entered the HJ until he became a soldier or an SS man. He was equipped not only with a uniform, but with a bayonet as well. When boys reached nineteen, they were drafted into the Reichsarbeitsdienst (Reich Labor Service), which stressed physical work and iron discipline, with thousands of the youngsters put to work on the land. As soon as they had completed the compulsory term in the Labor Service, the young men enlisted in the armed forces. This process enabled the Nazi party to control and supervise German youth from age ten to age twenty-one.

The objectives of the BDM were based on the Nazi ideal woman—in other words, the racist ideal. The values that were to be implanted in the girls by their training were obedience, performance of duty, self-sacrifice, discipline, and physical self-control. Two-thirds of the time the girls spent in the BDM was taken up with sports, and one-third with ideology. The main goal for which the girls were trained was to become mothers of genetically healthy children, whom they would in turn educate in the spirit of National Socialism. The BDM members were indoctrinated with "racial pride" and the consciousness of being "German women," who would shun any contact with Jews.

Hitler Youth identification card. [A Living Memorial to the Holocaust—Museum of Jewish Heritage, New York]

During the war the BDM became increasingly involved in the war effort, at the expense of ideological training. Political and ideological indoctrination in the HJ played a much larger role than in the BDM. The activities in which the HJ members were engaged overshadowed the formal education they were receiving and estranged them from their families; quite often the youngsters became their family's Nazi propagandists—and ideological supervisors. The propaganda used for the implanting of Nazi ideas also drew on the mass media, and sophisticated methods were employed to gain German youth's support for the HJ ideals. The film *Hitlerjunge Quex* (Hitler Boy Quex) is a typical example of the Nazi style of brainwashing. Produced in 1933, the film tells the life story of a boy imbued with Nazi ideas.

Many of the young men who were converted to Nazi ideology during their membership in the HJ absorbed the poison of Jew hatred through their training and activities, and when they grew up became agents of the "Final Solution"—murderers by conviction.

BIBLIOGRAPHY

Klönne, A. *Hitlerjugend: Die Jugend und ihre Organisation im Dritten Reich.* Hannover, 1956.

Koch, H. W. *Hitler Youth: Origins and Development, 1922–1945.* New York, 1975.

Noakes, J., and G. Pridham, eds. *Documents on Nazism, 1919–1945.* New York, 1975.

Walker, L. D. *Hitler Youth and Catholic Youth.* Washington, D.C., 1970.

ZVI BACHARACH

HITLER YOUTH. *See* Hitlerjugend.

HIWIS. *See* Hilfswillige.

HLINKA, ANDREJ (1864–1938), Slovak cleric and political leader. Born in a village in northern SLOVAKIA, Hlinka became a Catholic priest and also a fanatic nationalist. The spiritual and secular Hungarian authorities alike were outraged by his propagandist activity, accusing him of violating the civil as well as the canon law; he was jailed and deprived by his bishop of priestly authority. During Hlinka's absence a new church was constructed in his village, and the villagers asked that Hlinka, as a native son, be permitted to consecrate it. In the clash that ensued with the local gendarmerie, dozens of people were killed or wounded. The incident made Hlinka's name known all over Europe and drew attention to the tribulations of the minorities living in the kingdom of Hungary.

When Czechoslovakia was founded as a republic in 1918, Hlinka welcomed it and supported Slovakia's joining the new state. Both he and the Slovak clergy, however, were troubled by the separation of church and state, and particularly by the laws that secularized education, taking the schools out of their hands. Disappointed by these developments, Hlinka decided to reestablish the Slovak People's Party (Slovenská Ľudová Strana), originally founded in 1905, and lead

Andrej Hlinka.

it in a struggle for Slovak autonomy within the framework of the Czechoslovak republic. Before long, Hlinka and his party clashed with the authorities, whose policy was based on belief in a single Czechoslovak people. This policy—in addition to a sense that anti-Slovak discrimination existed in economic and cultural affairs and in the local Czechoslovak administration—antagonized many Slovaks and led them to support Hlinka's party, which was eventually named after him. The party platform, nationalist and Catholic-oriented, came to represent the voice of Slovak nationalism. Hlinka was not always able to force his views on his aides and advisers; the party became increasingly hard-line, and after 1935 some of its sectors were inclined to cooperate with extreme right-wing movements. The radicals in the party, especially the younger members, aspired to the dismemberment of Czechoslovakia, whereas Hlinka himself continued to adhere to the more limited demand for Slovak autonomy. When the German-sponsored Slovak republic was created in 1939, after Hlinka's death, his party became the predominant political force and his memory became the symbol of a Slovak national renaissance.

In his youth Hlinka had spread anti-Jewish propaganda, and his party too used antisemitism to attract followers; among the younger generation it became an unbridled incitement to violence. Hlinka himself assured the Jews that he disapproved of antisemitism and discrimination against Jews, calling on them to support the Slovaks' national struggle.

A fervent nationalist who was utterly devoted to his people, Hlinka is regarded as the outstanding Slovak personality of the twentieth century.

BIBLIOGRAPHY

Fagula, L. G. *Andrej Hlinka*. Bratislava, 1943.
Hoensch, J. K. *Die Slowakei und Hitlers Ostpolitik: Hlinkas Slowakische Volkspartei zwischen Autonomie und Separation, 1938–1939*. Cologne, 1965.
Jelinek, J. *The Parish Republic: Hlinka's Slovak People's Party, 1939–1945*. New York, 1976.

YESHAYAHU JELINEK

HLINKA GUARD (Hlinková Garda), the militia maintained by the Slovak People's Party in the period from 1938 to 1945; named after Andrej HLINKA.

The Hlinka Guard was preceded by the Rodobrana (People's Defense) organization, which existed from 1923 to 1927, when the Czechoslovak authorities ordered its dissolution. During the crisis caused by Hitler's demand for the Sudetenland (in the summer of 1938), the Hlinka Guard emerged spontaneously, and on October 8 of that year, a week after Hitler's demand had been accepted at the MUNICH CONFERENCE, the guard was officially set up, with Karol Sidor (1901–1953) as its first commander.

The guard was the Hlinka party's military arm for internal security, and it continued in that role under the autonomous government of SLOVAKIA in federated Czechoslovakia. It operated against Jews, Czechs, the Left, and the opposition. By a decree issued on October 29, 1938, the Hlinka guard was designated as the only body authorized to give its members paramilitary training, and it was this decree that established its formal status in the country. Hlinka guardsmen wore black uniforms and a cap shaped like a boat, with a woolen pom-pom on top, and they used the raised-arm salute.

Until March 14, 1939, when Slovakia declared its independence, the Hlinka Guard attracted recruits from all walks of life. On the following day, March 15, Alexander MACH became its commander, retaining the post up to the collapse of the pro-Nazi regime in Slovakia in 1945. Its functions were laid down in a series of government decrees: it was to be a paramilitary organization attached to the party, fostering love of country, providing paramilitary training, and safeguarding internal security. By assuming these tasks, the guard was meant to counterbalance the army and the police. In 1941 Hlinka Guard shock troops were trained in SS camps in Germany, and the SS attached an adviser to the guard. At this point many of the guardsmen who were of middle-class origin quit, and thenceforth the organization consisted of peasants and unskilled laborers, together with various doubtful elements. A social message was an integral part of the radical nationalism that it sought to impart.

In 1942, the Hlinka Guard joined the police and the storm troopers of the local German population in deporting Jews to camps in Poland. Over the course of time, the guardsmen prospered financially and their zeal abated. Leadership passed into the hands of elements close to the Hlinka party. A small group called Nas Boj (Our Struggle), which operated under SS auspices, was the most radical element in the guard. Throughout its years of existence, the Hlinka Guard competed with the Hlinka party for primacy in ruling the country. After the SLOVAK NATIONAL UPRISING in August 1944, the SS took over and shaped the Hlinka Guard to suit its own purposes. Special units of the guard (Pohotovostne Oddiely Hlinkovej Gardy) were employed against partisans and Jews.

BIBLIOGRAPHY

Jelinek, Y. *The Parish Republic: Hlinka's Slovak People's Party, 1939–1945.* Boulder, 1976.
Jelinek, Y. "Storm-Troopers in Slovakia: The Rodobrana and the Hlinka Guard." *Journal of Contemporary History* 6/3 (1971): 97–119.
Susko, L. "Hlinková Garda od svojho vzniku az po salzburske rokovanie (1938–1940)." *Zbornik Muzea Slovenskeho Narodneho Povstania* 11 (1969): 167–262.

YESHAYAHU JELINEK

HOLLAND. *See* Netherlands, The.

HOLOCAUST (Heb., *sho'ah*). The word "holocaust" is derived from the Greek *holokauston*, which originally meant a sacrifice totally burned by fire; it was used in the translation of 1 Samuel 7:9, "a burnt offering to God." In the course of time it came to. be used to describe slaughter on a general or large scale, and, especially, various forms of the destruction of masses of human beings. In the 1950s the term came to be applied primarily to the destruction of the Jews of Europe under the Nazi regime, and it is also employed in describing the annihilation of other groups of people in World War II. The mass extermination of Jews has become the archetype of GENOCIDE, and the terms *sho'ah* and "holocaust" have become linked to the attempt by the Nazi German state to destroy European Jewry during World War II.

The use of the Hebrew word *sho'ah* to denote the destruction of Jews in Europe during the war appeared for the first time in the booklet *Sho'at Yehudei Polin* (The Holocaust of the Jews of Poland), published by the United Aid Committee for the Jews of Poland, in Jerusalem in 1940. The booklet contains reports and articles on the persecution of Jews in eastern Europe from the beginning of the war, written or verbally reported by eyewitnesses, among them several leaders of Polish Jewry. Up to the spring of 1942, however, the term was rarely used. The Hebrew term that was first used, spontaneously, was *hurban* (lit., "destruction"), similar in meaning to "catastrophe," with its historical Jewish meaning deriving from the destruction of the Temple. It was only when leaders of the Zionist movement and writers and thinkers in Palestine began to express themselves on the destruction of European Jewry that the Hebrew term *sho'ah* became widely used. It was still far from being in general use, even after the November 1942 declaration of the Jewish Agency that a *sho'ah* was taking place. One of the first to use the term in the historical perspective was the Jerusalem historian Ben-Zion Dinur (Dinaburg), who, in the spring of 1942, stated that the Holocaust was a "catastrophe" that symbolized the unique situation of the Jewish people among the nations of the world.

BIBLIOGRAPHY

Eliach, Y. "Defining the Holocaust: Perspectives of a Jewish Historian." In *Jews and Christians after the Holocaust*, edited by A. J. Peck, pp. 11–23. Philadelphia, 1984.
Tal, U. "On the Study of the Holocaust and Genocide." *Yad Vashem Studies* 13 (1979): 7–52.

URIEL TAL

HOLOCAUST ART. *See* Art of the Holocaust.

HOLOCAUST, DENIAL OF THE. Denying the Holocaust includes attempts to deny the fact that the extermination of the Jews by the Nazis ever took place; contentions that Jewish losses have been grossly exaggerated; denials that the Holocaust was the result of a deliberate policy; and the tendentious and trivializing claim that the Holocaust was not unique and that there had been precedents, even precedents that had served as models for the Holocaust.

Such attempts began even before the conclusion of World War II and have since been systematically spread, in various ways, in many countries. The phrase "denial of the Holocaust," however, should not be restricted to the false accusations or the distortions of historical fact that began to appear as early as 1945, with the collapse of the Nazi regime. It also refers to the suppression of facts and the disavowal and destruction of pieces of evidence that were an integral part of the murder action and its implementation. The German bureaucracy entrusted with the task of carrying out the different stages of the "FINAL SOLUTION" used a variety of euphemistic terms to cover up the mass killings. The transports of Jews to AUSCHWITZ-Birkenau— where some or all of them were destined to be killed in gas chambers—were accompanied by a document stating that they were to undergo "special treatment" (*Sonderbehandlung; see* SPRACHREGELUNG). SS men and police who handled the deportations and operated the extermination camps, such as the AKTION REINHARD teams, were sworn to secrecy and committed themselves not to reveal anything about their actions, even after their mission had been accomplished. In an address made by Heinrich HIMMLER in October 1943 to an assembly of senior SS officers in Posen (Poznán), the SS chief said that the mass murder of the Jews was an operation "of which we shall never speak publicly." In July 1943, Martin BORMANN issued an order in Adolf HITLER's name prohibiting public reference to the "total solution" (*Gesamtlösung*) that was under way, and instructing that the treatment of the Jews be described as their "collective draft for a planned labor program." During the last two years of the war, special SS units were formed whose task was to remove the corpses of Jews from the pits where they had been buried and to burn them, so as to eradicate all traces of the massacres that had taken place. Paul BLOBEL, the commander of the units formed to carry

out AKTION 1005, testified at Nuremberg (in June 1947) that "in June 1942 Gruppenführer [Heinrich] MÜLLER instructed me to obliterate traces of the massacres carried out by the EINSATZGRUPPEN in the east."

Some of the Jewish victims were well aware of the Nazis' intention to deny the murders and their responsibility for them. The diarists of that period stated that they felt it their duty to make a written record of what was taking place, so that the world and the future generations would know the truth. Thus, Itzhak KATZENELSON, the poet who was imprisoned in the VITTEL camp in France and later killed at Auschwitz, wrote in his diary on the eve of his deportation:

They will never believe. They will never believe that the people of Adolf Hitler set up a slaughterhouse and massacred seven million Jews. They won't believe it, and worse: they will pretend to accept the big lie which that loathsome people has spread throughout the war years: "We did not kill the Jews. The Jews died on the way when we were taking them to the concentration camps. This was what was ordained for them. . . . They succumbed because they were weak, a weak and feeble people." They invented these terrible lies for the sake of their allies, to serve as an excuse, an alibi.

Leib Langfuss, one of the Jews working for the SONDERKOMMANDO in Auschwitz, wrote (on pages that were found in the vicinity of the Birkenau crematoria) that even those who witnessed what was happening in the ghettos could only tell the truth that they knew, but that "the real truth is far more tragic and dreadful."

Those who deny the Holocaust exploit various versions and methods. The most extreme among them claim that the Third Reich authorities never planned to murder the Jews of Europe, that no extermination camps were built and operated, and that there is no truth to the allegations that a murder apparatus run by the Nazis exterminated five million to six million Jews by deliberate, sophisticated methods. Others do not resort to a total denial of the facts, but they deny that the murder was as thorough and as extensive as it actually was. Also to be included among those who seek to deny the whole truth of the Holocaust are revisionists, among them genuine scholars and historians, who do not disclaim proven facts, but seek to reduce the degree of responsibility that the top Nazi echelon and Hitler himself bore. They depict the Holocaust as an occurrence that was essentially no different from earlier mass slaughters, such as those perpetrated by Stalin in the Soviet Union, which even served the Holocaust as models.

According to the most extreme version, the Holocaust never took place and is to be seen as a Zionist-Communist fabrication designed to besmirch Germany's reputation. In *The Lie about Auschwitz*, Thies Christophersen, an SS man who had been stationed in one of the Auschwitz satellite camps, claims that there were no gas chambers in Birkenau; he had personally investigated such "rumors" during his stay in Auschwitz, and they turned out to have no basis in fact. Another German, Wilhelm Staeglich, a Wehrmacht officer who served in the Auschwitz area, also claims to know that no murder by gassing took place in the Auschwitz-Birkenau camp. (After the war, Staeglich was a judge in the Federal Republic for twenty years, until he was ousted.) According to these claims, a Zionist-Communist conspiracy concocted the Holocaust. The Communists, it is alleged, seek to undermine Germany, which constitutes the main obstacle to Communist expansion in Europe, while the Zionists want Germany and the rest of Europe to suffer guilt feelings toward the Jews so that the Zionists can exploit these feelings, materially and politically, for the promotion of their own aims. The anti-Zionist policies of the Communist camp have, however, made the charge of a "Zionist-Communist conspiracy" ludicrous, although the charge is still being raised, separately, against each of the "partners" in this "conspiracy." In some of the printed material put out by the revisionists, the claim is made that it was no accident that the extermination camps were situated in areas that are now under Communist control, where no reliable on-the-spot investigation can be made. These extreme revisionists are not deterred by the evidence given by Polish emigrants in the West, who cannot be suspected of sympathy with the regime in their native country —evidence that confirms the existence and operation of Nazi extermination camps on Polish soil. Nor are the revisionists impressed

by the thousands of documents and testimonies given by victims of the Holocaust, as well as by men who were in charge of the murder operations; or by important public acts such as Pope John Paul II's praying on the murder sites and branding the murders as such. On the basis of the authentic documents and proven testimonies now available, it is possible to reconstruct almost everything that went on in the extermination camps, and to follow the tracks of every transport that reached them from every part of occupied Europe. To this large body of incontrovertible evidence the inveterate revisionists turn a deaf ear.

More sophisticated, and therefore more dangerous, is the partial denial—the attempt to undermine the validity of historical facts by casting doubts on the numerical data, the credibility of documents and witnesses, and so forth. Those who adopt this approach also aim at total denial of the Holocaust, but they believe it is easier to attain their objective by questioning the reliability of various details in the total historical picture. This method is deemed more effective, since it poses as a revisionist approach that examines each event on its own merits. This group of "partial revisionists" includes some who regard the total denial as ineffective and damaging, and others who believe that while the propaganda material circulated by the radicals addresses itself to the ignorant as well as to the extreme right, articles posing as respectable theoretical discussions will reach an intelligent sector interested in studying the subject.

One of the most widespread tactics in the writings of the revisionists is to question the legitimacy of the NUREMBERG TRIAL, which is attacked from various legal angles, some of them taken from critics who did not question the facts of the Holocaust. One major approach relates to the Soviet participation in the Nuremberg Trial and the ban on the introduction of crimes committed by the Soviets. This argument was raised by many critics of the International Military Tribunal, and the revisionists exploit it to cast doubt on the reliability of the many documents that served the prosecution as the basis for its case. In actuality, the documents collected for the trial and published in numerous volumes together with the proceedings of the trial represent one of the best-known, most widely circulated, and most credible source collections.

Another issue often raised by the revisionists is the number of victims. The radicals propagate the thesis put forward by a veteran Nazi, Wolf Dieter Rothe: "I am firmly convinced that not a single Jew was liquidated with the knowledge of the Reich government, of Adolf Hitler, who was then the Führer, and of the German people, simply because he was Jewish." In their attempt to refute the real number of victims and to sow doubt and confusion on this issue, the revisionists quote misleading prewar figures, or invent new ones, to demonstrate that the millions of Jews who were murdered during the war were a figment of the imagination. They have also proposed a variety of theories concerning the present whereabouts of the Jews from Nazi-occupied Europe. According to Paul Rassinier, a Frenchman who is one of the founders of the revisionist school, between half a million and a million Jews perished during the war, mostly as the result of the prevailing bad conditions and the Jews' inability to adapt to the changes that were taking place. Those who pursue this line of argument, however—that those Jews who died perished gradually—are faced with an irrefutable counterargument in the case of HUNGARY. There the Jews fell into the Nazis' clutches only in March 1944, and the destruction of most of the community was complete by early July of that year. Here a slow attrition cannot account for their disappearance. Rassinier "discovers" the millions of Jews who disappeared from Europe in various places. He claims, for example, that the masses of North African Jews who settled in Israel before and after its establishment as a state were not necessarily native North Africans but that many were Jews who had escaped from Europe. A prominent American revisionist, Arthur R. Butz, author of *The Hoax of the Twentieth Century*, claims that no more than 350,000 Jews are missing; some of them, according to Butz, lost touch with their relatives and are not really missing, and about 200,000 were executed by the German authorities on various grounds. Butz also "reveals" that large numbers of Jews entered the United States as illegal immigrants, assumed a new identity, and were swallowed up in the vast urban concentrations of America without leaving a trace.

Another piece of Butz's "evidence" that the figure of 6 million Jews who were murdered is nothing but a myth willfully spread by the Zionists is that YAD VASHEM (an institution that, Butz claims, was established for the very purpose of spreading the "trumped-up Jewish version" of the Holocaust, and has collected memorial pages for "every victim" of the Holocaust) has not been able to discover more than 2.5 million to 3 million names. Butz does not explain why the institution that purportedly has the task of spreading a myth did not also fabricate a few million names in order to produce the required figures.

Another target for the revisionists is the enormous wealth of material examining and documenting the Holocaust years and the Nazi crimes, down to the last detail—including official papers and thousands of diaries, testimonies, and memoirs. Very few events of historical dimensions have left behind such an enormous mass of documentation. The Nazis habitually put everything on paper, whatever the subject, even the most confidential issues, and although part of the documentation was destroyed in the last stages of the war, large quantities fell into the hands of the victorious powers. Contrary to the usual practice with official records, this material was not subjected to a long freeze before its release to the general public, and it has been readily available for research and publication. Among the most revealing documents are those from the war itself; the office diary kept by Hans FRANK, the head of the GENERALGOUVERNEMENT; a book written by Hitler in 1928 and shelved (*Hitler's Second Book*); the diaries of Joseph GOEBBELS; the speeches of Heinrich HIMMLER; and the minutes of the WANNSEE CONFERENCE on the implementation of the "Final Solution." Among the important sources of information from after the war are the statements made by the many thousands of Nazi criminals in their interrogations and during their court trials, and the autobiography and other notes of Rudolf HÖSS, the commandant of Auschwitz.

The revisionists become trapped in their attempts to explain or reject this huge accumulation of documents. The diaries and testimonies of Jews are rejected as not credible, because Jews are an interested party, and whatever they said or wrote down is dismissed as one big after-the-fact lie. Testimonies given by non-Jews, and documents forwarded from the occupied countries during the war (especially from Poland), which provide a record of the events that were taking place from non-Jewish and sometimes even anti-Jewish sources, are rejected as biased and written under pressure from Jews. The revisionists ingeniously exploit any contradiction or distortion in the documentation. Thus, when some witnesses let their imagination run free and incorrectly claim that the DACHAU concentration camp had working gas chambers, the revisionists pounce on this discrepancy to assert that if some details in the evidence given by witnesses are incorrect, then the whole story of the Holocaust must be nothing but a pack of lies. Generally, however, the revisionists realize that such wholesale denials on their part weaken their case, and so they concentrate on seeking to discredit particular aspects. For example, Robert Faurisson has argued that it was impossible to use ZYKLON B gas regularly in one place, as was the case in Auschwitz, and that therefore the story of the use of gas in Auschwitz is not true. An American colleague of Faurisson's, Reinhard K. Buchner, has sought to prove that it is impossible to cremate human bodies at the rate that this was done in the extermination camps, basing his conclusion on a comparison with the time it takes to cremate bodies in ordinary crematoria operating under normal conditions.

A vexing question in this denial of the Holocaust is the identity and nature of the people involved and their motivations. Another question is whether they know the truth and deliberately fabricate their web of lies. A careful analysis of their writings indicates that prominent revisionists know the truth. Their arguments carefully avoid the obvious weak points that could reveal them as liars, and the construction of their arguments discloses that they are aware of the truth, but are trying to distort and suppress it. Altogether, only a few dozen people are involved in this enterprise—writing books and articles, holding conferences, and quoting one another to create the impression that they represent a historical school. There are no historians among them: Butz is a professor of electronics; Faurisson was a professor of literature; Rassinier, a teacher of geography; some are journalists. They have an international orga-

nization of sorts coordinating their activities, distributing books and pamphlets from country to country and from continent to continent, operating cells in different countries, and establishing channels to reach various sectors of the population. One of the revisionists' major problems is obtaining serious academic status for their arguments and their publications, so as to gain entry to universities and colleges and capture the attention of students and educators. Their center in California specializes in these efforts. It conducts international conferences of revisionists and seeks to have them invited to prestigious universities. The revisionist *Journal of Historical Review* is published in Torrance, California, with a format like that of an authentic scholarly journal. Other centers of revisionist activities are in Sweden, Germany, France, England, Argentina, and Australia.

The revisionists' motivations are varied. Some are Nazi activists who are using the denial of the Holocaust to repair the Nazi image. Rassinier, and perhaps others like him, have joined because of their bitter hatred of communism and Communists, which is so extreme that it forces them to adopt an apologetic position on Nazism. Rassinier was formerly a Socialist, was himself a prisoner in a Nazi concentration camp, and at first recognized that the Holocaust had taken place; but his clash with communism became a deep-rooted phobia. Some of the revisionists are arch-antisemites who are ready to adopt any means to attack Jews. Most of them belong to neo-Nazi and neofascist movements, which have received little credence, largely because of the revelation of the horrors of the Holocaust. It is not surprising, therefore, that the present-day fascists and their sympathizers seek to hide or obliterate the truth about the Holocaust, which blocks their quest for power.

The writings of some reputable scholars and authors are utilized and recommended by the revisionists. One example is *The Origins of the Second World War*, by A. J. P. Taylor. This controversial book, written by a respected historian, apportions the blame for the outbreak of World War II in equal measure among all the parties involved in the conflict, and regards Hitler as just one more bad German leader; that in itself is seen by the revisionists as a support for their views. In his book

Der erzwungene Krieg (The Forced War; 1961), David Hoggan, who is scarcely a historian on a par with Taylor, tries to present a revisionist interpretation of the causes of World War II. David Irving's book *Hitler's War* propounds the view—completely baseless—that until the fall of 1943 Hitler had no knowledge of the mass murder of Jews, which was being carried out behind his back. The inference drawn is that neither Hitler nor some of his close confidants bear responsibility for the crime. Irving is a deliberate and consistent apologist for the Nazis and has contacts with the revisionists and their conferences. Professor Ernst Nolte, a respected German scholar and student of political movements, especially in the field of fascism, National Socialism, and totalitarian regimes, has made statements in his writings that contain elements taken from the revisionist trends and arguments. Of course, Nolte does not deny that there was a Holocaust, but he argues that Hitler had reason to be wary of the Jews. Some of them, like Chaim WEIZMANN, president of the World Zionist Organization and the Jewish Agency, had declared at the outbreak of the war that the Jews considered themselves part of the democratic camp that was fighting the Nazis and therefore the Jewish people had declared war on Hitler. Moreover, Nolte believes that the Holocaust was no different from other mass murders carried out in the twentieth century, the only unique feature being the use of gas for the murders. He points out that Hitler's massacres were preceded by those of Stalin and that these may have been not only a model, but also a motive for the Holocaust. The publication of Nolte's controversial ideas sparked a sharp and widespread debate in which many leading German historians participated; quite a few were inclined to justify Nolte's assumptions or even to agree with him. In Nantes, France, a doctoral dissertation justifying the denial of the Holocaust was submitted to the local university, and was approved. Because of public pressure, the approval of the dissertation was canceled, as was the academic degree awarded on its basis.

The historiography of the Soviet Union has seen no denial of the Holocaust as far as the facts are concerned. Soviet historians, however, refer to the victims as citizens of the Soviet Union or of the other states from which they came; the Soviets do not identify the Jewish victims as such, and do not make it unequivocally clear that the Jews were massacred only because they were Jews, not because they were Russians, Ukrainians, or citizens of the European countries. Soviet writings on the subject also overlook the role played by the peoples of the Soviet border regions in the persecution of the Jews, in collaboration with the Germans.

The arguments of the revisionists have won attention and acquired influence. In some quarters their impact may grow among young people who learn nothing about the Holocaust. It is natural that such persons, hearing about the Holocaust for the first time, refuse to believe that such incredible events could have occurred. Consequently, those who seek to deny that such events did take place, or to discredit them in one way or another, find a ready audience. Moreover, at some academic institutions the presentation of revisionist ideas has been legitimized by holding them forth as counterarguments to accepted historical facts concerning the Holocaust. The revisionists also claim the right to be given access to the media, and when no notice is taken of them, they complain that the principles of democracy and freedom of speech are being violated and that they are the victims of a conspiracy. In some instances, when the revisionists used provocative means to promote their ideas, their attempts failed. In California, for example, they announced in 1980 and 1981 that they would give a prize to any person who could prove that murder by gassing was committed at Auschwitz; they were brought to court and sharply reproved for their action. Some countries have outlawed the revisionists' publications. Revisionists have also been put on trial in some places, and in most cases, the judgment has gone against them. But there have also been instances when judicial authorities refused to take a clear stand on such issues as the murder methods used in the Holocaust or the dimensions of the Holocaust, on the ground that these are historical matters that a court of law is not competent to judge.

Attempts to deny the Holocaust have also led to vigorous counteraction. The denial attempts have had the unintended effect of arousing interest in the subject and a desire to learn more about the Holocaust and its meaning. They have spread awareness of the Holocaust and of the need to protect humanity from the scourge of racism and genocide.

[*See also* Historiography of the Holocaust.]

BIBLIOGRAPHY

Gutman, Y. *Denying the Holocaust.* Jerusalem, 1985.

Kampe, N. "Normalizing the Holocaust? The Recent Historians' Debate in the Federal Republic of Germany." *Holocaust and Genocide Studies* 2/1 (1987): 61–80.

Klarsfeld, S., ed. *The Holocaust and the Neo-Nazi Mythomania.* New York, 1978.

Kulka, E. *The Holocaust Is Being Denied: The Answer of Auschwitz Survivors.* Tel Aviv, 1977.

ISRAEL GUTMAN

HOLOCAUST EDUCATION. *See* Education on the Holocaust.

HOLOCAUST FILMS. *See* Films on the Holocaust.

HOLOCAUST LITERATURE. *See* Literature on the Holocaust.

HOLOCAUST MARTYRS' AND HEROES' REMEMBRANCE AUTHORITY. *See* Yad Vashem.

HOLOCAUST MEMORIAL COUNCIL. *See* U.S. Holocaust Memorial Council.

HOLOCAUST SURVIVORS. *See* Survivors, Psychology of; United States Army and Survivors in Austria and Germany.

HOME ARMY. *See* Armia Krajowa.

HOMOSEXUALITY IN THE THIRD REICH. In 1871, when the Prussian-dominated German Empire was established, the Reich penal code had a paragraph (para. 175) that classified homosexuality as "an unnatural form of licentiousness," carrying a prison term for persons caught in such an act. Under the Weimar Republic (1919–1933), the issue became a subject of free public discussion, and the Wissenschaftlich-Humanitäres Komitee (Scientific-Humanitarian Committee) was established for the defense of homosexuals. Even in that period the Nazi party denounced homosexuality in no uncertain terms, declaring it a deviation from normal sexual behavior that placed the main emphasis on the sensual, pleasurable element of sex life to the detriment of the natural increase in population, the nation's strength, and a proper family life. Sexual relations, according to the Nazi view, "serve the reproductive process, their purpose being the preservation and continued existence of the *Volk*, rather than the provision of pleasure to the individual." Homosexuality, in males and females, was not only an egotistic form of sex life; it also harmed the strength of the *Volk* and the race, and was therefore incompatible with the ideal of racial purity.

The wave of "protective custody" (*Schutzhaft*) of hostile political elements that was launched in the middle of March 1933 also included persons who were known for their activities in behalf of homosexuals. In 1935, paragraph 135 of the penal code was made more stringent when the promotion of friendship between males that was based on homosexuality, even without actual homosexual acts being performed, was made an offense. In August 1936 arrests were carried out in several large cities, in places where homosexuals were known to congregate. The attitude toward homosexuals was that they were asocial elements who should be put in prison. Persons who were found to be "recidivist" and "chronic" homosexuals were incarcerated in concentration camps.

The Nazi position on homosexuality, however, was inconsistent, and the approach to it was tactical in nature. Officially, homosexuality was sharply denounced, but its practice in certain Nazi circles was tolerated or ignored. This was the case with Ernst RÖHM, chief of the SA (Sturmabteilung; Storm Troopers) and a Hitler confidant, who was a known homosexual, as were several of his aides in the SA command. Political opponents took the Nazis to task over Röhm's homosexuality, but Hitler chose to ignore his close aide's sexual preference. It was only after the "Night of the Long Knives" (June 30–July 1, 1934), when Röhm and a group of his SA cohorts were murdered in the wake of a political confrontation in the Nazi leadership, that Röhm's homosexuality was mentioned as one of the reasons for his murder.

The charge of homosexuality was also used to get rid of prominent figures who were no longer regarded as desirable. Thus, in 1938, the chief of the general staff, Gen. Werner Freiherr von Fritsch, was dismissed from his post because he disagreed with Hitler's political and military plans. The official reason given, however, was that he had been discovered to be a homosexual—a libel invented by the Gestapo.

Under Nazi rule, tens of thousands of persons were punished on the charge of homosexuality. Thousands of them (some sources put the figure at ten thousand or more, but no precise figure is available) were imprisoned in concentration camps, where they had to wear a pink triangular patch (*rosa Winkel*). Many of the homosexuals imprisoned in the camps perished there. Shortly before the end of the war, some of them were set free and drafted into frontline service with the Wehrmacht. This step, of course, violated the Nazi principle on the issue.

Persecution of homosexuals was restricted to the Reich and the areas annexed to it. There is no evidence of Nazi-instigated drives against homosexuality in the occupied countries.

BIBLIOGRAPHY

Heger, H. *The Men with the Pink Triangle.* Boston, 1980.
Plant, R. *The Pink Triangle: The Nazi War against Homosexuals.* New York, 1986.
Rector, F. *The Nazi Extermination of Homosexuals.* New York, 1981.

ELISHEVA SHAUL

HORODENKA. *See* Gorodenka.

HORST WESSEL SONG, Nazi anthem. Horst Wessel (1907–1930) was a member of the SA (Sturmabteilung; Storm Troopers) who was shot dead by a Communist in a private vendetta. His killing was depicted by Nazi propaganda as a political assassination, and he became a Nazi hero and political symbol. The lyrics of a poem he published in 1929 in Joseph GOEBBELS's newspaper, *Der Angriff* (The Attack), set to the tune of a sailors' marching song, became the official song of the Nazi party and the second song of the Third Reich, after the national anthem, *Deutschland über Alles.* The lyrics were:

Die Fahne hoch!
Die Reihen dicht geschlossen,
SA marschiert
Mit ruhig festem Schritt.
Kameraden, die Rote Front und
Reaktion erschossen,
Marschieren im Geist in unsern Reihen mit.

Die Strasse frei den braunen Bataillonen!
Die Strasse frei dem Sturmabteilungsmann!
Es schaun aufs Hakenkreuz voll
Hoffnung schon Millionen.
Der Tag für Freiheit und für Brot bricht an.

Zum letzten Mal wird zum Appell geblasen!
Zum Kampfe stehn wir alle schon bereit.
Bald flattern Hitlerfahnen über allen Strassen,
Die Knechtschaft dauert nur noch kurze Zeit!

Banner up! With ranks tightly closed,
The SA marches with calm, firm step.
Comrades shot by the Red Front and
   reactionaries
March with us in spirit.

Clear the streets for the brown battalions,
Clear the streets for the storm troopers.
Filled with hope, millions already look toward
   the swastika.
The day of freedom and bread dawns.

Blow the roll call for the last time,
We all stand ready for the fight.
Soon Hitler flags will flutter over all streets,
Servitude will only last a short time longer.

DAVID BANKIER

HORTHY, MIKLÓS (1868–1957), regent of HUNGARY from 1920 to 1944. In 1919 Horthy was the military leader of the counterrevolutionary "white terror" campaign against the short-lived Béla Kun Socialist-Communist regime, and after the evacuation of the Romanian occupying forces, he became regent of the Hungarian kingdom (March 1, 1920).

1943, while facing Hitler's challenge, he rejected German pressure to impose even harsher measures, such as the exclusion of Jews from all economic activities, enforcement of wearing the Jewish BADGE, ghettoization, and the deportation of all Jews to concentration and extermination camps.

After the German occupation of Hungary (March 19, 1944), Horthy nominated a government totally subservient to the Nazis, giving it unlimited authority for all anti-Jewish measures. Some 500,000 Jews never returned from the deportations. On July 7, 1944, with over 150,000 Budapest Jews and several thousand men in labor service still in the country, Horthy ordered the deportations stopped. On October 15, after an aborted armistice attempt, he was deposed by the Germans and replaced as head of state by Ferenc SZÁLASI, the leader of the fascist ARROW CROSS PARTY. After the war, the Allied powers allowed Horthy to go to Portugal, where he wrote his memoirs, which were published in 1965.

BIBLIOGRAPHY

Braham, R. L. "The Rightists, Horthy and the Germans: Factors Underlying the Destruction of Hungarian Jewry." *Jews and Non-Jews in Eastern Europe*, edited by B. Vago and G. L. Mosse, pp. 137–156. New York, 1974.

Fenyo, M. D. *Hitler, Horthy, and Hungary: German-Hungarian Relations, 1941–1944.* New Haven, 1972.

Katzburg, N. *Hungary and the Jews: Policy and Legislation, 1920–1943.* Ramat Gan, Israel, 1981.

Macartney, C. A. *October Fifteenth: A History of Hungary, 1929–1945.* New York, 1957.

ASHER COHEN

Miklós Horthy (November 1938).

His initial, aggressively antisemitic regime was gradually moderated, especially after the debate on the first anti-Jewish *numerus clausus* (quota) laws (September 22, 1920). In general, Horthy's rule was characterized throughout by constant official and semiofficial antisemitism. Throughout the 1920s and 1930s, he conducted a conservative internal policy, relying on the traditional aristocracy and on certain modern capitalist elements, and was a widely popular leader. The main objective of his foreign policy was the revision of the Treaty of Trianon (concluded in Versailles in 1920, when Hungary ceded about two-thirds of its prewar territory), which brought him to an ever-growing cooperation with Hitler's Germany.

Between 1938 and 1941, Horthy authorized three increasingly harsh and comprehensive anti-Jewish laws. Nevertheless, in 1942 and

HORTHY OFFER, proposal made public by the Hungarian regent, Adm. Miklós HORTHY, in July 1944, recommending that several categories of Jews in HUNGARY be allowed to emigrate, primarily to Palestine. The public offer was made soon after Horthy halted the deportations of Jews from Hungary early that month, partly because of Allied pressure. The Swedes and the Americans in particular had appealed to Horthy to ameliorate the suffering of the remaining Hungarian Jews (in effect, the Jews of BUDAPEST), and among other steps had called for Hungarian permission to allow Jews to emigrate to Palestine. As a result, some ten days before he stopped the deportations, Horthy submitted his proposal to the Germans for their approval. The plan proposed that 1,000 children under the age of sixteen, plus 100 adult chaperons and an additional nine families per week, would emigrate to Palestine. Three weeks later, the Germans allowed the Hungarians to inform the western Allies and neutral nations of the offer.

The first news of the offer was sent to Haim Barlas, of the Jewish Agency delegation in Istanbul, by the head of the Palestine Office in Budapest, Moshe (Miklós) Krausz, on July 13. According to Krausz, 1,000 children, as well as 8,243 holders of immigration certificates to Palestine and their families, would be allowed to leave Hungary for Palestine. Four days later the Hungarian chargé d'affaires in Bern, Imre Tahy, informed Carl Burckhardt of the International RED CROSS about the offer in similar terms. He added two important clauses: Jews who had parents in Sweden or who maintained business relations with Sweden could go either to Palestine or to Sweden; and the Germans had agreed to the offer. In actuality, the Germans were not at all willing to allow substantial emigration from Hungary.

The British, the Americans, and the Jewish Agency took the offer at face value, and the Jewish Agency urged the western Allies to accept it. The official response of the Americans and the British to the offer was published on August 18, 1944:

> Because of the desperate plight of the Jews in Hungary and the overwhelming humanitarian considerations involved, the two governments are informing the government of Hungary through the International Red Cross that despite the heavy difficulties and responsibilities involved they have accepted the offer of the Hungarian government for the release of the Jews and will make arrangements for the care of such Jews leaving Hungary who reach neutral or United Nations territory, and also that they will find temporary havens of refuge where such people may live in safety. . . . The governments of the United Kingdom and the United States emphasize that in accepting the offer which had

been made, they do not in any way condone the action of the Hungarian government in forcing the emigration of Jews as an alternative to persecution and death.
> (*New York Times*, August 18, 1944)

The United States was the motivating force behind this declaration, to which the British agreed primarily because of American pressure. Throughout the summer and fall, the United States sought to convince neutral governments in Europe and Latin America to provide a haven for any Jews who might succeed in leaving Hungary. Most of the Latin American countries eventually made only minimal concessions to this pressure. The Swiss and the Swedes, however, both promised to allow into their countries several thousand Jews. For their part, the British agreed to allow into Palestine those Jews who had immigration certificates. As a result, *Schutzpasse* (safe-conduct passes issued by the neutral governments), which had already surfaced in Budapest, were issued by the neutral representatives to tens of thousands of Jews there who were considered potential citizens of a number of neutral and Western countries, including Palestine. No Jews, however, would leave Hungary during the summer and early fall through the Horthy offer, owing to German opposition. With the ousting of Horthy on October 15 and his replacement by the ARROW CROSS PARTY regime of Ferenc SZÁLASI, the offer seemed to have lost its validity.

However, the repercussions of the offer continued to have an effect throughout the last months of the German occupation of Hungary. Shortly after the Arrow Cross coup, in a meeting between Friedrich Born, the International Red Cross representative in Budapest, and Edmund VEESENMAYER, the German plenipotentiary for Hungary, an offer similar to Horthy's was discussed. On October 23, 1944, as a result of this meeting, the Germans declared that they would allow Jews to leave Hungary, and on November 15, they set the number of emigrants at 8,000. Once again, none of these Jews were allowed to leave, but the mere discussion of emigration gave value to the *Schutzpasse* and contributed to the rescue activities in Budapest of neutral diplomats such as Raoul WALLENBERG, Carl LUTZ, and Born, as well as of the Zionist youth and

the RELIEF AND RESCUE COMMITTEE OF BUDA-
PEST during the Szálasi regime.

BIBLIOGRAPHY

Vago, B. "The Horthy Offer: A Missed Opportunity
for Rescuing Jews in 1944." In *Contemporary
Views of the Holocaust*, edited by R. L. Braham,
pp. 23–45. Boston, 1983.

ROBERT ROZETT

HÖSS, RUDOLF (1900–1947), camp commandant of AUSCHWITZ. Höss was born in Baden-
Baden; his father was an officer in the German colonial army in southeast Africa. When
World War I broke out Höss volunteered for
service, even though he was underage. On his
return to Germany after the war he joined
the Freikorps in East Prussia, then the Rossbach Freikorps in the Baltic states, and later
participated in terrorist actions against the
French occupation forces in the Ruhr and
against the Poles in the struggle for Silesia
(1921).

In November 1922, Höss joined the Nazi
party while attending a reunion of members
of the Rossbach Freikorps in Munich. In June
1923 he was arrested in the Ruhr district and
sentenced to a ten-year prison term, for participating in the murder by a Freikorps underground group of a German teacher who
had collaborated with the French. By 1928
Höss was pardoned, and as soon as he was
released he joined the Artamanen Society,
a nationalist-*völkisch* group that advocated
work on the land and settlement in the east,
on Polish territory. Höss and his wife, Hedwig, who was also a member of Artamanen,
worked for various groups of the society's *Ar-
beitsdienst* (labor service), which was a device
for recruiting members for militant Nazi organizations, mainly the SS.

In 1933, on instructions from the Nazi
party and local estate owners, Höss formed
an SS cavalry unit that was based on the
Sullentin estate in Pomerania. In June 1934
he joined the SS for active service, at the
suggestion of Heinrich HIMMLER, who was
one of the leaders of the Artamanen Society.
From December 1934 until May 1938 Höss
held various appointments in the administration of the DACHAU concentration camp,
where he trained under Theodor EICKE, the
first commandant of the camp. In May 1940
Höss was posted to Auschwitz, appointed
Obersturmbannführer, and became the actual
founder of the camp and its first organizer
and commandant. In the summer of 1941,
Höss began readying the camp under his
command for the extermination of masses of
human beings, and as of January 1942 he was
at the helm of the killing operation in the
installations set up for this purpose in
Auschwitz-Birkenau.

A report on the extermination in Auschwitz
that Höss wrote while under investigation after the war in a Kraków jail opens with the
following words:

> In the summer of 1941—I cannot state the
> precise date—I was summoned by the adju-
> tant's office to Berlin, to report to Reichsführer-
> SS [Chief of the SS] Himmler. Without his
> aide-de-camp present—contrary to his usual
> practice—Himmler said to me: "The Führer has
> ordered the 'Final Solution of the Jewish Ques-
> tion.' We, the SS, are charged with the execu-

Rudolf Höss, former commandant of Auschwitz,
during his trial in Poland.

tion of this task. I have chosen the Auschwitz camp for this purpose, because of its convenient location as regards transportation and because in that area it is easy to isolate and camouflage the camp. I first thought to appoint one of the senior SS officers to this task, but then I changed my mind because of the problems of the division of authority that such an appointment would run into. I am herewith charging you with this task. This is a strenuous and difficult assignment that calls for total dedication, regardless of the difficulties that will arise. Further practical details will be conveyed to you by Sturmbannführer Adolf Eichmann of the Reichssicherheitshauptamt, who will soon get in touch with you. The offices concerned will hear from him at the appropriate time. You must keep this order absolutely secret, even from your own superiors. After your talk with Eichmann let me know what arrangements you propose to be made."

On December 1, 1943, Höss was appointed chief of Section 1D of the SS WIRTSCHAFTS-VERWALTUNGSHAUPTAMT (Economic-Administrative Main Office; WVHA). In late June of 1944 he was sent back to Auschwitz, on a temporary assignment, to preside over the murder of the Jews of Hungary. In that operation—Aktion Höss, as it was named—430,000 Jews were brought to Auschwitz in fifty-six days, to be annihilated there. In recognition of his "outstanding service" in the concentration camps, Höss was awarded war crosses classes I and II, with swords. After the fall of the Reich, Höss assumed the name Franz Lang; he was released from a prisoner-of-war collection point and put to work in agriculture.

In March 1946 Höss was recognized, arrested, and handed over to the Polish authorities, in keeping with the agreement on the EXTRADITION OF WAR CRIMINALS. He was taken to Warsaw and from there to Kraków, where his case was investigated. In the Kraków jail where he was held in 1946 and 1947, Höss wrote an autobiography and a series of notes about the SS commanders in the concentration camp and those who were in charge of putting the "Final Solution" into effect, including a profile of Eichmann (published in English as *Commandant of Auschwitz: The Autobiography of Rudolf Hoess*; 1960). The supreme court in Warsaw sentenced Höss to death, and he was hanged in Auschwitz on April 16, 1947.

BIBLIOGRAPHY

Frankel, T. "The Good German of Auschwitz." *Midstream* 6/3 (Summer 1960): 16–24.
Tenenbaum, J. "Auschwitz in Retrospect: The Self Portrait of Rudolf Hoess, Commandant of Auschwitz." *Jewish Social Studies* 15/3–4 (July–October 1953): 203–236.

JOZEF BUSZKO

HOTEL POLSKI, hotel in Warsaw. In mid-1943 the Gestapo lodged in the Hotel Polski Jews holding citizenship papers of neutral —primarily South American—countries, who were to be exchanged for German nationals interned by the Allies.

Most of these papers were fictitious documents made out by consulates in Europe. Some Jews who had gone into hiding acquired the documents, at great cost. With the papers in their possession, they left their hiding places, despite warnings they were given by the underground and the great risk involved, because they felt that they could not hold out for long in their temporary refuge.

Eventually the Jews in the hotel were taken to the VITTEL camp (300 persons) or to BERGEN-BELSEN (2,000 to 2,500). Some of the people on the last transport, which was made up of 420 persons, were shot to death in the PAWIAK PRISON. The South American countries did not honor the documents issued by their consulates, and as a result 2,500 holders of such documents were deported to AUSCHWITZ, in the fall of 1943 and spring of 1944, where they perished. Several hundred Jews were saved, most of them candidates for exchange with German nationals interned in Palestine.

BIBLIOGRAPHY

Shulman, A. *The Case of Hotel Polski*. New York, 1982.

TERESA PREKEROWA

HTO. See Haupttreuhandstelle Ost.

HUGO SCHNEIDER AKTIENGESELL-SCHAFT METALWARENFABRIK, LEIPZIG. See HASAG.

HULL, CORDELL (1871–1955), United States secretary of state from 1933 to 1944. Hull entered the State Department with little foreign-policy experience from his years in the House of Representatives (1907–1921 and 1923–1931) and Senate (1931–1933).

During the prewar years, Hull's interest lay in international trade and relations with Latin America. The former led him to oppose both an economic boycott of Germany and increased tariffs on German imports. His knowledge of the Nazi persecution of the Jews was limited, although he expressed his disapproval to German ambassador Hans Luther in May 1933. Generally, Hull declined to intercede in what he regarded as Germany's internal affair, but he supported the recall of the United States ambassador to Germany, Hugh Wilson, on November 15, 1938, in protest against KRISTALLNACHT. Throughout his tenure, Hull opposed any relaxation of American immigration regulations.

Hull presided over his department while its influence was declining during the war. He was preoccupied with laying the groundwork for a postwar United Nations, for which he received the Nobel Peace Prize in 1945, and he left rescue and refugee matters to his subordinates, particularly Breckinridge Long. When Treasury secretary Henry MORGENTHAU, Jr., confronted Hull, in December 1943, with the State Department's obstruction of information about and rescue efforts for Jews, he found Hull uninterested and uninformed. The subsequent creation of the WAR REFUGEE BOARD effectively took rescue activities out of the State Department.

Ill-health forced Hull to resign in November 1944. He was replaced by the more interested and energetic Edward R. Stettinius, Jr.

BIBLIOGRAPHY

Feingold, H. L. *The Politics of Rescue: The Roosevelt Administration and the Holocaust, 1938–1945.* New York, 1980.
Pratt, J. W. *Cordell Hull, 1933–1944.* 2 vols. New York, 1964.
Wyman, D. S. *The Abandonment of the Jews: America and the Holocaust, 1941–1945.* New York, 1984.
Wyman, D. S. *Paper Walls: America and the Refugee Crisis, 1938–1941.* Amherst, Mass., 1968.

DAVID SILBERKLANG

HUNGARIAN LABOR SERVICE SYSTEM.
See Munkaszolgálat.

HUNGARY. [*This entry consists of an overview of Hungary's history and policies from the early 1930s to the end of World War II, followed by a history of Hungarian Jewry focusing on the Holocaust period.*]

General Survey

Following Adolf Hitler's rise to power in 1933, the Hungarian leadership became interested in forming an alliance with Nazi Germany. An alliance attracted Hungarian leaders for three main reasons: Nazi Germany offered Hungary a market for its agricultural goods; it would be a strong ally in the struggle for revision of the Treaty of Trianon, which had deprived Hungary of more than two-thirds of its territory and about 60 percent of its population after World War I; and it offered an element of political and ideological kinship, since Hitler's government was fascist and regent Miklós HORTHY's government was chauvinistic and authoritarian. As time passed, Hungary was drawn increasingly closer to Nazi Germany, but eventually elements in the Hungarian ruling circle sought a way to distance their nation from Hitler.

As early as 1923, the Hungarian racist Gyula Gömbös had established a mutual rapport with Hitler. Gömbös, who became Hungarian prime minister in 1932, resumed his personal relationship with Hitler after the Nazis came to power. Tangible cooperation between the two nations, however, began in the economic sphere. Germany wanted to expand its interests in east-central Europe, whereas Hungary eagerly sought markets for its agricultural surplus in the wake of the worldwide depression. Against this background, Germany soon became Hungary's foremost trading partner.

By the mid-1930s, political considerations began to rival economic interests in drawing the two countries together. Nazi Germany's growing strength and audacious behavior in the international arena whetted Hungary's appetite for the return of its lost territories and peoples. Understanding Hungary's revisionist desires, Hitler offered German support for territorial revision from 1937 onward. In return, Hungary offered Nazi Germany economic and political concessions.

With the 1938 Munich agreement, the courting of Hitler paid off, as Hungary received part of a former territory from Czechoslovakia. This convinced some Hungarian politicians that the Axis would play a leading role in Europe for the next several decades.

Gyula Gömbös (center), Hungarian racist and prime minister, at the Reich Chancellery with Adolf Hitler (left) and Hermann Göring (right) during a visit to Germany in 1934.

Others, however, harbored the traditional Hungarian fear of a strong Germany, which was exacerbated by the inherent brutality of the Nazi system. Count Pál Teleki, who became Hungary's prime minister in March 1939, retained this traditional fear to a certain extent. He tried to maintain some distance from Hitler and did not join the war effort in 1939. Teleki sought to strike a balance between Hungary's desire for territory and its desire for a degree of political independence.

Nazi successes in Poland and western Europe in the early stages of the war confirmed the belief of many politicians that to achieve their political goals, they should cooperate with Germany. Nevertheless, the long-standing traditions of fear of Germany and sympa-

thy for Poland were not totally forgotten. During the first months of the war, the Hungarian government allowed more than one hundred thousand Polish refugees to find shelter in Hungary, which did not help it to ingratiate itself with Hitler.

Throughout the interwar period, one of Hungary's foremost desires had been for the return of TRANSYLVANIA, which was 33 percent Hungarian and about 55 percent Romanian. Hitler, who sought to dominate southeastern Europe, wanted to be the supreme judge of the fate of this area. In August 1940, the foreign ministers of Germany and Italy (Joachim von RIBBENTROP and Count Galeazzo Ciano) signed an agreement, the second Vienna Award, which allowed the Hungarians to take possession of northern Transylva-

HUNGARY

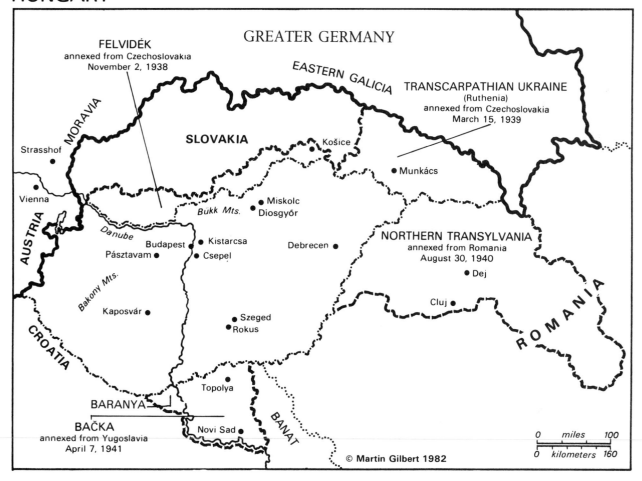

GREATER GERMANY

FELVIDÉK
annexed from Czechoslovakia
November 2, 1938

EASTERN GALICIA

TRANSCARPATHIAN UKRAINE
(Ruthenia)
annexed from Czechoslovakia
March 15, 1939

MORAVIA

SLOVAKIA

Košice

Munkács

Strasshof

Vienna

AUSTRIA

Bükk Mts.

Miskolc

Diosgyőr

Danube

Budapest

Kistarcsa

Debrecen

NORTHERN TRANSYLVANIA
annexed from Romania
August 30, 1940

Pásztavam

Csepel

Bakony Mts.

Dej

Kaposvár

Cluj

ROMANIA

Szeged

Rokus

CROATIA

Topolya

BARANYA

BANAT

BAČKA
annexed from Yugoslavia
April 7, 1941

Novi Sad

© Martin Gilbert 1982

0   miles   100

0   kilometers   160

nia and its 2.5 million inhabitants. Most Hungarians regarded this as a major foreign-policy success.

Teleki, however, saw quite clearly that Hungary would have to pay a further price for northern Transylvania. Part of the price had been spelled out at the time of the award. Hungary was to allow the Nazi Volksbund to be the sole representative of the VOLKSDEUTSCHE (ethnic Germans) in Hungary. Soon afterward, through the Hungarian ambassador in Berlin, Döme SZTÓJAY, it also was made clear that Hungary was to integrate itself more fully into the new German order. On October 10, 1940, an accord was reached, calling for better coordination between Hungarian agricultural production and German needs. Moreover, Hungary was allowed to join the recently concluded Tripartite Pact binding Germany, Italy, and Japan. This sealed its formal military and political alliance with Nazi Germany.

Domestically, concessions were also made. The fanatic leader of the ARROW CROSS PARTY, Ferenc SZÁLASI, was released from prison; the ban prohibiting civil servants from joining extremist parties was lifted; and a new political party, which adhered strongly to the Nazi political platform, was formed.

In the first year of the alliance, three major foreign-policy decisions further subordinated Hungarian interests to those of Nazi Germany. In December 1940, as a show of its desire for a modicum of independence, Hungary signed a pact of "eternal friendship" with Yugoslavia, which, except for the Soviet Union, was its only neighbor not yet dominated by Hitler. But in March 1941, following a military coup there by anti–Tripartite Pact forces, Hitler decided to invade Yugoslavia. He offered Horthy territorial rewards if he would join the fray, and the Hungarians accepted. In the wake of the events, Teleki committed suicide, and the new prime minister, László Bárdossy, sent Hungarian troops to Yugoslavia a few days after the German attack. As a result, Hungary received territory with a population of over one million (36 percent Hungarian).

The second major decision was to join the Germans in their war against the Soviet Union. The bombing of several Hungarian towns, pressure from the German and Hungarian military, and the government's perception of domestic and foreign-policy considerations all combined to catapult the nation into the new offensive on June 26, 1941. In particular, the government feared that by not joining Romania and Slovakia, which were already fighting, Hungary would look bad to the Germans.

The last fateful move was the declaration of war on the United States in December 1941. This led to a British declaration of war on Hungary and the severance of all major links with the West. The ill-fated Hungarian declaration came while the Axis was suffering its first significant defeat in the Soviet Union. Hungary soon saw itself isolated, committed to a long war, and at the mercy of increasing Nazi coercion. Instead of being a partner, the nation was becoming more and more a satellite of Germany. In January 1942, the Germans pressed Hungary to send most of its troops to the Soviet Union, and the Hungarians complied.

Elements of the Hungarian ruling elite began to regard Bardossy as too subservient to Germany, and in March 1942 a new prime minister, Miklós KÁLLAY, was appointed by Horthy. A conservative politician, with neither personal nor political affiliations with Germany, he pursued a more cautious policy.

With the Axis defeat at STALINGRAD and with the debacle at Voronezh on January 13, 1943, when the Red Army broke through the Hungarian lines and caused the loss of 150,000 of the 200,000 Hungarian soldiers, Kállay began to work toward extricating Hungary from its alliance with Nazi Germany. No more troops were sent to the Russian front in 1943, and preparations were made to allow more political freedom at home. Peace feelers were put out to the West and a preliminary agreement was signed in Istanbul, stating that Hungary would change sides when British and American forces reached the Hungarian frontier. The Germans were aware of this change in attitude, but they were not inclined to intervene as long as Hungary maintained its economic agreements and as long as the British and United States armies were far from its borders. Still, as early as September 1943, the German general staff prepared a contingency plan for the military occupation of Hungary.

The Hungarian Gendarmerie, which after the German occupation of Hungary on March 19, 1944, became the major instrument of state power in the ghettoization and deportation of approximately 440,000 Jews.

At the end of the year, as a gesture of goodwill toward the Allies, Hungary tried the officers responsible for the massacres that had taken place in January 1942 in the Délvidék region. At the same time, plans were made to welcome the American and British envoys, and Horthy personally requested the withdrawal of Hungarian troops from the Soviet Union.

With the Red Army approaching the Carpathian Mountains, Hitler decided to move against Hungary in March 1944. On March 18, he invited Horthy to Germany and told him of the imminent occupation. Because Horthy feared that if he did not comply Romania would take part in the occupation, the Hungarians did not resist the Germans. On March 19 German soldiers entered Hungary, and a government that the Nazis considered reliable was set up under the former Hungarian ambassador in Berlin, Sztójay. Horthy himself withdrew from public affairs, and various "experts" arrived from Germany to put Hungary back on a pro-German course.

Sztójay's government began carrying out the directives of the German plenipotentiary, Edmund VEESENMAYER. All anti-Nazi parties and politicians were eliminated. After some hesitation, the government also mobilized 300,000 soldiers to try to thwart the advance of the Red Army, which was less than 62 miles (100 km) from the Hungarian border.

In August, Horthy replaced Sztójay with Gen. Géza Lakatos. Lakatos's government continued the earlier policy of seeking a way for Hungary to pull out of the war. This was complicated by Romania's successful reversal at the end of the month. On the one hand, the Romanian example bolstered the anti-German forces in Hungary, while on the other, it worsened their diplomatic position and contributed to actual fighting on Hungarian soil. After a few failed attempts to extricate Hungary from the war, through contacts with only the western Allies, a secret Hungarian armistice delegation arrived in Moscow on October 1. A preliminary agreement was reached, according to which Hungary would give up territories gained through its alliance with Germany and would turn against the Nazis.

On October 15, 1944, Horthy decided to carry out his planned change of course. The announcement was made, but the Germans had made contingency plans. They blocked Horthy's move, taking his son Miklós (Nikki) prisoner and threatening Horthy with the latter's death if the reversal were carried out. The Germans replaced Horthy with the Arrow Cross party leader Szálasi, and Arrow Cross men took over strategic positions throughout the country.

Total chaos seized Hungary. The Arrow Cross began a reign of terror, plundering, pillaging, and murdering. Szálasi promised to send 1.5 million soldiers to the Russian front, intending to draft all males and females between the ages of twelve and seventy into the army or labor brigades. The Nazis and the Szálasi government proposed to follow a scorched-earth policy. Factories were dismantled and sent to Germany, along with livestock. Many train cars and a large part of the precious-metal reserves in the National Bank of Hungary were also dispatched to Germany. The population was ordered to retreat with the fascist troops in the direction of Germany. Whatever could not be sent to Germany was to be destroyed. In November, political prisoners were turned over to the Nazis, who sent them to concentration camps, where most of them died.

As the Red Army overran Hungary, a handful of complete troop formations went over to the Soviets; tens of thousands more Hungarians dodged conscription and deserted from the army. To stem the tide, Szálasi decreed summary trials and executions. Signs of active opposition also increased by November, when the Soviets had taken two-thirds of the country. The Magyar Front (which had been formed in May under the leadership of the Social Democrat Arpad Szakasits) and the Committee of Liberation (headed by Endre Bajcsy-Zsilinsky and Lt.-Gen. János Kiss), which incorporated the Front in November, made plans to foment armed resistance. But before they could put their plans into operation, Bajcsy-Zsilinsky and Kiss were captured by the Arrow Cross and executed. The Rákosi brigade fought the Germans in the Carpathians, and the Petőfi group resisted in Slovakia. Several smaller groups, like Szir, Marot, and Laci, committed acts of sabotage in the capital. Similar groups functioned in the Bukk and Bakony mountains. But on the whole, even at this late date, organized Hungarian armed resistance was negligible.

In January 1945, a Hungarian armistice was signed with the Soviet Union. On January 17 Pest fell to the Red Army, and less than a month later Buda followed. By April 4, 1945, no more Germans were fighting in Hungary.

[See also Gendarmerie, Hungarian; Trials of War Criminals: Hungary.]

BIBLIOGRAPHY

Fenyo, M. D. *Hitler, Horthy, and Hungary: German-Hungarian Relations, 1941–1944.* New Haven, 1972.

Lacko, M. *Arrow Cross Men, National Socialists, 1935–1944.* Budapest, 1969.

Macartney, C. A. *A History of Hungary, 1929–1945.* New York, 1957.

Ranki, G. *1944: Marcius 19.* Budapest, 1978.

Sakmyster, T. L. *Hungary: The Great Powers and the Danubian Crisis, 1936–1939.* Atlanta, Ga., 1980.

Vago, B. *The Shadow of the Swastika: The Rise of Fascism and Anti-Semitism in the Danube Basin, 1936–1939.* London, 1975. See pages 115–154.

GYÖRGY RANKI

Jews during the Holocaust

According to the census of 1941, Hungary had a Jewish population of 725,007, representing 4.94 percent of its total population of 14,683,323. Of the country's Jews, 401,000 lived in Trianon Hungary (Hungary according to the Treaty of Trianon, which deprived it of much of its territory); more than 67,000 in the Felvidék (Upper Province), the area acquired from Czechoslovakia in November 1938; 78,000 in Carpathian Ruthenia (*see* TRANSCARPATHIAN UKRAINE), the territory acquired from Czechoslovakia in March 1939; 150,000 in northern TRANSYLVANIA, the area acquired from Romania in August 1940; and 14,000 in the Délvidék, the area conquered from Yugoslavia in April 1941. In addition, there were approximately 100,000 converts and Christians of Jewish origin, who were racially identified as Jews according to a 1941 law and subjected to the anti-Jewish measures, although they occasionally had certain privileges exacted of the government by the Christian churches.

Jewish settlement in the area of what is now Hungary goes back to Roman times. In the modern period, the Jewish community of

Hungary became highly integrated into the economic and cultural life of the country. Especially from the second half of the nineteenth century until World War I, Hungarian Jews became willing partners in the struggle of the Magyars (Hungarians) to strengthen their language and culture in a land populated by diverse minority groups. As a result most Hungarian Jews felt very Hungarian, especially those living in the truncated area left to Hungary by the Treaty of Trianon at the close of World War I. For the most part, this Hungarian national identification remained quite firm despite the increased antisemitism that marked the interwar years, and it continued to influence the response of Hungarian Jews to their evolving situation during World War II.

The "Jewish question," which came to the fore during the counterrevolution that followed the short-lived proletarian dictatorship of Béla Kun (1919), acquired a special momentum during the 1930s. Demands for its solution emanated from a variety of pro-Nazi rightist political parties and movements and from the heads of the Christian churches. The anti-Jewish climate was fanned by the mass media, especially the largely German-financed press. In addition, the Honvédseg, the Hungarian armed forces, was one of the most radical and aggressive hotbeds of antisemitism in Hungary. Shortly after the AN-SCHLUSS, Hungary adopted the first major anti-Jewish law (May 1938), which restricted the Jews' role in the professions and the economy to 20 percent. The second anti-Jewish law (May 1939) further restricted the Jewish role in the economy to 6 percent and identified the Jews in racial terms—a process that culminated in the racial law of 1941, which resembled the NUREMBERG LAWS. Hungary also introduced (1939–1940) a unique labor service system designed for Jewish men of military age: the MUNKASZOL-GÁLAT, which was under the command of the Honvédseg. The Jews in the service were not allowed to bear arms or, after a while, to wear military uniforms. Once drafted, they

A group of Jews from the forced-labor camp in Bogdany, a town about 3 miles (5 km) north of Budapest (1941). [Beth Hatefutsoth]

were organized into battalions and companies and assigned primarily to war-related work projects. These included building and repairing roads, clearing forests, digging trenches, and building tank traps, at home and along the fronts in the Ukraine and Serbia. Close to forty-two thousand Hungarian Jews perished in these mobile forced-labor units before the German occupation of Hungary on March 19, 1944.

Prior to the occupation, Hungarian Jewry also suffered as many as eighteen thousand other casualties. Of these, around seventeen thousand were "alien" Jews seized by the Hungarian authorities in July and August 1941 and deported to a site near KAMENETS-PODOLSKI, where the majority of them were massacred, together with the indigenous Galician Jews, by SS troops under the command of SS-Obergruppenführer Friedrich JECKELN. More than one thousand Jews were murdered in Novi Sad (Ujvidék) and other areas of the Délvidék region in January and February 1942 by Hungarian military and gendarmerie units "in pursuit of partisans." Except for these tragedies, the Hungarian Jews continued to live in safety, although considerably restricted in their civil rights and economic opportunities, until the German occupation. Miklós KÁLLAY's government (March 1942 to March 1944) consistently rejected the repeated German demands that Hungary emulate the other Nazi-dominated countries in Europe by implementing the "FINAL SOLUTION" program. It was for this reason, among others, that the Jewish leadership pinned its hopes on the conservative aristocratic regime, mistakenly convinced that Hungary, a member of the Axis, would retain its sovereignty to the end.

These illusions were shattered when the Third Reich, aware of the Kállay government's "secret" efforts to have the western Allies extricate Hungary from the war, decided to intervene militarily. Kállay was replaced by the pro-German Döme SZTÓJAY. The occupation forces included a Sonderkommando (Special Commando) headed by Adolf EICHMANN, which provided guidance and technical assistance for the speedy implementation of the "Final Solution" program. The quisling regime adopted an avalanche of anti-Jewish decrees and placed the instru-

mentalities of state power at the disposal of a special "de-Judaizing" group, which included László BAKY and László ENDRE, the notorious antisemites serving as undersecretaries of state in the Ministry of the Interior. This group also included László Ferenczy, the gendarmerie officer in charge of the roundup, concentration, entrainment, and deportation of the Jews.

On April 15, 1944, leading antisemites, including Endre, established the Zsidókérdest Kutató Magyar Intézet (Hungarian Institute for the Researching of the Jewish Question), under the direction of Zoltán Bosnyák in Budapest. Advised and guided by SS-Hauptsturmführer Heinz Ballensiefen, a Nazi expert on anti-Jewish propaganda, the institute was modeled after the Institut zum Studium der Judenfrage, Berlin (the Rosenberg Institute). According to the bylaws, its task was "to study the Jewish question in Hungary in a systematic and scientific manner, to collect and scientifically process the related data, and to inform Hungarian public opinion about the Hungarian and general Jewish question." To further this goal, the institute published the newspaper Harc (Battle), which was modeled after Julius STREICHER's Der STÜRMER (The Attacker).

The anti-Jewish decrees provided, among other things, for the isolation, marking, plundering, ghettoization, concentration, and deportation of the Jews. The isolation of the Jews, which began with the imposition of travel restrictions and the confiscation of telephones and radios, was completed with their marking: after April 5, when the compulsory wearing of the yellow badge (a 3.8 × 3.8 inch, or 9.65 × 9.65 cm, Star of David) was introduced (see BADGE, JEWISH), the Jews became easy targets for the antisemites. This measure was followed by the confiscation and expropriation of Jewish-owned businesses, industrial enterprises, financial establishments, and professional offices. Jews were deprived of their personal property, including their valuables, bank accounts, and jewelry. Although the decree for the ghettoization of the Jews was published only on April 28, the Jews of Carpathian Ruthenia and northeastern Hungary were ordered into ghettos on April 16, the first day of Passover. They were ordered at the crack of dawn to pack and leave their homes within a half hour. Their homes were usually looted shortly after the owners' transfer.

In the rural areas, the Jews were normally first ordered into the local synagogues or community centers, and a few days later transferred to ghettos in the county seats. In some cities, the ghettos were established in the Jewish sections; in others, in brickyards or idle factories; in still others, the Jews were compelled to "set up camp" in neighboring forests under the open sky. The ghettos were hermetically sealed and were guarded by both local policemen and gendarmes brought in from other parts of the country. Internally, each ghetto was administered by a Zsidó Tanács (Jewish Council), which usually consisted of the traditional leaders of the communities. The Jewish councils were associated with the Central Jewish Council in Budapest, which was headed by Samu STERN, leader of the Budapest Neolog (Reform) community and a counselor to the royal court. The ghettos were short-lived, lasting only from two to six weeks. In addition to suffering from the horrible conditions, including the lack of food and adequate sanitary facilities, the Jews, especially those perceived as well off, were subjected to barbaric treatment by police and gendarmes searching for "hidden wealth."

The entrainment and deportation of the Jews proceeded according to a territorial order of priority. Because of the rapidly deteriorating military position of the Axis (the Soviet forces were about to cross the Romanian frontier), the "de-Judaizers" proceeded at lightning speed, focusing first on the liquida-

In the spring of 1944 the Jews of Kőszeg, a town in western Hungary near the Austrian border, were rounded up by the Hungarian Gendarmerie and ghettoized in a building that was formerly used for grain storage. Jews from the ghetto were tortured by the gendarmerie on June 18 so that they might reveal where they had hidden valuables. On July 4 the Jews were all deported to Auschwitz. The photo shows the deportation.

A stream of Hungarian Jewish refugees, survivors of the Holocaust (1946). [JDC Archives, New York]

tion of the largely Orthodox and Hasidic Jewish communities of Carpathian Ruthenia and northeastern Hungary. Then there followed the entrainment and deportation of the Jews of northern Transylvania, who in turn were followed by those living in the northern, southern, and western parts of the country.

The 434,351 Jews who were deported mostly from the countryside ended up in AUSCHWITZ. (In contrast to this figure, cited in László Ferenczy's report, Edmund VEESEN-MAYER, the German plenipotentiary in Hungary, cited the number of deportees as 437,402.) They were deported between May 15 and July 9, 1944, from fifty-five major ghettos and concentration centers, in 147 trains composed of hermetically sealed freight cars. Most of the Hungarian Jews were gassed in Birkenau shortly after their arrival. By July 7, when Miklós HORTHY halted the deportations (the "de-Judaizers" continued their operations for two days, liquidating the Jewish communities in western Hungary and around the capital), Hungary was already *judenrein* ("cleansed of Jews"), with the exception of BUDAPEST. A few trans-

ports, with about 21,000 Jews from the southern part of Hungary, were directed to STRASSHOF, near Vienna, to be "put on ice" pending the outcome of Zionist-SS negotiations (*see* RELIEF AND RESCUE COMMITTEE OF BUDAPEST). Most of these Jews survived the war.

The anxiety-filled but relatively safe period for Budapest's Jewry—confined since June 1944 to living in special buildings designated with a yellow star (*csillagos házak*)—ended on October 15 of that year. On that day the Hungarian Nazis, the ARROW CROSS PARTY, came to power with the aid of the Germans in the wake of Horthy's unsuccessful attempt to extricate Hungary from the war. Thousands of Jews, mostly women, were forcemarched to Hegyeshalom and its environs near the Reich to build fortifications for the defense of Vienna. Most of them were first concentrated in the Óbuda brickyards. Terror was rampant, with armed Arrow Cross gangs roaming the streets, robbing and killing Jews. Many of the victims were taken to the banks of the Danube, where they were shot and thrown into the river. Early in December, during the Soviet siege of Budapest, close to seventy thousand Jews were ordered into a ghetto that was established in the Jewish section, near the Dohány Street synagogue. Although relatively short-lived (it was liberated on January 17–18, 1945), the ghetto suffered horribly. Thousands died as a result of disease, starvation, and the cold.

The plight of the Jews during the Arrow Cross era was eased by the heroism of many. It was at this time that the young Zionist pioneers saved many lives by forging and distributing various types of documents, and by supplying the ghetto with food. Similar rescue activities were undertaken by the representatives of the neutral states, above all Raoul WALLENBERG of the Swedish legation and Carl LUTZ of the Swiss legation. Many Jews, especially children, owed their lives to the activities of those associated with various Christian orders and agencies of the International RED CROSS, headed by Friedrich Born.

The Hungarian Jewish community lost 564,500 lives during the war, including 63,000 before the German occupation. Of the 501,500 casualties of the post-occupation era, 267,800 were from Trianon Hungary—85,500 from Budapest and 182,300 from the provinces—and 233,700 from the territories acquired from Czechoslovakia, Romania, and Yugoslavia during the period from 1938 to 1941.

[See also Youth Movements: Hungary.]

BIBLIOGRAPHY

Braham, R. L. *The Politics of Genocide: The Holocaust in Hungary.* 2 vols. New York, 1981.
Braham, R. L., ed. *Hungarian Jewish Studies.* 3 vols. New York, 1966–1973.
Katzburg, N. *Hungary and the Jews: Policy and Legislation, 1920–1943.* Jerusalem, 1981.
Lévai, J. *Zsidósors Magyarországon.* Budapest, 1948.

RANDOLPH L. BRAHAM

HUSSEINI, HAJJ AMIN AL- (1895–1974), Grand Mufti of Jerusalem; one of the most prominent Arab leaders in Palestine and the Middle East. Husseini was born in Jerusalem, into a well-connected and wealthy family from whose ranks, for many generations, had come religious leaders and public per-

sonalities. During World War I Husseini was an officer in the Turkish army. In 1920 he helped to organize and incite the anti-Jewish riots that took place in Palestine; he was sentenced to fifteen years in prison, but was pardoned. The following year the British appointed him mufti (Muslim religious head) of Jerusalem, and in 1922 he was elected head of the Supreme Moslem Council, a British-created body. Husseini gradually became the top leader of the Palestinian Arabs, a status he achieved by exploiting his clerical position and his family connections, as well as by using terror against his rivals and by taking the most radical and uncompromising position against the settlement of Jews in Palestine. At the beginning of the Palestine riots of 1936 to 1939, Husseini was elected chairman of the Arab Higher Committee. The British outlawed that committee in October 1937 and disbanded the Supreme Moslem Council, but they let Husseini flee the country for Lebanon, where he remained until October 1939.

The story of Husseini's ties with the Axis powers, and especially with Nazi Germany, covers only a fraction of his far-flung political activities, but it has been the subject of much speculation and a variety of interpretations. Some believe that Husseini's collaboration with the Germans was designed to obtain support for Arab national goals from a power that seemed to have very good prospects of winning the war and that had no colonial past in the Middle East. According to this view, Husseini mainly sought a strong ally to replace the consistent support he had had from the British in the 1920s and 1930s.

Others link Husseini's sympathy for Nazi Germany to his enthusiasm for its policy on the Jews, and particularly its plan for the "FINAL SOLUTION." Husseini did not confine himself to the struggle against a Jewish national home in Palestine, but set "world Jewry" as the target of his fight, because in his opinion the solution of the "Palestine question" depended upon a solution of the entire "Jewish question."

Some go further and perceive a general ideological affinity between the totalitarian Fascist and Nazi theories and Islam, as conceived by Husseini. Hitler's unchallenged position of central leadership and authority may have appeared to Husseini to have much in

Hajj Amin al-Husseini, mufti of Jerusalem, inspecting troops in Bosnia (1943).

common with the all-embracing leadership that the caliph had exercised in the Muslim world, and it may have inspired him to seek a similar position of leadership for himself. Most importantly, National Socialism's world view corresponded to Husseini's Pan-Arabic policy (and also to his Pan-Islamic views for the more distant future). Paradoxically, this basic ideological affinity may account for Husseini's relatively small success with the Nazi and Fascist leaders; his global ambitions, even though restricted to Muslims, had a negative effect on government circles in Berlin.

Husseini made his first approach to the Nazis immediately after their victory in the March 5, 1933, elections, when he called on the German consul in Jerusalem to congratulate him on the new regime. It was only in late 1937, however, after he had broken with Britain and had launched an open struggle against British policy in Palestine, that Husseini made concrete proposals to the Germans for collaboration with them. Prior to the outbreak of the war, Husseini sent two emissaries to Berlin; the first, in December 1937, was Dr. Said Abd-al-Fattah Imam, and the second, in May 1939, was a close confidant, Awni-bey Abd-al-Hadi. Both asked for German aid, in the form of financial support and military arms, for the Arab rebellion in Palestine; they also sought public German support for the independence of Arab countries. Official German reaction to these re-

quests was reserved, but Adm. Wilhelm CANARIS, chief of the ABWEHR, gave financial support for the Arab uprising in Palestine from 1936 to 1938. Later, too, the Abwehr—as well as the REICHSSICHERHEITSHAUPTAMT (Reich Security Main Office; RSHA) and the SS—displayed more interest in Husseini's ambitions than did the German Foreign Office.

When World War II broke out Husseini, together with other exiles from Palestine, fled to IRAQ. There he contributed much to the planning and organization of the pro-Nazi revolt headed by Rashid Ali al-Kailani, in April 1941. Husseini also engaged in propaganda activities among the nationalist fascist circles in Iraq who in early June of that year launched a pogrom against the Jews of Baghdad.

When the revolt in Iraq was quelled, Husseini lost his Middle Eastern base and went into exile, first in Fascist Italy and then in Nazi Germany. From October 1941 to the end of the war, Husseini linked his fate to that of the Axis powers. His first meeting with Benito MUSSOLINI took place on October 27, 1941, and with Adolf Hitler, on November 28, 1941. He maintained regular contact with the German Foreign Office, as well as with the top echelons of the SS and the Gestapo, which appointed special liaison officers for these contacts and paid Husseini and his entourage a monthly stipend of tens of thousands of reichsmarks. Husseini was also in touch with the Japanese authorities. Throughout this period he operated on two major levels simultaneously: pursuing Arab national political goals and lending his support to the "Final Solution."

In his efforts on behalf of the Arab cause, Husseini did not separate the national goals from his own personal ambitions. He sought to gain recognition as the undisputed leader of the Arabs of Palestine and the whole of the Middle East, and eventually, as the spokesman of all the Muslims of the world. For this purpose he set himself three goals: (1) the issuance of a German-Italian joint declaration recognizing the independence of the Arab countries and their unity in a federation; (2) the establishment of a center for pro-Axis propaganda and sabotage, under his control, in one of the Arab countries; and (3) the formation of an Arab army, wearing Arab national insignia, that would fight together with the Axis forces, and whose military objectives would be determined in consultation with himself.

Husseini made a special effort to obtain the joint declaration, only to have one disappointment after the other. Its first version, officially published in October 1940, was nothing more than an expression of general support for the Arab cause, and contained no provision recognizing the independence of Arab states or their unity. A second version, which came much closer to the text that Husseini had in mind, was contained in a letter that the German foreign minister, Joachim von RIBBENTROP, sent to Husseini on April 28, 1942. This, however, was a secret and personal letter, and was addressed both to the "Grand Mufti of Palestine" (Husseini) and to Rashid Ali al-Kailani, Husseini's rival for Nazi favor, whom Ribbentrop referred to as the "prime minister of Iraq." The declaration in the letter, moreover, related only to "Arab states suffering under the yoke of British oppression," which meant that it did not cover even the mufti's minimal program.

Husseini's proposal to establish a Nazi-Fascist propaganda and sabotage center was intended to enable him to restore, with the help of German and Italian bayonets, the support base that he had lost in Iraq. In order to convince his interlocutors in Berlin and Rome of the feasibility of his proposal, Husseini presented himself as chief of a secret organization, the Arab People's Party, which, he claimed, had had branches in all the Arab countries since its founding in Iraq, in the summer of 1940. The Germans had justifiable doubts about the effectiveness of this organization (of whose existence there is no clear-cut evidence). Still, the mufti did succeed in linking himself with the German intelligence network in the Middle East, whose outstanding contribution was to give a precise advance warning of the timing of the Allied invasion of North Africa in November 1942, as well as information about its objectives.

The Italians too came to realize Husseini's potential for intelligence assistance. In September 1942 the chief of Italian intelligence, Gen. Cesare Ame, drew up with Husseini a plan for the establishment of an intelligence and sabotage center in Libya, to be headed by Husseini. The British victory at Al-Alamein, in October and November 1942, put an end to that plan. In the fall of 1944 the Germans made another gesture to indicate their interest in an Arab intelligence and sabotage center (even though they do not seem to have had any confidence in its possible effectiveness). In October 1944 they dropped five parachutists (three Germans and two Arabs) over Jericho, and in November, four parachutists—all Arabs—over Mosul in Iraq. Most of them were caught; the Arabs among them were all Husseini supporters who had been in his entourage in Palestine and Iraq.

Husseini's plan to form an Arab national legion, within the structure of the Axis forces, also failed to gain much of a response. In late 1941 the Deutsch-Arabische Lehrabteilung (German-Arab Training Section) was created, under the German general Helmuth Felmy, with its base at Cape Sounion (Cape Colonna) in Greece. By the end of 1942 it consisted of no more than 130 men. The mufti made efforts to enlarge this unit, and called for the establishment of regular Arab formations, which would fight under his command and under the Arab flag. He also complained about Muslim units being sent to fight in the Caucasus rather than in the Western Desert, seeing this as a waste of their potential propaganda value. On this occasion, too, the mufti sent one of his confidants to act as a liaison officer between the Muslim population in the Caucasus and the German command. It was only in November 1944 that an announcement was published on the establishment of an Arab Legion in Germany, which would wear a patch with the words "Free Arabia" and would be manned by Arab students in Germany, Arab volunteers, released Arab prisoners of war, and soldiers who had previously served in the French Foreign Legion. This plan, too, existed for the most part only on paper.

It so happened that Husseini made his contribution to the Axis war effort in his capacity as a Muslim, rather than as an Arab leader, by recruiting and organizing in record time, during the spring of 1943, Bosnian Muslim battalions in CROATIA comprising some twenty thousand men. These Muslim volunteer units, called Handjar (Sword), were put into the Waffen-SS, fought Yugoslav partisans in Bosnia, and carried out police and security duties in Hungary. They participated in the massacre of civilians in Bosnia and volunteered to join in the hunt for Jews in Croatia. A German general named Berger was the special liaison officer between Husseini and the SS. The Germans made a point of publicizing the fact that Husseini had flown from Berlin to Sarajevo for the sole purpose of giving his blessing to the Muslim army and inspecting its arms and training exercises.

Husseini also helped boost the fighting morale of the OSTBATAILLONE, Muslim auxiliary units of the Wehrmacht that had been formed in early 1942 and had fought bravely against the Soviet army. They had been recruited among the Tatars in the Crimea and Caucasia and among Muslim volunteers in prisoner-of-war camps whose ethnic origins were in Turkistan, Azerbaijan, and other parts of Central Asia. The ethnic leaders and officers of these Ostbataillone attended training courses at the Islamic Institute that Husseini had established in Dresden for this purpose. One of the men who underwent this training was Ahmed Osenbashli, leader of the Tatars in the Crimea and the Volga region, who was the German candidate for the post of mufti in the Muslim areas of the Soviet Union. Husseini also appointed a chief imam for the Turkish units of the Ostbataillone, Mullah Mussayev Uthman.

Other plans hatched by Husseini were not adopted. One such proposal was to appoint a grand mufti for the German-occupied areas, to counterbalance the mufti of the Soviet areas, based in Tashkent. Husseini also proposed that an Islamic training center be established with an integrated military, religious, and political training program, the graduates of which would serve as soldier-preachers in the various Muslim units.

The postwar demand by Jewish representatives to put Husseini on trial as a war criminal was based, in part, on his role in the "Final Solution" of European Jewry. Husseini's men attended SS training courses and even visited the SACHSENHAUSEN concentra-

tion camp. At an early stage the mufti was aware of the enormous extent to which the Jews of Europe were being exterminated. He tried to persuade the Axis powers to extend the extermination program to include the Jews of Palestine, the Middle East, and North Africa. As part of his general struggle against world Jewry, Husseini repeatedly proposed that the Luftwaffe bomb Tel Aviv. From late 1942 to early 1943, when the Axis forces were about to evacuate Libya, he asked that Tripoli be "purged" of its Jews and that their property be confiscated.

When Husseini found out that efforts were under way to save Jews by means of various barter arrangements, he did all he could to foil them. He appealed to the foreign ministers of Romania, Bulgaria, and Hungary, to the German Foreign Office (Ribbentrop), and to the RSHA (Heinrich HIMMLER) to cancel emigration permits given to Jews, on the ground that letting them leave these countries for Palestine would not only impair Arab interests but would also harm the war effort. The proper solution, he argued, would be to send these Jews "to a place where they would be under strict supervision," such as Poland—that is, to exterminate them. German Foreign Office correspondence on this issue reveals that the mufti's pressure had a considerable influence on German thinking. Adolf EICHMANN was the mufti's most devoted ally in trying to persuade the Foreign Office to delay the negotiations on rescue arrangements for as long as possible. These delaying tactics usually achieved their goal.

In late 1943 the mufti, as part of his propaganda drive against the Jewish people and the Jewish religion, established the Arab Institute for Research into the Jewish Question in Berlin, for which the Germans provided the financing. This was an Arab version of a similar institute in Frankfurt, inspired by Alfred ROSENBERG, which the mufti inspected in the spring of 1943.

Although there was ample evidence to declare Husseini a war criminal, the Allies made no effort to arrest him and to put him on trial after the war. The British and the French were deterred from doing so by Husseini's prestige in the Arab world—which persisted in spite of his political failures—

and by their concern that his arrest and trial might compromise their long-standing interests in the Middle East and North Africa. The United States and the Soviet Union did not want to risk their own chances of gaining a foothold in that area. In 1946 the Yugoslav government asked for the mufti's extradition as a war criminal, but the chairman of the Arab League and the government of Egypt succeeded in having that demand tabled. In the British Parliament and the UNITED STATES DEPARTMENT OF STATE, the issue was taken off the agenda for "technical reasons." The argument was that Husseini could not be regarded as a war criminal because he was not the national of an enemy state (Germany or Italy) and had not been on active service in the Axis forces.

When the war ended Husseini was arrested in France, but in June 1946 he managed to escape and was given asylum in Egypt. In the autumn of 1948 he formed the All-Palestine Government in Gaza, but it did not gain any real influence. During the rest of his life he resided in various Arab capitals, primarily in Beirut.

BIBLIOGRAPHY

Carpi, D. "The Mufti of Jerusalem: Amin el-Husseini and His Diplomatic Activity during World War II (October 1941–July 1943)." *Zionism* 9 (1984): 285–316. (In Hebrew.)

Cooper, E. "Forgotten Palestinian: The Nazi Mufti." *American Zionist* 68/4 (March–April 1978): 5–39.

Hirszkowicz, L. *The Third Reich and the Arab East.* London, 1966.

Nevo, J. "Al-Hajj Amin and the British in World War II." *Middle Eastern Studies* 20/1 (January 1984): 3–16.

Nicosia, F. *The Third Reich and the Palestine Question.* London, 1985.

Pearlman, M. *Mufti of Jerusalem: The Story of Haj Amin el-Husseini.* London, 1947.

Schechtman, J. B. *The Mufti and the Fuehrer: The Rise and the Fall of Haj Amin el Husseni.* New York, 1965.

IRIT ABRAMSKI-BLIGH

I

IAŞI (Ger., Jassy), regional capital of northeastern ROMANIA. In 1565, Iaşi became the capital of Moldavia. The presence of Jews there was first mentioned in the fifteenth century. A Jewish community was established in Iaşi in the sixteenth century, and the town was known for its rabbis, its Jewish intellectuals, its Jewish theater, and its Zionist activity. In 1930, 35,462 Jews lived in Iaşi, and their numbers increased to 51,000 after Jews were excluded from the surrounding villages and towns in 1941. The city was known as a center for antisemitic activity; the Jews there suffered from pogroms initiated by Romanian students in 1899 and 1923. In 1923 the Christian National Defense League was created, headed by the progenitor of modern antisemitism in Romania, Alexandru CUZA. It was the forerunner of the IRON GUARD, founded in 1930.

When Ion ANTONESCU came to power, Iaşi was proclaimed the "capital of the Iron Guard" (September 8, 1940), and organized persecutions of the city's Jews began—arbitrary arrests, oppression, extortion, property confiscations, seizure of businesses and factories, staging of trials of suspects charged with belonging to the Communist party, and the like. In November 1940 two of the splendid synagogues were destroyed on the orders of members of the Iron Guard. The leaders of the anti-Jewish agitators included priests who belonged to the Iron Guard. The Jews tried to defend themselves; the heads of the community did not hesitate to lodge complaints about the acts of the "Legionnaires"

(another name for the Iron Guard), and in several quarters the Legionnaires who came to carry out pogroms were beaten. In defiance of an express order, the Jewish merchants refused to open their shops and factories on the Day of Atonement, 1940. The principal activity of the Iron Guard members in the city between September 1940 and January 1941 centered on the "struggle" to acquire the shops and houses owned by the "Yids." The heads of the Jewish community bribed the heads of the Iron Guard, and first and foremost their leader, Ilie Vlad Sturza, so that quiet reigned in Iaşi during the Iron

IAŞI

Annexations from June to September 1940: (1) Bessarabia and (2) N. Bukovina to USSR; (3) N. Transylvania to Hungary; (4) S. Dobruja to Bulgaria.

On June 29, 1941, 2,430 Jews from Iaşi were brought to the railway station and packed into freight cars, which were then locked and sealed and the windows boarded over. The prisoners in the train were not given food or water, and the heat and overcrowding were unbearable. After making many stops for removal of the dead bodies, the train arrived at Călăraşi, 63 miles (101 km) southeast of Bucharest—a distance of about 265 miles (428 km) from Iaşi—on July 6, having traveled six days and seven nights. The survivors were billeted in the yard of an army camp and were assisted by the local Jewish community. On August 30, 980 survivors of the original 2,430 were returned to Iaşi.

The dead bodies were thrown out of the train along the tracks at each of the stops. Here, local Romanian farmers rummage among the bodies for clothes and other valuables, including gold teeth.

Guard's revolt against Antonescu and its attempt to seize power (January 21 to 23, 1941).

On the eve of the war against the Soviet Union, Iaşi was an assembly point of Romanian and German army units, and the tension between non-Jews and Jews increased. Pogroms in the city were organized by members of the Romanian Special Intelligence Service, the liaison office with the German army, the heads of the Romanian military and civil authorities in the city, and Romanian and German army units stationed there. Following the circulation of rumors that Jews had signaled to Soviet planes which bombed the city, assaults on the Jews began on the eve of June 28, 1941, with the participation of Romanian and German soldiers, policemen, and many residents. Thousands were killed in their homes and on the streets, and thousands more were arrested by Romanian and German army patrols and brought to police headquarters. In the homes of Christians, crosses and icons appeared, as well as signs reading: "Here live Christians, not Yids."

On June 29, 1941, dubbed "Black Sunday" by the Jews, of the thousands of Jews assembled in the courtyard of the police headquarters, many were shot by Romanian soldiers; 4,330 of the surviving Jews, as well as Jews collected from all parts of the city, were placed in closed cargo vans and crowded into train cars; 2,650 of them suffocated or died of thirst. Many lost their sanity. On July 2, the police reported to Antonescu that more than 8,000 Jews had been killed in the disturbances. The court that tried the Romanian war criminals in 1948 determined that over 10,000 Jews had been murdered in Iaşi.

BIBLIOGRAPHY

Carp, M. *Pogromul dela Iaşi.* Vol. 2A of *Cartea Neagră.* Bucharest, 1948.

Karetki, A., and M. Covaci, eds. *Zile insingerate la Iaşi, 28–30 Iunie 1941.* Bucharest, 1978.

Lavai, T., ed. *Romania,* vol. 1. In *Pinkas Hakehillot; Encyclopaedia of Jewish Communities.* Jerusalem, 1969. See pages 141–176. (In Hebrew.)

Zaharia, G. "Quelques données concernant la terreur fasciste en Roumanie (1940–1944)." In *La Roumanie pendant la Deuxième Guerre Mondiale: Études,* pp. 9–36. Bucharest, 1964.

JEAN ANCEL

IEQJ. *See* Institut d'Etude des Questions Juives.

IGCR. *See* Intergovernmental Committee on Refugees.

I.G. FARBEN (IGF), German limited company that was a conglomerate of eight leading German chemical manufacturers, including Bayer, Hoechst, and BASF (Badische Anilin- und Sodafabrik), which were the largest such firms in existence at the time. As early as World War I these firms had established a "community of interests" (*Interessengemeinschaft;* hence the initials I.G.), which merged into a single company on December 25, 1925, constituting the largest chemical enterprise in Europe and, indeed, the whole world. Its share capital in 1926 was 1.1 million reichsmarks; its turnover increased from 1.2 million reichsmarks in 1926 to 3.1 billion in 1943. On the German market IGF had a monopoly, and it was the country's largest single exporter. The first chairman of its board was Dr. Karl Bosch, who had previously been the chief executive officer of BASF.

Costly innovations, such as the production of synthetic fuel from coal and of synthetic rubber (Buna) from coal or gasoline, persuaded IGF, at the time the economic crisis came to an end, that the company ought to establish close ties with Hitler. At an early stage Hitler had become aware of the opportunity for Germany to become independent of imports of raw materials, by means of the production processes in IGF's possession. In order to be profitable, the new IGF products needed an assured market, and Hitler indicated that he would be ready to give guarantees for the purchase by the state of these products, in appropriate quantities. At a meeting of leading German industrialists with Hjalmar SCHACHT, Hermann GÖRING, and Heinrich HIMMLER, held on February 20, 1933, IGF contributed 400,000 reichsmarks to the Nazi party, the largest single amount in the total sum of 3 million reichsmarks raised at this meeting by German industrialists for the Nazi party's election campaign. Notwithstanding the presence on the IGF board of several Jewish members, and the fact that even after 1933 Nazi propaganda continued for a time to attack IGF as an example of an international Jewish firm that was exploiting its workers, the contacts between IGF's management and the government became increasingly close, since the products of the great chemical conglomerate were an indispensable element in the Nazi rearmament program.

The FOUR-YEAR PLAN, proposed by Hitler in 1936, which intended to put the entire German industry on a war footing, further enhanced IGF's influence. A member of its board, Carl Krauch, was given a leading position in the organization headed by Göring that had the task of implementing the Four-Year Plan. By this time the company was also adapting itself to the regime's ideological requirements; in 1933 Bosch had still objected—although in vain—to the removal

Heinrich Himmler (front, left), with Walter Dürr-feld and other I.G. Farben representatives, during Himmler's March 1941 inspection of the Auschwitz plant. [YIVO Institute for Jewish Research]

of Jewish scientists from the company and from various scientific institutions, but by 1937 no Jews were left in the IGF executive or on its board of directors. The majority of the board members joined the Nazi party. By means of economic and political blackmail, IGF took over important chemical factories in the areas annexed to the Reich or occupied by it. Bosch resigned his post as chief executive officer in 1935 and was instead elected chairman of the board. His successor as chief executive officer was Hermann Schmitz, a member of the BASF board. After Bosch's death (April 26, 1940), Krauch took his place as board chairman, adding this position to the different posts he held in the Four-Year Plan administration. More than anyone else, Krauch personified the link between private industry and the growing government involvement in economic life during the Nazi period.

In connection with the economic preparations for the forthcoming war against the So-viet Union, the IGF board, with government support, decided to establish an additional Buna works and installations for the production of synthetic fuels. The board decided on AUSCHWITZ, in Upper Silesia, as the place where the new installations were to be located, not only because of its convenient closeness to the railway and to coal mines but, primarily, because the concentration camp then being constructed on the site offered the company up to ten thousand prisoners for work on the construction of the new plant. Board members Otto Ambros and Heinrich Bütefisch were responsible for the Auschwitz plant in their capacity as the officers in charge of Buna and gasoline, respectively. Dr. Walter Dürrfeld became general manager. At first, the plant management protested against the maltreatment of the prisoners working in the plant and their poor physical condition, but Dürrfeld eventually went along with the SS policy, in order to speed up the work. In the middle of 1942 a new section of the concentration camp (Auschwitz-Monowitz) was established, close to the site of the IGF works, to house the prisoners working there and thereby save the time-consuming daily march from and to the main camp. The prisoners' performance, however, never came close to IGF expectations and was always considerably inferior to that of free workers. The Buna production never got started—in part because of the Allied air attacks—and only small quantities of synthetic fuel were actually produced. ZYKLON B gas, used in Auschwitz for the killing of Jews, was a product of DEGESCH, a firm in which IGF had a decisive share.

In the SUBSEQUENT NUREMBERG PROCEEDINGS, which were tried by the Nuremberg Military Tribunals, the United States, as the occupying power, conducted trials against (among others) the top officers of three major industrial concerns—Krupp, Flick, and I.G. Farben. In the IGF trial the accused were the chairman of the board, Carl Krauch, and several of his associates, including Dürrfeld. The major charges were: (1) preparing and waging aggressive war; (2) crimes against humanity, by looting the occupied territories; and (3) enslaving and murdering civil populations, prisoners of war, and prisoners from the occupied territories. All the defendants were acquitted of the first count; nine were found guilty of the second; Krauch, Fritz ter Meer (the board member responsible for the entire Buna production), Ambros, Bütefisch, and Dürrfeld were found guilty of the third. Against the last four defendants, the decisive factor was their role in the construction of the Auschwitz installations. The tribunal did not find the IGF board criminally involved in the poison-gas deliveries made by the DEGESCH company. The sentences imposed on Ambros and Dürrfeld were the most severe (eight years each). By 1951, however, all the IGF officers convicted had been released from prison.

Under Allied Control Council Law No. 9, of November 30, 1945, IGF assets were seized by the Control Council, which in turn handed them over to the four occupying powers, instructing them that installations for the manufacture of war material were to be destroyed, certain plants were to be appropriated as war reparations, and the entire conglomerate was to be broken up. The IGF plants existing in the Soviet zone of occupation were nationalized. In the Western zones, however, no change of ownership took place in the end. Basically, the conglomerate was broken up into its original three major component parts—Bayer, BASF, and Hoechst—whose balance sheet, by the end of the 1950s, already exceeded that of the original IGF. The final IGF Liquidation Act, of January 21, 1955, removed all the remaining restrictions

The Subsequent Nuremberg Proceedings. Trial 6, The I.G. Farben Case, May 8, 1947–July 30, 1948. Fritz ter Meer, the highest-ranking scientist on the I.G. Farben managing board, being sentenced to seven years' imprisonment for his part in the Auschwitz operation.

The Subsequent Nuremberg Proceedings. Carl Krauch, Nazi plenipotentiary for chemical production, who praised the efficiency of the Auschwitz solution of the labor problem, being sentenced.

imposed by the Allies; many of the former top officers of IGF, including Ter Meer and Ambros, were soon again in leading positions in the German chemical industry.

A court of the Federal Republic of Germany in a 1953 decision established the principle that a Jewish prisoner who had been forced to work for IGF in Monowitz had a right to sue the company for compensation. In the wake of this decision and after prolonged negotiations, the residual company—I.G. Farben in Liquidation—agreed to put 27 million deutsche marks at the disposal of the Jewish Material Claims Conference to cover the claims of all Jewish forced laborers and prisoners who had been compelled to work at Monowitz. The payment was described as having been made on a purely voluntary basis and was not to be interpreted as an admission of guilt. IGF did not pay any com-

pensation to non-Jewish forced laborers and prisoners.

[*See also* Forced Labor.]

BIBLIOGRAPHY

Borkin, J. *The Crime and Punishment of I.G. Farben.* New York, 1979.
Ferencz, B. *Less Than Slaves: Jewish Forced Labor and the Quest for Compensation.* Cambridge, Mass., 1979.
The I.G. Farben Case. Vols. 7 and 8 of *Trials of War Criminals before the Nuremberg Military Tribunals under Control Council Law No. 10.* Washington, D.C., 1952.

FALK PINGEL

IMMIGRATION TO PALESTINE. *See* Aliya Bet; Exodus 1947; HICEM; Mauritius; St. Louis; Struma; Yishuv; Youth Aliya.

IMT. *See* Trials of War Criminals: Nuremberg Trial.

INSTITUT D'ETUDE DES QUESTIONS JUIVES (Institute for the Study of the Jewish Problem; IEQJ), anti-Jewish institution that existed in FRANCE from 1941 to 1943. The IEQJ was founded in May 1941, and financed by the German occupation authorities. Its purpose was to encourage anti-Jewish propaganda under a French label.

The institute, headed first by René Gérard and then by Paul Sézille, engaged in general anti-Jewish propaganda, in promoting the "Aryanization" of French economic and cultural life, and in encouraging the French population to inform on Jews and hand them over to the authorities. Its most significant operation was the exhibition "Le Juif et la France" (The Jew and France), which was housed in the Palais Berlitz and opened on September 5, 1941. Aimed at demonstrating to the public in visual form the destructive and disastrous role that Jews and "Judaizers" had played in French history, the exhibition had widespread success. In Paris alone, five hundred thousand persons attended it, before it moved on to Bordeaux and Nancy. Apart from this, the institute also spent much effort and money on the publication and distribution of anti-Jewish literature, especially the bimonthly *Le Bulletin* and *Le Cahier Jaune*, both modeled on Julius STREICHER's *Der* STÜRMER.

In May 1942 the COMMISSARIAT GÉNÉRAL AUX QUESTIONS JUIVES was entrusted (by Pierre LAVAL) to Louis DARQUIER DE PELLE-POIX, an event implying that closer collaboration with Nazi designs had been adopted by the highest echelons of French officialdom and making the IEQJ superfluous and indeed embarrassing, from the German point of view. In June 1942 the institute's director, Paul Sézille, decided to attach it to Darquier's commissariat. Within its new framework, the institute (renamed the Institut d'Etude des Questions Juives et Ethno-Raciales, or Institute for the Study of Jewish and Ethno-Racial Problems) was headed by Georges Montandon, an anthropologist who tried to uncover Jews by means of physical criteria. The institute was officially inaugurated on February 24, 1943, but, except for Montandon's spurious research, it existed on paper alone, and by July of that year it had disappeared altogether.

BIBLIOGRAPHY

Billig, J. *Le Commissariat général aux questions juives, 1941–1944*. 3 vols. Paris, 1955–1960.

Billig, J. *L'Institut d'étude des questions juives, officine française des autorités nazies en France: Inventaire commenté de la collection de documents, provenant des archives de l'Institut conservés au C.D.J.C.* Paris, 1974.

Cotta, M. *La collaboration, 1940–1944*. Paris, 1964.

Marrus, M. R., and R. O. Paxton. *Vichy France and the Jews*. New York, 1981.

Polonski, J. *La presse, la propagande et l'opinion publique sous l'occupation*. Paris, 1946.

ADAM RUTKOWSKI

INTERGOVERNMENTAL COMMITTEE ON REFUGEES (IGCR), committee created at the EVIAN CONFERENCE in July 1938 with the intent of solving the growing problem of REFUGEES in Europe. Its first director, George Rublee, an American lawyer, approached the German government to negotiate the orderly transfer of Jews, with their property, in order to facilitate resettlement. In December 1938, Rublee began negotiations with Dr. Hjalmar SCHACHT, president of the Reichsbank. After Schacht's dismissal the following year, Rublee continued negotiations with Helmuth Wohlthat, an official of the Reich Ministry of Economics. The Rublee-Wohlthat plan that emerged envisaged the establishment of a trust fund, based on Jewish property in Germany, to finance the eventual departure of 400,000 Jews from the Reich. The plan also called for the creation of an international corporation, the Coordinating Foundation, to assist in the project. Though most Jewish organizations opposed the plan, labeling it Nazi blackmail, it was supported by President Franklin D. ROOSEVELT and by several prominent Jews.

The Coordinating Foundation was established in July 1939. However, the outbreak of war put an end to its activities. The attempts of the IGCR to find places of refuge, particularly in undeveloped countries, were also unsuccessful. In the first years of the war the IGCR, now directed by Sir Herbert Emerson, ceased to function in all but name. At the BERMUDA CONFERENCE of April 1943, a decision was made to revitalize the IGCR and grant it greater authority and financing. The reorganization of the committee dragged on for months, and the ineffective IGCR played only a minor role in the rescue of refugees.

During the postwar years the IGCR fulfilled an important role in the resettlement of DISPLACED PERSONS. In June 1947 it was disbanded, and its functions were assumed by the International Refugee Organization.

BIBLIOGRAPHY

Bauer, Y. *American Jewry and the Holocaust*. Detroit, 1981.

Feingold, H. L. *The Politics of Rescue: The Roosevelt Administration and the Holocaust, 1938–1945*. New York, 1982.

Wyman, D. S. *The Abandonment of the Jews*. New York, 1984.

Wyman, D. S. *Paper Walls: America and the Refugee Crisis, 1938–1941*. New York, 1968.

ARIEL HURWITZ

INTERNATIONALE BIBELFORSCHER VEREINIGUNG. *See* Jehovah's Witnesses.

INTERNATIONAL MILITARY TRIBUNAL. *See* Trials of War Criminals: Nuremberg Trial.

INTERNATIONAL RED CROSS. *See* Red Cross, International.

IRAQ. The Jewish community of ancient Babylonia—whose territory was part of what is now Iraq—dates back to the period of the First Temple. For hundreds of years the Jews of Babylonia constituted the largest and most important Jewish community in the world, containing the leadership of the Jewish people as a whole.

In the late 1920s the Jewish community of Iraq numbered some 120,000, most of them living in Baghdad (90,000) and Basra (10,000), and the rest in Mosul, Kirkuk, Sulaimaniyah, Irbil, and various small towns and villages, representing 2.5 percent of the total population (25 percent of the population of Baghdad). By the 1930s, the community was well organized and played an active part in the economy and the general life of the country—more so than the Jews of other countries in the East.

A critical juncture in the situation of the Jews occurred in October 1932, when the British Mandate came to an end and Iraq declared its independence. This was a turn for the worse, which was exacerbated with the death of King Faisal I, in September 1933. In the eight years that followed Faisal's death, Iraq experienced five military coups. Iraqi nationalism was on the rise and consolidating its strength, and it was marked by hatred of foreigners and members of the minorities. One of the manifestations of this attitude was the brutal slaughter of the Assyrian Christian minority in Iraq, in the summer of 1933.

The internal upheavals taking place in Iraq coincided with the Nazi rise to power in Germany, Nazi propaganda in Iraq, and the growing tension in Arab-Jewish relations in Palestine. In October 1932 Fritz Grobba, an Orientalist, was appointed German minister to Baghdad, and he succeeded in skillfully adapting Nazi propaganda to the Iraqis' expectations. The German legation acquired an Iraqi daily, *Al-Alim al-Arabi*, which, beginning in October 1933, serialized Hitler's book MEIN KAMPF, and published propaganda pieces praising the fascist regimes. Members of the intelligentsia and army officers were invited to Germany as guests of the Nazi party. Radical nationalist organizations inspired by fascist ideology were established, such as the Arab Cultural Society, in 1931, and the Mutana Ibn Hartha Society in 1935 (the latter named after the commander of the first Muslim force that invaded Iraq). In 1938 the Al-Futuwwa youth organization sent a delegate to the Nuremberg Nazi party rally, and in turn hosted the Hitler Youth leader Baldur von Schirach in Baghdad. In 1939 all students attending secondary schools, as well as their teachers, were obliged to join Al-Futuwwa, and its membership grew to sixty-three thousand. It was this movement that produced the men who were to stage the pogrom against Baghdad Jews in 1941.

The Arab riots that took place in Palestine between 1936 and 1939 gained wide publicity in Iraq, thanks to efforts made by Palestinian and Syrian exiles and refugees who came to Iraq after participating in them. In October 1939 they were joined by the mufti of Jerusalem, Hajj Amin al-HUSSEINI.

Official discrimination against Jews was introduced in Iraq in 1934, when dozens of Jewish civil servants were dismissed from the ministries of economic affairs and transportation. In 1935 an unofficial *numerus clausus* (quota) made its appearance in government schools. Jews who wanted to travel to Palestine ran into bureaucratic problems and had to pay a deposit of 50 dinars, to be held until their return to Iraq; as time went on, the sum of this compulsory deposit grew to 3,000 dinars. In February 1936, some three hundred Jewish officials—most of them holding senior posts—were dismissed. That same year, when the Arab riots broke out in Palestine, physical assaults on Jews were launched. On the eve of the Jewish New Year in 1936, three Jews were murdered. A few days later, on the Day of Atonement, a bomb was thrown into a Baghdad synagogue, and only by pure luck was a catastrophe averted. Anti-Jewish incitement in the form of demonstrations, newspaper articles, and posters became commonplace. A Jewish-owned newspaper, *Al-Hassad,* was closed down in 1938. Antisemitic incidents grew in violence and frequency, culminating in the Baghdad pogrom.

German victories in Europe in the early years of World War II raised new hopes among the Iraqi nationalist movement. On April 1, 1941, four colonels (dubbed the "Golden Square"), led by Rashid Ali al-Gaylani, a lawyer by profession and a radical nationalist, seized power in the country and established a pro-Nazi "government of national defense." In the two months that the pro-German government was in power, the Jews lived with fear and terror in their hearts. No blood was shed, but the war against the British, who had reoccupied Iraq to prevent Nazi control, also singled out the Jews as its target, and the presence of Germans made itself felt in the country. Anti-British and anti-Jewish propaganda was disseminated in the media and at public assemblies. Anti-Jewish demonstrations took place in Baghdad, Mosul, Kirkuk, Irbil, and Amara, often ending in violence. Much money was extorted from the Jewish community, and considerable Jewish property was confiscated to service the needs of the war against the British. Jews were arrested and tortured on charges of spying for the British and giving signals to British aircraft hovering over Baghdad. Police duties and the maintenance of public order were put into the hands of Al-Futuwwa members, organized into armed gangs under the name of Ketaib a-Shabab (Youth Battalions). These battalions were under the authority of the nationalist lawyer and translator of *Mein Kampf* Yunis es-Sebawi, a government minister holding several portfolios, including those of propaganda and internal security, who was pro-Nazi and radically antisemitic. In Baghdad the Ketaib took over two Jewish schools and launched attacks on Jews and violent break-ins to Jewish houses.

The great pogrom and slaughter of Jews in Baghdad and the pillage of Jewish-owned stores in Basra took place after officials of the Rashid Ali regime had fled and before another regime had been installed in its place. Basra was taken by the British on May 16, 1941, but in order to interfere as little as possible with Iraq's internal affairs, the British forces were encamped on the outskirts of the city. This situation was exploited by mobs that on May 19 broke into the commercial quarters to pillage and destroy Jewish shops and businesses. No loss of life was recorded.

Baghdad was taken by the British on May 30, and here too the British troops stayed outside the city. That same day Rashid Ali, the mufti Husseini, and their close associates escaped to Iran. The only member of the pro-Nazi regime to stay behind was es-Sebawi, who appointed himself military governor. According to some versions, es-Sebawi planned the organized slaughter of Jews. He held power, however, for a few hours only, and was replaced by a Committee of Public Order. The rioting began on the Jewish Festival of Weeks (Shavuot), June 1, 1941, when Iraqi soldiers, frustrated by their defeat at the hands of the British, encountered a group of Jews in festive attire at the Al-Har bridge; the Jews were on their way to welcome Abdul Illah, the pro-British regent, on his return to the capital. The soldiers were joined by a mob, and within a few hours the rioting spread to various other parts of the city. Leading the mobs were the Ketaib a-Shabab, which had been trained by es-Sebawi. All this happened at a time when actual control was in the hands of the British. The rioting mobs were made up of Muslims from the lower classes, a few Christians who guided the mob to the Jewish houses, and Bedouin from outside the city. The police took no action, and the Committee of Public Order apparently intervened only when it seemed that the riots might spread and endanger non-Jewish property as well. In all, 179 persons were killed in the riots and 2,118 were injured; 242 Jewish children were orphaned. The number of persons whose property was looted was put at 48,584. Unspeakable brutalities were committed in the pogrom: rape, murder, and the crushing of body organs of babes in arms, women, and men, young and old. Synagogues were profaned and Torah scrolls defiled.

Once a permanent government was installed, order was restored. On June 8, a commission of inquiry into the events was appointed; its findings called for the punishment of the leaders of the rioting. Pro-Nazi elements were arrested and exiled, and the

Jews were even awarded a rehabilitation grant. Nevertheless, the pogroms had created a new situation, as far as the Jews were concerned. True, the traditional Jewish leadership still believed that the 1941 pogroms had been an exceptional occurrence and that the Jews had to integrate into Iraqi society. The leadership was also influenced by the promise of easy enrichment held out by the economic boom that followed the British victory. It even withheld publication of the inquiry commission's report. The Jewish youth, however, looked for new paths to follow. Most of the young people turned to Zionism, and the first Jewish youth organizations, such as Youth for Rescue, Unity and Progress, and the Society of Free Jews, were founded; in April 1942 a Hagana organization came into being, with the help of Jewish emissaries from Palestine. Some of the Jewish youth joined the Communist party, whose prestige had risen, especially after the great victories that the Soviets had scored in the war. Both the Zionist movement and the Communist party operated as underground organizations.

There were more sporadic attacks on Jews in Iraq during the war years, in remote places. Thus, on December 17, 1942, eight Jews were murdered in Sandur, in the Kurdish area of northern Iraq, by Arabs from a neighboring village. The murderers were not punished.

BIBLIOGRAPHY

Goldstein-Meir, A. "Pogroms against the Jews of Baghdad." *Pe'amim* 8 (1981): 21–37. (In Hebrew.)

Hirszowicz, L. *The Third Reich and the Arab East.* London, 1966.

Kazaz, N. "The Influence of Nazism in Iraq and Anti-Jewish Activities, 1933–1941." *Pe'amim* 29 (1986): 48–71. (In Hebrew.)

Kazaz, N. "The Report of the Government Committee of Investigation of the Occurrences of 1–2 June 1941." *Pe'amim* 8 (1981): 47–59. (In Hebrew.)

IRIT ABRAMSKI-BLIGH

IRGUN BERIT ZION (United Zion Organization; IBZ), secret Zionist organization founded in KOVNO, Lithuania, at the end of 1940. Its goal, at the time it was founded, was to foster Jewish national culture and Zionism, which was jeopardized after the incorporation of Lithuania into the Soviet Union earlier that year. The emphasis was on "general" Zionism, the founders of IBZ disapproving of the proliferation of organizations in the Jewish community at the time.

The activists in the organization, including its founder and first leader, Shimon Grau, came from among the older former students of the Hebrew secondary schools, which had been closed down by order of the Communist authorities. Some of the pupils, but not all, had belonged to Zionist youth movements, mainly to Ha-No'ar ha-Tsiyyoni, Maccabi ha-Tsa'ir, and Bnei Akiva. Under Soviet rule, during 1940 and 1941, the organization operated on the basis of underground cells and never had more than one hundred members. Its main activities were the publication of a Hebrew magazine, *Nitsots* (Spark), at regular intervals, and the operation of study groups. Later, when Lithuania was under German occupation and the Jews of Kovno were ghettoized, IBZ also sought to recover the Hebrew books that the Soviet authorities had confiscated.

IBZ was at its most successful in 1943, when it numbered from 150 to 200 members, most of the newer ones between the ages of twelve and fifteen. The members were enrolled in permanent organizational units—companies, battalions, and the like—which bore Hebrew names such as He-Atid, Nili, and Ma'apilim. In the three years of its existence in the ghetto IBZ was headed, at various times, by Yitzhak Shapira, Avraham Melamed, and Aryeh Cohen. In addition to *Nitsots*, which became a monthly in the ghetto, IBZ produced other publications, such as *Shalhevet* and the almanac of the Ma'apilim battalion. Its main emphasis was on ideological and educational activities.

IBZ did not discourage those of its members who were set on escaping from the ghetto to join the partisans or to go into hiding in the villages. In the final months of the ghetto's existence, IBZ concentrated on preparing hideouts in the ghetto, but these did not stand the test when it came during the liquidation of the ghetto in July 1944, and many IBZ members met their death there. The remaining members, together with the

A group of Irgun Berit Zion members in Kovno. Standing, left to right: Lalka Kilson, Shlomo Frankel-Shafir, Sarah Petrobolski, Zerubavel Rosenzweig. Seated, left to right: Sasha Gurewitz, (?), Fima Shtrofan.

other survivors of the ghetto, were sent to concentration camps in Germany, mainly to DACHAU and KAUFERING. Even there, some IBZ members continued to publish *Nitsots*, until their liberation in April 1945. Four months earlier, the IBZ in the camps had united with the underground Masada organization from ŠIAULIAI and with other Zionist groups into a new framework that they called Hitahdut ha-No'ar ha-Yehudi (Jewish Youth Association). Some fifty IBZ members survived the war; most of them settled in Israel.

BIBLIOGRAPHY

Levin, D. *Between a Spark and the Flame*. Ramat Gan, Israel, 1987. (In Hebrew.)

DOV LEVIN

IRON GUARD (Garda de Fier; also called Totul Pentru Ţară, "All for the Fatherland"), Romanian fascist and antisemitic movement.

It was established in July 1927 by Corneliu Codreanu under the name of Legiunea Arhangehelului Mihail (Legion of the Archangel Michael), which was changed to Iron Guard in 1929. An extremist antidemocratic movement, the Iron Guard gained support among college and high school students, and its activity marked a milestone in the annals of the Jews of ROMANIA. On December 9, 1927, during a convention of Christian students in ORADEA MARE, a pogrom took place in which five of the city's synagogues were destroyed and twenty-eight Torah scrolls were desecrated and burned; in CLUJ, eight synagogues were destroyed and forty-six Torah scrolls defiled. Acts of vandalism also occurred in other Transylvanian cities, as well as in IAŞI. The members of the Iron Guard—who were also called "Legionnaires"—were organized into paramilitary units and operated in party cells.

Before long, the Iron Guard became a fascist movement with original Romanian characteristics, based on Christian mysticism, the cult of death, antidemocratic principles, absolute obedience to the "leader," and rejection of the parliamentary system of government. It also aimed at excluding Jews from all spheres of the country's life, abrogating their civil rights, and, if possible, "purging" Romania of their presence, out of the belief that Jews were the major cause of the crises besetting Romanian society. The Iron Guard leaders succeeded in turning their organization into a mass movement by exploiting the peasants' devotion to the Christian faith and fanning their antisemitism, which the movement's leaders depicted as an integral part of that faith—an ideology that gained them the support of the clergy in the rural, as well as the urban, areas.

Close ties with the Nazis came relatively late, only in 1936, and the Iron Guard leaders prided themselves on having anticipated their Nazi friends, mainly on the issue of Jew-hatred. The growth of the Iron Guard's power was also facilitated by the leniency with which it was treated, and by the support given by various Romanian governments to antisemitic movements—sometimes in the form of financial subsidies—in the hope that the governments could exploit these movements when the need arose.

Under pressure from France, its patron power, the Romanian government dissolved the Iron Guard at the end of 1933. The movement reacted by launching a murderous political terror campaign, in the course of which it assassinated two prime ministers and dozens of other political adversaries. Despite its official dissolution, the Iron Guard took part in the 1937 elections (the last democratic elections held in Romania), under the name Totul Pentru Ţară; the election results made it the third largest political party in the country. In 1938 King Carol II banned all political activity, by which ruling Iron Guard activities were also outlawed. On a visit to Germany, the king realized that the Iron Guard had become the most powerful pro-Nazi element in Romania and was a threat to his regime, and he ordered the execution of its leaders, including Codreanu.

In the summer of 1940 the king became reconciled with Horia SIMA, Codreanu's successor, and appointed him to the Cabinet. On September 6 of that year, Ion ANTONESCU and Sima formed a National Legionary government, which put into practice parts of the Iron Guard's antisemitic platform. The members of the movement, within the government as well as outside it, set up a regime of terror in the country against their political adversaries and against the Jews. Their major goal was to strip the Jews of their property and eliminate them from economic and cultural life; to achieve their purpose they applied both racist legislation and violence. Romania's ties with Nazi Germany and Fascist Italy were greatly strengthened, and the country's leaders went out of their way to please Nazi emissaries in Romania. From January 21 to 23, 1941, Horia Sima staged a coup against Antonescu, which failed because the army remained loyal and because Hitler too supported Antonescu and ordered Nazi units in Romania to place themselves at the prime minister's disposal. The abortive coup was accompanied by anti-Jewish riots in Bucharest in which 123 Jews were killed. The Iron Guard leaders took refuge in Germany, where they became bargaining cards for the Germans in their dealings with Antonescu.

In December 1944, following Romania's surrender, the Nazis formed a Romanian government-in-exile in Vienna, made up of Iron Guard men, with Sima at its head. When the war ended the Iron Guard leaders dispersed all over the world, mainly to Spain and Portugal. They were able to avoid being tried as war criminals, since during most of the war they had not been in Romania and were not there when the Antonescu regime committed its great crimes against the Jewish people. These included the annihilation of the Jews of BESSARABIA and BUKOVINA, the massacre of the Jews of ODESSA, and the deportation of Jews to TRANSNISTRIA. Groups of former Iron Guard men are to be found in Spain, the United States, Canada, and some countries in Latin America.

BIBLIOGRAPHY

Codreanu, C. Z. *Eiserne Garde.* Berlin, 1939.
Palaghita, S. *Garda de Fier: Spre reinvierra Romaniei.* Buenos Aires, 1951.
Patrascanu, L. *Sous trois dictatures.* Bucharest, 1946.
Vago, B. *The Shadow of the Swastika: The Rise of Fascism and Antisemitism in the Danube Basin, 1936–1939.* London, 1975.

JEAN ANCEL

ISRAEL. *See* Yishuv.

ITALY. [*This entry consists of three articles. The first is a general survey of Italy and Italian Jewry in the Fascist era. The second article deals with the concentration camps set up in Italy by the Fascist regime and used later by the Nazis. The third focuses on the aid offered to Jews during the Holocaust by the Italian people.*]

General Survey

The Italian Jewish community is the oldest continuous settlement of the European Diaspora; its annals span well over twenty centuries. The emancipation of Italian Jewry, first granted in the kingdom of Sardinia in 1848 and extended to the whole of the Italian peninsula by 1870, was a unique achievement, in both its positive and its negative aspects: in the security, opportunities, and acceptance accorded the Jewish minority on the one hand and in the progressive erosion of Jewish identity on the other. Jews were fully integrated into Italian society and politics and had access to careers in the diplomatic corps, the civil service, and the army—careers generally closed to them elsewhere in the West.

Until 1936, fourteen years after Benito MUSSOLINI's seizure of power, antisemitism on the peninsula was a marginal phenomenon, isolated from the mainstream of Italian life, and the clerical campaign against the Jews (1883–1903) served only to increase the isolation of the Catholic church from the political life of the kingdom. On the other hand, the post-risorgimento period was marked among Jews—at least up to 1938—by progressive assimilation, ever-increasing secularization, widespread intermarriage, and a sharp drop in the Jewish birthrate. Assimila-

ITALY

▲ Concentration Camp

0   miles   80

0   kilometers   120

© Martin Gilbert 1982

tion was facilitated by several factors particular to Italy (at least in their convergence): the numerical insignificance of the Jewish nucleus (about one tenth of one percent of the total population); the virtual absence of Jewish immigration from eastern Europe; the liberal ideology of the Italian state; the "universalistic" nature of Italian nationalism itself (which, until 1938, was defined in cultural and not in "racial" terms); and, last but not least, a curious blend of respect for individual Jews and disregard for Judaism as a religion and as an ethical system, a combination that subtly encouraged irreligion and apostasy among Italian Jews.

Countercurrents of Jewish revival surfaced in the first two decades of the twentieth century, with the emergence of Zionism, the formation of a school of historical studies at the Rabbinical College of Florence, the Pro Cultura circles, the proliferation of Jewish periodicals, and the founding of a Jewish youth movement. These manifestations of Jewish "separatism" gave rise to criticism, given the liberal assumption that emancipation would be followed by the disappearance of the Jewish minority. The advent of FASCISM gave a fresh impetus to this criticism, largely owing to Fascist suspicions of Jewish internationalism and the danger it was believed to represent to the "monolithic unity" of the future Fascist state. Mussolini himself repeatedly denounced "Jewish" Bolshevism and "English" Zionism in his newspaper *Il Popolo d'Italia* between 1919 and 1922; he also warned the Italian Jews not to stir up antisemitism in the only country where it had never existed, adding that the "New Zion" of Italian Jewry was not in Palestine, but in Italy.

The Fascists Seize Power. The Fascist seizure of power on October 30, 1922, evoked a certain alarm among the leaders of Italian Jewry, owing as much to Mussolini's previous invectives against the Jews as to the general enthusiasm that the March on Rome aroused among foreign antisemites. Simultaneously, charges of antisemitism were leveled against the new regime in the international Jewish press; and on March 26, 1923, the president of the World Zionist Organization, Chaim WEIZMANN, repeated these charges in a public speech in New York. The Fascist

reaction was swift; immediately after the March on Rome, a member of the Italian government assured the Chief Rabbi of Rome, Angelo Sacerdoti, that Fascism was entirely free from antisemitic tendencies. A year later Mussolini received Sacerdoti in order to repeat these assurances as publicly and as emphatically as possible:

As Dr. Sacerdoti in the ensuing conversation drew the Hon. Mussolini's attention to the fact that the antisemitic parties abroad desire in some fashion to find an accession of strength to their antisemitic policy in an alleged antisemitic attitude on the part of Italian Fascism, on which they wish to model themselves, His Excellency declared formally that the Italian government and Italian Fascism have never had any intention of following, nor are following, an antisemitic policy, and further deplore that foreign antisemitic parties should desire to exploit in this manner the spell which Fascism exercises in the world.

This public declaration was followed by a confidential remark about the kindred movement in Germany: "I have refused to receive Hitler, and the Bavarian papers have accused me of being a tool of the Jews; when they hear what I am telling you now, they will say that I have myself become a Jew."

The evolution of Fascist policy toward the Jews may be divided into four periods: (1) a "honeymoon period" of outwardly cordial relations, during which some sort of symbiosis developed between the regime and Italian Jewry (1922–1932); (2) a transitional phase of ambivalent posturing, during which Mussolini performed a "balancing act" between Hitler's Germany and the Western democracies (1933–1936); (3) a six-year span of increasingly violent antisemitism, beginning with racist propaganda and culminating in discrimination and persecution (1937–1943); and (4) the final period of German domination, during which Hitler's Jewish-affairs experts applied the "Final Solution" of the Jewish problem to the German-occupied part of the Italian peninsula (1943–1945).

Cordial Relations. In the decade following the March on Rome, the civil and religious rights of the Jewish minority were respected. Mussolini publicly condemned racism and antisemitism, had cordial talks with Zionist leaders, and encouraged (up to a certain point) the activities of the Italian Zionist Federation, despite his objections to Jewish "separatism." It was during this phase that the Fascist dictator began to use the Jews as a vehicle for the extension of Fascist power at home and for the expansion of Fascist influence abroad. This policy found expression in the most important act of Fascist legislation regarding the Jews before the racial laws of 1938: the establishment in 1930 and 1931 of the Union of Italian Jewish Communities, as an officially recognized representative and administrative body, by a series of royal decrees that gave a coherent and unified legal status to Italian Jewry and provided a stable financial base for Jewish religious, cultural, and charitable activities. By the same decrees, the Jewish communities of LIBYA and RHODES were aggregated to the union and placed under its jurisdiction, thereby accelerating their Italianization and "Fascistization."

Transitional Phase. Hitler's rise to power in 1933 marked the beginning of a reorientation. For the next three years, until the outbreak of the Spanish Civil War, Mussolini alternated declarations and acts in favor of the Jews with (strictly unofficial) antisemitic moves and expressions of sympathy for the German position. The Ethiopian war gave rise to fresh polemics against "international Jewry," accused of being the occult power behind Anglo-French "sanctionism." Throughout this transitional phase, however, no alteration in the favorable legal status of Italian Jewry was either effected or contemplated, and no anti-Jewish measures, official or unofficial, were taken by the regime. Mussolini even tried to win laurels as a mediator between Jews and Germans. He also called for the establishment of a Jewish state in Palestine and had "cordial" talks with the Zionist leaders, Chaim Weizmann, Nahum Sokolow, and Nahum GOLDMANN. As late as July 1936 his agents made advances to Zionist leaders.

Antisemitism Increases. German-Italian intervention in Spain put an end to these ambivalent developments. After the German-Italian rapprochement of October 1936, the evolution of the Jewish question in Italy was determined by the exigencies of Axis policy, despite the fundamental conflict of interest between the Axis partners and the divergence of views on Hitler's doctrine of Nordic superiority (which had anti-Italian as well as anti-Jewish implications). In the fall of 1936 Mussolini launched an antisemitic press campaign that, unlike previous anti-Jewish polemics, was explicitly directed against Italian Jewry as a whole. The promulgation of discriminatory legislation was delayed because of the need to prepare Italian public opinion, the desire to avoid a premature clash with the Vatican, continued friction between Rome and Berlin, and a lingering fear of negative repercussions in the Western democracies. When the racial laws were finally issued in the autumn of 1938, it was clear to all concerned that Mussolini had burned his bridges with the West and committed himself to the Rome-Berlin Axis.

With Italy's entry into World War II on June 10, 1940, new anti-Jewish measures were decreed and the anti-Jewish press campaign was intensified. However, though side by side, the two allies never marched in step, and this was again reflected in the field of Fascist Jewish policy. Given his military and economic dependence on the Germans, Mussolini could not back away from his anti-Jewish legislation, nor could he mitigate his racist ideology. On the other hand, the Jewish question outside Italy served the Fascists as a means of asserting what little freedom of action from their Axis partners they were able to maintain. Together with genuine expressions of spontaneous humanitarianism, this eminently political consideration explains why the Italian-occupied territories in FRANCE, YUGOSLAVIA, and GREECE became havens of refuge for persecuted Jews. It also explains why Mussolini, while approving of security measures against hostile Jewish elements, would never agree to the deportation of Italian citizens to the east. Hitler was determined to impose his anti-Jewish obsession on the whole of Europe, including Italy; but until Italy's surrender to the Allies, he was not prepared to jeopardize relations with Rome on a question of extending the "Final Solution" to the Italian sphere of influence. It was only after the Italian armistice with the Allies on September 8, 1943, that he decided to treat the part of Italy under German control as conquered as well as occupied territory, and to include Jews of Italian nationality in the "racial" measures from which they had hitherto been exempt.

"Final Solution" Applied to Italy. In assessing the impact of the German occupation on the Holocaust in Italy, three basic facts must be borne in mind. First, there was the geographical distribution of Italian Jewry. Ever since the expulsions of 1492 and 1541, Italian Jewish life had been confined to the north of the country, that is, the part of Italy that came under German control. Second, there was Hitler's decision (taken against the advice of his experts) to restore Mussolini to power in 1943. Since the success of the anti-Jewish policy depended largely on Italian cooperation, the creation of a Fascist puppet republic had the effect of facilitating the implementation of the "Final Solution" in Italy. And third, there was Hitler's change of mind with regard to the projected occupation of the Vatican. Of all the decisions taken by the German dictator after the Italian "betrayal,"

this was the only one that benefited the Jews, for it enabled the Catholic church to save thousands of Jewish lives.

Fascist antisemitism was neither a logical development of the Fascist creed nor a logical extension of the racial measures adopted in Africa after the Ethiopian campaign. It was, however, a logical consequence of Mussolini's alliance with Hitler; it was implicit in Fascism because the Rome-Berlin Axis was implicit in the "totalitarian" pretensions of the movement, with particular reference to the Fascist pursuit of empire. The Fascist race laws were neither an original Italian creation (as Mussolini asserted) nor a slavish imitation of the German model (as his opponents claimed) but an unsuccessful attempt to adapt the German racial theories to Italian conditons. The result was a watered-down version of Hitler's NUREMBERG LAWS that antagonized Italian and Western opinion, displeased the Germans, and alienated the Cath-

Jewish forced laborers in the town of Gorizia, on the Yugoslav border, 23 miles (37 km) northwest of Trieste (September 1942).

The memorial at the Ardeatine Caves, outside Rome. Here, on March 24, 1944, the Germans massacred 335 men and boys (of whom 78 were Jews) in retaliation for the killing of thirty-three German SS police by Italian partisans in Rome on the previous day, March 23. The victims were taken to the caves and made to wait outside while groups of three were taken inside, forced to kneel, and shot in the back of the head.

olic church. Far from strengthening the Axis alliance, it added a new dimension to the conflict of interest between the two countries. Worse still, it marked the beginning of a rupture between the Fascist regime and the Italian people, as well as the end of the idyll between Italy and the Holy See.

Between September 15, 1943, and January 30, 1944, at least 3,110 persons of Jewish "race" were shipped from Italy to AUSCHWITZ, 2,224 of whom are known to have perished in the Holocaust. Between February and December 1944, at least another 4,056 were deported to the east on orders from Friedrich Robert Bosshammer, Adolf EICHMANN's Jewish-affairs expert in Italy; 2,425 of these are known to have lost their lives. About 2,700 Italian Jews were deported from areas outside of Bosshammer's jurisdiction—837 from Trieste to Auschwitz, Ravensbrück, and Bergen-Belsen, in which places all but 77 met their end; over 1,800 from Rhodes to Auschwitz, where 1,622 of them died; and at least 82 from foreign countries under Ger-

man rule, only 9 of whom survived the war. At least 44 were deported for reasons unconnected with their "race"; 25 of these are known to have lost their lives. There were 387 deportees whose date of departure has not yet been ascertained; and 334 of them are known to have perished. In addition, at least 173 Jews were murdered on Italian soil between the Italian armistice and the collapse of the Fascist republic, including 78 who were butchered at the Ardeatine Caves near Rome on March 24, 1944, in retaliation for the ambush of an SS detachment in Rome. As late as April 26, 1945, three days before the collapse of Hitler's hold on Italy, 6 Jews (all of them foreigners) were killed by the SS at Cuneo; and at least 119 persons of Jewish "race" perished in Italian prisons and internment camps during the twenty months of the German occupation.

Collaboration and Aid Given. At the trial of Eichmann in 1961, it was stated that "every Italian Jew who survived owed his life to the Italians." But while it is true that most of the

Jewish survivors were saved by Italian "Aryans" of all classes, it is no less true that such "successes" as Bosshammer was able to achieve were largely owing to (willing or unwilling) Italian collaborators. Thousands of Jews were arrested and interned by the Fascist police to be deported and killed by Himmler's subordinates. Others were denounced by Italian agents of the SS; still others were tracked down by Fascist squads headed by notorious thugs. Not a few Jews had their hiding places betrayed by Italian civilians who were motivated by greed, the Germans having offered rewards for the denunciation of Jews. There were even a few renegade Jews who made common cause with the enemies of their people, the most notorious being Celeste di Porto, a Roman Jewish woman who turned over dozens of fellow Jews to the Italian agents of the SS for 5,000 lire each.

At the time of the Italian armistice there were some 44,500 Jews in Italy and Rhodes, about 12,500 of them foreigners. By the end of the war, at least 7,682 of these had perished in the Holocaust. Of the 8,369 deportees who have so far been identified, only 979 returned to Italy after the war, including a baby born at Bergen-Belsen. In addition, at least 415 Jews survived imprisonment or detention in Italy proper, and a few leaped to freedom while on their way to the extermination camps.

But although approximately four-fifths of the Jews of Italy survived the war, Italian Jewry suffered a blow from which it is unlikely to recover in the foreseeable future. Thousands had abandoned the community, and some six thousand had emigrated; many of those who remained were physically and spiritually broken. The habit of Jewish life had been interrupted, and in many places its very setting had disappeared. Italian Jewry remains only a shadow of its former self.

BIBLIOGRAPHY

Carpi, D. "The Origins and Development of Fascist Anti-Semitism in Italy (1922–1945)." In *The Catastrophe of European Jewry*, edited by I. Gutman and L. Rothkirchen, pp. 283–298. Jerusalem, 1976.
Michaelis, M. *Mussolini and the Jews: German Italian Relations and the Jewish Question in Italy, 1922–1945.* Oxford, 1978.
Zuccotti, S. *The Italians and the Holocaust: Persecution, Rescue, and Survival.* New York, 1987.

MEIR MICHAELIS

Concentration Camps

Before the outbreak of World War II, concentration camps, as an institution for the systematic isolation and liquidation of political opponents, did not exist in Italy. Persons suspected of being engaged in hostile actions against the Fascist regime were restricted to residence in remote villages, chiefly in the central or southern parts of the country. Political prisoners who had been tried and sentenced served their terms in regular prisons or special wings of such prisons.

This situation changed on the eve of Italy's entry into the war (June 10, 1940), with mass arrests of the foreign nationals among the Jews who had not complied with the expulsion order issued in 1938. Men, women, and children were thrown into jail with no charges brought against them, and were often held under appalling conditions. Three months later, on September 4, the Ministry of the Interior ordered forty-three concentration camps to be established, for the imprisonment of enemy aliens and of Italians suspected of subversive activities. Among the prisoners in these camps were thousands of Jews who were foreign nationals or stateless persons, and 200 Italian Jews who were known to oppose the Fascist regime.

With respect to the prisoners' physical safety and living conditions, there was no comparison between the concentration camps in Italy and those set up by the Nazis in Germany and in the countries they occupied. In the Italian concentration camps, families lived together; there were schools for the children and a broad program of social welfare and cultural activities. For the most part, the work imposed on the prisoners involved only services required for the camp itself. As time went on, more camps were set up, for Allied prisoners of war; one of these camps, Fossoli di Carpi, later became a concentration and transit camp for thousands of Jews who were designated for deportation.

The fall of the Fascist regime on July 25, 1943, and Italy's surrender to the Allies on September 8, 1943, were dramatic turning points. King Victor Emmanuel and the prime minister, Pietro BADOGLIO, fled to the south; the army disintegrated; and the country was divided into two, the south in the hands of the Allies and the central and northern parts in the hands of the Germans. For many Jews, who had been imprisoned in Fascist concentration camps, this meant liberation, since most of the camps were situated in the southern districts that were the first to be set free. This included the largest camp, at FERRAMONTI DI TARSIA. On the other hand, the bulk of the Jewish population of Italy, which for historical reasons was concentrated in Rome and the north, was caught in the German-occupied part. It was in this section that the Fascist satellite state, the Italian Socialist Republic, was set up.

After the north fell under German rule, seizures of Jews took place in all the major cities, where the Jews were still living peacefully in their homes. The German raiding parties had lists of the names and addresses of the Jews and were assisted, passively or actively, by the Italian Fascist armed forces. In Rome, the Germans cordoned off the Jewish quarter, and in a single day—October 16, 1943—arrested more than one thousand persons. Similar actions took place in Trieste (October 9), Genoa (November 3), Florence (November 6), Milan (November 8), Venice (November 9), Ferrara (November 14), and other places. After being held in local jails for a while, the Jews were confined to concentration camps, usually in Fossoli and Bolzano; from there, when a certain number of prisoners had been collected, they were deported to extermination camps, mainly to AUSCHWITZ.

The Fascist satellite state under Mussolini at first contented itself with issuing a declaration of principles, which laid down that "the members of the Jewish race" were aliens who "in this war are regarded as belonging to an enemy nation." Before long, however (on November 30, 1943), this declaration was followed up by an order from the minister of the interior, G. Buffarini Guidi, requiring all Jews, without exception, to be put in concentration camps and their property to be confiscated. Other orders in this vein, issued by various branches of the Fascist government, dealt mainly with procedural matters regarding the confiscation of

Jewish property. But these did not affect the situation of the Jews, who by then had either abandoned their property and fled for their lives or had been imprisoned in concentration camps or deported to eastern Europe. In Italy, the Germans—who bore the main responsibility for actions against the Jews and, for the most part, also carried them out—carefully abstained from issuing special anti-Jewish decrees, such as the wearing of the yellow badge (see BADGE, JEWISH) or the establishment of ghettos and Judenräte (Jewish councils). They concentrated on seizing Jews, imprisoning them in jails or special concentration camps, and deporting them from Italy.

This last period, from September 8, 1943, to April 1945, can be described as the period of the manhunts for Jews. In these manhunts, more than 20 percent of Italy's Jews (who numbered thirty-seven thousand on the eve of the German occupation) were imprisoned in jails and concentration camps in Italy, and kept there for weeks or months prior to being deported to the extermination camps. The conditions that prevailed in transit and concentration camps were not uniform. Some were under German command from the beginning, others had a mixed German-Italian command, and a third group was handed over to the Germans by their original Italian commands. Some were labor camps; others were transit camps where the Jews were held pending deportation. In one camp, San Sabba, near Trieste, killings took place and a crematorium was set up.

The Fossoli camp, established in 1940 to house prisoners of war, was located near the town of Carpi, 12.5 miles (20 km) north of Modena. In the initial stage it consisted of several large barracks, surrounded by a triple-apron barbed-wire fence and guard towers. Following Italy's surrender, Fossoli was handed over to the Germans and soon began to be filled with Jews—individuals and families; men, women, and children—who had been seized in their homes during the systematic manhunts and designated for deportation. Also held in the camp, in barracks of their own, were political prisoners and Italian army personnel who refused to serve under the flag of the Fascist satellite state. The number of persons belonging to either of these groups varied according to the type of transport that was being readied, either Jewish transports (which went chiefly to Auschwitz, though one transport of Jews, nationals of neutral countries, was sent to BERGEN-BELSEN) or those of political prisoners, which went mainly to MAUTHAUSEN.

Initially, the camp was able to hold 800 prisoners, but by the end of 1943 its capacity was enlarged. Between November 1943 and the end of 1944, at least 3,198 Jews are known to have passed through Fossoli—in other words, more than a third of the number deported from Italy. Fossoli was at all times under the command of German officers, who were assisted by SS men and Fascist militia.

Conditions in the camp were a strange mixture of callousness, starvation, and violence on the one hand, and, on the other, some "humane" habits that did not exist in other German camps. The Jewish prisoners lived together in several barracks, men and women separately; they were allowed to take care of the children, even the infants and those who were without parents. The few possessions that the prisoners had brought along were not confiscated, nor did they have to wear prison garb.

The Bolzano camp was established by the Germans in late 1943 or early 1944 in Gries, a suburb of Bolzano. It had the largest capacity of all the concentration camps in Italy, housing as many as three thousand prisoners at a time. The Jews in the camp never numbered more than 20 percent of the prisoner population. Beginning in early August 1944, most of the prisoners and the entire administrative staff of the Fossoli camp were moved to Bolzano; Fossoli was no longer regarded as safe because of the advancing front line and the rise of partisan operations in the area. Several transports left Bolzano for Auschwitz (the last on October 24, 1944) and then for concentration camps in Germany (RAVENSBRÜCK and Flossenbürg). The last transport from Bolzano apparently left on January 25, 1945; thereafter, no more than eight hundred prisoners remained, including several dozen Jews. The Germans had planned to deport them on February 25, 1945, but they missed the opportunity: the Alpine passes were being bombed from the air, disrupting all traffic with Germany. The prisoners, who were already on their way there, were taken back to Bolzano, where they remained until they were liberated at the end of April 1945.

In its layout and established procedures, Bolzano resembled a typical German labor camp, more than any other camp in Italy. On arrival, the prisoners had to go through the usual routine: their hair was shaved, their possessions were confiscated, and their clothes were exchanged for prison uniforms. Every prisoner had to sew a triangular patch on his or her clothing displaying a registration number. The patches were in different colors—red for dangerous political prisoners, pink for ordinary political prisoners or military personnel, yellow for Jews.

The prisoners were put on hard forced labor inside and outside the camp, working in the fields, making railway repairs, digging tunnels near the camp, and so on. Only the political prisoners classified as "dangerous" were not put to work, for security reasons, and were restricted to their block.

Escape attempts were rare, one reason being that the German South Tyrol minority was hostile to all Italians and especially to Italian Jews. The few prisoners who did escape from the camp and were caught by these local inhabitants were handed over at once to the camp guards and executed, after undergoing cruel torture. An organized escape attempt, through a tunnel that was dug in the block of the dangerous political prisoners, was also doomed to failure.

The La Risiera di San Sabba camp was not an extermination camp in the standard meaning of the term, but it had a crematorium that was used for burning the corpses of prisoners who had been executed or had died under torture. The original structure had been built at San Sabba, near Trieste, in 1913 by the Austrian authorities who were then in control of the area, to serve as a plant for separating rice from chaff (hence the name Risiera). This large structure also contained a furnace and a high chimney, for drying the rice. By the 1920s the structure was no longer in use for its original purpose and was only temporarily occupied, from time to time, by Italian army units.

After the Italian surrender to the Allies, Trieste became part of a special district, separate from the rest of Italy, that was put under the direct and exclusive control of the German security authorities—the Adriatisches Küstenland Operationszone (Adriatic Coastal Area Operational Zone). Two notorious SS officers, Odilo GLOBOCNIK (who was a native of Trieste) and Franz STANGL, operated in this zone at different times.

Shortly after they had taken control of the area, the Germans seized the abandoned structure and made it into a transit camp, bringing Slovenian partisans there for questioning, torture, and execution. Also brought to La Risiera were political prisoners and Jews, for questioning and detention pending their dispatch to the north. Commandants of the camp, successively, were SS-Obersturmbannführer Christian WIRTH (from the fall of 1943 to May 1944) and SS-Obersturmbannführer Dietrich Allers, who had been director of the German euthanasia campaign in 1939 (June 1944 to April 1945). The camp staff was all German, except perhaps for a few Ukrainian auxiliaries. In the period of its existence, more than twenty thousand prisoners passed through La Risiera. Several thousand persons were murdered—generally by having their skulls cracked with heavy clubs—and their bodies were burned in the crematorium (which had been constructed by enlarging the old furnace and also utilizing the existing chimney). Several dozen Jews were among those killed at La Risiera, and their bodies, too, were cremated; some six hundred and fifty were deported to Auschwitz or, as of the end of 1944, to camps in Germany. The last transport left the camp on January 11, 1945.

Apart from these three camps—Fossoli, Bolzano, and San Sabba—the main assembly points for Jews in Italy were in Mantua, in a building that had belonged to the Jewish community; in the San Vittore prison in Milan; and in Borgo San Dalmazzo.

BIBLIOGRAPHY

Baccino, R. *Fossoli.* Modena, 1961.
Folkel, F. *La Risiera di San Sabba.* Milan, 1979.
Levi, P. *Survival in Auschwitz.* New York, 1959.
Liggeri, P. *Triangolo rosso.* Milan, 1963.
Michaelis, M. *Mussolini and the Jews: German-Italian Relations and the Jewish Question in Italy, 1922–1945.* London, 1978.

DANIEL CARPI

Aid to Jews by Italians

During World War II the Italians, more than most other peoples in Europe, extended aid to the Jews. These rescue efforts took different forms and sprang from a variety of motives. The period during which they occurred may be divided into three different stages.

In the first stage, from the beginning of the war to mid-1942, the Italian authorities, and particularly Foreign Ministry officials, gave protection to Jews of Italian nationality living in German-occupied territories or in countries in the German sphere of influence. Particularly outstanding in their range and forcefulness were the actions taken by the Italians in occupied FRANCE, where there were fifteen hundred Jews of Italian nationality, and in TUNISIA, where they numbered fifty-five hundred. Jews were also protected in SALONIKA and in satellite states in the Balkans and the Danube basin. With these actions the Italians safeguarded their own interests, maintaining their presence and their social and economic position, since more often than not it was Italian Jews living in these areas who served these interests, especially in the Mediterranean countries. Moreover, in this period the Italians were still on an equal footing with the Germans and were not prepared to tolerate discrimination of their nationals, irrespective of the "race" to which they belonged.

The second stage extended from mid-1942 to September 1943. During this period, the Italians witnessed the arrest, roundup, and deportation to the east of entire Jewish populations in France, Belgium, and Greece, and saw with their own eyes the unspeakable atrocities committed against Jews in CROATIA. Moreover, rumors of what was happening in eastern Europe had come to their attention. Many of the Italian military personnel and Italian diplomats serving in these places were outraged, and persuaded their superiors in the Foreign Ministry and the General Staff in Rome to give aid to Jews, regardless of their nationality, who were seeking asylum in the Italian zones of occupation. As a result a genuine rescue operation was launched in areas under the supervision or control of the Italian army: in Dalmatia-

Croatia, where five thousand Jews found refuge; in southern France, where approximately twenty-five thousand had gathered (the Germans cited a figure of fifty thousand); and in ATHENS and the Greek islands, where thirteen thousand Jews had congregated. In this way, at least forty thousand Jews who were not Italian nationals were given refuge in the Italian-occupied areas. The Italians treated these Jews in a humane manner and did not hand them over to the Croats, the Vichy police, or the Germans, despite unceasing demands and protests.

The Germans, in particular, brought tremendous pressure to bear upon Italy, on different military and diplomatic levels—all the way up to Mussolini—to have the Jews handed over to them. On at least two occasions, Mussolini was ready to yield to the German pressure, and he even gave his agreement to surrender the Jewish refugees from Croatia. But the high-ranking diplomats and officers in his entourage who would have had to implement this order refused to do so, and by various means succeeded in thwarting this act.

Italian diplomats who distinguished themselves in this effort included Luigi Vidau, Leonardo Vitetti, Luca Pietromarchi, Giuseppe Bastianini, and Blasco Lanza d'Ajeta in Rome; Giuseppe Castruccio, Guelfo Zamboni, and Pellegrino Ghigi in the Italian mission in Athens; Vittorio Zoppi, Alberto Calisse, Gustavo Orlandini, and Gino Buti among the diplomats serving in France; and Vittorio Castellani in Croatia. Among the army officers, Generals Giuseppe Pièche, Giuseppe Amico, Carlo Avarna di Gualtieri, Mario Roatta, Carlo Geloso, and Mario Vercellino were prominent. Also outstanding in this effort was Guido Lospinoso, an Italian police inspector serving in southern France. In addition, during this period thousands of Jews infiltrated into Italy itself, especially from Yugoslavia and with the assistance of the Italian military, and found refuge there from their persecutors.

The third and last stage was ushered in on September 8, 1943, when the Italian government surrendered to the Allies. From then on, until the day of liberation, the Jews were hunted down mercilessly in every place. In this period of endless terror, during which every Jew was in danger of his life, each Jew, whether an Italian or an alien, was in desperate need of help from the Italian people. In most instances the Jews were given such help, by people from all walks of life. On the other hand, Italy had its collaborators with the Germans, the men of the Fascist Black Brigades and the volunteers of the Italian SS. These men represented a constant threat to the Jews, for they did not have the slightest compunction about helping the Germans to round up the Jews, question them, and deport them to their deaths. There were also informers among the Italians.

The great majority of the people of Italy, however, including a substantial part of the Italian clergy, gave aid to the Jews and helped them go into hiding, in the homes of "Aryan" friends, in remote villages, and in monasteries. It was thanks to this aid, as well as to other possibilities (such as crossing into Switzerland or to southern Italy, which had already been liberated by the Allies), that the greater part of the Jews of Italy were saved.

BIBLIOGRAPHY

Carpi, D. "Notes on the History of the Jews in Greece: Attitude of the Italians (1941–1943)." In *Festschrift in Honor of Dr. George S. Wise*, pp. 25–62. Tel Aviv, 1981.

Carpi, D. "The Rescue of Jews in the Italian Zone of Occupied Croatia." In *Rescue Attempts during the Holocaust*. Proceedings of the Second Yad Vashem International Historical Conference, edited by Y. Gutman and E. Zuroff, pp. 465–526. Jerusalem, 1972.

Poliakov, L., and J. Sabille. *Jews under Italian Occupation*. Paris, 1955.

Zuccotti, S. *The Italians and the Holocaust: Persecution, Rescue, and Survival*. New York, 1987.

DANIEL CARPI

IVANO-FRANKOVSK. *See* Stanisławów.

J

JABOTINSKY, VLADIMIR (Zeev; 1880–1940), Zionist leader and author. Jabotinsky was born in Odessa, studied law in Italy, and became a journalist and writer. He was one of the founders of the Jewish battalions in World War I and fought in their ranks. In 1920 he was sentenced to jail for participating in the defense of Jerusalem during bloody riots that took place in the city, but was pardoned. Jabotinsky was a member of the Zionist Executive but resigned. In 1925 he established the Revisionist movement, becoming its leader and the head of Betar, the Revisionist youth movement. From 1936 he was also supreme commander of Irgun Tseva'i Le'ummi.

When Hitler came to power in Germany, it was Jabotinsky's view that Nazi antisemitism was "the most significant component" in the Nazi party's collective soul. Like other Jewish leaders, however, he did not consider Hitler's MEIN KAMPF a blueprint for extermination, although he was not at all optimistic about the Nazi regime and did not exclude the possibility that it would maintain itself for a long time. Jabotinsky was inclined to regard the Hitler regime as based on weak foundations resting solely on Jew-hatred, and incapable of realizing its dream of a Greater Germany. The Third Reich, he thought, was "no more than a trite episode in the story of Jewish suffering." Jabotinsky felt that the Nazis' aim was to gain the support of the *petite bourgeoisie* (lower middle class) and the German intelligentsia by destroying the role played by the Jewish merchants and the Jew-

Vladimir Jabotinsky. [Central Zionist Archives, Jerusalem]

ish intelligentsia. When the anti-Nazi boycott movement was launched (*see* BOYCOTTS, ANTI-NAZI), Jabotinsky assumed that it would turn international public opinion against the Nazis and might lead to Hitler's downfall. Consequently, he was strongly opposed to the

HAAVARA AGREEMENT, which was intended to facilitate the emigration of Jews from Germany and enable them to take out part of their assets.

All his life Jabotinsky believed in a theory of antisemitism that he had developed, following in the footsteps of Theodor Herzl and Max Nordau. According to this theory there were two kinds of antisemitism: the "subjective antisemitism of people" and the "antisemitism of objective reality." The latter was represented by Polish antisemitism, which was the most threatening and foreshadowed a "social earthquake"; on the other hand, the antisemitism found in Germany, Romania, and Hungary was "subjective antisemitism," a form of virulent animosity with its ups and downs. But even when it is on the rise only a minority pursues it actively, while the rest are pulled along. This antisemitism is flexible, and when its protagonists are ordered to cease and desist, they obey.

There is no truth to the widely held belief that Jabotinsky foresaw the extermination of the Jews, from either "subjective antisemitism" or "antisemitism of objective reality." In his opinion, the solution to the question of the Jews of Europe lay in "evacuation": the transfer, within ten years, of 1.5 million Jews from eastern Europe to Palestine—on both banks of the Jordan—so as to save them from the ongoing erosion of their social and economic status. The deterioration of the situation of the Jews following KRISTALLNACHT caused Jabotinsky to revise his "Ten-Year Plan," and he called for the immediate emigration to Palestine of a million Jews. He did not expect a second world war to break out; when Hitler occupied Prague in March 1939, Jabotinsky said that war between the great powers was impossible, except for a war between Japan and the Soviet Union. When war did begin, he realized that he had erred in not foreseeing it, but he doubted that the war would widen and (in January 1940) expected that the warring powers would enter negotiations.

Jabotinsky kept careful track of the Nazi massacres of Jews in Poland that the Jewish Telegraphic Agency was reporting, while the general press was ignoring some of these reports. He collected the reports, but did not revise his theory of differentiating between "objective" and "subjective" antisemitism—

despite his finding that the loss of life suffered by the Jews was higher than that of the combined losses of the Polish and German armies (except for the losses in actual combat) and that the agony the Jews were experiencing was worse than that of any other people.

After war had broken out, Jabotinsky concentrated mainly on raising the demands of the Jewish people, as conceived by the Zionist Revisionist movement, and obtaining the recognition of these demands as war aims by the Allies that were at war with Hitler. The Lublin Reservation project (see NISKO AND LUBLIN PLAN) was in his eyes a "confused improvisation" by the Germans that might vanish from the scene, but that might also develop into a broad solution. Jabotinsky's estimate of the Nazi murders in Poland was that they did not exceed the usual pattern of pogroms; hence his demand that after the war the Jews of Poland be granted equal rights, but that the Allied powers had to realize that Poland alone could not be expected to bear the whole burden of the Jewish problem on its shoulders. In sum, Jabotinsky did not consider Nazi antisemitism as a new phenomenon, but rather as part of nineteenth-century German antisemitism, a tradition that claimed adherents from Arthur Schopenhauer to Houston Stewart CHAMBERLAIN, which political parties had turned into a political doctrine. On the eve of his death Jabotinsky was of the belief that most of the Jews of Europe would survive.

Jabotinsky died when the war had been in progress for only eleven months. At that point, only a very few envisaged the possibility of a holocaust on the scale that in fact took place.

BIBLIOGRAPHY

Jabotinsky, V. *The Jewish War Front.* London, 1940.
Schechtman, J. B. *The Vladimir Jabotinsky Story.* 2 vols. New York, 1956, 1961.

JOSEPH HELLER

JÄGER, KARL (1888–1959), SS officer. Jäger was born in Schaffhausen, Switzerland, and engaged in commerce. He joined the Nazi

Karl Jäger. [National Archives]

party in 1923 and the SS in 1932. Beginning in 1935 he served in Ludwigsburg, Ravensburg, and Münster, successively. In Münster, where he was assigned in 1938, he was appointed chief of the SD (Sicherheitsdienst; Security Service). After serving in the occupied Netherlands for a time, Jäger was appointed commanding officer of Einsatzkommando 3 in Einsatzgruppe A, which was attached to an army corps in northern Soviet Russia. He later became commander of the Sicherheitspolizei (Security Police) and SD for the General Commissariat of LITHUANIA in Kovno, with the rank of SS-*Standartenführer.*

In this capacity, Jäger was in charge of the extermination of Lithuanian Jewry, as witnessed by the reports that he submitted. In a report dated December 1, 1941, Jäger stated: "There are no more Jews in Lithuania, except for those in three small ghettos, ŠIAULIAI, KOVNO, and VILNA." In another report, of February 9, 1942, Jäger summed up the killings accomplished by the unit under his command: 136,421 Jews, 1,064 Communists, 653 mentally ill persons, and 134 others. Among the 138,272 victims there were 55,556 women and 34,464 children.

In the fall of 1943 Jäger was reassigned to Germany and was appointed chief of police in Reichenberg, in the Sudetenland. When the war ended he succeeded in assuming a false identity and became a farmer. In April 1959 he was arrested, and on June 22 of that year he committed suicide in his cell.

BIBLIOGRAPHY

Krausnick, H., and H.-H. Wilhelm. *Die Truppe des Weltanschauungskrieges: Die Einsatzgruppen der Sicherheitspolizei und des SD, 1938–1942.* Stuttgart, 1981.

YAACOV LOZOWICK

JANÓWSKA, labor and extermination camp situated in the suburbs of LVOV, in the Ukrainian SSR. In September 1941 the Germans set up a factory on Lvov's Janówska Street, to service the needs of the German army. Soon after, they expanded it into a network of factories as part of the DEUTSCHE AUSRÜSTUNGSWERKE (German Armament Works), a division of the SS. From their inception, these factories used the Jews of Lvov as forced labor; in September 1941, 350 Jews were employed there, and by the end of October their number had risen to 600. At that point the factories' status underwent a change: the area in which they were located became a restricted camp, enclosed by barbed wire, which the Jews were not permitted to leave. In 1942 the labor in the camp was intensified and its inmates were employed in metalwork and carpentry. They were also given jobs with no practical purpose, such as digging trenches and moving loads from one place to another, in order to break the prisoners in body and spirit before dispatching them to their death.

At the beginning of November 1941, the Germans asked the Lvov JUDENRAT (Jewish Council) to supply more workers for the camp, but the Judenrat chairman, Dr. Joseph Parnes, refused to comply. As a result, he was executed. In the wake of an *Aktion* against the Jews of the city in March 1942, several hundred more Jews were put into the camp. When the mass deportation of Jews from Eastern Galicia to the BEŁŻEC extermination camp began during that month, the role of the Janówska camp changed: from time to time, groups of Jews from towns and villages in the area were interned there before being sent on to their death. Inside the camp, *Selektionen* classified some as fit for work; these stayed behind, while the others were dispatched to Bełżec. Later in the spring of that year the camp was enlarged and took on the character of a concentration camp, with beatings and killings, starvation and disease becoming the lot of its prisoners. In an effort to ease their plight, the Lvov Judenrat, together with the prisoners' families, organized a committee that sent food to the camp. Only a fraction of it reached the prisoners, however, the bulk being confiscated by the camp staff.

Following *Aktionen* in Lvov in the summer of 1942, thousands more Jews were put into the camp. By mid-1943 Janówska, while still functioning as a labor camp, was being turned into an extermination camp. Fewer prisoners were employed in the factories inside the camp and in the city and the length of stay of newcomers was shortened, most being taken directly to places of execution on the city outskirts. In the middle of May 1943 over six thousand Jews were murdered. The harassment and killing of Jews were directed by the exceptionally cruel German camp commanders and staff, among them Obersturmführer Fritz Gebauer, Untersturmführer Gustav Wilhaus, Hauptscharführer Joseph Grzimek, and Obersturmführer Wilhelm Rokita.

Despite the reign of terror in the camp, there were cases of mutual help and even efforts at organizing resistance. In particular, the prisoners tried to help those who were ill, so that they would not be put to death immediately. In the middle of 1943, attempts were made to form resistance groups in the camp. Underground activists among the prisoners smuggled in arms with the help of prisoners whose place of work was on the outside; the aim was to offer armed resistance when the camp was about to be liquidated. The liquidation did in fact begin in November 1943, and it has been suggested that the Germans advanced the date in order to preempt a general uprising in the camp. While the Jewish underground did not have the time to organize such an uprising, there were instances when prisoners at-

The Janówska camp orchestra played while the inmates set out to work and when they returned. It was established by the Germans, who amused themselves by mocking and humiliating the inmates.

tempted armed resistance while being taken to the execution sites. On November 19, a revolt broke out among the group of prisoners known as Sonderkommando 1005 (*see* AKTION 1005), who had the task of collecting and cremating the bodies of the victims. Several of the guards were killed and some among the Sonderkommando escaped, although most were caught and executed.

No precise figures are available on the number of Jews who perished in the Janówska camp, but it is estimated that tens of thousands of Jews from Lvov and Eastern Galicia met their death there.

BIBLIOGRAPHY

Kahana, D. *Lvov Ghetto Diary*. Jerusalem, 1978. (In Hebrew.)
Schoenfeld, J. *Holocaust Memoirs: Jews in the Lwow Ghetto, the Janowski Concentration Camp, and as Deportees in Siberia*. Hoboken, 1985. See pages 125–153.
Wells, L. *The Janowska Road*. New York, 1963.
Zadereczki, T. *When the Swastika Ruled in Lvov: The Destruction of the Jewish Community as Seen by a Polish Author*. Jerusalem, 1982. (In Hebrew.)

AHARON WEISS

JAPAN. Japan's policy toward the Jews during the Hitler era was anomalous. A full partner in the Berlin-Rome Axis, and greatly influenced by Nazi propaganda, Japan had its own influential "experts on Jewish affairs" who wrote as well as translated antisemitic works and sponsored antisemitic fairs that were subsidized by the German Ministry of Foreign Affairs. Yet the fifteen thousand or so stateless Russian Jews living in eight communities of northern China and Manchuria under Japanese control were granted legal status. Within this status, the Jewish refugees were recognized as one of the Manchurian nationalities and were enabled to carry out their autonomous community affairs within the laws of the country. As part of this, the Japanese government officially recognized their Zionist organization. Moreover, during this period, Japan provided a haven from Hitler's clutches for about seventeen thousand Jewish refugees from Germany, Austria, and Poland, in SHANGHAI.

At a secret Five Ministers' Conference on December 6, 1938, only a few weeks after the KRISTALLNACHT pogrom, when thousands of central European Jews were seeking refuge, Japan formulated a pro-Jewish policy enabling thousands of Jews to immigrate to the Japanese-occupied sector of the International Settlement in Shanghai, without visas or papers of any kind. This was at a time when the world's doors were virtually closed to Jewish refugees.

This singular behavior can be explained by the influence on Tokyo of Japanese "experts on Jews": middle-echelon officers in the Japanese army and navy, such as Col. Senko Yasue and Capt. Koreshige Inuzuka. Yasue, Inuzuka, and their dozen or so colleagues sincerely believed the canard, found in the PROTOCOLS OF THE ELDERS OF ZION and other antisemitic books, that world Jewry had conspired to bring about the downfall of the Russian, German, and Austro-Hungarian empires during World War I and wielded decisive financial and political power on the international scene, especially in Western countries such as the United States and Great Britain.

To the Japanese "experts," the validity of the notion of the Jews as rich, influential financiers was confirmed by the one Jew familiar to every Japanese: Jacob Schiff, the head of Kuhn, Loeb and Company, a New York–based banking firm. With the help of the Jewish banking firm M. M. Warburg and Company, of Germany, and of Sir Ernest Cassel in England, Schiff floated four crucial loans for Japan during the Russo-Japanese War (1904–1905). Schiff was the first Westerner to be honored by the emperor, and his name became a household word in Japan.

Throughout the 1920s and 1930s, Inuzuka, Yasue, and their fellow "experts on Jews" wrote books containing such statements as:

The Bolshevik Revolution is part of the Jewish plot. . . . Zionism seems to be the goal of the Jews, but they actually want to control the world's economy, politics, and diplomacy. . . . The Jewish plot must be destroyed by force. . . . The Jews are responsible for the American and European control of the Chinese Nationalist government. . . . The Jews control the American press and thereby public opinion, turning it against Japan. . . . They are responsible for the immorality of the Japanese youth.

The existence of such antisemitism among the Japanese, who were barely aware of the existence of Jews, can be understood only in light of Japan's painful process of modernization in the late nineteenth and early twentieth centuries. Along with industrial, technical, and military innovations came the inevitable flood of Western concepts, which were in direct conflict with Japan's ancient culture and traditional values. The sacrosanct nature of family and nation headed by a revered emperor was antithetical to democracy's emphasis on the individual. Especially disturbed were the ultranationalists, both military and civilian, who resented this "intrusion" from the West. Imbued with the agrarian myth of an earlier, more innocent age, they sought, unsuccessfully, to hinder technological progress, which must inevitably lead to social acculturation as well. Like their counterparts in Russia, Germany, and even the United States, they truly believed in the canards of the *Protocols* or *The International Jew*, which portrayed the Jew as the ultimate cause of international and domestic problems. In the minds of the less sophisticated Japanese, it appeared only logical that since Jews controlled the United States and Britain, which represented the West, the Jews and the West were synonymous. Thus, antisemitic books were written with "Jew" in the title, but nowhere in the entire text were Jews mentioned.

In contrast to the Western tradition of antisemitism, however, the Japanese lacked two millennia of hatred of the Jews as "perpetrators of deicide," and this gave their antisemitism its peculiarly Japanese pragmatic twist. Japanese ultranationalists intended to apply the Western version of antisemitism and "Jewish power" to Japan's "New Order" in East Asia. But while writing the most vicious antisemitic works, in practice they inspired Japan's pro-Jewish policy and personally treated Jews well.

The transition from theory to practice began to take shape after Japan occupied Manchuria in 1931 and 1932. Yasue, Inuzuka, and their dozen or so colleagues were leaders of the military and civilian political clique, known as the Manchurian faction, that pushed for the Manchurian takeover. Its goal was the development of Manchuria and its vast resources, which were vital to Japan's defense. Two to three billion dollars were required to finance the Manchurian project, and their assumption was that if Japan treated the Jews in East Asia well, the Jews in turn would convince their rich and influential co-religionists in the United States to emulate Schiff's loans.

Moreover, these Russian or Sephardic Jews, or German refugees, residing peacefully under benign Japanese rule, would also, through their influential fellow Jews, mitigate America's negative policy toward Japan. After Japan occupied Manchuria, and especially after the start of hostilities with China in 1937, United States policy toward Japan was extremely harsh and inflexible. For example, in 1938 the United States established an embargo against Japan that withheld scrap iron and oil crucial to Japan's industrial and military needs. The Japanese also looked on the refugees from Germany as potential hostages and as possessing the scientific knowledge necessary for Manchurian development. At the same time, to counterbalance the Soviet Jewish "homeland" in nearby Birobidzhan, these Jewish inhabitants of Manchuria would be offered a Zionist state of their own.

Around 1936, Gisuke Ayukawa, the industrialist member of the Manchurian faction, formulated his plans for the industrialization of Manchuria, to be underwritten by American capital. Thus, the pro-Jewish policy received a further stimulus. It came to full fruition at the Five Ministers' Conference of 1938, which resulted in an open-door policy for central European refugees fleeing to Shanghai and opened an era of goodwill toward Jews that lasted until the outbreak of the war in the Pacific, on December 7, 1941.

The first beneficiaries of the pro-Jewish policy were the stateless Russian Jews living under Japanese hegemony in Manchuria, who suffered from White Russian antisemitism and from economic pressure exerted by the Japanese during the early 1930s. Though many were impelled to leave for the freer economic atmosphere of Shanghai and Tientsin, those who remained finally achieved legal status and protection. None other than Colonel Yasue was made the liaison between the Japanese authorities and the Jews. He promptly closed *Nash Put,* the White Russian antisemitic newspaper, and in 1937 he helped organize the first of three annual Far Eastern conferences of Russian Jewish communities. These conferences were attended by a thousand delegates, and the Zionist flag flew alongside the flags of Japan and Manchuria, while uniformed members of the Zionist youth movement Betar joined Japanese soldiers in standing guard. In 1941 Yasue went to Palestine, where he was inscribed in the Golden Book of the Jewish National Fund. He is remembered fondly by Jews of that era—all this while pseudonymously writing books such as *The Jewish Control of the World* and translating the *Protocols of the Elders of Zion.*

At the same time, Captain Inuzuka served as his counterpart in Shanghai, where he headed the Bureau of Jewish Affairs and tried to effect his goal of a Jewish settlement in Shanghai, instead of in Manchuria. His objectives came somewhat closer to fruition with the arrival of the Jewish refugees from 1938 to 1941. They were permitted entry into Shanghai despite efforts by the Western members of the governing body of the International Settlement, including the United States and Britain, to keep them out.

In November 1940, soon after the signing of the Tripartite Pact between Germany, Italy, and Japan, and to the consternation of the German Ministry of Foreign Affairs, Inuzuka broadcast a pro-Jewish message on the Tokyo radio, in which he contrasted Japan's favorable treatment of the Jews with that of the Nazis. At the same time, under a pseudonym, he published a translation of the *Protocols,* lauded by the same unwitting Germans.

Then, in early 1941, when more than a thousand Polish Jewish refugees found themselves stranded in Kōbe, Japan, with Curaçao visas of questionable validity and expired Japanese transit visas, Foreign Minister Yotsuke Matsuoka (the former governor of Manchuria) approved the extension of their transit visas (*see* RESCUE OF POLISH JEWS VIA EAST ASIA). This was just prior to his trip to Berlin to cement relations with Hitler. With the approach of war, the Japanese relocated the Polish refugees—among them writers, artists, Socialist leaders, Talmudic students,

and rabbis—to their sector of Shanghai. For his help in providing this new home, the Union of Orthodox Rabbis of the United States and Canada sent an inscribed silver cigarette case to Captain Inuzuka (which was to help him obtain release from a trial of war criminals in Manila after the war).

With the beginning of the war in the Pacific, the Japanese became more susceptible to Nazi influence. The "pro-Jewish" Bureau of Jewish Affairs was disbanded, and Inuzuka was shipped to the Philippines. By February 18, 1943, the Japanese finally gave in to German demands to set up a ghetto for the Jews. Only the German, Austrian, and Polish refugees were relocated, to a ghetto of 2 square miles (5 sq km), which included thousands of Chinese. Because of Japan's sensitive relationship with the Soviet Union, the three thousand to four thousand stateless Russian Jews remained free, as did the few hundred Sephardic Jews (the wealthy ones were interned as British "enemy nationals").

While the ghetto posed great economic and psychological hardship, in no way did it resemble its European counterparts. Although Japanese soldiers, with the help of unarmed Pao Chia (Jewish auxiliary police), guarded entry to and exit from the ghetto, no walls or even barbed wire surrounded it. The Japanese authorities generally left the community alone—with all its cultural, religious, and educational activities intact—and engaged in no random torture or shooting, along Nazi lines. Thus, the refugees lived in relative peace throughout the war, though with not too much to eat. Only if a refugee required a pass to leave the ghetto for business or medical reasons would he possibly encounter trouble with the Japanese officials. Okura might throw one in jail, or Ghoya, who called himself "King of the Jews," might slap or even kick the refugee standing on line one minute, and behave like a gentleman the next. But unlike the Americans, with their stringent wartime communication laws, the Japanese never prevented the sending of money by Jewish organizations via neutral countries to support most of the indigent refugees in Shanghai. By the end of 1943, in response to pressure by the VA'AD HA-HATSALA (Rescue Committee of United States Orthodox Rabbis), the United States permitted such money transfers, and conditions improved for the refugees.

The Japanese, even in the midst of war, were still under the illusion of a potent "Jewish power" in the United States. They tried several times, unsuccessfully, to send out peace feelers to the United States by means of unsuspecting Jews in Shanghai or Tientsin. Ironically, throughout the period of the Holocaust, it was this type of Japanese antisemitism that served to protect, rather than hurt, some Jews.

[*See also* Sugihara, Sempo.]

BIBLIOGRAPHY

Kranzler, D. "The Japanese Ideology of Antisemitism and the Holocaust." In *Contemporary Views of the Holocaust*, edited by R. L. Braham, pp. 79–107. Boston, 1983.

Kranzler, D. "Japanese Policy toward the Jews, 1938–1941." *Japan Interpreter* 11/5 (1977): 493–527.

Kranzler, D. *The Japanese, the Nazis, and the Jews.* New York, 1976.

DAVID KRANZLER

JARBLUM, MARC (1887–1972), Jewish leader in Vichy France. Born in Warsaw, Jarblum came to Paris at the age of twenty and soon became a central figure in Po'alei Zion, a Socialist Zionist movement. In the interwar period he was also active in various immigrant organizations, while maintaining close ties with the French Socialist movement. After the fall of France, Jarblum attempted to coordinate welfare activity in the occupied zone and supported the creation of the Commission Centrale des Organisations Juives d'Assistance, attempting unsuccessfully to make it the political representative of the Jewish community in France. Jarblum found himself at odds with the French-born Jewish leaders and often condemned their lack of concern for the immigrant Jews in France. When the UNION GÉNÉRALE DES ISRAÉLITES DE FRANCE (UGIF) was proposed, he immediately opposed it, led the campaign against its creation, and refused to be nominated to its council.

Following the deportations from France in the summer of 1942, Jarblum channeled the activities of the FÉDÉRATION DES SOCIÉTÉS

Marc Jarblum speaking before a displaced persons' demonstration in the Bergen-Belsen camp that called for free immigration to Palestine.

JUIVES DE FRANCE into "illegal" welfare work, though the federation continued to maintain an official position within the UGIF. He also encouraged Jews to flee to the Italian zone after November of that year, when the south of France was conquered by Germany and Italy; he himself was pursued by the Nazi-sponsored French militia and the SS for his anti-Vichy activity and escaped to Switzerland in spring 1943. While in Switzerland, Jarblum collected funds for Jewish organizations in southern France to enable them to extend their illegal work and free themselves from the UGIF's guardianship. Various projects to save Jewish children, either by hiding them in France or by helping them escape to Spain, were high on the list of his priorities. Jarblum survived the war and continued his Zionist activity in France before immigrating to Israel in 1955. His writings include *La lutte des Juifs contre les Nazis* (1945).

BIBLIOGRAPHY

Bauer, Y. *American Jewry and the Holocaust: The American Jewish Joint Distribution Committee, 1939–1945.* Detroit, 1981.

Cohen, R. I. *The Burden of Conscience: French Jewish Leadership during the Holocaust.* Bloomington, 1987.

Weinberg, D. H. *A Community on Trial: The Jews of Paris in the 1930s.* Chicago, 1977.

RICHARD COHEN

The former priest Miroslav Filipović-Majstorović, a member of the Jasenovac camp staff, in his Ustaša uniform.

there. Scores of Ustaše (Croatian fascists) served in the camp; the cruelest was the former priest Miroslav Filipović-Majstorović, who killed scores of prisoners with his own hands.

JASENOVAC, the largest concentration and extermination camp in CROATIA. Jasenovac was in fact a complex of several subcamps, in close proximity to each other, on the bank of the Sava River, about 62 miles (100 km) south of Zagreb. The women's camp of Stara Gradiška, which was farther away, also belonged to this complex.

Jasenovac was established in August 1941 and was dismantled only in April 1945. The creation of the camp and its management and supervision were entrusted to Department III of the Croatian Security Police (Ustaška Narodna Služba; UNS), headed by Vjekoslav (Maks) Luburić, who was personally responsible for everything that happened

The Jasenovac camp.

JASENOVAC

Some six hundred thousand people were murdered at Jasenovac, mostly Serbs, Jews, GYPSIES, and opponents of the USTAŠA regime. The number of Jewish victims was between twenty thousand and twenty-five thousand, most of whom were murdered there up to August 1942, when deportation of the Croatian Jews to AUSCHWITZ for extermination began. Jews were sent to Jasenovac from all parts of Croatia—from Zagreb, from Sarajevo, and from other cities and smaller towns. On their arrival most were killed at execution sites near the camp: Granik, Gradina, and other places. Those kept alive were mostly skilled at needed professions and trades (doctors, pharmacists, electricians, shoemakers, goldsmiths, and so on) and were employed in services and workshops at Jasenovac. The living conditions in the camp were extremely severe: a meager diet, deplorable accommodations, a particularly cruel regime, and unbelievably cruel behavior by the Ustaše guards. The conditions improved only for short periods—during visits by delegations, such as the press delegation that visited in February 1942 and a Red Cross delegation in June 1944.

The acts of murder and of cruelty in the camp reached their peak in the late summer of 1942, when tens of thousands of Serbian villagers were deported to Jasenovac from the area of the fighting against the partisans in the Kozara Mountains. Most of the men were killed at Jasenovac. The women were sent for forced labor in Germany, and the children were taken from their mothers; some were murdered and others were dispersed in orphanages throughout the country.

In April 1945 the partisan army approached the camp. In an attempt to erase traces of the atrocities, the Ustaše blew up all the installations and killed most of the internees. An escape attempt by the prisoners failed, and only a few survived.

BIBLIOGRAPHY

Romans, J. *Jews of Yugoslavia, 1941–1945: Victims of Genocide and Freedom Fighters.* Belgrade, 1982.

Sindik, D., ed. *Secanja Jevreja na logor Jasenovac.* Belgrade, 1972.

MENACHEM SHELAH

JASSY. *See* Iaşi.

JDC. *See* Joint Distribution Committee.

JECKELN, FRIEDRICH (1895–1946), SS commander. Born in Hornberg, Jeckeln joined the Nazi party in the 1920s; by 1930 he was an SS-*Obergruppenführer*. Following the German invasion of the Soviet Union in June 1941, Jeckeln was appointed *Höherer SS- und Polizeiführer* (Higher SS and Police Leader; HSSPF) on the southern front, which included the occupied areas of the Ukraine. On September 1, 1941, the units under his command slaughtered at least fourteen thousand Hungarian Jews who had been deported to the KAMENETS-PODOLSKI area. From July to October of that year they participated in the massacre of the Jews of Kiev at BABI YAR and in the mass killings at ROVNO and DNEPRO-PETROVSK. On October 11, Jeckeln was appointed HSSPF on the northern front and in Ostland, which encompassed the Baltic countries (Lithuania, Latvia, and Estonia) and parts of Belorussia. Jeckeln was in charge of the annihilation of the Jews of RIGA in November and December 1941, including the Jews from Germany and Austria who were sent to that city in the last months of 1941. In Aktion Sumpffieber (Operation Malaria), carried out in early 1942, the anti-partisan units under his command in Belorussia liquidated many ghettos and slaughtered tens of thousands of Jews.

After the war, Jeckeln was arrested by the Allies and handed over to the Soviet Union. He was tried in Riga before a Soviet military court, which sentenced him to death by hanging on February 3, 1946. The sentence was carried out immediately.

BIBLIOGRAPHY

Hilberg, R. *The Destruction of the European Jews.* New York, 1986.

Krausnick, H., and H. Wilhelm. *Die Truppe des Weltanschauungskrieges: Die Einsatzgruppen der Sicherheitspolizei und des SD, 1938–1942.* Stuttgart, 1981.

YITZHAK ARAD

Friedrich Jeckeln.

JEFROYKIN, JULES ("Dika"; 1911–1987), Jewish resistance leader in Vichy France. The son of Israel Jefroykin, a prominent figure in the eastern European Jewish community in interwar France, Jules Jefroykin, together with Simon LEVITTE, was instrumental in organizing the Mouvement de la Jeunesse Sioniste (Zionist Youth Movement; MJS) in the winter of 1941–1942. Open to Jewish youth of every persuasion, the MJS spearheaded cultural and social work in southern France, both officially and clandestinely. Jefroykin later became the JOINT DISTRIBUTION COMMITTEE's representative in southern France and was, with Maurice Brener, responsible for diverting the Joint's funds to "illegal" work. Jefroykin also participated in the underground operations of the Organisation Juive de Combat, most daringly in efforts to smuggle Jewish children and youth across the Pyrenees into Spain.

BIBLIOGRAPHY

Avni, H. "The Zionist Underground in Holland and France and the Escape to Spain." In *Rescue*

Attempts during the Holocaust. Proceedings of the Second Yad Vashem International Historical Conference, edited by Y. Gutman and E. Zuroff, pp. 555–590. Jerusalem, 1977.

Bauer, Y. *American Jewry and the Holocaust: The American Jewish Joint Distribution Committee, 1939–1945.* Detroit, 1981.

RICHARD COHEN

JEHOVAH'S WITNESSES (Ger., *Bibelforscher*, or "Bible Students"), religious sect organized in Germany as the Internationale Bibelforscher Vereinigung (International Bible Students' Association), affiliated with the Watchtower Bible and Tract Society of New York, Inc., whose main task is to distribute the sect's printed material. In 1933 the sect had about twenty thousand members in Germany.

The Jehovah's Witnesses' faith is based on an eschatological doctrine; in every generation they expect the "end of days," which will be inaugurated by a great trial of all people who do not belong to the sect. The "end of days" will be preceded by political catastrophes, such as war, revolution, or economic crisis. Obviously, the Nazi policy of persecution and war could be interpreted as heralding the approach of the "end of days."

While the Witnesses were among the early victims of Nazism, their initial attitude toward the Nazi regime was ambivalent. There is no evidence of concrete action on their part against the regime in its early period. In Bavaria the sect was outlawed in April 1933, and other provinces followed suit. Relations between Nazi Germany and the Catholic church seem to have been a decisive consideration for this step, in view of the extremely tense relationship between the sect and the Catholic church. An additional consideration was the existence of a tight international organization of Witnesses, and their refusal to officially renounce religious meetings, Bible evenings, and the recruitment of new members. The day after Prussia issued its prohibition of the sect (June 24, 1933), a convention of the Witnesses in Germany was still able to declare that essentially it had no quarrel with the National Socialist government, and

in principle shared its hostile attitude toward Bolshevism and the church, and its antisemitism. It was only when the Witnesses refused to make the "Heil Hitler" salute, and, beginning in 1935, to serve in the army, that the sect's officials and large parts of its membership adopted a clear posture of opposition to the regime. This led to the first wave of arrests of Witnesses in 1936 and 1937, which in many cases led to imprisonment in concentration camps. An international convention of the Witnesses, held in Lucerne, Switzerland, in September 1936, reacted by issuing a resolution condemning the entire Nazi regime. Although at the time the sect's leading officials in Germany were under arrest, it found a way of distributing the text of the "Lucerne Resolution" among its members in Germany (as it did in the rest of the world). More large-scale waves of arrests were recorded after the outbreak of the war, and again in 1944.

At all times, however, the Witnesses in the concentration camps were a relatively small group of prisoners (not exceeding several hundred per camp) and mostly of German nationality. As a rule the Witnesses imprisoned in the camps refused to renounce their convictions. Even though they could obtain their release, or could have escaped imprisonment in the first place, by signing a declaration that they would no longer be active on behalf of their organization, most of the Witnesses refused to do this. Inside the concentration camps the Witnesses were a relatively compact group, supporting one another and conspicuous by the order, cleanliness, and discipline that they maintained in their barracks. Their helpfulness also benefited other groups. The Witnesses' behavior, however, was determined by their religious beliefs; they did not cooperate with the illegal political groups, and refused to try to escape from the camps or to offer active resistance to the SS.

At first, the SS used special methods of harassment, their purpose being to break up the Witnesses' internal solidarity. The SS also sought to keep the Witnesses apart from other prisoners lest they gain new converts to their faith. At a later stage, the SS made a conscious effort to disperse the Witnesses in the camps and thereby to break up their cohesive groups. Finally, the SS exploited the Witnesses' exceptional behavior for its own purposes. On Heinrich HIMMLER's orders, for example, it was permitted to use the Witnesses for gathering mushrooms and fruit outside the camp, since there was no danger of their trying to escape or attacking the SS. As a result of this change in SS policy, the situation of most of the Witnesses in the concentration camps was changed for the better.

BIBLIOGRAPHY

"The Holocaust: Why Did God Allow It? Will Those Dead Return?"*Awake!* (8 April 1989): 1–20.

King, C. E. *The Nazi State and the New Religions: Five Case Studies in Non-Conformity.* Vol. 4 of *Studies in Religion and Society.* New York, 1984.

FALK PINGEL

JEWISH AGENCY FOR PALESTINE. *See* Yishuv.

JEWISH ANTIFASCIST COMMITTEE (Evreiski Antifashistski Komitet), Soviet Jewish institution founded in 1942 that functioned in the SOVIET UNION throughout World War II and until 1948. Its offices were first in Kuibyshev (to which several government ministries had moved in October 1941, when the battle of Moscow began) and later in Moscow. It was one of several antifascist committees that were part of the Soviet Propaganda Office (Sovinformbiuro).

In 1938, in the wake of KRISTALLNACHT, Soviet Jewish personalities were recruited to take part in Soviet antifascist propaganda. In August 1941, following the German invasion, a public meeting was held in Moscow (and broadcast on Soviet radio) in which the unity of the Jews of the Soviet Union with their Jewish brethren the world over was upheld. Among those who addressed the meeting were the actor Shlomo Mikhoels, director of the Moscow Jewish Theater, and the writers Peretz Markish, David Bergelson, Ilya EHRENBURG, and Shmuel Marshak. The meeting was followed, in September through November of that year, by an effort to establish an Anti-Hitler Jewish Committee, initiated by Henryk Erlich and Wiktor Alter, BUND leaders from Poland who had taken refuge in the Soviet Union and had been jailed but subsequently released. This attempt, which was unsuccessful, went through various phases and its full story is yet to be revealed; Erlich and Alter were rearrested at the beginning of December, and were put to death.

In April 1942, Moscow announced the formation of several antifascist committees, among them the Jewish Antifascist Committee—the only one to speak on behalf of a national group. The committee addressed itself to the Jews of the world—with American Jewry as its main target—and called on them to join the struggle against Nazi Germany. Its appeals made use of Jewish themes, Jewish symbols, and the names of Jewish personalities. During the war, some one hundred Soviet Jews lent their names to these appeals. Heading the committee was an executive council made up of twenty prominent Soviet Jews from all walks of life. Shlomo Mikhoels was the council's chairman, and its active members included the poet Itzik Fefer and the journalist Shakhno Epshtein, who was the committee's secretary and editor of its newspaper, EYNIKEYT.

The committee's declared purpose was to disseminate antifascist propaganda, primarily among world Jewry, but its members and leaders did not disregard the current needs of the Soviet Jewish population. From time to time distinctively Jewish topics were raised, such as the return of the Jews to the liberated areas of Europe and their resettlement there; antisemitism among the non-Jewish Soviet population; and the difficulties encountered in the effort to revive Jewish culture. A major issue that came up for discussion was the murder of Jews by the Nazis and the Jewish fight against the Nazis. The committee was one of the first organizations to document the Holocaust and the heroism of Jewish resistance, setting up a special subcommittee for this purpose. *Eynikeyt* published reports, articles, and testimonies on the murder of Jews in German-occupied Soviet territory, and it had a regular feature on Jewish soldiers who had distinguished themselves in the Red Army. The committee maintained contact with the Soviet Government Commission for

Members of the Jewish Antifascist Committee. Far left: Itzik Feffer, Yiddish poet, executed in 1952 during Stalin's anti-Jewish purges. Third from left: Shlomo Mikhoels, actor and manager of the Moscow Jewish Theater, killed by the Soviet secret police in 1948. Far right: Peretz Markish, Yiddish writer, executed in 1952 during the anti-Jewish purges. [Ben-Zion Goldberg]

the Investigation of Nazi Crimes, and its major enterprise was compilation of the *Chernaia kniga* (The BLACK BOOK OF SOVIET JEWRY), which aimed to document the fate of the Jews in the occupied areas of the USSR. Il-ya Ehrenburg was the first to oversee this project, followed by another writer, Vasily Grossman; the book, however, was not published in the Soviet Union, owing to the change in Soviet policy after the war. The Jewish Antifascist Committee maintained contact with Jewish organizations and prominent Jews outside the Soviet Union, and it supplied material relating to the Holocaust to Jewish institutions and newspapers abroad. These contacts reached their high point when Mikhoels and Fefer visited the United States, Canada, Mexico, and Great Britain in 1943. Efforts to arrange a visit to Palestine of a delegation from the committee did not succeed.

When the war was coming to an end, and in the immediate postwar period, the commit-tee, on its own initiative, submitted proposals to the Soviet authorities concerning the restoration and expansion of Jewish cultural institutions and activities, and the creation of new possibilities for the settlement of Jews. In 1944 it proposed the establishment of a Soviet Jewish republic in the Volga region, from which the German population had been removed, or in the Crimea, from which the Tatars had been expelled. All these plans came to nothing. The committee also supported the renewed settlement of Jews in the Jewish Autonomous Oblast of Birobidzhan.

During its existence, the committee was regarded as the central Jewish institution in the Soviet Union, a representative body to which Jewish requests for advice and support could be directed. Many Soviet Jews also saw in it an appropriate repository for complaints and for the expression of their hopes and expectations. Mikhoels, its chairman and moving spirit, was asked for help by Jews in personal affairs as well as matters of Jewish public interest. The committee kept in contact with Yiddish writers, both native Soviet Jews and those who were refugees in the country. Throughout its existence, but especially from 1944–1946, the committee served as a meeting place for Jewish writers, artists, soldiers, and partisans, and from 1943 to 1948 it had a regular evening program on literature and art.

The Soviet authorities had an ongoing interest in the existence of a specifically Jewish institution and supported the committee's worldwide information and propaganda campaign. This kept the committee in existence even after the war come to an end. Gradually, however, the discrepancy between the official purpose for which the committee had been created and the hopes that some Soviet Jews pinned on it widened, while the oppressive character of the Soviet regime and the cold war increased. The authorities were also taken aback by the enthusiasm displayed by part of the Soviet Jewish population over the establishment of the state of Israel and the arrival of its diplomatic representatives in Moscow. As a result, the committee's activities were curbed and eventually, in November 1948, it was abolished. Earlier, in January 1948, Shlomo Mikhoels had been killed in Minsk, on STALIN's orders. Before long, most of the committee members were imprisoned. The more prominent among them were put to death in the course of Stalin's anti-Jewish campaign (1949–1952).

BIBLIOGRAPHY

Altshuler, M. "The Jewish Antifascist Committee in the USSR in the Light of New Documentation." *Studies in Contemporary Jewry* 1 (1984): 253–291.
Redlich, S. *Propaganda and Nationalism in Wartime Russia: The Jewish Antifascist Committee in the USSR, 1941–1948.* Boulder, 1982.

SHIMON REDLICH

JEWISH ARMY. *See* Armée Juive.

JEWISH BADGE. *See* Badge, Jewish.

JEWISH BRIGADE GROUP, a brigade group of the British army, composed of Jewish volunteers from Palestine, that was formed in September 1944 and fought in the Italian theater of war from March to May 1945.

The origins of the brigade can be traced back to the earlier stages of World War II. Upon the outbreak of hostilities, Chaim WEIZMANN, as president of the World Zionist Organization, offered the British government the full cooperation of the Jewish people in the war effort, and began negotiations on the creation of a Jewish fighting force within the British army. The British were at first reluctant, but in the summer of 1940 they changed their minds, hoping to achieve by the formation of a Jewish force greater support in American public opinion for a policy of assistance to isolated Britain. In October 1940 the War Cabinet decided to establish such a force, amounting initially to one division. Most of the recruits were to come from the neutral United States and from refugees. Palestine would provide this division with a nucleus of commanding staff to safeguard its national-Zionist character.

The actual talks with Weizmann on the establishment of the division were put off until the American presidential elections in November 1940, and then they dragged on inconclusively until March 1941. In the interval the war situation changed considerably. The threat of invasion to the British Isles receded, while the Middle East and the Balkans became Britain's principal theater of war. The British generals in the Middle East were apprehensive of the likely Arab reaction to the establishment of a Jewish division, and Winston CHURCHILL was persuaded by his ministers and generals first to postpone the execution of the War Cabinet decision for a few months, and then to cancel it altogether in October 1941.

With the occupation of Europe by the Nazis and the imminent entrance of the United States into the war, the whole idea of a Jewish formation within the British army had to be modified. It was now completely based on volunteering in Palestine. In July 1940 the British renounced their earlier idea of mixed Jewish-Arab units, and accepted the principle of Jewish companies in most ancillary corps of the ground forces. At the same time,

A party given by Jewish Brigade Group soldiers in Nijmegen, 12 miles (19 km) south of Arnhem, for Jewish children who had been hidden in monasteries and Christian homes (1946). [Beth Hatefutsoth]

the Jewish Agency agreed to cooperate in the recruitment of 2,500 individuals for ground crews of the Royal Air Force and in the formation of Jewish Auxiliary Military Pioneer Corps companies. In September 1940, the British responded to another Jewish request and created the Jewish infantry companies known as the "Buffs" and several Jewish anti-aircraft and coastal artillery batteries as a part of the garrison in Palestine, where they officially promised these units would serve.

About three thousand of the volunteers who had enlisted at the beginning of the war were dispatched in early 1941 to Greece. About one hundred were killed in action and seventeen hundred were captured by the Germans in the campaigns of Greece and Crete. The remainder were evacuated to Egypt. Under the growing threat to Britain's position in the Middle East, enlistment increased in the spring of 1941.

The recruitment campaign reached its peak in July 1942, when German general Erwin Rommel's troops arrived at El Alamein in Egypt and the British position in the Middle East seemed to collapse. Under pressure from American and local public opinion, the British on August 6, 1942, declared the establishment of the Palestine Regiment, consisting of three Jewish battalions and one of Arabs. The low status of the Palestine Regiment disappointed the YISHUV (the Jewish population in Palestine); recruitment began to dwindle, and many soldiers asked for transfer into ancillary units, which at least served nearer the front lines in Egypt and the Western Desert, and sometimes participated in the fighting.

The news of the extermination of the Jews in Europe, which reached Palestine in November 1942, had little influence on enlistment in the army. Eighty percent of the thirty thousand recruits joined the army in the first half of the war, and only one-fifth enlisted in the following years. The Holocaust had more impact within the ranks, particularly among the soldiers of the infantry battalions and artillery batteries stationed in Palestine. Against the official stance of the Jewish Agency, they now demanded to be dispatched out of the country and sent to the front, where they would be able to take their revenge on the Nazis and assist the surviving remnant of European Jews upon its liberation. The demand persisted throughout 1943, and was nourished by the news of the participation of Jewish transport and engineers' companies in the landings in Italy and their assistance to the liberated Jewish inmates of FERRAMONTI DI TARSIA and other camps, as well as to refugees who crossed the Adriatic from Yugoslavia.

New Zionist proposals in the summer of 1943 for the creation of a fighting force were not connected with the Middle East and its sensitive equilibrium between Arabs and Jews, and the British were this time more responsive. Though the generals still had several misgivings, moral considerations carried more wieght than before. It seemed unjustifiable to deny the Jews the right to revenge and fight their oppressors, when the Allies were doing practically nothing to stop the mass murder. Churchill exercised all his personal authority in favor of accepting the Zionist proposal and urged his colleagues to approve it. On July 3, 1944, the British War Cabinet decided that although the formation of a Jewish division was not feasible on practical grounds, the creation of a brigade should be immediately and positively examined.

The cabinet decision opened the way to intensive talks, culminating in an official communiqué by the War Office on September 20, 1944, announcing the formation of the Jewish Brigade Group. Brigadier Ernst Benjamin was appointed its commanding officer, and the Zionist flag was officially approved as its standard.

The three infantry battalions of the brigade assembled near Alexandria; in early November they sailed for Italy. The brigade took part in the early stages of the final Allied offensive in Italy in April 1945 and then was withdrawn for reorganization. Its casualties at the front totaled fifty-seven killed and about two hundred wounded (including non-Jewish personnel). Although the brigade was not the first Jewish unit to take part in combat, it was the first and only Jewish formation to fight in World War II under the Jewish flag, recognized as representing the Jewish people.

After the termination of hostilities, the brigade was stationed in Tarvisio, near the border triangle of Italy, Yugoslavia, and Austria. Several missions set out from Tarvisio to eastern Europe and to the DISPLACED PERSONS' camps in Austria and Germany, and soon the brigade became a source of attraction for the surviving Jewish youth from all over the continent. During its two months' sojourn in the region, about one hundred fifty thousand Jews were smuggled to Tarvisio, where they were hospitalized and fed by the soldiers until their eventual transfer by the Jewish transport units to the refugee centers farther south.

In July 1945, the brigade moved to Belgium and the Netherlands. About one hundred and fifty soldiers were clandestinely dispatched to conduct organizational and educational work in the displaced persons' camps, to organize the BERIHA stations in Austria and Germany, and to assist in the preparations for "illegal" immigration to Palestine. Other soldiers concentrated on illegal arms purchase for the Hagana (the Jewish underground military organization in Palestine). Despite last-moment attempts by the Jewish Agency to prolong the brigade's existence, the British were determined to disband it according to their demobilization plan, and this was accomplished in June and July of 1946.

Thirty thousand Jews volunteered in Palestine for service in the British army between 1939 and 1946. They sustained 700 fatalities; 1,769 were taken prisoner; several thousand were wounded; and 323 were decorated or mentioned in dispatches. Five thousand served in the Jewish Brigade.

[See also Resistance, Jewish.]

BIBLIOGRAPHY

Casper, B. M. *With the Jewish Brigade.* London, 1947.

Gelber, Y. *History of Volunteering.* 4 vols. Jerusalem, 1979–1984. (In Hebrew.)

Penkower, M. N. "The Struggle for an Allied Jewish Fighting Force during World War II." In *Contemporary Views of the Holocaust*, edited by R. L. Braham, pp. 47–75. Boston, 1983.

Rabinowitz, L. *Soldiers from Judea: Palestinian Jewish Units in the Middle East, 1941–1943.* New York, 1945.

YOAV GELBER

JEWISH CENTER FOR ADULT EDUCATION. *See* Mittelstelle für Jüdische Erwachsenenbildung.

JEWISH CENTER IN ROMANIA. *See* Centrala Evreilor.

JEWISH CENTER IN SLOVAKIA. *See* Ústredňa Židov.

JEWISH COUNCIL. *See* Judenrat.

JEWISH COUNCIL IN THE NETHERLANDS. *See* Joodse Raad.

JEWISH FIGHTING ORGANIZATION. *See* Żydowska Organizacja Bojowa.

JEWISH GHETTO POLICE. *See* Jüdischer Ordnungsdienst.

JEWISH HISTORICAL INSTITUTE. *See* Documentation Centers: Żydowski Instytut Historyczny.

JEWISH LABOR COMMITTEE (JLC), organization formed in New York City in 1934 to represent Jewish trade union interests, mainly in the then predominantly Jewish needle trades. Rapidly recognized as a major American Jewish organization, it took an active part in the movement to boycott German goods, and was the most outspoken of all Jewish organizations in the struggle to increase the number of Jewish refugees allowed to enter the United States.

Through its close ties to the Jewish Labor BUND in Poland, the JLC was the first group to receive news of the massacre of Polish Jewry, in May 1942. It was able to use its contacts with the POLISH GOVERNMENT-IN-EXILE to send funds to the Bund underground. The JLC also used its strong position in the American trade union movement to enlist the support of the American labor leadership to pressure the United States government to aid in the rescue and relief of European Jewry. Having easy access to the large numbers of Jewish workers at their factories, the JLC was able to mobilize large numbers of Jewish workers for demonstrations. Among these was the work stoppage on December 2, 1942, which was called to commemorate the Jewish people who had been massacred in Europe. This event was intended to create pressure for American intervention to save European Jewry.

The JLC often found itself working closely with the ultra-Orthodox VA'AD HA-HATSALA because of the readiness of both groups to take steps that were illegal to aid or rescue the beleaguered Jews in Europe. As one of the major American Jewish organizations, the JLC participated in all the joint rescue endeavors of the American Jewish community, and was critical of the failure of the short-lived Joint Emergency Committee for European Jewish Affairs (comprising various leading United States Jewish organizations) to carry out a forceful struggle for rescue. The JLC was at first a participant in the AMERICAN JEWISH CONFERENCE, but left when the conference accepted to membership the pro-Communist Jewish People's Fraternal Order.

BIBLIOGRAPHY

Finger, S., ed. *American Jewry during the Holocaust.* New York, 1984.

ARIEL HURWITZ

JEWISH MILITARY UNION. *See* Żydowski Związek Wojskowy.

JEWISH PHILOSOPHICAL AND THEOLOGICAL RESPONSES TO THE HOLOCAUST. The overwhelming reality of the destruction of European Jewry has, of necessity, elicited a wide variety of philosophical and theological reflections. Contemporary thinkers have sought to give some response to the radical happenings associated with this event, either through recycling, often with special emphases, classical "answers" to the problems of theodicy and human suffering, or through innovative conceptual analyses. All of these responses remain problematic.

Traditional Answers. Jewish history is no stranger to national calamity, mass death, and immense human suffering. In response the Jewish tradition has, with varying degrees of success, formulated a series of replies that seek both to explain what has happened and to comfort the victims. Though perhaps the least appealing from the modern perspective, the ascription of the tragedy to the sinfulness of the Jews is historically primary among these theological paradigms, and the most deeply rooted in the biblical sources. Given this explanation, the horrific actuality of Auschwitz raises no special dilemmas for faith: the Jews were untrue to their covenantal obligations and God responded by punishing them. There is no need to look further for reasons, or to question either God's existence or the reality of the Jews' covenantal faith. As an explanation applied to the events of the 1930s and 1940s specifically, this accusation has taken three forms among the more Orthodox Jews. The first lays the general charge of infidelity and sinfulness against the Jews but eschews further specificity (the view of Rabbi Isaac Hutner); the second causally connects the Holocaust with the rise of Reform and other non-Orthodox forms of Judaism (the view of Rabbi Elhanan Wasserman, among others); the third cites Zionism as the culprit because it sought to reject the Exile, not being content to wait on God's messianic redemptive act (the position of Rabbi Joel Teitelbaum). All three forms of this response are problematic, not least because of the sort of God they picture, that is, one who would find it necessary for a million Jewish children to be murdered for any or even all of these "sins."

Four other biblically grounded doctrines or models that have been called into service to respond to the annihilation of European Jewry are (1) the *Akeda*—the Binding of Isaac; (2) the "Suffering Servant" of Isaiah; (3) *Hester Panim*—the "Hiding" of God's countenance; and (4) Job. The *Akeda* paradigm likens the victims to Isaac, innocent victims who are sacrificed (unlike the biblical Isaac) as a test of faithfulness. Bearing no sin, free of all imputation of guilt, they die as an act of ultimate fidelity to Jewish tradition, to Torah, to the God of Israel. This paradigm has long been hallowed in Jewish life. Its appositeness with regard to the Nazi extermination camps, however, is questionable, not least because the SS are not Abraham and their

victims not martyrs in the classical sense of having freely chosen their fate.

The Suffering Servant model, drawing primarily on Isaiah 53, has also found a significant place in post-Holocaust reflections. Like the *Akeda*, it is an appealing form of response and explanation because it lays no blame on the victims, seeing their suffering rather as a vicarious, if mysterious, means by which God balances the forces of creation and brings salvation to the wicked while assuring His special love, even sharing in the suffering of the righteous victims whom He rewards in the hereafter. As employed in modern times (by Hasidic leaders, by Abraham Joshua Heschel, by the Orthodox thinker Eliezer Berkovits, and by the Reform theologian Ignaz Maybaum, among others) to answer the theological dilemma, it has been criticized, not least because it evokes a doctrine of vicarious suffering, which itself needs to be deciphered. Moreover, it raises the difficult question of why God—and what sort of God—would require such sacrifices to regulate His universe.

Hester Panim, appealing to the Divine hiddenness, is explained in the Bible as being due to sin (as in Dt. 31:17–18) and also and quite differently as a mysterious, inexplicable happening for which no clear reason can be given (as in Psalm 44, Psalm 13, Is. 8:17, and Is. 45:5). This concept is connected in some theological accounts to God's quality of "long-sufferingness"; that is, His gracious toleration of the sinner means that He must allow sin to occur, which necessarily creates victims. This "explanation" ultimately falters, for it explains one conundrum, the reality of evil, by creating another—Divine hiddenness. Thus, when employed by contemporary theologians in response to Auschwitz (as for example in Martin Buber's *Eclipse of God*), it explains too little.

Finally, the Job paradigm, while widely invoked and appealing because Job is known not to be a sinner, appears both theologically and methodologically unsatisfactory. Whereas the biblical Job is protected by God as a condition of this test (see Job, "Prologue"), the Jewish people in our time knew no such protection. Nor, again, did the Divine reveal itself in an unambiguous theophany after the "test," confirming His existence and control of the cosmos (even if in a manner that transcends human understanding), as He did to Job. However, this issue is complex, for some credit the creation of the state of Israel as such a theophany, even though it is not an "unambiguous" revelation as occurs in the book of Job.

Modern Responses. In contrast to these well-worked replies to calamity, other Jewish thinkers have creatively, if not altogether satisfactorily, responded to the Holocaust with original and thought-provoking explanations. The most extreme, if also the least satisfactory, has been that offered by Richard Rubenstein in *After Auschwitz* (1966). Rubenstein argued that the Holocaust decisively disproves the existence of God and proves the bankruptcy of traditional Jewish theology. The universe is absurd, without meaning or purpose, and in such a universe it is not surprising that obscenities like Auschwitz exist. Accordingly, Jews should turn away from their ancient theological myths of transcendence and salvation and recognize instead a new immanent, naturalistic system of values, which alone can provide what happiness and solace there can be in this world. As developed by Rubenstein, however, this thesis is riddled with logical and methodological difficulties that undermine its coercive force.

Another approach is the "free-will defense," a revised version of a classical argument that sought to account for the existence of human evil in God's creation. Here evil is logically legitimized through the contention that for human beings to be free and hence majestic, they must also be free to sin and hence create evil consequences for others (see especially the employment of this thesis in the works of Eliezer Berkovits and Arthur A. Cohen). Not God but human beings are the cause of evil. This view too lacks complete plausibility, for it fails to grapple sufficiently with alternative metaphysical possibilities, for example, the possibility that God could have created a world with freedom and less or no evil; or that He could have at least created human beings with a stronger disposition toward good and with a more receptive capacity for moral education.

The third novel position concerning the Holocaust has been advanced by Emil Fackenheim, who has argued that it should be understood as a new occasion of Divine revelation. God was at Auschwitz, though we cannot understand exactly what He was doing there. And out of the cataclysm has emerged a new 614th commandment (in addition to the traditional 613 commandments): "Jews, do not give Hitler a posthumous victory." By speaking of this commandment, Fackenheim intends to convey that Jews should understand themselves as being under a sacred obligation to survive so as to ensure that Hitler, with his genocidal frenzy aimed at the Jewish people, does not ultimately succeed. Above all, this commandment entails both Jewish survival and the dialectical obligation that Jews are "forbidden to despair of the God of Israel, lest Judaism perish." Philosophical difficulties, however, ensue from adopting this position, and revolve around certain elemental problems in Fackenheim's notions of revelation and commandment.

An even more radical position has been proposed by Irving (Yitzchak) Greenberg. He has made the observation that the Holocaust shattered the covenant between God and Israel. Describing the terms of the traditional covenantal relationship as a "suicide mission" that can no longer be commanded, even by the Almighty, Greenberg advances the provocative thesis that while the old terms of Israel's relation to God are at an end, Israel has now voluntarily entered into a new and more equal relationship with God as a result of what took place. This sidesteps the reason why the Holocaust happened and focuses instead on the proper post-Holocaust response to be adopted by the Jewish people. While it is an intriguing proposal, the logic of the position, especially its use of basic theological terms and concepts such as "covenant," "commandments," "revelation," and "God," is open to interrogation, as is the centrality it gives to Hitler in defining a post-Holocaust Jewish theology.

Moving in a still more novel direction, Arthur A. Cohen, in *The Tremendum: A Theological Interpretation of the Holocaust* (New York, 1981), has suggested that the only way to resolve the many fundamental theological issues emerging from the Holocaust is to redefine God, that is, to recognize that our older notion of the Divine, replete with all the omni-predicates (omniscience, omnipotence, and so on), is mistaken. There is a God, but He does not have the power to interfere in human affairs, as previous generations have thought. Our understanding of Him as the all-powerful providential orderer of history and nature has to be scrapped and a more modest conception of Divinity substituted in its place. But this raises the question as to whether God is still God if He is no longer the providential agency in history. And even if one could defend this minimalizing conceptualization in general philosophical terms, can such a "reduced" divinity be the God of Torah and covenant, of prayer and redemption—the God of Israel?

There are, finally, those who have championed silence as the most appropriate response to the genocidal horrors of our time: not the silence of the agnostic, but rather the silence of those who have wrestled with the abyss, of those who, having pushed reason to its limits, recognize the limits of reason.

BIBLIOGRAPHY

Berkovits, E. *Faith after Auschwitz.* New York, 1973.

Berkovits, E. *God, Man, and History: A Jewish Interpretation.* New York, 1959.

Berkovits, E. *With God in Hell.* New York, 1979.

Cohen, A. A. *Arguments and Doctrines: A Reader of Jewish Thinking in the Aftermath of the Holocaust.* New York, 1970.

Cohen, A. A. *The Tremendum: A Theological Interpretation of the Holocaust.* New York, 1981.

Fackenheim, E. *God's Presence in History: Jewish Affirmation and Philosophical Reflections.* New York, 1972.

Fackenheim, E. *The Jewish Return into History: Reflection in the Age of Auschwitz and a New Jerusalem.* New York, 1978.

Fackenheim, E. *To Mend the World.* New York, 1982.

Greenberg, I. "Religious Values after the Holocaust: A Jewish View." In *Jews and Christians after the Holocaust,* edited by A. J. Peck, pp. 63–86. Philadelphia, 1982.

Katz, S. T. *Post-Holocaust Dialogues: Critical Studies in Modern Jewish Thought.* New York, 1983.

Maybaum, I. *The Face of God after Auschwitz.* New York, 1976.

Rubenstein, R. L. *After Auschwitz: Radical Theology and Contemporary Judaism.* Indianapolis, 1966.

STEVEN T. KATZ

JEWISH POLICE. *See* Jüdischer Ordnungsdienst.

JEWISH RESCUE COMMITTEE. *See* Pracovná Skupina.

JEWISH RESISTANCE MOVEMENT IN FRANCE. *See* Armée Juive.

JEWISH SCOUTS, FRENCH. *See* Eclaireurs Israélites de France.

JEWISH YOUTH FRONT. *See* Front of the Wilderness Generation.

JEWISH YOUTH MOVEMENTS. *See* Youth Movements.

JODENVEREENIGING VAN BELGIE. *See* Association des Juifs en Belgique.

JODL, ALFRED (1890–1946), German military commander; Hitler's chief adviser on strategy and operations throughout World War II. Born in Würzburg, Bavaria, Jodl served in World War I mainly in staff assignments. After the war, he served until 1938 as *Chef der Abteilung Landesverteidigung* (Head of the Defense Department) in the General Staff. On August 22, 1939, he was appointed *Chef des Wehrmachtführungsstabes im OKW* (Chief of the Armed Forces High Command Operational Staff), a post he held until the end of World War II. In this capacity he directed, under Adolf HITLER and Field Marshal Wilhelm KEITEL, all the campaigns except that against the Soviet Union, which was conducted by the Oberkommando des Heeres (Army High Command; OKH), and countersigned many orders to shoot hostages and to execute other war crimes contrary to international law. He was promoted in 1940 to the rank of general of artillery, and in 1944 to *Generaloberst* (senior general).

On May 7, 1945, Jodl signed, by order of

Alfred Jodl, general in the German High Command, arriving at Lüneburger Heide to surrender to the British (May 1945). [National Archives]

Adm. Karl Dönitz, Hitler's successor, the general capitulation of the German armed forces at Reims, France. He was sentenced to death for war crimes by the International Military Tribunal (*see* NUREMBERG TRIAL) on October 1, 1946, and was hanged on October 16.

During Jodl's imprisonment in Nuremberg, he dictated a number of memoranda, including "Betrachtungen über den Einfluss Hitlers auf die Kriegsführung" (Reflections on Hitler's Impact on the Conduct of War). Though a stout believer in Hitler's genius, Jodl came to believe while in prison that he had in fact been exploited by the Nazi leader.

BIBLIOGRAPHY

Brett-Smith, R. *Hitler's Generals.* San Rafael, Calif., 1977.
Jodl, L. *Jenseits des Endes: Leben und Sterben des Generaloberst Alfred Jodl.* Vienna, 1976.
Kriegstagebuch des OKW. Frankfurt, 1961.

JEHUDA L. WALLACH

JOINT BOYCOTT COUNCIL (JBC), American organization founded in 1936 to coordinate Jewish anti-German boycott groups. In March 1933, boycott actions against Germany were undertaken in the United States, with the Jewish War Veterans of the United States

of America taking the initiative. The campaign, however, was conducted by several organizations, each acting individually, a situation that resulted in lack of coordination and duplication of efforts. The first committee to be established was set up by Abraham Coralnik, a Yiddish journalist, and was called the American League for the Defense of Jewish Rights. Three months later the American Jewish Congress set up its own boycott committee, and when the JEWISH LABOR COMMITTEE was founded in 1934, it too engaged in boycott activities. In 1936, the Jewish Labor Committee's boycott committee joined forces with that of the American Jewish Congress, forming the Joint Boycott Council in order to coordinate activities.

The league that Coralnik had founded—now headed by Samuel Untermyer—did not join the JBC; it had become a general American rather than a Jewish organization, and had changed its name to the Non-Sectarian Anti-Nazi League to Champion Human Rights. The two bodies—the JBC and the league—continued to function independently of each other.

Throughout its existence, the JBC was headed by Dr. Joseph Tennenbaum, who proposed the pro-boycott resolution passed by the World Jewish Congress in 1936. When the B'NAI B'RITH lodges in Germany were closed down, in January 1939, the parent organization in the United States also joined the JBC. The council kept up its work up until the end of 1941, when the United States entered the war.

[*See also* Boycotts, Anti-Nazi.]

BIBLIOGRAPHY

Gottlieb, M. "The Anti-Nazi Boycott Movement in the United States: An Ideological and Sociological Appreciation." *Jewish Social Studies* 35/3–4 (July–October 1973): 198–227.
Gottlieb, M. "In the Shadow of War: The American Anti-Nazi Boycott Movement." *American Jewish Historical Quarterly* 62/2 (December 1972): 146–161.

DAVID H. SHPIRO

JOINT DISTRIBUTION COMMITTEE (JDC; full name, American Jewish Joint Distribution Committee; also known as the Joint), American Jewry's overseas relief and rehabilitation agency, founded in 1914. As early as 1930, the JDC's European director, Bernard Kahn, had foreseen the need for mass emigration of German Jews, but the decrease in income of American Jews following the 1929 economic crisis and the inbuilt German Jewish ideology of the JDC's lay leaders, who could not conceive of a catastrophe of the kind that befell German Jewry after 1933, prevented proper preparation for what then happened. Nevertheless, once the calamity came about, the JDC became a major factor in an overall effort to help German Jews find new bases for economic survival in Germany. At the same time, it aided in the emigration of those who could not stay there in what it hoped would be an organized exodus. The JDC supplied between 28.7 percent and 36.3 percent of the budget of the ZENTRALAUSSCHUSS DER DEUTSCHEN JUDEN FÜR HILFE UND AUFBAU (Central Committee of German Jews for Relief and Reconstruction) between 1934 and 1937 —a sum equivalent to $4.6 million. This was about 64 percent of the total expenditure of the JDC in those years. The rest went mainly to support the eastern European communities, which were in a far worse economic situation than even German Jewry during the first years of Hitler's regime. The JDC also funded HICEM, the Jewish emigration organization, as well as helping to support emigration directly.

The committee's leaders from 1914 to 1937 were Felix M. Warburg, born in Hamburg (his son, Edward M. M. Warburg, was to become the leader in later years), and Paul Baerwald, also originally a German Jew. However, as time went on, professional fund-raisers played an increasingly central part in the JDC's operations, especially Joseph C. Hyman in the early 1930s, and after him Moses A. Leavitt. During World War II, the central figure was Joseph J. SCHWARTZ, who became head of the JDC's European operation.

During the Holocaust, the JDC maintained three types of policies: (1) the central office in New York followed American official policy to the letter; (2) Schwartz, in neutral Lisbon, stretched that policy so that the JDC's operations in Europe verged on, and sometimes went beyond, the boundaries of legality (in American terms); (3) the JDC's local offices in Nazi-occupied Europe often became foci of self-help and underground activity, and even supported armed resistance. Expenditures

Distribution of basic food products (milk, flour, fats) to the needy Jewish population of Żelechów, about 50 miles (80 km) northwest of Lublin, by the Joint Distribution Committee.

came to $12.29 million in 1938–1939, and $11.9 million in 1940–1941. The decrease was due to the American Jews' disinterest in what was happening in Europe, despite strenuous fund-raising efforts by the JDC. In 1942, the crucial year of the Holocaust, the committee had $6 million at its disposal for European relief, but funds could no longer be transferred to Europe except under crippling conditions. In Switzerland, which could have been the main center for distribution of funds, the JDC nominated Saly MAYER, who was to resign soon from the presidency of the Federation of Swiss Jewish Communities (Schweizerischer Israelitischer Gemeindebund; SIG) as its representative. But in 1942–1943, owing to disagreements between the American and Swiss governments, no funds could be transmitted to that country. Global expenditures

increased in 1943 to $8.9 million, to $14.8 million in 1944, and to $26.8 million in 1945, but by that time most of European Jewry had been murdered, though the funds helped some of those who had a chance of survival.

The JDC funds were used to provide aid to French Jews, partly by means of the UNION GÉNÉRALE DES ISRAÉLITES DE FRANCE and partly through underground channels, among them the FÉDÉRATION DES SOCIÉTES JUIVES DE FRANCE. Orphanages, hospitals, and public kitchens were supported by JDC funds. Schools, theaters, and study groups received JDC aid, as did efforts to help Jews obtain false identity papers and cross international borders. Small groups of surviving Jews were supported in Berlin in 1944, and the remnants of the community in Zagreb were helped. Parcels were sent to a number of concentra-

A meeting in Paris (1939) of the heads of the Joint offices in Europe, chaired by Morris C. Troper of New York, the European director of the JDC. On September 9, 1940, Troper addressed the board of directors of the JDC in New York as follows: "[The Jews in Europe] have nothing to look forward to except starvation, disease, and ultimate extinction. . . . Ours is the sacred task of keeping our brethren alive— if not all, then at least some. . . . The problem is one and indivisible for all the Jews of the world." [JDC Archives, New York]

tion camps and to the ghetto of Theresienstadt; aid was sent to the so-called Jüdische Soziale Selbsthilfe (directed by Michael Weichert) in Kraków during the late stage of the war, a controversial social-aid operation under German surveillance.

Until the United States entered the war, in December 1941, the JDC sent food and money by various means to Poland (after the American entry into the war, the committee was forbidden to help "enemy" countries). Several thousand Jews were evacuated from Lithuania to East Asia, largely with JDC support. In Warsaw, a very active JDC committee under the leadership of Yitzhak GITTERMAN raised funds (against the instructions it received from New York, but with Schwartz's tacit approval) by promising repayment in dollars after the war (these promises were later honored). Children's centers, hospitals, and house committees providing social, cultural, economic, and moral support were established under the JDC's supervision in the Warsaw ghetto. Educational efforts were made on a large scale, again by the JDC. Finally, the JDC office in Warsaw provided funds for armed resistance, both in Warsaw and in Białystok.

Owing again to the initiative of a local JDC leader, Gisi FLEISCHMANN, the JDC became a very active participant in the attempts to rescue Slovak Jewry. From Switzerland, Mayer could not supply the large sums that were needed in Slovakia, because he did not receive them from New York or from the committee's European office in Lisbon, but some funds were sent and others raised locally. Some Polish Jews were smuggled into Slovakia, where the JDC supported work camps that were to provide relative safety for their inmates. In Hungary, after the March 1944 occupation of that country by the Germans, the JDC supplied large sums of money. These funds were used to establish children's shelters (later under international protection) and were given to neutral diplomats to provide aid to Jews. Raoul WALLENBERG received the money he needed from the JDC, as did Carl LUTZ, the Swiss vice-consul in Budapest. In Hungary, particularly in late 1944, when the fascist SZÁLASI government took over (October 15), the JDC's help became crucial in

saving the remnants of Hungarian Jewry until Budapest was liberated.

The JDC supplied large sums of money, channeled through Switzerland, to aid Romanian Jewry. Wilhelm FILDERMAN, the acknowledged leader of the Jewish community in Romania, was also the JDC representative. JDC funds also went to save what was left of the Bessarabian and Bukovina Jews who had been expelled to the southern Ukraine (TRANSNISTRIA) in 1941.

The JDC's operations, on the whole, were the main way in which American Jewry aided their European brethren during the Holocaust. Some of this was not actually American help but locally organized actions using the name of the Joint. In sum, the various aspects of the JDC's material succor aided a large number of Jews and helped an undetermined number of them to survive.

After the war, the conscience of American Jews was aroused, and self-accusations were made regarding what had not been done during the Holocaust. Perhaps as a result of this, the JDC, working together with the (Zionist) Jewish Agency, the United HIAS Service, and other organizations, became the central Jewish agency supporting survivors in the DISPLACED PERSONS' camps in Germany, Austria, and Italy, and in Poland, Hungary, Romania, and elsewhere. Between 1946 and 1950, the sum of $280 million was spent (compared to $169 million between 1914 and 1945), and quantities of food to augment the official rations; clothing, books, and school supplies for children; cultural amenities; religious supplies; and much more were provided. Vocational training centers were aided, and after the establishment of Israel in May 1948 the JDC became responsible for bringing immigrants there. Until 1949, it also supported the social activities in the detention camps that the British had set up in Cyprus. The JDC's work with survivors terminated with the closing of the last displaced persons' camp (Föhrenwald) in 1957, and with the committee's participation in the Claims Conference (see REPARATIONS AND RESTITUTION), which received and administered German reparation funds to Holocaust survivors after 1953. Without the JDC, the survivors' fate would have been much harder than it was.

BIBLIOGRAPHY

Bauer, Y. *American Jewry and the Holocaust: The American Jewish Joint Distribution Committee, 1939–1945.* Detroit, 1981.

Bauer, Y. *My Brother's Keeper: A History of the American Joint Distribution Committee, 1929–1939.* Philadelphia, 1974.

YEHUDA BAUER

JOINT RESCUE COMMITTEE (also known as the Committee for the Jews of Occupied Europe), a committee within the Jewish Agency established by the institutions of the YISHUV, the Jewish community of Palestine, to find ways of helping the Jews of Europe during the war.

When World War II broke out, a four-man committee was set up by the Jewish Agency in Jerusalem, made up of members of the Executive—Itzhak GRUENBAUM, Moshe Shapira, Eliyahu Dobkin, and Dr. Emil Schmorak. Known as the "Committee of Four" or the "Committee for Polish Jewry," its task was to gather the reports that were coming in from the Jews in the Polish ghettos and to extend aid to these Jews, by obtaining immigration certificates to Palestine for them, sending them food parcels, and maintaining contact with them. Before 1942 the aid provided by the committee (which operated together with a body representing Polish Jewry) was modest and was extended primarily to veteran Zionists and to relatives of Jews living in Palestine. At the end of 1942, when it became clear that systematic physical extermination of Jews was being carried out in Europe, the Jewish public in Palestine demanded that a body be set up that would represent the entire Yishuv, with the authority and means to serve as the central agency for the rescue efforts.

As a result, in January 1943 the board of a Rescue Committee was appointed. It consisted of twelve members: the original four, together with Bernard (Dov) Joseph, also a member of the Jewish Agency executive board; Itzhak Ben-Zvi, Shlomo Zalman Shragai, and Yehoshua Suprasky, all three members of the Va'ad Le'ummi, the Nation-al Council of Jews in Palestine; Binyamin Mintz and Rabbi Isaac Meir Levin, representing the religious movement Agudat Israel; and Joseph Klarman and Zvi (Herman) Segal, of the nationalist Revisionist party. Itzhak Gruenbaum was appointed chairman of the board. A council was also elected consisting of thirty members, most of them representing the various immigrants' associations, as well as institutions and political parties. The three-man secretariat consisted of Maximilian Apolinary Hartglas (the last chairman of the Zionist organization of Poland) as political secretary; Avraham Haft, a member of Kibbutz Deganya Aleph, as treasurer; and Joseph Kleinbaum as secretary-general.

From the very beginning, the committee was subject to public attack because of its composition. Its members had many other responsibilities and could not devote all their time to the rescue efforts. Moreover, it had no authority of its own, since the operations of other departments of the Jewish Agency deprived it of any real power. Public demonstrations and petitions were handled by the Va'ad Le'ummi, and other Agency bodies gathered information. These misgivings about the committee were shared by all of its members except for the five who were on the Jewish Agency executive board.

The committee's chairman, Itzhak Gruenbaum, was the target of especially severe criticism and was repeatedly called upon to resign. In 1942, Gruenbaum refused to lend credence to the reports of systematic murders and extermination camps. By early 1943 Gruenbaum despaired of the success of any large-scale rescue efforts, in view of the Yishuv's lack of resources and the indifference displayed by the Allies, and he stated that the Yishuv's main role was to establish in Palestine a place of refuge for those Jews who survived the war. He did not hesitate to speak his mind in no uncertain—and even provocative—terms, as when he stated that the needs of Palestine and of the Yishuv took priority over the needs of the Diaspora. Nevertheless, Gruenbaum collected large sums of money for the rescue efforts from non-Agency sources, and he conducted a far-flung correspondence with statemen and organizations in many parts of the world, urging them to participate. He also came up with a variety of ideas and proposals for saving Jewish lives and for bringing Jews out of Europe, although not necessarily to Palestine.

The tense relations between Gruenbaum and David BEN-GURION, the chairman of the Jewish Agency, made it difficult for Gruenbaum to carry out his function as chairman of the Rescue Committee, and contributed to the committee's lack of any real power. Its activities remained primarily marginal: it collected information, sounded out new ideas, dispatched cables, and appealed for aid. Most of the Yishuv's rescue efforts were carried out by other bodies, such as the Mosad le-Aliya Bet (Organization for "Illegal" Immigration), by leading figures in the Hagana (the underground Jewish army) and Histadrut (the Trade Union Federation), and by Yishuv representatives in Istanbul and Geneva. The operations of these institutions and individuals were confidential and therefore not known to the public at large, leaving the Rescue Committee as the only target for the Yishuv's profound dissatisfaction with the modest rescue efforts in 1943 and 1944.

Nevertheless, the committee remained in existence for a year and a half, mainly because the participating organizations realized that the situation in Europe was far too complex for any one of them to operate on its own, and also because of the high respect that they had for Gruenbaum's integrity and personal stature. In June 1944 the Revisionist representatives on the committee were dismissed, their party was conducting its own fund-raising for rescue operations, and their relations with the Yishuv's official institutions were deteriorating. In 1945 the Rescue Committee's main efforts were devoted to aiding the war refugees. As the time drew near for the establishment of the Jewish state, the committee ceased its operations.

BIBLIOGRAPHY

Gruenbaum, Y. *In the Days of Destruction and Holocaust, 1939–1945.* Jerusalem, 1950. (In Hebrew.)
Morgenstern, A. "The Jewish Relief Committee Attached to the Jewish Agency, 1942–1945." *Yalkut Moreshet* 13 (June 1971): 60–103. (In Hebrew.)

Porat, D. *An Entangled Leadership: The Yishuv and the Holocaust, 1942–1945.* Tel Aviv, 1986. (In Hebrew.)

DINA PORAT

JOODSE RAAD, the Jewish Council (JUDENRAT) in the NETHERLANDS, in existence from 1941 to 1943. The Joodse Raad was established in the wake of the riots caused by Dutch Nazi units in the Jewish quarter of Amsterdam in early February 1941, and of the ensuing clashes between Jews and non-Jews. One of the means to which the Germans resorted to reestablish order according to their needs was the creation of a Judenrat, on the model existing in other occupied countries. A German official on the staff of Arthur SEYSS-INQUART, the Reichskommissar for the Netherlands, summoned three Jews to his office, one of whom was Abraham ASSCHER, a well-known public figure (the other two were rabbis). Asscher agreed to set up a seventeen-member Judenrat for Amsterdam, with the aid of his close friend David COHEN.

Most of the men invited by Asscher and Cohen to join the Joodse Raad had worked with them for years in various Jewish institutions. Professionals and wealthy businessmen were in the majority, and the others were representatives of the Ashkenazic and Sephardic communities; religious leaders and Socialists were a very small minority. The day after receiving the German "invitation," the prospective members held their first meeting, on February 13, 1941. One of those present, Dr. Isaac Kisch, expressed his misgivings about the establishment of a Joodse Raad and spoke of the risks that the Jews would be taking if they agreed to set up such a body. Kisch was a member of the Jewish Coordination Committee, which the Jewish community organizations had formed at the end of 1940 to deal with problems created by the occupation and the German authorities' anti-Jewish policy. The chairman of that committee, Lodewijk Ernst VISSER, was totally opposed to the policy of cooperation with the Germans that Asscher and Cohen were advocating, and argued that the Jews should not negotiate with the Germans but should call on the

Dutch administration to protect the Jews as Dutch nationals. The co-chairmen of the Joodse Raad, Asscher and Cohen (especially the latter), were of the contrary opinion that the Jews had to accept the facts that the Germans were in power in the Netherlands, that it was they who determined policy toward the Jews, and that only by cooperating with them would it be possible to exert influence and gain some concessions. Within a short while Asscher had the opportunity of testing the validity of this view. When Dutch workers went on strike in February to protest Nazi brutalities, he appealed to employers to help prevent the strike from spreading to their own enterprises, and was permitted to go on the local radio station to call on the Jews to calm down.

The Joodse Raad rapidly became a strong, authoritative body, mainly owing to its large and efficient staff—the staff of the Comité voor Bijzondere Joodse Belangen (Committee for Special Jewish Affairs), which Asscher and Cohen had formed in 1933 to aid Jewish refugees from Germany. The Joodse Raad's prestige also benefited from its success in obtaining a permit to publish a weekly for the Jewish population, *Het Joodse Weekblad* (The Jewish Weekly). For a while the Germans considered setting up a national Jewish body to represent all the Jews of the Netherlands, and giving it legal status. At the end of 1941, however, Seyss-Inquart decided to have the Amsterdam Joodse Raad deal with all Jewish affairs in the country without changing its name or giving it such status. This decision also meant that the Jewish Coordination Committee had to be disbanded. While that committee cooperated with the Joodse Raad in some areas, it was basically at odds with it, with Visser attacking Asscher and Cohen for taking (in his view) too submissive a line toward the Germans.

Expansion of Activities. In the course of 1941, the range of the Joodse Raad's activities grew and its staff took on the size of a government department. The main cause of this phenomenal growth was the anti-Jewish policy of the occupying authorities. The Jews were dispossessed of their businesses and livelihood, and their economic contacts were restricted to other Jews; as a result, a large part of the community was in need of financial assistance. Public institutions and parks were placed out of bounds, and the Jews had to expand their existing institutions or create others from scratch.

Some one thousand Jewish companies and societies were dissolved or broken up in 1941; in most instances their property was confiscated and their obligations were passed on to the Joodse Raad. An umbrella organization, financed by the Joodse Raad, was founded to include all social-welfare agencies. Another expansion of the Joodse Raad's size and responsibilities was caused by the exclusion, in the summer of 1941, of all Jewish children from public schools. At first, local government authorities assumed the task of establishing schools for the Jewish children, but since these authorities required the Joodse Raad's advice and assistance, the council created a special bureau for this purpose. After the first school year was over, the entire Jewish educational system was put into the hands of the Joodse Raad, and all the teachers in the system became its employees. In February 1942, its educational network consisted of 111 schools in 36 cities, with a staff of 758 teachers and a student body of 14,500. The staff of the central school administration also dealt with school buildings, teaching aids, and supervision. Apart from its responsibilities for education and social welfare (which included supervision of hospitals and their staff), the Joodse Raad also was in charge of food distribution to the Jews of Amsterdam and the issuance of various types of certificates, such as travel permits. This meant a corresponding growth in the size of the staff; at its height, it numbered seventeen thousand. Some of these workers were unpaid, their employment by the council providing assurance—for a while— that they would not be sent to labor camps and from there deported to Poland.

Taxes and Money Collection. Even before the Joodse Raad was created, a finance committee for Jews in the Netherlands had been formed, under the auspices of the Committee for Special Jewish Affairs. On German orders, that finance committee was taken over by the Joodse Raad. Shortly after the occupation of the country in May 1940, the finance committee imposed a "voluntary" tax on all Jews in order to fund educational and other activities. It also determined the amount to be paid by

The Joodse Raad. Seated at the far left is Abraham Asscher, co-chairman; next to him is Professor David Cohen, co-chairman. Chief Rabbi Philip Frank is seated sixth from the left.

every Jew out of his income and his financial assets. By the time the committee was taken over by the Joodse Raad, the tax had become compulsory; anyone who did not pay was not issued a "gray card." This card, certifying that the bearer had fulfilled his financial obligation, had to be produced by every Jew who applied to the Joodse Raad for aid. The substantial sum of 6 million gulden was collected in this manner.

On August 8, 1941, the Germans published an order according to which all Dutch Jews had to deposit their money in a single bank, Lippmann-Rosenthal—a Jewish bank that became a de facto extension of the German administration. From then on, all contributions to the Joodse Raad had to be paid through this bank. On January 1, 1943, all individual Jewish accounts were abolished and their balances were absorbed into a single general account, from which the Joodse Raad received a monthly allocation to cover its expenses. According to its section, monthly costs for the four permanent outlays—education, organizations, welfare, and general expenses—amounted to 945,000 gulden. As of that month, however, the German administration demanded that the Joodse Raad also finance the monthly allocations that individual account-holders had hitherto been permitted to withdraw; these added up to 600,000 gulden a month. This meant that the council required over 1,500,000 gulden a month to meet its obligations. The German administration, however, transferred only 800,000 gulden a month and was generally late with that. The Joodse Raad's expenditures therefore had to be reduced by nearly 50 percent.

The "Final Solution." In summer 1941 the German authorities in the Netherlands embarked on preparations for the "Final Solution" and assigned new tasks to the Joodse

Raad. Of these, the most difficult to implement was the concentration in Amsterdam of Jews from the rest of the Netherlands (except for those who were taken to the VUGHT camp) and the supplying of Jews to the labor camps that were being set up. The German administration ordered the Joodse Raad to provide it with lists of all unemployed Jews—after first depriving many Jews of their work permits so as to render them unemployed. The council also had to deal with the administrative aspects of moving Jews to the labor camps, the latter ostensibly being run by the Dutch authorities. The fact that the Joodse Raad agreed to select the candidates for the labor camps caused great resentment among Jews. Both the men who were sent to the camps and the families they left behind suffered severely. Especially after April 1942, conditions in the camps were harsh, and Jewish laborers were treated worse than the non-Jewish unemployed.

On May 3, 1942, the yellow badge (see BADGE, JEWISH) was introduced in the Netherlands, with the Joodse Raad actively participating in its distribution. On June 26 of that year, the council was told of the deportations to eastern Europe, where, it was explained, the deported Jews would be asked to perform "police duties in German labor camps." In order to turn the Joodse Raad into an effective instrument in the operation, the Germans promised its staff that "until further notice" they would be exempt from the deportations. As it turned out, however, the Joodse Raad could not force the Jews to report for the transports of their own free will. The German and Dutch police had to seek them out and arrest them, using for this purpose lists based on the council's card index.

Throughout the period of the deportations, the Joodse Raad sought to keep up its educational and social-welfare functions, but in practice most of its efforts were related to the deportations. It attempted to negotiate the release of Jews, either as members of its staff or on the basis of documents it submitted to the Nazis trying to prove that the persons threatened were "Aryans" or were making an essential contribution to the German war effort. The Joodse Raad also tried to help Jews who were about to be deported, mainly by providing them with warm clothing.

For about ten months it was found possible to fill the trains that left the WESTERBORK transit camp for the extermination camps in Poland without touching the Joodse Raad staff to any appreciable extent. But their turn came. In May 1943, the Joodse Raad leaders were told to provide a list of 7,000 of the council's employees and their families (some 40 percent of the total protected staff) for deportation to the east. Once again the leaders gave in. In a single day, a small select team drew up a list of candidates for deportation, filled in the individual "invitations" to report for expulsion (over David Cohen's signature), and had runners deliver them to the victims. However, only about 10 percent of the candidates reported at the specified time and place, indicating that the Joodse Raad no longer had control over the Jews.

The reaction of the German administration came the very next day (May 26), when a major raid was launched in the old Jewish quarter of Amsterdam and its vicinity. On June 20 a similar raid was made in other parts of the city inhabited by Jews; 8,850 Jews were seized in the two raids and taken to Westerbork. What remained of the Joodse Raad continued to function until September 29, 1943, when most of the remaining Jews—numbering some two thousand persons—were taken to Westerbork. Asscher and Cohen, the two chairmen, were among them, and in Westerbork they were informed that the Joodse Raad had ceased to exist.

After the war, when members of the Joodse Raad returned to the Netherlands, both the surviving Jewish public and the Dutch authorities raised grave accusations against them. Cohen and Asscher were arrested and were to stand trial. The trial, however, never took place, partly because of evidence that came to light of the enormous role played by non-Jewish administrators in the crimes against the Jews. A "court of honor" that the Jews set up found Asscher and Cohen guilty on five counts: (1) the very establishment of the Joodse Raad; (2) the publication of a weekly paper that disseminated their course of action; (3) the giving of instructions concerning the deportations to eastern Europe; (4) the participation in handing out the yellow badge; and (5) the selection of 7,000 names for deportation. The sentence, issued in 1947, was intended to bar the two from serving in any honorary post in a Jewish institution. In 1950 the Union of Ashkenazic Congregations quashed the sentence.

BIBLIOGRAPHY

De Jong, L. *Het Koninkrijk der Nederlanden in de Tweede Wereldoorlog.* Vols. 4–8. The Hague, 1972–1978.

Herzberg, A. J. *Kroniek der Jodenvervolging.* Amsterdam, 1978.

Michman, J. "The Controversial Stand of the Joodse Raad in the Netherlands." *Yad Vashem Studies* 10 (1974): 9–68.

Michman, J. "The Controversy Surrounding the Jewish Council of Amsterdam." In *Patterns of Jewish Leadership in Nazi Europe, 1933–1945.* Proceedings of the Third Yad Vashem International Historical Conference, edited by Y. Gutman and C. J. Haft, pp. 235–258. Jerusalem, 1979.

Michman, J., H. Beem, and D. Michman, eds. *The Netherlands.* In *Pinkas Hakehillot; Encyclopaedia of Jewish Communities.* Jerusalem, 1985. See pages 79–138. (In Hebrew.)

Presser, J. *The Destruction of the Dutch Jews.* New York, 1969.

JOZEPH MICHMAN

JOYCE, WILLIAM ("Lord Haw-Haw"; 1906–1946), British fascist; broadcaster of Nazi propaganda from Germany to the British Isles during World War II.

Joyce was born in New York into an Irish family. His father was a Catholic and his mother a Protestant. The family became American nationals, but returned to Ireland in 1909. Joyce's parents were loyal British subjects and educated him to be the same. In 1921 they moved to England, and Joyce engaged in university studies in London.

In 1923 Joyce joined a small group of anti-Communist British fascists. He became a member of the British Union of Fascists (BUF) when it was founded in 1932, under the leadership of Sir Oswald MOSLEY. By virtue of his talents and zeal, Joyce was put in charge of the party's political propaganda machine, and achieved a reputation as a fiery speaker who aroused audiences with his radical ideas. He failed to be elected to a local council in London and fell out with Mosley, whose anti-Jewish policy he considered too moderate. For these reasons, and also because of the current financial crisis, in 1937 Joyce left the BUF. Together with former member of Parliament John Beckett, who had also broken with the BUF, he established the National Socialist League. The league was close to German Nazism; Joyce admired Adolf HITLER, and aspired to escalate the struggle against capitalism and the Jews. It remained a small group of extremists and made no impression on the political life of Britain.

In August 1939, on the eve of the outbreak of war, Joyce decided to go to Germany together with his second wife. Shortly after the war began, he began to make propaganda broadcasts, including attacks on the Jews, to Britain on behalf of the Germans, in the program "Germany Calling," which attracted many listeners. Estimates differ as to the impact of these broadcasts. Some observers claim that the British public considered them a kind of wartime entertainment, while others have suggested that the broadcasts helped to spread defeatist rumors, arguing that they always included a certain amount of genuine information together with falsehoods and provocations. The nickname "Lord Haw-Haw" originated in the British press before Joyce's true identity was known. He was hated by the British people and considered a traitor. Joyce himself wrote the majority of the material he broadcast.

During the war Joyce was granted German citizenship, and after the defeat of the Nazis he tried to escape under an assumed name, but he was discovered and arrested at the end of May 1945. He was brought to Britain and charged with treason in time of war. In his defense Joyce argued that he was not a British national, that he was an American citizen by birth, and that during the war he had received German citizenship. However, it was discovered that in 1933 Joyce had applied for and received a British passport, claiming British nationality; that the validity of the passport had been extended; and that he had used it to travel to Germany. The trial evoked tremendous public interest. He was found guilty, and in January 1946 he was executed.

Joyce's last public statement was: "During

my life and at my death I fought against the Jews, who were the cause of the war and who represent the forces of evil."

[*See also* Great Britain: Fascism in Great Britain.]

BIBLIOGRAPHY

Cole, J. A. *Lord Haw-Haw—William Joyce.* New York, 1965.
West, R. *The Meaning of Treason.* London, 1952.

JACQUELINE ROKHSAR

JUDENRAT [*This entry is a survey of the Jewish councils created by the Nazis to administer the internal life of the ghettos of eastern Europe and the regional Jewish populations in western Europe. See also* Ghetto; *for more information about specific Judenräte, see the headings in the encyclopedia by country and place. See in addition the biographies of individual heads of Judenräte.*]

The name "Judenrat" (pl., Judenräte) refers to the Jewish councils established on German orders in the Jewish communities of occupied Europe. Judenräte were first instituted in occupied Poland, on instructions issued by Reinhard HEYDRICH on September 21, 1939, and through an order promulgated by Hans FRANK, the head of the GENERALGOUVERNEMENT, on November 18, 1939, and subsequently in other countries conquered by Germany. The Judenräte did not have a uniform structure; some of them held authority in one location only, while others administered Jewish communities throughout a district or even an entire country. The role played by the Judenräte in Jewish public life during the Holocaust is one of the most controversial issues relating to the period; some historians believe that the institution of the Judenrat had a debilitating effect on the inner strength of the Jewish communities, whereas others maintain that the Judenräte reinforced the Jews' power of endurance in their struggle for survival.

On the basis of Heydrich's instructions of September 21, Judenräte were set up over the course of a few weeks in September and October 1939 in the communities of central and western Poland. The guidelines stipulated that the Judenräte would be fully responsible for the implementation of German policy regarding the Jews and would be made up, "as far as possible, of influential people and rabbis." In this way, the Jewish communities had forced on them a body whose function was to receive German orders and decrees and be responsible for carrying them out. The inclusion of prominent personalities in the Judenräte had a dual purpose: to ensure that

Members of the Kovno Ältestenrat (Council of Elders). Dr. Elchanan Elkes is in the center.

The Judenrat of the town of Checiny, 9 miles (14.5 km) southwest of Kielce, in Poland. The German army entered the town on September 5, 1939. On September 13, 1942, the ghetto was liquidated and the remaining Jews deported to Treblinka.

German orders were implemented to the fullest possible extent, and to discredit Jewish leadership in the eyes of the Jewish population.

Under Frank's order, in places where the Jewish population did not exceed ten thousand the Judenrat was to have twelve members, and in the larger towns or cities it was to consist of twenty-four members. The councils were to be elected by the members of the community and were themselves to elect their chairman and vice-chairman. The process of electing the Judenräte and their two top officers was to be completed by December 31, 1939; the results were subject to the approval of the German *Kreishauptmann* (chief district official) or, in the cities, of the German *Stadthauptmann* (chief city official). This last provision meant in effect that the elections provided for in Frank's order were quite

meaningless, and that the Germans never did intend to have the Judenräte's composition determined by elections. German intervention in the process, however, was not absolute, and on a number of occasions active members of the Jewish community had a say in determining the composition of the council. In some cases, Jewish activists refused to join the Judenrat, because they were suspicious of the use that the Germans would make of the institution. Generally, however, local Jewish leaders did become members of the councils. This corresponded to the wishes of the Jewish population, which felt that it was precisely the traditional leaders of the community who were best equipped to represent it vis-à-vis the German authorities in the critical and perilous situation that had arisen. Thus, paradoxically, the two conflicting purposes, of the Jews and the Germans, ensured that in the

Members of the Kraków Judenrat.

early stages of their existence, the Judenräte preserved the continuity of local leadership. However, even in the first councils to come into being, some of the members had no previous experience in public affairs.

Decisions on Implementation. Once the Judenräte were established, the Germans lost no time in presenting them with urgent tasks: drafting people for forced labor, taking a census of the Jewish population, evacuating apartments and handing them over to Germans, paying fines or ransoms, confiscating valuables owned by Jews, and so on. In most cases, the Judenrat members tried to delay the administrative and economic measures that the Germans were imposing, or at least to alleviate them. However, the traditional methods employed by Jews for dealing with the authorities, such as lobbying officials and utilizing personal contacts, were not applicable under the new conditions. The Judenräte did try to exploit the rivalry among the various branches of the German administration in order to lighten the burden imposed on the Jews, but their success here was minimal.

The Judenräte believed that by complying with the German demands they would impress upon the Nazis the vital importance to the Germans of the Jewish community. In this way they hoped to avert or moderate some of the blows, to gain time, to ward off or delay collective punishments, and perhaps even to persuade the Germans to reconsider their policy in view of the benefit they could derive from the Jews, as a reservoir for the manpower the Germans sorely needed; in the meantime, the Jews hoped, the war would end in a German defeat. It took a while before these theories and assessments were put to the test—until the mass deportations of 1942, when the true nature of German policy became increasingly obvious.

Providing Basic Needs. Judenrat members were also involved in providing the community with its basic needs. The German invasion of Poland, and subsequently of other countries, destroyed the existing Jewish economic structure, which even before the war had been shaky. Jewish society had always included groups requiring public assistance, but the problems created by the German occupation were of unprecedented dimensions. Various measures imposed upon the Jewish community caused a further deterioration of their economic condition. Tens of thousands of Jews were displaced from their homes and became refugees, without a place to live or a source of food. Jews were no longer covered by the general public services and required their own health services and public institutions, such as homes for the aged, orphanages, and, in part, educational institutions. In coping with this daily struggle for the survival of the community, the Judenrat members drew upon their experience gained in Jewish welfare activities before the war, even though there was no comparison between conditions in the two eras. The Judenrat's efforts to ease the plight of the Jewish population were among of the ways in which it sought to counter the Nazi policy of starving the communities and breaking their power of resistance. Even in that first stage, however, some of the Judenrat activities were not without instances of protectionism, favoritism, misuse of positions of public trust for personal advantage, and so on. Such practices caused bitter resentment in the communities and were harshly criticized.

More functions were imposed upon the Judenräte by the Germans with the ghettoization of the Jews of occupied Poland and, following the invasion of the Soviet Union, the Jews of other countries of eastern Europe. The Judenräte were made responsible for transferring Jews from their homes into the areas allotted for the ghettos, for providing accommodation in the ghettos for the new inhabitants, for maintaining public order in the ghettos, and for preventing smuggling. Some of these duties were carried out by the Jewish police (see JÜDISCHER ORDNUNGSDIENST).

Under ghetto conditions, which separated the Jews from the general population, the hardships became much worse. Large sections of the Jewish community faced starvation. It was the Judenrat's responsibility to distribute the food rations permitted by the Germans, but usually these did not constitute even the barest minimum needed for survival. In a number of ghettos, the Judenräte sought to obtain more food by buying provisions on the black market or on the "Aryan" side, or by bartering products manufactured in the ghetto. The Judenräte also established organizations for mutual help, thereby providing some relief from the suffering.

Self-Help. As a result of starvation, overcrowding, and the lack of basic sanitary facilities, diseases spread in the ghetto. The Germans held the Judenrat responsible for ensuring that contagious diseases did not cross the ghetto borders, but they regarded the growth of the death rate in the ghettos as a welcome addition to their own measures taken against the Jews. The Judenrat, for its part, set up hospitals and clinics and organized other forms of medical aid in order to reduce, as much as possible, the dimensions of the diseases and epidemics. In many ghettos, community forces other than the Judenrat waged war on starvation and disease through such unofficial frameworks as political organizations and youth movements. In Poland, the Żydowska Samopomoc Społeczna (Jewish Self-Help Society), an organization recognized by the Germans, sought to provide help to the needy. In some cases the Judenrat and the voluntary organizations cooperated with one another, but there was friction between them when the Judenrat wanted to exercise supervision over all welfare and medical-aid operations among the Jewish population.

Beginning in 1940, the Judenräte were given the task of providing forced labor for the camps that were being set up, first in occupied Poland and later in other occupied areas. This was a fundamental change from the Judenrat's previous assignments. It did not mean sending people on forced labor in or near their place of residence, where they could return in the evening to their community and family; it meant total separation and transfer to remote locations where a much harsher regime was in force—a regime that many prisoners could not endure for long.

Compliance or Refusal. The Judenräte had to make a decision whether to comply with this German demand. In most instances they did supply the required quota of able-bodied young men as workers for the labor camps, causing friction with the community when the latter had to be seized on the streets for deportation to the camps. In the initial stages of forced-labor deportations, the Judenräte tried to maintain contact with the members of their community imprisoned in the camps, sending them food, clothing, and medicines, but when German policy took a turn for the worse, the contact was broken off. In some cases councils refused to supply quotas for the labor camps. When Joseph Parnes, chairman of the Judenrat in LVOV, refused to send men to the JANÓWSKA camp, he forfeited his life.

As time went on, however, and Nazi policy

approached the next phase, that of mass extermination of Jews, the Judenräte had very little room left for maneuvering between the needs of the Jewish population and the demands made by the Germans. Judenrat members had to confront the question of where to draw the line—to decide whether compliance with German orders was still to be regarded as a contribution to the community's struggle for survival. On this issue there were bitter discussions within and outside the Judenräte. The decisions taken by the council members and the answers they gave to this crucial question differed in substance, and also depended on the specific moment when they had to be made. It is these decisions and answers that form the basis for value judgments of the Judenrat.

The pattern of behavior of Judenrat members falls into four categories:

1. Refusal to cooperate with the Germans, even with regard to economic measures or other relatively mundane issues;
2. Acquiescence with extreme measures of a material nature, such as the seizure of property, but absolute refusal to hand over human beings;
3. Resignation to the destruction of parts of the Jewish community, on the assumption that this would enable other segments to be saved;
4. Compliance in full with all German orders, without any consideration for their effect on the Jewish public, and with concern only for one's own personal interests.

Isaiah Trunk, in his 1972 study on the Judenrat, provides data on the fate of 720 Judenrat members in eastern Europe, summarized in Table 1. These figures show that close to 80 percent of Judenrat members died either before the mass *Aktionen* took place or in the course of the deportations to extermination camps. In very many cases, they lost their lives as a result of their failure to comply with German orders. The conduct of 146 Judenrat chairmen, the first to be appointed to their posts in the Generalgouvernement, is shown in Table 2, a summary of data in Aharon Weiss's 1977 study.

It can be seen that in the first phase of the Judenrat's existence, the chairmen looked after the interests of their community and did not give in to German pressure. Those who followed—that is, those who assumed their posts after the original chairmen had been dismissed or killed—were, for the most part, German appointees, and their conduct in office shows a different pattern. For that final phase, Table 3 summarizes data (in Weiss's study) on 101 communities in the Generalgouvernement.

The outstanding feature of these data is the sharp rise in the figures that indicate obedience to the Germans and yielding to their pressure. Whereas in the first phase the Judenrat chairmen (or at least some of them) had been responsible Jewish leaders, their successors were less sensitive to public interests; in the final stages of mass extermination and relentless terror, these Judenrat chairmen almost invariably carried out Nazi orders.

In their search for ways to prevent, slow down, or reduce the onslaught upon their communities, many Judenräte adopted a pol-

TABLE 1. *Fate of 720 Judenrat Members in Eastern Europe*

	NUMBER	PERCENTAGE
Relinquished their membership	21	2.9
Were removed from the Judenrat or arrested	13	1.8
Were murdered before the deportations to extermination camps	182	25.3
Went to their death during the deportations (either murdered on the spot or deported)	383	53.2
Committed suicide	9	1.2
Died a natural death	26	3.6
Survived	86	12.0
Total	720	100.0

TABLE 2. *Conduct of 146 Judenrat Chairmen in the Generalgouvernement*

	NUMBER	PERCENTAGE
Extended help to the community, refused to carry out economic measures, warned of *Aktionen* that were being prepared	45	30.8
Resigned from their posts because they could not accept Nazi policy	11	7.5
Were dismissed by the Germans after failing to carry out orders	26	17.8
Were killed by the Germans after refusing to hand over members of the community	18	12.3
Committed suicide	5	3.4
Maintained contact with the underground	2	1.4
Died at beginning of term	4	2.7
Were replaced by the Jews themselves	1	0.7
Opinions differ on their conduct in office	13	9.0
Complied with German orders	21	14.4
Total	146	100.0

icy of "rescue by labor." The Judenrat members who supported this policy saw in it one of the few realistic alternatives they had to convince the Germans of the importance, for Germany, of the continued existence of the community. And, as the war went on and the economy required additional manpower, certain German circles, on both the central and the local level, were inclined to utilize Jewish manpower. These were primarily officials in charge of the production of arms and other military equipment and supplies. Their view was not a deviation from the "Final Solution" policy; it represented no more than a pragmatic consideration dictated by the prevailing conditions. But there were Judenräte that saw in such German needs openings that could be exploited to save Jews. The Judenräte that applied this policy were in fact resigned to the hopelessness of trying to save their entire community, but they felt they might salvage a part of it. Prominent among

TABLE 3. *Conduct of 101 Later Judenrat Chairmen in the Generalgouvernement*

	NUMBER	PERCENTAGE
Helped the community, refused to comply with economic decrees, warned of impending *Aktionen*	16	15.8
Could not accept Nazi policy and resigned from their posts	4	3.9
Were dismissed by the Germans for failing to carry out orders	8	7.9
Were killed by the Germans after refusing to hand over members of the community	2	2.0
Committed suicide	1	1.0
Maintained contact with the underground	1	1.0
Died a natural death	1	1.0
Opinions differ on their conduct	7	7.0
Complied with German orders	61	60.4
Total	101	100.0

members who supported this line were Mordechai Chaim RUMKOWSKI of Łódź, Jacob GENS of Vilna, Moshe MERIN of SOSNOWIEC, in Eastern Upper SILESIA, and Efraim BARASZ of BIAŁYSTOK.

Resistance. Relations between the Judenrat and the Jewish underground and fighters' organizations in the ghettos were highly complex and did not follow a uniform pattern. A substantial number of Judenräte were opposed to the idea of armed resistance or of fleeing to the forests to join the partisans. Some council members believed that underground activities in the ghetto would endanger the entire community and hasten its liquidation, in view of the rule of "collective responsibility" that the Nazis had introduced. This was the background to the tension in many ghettos where the Judenrat and the underground competed for influence. In some places, feelings ran high enough for violent clashes to erupt: in WARSAW, where the ŻYDOWSKA ORGANIZACJA BOJOWA (Jewish Fighting Organization; ŻOB) attacked the Jewish police, and in VILNA, where a dispute erupted over the Yitzhak WITTENBERG affair. In Eastern Upper Silesia, Judenrat chairman Moshe Merin waged all-out war against the underground; similar situations existed in Kraków and other places.

Some Judenräte did not have a clear-cut position on the issue of resistance. They accepted the presence of an underground and even gave it help, but argued that if active resistance were offered prematurely, it would interfere with the Judenrat's policy, the main purpose of which was to gain time in the hope that developments in the war situation would bring rescue for the Jews. While supporting the concept of resistance, they felt it should be implemented only when it was clear that the community was about to be liquidated. This was the position held by Efraim Barasz, chairman of the Judenrat in Białystok.

In other ghettos, such as those of KOVNO and (at one period) MINSK, Judenrat members assisted the underground without reservations of any kind. There were also instances when Judenrat members headed underground activities and took a leading part in uprisings. Dov Lopatyn, the Judenrat chairman in LACHVA, was one of the leaders of the uprising there, in which the whole community took

part; in DIATLOVO, the Judenrat members organized a partisan unit; and council members played a central role in the uprising in TUCHIN.

National and Local Function. As the war progressed and German power increased, the Germans and their allies continued to establish Judenräte. The problems facing these Judenräte had much in common with those of eastern Europe. But there were also differences, which depended on local conditions, on the structure of the Jewish communities and the standing of their leaders, and on the policies pursued by the German government and the governments of the satellite and German-protected states. Thus, for example, in the areas of eastern Europe where the Germans exercised direct control, the Judenräte were local institutions and, for the most part, had no contact with one another. In other parts of Europe, the councils were set up as country-wide institutions, and this affected the way they functioned, their relations with the Germans and the local governments, and their ties with the Jewish population.

Germany. In 1933, when the Nazis came to power in GERMANY, the Jews, on their own initiative, established an umbrella organization, the REICHSVERTRETUNG DER DEUTSCHEN JUDEN (Reich Representation of German Jews), a voluntary federation of Jewish communities and large organizations. Its purpose was to deal with the major problems that German Jewry was facing under the Nazi regime. In 1939 the Reichsvertretung became the official central organization of the Jews, with its name changed to the Reichsvereinigung der Juden in Deutschland (Reich Association of Jews in Germany). It was headed by the same men who had been the leaders of the Reichsvertretung, Rabbi Leo BAECK and Otto HIRSCH.

Until recently, the prevailing opinion of scholars was that the change from a voluntary to a centralist and compulsory organization had been instigated by the Germans to facilitate the implementation of their steadily hardening policy toward German Jewry. A large number of scholars considered that the Reichsvereinigung was the prototype of the Judenräte which the Germans were to set up in the areas they occupied during the war. Current research, however, has revealed that the changeover from Reichsvertretung to Reichsvereinigung was largely initiated by the Jewish leadership itself, which sought to strengthen its influence on the Jewish population in view of the Nazi decision, in 1938, to abolish the legal status of the Kultusgemeinde (local Jewish community organizations). Coincidentally, the Germans were also interested in establishing a central Jewish body—their purpose indeed being to turn it into an instrument for implementating measures against the Jews that was more efficient and easier to control than its predecessor. In due course, the Germans were to apply the same principles in the creation of the Judenräte.

Other Countries. In FRANCE, a central Judenrat, the UNION GÉNÉRALE DES ISRAÉLITES DE FRANCE (UGIF), was set up on November 29, 1941. It consisted of two branches, one in German-occupied northern France and the other in Vichy France, in the south. All other political and public Jewish organizations were closed down, though most continued to operate as independent bodies under the cover of UGIF departments, which enabled them to combine their legal functions with their clandestine aid and rescue operations. The UGIF was headed by prominent prewar Jewish leaders who took no part in the arrest, imprisonment, and deportation of Jews, and who tried to ease the overall lot of the French Jews.

In BELGIUM, the order for the establishment of a Judenrat was announced on November 25, 1941. It was named the ASSOCIATION DES JUIFS EN BELGIQUE (AJB), and the Chief Rabbi of Belgium, Solomon Ullman, was appointed its chairman. The AJB, with local branches in the Belgian cities, was charged with setting up a register of the Jewish population that the Germans planned to use in drafting Jews for forced labor and for deportation. Most of the time the AJB complied with the orders it was given by the Germans, thus causing bitter resentment and resistance among the Jews. In the summer of 1942, Judenrat members delivered to the Jews German notices ordering them to report for forced labor—in actuality, a cover for deportation to "the east." As a result, other Jews who had been working for the Judenrat decided to resign. The phenomenon of AJB members giving in to German decrees repeated itself in 1943 and 1944, but

there were also many AJB people who established ties with the Jewish underground and general Jewish organizations during that period and who made their contribution to the resistance and rescue efforts.

The Germans established a Judenrat, the JOODSE RAAD, in the NETHERLANDS in early 1941. Its authority was restricted at first to Amsterdam, but within a short time was extended to the entire country. David COHEN and Abraham ASSCHER, two veteran leaders of the community, were appointed as the Judenrat heads. In the first phase of its existence, the Joodse Raad organized services needed by the community, but it was also charged with various tasks that served German measures against the Jews, such as registering the Jewish population of the country. In summer 1942 the Joodse Raad was ordered to draw up lists of persons who were to be sent "to work in the east." Following a sharp internal debate, the council agreed to provide the Germans with 7,000 names. For this action and for other instances of compliance with German orders, the Judenrat in the Netherlands was severely criticized at the time, and also in the postwar years.

In SLOVAKIA, a central Judenrat, the ÚSTREDŇA ŽIDOV (Jewish Center), was set up in September 1940, with headquarters in the capital, Bratislava, and branches in other cities. It was the only institution authorized to represent the Jews, and its officers were well-known public figures. The council sought to provide the Jewish population with essential services, give aid to the needy, create employment, and establish vocational training courses. Following the 1942 deportations from Slovakia, it increased its activities in the labor camps, setting up workshops and organizing construction crews, with the object of demonstrating that the Jews played a vital role in the country's economy. Some members were inclined to submit to German demands; one of these was Karel Hochberg, who wielded considerable influence in the Ústredňa Židov. During the deportations an underground group, the PRACOVNÁ SKUPINA (Working Group), was formed within the council, under the leadership of Gisi FLEISCHMANN and Rabbi Michael Dov WEISSMANDEL, who did not belong to the latter. In addition to their official duties in the Ústredňa Židov, the

An Ústredňa Židov (Jewish Center) workshop in Slovakia for vocational retraining.

Pracovná Skupina members initiated aid and rescue efforts, in the course of which they made contact with elements outside Slovakia; it was they who put forward the so-called EUROPA PLAN, a proposal for rescuing the surviving remnants of European Jewry.

A central Judenrat for HUNGARY was instituted in Budapest in March 1944, under the name of Zsidó Tanács (Jewish Council). Its chairman was Samu STERN, a leader of the Neolog (progressive Judaism) movement in Hungary and the president of the Jewish community in Pest. Local councils were formed in other Hungarian cities. Both the central and local councils in Hungary complied with the administrative and economic measures that were imposed on the Jews. Researchers of the Holocaust in Hungary stress that the Judenrat members gave no warning to the communities in which they operated of the dangers in store for them, although they themselves were well aware of what had happened to the Jews in other countries under German occupation. The legalistic-traditional approach of the Hungarian Judenrat leaders was unsuitable for the conditions that prevailed in the Holocaust era: they expected that Hungarian political forces would rally to their defense, but these, for the most part, turned their backs on the Jews. The Judenrat members in Hungary have been accused of failing to exercise proper leadership of the community in that grim period.

In ROMANIA, the CENTRALA EVREILOR (Jewish Center) went into operation in Bucharest at the beginning of 1942, with branches in various Romanian cities. The Union of Jewish Communities (Federatia Uniunilor de Comunitati Evreesti), which until then had administered Jewish community life in the country, was disbanded. Nandor Ghingold, a baptized Jew who was totally unknown among the Jewish population, was appointed chairman of the council, which was directly subordinated to Radu LECCA, the Romanian official in charge of Jewish affairs. The council operated in four areas: preparing surveys of the Jewish population, drafting Jews for forced labor, collecting fines imposed on the Jews, and organizing welfare assistance. The Germans kept track of the council's activities and exerted pressure on the Romanian government to use it in a manner designed to weaken the public standing and influence of Dr. Wilhelm FILDERMAN, who had been the head of the Union of Communities, and of other traditional Jewish leaders. The attempt failed, and Filderman and the other veteran leaders worked to block the designs of the Germans and the Romanian antisemites. The Centrala Evreilor, on the other hand, did not gain the recognition of the Jewish population.

In GREECE there was no overall Judenrat per se. The Germans took SALONIKA on April 9, 1941, two months before all of Greece was occupied (on June 2) and divided among Germany, Italy, and Bulgaria. The Gestapo immediately seized some of the Jewish community leaders of Salonika—whom they considered possible sources of resistance—and appointed Shabbetai Shealtiel, an employee of the Jewish community association, as head of a newly constituted community board. The board was ordered to supply men for forced labor and to implement anti-Jewish economic measures. It complied with these demands.

Shealtiel proved to be inefficient, and in December 1942 he was dismissed and the Chief Rabbi of Salonika, Zvi KORETZ, was appointed in his place. From this point on, the board lost all autonomy, rapidly assumed the characteristics of a Judenrat, and was forced to carry out German orders to the letter. When deportations from Salonika to the extermination camps in Poland were launched in March 1943, Koretz tried to stop them, appealing to the Greek authorities to intervene on behalf of the Jews, but his efforts failed. Opinions differ as to Rabbi Koretz's actions; some historians point to the exertions he made to assist the Salonika community in critical days, while others emphasize his submission to German pressure.

Historical View. Research on the Judenrat phenomenon has been gradually abandoning the earlier indiscriminate condemnation of the Judenräte, and there is now a sharper discernment of the various elements that made up their activities. This view of the Judenrat takes into account the different phases that Nazi policy on the "Final Solution" went through and the changes that took place in the composition of the Judenräte, and examines the effect of these changes on the conduct of Judenrat members. Efforts have been made to understand the Judenrat by ascertaining how it used its limited authority—given to it by the Germans with the sole aim of enabling it to carry out German orders—for the good of the Jewish population; to what extent it achieved a fair distribution of the burden among the Jews; how it acted during the mass deportations to the extermination camps; the attitude of Judenrat members toward the deportations before it was known what fate awaited the deportees, and their actions once that fate was discovered; how the Judenrat viewed rescue efforts and the underground. An objective assessment of all these elements permits a more realistic and accurate historical evaluation of the Judenrat.

BIBLIOGRAPHY

Bauer, Y., and N. Rotenstreich, eds. *The Holocaust as Historical Experience: Essays and Discussion.* New York, 1981.

Friedman, P. "The Messianic Complex of a Nazi Collaborator: Moses Merin of Sosnowiec." In *Roads to Extinction: Essays on the Holocaust,* edited by Ada J. Friedman, pp. 353–364. Philadelphia, 1980.

Gutman, Y., and C. J. Haft, eds. *Patterns of Jewish Leadership in Nazi Europe, 1933–1945.* Proceedings of the Third Yad Vashem International Historical Conference. Jerusalem, 1979.

Klein, B. "The Judenrat." *Jewish Social Studies* 22/1 (1960): 67–84.

Trunk, I. *Judenrat: The Jewish Councils in Eastern Europe under Nazi Occupation.* New York, 1972.

Weiss, A. "Jewish Leadership in Occupied Poland: Postures and Attitudes." *Yad Vashem Studies* 12 (1977): 335–365.

AHARON WEISS

JÜDISCHER CENTRALVEREIN. *See* Centralverein Deutscher Staatsbürger Jüdischen Glaubens.

JÜDISCHER ORDNUNGSDIENST (Jewish GHETTO police, referred to by the Jews as the "Jewish police"), Jewish police units established by the Germans in certain places in the areas under their occupation. A relatively short time after their establishment, the Judenräte (Jewish councils) in eastern Europe were ordered to organize these units, usually in anticipation of the ghettoization of the Jews.

Whereas the JUDENRAT itself, although also

Jewish police in Lublin.

created on German orders, often contained elements of voluntary association, the Jewish police came into being only on German orders. There was no precedent in the life of the Jewish community for the existence of a Jewish police force, and no indication that independent initiative by Jews in any way played a part in the establishment of the ghetto police.

The Germans set guidelines according to which the Judenrat was to recruit the police personnel—physical fitness, military experience, and secondary or higher education. In practice, these guidelines were not always observed. Formally, the Jewish police constituted one of the Judenrat departments, but from the very beginning many Judenräte were apprehensive about the police department's public character and the way it would function. They suspected that the Germans would have direct supervision of the police

and use it for the implementation of their policies. Aware of this danger, many Judenräte sought to establish their own means of controlling the police and the standards of its behavior, and tried to attract to the police young Jews who would be trustworthy. At first, some of the recruits did indeed believe that joining the police gave them an opportunity to serve the community. But there were other reasons for joining. Belonging to a protected organization, provided immunity from being seized for forced labor. Police service also offered greater freedom of movement and possibilities of obtaining food.

A study of the records of over one hundred Jewish police officers in the GENERALGOUVERNEMENT reveals that the Judenräte did not succeed in their efforts to ensure that the police had public credibility. Seventy percent of the men who served in the police force had taken no part in political and community life before the war, and some 20 percent were refugees and strangers to the ghetto population; only 10 percent had participated in community affairs in the prewar period. The Germans themselves often made sure, when the police was set up, that it would be headed by men who would blindly follow their orders. Some circles in the ghetto population who were not associated with the Judenrat regarded the Jewish police from the outset as an alien body and a potential danger to the community. In many places, youth movements and Jewish political parties did not permit their members to enlist in the police.

The size of the Jewish police force was not fixed but depended on the size of the Jewish community. Thus, in Warsaw the Jewish police at first numbered 2,000, in Lvov 500, in Łódź 800, in Kraków 150, and in Kovno 200. There was no uniform structure for the police units. In the large ghettos, the commanders held officer rank and the units were made up of subdivisions and district stations. The policemen were identified by the different caps they wore and by the unit's designation inscribed on their armband, the yellow badge that they, like all other Jews, had to wear (see BADGE, JEWISH). In the small ghettos where the police consisted of a few men only, no such organizational differentiations were made.

Jewish police in the Warsaw ghetto.

Police Duties. The duties carried out by the Jewish police can be divided into three categories:

1. Duties in response to specific German demands as conveyed to the police by the Germans, via the Judenrat
2. Duties related to the Judenrat's activities among the Jews that were not directly related to German demands
3. Duties related to the Jewish population's needs

The first two categories included collecting ransom payments, personal belongings and valuables, as well as taxes; fetching people for forced labor; guarding the ghetto wall or fence and the ghetto gates; escorting labor gangs who worked outside the ghetto; and, as time went on, conducting random seizures of persons to be sent to labor camps and participating in the roundup of Jews for mass deportations.

The exclusion of the Jewish population from public services and their isolation in ghettos created serious problems. In the early stage of its existence, the Jewish police attended to sanitary conditions and assisted in the distribution of food rations and aid to the needy. It also helped in the control of epidemics, and the settling of disputes—all this, of course, in addition to complying with German demands. The ghetto population appreciated the Jewish police for these public-welfare activities. However, already at this stage, there were instances of corruption and misconduct among the police.

Dilemmas. As time went on, the role of the Jewish police in alleviating living conditions in the ghetto was considerably reduced. The mass deportations to extermination camps, beginning in 1942, affected the families of the men serving in the police, their friends, acquaintances, and fellow Jews, and they had to decide whether or not to stay at their posts. Many decided to quit the force, some in an overt manner, so as to express their identification with their families and with the Jewish population as a whole. Most of the Jewish policemen who made such a decision were subsequently included in the transports that left for the extermination camps. But there were also Jewish police who stayed on their jobs up to the final phases of the ghettos' existence, submitting to German pressure and obediently following orders. At that stage the Jewish police took on a different complexion. Directly intervening in its administration, the Germans recruited new men into the force, both as officers and rank and file, who had no commitment at all to the Jewish population. Among the new Jewish police personnel were many refugees with no ties to the surviving remnants of the local Jewish community, as well as men of dubious reputation. In numerous ghettos where the Judenrat was not prepared to submit blindly to German orders, it was the Jewish police who gained in strength, to the extent that it was able to control the Judenrat or simply take its place.

The Underground. The attitude of the Jewish police toward the ghetto underground took on three different forms:

1. The most common relationship was one of tension. In several ghettos—such as those of BĘDZIN, SOSNOWIEC, KRAKÓW, and WARSAW—the Jewish police tried to do away with the underground (which is not to say that all members of the police in these places took part in such efforts). In Warsaw, in August 1942, during the mass deportations, the Jewish police commander, Joseph Szerynski, was attacked by the underground and seriously wounded. His successor, Jacob Lejkin, was assassinated in October of that year, on orders of the ŻYDOWSKA ORGANIZACJA BOJOWA (Jewish Fighting Organization; ŻOB).

2. There were instances when the Jewish police followed a policy of nonintervention in the activities of the underground that sometimes took on the form of "benign neglect."

3. In some ghettos, such as that of KOVNO, the Jewish police gave active help to the underground, and some policemen were also members of clandestine organizations.

Conclusion. When the war ended, the conduct of the Jewish police in the ghettos came under investigation by groups of survivors. In Munich (which was in the American zone), forty Jewish policemen were found guilty of improper conduct and were ostracized by the Jewish public. In Israel, several policemen were charged under the Nazis and Nazi Collaborators (Punishment) Law; a few were convicted but most were acquitted, the courts taking into account, *inter alia*, the extraordinary circumstances under which the Jewish policemen in the ghettos had had to function.

BIBLIOGRAPHY

Trunk, I. *Judenrat: The Jewish Councils in Eastern Europe under Nazi Occupation.* New York, 1972. See pages 475–569.

Weiss, A. "The Relations between the Judenrat and the Jewish Police." In *Patterns of Jewish Leadership in Nazi Europe, 1933–1945.* Proceedings of the Third Yad Vashem International Historical Conference, edited by Y. Gutman and C. Haft, pp. 201–217. Jerusalem, 1979.

AHARON WEISS

JUD SÜSS. *See* Films, Nazi Antisemitic.

JURISPRUDENCE IN NAZI GERMANY. *See* Law and Judiciary in Nazi Germany.

K

KACZERGINSKI, SHMARYAHU (Shmerke; 1908–1954), Jewish writer, poet, and partisan. Kaczerginski attended the Talmud Torah (religious school) in Vilna and then received vocational training, becoming a lithographer. While still at school he wrote poems and stories, and in the late 1920s was one of the founding members of Yung-Vilne (Young Vilna), a group of modernist Yiddish writers. He was arrested a number of times for his activities among the underground Communist youth. His revolutionary poems became popular folk songs in Poland, and prior to World War II he published poems, stories, a novel (*Yugnt on Freyd* [Youth without Joy]), and articles. He was also a correspondent of *Morgn Frayhayt,* the New York Yiddish daily.

After the German invasion of the Soviet Union in June 1941, Kaczerginski tried unsuccessfully to escape to the Soviet interior, and for a year he roamed about Vilna, posing as a deaf-mute. In the spring of 1942 he entered the Vilna ghetto and took an active part in its cultural life and the education of the youth. He directed the programs of the Yugnt Klub, a club for youth of school age. He also joined in the preparations for the formation of the FAREYNEGTE PARTIZANER ORGANIZATSYE (United Partisan Organization; FPO), the ghetto's movement for armed resistance to the Nazis. The poems that Kaczerginski composed at the time relate to these activities. Some of them became popular in the ghetto and have survived, such as the lullaby "Shtiler, shtiler" (Softly, Softly) and "Yugnt-Himen" (Youth Anthem). In addition to poems, Kaczerginski wrote articles and lectured extensively to ghetto audiences. His writings include an essay on the poet Abraham SUTZKEVER and a 300-page monograph on Chaim Grade, the Yiddish poet and novelist.

The Germans made use of Kaczerginski in sorting out valuable books (*see* EINSATZSTAB ROSENBERG) in the library of Vilna's Yivo Institute for Jewish Research (YIVO) for confiscation by them. The library was situated outside the ghetto; this enabled Kaczerginski to establish contacts for obtaining arms and smuggling them into the ghetto, and also to save books and manuscripts from the Germans. Together with Sutzkever and others, Kaczerginski saved some eight thousand items in the Vilna ghetto archives, among them the diary of Herman KRUK. This collection is now in the possession of YIVO in New York.

On September 12, 1943, Kaczerginski, together with a group of FPO members, succeeded in leaving the ghetto clandestinely. For ten months, until the liberation of Vilna (July 13, 1944), he served with the partisans of the Voroshilov Brigade in the Naroch Forest. The brigade commander appointed Kaczerginski and Sutzkever official historians of the partisan movement in the region; their task included interviewing partisans and recording their statements on the partisan operations. Among those they interviewed were Jews who had taken refuge in the forest or were serving in the brigade. The impression made by these encounters is reflected in poems and stories about partisans that Kaczerginski wrote, especially in 1943.

Shmaryahu Kaczerginski.

He also made translations from Russian into Yiddish.

In 1948 Kaczerginski published a collection of 250 Yiddish poems that had been composed in the ghettos and the camps, including notes on the fate of the authors, music to about 100 songs, and his own introduction. This is still the largest and most important collection of its kind. In 1950 Kaczerginski emigrated to Argentina, where he lost his life in an airplane accident.

BIBLIOGRAPHY

Kaczerginsky, S. *Songs of the Ghettos and Concentration Camps.* New York, 1948. (In Yiddish.)

Kalisch, S. *Yes, We Sang: Songs of the Ghettos and Concentration Camps.* New York, 1985.

Niger, S. "Yiddish Poets of the Third Destruction." *Reconstructionist* 13/10 (June 27, 1947): 13–18.

Rubin, R. "Yiddish Folksongs of World War II: A Record of Suffering and Struggle." *Jewish Quarterly* 11/2 (Summer 1963): 12–17.

YEHIEL SZEINTUCH

KAHN, FRANZ (1896–1944), Czechoslovak Zionist leader, born in Plzeň (Pilsen), in Bohemia. In 1916, while serving as a captain in the Austro-Hungarian army on the Russian front, Kahn was wounded and lost his left arm. After World War I he became active in the Zionist Tekhelet-Lavan (Blue-White) movement, and completed his law studies. In 1921, when the Zionist Organization of Czechoslovakia moved its headquarters to Moravská Ostrava, Kahn also moved to that city as the organization's secretary, and later became one of the leaders of Zionism in the country. At the end of 1938, following the MUNICH CONFERENCE and the truncation of Czechoslovakia, Kahn returned to Prague and was co-opted to the Zionist Action Committee.

Franz Kahn.

When BOHEMIA AND MORAVIA were occupied by the Germans in March 1939, Kahn, unlike other members of the Zionist leadership, refused to abandon Protectorate Jewry and save himself by leaving the country; nor did he seek to exploit his privileged status as a disabled war veteran. He did arrange for his son and daughter to immigrate to Palestine. As the son of an American citizen, Kahn could have applied for repatriation to the United States, but he refused to affix his signature to such a request. He believed that this step might bar him from representing the Jews vis-à-vis the Germans, which he felt to be his duty, despite the loathing he felt whenever he had to meet with Germans.

In January 1943, Kahn and his wife were moved to the THERESIENSTADT camp. He did not join the camp's Ältestenrat (Council of Elders), but accepted the post of director of the cultural section and devoted himself to work among the youth in the camp. The many efforts made to rescue Kahn, by Nahum GOLDMANN and Stephen S. WISE in the United States, and by Chaim WEIZMANN and Moshe Shertok (Sharett) in London and Jerusalem, were of no avail. In October 1944 he was deported to AUSCHWITZ, as were most of the other Jewish leaders in Theresienstadt and their families, although as a rule, disabled war veterans in Theresienstadt were not subject to further deportation. That same month he was killed in Birkenau.

BIBLIOGRAPHY

Bondy, R. *"Elder of the Jews": Jakob Edelstein of Theresienstadt.* New York, 1989.
Dagan, A., ed. *The Jews of Czechoslovakia: Historical Studies and Surveys.* Vols. 2, 3. Philadelphia, 1971, 1984.

SEEV GOSHEN

KAIDAN. *See* Kėdainiai.

KAISERWALD (Latv., Meza-Park), concentration camp in LATVIA. Kaiserwald was set up in March 1943 in a recreation village near RIGA. Its first inmates were several hundred German convicts. From June 1943 the majority of the Jews expelled from Riga were sent to Kaiserwald. In November of that year, the remainder of Latvian Jewry was taken to Kaiserwald from the liquidated ghettos of Riga, LIEPĀJA, and DVINSK, as were survivors of the VILNA ghetto. A few Jews from the Riga ghetto were sent to labor camps to work at the Lentta factory, the Strazdenhof (Strazdemuiza) camp, the German government railways (the Reichsbahn), and German military and police bases such as the Heeres Kraftfahrpark (the military vehicle maintenance services) and the Armeebekleidungsamt (the military clothing stores). Over the course of time these camps were brought under the jurisdiction of the Kaiserwald camp, and all the Jews living on Latvian soil were incarcerated there. In 1944, thousands of Jewish women were brought to Kaiserwald from Hungary, as was a group of Jews from ŁÓDŹ. In March of that year there were 11,878 inmates in the camp and its subsidiaries, 6,182 males and 5,696 females. Only 95 were non-Jews. A small number of Jewish children who had succeeded in escaping the *Aktionen* lived in the camp unofficially.

The Kaiserwald camp was planned to exploit the labor potential of the inmates. The majority worked in factories, mines, and farms. A large group of women worked in the gigantic A.E.G. (Allgemeine Elektrizität Gesellschaft; the German industrial electric corporation), and a few Jews were employed in the camp kitchen, clothing stores, workshops, and medical services. Kaiserwald's organization was like that of the other concentration camps: uniform clothing, identification numbers, separate housing for men and women, hard labor, rigid discipline, and brutal punishment. The inmates suffered from hunger, cold, and overcrowding. The camp commandant was an SS-*Obersturmführer* named Zauer.

In July 1944, as the Soviet army approached the Latvian border, the Germans began gradually to evacuate the inmates. Prior to the evacuation, vicious *Aktionen* were carried out in which thousands of Jews who were unfit for work—the ill, the frail, and the young—were put to death. In one of the subsidiary camps of Kaiserwald, all the Jewish prisoners who had been convicted of offenses during their internment were put to death. In another, all the Jews except those between the ages of eighteen and thirty were massacred. The evacuation was completed in September 1944, except for a few dozen Jews left by the Germans to perform various tasks. The evacuees were transferred by ship and train to the STUTTHOF camp near Danzig, and in the course of time were dispersed among a number of camps inside Germany.

BIBLIOGRAPHY

Levin, D., ed. *Latvia and Estonia.* In *Pinkas Hakehillot; Encyclopaedia of Jewish Communities.* Jerusalem, 1988. (In Hebrew.)

ESTHER HAGAR

KÁLLAY, MIKLÓS (1887–1967), Hungarian statesman. The scion of an ancient family of the nobility, Kállay held leading positions in various governments. He succeeded László Bárdossy as prime minister on March 9, 1942, and held this position until March 19, 1944, when the Germans occupied the country. A number of anti-Jewish measures were adopted during Kállay's tenure; for example, tens of thousands of Jewish men in the Hungarian labor service system (MUNKASZOLGÁLAT) were assigned to the Ukrainian front, where many of them were subsequently killed. Yet he successfully resisted the Third Reich's pressures on Hungary to resolve its "Jewish problem." After Italy's attempt to break away from the Germans in 1943, he tried to find an honorable way out of the war, and this induced the Germans to occupy Hungary. Kállay found haven in the Turkish legation, but he was compelled to leave his refuge following the fascist ARROW CROSS PARTY coup of October 15, 1944. He was subsequently deported to MAUTHAUSEN. After the liberation of the camp, Kállay went to Rome, and in 1951 he settled in New York. In 1954 he wrote *Hungarian Premier: A Personal Account of a Nation's Struggle in the Second World War*, which tells of his term of office.

Miklós Kallay (right) with Joachim von Ribbentrop. [National Archives]

BIBLIOGRAPHY

Braham, R. L. *The Politics of Genocide*. New York, 1980.

Katzburg, N. *Hungary and the Jews: Policy and Legislation, 1920–1943*. Ramat Gan, Israel, 1981.

Macartney, C. A. *October Fifteenth: A History of Hungary, 1929–1945*. New York, 1957.

RANDOLPH L. BRAHAM

KALMANOWITZ, ABRAHAM (1891–1964), rabbi of Tiktin, Poland. Kalmanowitz played a leading role in the rescue from Vilna to Shanghai of the Mir yeshiva (rabbinical academy) and in the activities of the VA'AD HA-HATSALA of the Orthodox rabbis in the United States. After the outbreak of World War II he escaped to Vilna, and from there he went to the United States in early 1940. Immediately upon his arrival in America, he assumed a leadership role in the Va'ad ha-Hatsala and traveled to numerous cities to raise funds for its work. After the United States entered World War II, he maintained contact with and sent relief to the hundreds of rabbis and yeshiva students stranded in Shanghai, by means of clearance arrangements via Uruguay and Argentina. Kalmanowitz was recognized for his expertise in influencing government officials and political leaders. He was also known for the fact that on several occasions he publicly rode vehicles on the Sabbath to stress the urgency of the predicament of European Jewry under Nazi rule.

BIBLIOGRAPHY

Kranzler, D. *Thy Brother's Blood*. Brooklyn, N.Y., 1987.

Zuroff, E. "Rescue Priority and Fund Raising as Issues during the Holocaust: A Case Study of the Relations between the Vaad Ha-Hatzala and the Joint, 1939–1941." *American Jewish History* 68/3 (1979): 305–326.

Zuroff, E. "Rescue via the Far East: Attempt to Save Polish Rabbis and Yeshivah Students, 1939–1941." *Simon Wiesenthal Center Annual* 1 (1984): 153–184.

EFRAIM ZUROFF

KALTENBRUNNER, ERNST (1903–1946), Nazi politician. Born in Ried im Innkreis (Upper Austria), Kaltenbrunner attended school in Linz. After studying chemistry and law in Prague and elsewhere, he practiced as a lawyer. He joined the National Socialist party and the SS in 1932. In 1934 and 1935, Kaltenbrunner was imprisoned in Austria on a charge of high treason. He headed the SS in that country from 1935 until 1938.

After the ANSCHLUSS, Kaltenbrunner, now an SS-*Gruppenführer*, was promoted to the post of under secretary of state for public security in the Ostmark (as Austria was renamed by the Nazis). He remained there until 1941, and at the same time was a member of the Reichstag. Together with Gauleiter Josef Bürckel, Kaltenbrunner was responsible for the ZENTRALSTELLE FÜR JÜDISCHE AUSWANDERUNG (Central Office for Jewish Emigration) in Vienna, headed by Adolf EICHMANN. Up until Eichmann's transfer to Prague in April 1939, 150,000 Jews emigrated from Austria. After the attempt on Reinhard HEYDRICH's life on May 27, 1942, Kaltenbrunner was appointed head of the REICHSSICHERHEITSHAUPTAMT (Reich Security Main Office; RSHA). Heydrich died on June 4, and Kaltenbrunner was formally named his successor as

Heinrich Himmler visiting the Mauthausen concentration camp in April 1941. From left: Himmler; Sturmbannführer Franz Ziereis (1905–1945), commandant of Mauthausen from August 1939 to May 1945, when the camp was liberated; and SS-Gruppenführer Ernst Kaltenbrunner.

chief of the Sicherheitspolizei and the SD (Sicherheitsdienst; Security Service) on January 30, 1943.

In addition to Heinrich HIMMLER, Kaltenbrunner was one of the main initiators of AKTION REINHARD and bore much of the responsibility for the implementation of the "FINAL SOLUTION" from 1942 to 1945, although few contemporary documents record his activities in this connection. The same holds true for his participation in the EUTHANASIA PROGRAM. This may be partly attributed to Himmler's growing tendency to reserve the credit for himself. There exists evidence, however, of Kaltenbrunner's role as instigator of the deportation from THERESIENSTADT in the spring of 1943 of Jews unfit for work, and of Bulgarian Jews in the summer of 1943. In 1945 Kaltenbrunner took as his personal adjutant an SS officer who in 1941 had been responsible for the murder of at least sixty thousand Jewish men, women, and children in Lithuania.

Because of Kaltenbrunner's personal reserve, many of his department heads appeared to be more important than they actually were in the power structure of the RSHA. This may have been connected with Kaltenbrunner's belief that, in contrast to many of his subordinates, he had a very real chance to survive after the end of the war. Even at Nuremberg (see NUREMBERG TRIAL), he attempted to play the part of someone who "had absolutely no idea." Nevertheless, on October 9, 1946, the International Military Tribunal sentenced him to death by hanging, and the sentence was carried out on October 16.

The so-called Kaltenbrunner reports are a collection of reports on the Gestapo interrogations conducted after the attempt on Hitler's life of July 20, 1944. They were drawn up for Martin BORMANN, on Kaltenbrunner's orders, by an ad hoc RSHA unit headed by SS-Obersturmbannführer Walter von Kielpinski. According to the historian Hans-Adolf Jacobsen, they were the result of "thousands of investigations" carried out by some four hundred RSHA officials operating in eleven groups—the Sonderkommandos 20 Juli—who took part in suppressing the attempted coup.

BIBLIOGRAPHY

Black, P. R. *Ernst Kaltenbrunner: Ideological Soldier of the Third Reich*. Princeton, 1984.

Krausnick, H., and H. Wilhelm. *Die Truppe des Weltanschauungskrieges: Die Einsatzgruppen der Sicherheitspolizei und des SD, 1938–1942*. Stuttgart, 1981.

HANS-HEINRICH WILHELM

KAMENETS-PODOLSKI, city in the Ukrainian SSR where mass killings of Jews, mostly from HUNGARY, took place in August 1941. Shortly after Hungary declared war on the Soviet Union, on June 27, 1941, a plan was devised by Ödön Martinides and Árkád Kiss, two leading officers of the National Central Alien Control Office (Külföldieket Ellenórzó Országos Kozponti Hatosag; KEOKH), the agency with jurisdiction over foreign nationals living in Hungary, to "resettle" the Polish and Russian Jews in the Hungarian-administered part of "liberated" Galicia. Under Decree No. 192/1941, adopted on July 12, and a subsequent secret directive of the KEOKH, a drive was begun to deport "the recently infiltrated Polish and Russian Jews in the largest possible number and as quickly as possible." Among the "alien" Jews rounded up that month were also a considerable number of Hungarian Jews who could not prove

Bodies of Jews massacred at Kamenets-Podolski.

their citizenship simply because their papers were not immediately available. Other Hungarian Jews were merely caught up in the maelstrom. In the TRANSCARPATHIAN UKRAINE, an area inhabited by Orthodox and Hasidic Jews, many Jewish communities were uprooted in toto. Since the Jews were rounded up at great speed, usually under cover of darkness, very few of them could take along adequate provisions.

The "alien" Jews were packed into freight cars and taken to Körösmezö, near the Polish border. From there, they were transferred across the border at the rate of about 1,000 a day. By August 10, approximately 14,000 Jews had been handed over to the SS. An additional 4,000 were transferred by the end of the month, when the operation was completed. From Körösmezö the Jews were first taken to KOLOMYIA, and then marched in columns of 300 to 400 to Kamenets-Podolski. Their fate was decided on August 25 at a conference held at the Vinnitsa headquarters of the *General-quartiermeister-OKH*, where SS-Obergruppenführer Friedrich Jeckeln assured the conferees that he would complete the liquidation of the Jews by September 1, 1941. The *Aktion* took place on August 27 and 28 near the city and claimed (according to Jeckeln's Operational Report USSR No. 80) 23,600 Jewish lives— the first five-figure massacre in the Nazis' "FINAL SOLUTION" program. Of these, 14,000 to 18,000 Jews were from Hungary; the remainder were local.

BIBLIOGRAPHY

Braham, R. L. "The Kamenets Podolsk and Delvidek Massacres: Prelude to the Holocaust in Hungary." *Yad Vashem Studies* 9 (1973): 133–156.

RANDOLPH L. BRAHAM

KAMINSKI BRIGADE. *See* Russkaya Osvoboditelnaya Armiya.

KAPLAN, CHAIM AARON (1880–1942), author of a WARSAW ghetto diary. Born in a village near Baranovichi, Belorussia, Kaplan became the principal of a Hebrew school in Warsaw. He kept a detailed personal diary (starting apparently in 1933) written in Hebrew, which is one of the rare original documents of its kind that has survived the Nazi era. It describes the decline of Jewish Warsaw and the Holocaust period in general. The diary, as Kaplan put it, became "my soul brother, my colleague and companion." Until the beginning of World War II it was a private personal account; but when the war broke out the diary changed its character, and in addition to his own experiences and troubles, Kaplan recorded the story of the Jews of Warsaw, his own speculations on future developments, the behavior and policies of the Germans as they unfolded before his eyes, and his opinions about the Poles.

Kaplan had a penetrating mind and a sharp eye, and his diary faithfully reflects the events of most of the ghetto's existence. The war diary begins on September 1, 1939, and ends on August 4, 1942, the day when the mass deportation was at its height. Kaplan evidently made his final entry a day or two before his own deportation to TREBLINKA. "When my end comes—what will happen to the diary?" reads the last sentence.

Kaplan's war diary was discovered almost intact after the war on a farm outside Warsaw, preserved in a kerosene can; the notebooks were legible and in good condition. The diary was published in Hebrew (*Megilat Yisurin, Yoman Geto Varsha—September 1, 1939–August 4, 1942*, with introduction and notes by A. I. Katsh and N. Blumental; Tel Aviv and Jerusalem, 1966) and in two English editions. The second contains all the pages of the diary that were recovered (*The Warsaw Diary of Chaim A. Kaplan*, translated and edited by A. I. Katsh; New York, 1965, 1973).

BIBLIOGRAPHY

Gutman, Y. *The Jews of Warsaw, 1939–1943: Ghetto, Underground, Revolt.* Bloomington, 1982.

ISRAEL GUTMAN

KAPLAN, JOSEF (1913–1942), a leader of the WARSAW Jewish underground and a founder of the ŻYDOWSKA ORGANIZACJA BOJOWA (Jewish Fighting Organization; ŻOB). Kaplan was

Josef Kaplan.

born in Kalisz, in western Poland, into a poor family and a strict religious atmosphere. Early in his youth he was drawn to secular education and culture and joined the Ha-Shomer ha-Tsa'ir Zionist youth movement in the town. In the late 1930s he was one of the leaders of that movement in Poland. During the first few days of World War II, in September 1939, Kaplan joined the flood of refugees to the east, and took charge of the illegal border-crossing point at Lida on the Polish-Lithuanian border. At the beginning of 1940 he returned to Nazi-occupied Poland from Vilna (which in the meantime had been incorporated into Lithuania), in order to take charge of the underground Ha-Shomer ha-Tsa'ir movement. From that moment on, Kaplan devoted all his time to the underground. He consolidated the movement's structure in the various ghettos and ensured the continuation of agricultural training even on a clandestine basis; he published and distributed underground newspapers, and was his movement's representative in the overall Jewish underground organizations and institutions.

In the spring of 1942, Kaplan embarked upon the formation of a Jewish body that would fight against the Nazis. He took part in the activities of the Antifascist Bloc in Warsaw and, in July of that year, in establishing the ŻOB in Warsaw. On September 3, 1942, in the midst of the mass deportation of Jews from Warsaw, the Nazis caught Kaplan in the act of preparing forged documents for a group of fighters who were about to join the partisans, and he was killed.

Kaplan kept a diary, but it was not preserved. Irena ADAMOWICZ, who knew him well, described him in the following terms: "The activist who had been likable but quite average turned into a great man, very strong . . . and very calm. He was an excellent organizer and an ideal underground operator, painstaking and resourceful in all humdrum day-to-day affairs, and with a clear and inspiring approach to matters of principle, of life and death."

BIBLIOGRAPHY

Gutman, Y. *The Jews of Warsaw, 1939–1943: Ghetto, Underground, Revolt.* Bloomington, 1982.
Gutman, Y. *The Revolt of the Besieged: Mordehai Anilevitch and the Uprising of the Warsaw Ghetto.* Merhavia, Israel, 1963. (In Hebrew.)

ISRAEL GUTMAN

KAPLINSKI, HIRSCH (Zvi; 1910–1942), underground leader and partisan commander. Born in DIATLOVO (Zhetl), in the NOVOGRUDOK district of Poland, Kaplinski was the secretary of the local Tarbut (Zionist-oriented) school and took an active part in Zionist and Jewish public life in the town. After World War II broke out, he served as a sergeant in the Polish army and then joined the underground in the Diatlovo ghetto. His parents, wife, and son were killed in the second *Aktion,* on August 5, 1942; together with comrades Kaplinski escaped from the ghetto to the Lipiczany Forest.

Kaplinski was a founder and commander of the Jewish partisan battalion known as the "Kaplinski Battalion." Consisting of 120 men, it was later incorporated in the Borba (Struggle) unit, as a company. The battalion took punitive action against peasants who had collaborated with the Nazis, fought the German militia in Mirovshchina, Zykovshchina, Nakryshki, and Mutsevichi, blew up bridges, and collected captured arms (in the Ruda-Jaworska battle).

During the German attack on the Lipiczany Forest, on December 10, 1942, Kaplinski was ambushed while on his way to division headquarters, and in the course of the fight was severely wounded. Apparently, the Russian partisans whom Kaplinski asked for help disarmed and killed him.

BIBLIOGRAPHY

Kahanovich, M. *The War of the Jewish Partisans in Eastern Europe.* Tel Aviv, 1954. (In Hebrew.)
Kaplinski, B. *Pinkas Zetel [Zetel Record]; A Memorial to the Jewish Community of Zetel.* Tel Aviv, 1957. (In Hebrew.)

SHALOM CHOLAWSKI

KAPO (from Ital. *capo,* "chief," "boss"), term used in the Nazi CONCENTRATION CAMPS for an inmate appointed by the SS men in charge to head a *Kommando* (work gang) made up of other prisoners. The term "Kapo" is sometimes also used for any prisoner who was given an assignment and collaborated with the Nazis, and, beyond that, for any Nazi collaborator. In the German-occupied countries and in the camps, however, only the "bosses" of prisoner work gangs were referred to as "Kapos."

Generally, the Kapo was not a skilled worker, and his job was to escort the prisoners to their place of work and ensure that they performed their tasks properly and met the quotas. But work as such was not the major objective in the concentration camps; the real purpose was to break the prisoners in mind and spirit. The Kapo, therefore, became the instrument by which a regime of humiliation and sheer physical cruelty was imposed upon the prison population. At the workplaces, the work gangs were split up into smaller groups, each headed by a *Vorarbeiter* (foreman) responsible to the Kapo.

In 1942 there was a slight improvement in the regime prevailing in the camps, because the Germans became interested in exploiting the prisoners' productive capacity, which meant that they had to treat them better. In many instances, the Kapos—

especially those who were political prisoners in the camps—pretended to be strict with the prisoners, when in fact they tried to handle them as moderately as possible. At all times a deep gulf divided the rank-and-file prisoner from the Kapo and other supervisors, affecting the human relationship between them and the conditions under which they lived. The Kapos' clothing was relatively warm, they had enough to eat, and they enjoyed their own reserved section in the prison barrack (the "block"), whereas such amenities were privileges unthinkable for the regular prisoners. In many instances Kapos mistreated prisoners in a criminal fashion and were put on trial after the war.

BIBLIOGRAPHY

Cohen, E. A. *Human Behavior in the Concentration Camp.* New York, 1953.

Col. Herbert Kappler of the German army, in custody. Kappler carried out the massacre of Italian civilians at the Ardeatine Caves near Rome on March 24, 1944. [National Archives]

Glicksman, W. "Social Differentiation in the German Concentration Camps." *YIVO Annual* 8 (1953): 123–150.
Kogon, E. *The Theory and Practice of Hell: The German Concentration Camps and the System behind Them.* New York, 1950.

ISRAEL GUTMAN

KAPOSVÁR, capital of Somogy county, in southwestern Hungary. In 1941, it had a Jewish population of 2,346, representing 7.1 percent of the total. The community was headed by Ödön Antl, who also served as the chairman of the sixteen-member JUDENRAT (Jewish Council) that was established after the Jews were ordered into a ghetto in May 1944. The ghetto was located in and around Berzsenyi and Kanizsai streets, the central thoroughfares of the community. Toward the end of June, the ghetto population was transferred to an artillery barracks near the railway lines. The barracks, which served as the main entrainment center, already "housed" the slightly more than 2,500 Jews brought in from the smaller towns and rural communities in Somogy county. The liquidation of the ghetto took place when 5,159 Jews were deported to AUSCHWITZ, on July 4, 1944. In 1946, Kaposvár still had 439 Jews, representing 1.3 percent of the population. Many of them were survivors who had moved into the city from neighboring rural communities.

RANDOLPH L. BRAHAM

KAPPLER, HERBERT (1907–1978), official in the Nazi SD (Sicherheitsdienst; Security Service). When he was sent to ROME in 1939, Kappler was an SS-*Obersturmbannführer.* As head of the SD in Rome, he cooperated closely with the Italian Fascist police. In 1944 he became head of the Gestapo in Rome.

Kappler began to play a more significant role after September 8, 1943, when the Germans took over the control of Rome. That month he helped organize the rescue of Benito MUSSOLINI by SS commandos. He planned and executed the deportation of about ten thousand Jews of Rome after the extortion of their gold. During the night of October 15–

16, 1943, the *Aktion* started, and 1,259 Italian Jews were arrested. On October 18, 1,007 were sent to AUSCHWITZ; only about 10 came back alive.

On March 23, 1944, Italian partisans killed thirty-three Germans with a bomb on Via Rasella in Rome. An order was received from Adolf Hitler to kill 10 Italians for each German soldier. Kappler, together with Pietro Caruso, the chief of the Italian police, was responsible for selecting the victims. People arrested on the spot, political prisoners, and Jews were sent to the Ardeatine Caves near Rome, shot in the neck in small groups, and buried under the sand; the entrances were subsequently sealed by exploding charges. Altogether, 335 Italians were killed at the Ardeatine Caves, among them seventy-eight Jews.

After the war Kappler was held by the British and then handed over to Italian authorities in 1947. He was put on trial before an Italian military tribunal and given a life sentence. In 1977, he fell ill and was taken to a hospital in Rome, from which he managed to escape. He died a year later in his own home in Germany.

BIBLIOGRAPHY

Michaelis, M. *Mussolini and the Jews: German-Italian Relations and the Jewish Question in Italy, 1922–1945.* Oxford, 1978.

Piscitelli, E. *Storia della resistanza romana.* Bari, 1965.

Zuccotti, S. *The Italians and the Holocaust: Persecution, Rescue, and Survival.* New York, 1987.

SERGIO I. MINERBI

KARAITES. The Karaites were members of a Jewish sect that emerged in the eighth century in Babylon, and spread from there to the countries of the Middle East. In the thirteenth and fourteenth centuries Karaites migrated to the Crimean peninsula. The Lithuanian prince Vytautus (Witold) the Great (r. 1386–1430) moved hundreds of Karaites from the Crimea to the north and settled them in Troki, Lutsk, and Galich (Pol., Halicz). From the early nineteenth century Karaites in Russia demanded equal rights, and several of their scholars (such as Abraham Firkovich) claimed that their origins were not Jewish. In the second half of the nineteenth century this claim was accepted; the Karaites were accorded the same rights as the Russians, and were integrated into society, serving in the tsar's army and in government service. In the Civil War that followed World War I, Karaite officers fought in the White Army against the Bolsheviks. After the Bolshevik victory they emigrated to the West, settling in Warsaw, in Berlin, in France, and in Italy.

Between the two world wars, 9,000 Karaites lived in the Soviet Union, mostly in the Crimea (6,500). In eastern Poland there were Karaites in Troki (300), Vilna (200), Lutsk (50), and Galich (40 families). A few families lived in Ponevezh in Lithuania, in Riga in Latvia, in Warsaw and its vicinity, in Berlin (18), in France (250), and in Italy (a few score).

The Nazis first came up against the problem of the Karaites when they published the regulations for enforcement of the NUREMBERG LAWS. The heads of the small Karaite community in Berlin asked the authorities to exempt them from the regulations; on the basis of their legal status in tsarist Russia, they claimed that they were not of Jewish origin. After examination of the claim, on January 5, 1939, the Reichsstelle für Sippenforschung (Reich Agency for Investigation of Families) determined that the Karaite sect should not be considered part of the Jewish religious community with regard to those regulations, and that the racial classification of the Karaites should be decided not according to their attachment to a specific people, but according to their personal genealogy. That document became an edict, and from then on it served the Nazi authorities as the basis for dealing with the Karaites.

After the outbreak of World War II the Germans again encountered Karaites, first in occupied France, and then in occupied areas of the Soviet Union. The COMMISSARIAT GÉNÉRAL AUX QUESTIONS JUIVES (General Office for Jewish Affairs) in Vichy France required Karaites to be registered as Jews. But on the basis of memoranda and opinions of the heads of the Orthodox church there, the Karaites attempted to prove that they were not of Jewish origin. The journal of the UNION GÉNÉRALE

DES ISRAÉLITES DE FRANCE (General Council of French Jews) claimed that the Karaites were Jews, but eventually instructions arrived from Berlin to accept the Karaites' position.

In the USSR the first Germans to come across the Karaites were the EINSATZGRUPPEN. Although at that time the origins of this sect were not clear to the Nazis, the Einsatzgruppen attacked them in several localities, for instance in Kiev, where more than two hundred Karaites died at BABI YAR. When approaching the Crimea, the Einsatzgruppen sought clarification from Berlin, and received instructions not to harm the Karaites, since they were not of Jewish origin.

When members of the Nazi civilian government established their authority in the occupied areas of the USSR, they also met the Karaites. The heads of the Generalkommissariat of Lithuania encountered Karaites in Troki and in Vilna, among them the chief religious authority of the Karaites, Seraya Shapshal. The Generalkommissariat wrote to the REICHSKOMMISSARIAT OSTLAND, which passed on the inquiry to the Ministry for the Occupied Territories in the East, located in Berlin. An exchange of letters, opinions, and position papers ensued, containing frequent references to the edict of the Reich Agency for Investigation of Families. In those documents it was again decided that the Karaites were of Turkish-Mongolian extraction, and had adopted the Jewish religion from missionaries in the Kuzari kingdom in the eighth and ninth centuries. In the late summer of 1942 the Nazis addressed separate inquiries to Jewish scholars in three ghettos: Professor Meir Balaban and Dr. Ignacy SCHIPER in Warsaw, Selig Hirsh Kalmanowitz in Vilna, and Dr. Leib Landau and Dr. Yaakov Schall in Lvov. Wishing to save the Karaites from the fate of the Jews, the scholars expressed the opinion that the Karaites were not of Jewish extraction.

In May 1943 the Ministry for the Occupied Territories in the East finally determined that the Karaites were not part of the Jewish religious community, and that their origin was Turkish-Tatar-Mongolian. The determination of origin had been made, it was claimed, on the basis of racial examinations carried out among different groups of Karaites. The ministry demanded that the Karaites be treated like Turks and Tatars, in order not to anger those peoples. Politically, it was hoped that decent treatment of the Karaites would gain the sympathy of the Turks and Tatars, which the Germans needed at that time, since they were in general retreat from the USSR following the fall of STALINGRAD and the withdrawal from the Caucasian front. The ministry decision saved the Karaites from the fate of their Jewish brethren—annihilation in the framework of the "FINAL SOLUTION" to the Jewish problem.

In the second half of 1944 the problem of the Karaites again arose, when the heads of the SS realized that about five hundred to six hundred of the sect were serving in the Waffen-SS and the Tatar division of the German army. These must have been Karaites who served in the Crimea, in local government and police, and in various auxiliary army units, and who were retreating to the west. Their families settled in the vicinity of Vienna, and there, together with the Crimean Tatars, they created the Association of Tatars and Karaites from Crimea, an organization with social objectives.

The fact that Karaites were serving in the army disturbed SS circles, and correspondence began on this matter between the heads of Heinrich HIMMLER's personal staff and the head office of the SS responsible for the Waffen-SS. Again the question of the Karaites' religion and origin was raised, and the decision of the Ministry for the Occupied Territories in the East was again accepted. The political reasoning was also reendorsed: the Karaites must not be harmed because of their blood relatives, the Turks and the Tatars. The Jewish religion of the Karaites annoyed the SS circles, and it was therefore recommended not to publicize Karaite activity in the army. On December 7, 1944, Himmler approved these conclusions and recommendations, and the Karaites continued to serve in the German army until its surrender in early May 1945.

The relationship of the Karaites to the "Rabbanite" (non-Karaite) Jews is not easy to determine, in view of the dearth of evidence. Certainly, it was not uniform. In Lutsk the Karaites cooperated in the cruel treatment of the local Jews, and in Vilna and Troki they furnished precise lists of the members of their community, thereby frustrating an attempt to save hundreds of "Rabbanite" Jews who had obtained forged Karaite certificates. Those Jews were caught and killed. In other localities the Karaites helped the Jews, even providing original certificates and saving individual Jews.

After the war the number of Karaites in the USSR decreased. In 1959 there were 5,727 Karaites, mostly in the Crimea, and a minority in Lithuania (Troki, Vilna) and in the western Ukraine (Lutsk, Galich). In Poland there were about 600 Karaites in Warsaw, Szczecin (Ger., Stettin), and Silesia. A few hundred lived in Germany, France, and Italy, and several hundred in the United States. The largest community of Karaites (several thousand) is in Israel, and is of Egyptian origin.

BIBLIOGRAPHY

Friedman, P. "The Karaites under Nazi Rule." In *On the Track of Tyranny: Essays Presented by the Wiener Library to Leonard G. Montefiore, O.B.E., on the Occasion of His Seventieth Birthday*, edited by M. Beloff, pp. 97–123. London, 1960.

Green, W. P. "The Nazi Racial Policy Towards the Karaites." *Soviet Jewish Affairs* 8/2 (1978): 36–44.

Spector, S. "The Karaites in Nazi-Occupied Europe as Reflected in German Documents." *Pe'amim* 29 (1986): 90–108. (In Hebrew.)

SHMUEL SPECTOR

KARSKI, JAN (real surname, Kozielewski; b. 1914), Polish non-Jew who brought information on the Holocaust to the West. Born in Łódź, Karski completed his studies in demography at Lvov University in 1935 and worked in the Polish Foreign Office. After the occupation of Poland in September 1939, he joined the Polish underground and was a courier for the POLISH GOVERNMENT-IN-EXILE.

In 1942 Karski was sent on a mission to London, the headquarters of the government-in-exile, to transmit a report on the situation in occupied Poland, and in particular on the situation of the Jewish population there. To be able to give authentic testimony, Karski twice visited the WARSAW ghetto, where he met with two Jewish leaders, Menahem Kirschenbaum of the General Zionists and Leon FEINER of the BUND. They asked him to inform world leaders of the desperate situation of Polish Jewry.

In November 1942 Karski arrived in London, transmitted the report to the Polish government, and met with Winston CHURCHILL and other statesmen, journalists, and public figures. Basing itself on Karski's report, the Polish government-in-exile called on the Allied governments in December of that year to take steps that would compel Germany to halt the massacres of the Jews.

Following this mission, Karski left London for the United States. There he met with President Franklin D. ROOSEVELT and other statesmen, and tried to arouse public opinion against the massacres being carried out by the Germans. After the war, he remained in the United States.

Karski wrote a book about his experiences, *The Story of a Secret State* (1944). In 1982 he was awarded the title of "RIGHTEOUS AMONG THE NATIONS" by YAD VASHEM.

BIBLIOGRAPHY

Gilbert, M. *Auschwitz and the Allies*. New York, 1981.

Laqueur, W. *The Terrible Secret*. London, 1980.

ELISHEVA SHAUL

KASSA. *See* Košice.

KASZTNER, REZSŐ (Rudolf or Israel; 1906–1957), journalist, lawyer, and Zionist leader. Kasztner was a Labor Zionist activist, first in his hometown of Cluj and then, after the annexation of Transylvania by HUNGARY in 1940, in Budapest. In early 1943 he became the vice chairman, in fact the guiding spirit, of the RELIEF AND RESCUE COMMITTEE OF BUDAPEST of the Zionist movement, under Ottó KOMOLY. The committee maintained contact with the Slovak PRACOVNÁ SKUPINA (Working Group), which included Gisi FLEISCHMANN and Rabbi Michael Dov WEISSMANDEL; through it with Poland; and with a group of Palestinian emissaries in Istanbul, among whose founding members were Haim Barlas, Menachem Bader, and Venja Pomerantz.

The committee was well aware of the Holocaust in Poland and elsewhere, and tried to spread information about it, which was disbelieved in spite of the accounts of Polish Jewish refugees arriving in Hungary after 1942. In 1943 the committee was instrumental (through the work of Joel BRAND) in smuggling refugees from Poland and Slovakia into Hungary. Despite internal dissensions, the committee tried to prepare for the eventuality of German occupation, even attempting to organize armed resistance. Such resistance, however, proved illusory in Hungary, owing to pervasive anti-Jewish hostility on the part of the population, the lack of any local anti-German resistance, and the fact that most young Jewish men were compelled to serve in the labor service system (see MUNKASZOL-GÁLAT) under Hungarian army control.

When the Germans occupied Hungary in March 1944, the committee made contact with the SS group in charge of the future extermination program under Adolf EICHMANN. Similar contacts had led to ransom negotiations in Slovakia, where the Jewish negotiators believed they had resulted in the rescue of the remnant of Slovak Jewry and had led to the negotiations of the EUROPA PLAN. Kasztner believed that in Hungary, the only avenue for rescue was negotiation with the Germans. Consequently, sums of money were paid to the SS, and Joel Brand was sent to Istanbul in May to negotiate the release of large numbers of Jews in return for trucks and other materials (the operation was called "Blood for Goods"). Brand was accompanied by Andor (Bandi) Grosz, a quadruple agent who served German, Hungarian, and other masters.

Historians differ as to the seriousness of the proposal brought by Brand, but there is no doubt that it was originally formulated by Heinrich HIMMLER himself. When Brand was detained by the British and could not return as promised, his wife, Hansi, and Kasztner took over direct negotiations with Eichmann. At the end of June, a train with 1,684 Jews chosen by a committee headed by Komoly and Kasztner left Hungary, ostensibly for Spain or Switzerland; it was, however, directed to the BERGEN-BELSEN camp, where these Jews were interned. On the train were Kasztner's family and friends from Cluj, but in the main the group consisted of representatives from all political and religious factions, as well as wealthy people who had paid large sums subsidizing the others. Kasztner's idea was that this exodus would serve as a precedent for undoing the murder program, and that more trains would follow. However, none did.

In July an SS officer, Kurt BECHER, received Himmler's permission to negotiate with Kasztner. As a result, Brand's negotiations were continued with the JOINT DISTRIBUTION COMMITTEE representative in Switzerland, Saly MAYER, on the Swiss border. The first meeting, on August 21, 1944, led to Himmler's order to refrain from deporting the Jews of Budapest, and 318 Jews in Bergen-Belsen from the "Kasztner train" were released to Switzerland. In December of that year the remainder of the Bergen-Belsen internees were also sent to safety, and Becher became obligated to the Jews by his contacts with Kasztner. At Kasztner's prodding, he intervened in favor of the Budapest Jews. Becher appears to have acted from a variety of motives, but the outcome was an increase in Himmler's willingness to make some lifesaving gestures here and there, against the background of the approaching German defeat. The Jewish negotiators utilized the Germans' illusion that there might exist a possibility for negotiating with the West for a separate peace.

After the war, Kasztner was called to Nuremberg (see NUREMBERG TRIAL) to help the investigators in their work with Nazi criminals. His written testimony in favor of Becher undoubtedly helped to save the latter from a closer investigation into less savory aspects of his wartime career. (Becher had served in some notorious SS units in the Russian campaign in 1941 and 1942. He had confiscated the Manfred Weiss industrial concern, resulting in a huge sum paid to the SS, in return for allowing some members of the Weiss-Chorin family to escape to Lisbon.) Kasztner also testified in favor of other Nazis, such as SS-Obergruppenführer Hans Jüttner, chief of the SS-Führungshauptamt (SS

Jews from the "Kasztner train" arriving in Switzerland (1944). [Weiss family]

Operational Main Office), who had made the rather meaningless gesture of disapproving of the death march from Budapest in November 1944. Kasztner's line seems to have been one of *noblesse oblige*: once the war was over, any Nazi who had made a gesture or taken action in favor of Jews should be recognized for it.

In 1954, Kasztner brought a suit against one Malkiel Grünwald, who had accused him of being a traitor and causing the deaths of many Jews. The trial, in Israel, became instead a trial of Kasztner himself. Shmuel Tamir, Grünwald's attorney, steered the trial in the direction of an indictment of the Mapai Labor party, which had placed Kasztner on its list of candidates for the Knesset elections. The judge, Benjamin Halevi, accepted most of Tamir's arguments and summed up the court's opinion of Kasztner by accusing him of having "sold his soul to the devil." This referred both to the negotiations with the Nazis and to the train, which was seen as an avenue of rescue for Kasztner's relatives and friends and a German sop to Kasztner in return for his refraining from warning Hungarian Jewry of the impending disaster. The Israeli Supreme Court was debating Kasztner's appeal when he was murdered by na-

tionalist extremists who took Halevi's words literally. In a final verdict, the court exonerated Kasztner from all accusations except the charge that he had helped Nazis to escape from justice.

Given the conditions in Hungary at the time, negotiations with the Nazis were in actuality the only way in which Jews might have been saved. The train could just as well have arrived in Auschwitz, and perhaps by

Rezső Kasztner (left) and Ottó Komoly (1944). [Peretz Revesz]

putting his relatives on it, Kasztner persuaded many others to board it; in any case, he saw this as a breakthrough for future rescues. In the winter of 1944–1945, when he was already safe in Switzerland, Kasztner voluntarily returned to Germany, and with Becher went to Berlin to try and save the Jewish remnants in the concentration camps. His intervention was possibly instrumental in securing the surrender of Bergen-Belsen to the British without the bloodbath that could have taken place there.

The most difficult problem is the charge that he did not warn Hungarian Jewry. Kasztner was totally unknown, was not in control of the Hungarian Jewish Council (Zsidó Tanács), and was in no position to warn anyone. In Cluj, where he was known, a rescue committee composed of important local citizens failed to convince all but a very few to escape for their lives to neighboring Romania, a mere ten miles away. Kasztner's tragic figure has been the subject of plays and stories, and continues to engender heated controversy.

BIBLIOGRAPHY

Bauer, Y. *American Jewry and the Holocaust: The American Jewish Joint Distribution Committee, 1939–1945.* Detroit, 1981.

Bauer, Y. *The Holocaust in Historical Perspective.* Seattle, 1978.

Biss, A. *A Million Jews to Save: Check to the Final Solution.* Cranbury, N.J., 1975.

Kasztner, R., ed. *Der Bericht des jüdisches Rettungskomitees aus Budapest, 1942–1945.* Budapest, 1946.

                    YEHUDA BAUER

KATYN, town near Smolensk, in the USSR, in the vicinity of which Polish officers were murdered in large numbers. According to data in the possession of the POLISH GOVERNMENT-IN-EXILE, at the beginning of 1940 the Soviet Union held as many as 15,000 Polish prisoners of war, of whom 8,300 were officers. They had been taken prisoner by the Red Army in the second half of September 1939 and were interned in three camps: at Kozelsk, Starobelsk, and Ostashkov. Toward the end of 1940 there were reports that the three camps had

KATYN

been disbanded. Repeated requests for information on the fate of the prisoners made by the Polish government-in-exile to the Soviet Union in 1941 and 1942 were of no avail.

On April 13, 1943, the Germans announced that mass graves had been discovered in the Katyn forest, in their area of occupation, containing the bodies of thousands of Polish officers who had been shot in the head from behind. The Germans charged the Soviet authorities with murder and appointed a multinational medical commission to probe the matter. In May 1943, the commission reported that the graves contained the bodies of 4,143 officers, of whom 2,914 were identified by documents in their uniforms. It was the commission's opinion that the men had been shot to death in the spring of 1940. The Soviet authorities flatly rejected these charges made by a German-appointed commission; they claimed that the murder had been the work of Germans when they had occupied the area in July 1941.

In mid-April of 1943, when the Polish government-in-exile demanded that an investigation of the Katyn killings be made by the

International Red Cross, the Soviet Union reacted by severing relations with the government-in-exile, on April 25. This step was to have far-reaching effects on relations between the Soviet Union and Poland. In November of that year, several months after the Red Army had liberated the area, the Soviet Union appointed an inquiry commission of its own, which charged that the Katyn murders had been committed by the Germans. A United States congressional inquiry in the early 1950s concluded that the NKVD (Soviet secret police) was responsible, and most Western historians now believe that the massacre was ordered by the Soviet authorities. On March 8, 1989, the Polish government officially accused the NKVD of perpetrating the massacre.

BIBLIOGRAPHY

Fitzgibbon, L. *Katyn: A Crime without Parallel.* New York, 1971.
Mackiewicz, J. *The Katyn Wood Murders.* London, 1951.

SHMUEL KRAKOWSKI

KATZENELSON, ITZHAK (1886–1944), poet, playwright, and educator. Katzenelson was born in Korelichi, in the district of Minsk, Russia, where his father was a writer and teacher. In 1886 the family moved to Łódź. Katzenelson began writing poetry at an early age, and throughout his life he wrote in both Yiddish and Hebrew. His first book of Hebrew poems, *Dimdumim* (Twilight), appeared in 1910; earlier, in 1908, he had begun to write comedies in Yiddish, which he himself translated into Hebrew. Several of his Yiddish plays were performed in Łódź even before World War I. In 1912 he founded a theater, Ha-Bimah ha-Ivrit (The Hebrew Stage), in Łódź and took it on tours of cities in Poland and Lithuania. Before World War I Katzenelson undertook the creation of a network of Hebrew schools in Łódź, from kindergarten to high school, which functioned until 1939. He was the author of textbooks, biblical plays, and children's books. Beginning in 1930 he belonged to the Dror movement in Łódź and to the He-Haluts movement, the latter operating a training kibbutz (Kibbutz Hakhsharah) in Łódź.

82d Congress, 2d Session - - - - - House Report No. 2505

THE KATYN FOREST MASSACRE

———

FINAL REPORT

OF THE

SELECT COMMITTEE TO CONDUCT AN INVESTIGATION AND STUDY OF THE FACTS, EVIDENCE, AND CIRCUMSTANCES OF THE KATYN FOREST MASSACRE

PURSUANT TO

H. Res. 390

AND

H. Res. 539

(82d Congress)

A RESOLUTION TO AUTHORIZE THE INVESTIGATION OF THE MASS MURDER OF POLISH OFFICERS IN THE KATYN FOREST NEAR SMOLENSK, RUSSIA

DECEMBER 22, 1952.—Committed to the Committee of the Whole House on the State of the Union and ordered to be printed

———

UNITED STATES
GOVERNMENT PRINTING OFFICE
26668   WASHINGTON : 1952

Title page of the Congressional report on the Katyn Forest massacre. The report concluded: "This committee unanimously finds, beyond any question of reasonable doubt, that the Soviet NKVD (People's Commissariat of Internal Affairs) committed the mass murders of the Polish officers and intellectual leaders in the Katyn Forest near Smolensk, Russia."

Katzenelson's work in the interwar period was based on his sense that Jewish life in the Diaspora was incomplete; this belief also motivated his participation in cultural and other public affairs in those years. Such feelings appear in his works in the form of somber symbols of death, boredom, and silence. In his Yiddish play *Tarshish*, Katzenelson

Itzhak Katzenelson.

deals with the roots of antisemitism in Poland and with the utter hopelessness of Jewish life on Polish soil.

In late November 1939 Katzenelson fled from Łódź to Warsaw, where he lived and wrote (in Yiddish) until April 20, 1943, the day following the outbreak of the WARSAW GHETTO UPRISING. Then, for several weeks, he was in hiding on the "Aryan" side of Warsaw. In May the Germans discovered his real identity, but since he held a Honduran passport he was sent to the VITTEL camp in France, where he stayed for a year, keeping up his writing. In April 1944 he and his surviving son were deported to their death in AUSCHWITZ.

Katzenelson's work clearly reflects the shifts in the situation of the Warsaw ghetto; indeed, his literary output of that period reflects the events that were taking place. From the very first day of his stay in the ghetto, he contributed to the underground press and participated in educational and cultural activities —teaching in the high school and in the underground seminars conducted by Dror, founding and directing a Yiddish dramatic troupe and a Hebrew theater circle, advising the elementary-school teachers, involving himself in the cultural program of the orphanages, and so on. By public readings from his works, through the Bible study groups that he organized, and with the help of his close ties with Dror, Katzenelson was able to convey to the public his thoughts and feelings, as expressed in his poetry, plays, essays, and lectures. In this way his literary creations came to have an impact on day-to-day life in the ghetto.

Katzenelson spent much of his time in translating sections from the biblical prophetic books into Yiddish, for his reading public, and in writing plays for children or about children's life in the ghetto. In the first nineteen months of the Nazi occupation of Warsaw, Katzenelson sought to strengthen the ghetto population's resilience by interpreting contemporary reality in the light of the past history of the Jewish people—consoling them and offering the hope that "this too shall pass"—until the terrible truth dawned on him that the Nazis were aiming at the total destruction of the Jewish people.

In February and March of 1942, the mood of his writings became sharply more pessimistic, as reports came in of the mass murder being committed in the CHEŁMNO camp. After that, his writing addressed itself to the confrontation with death—the death, as he expected, of all the Jews of Poland. For the next two years, Katzenelson was the elegist of the Jewish people that was being driven to its death and also the prosecutor on its behalf, calling for the indictment of Western Christian civilization and for the punishment of the Germans, as a nation, for their crimes. Katzenelson's comprehensive reaction to the events finds its expression, above all, in the poem *Dos Lid funem Oysgehargetn Yidishn Folk* (The Song of the Murdered Jewish People; English ed., 1980), written in Vittel during the last year of his life. The poems that he composed in his last year in the Warsaw ghetto attempt to define and depict the essence of Jewish heroism (*Dos Lid vegn Shloyme Zhelichowski* [The Poem about Shlomo Zhelichowski] and *Dos Lid vegn Radziner* [The Poem about the Radzin Rebbe]). In that same year, he also elegized his wife and two of his sons, who had been deported to TRE-

BLINKA in the mass deportation of the summer of 1942 from the Warsaw ghetto.

Two days before that deportation was begun, Mordechai TENENBAUM hid portions of Katzenelson's works, together with the Dror archive, in a subterranean hideout; of the works that he composed in the Vittel camp, the Holocaust researcher Miriam Nowitz was able to save a part. The Ghetto Fighters' Museum (BET LOHAMEI HA-GETTA'OT) at Kibbutz Lohamei ha-Getta'ot in Israel is named after Itzhak Katzenelson. It has made extensive efforts to collect his manuscripts and to translate his works into English and other languages, and has published three editions of his last writings, consisting mostly of Hebrew translations of his Yiddish works and the Hebrew works that he wrote in the Holocaust period. Katzenelson's *Vittel Diary* was published in English (Tel Aviv, 1964).

BIBLIOGRAPHY

Even-Shoshan, S. *Yitzhak Katzenelson: Holocaust Mourner.* Naharia, Israel, 1964. (In Hebrew.)

Frank, M. Z. "Yitzhak Katzenelson, Martyred Poet." *Jewish Frontier* 30/9 (October 1963): 15–19.

Liptzin, S. *A History of Yiddish Literature.* New York, 1972.

Szeintuch, Y. "The Work of Yitzhak Katzenelson in the Warsaw Ghetto." *Jerusalem Quarterly* 26 (Winter 1983): 46–61.

Szeintuch, Y. *Yitzhak Katzenelson: The Last Writings in Hebrew and Yiddish from the Warsaw Ghetto and the Vittel Camp.* Jerusalem, 1989. (In Hebrew.)

Szeintuch, Y., ed. *Yitzhak Katzenelson: Yiddish Ghetto Writings; Warsaw, 1940–1943.* Naharia, Israel, 1984. (In Yiddish.)

YEHIEL SZEINTUCH

KATZMANN, FRITZ (1906–1957), SS officer. Katzmann joined the Nazi party in 1928 and the SS in 1930, eventually rising to the rank of SS-*Gruppenführer* and police lieutenant general. From November 1939 until August 1941 he was the SS and Police Leader of the RADOM district; he then became SS and Police Leader of the region of Galicia, overseeing the implementation of the "FINAL SOLUTION" for the Jews of that area. It was in the period of his command (which lasted until the fall of 1943) that most of the Jews of Eastern Galicia were murdered, with Katzmann bearing direct responsibility for the crime. In a report to his superiors dated June 30, 1943, he gave a detailed description of how he and the men under his command had purged the area of practically all the Jews who had lived there, either killing them on the spot or deporting them to forced-labor and extermination camps. Katzmann's report also referred to Jewish resistance in his area. In 1944 he became SS and Police Leader in Wehrkreis (military district) XX, with headquarters in DANZIG.

After the war, Katzmann went into hiding under an assumed name; he died in 1957. Nothing else is known of his fate.

BIBLIOGRAPHY

Hilberg, R. *The Destruction of the European Jews.* 3 vols. New York, 1985.

AHARON WEISS

KAUFERING, network of subsidiary camps of the DACHAU concentration camp in Germany. From June to October 1944, fifteen such subsidiary camps (eleven for men and four for women) were established around the village of Kaufering, about 25 miles (40 km) southwest of Munich. The inmates were used as part of the Jägerstab program, Albert SPEER's plan to bring Jewish slave labor to Germany to build underground fighter-aircraft factories inaccessible to Allied bombing attacks. The central camp administration was situated near Kaufering, about 4 miles (7 km) north of Landsberg. The commandant was subordinate to the commandant of Dachau.

The inmates of the Kaufering camps lived in huts half buried under the ground. Inadequate food, the absence of medical care, maltreatment, and extremely hard work for construction firms and armament industries caused a soaring death rate.

The first prisoners were Lithuanian Jews who arrived in June 1944. They were followed in October by large transports of Hungarian, Polish, Czechoslovak, and Romanian Jews, most of whom came from AUSCHWITZ. There are no exact statistical data as to how many

One of the subsidiary Kaufering camps was located at Landsberg, 3 miles (4.8 km) south of Kaufering. At this camp, called Lager No. 3, a Polish Jew who had been a prisoner for seven months looks at the bodies of his comrades, killed by the Germans. In an attempt to destroy the evidence the Germans had poured gasoline over the bodies and set them on fire (May 1, 1945). [United States Army]

prisoners were transported to Kaufering, how many perished there, or how many lived to see the liberation. Jules Jost, a French prisoner who helped keep the camp records, stated after the war that he had registered about twenty-eight thousand Kaufering inmates. At the beginning of December 1944, the fourth camp (No. IV) was put under quarantine because of an epidemic of typhus, and it became the sick bay for all the Kaufering camps.

A week before the liberation by American military units, evacuation of the Kaufering prisoners to Dachau and its subsidiary work camp at Allach began. When the Americans arrived on April 27, 1945, the camps were found abandoned, and many of the huts had been burned down by the SS guards. A few prisoners who had hidden in the woods returned to show the liberators burial pits containing thousands of bodies, and to bear witness to the crimes committed in these camps.

BIBLIOGRAPHY

Ervin-Deutsch, L. "About Those Who Survived and Those Who Died." *Dachau Review* 1 (1988): 116–156.

BARBARA DISTEL

KAUNAS. *See* Kovno.

KĖDAINIAI (Yi., Keidan), town located in the central part of the Lithuanian SSR. Jews lived in Kėdainiai beginning in the fifteenth century; from the sixteenth to the eighteenth century the town was an important trading center. On the eve of World War II it had a

Jewish population of three thousand, many of whom were truck farmers.

On June 24, 1941, two days after the German invasion of the Soviet Union, Kėdainiai was occupied. Only a few Jews managed to flee to the interior of the country. Upon the arrival of the Germans, the town's Lithuanian inhabitants began to harass and murder the Jews. At the end of July a ghetto was set up in Smilga Street, where all the Jews had to live; they were also forced to pay a heavy ransom. Two weeks later the Jews were taken to a nearby horse farm, where they were held under appalling conditions. On August 28, all the Jews—men, women, and children—were killed by firing squads made up of Lithuanians and men of Einsatzkommando 3. One of the Jews attacked two members of a firing squad, dragged them into a ditch, and choked one of them to death, but was himself immediately shot and killed.

Kėdainiai was liberated in the fall of 1944. Only 150 of its Jews survived, including those who had fled to the interior of the Soviet Union. After the war, a memorial was erected on the site of the execution.

BIBLIOGRAPHY

Chrust, J., ed. *Keidan Memorial Book.* Tel Aviv, 1977. (In Hebrew.)

DOV LEVIN

KEITEL, WILHELM (1882–1946), head of the Oberkommando der Wehrmacht (Armed Forces High Command; OKW) from 1938 to 1945. During World War I, Keitel fulfilled staff assignments and administrative duties in the Reichswehr. In 1934 he became closely associated with the Nazi party and advanced rapidly in his military career. When Hitler assumed personal command of the armed forces in February 1938, Keitel was appointed to the new post of chief of staff of the OKW, a post he held until the final surrender of Germany on May 8, 1945. In 1940 he was made a field marshal. Owing to his servile admiration for Hitler, Keitel was nicknamed by many German officers "Lakeitel" (from *Lakai*, "lackey").

Keitel signed a number of orders for the

Wilhelm Keitel in his prison cell in Nuremberg during his trial before the International Military Tribunal. [United States Army]

shooting of hostages, as well as for the wholesale murder of prisoners of war and civilians in occupied territories, including the notorious KOMMISSARBEFEHL and the *Nacht-und-Nebel-Erlass* (Night and Fog Decree; *see* NACHT UND NEBEL). After the July 20, 1944, attempt on Hitler's life by military conspirators, Keitel became a member of the "Court of Honor" (*Ehrengerichtshof*). This court stripped many high-ranking officers of their rank, leading to death sentences for them. On May 8, 1945, Keitel signed the document for the unconditional surrender of Germany.

At the NUREMBERG TRIAL, Keitel claimed that as an army officer he had served only to carry out orders of the state, but the tribunal declared that the defense of "superior order" did not apply to violations of international law. On October 1, 1945, Keitel was found guilty on all four counts of the indictment: conspiracy to wage a war of aggression; waging a war of aggression; war crimes; and crimes against humanity. He was sentenced to death and hanged on October 16, 1946. Keitel's memoirs, *In the Service of the Reich*, were published in 1979.

796   KHARKOV

BIBLIOGRAPHY

Davidson, E. *The Trial of the Germans.* New York, 1967.

Görlitz, W., ed. *Generalfeldmarschall Keitel: Verbrecher oder Offizier? Erinnerungen, Briefe, Dokumente des Chefs OKW.* Göttingen, 1961.

JEHUDA L. WALLACH

KHARKOV, second-largest city in the Ukrainian SSR. According to the 1939 census, the city had a Jewish population of 130,200, one-sixth of the total. In the summer of 1941, when the Germans were approaching the city, many of its inhabitants fled, including the bulk of the Jewish population. Kharkov was captured by the Germans on October 23, 1941, and became the headquarters of the German Sixth Army; it was under a military government throughout the German occupation and was not part of REICHSKOMMISSARIAT UKRAINE.

All the decrees concerning the city, including those affecting the Jews, were issued by the military government. Thus, on November 3, 1941, the military government announced the meager food rations, of which Jews were to receive only 40 percent; for example, the daily bread ration was set at 150 grams (5.25 oz), but Jews received only 60 grams (2 oz). Every day, hostages were taken, and, according to orders issued by the rear headquarters of Army Group South (to which the military government was subordinated), most were Jews; they were shot or hanged. On November 26, Sonderkommando 4a arrived in Kharkov, headed by Paul BLOBEL, and this meant the murder of more Jews. They were seized in groups from streets and houses; taken to the Hotel International, where they were tortured; and then murdered, mostly in GAS VANS.

On December 14, 1941, in an announcement published over the signature of the military governor of Kharkov, the city's Jews were ordered to assemble on the site of a nearby tractor plant by December 16. The plant was situated 7.5 miles (12 km) from Kharkov, and the Soviets had moved all its equipment to the east before their retreat. In order to terrorize the Jews, Sonderkommando 4a murdered 305

Jews, on the pretext that they had been spreading false rumors. The sheds in which the prisoners were housed had no doors, windows, or heating facilities, and the winter of 1941–1942 was severe. The number of people who were crowded in exceeded the sheds' capacity several times over. The prisoners were not permitted to fetch water or food and had to bribe the guards in order to obtain these basic needs. They were forbidden to leave the sheds at night, though there were no sanitary installations inside. There were many deaths from cold, disease, and hunger.

Only three weeks after the establishment of this ghetto, the liquidation of the Jews of Kharkov was set in motion. On the first day, "volunteers" were called for work in Poltava and Lubny, located west of Kharkov. The 800 men who reported for the trip were taken by truck to the Drobitski Ravine (Drobitski Yar), a nearby site, where they were murdered in pits that had been prepared in advance. In the following days more Jews were taken to the same ravine, by truck or on foot, and murdered. Gas vans were also used for killings. The mass slaughter was carried out by men of Sonderkommando 4a, assisted by members of German Police Battalion 314 and Waffen-SS

soldiers, who were probably from an SS Totenkopf (Death's-Head) unit (*see* TOTEN-KOPFVERBÄNDE).

A report issued by the special committee that after the war investigated Nazi crimes in Kharkov and opened the burial pits in the Drobitski Ravine stated that 15,000 people had been murdered there. However, according to evidence given at the trial of the officers and men of Sonderkommando 4a by the intelligence officer of the German Sixth Army (to which the Sonderkommando had been attached), the actual number of victims, as he had heard it from Blobel himself, was 21,685. This figure includes all the Jews killed from the beginning of the German occupation until early January 1942, when the liquidation of the Jews of Kharkov was completed.

The city was liberated on February 16, 1943, reconquered by the Germans, and liberated again on August 23. Only a few Jews survived; they had gone into hiding with the help of local inhabitants.

BIBLIOGRAPHY

Ehrenburg, I., and V. Grossman, eds. *The Black Book of Soviet Jewry.* New York, 1981.

SHMUEL SPECTOR

KHERSON, capital of the oblast (district) of the same name in the Ukrainian SSR. Kherson was founded in the eighteenth century. Jews lived there from the very beginning, and on the eve of World War II they numbered more than 15,000, out of a population of 167,108.

On August 19, 1941, Kherson was captured by the Germans; two-thirds of its Jewish population had by then been evacuated or had fled the city on their own. In the first few days of the occupation, the Jews were ordered to form a "Jewish committee," which was to register all the Jews from August 24 to 27. On August 25, the Jews were ordered to wear a Jewish star (*see* BADGE, JEWISH) on their chests (a yellow badge in the form of a Shield of David); they were also forced to hand over to the German administration all the money and valuables in their possession. When the registration was completed, the Jews were all concentrated in a ghetto. Between September 16 and 30, 1941, the five thousand Jews of Kherson were taken to an antitank ditch outside the city and murdered there.

The Kherson oblast contained the Jewish autonomous subdistricts of Kalinindorf, Stalindorf, and Nay Zlatopol. There were Jewish kolkhozes (collective farms) in these subdistricts, successors to the Jewish agricultural settlements that had been established there in the second half of the nineteenth century. On the eve of World War II, the three subdistricts had a Jewish population of thirty-five thousand, most of them farmers.

The fate of the Jews living in the kolkhozes can be deduced from the course of events in the Stalindorf subdistrict. In the second half of September 1941, *Aktionen* took place, and groups of Jewish men were murdered in several kolkhozes. Heavy collective fines were imposed on the Jews. They were robbed of their belongings, and the community property of the kolkhozes was confiscated. Early in the spring of 1942 the Jewish farmers were told to sow potatoes and grow vegetables for the German administration. In April, many Jewish men were drafted and put into eight labor camps, to work on the construction of the Dnepropetrovsk-Zaporozhye highway. The old men, women, and children left behind in the kolkhozes were rounded up and killed on May 29. On December 5, 1942, all the men were put into the Lyubimovka camp, where they were murdered or died as a result of hard labor and disease.

The Kherson region was liberated in mid-March 1944. Surviving Jewish farmers who returned, expecting to rehabilitate their farms, found them occupied by Russians and Ukrainians. The appeals that Jews made to the authorities in Kiev to restore the Jewish autonomous subdistricts were rejected, and when the war ended they were officially abolished.

SHMUEL SPECTOR

KIDDUSH HA-HAYYIM (lit., "sanctifying Life"), Hebrew term used during the Holocaust to refer to spontaneous, as well as planned, Jewish responses to the deadly objectives of Nazi Germany and its supporters by various means of resistance. The term is attributed to the European religious Zionist leader Rabbi Yitzhak Nissenbaum (1868–1942), who wrote, in the early months of the Warsaw ghetto: "This is the hour of *Kiddush ha-Hayyim* and not of KIDDUSH HA-SHEM by death. Formerly, our enemies demanded our soul, and the Jew sacrificed his body in sanctifying God's Name. Now the enemy demands the body of the Jew. This makes it imperative for the Jew to defend it and protect it."

The considerations and stimuli for *Kiddush ha-Hayyim* responses were varied and complex. For some they represented acts that sustained the morale of the individual, the family, and the community. For others, *Kiddush ha-Hayyim* was a new form of traditional Jewish response to crisis or a natural extension of genuine piety and belief. The psychologist Bruno Bettelheim, himself a prisoner in Dachau and Buchenwald in 1938 (whose harsh views on the passive response of Jewish victims have aroused indignation), states that expressions of *Kiddush ha-Hayyim* were the instinctive attempts of the victim to protectively insulate himself within the boundaries of "private behavior." In this manner, the person rejects traumatic forces that threaten the integrity and stability of the personality. This response, against unequal massive terror and the methods of its perpetrators, who sought to destroy the Jews, expressed the intention of the victim to live to the fullest, and, in the words of the Israeli Holocaust scholar Shaul Esh, "this often meant to live Jewishly." In raising the falling spirits of his flock in Zelichowo in June 1942, Rabbi Avraham Shalom Goldberg entreated: "Every Jew who remains alive sanctifies the Name of God among many."

There were numerous attempts to maintain independent Jewish community life in the face of hostility, intimidation, and risk. An early expression of group integrity and self-respect was the article "Wear the Yellow Badge with Pride," by Robert Weltsch, the editor of the Zionist *Jüdische Rundschau*, appearing in Berlin in April 1933. This audacious challenge to Jews to strengthen their ethnic and national commitments galvanized community efforts in Germany to enrich the internal Jewish fabric of their communities not only in terms of physical rescue efforts but also in the spiritual, cultural, and educational domains. Jewish and general education in independent school networks, cultural institutions, and YOUTH MOVEMENTS were activated in order to cope with entire populations who were suddenly disenfranchised educationally and professionally in their communities. Newspapers, at first tolerated and eventually prohibited, served as an important means of communication in the attempt to resume dignified communal life.

Though spiritual resistance included every

type of nonviolent act by secular as well as believing Jews who responded in terms of their own traditions, *Kiddush ha-Hayyim* is generally associated with the *Kiddush ha-Shem* world of belief, faith, and the Jewish life cycle. Roughly sketched calendars projected the Jewish religious year and the candle-lighting times for the Sabbath and festivals. They marked traditional days of joy and mourning. In the absence of Jewish ritual objects and facilities, the daily, weekly, monthly, and yearly events were commemorated symbolically. A glass of water could substitute for the mikva (ritual pool for immersion). Stale bread crumbs would serve instead of Sabbath wine and loaves. Potato peels would briefly provide the fuel for candles for Sabbath festivities. Scraps of prayers and study texts from the Talmud were circulated among camp inmates. The age-old tradition of rabbinic responsa to questions of Jewish law produced a genre of Holocaust responsa literature. The best known of these are in Rabbi Efraim Oshry's *Mi-Ma'amakim* (New York, 1949, 1963, 1969) and *Divrei Efraim* (New York, 1949), Rabbi Zvi Hirsh Meisels's *Mekadshei ha-Shem* (Chicago, 1955), and Rabbi Yehiel Weinberg's *Sifrei Esh* (Jerusalem, 1961–1969). They reflect the attempts of Jews of faith to continue to cling to ritual and tradition despite, or perhaps in response to, the declared objectives of Nazi Germany to destroy not only Jews but Judaism.

Kiddush ha-Hayyim, by means of benevolent acts toward others and steadfast faith in God (who is seen as suffering together with his people), is also conceived as the necessary catalyst for *tikkun* (reconstruction) within destruction in a rare work of rabbinic Hasidic theology written during the Holocaust. Rabbi Kalunimus Kalmish Shapiro, the Hasidic leader of Piaseczno, wrote in the Warsaw ghetto following Rosh Hashanah (New Year) of 1941: "When we undergo today these sufferings . . . we have to believe that out of our vast affliction will evolve a new creation by way of renewed penitence and good deeds."

The *tikkun* theme is central to Rabbi Issachar Shlomo Teichthal, who pleaded with the Jewish remnant in Hungary, in *Em ha-Banim Semeha* (Budapest, 1943), to dedicate itself to the return and rebuilding of the land of Israel. Only by re-creating an autonomous Jewish homeland—the ultimate reaffirmation of the sanctity of life for the Jew, the Jewish people, and the God of Israel—can the martyrdom of the Holocaust have any meaning. "If we shall move and ascend to Zion we will restore the Jewish souls who were murdered in acts of *Kiddush ha-Shem*. They with their lives will have compelled us to return to the estate of our forebears."

BIBLIOGRAPHY

Esh, S. "The Dignity of the Destroyed: Toward a Definition of the Period of the Holocaust." *Judaism* 11/2 (Spring 1962): 99–111

Oshry, E. *Responsa from the Holocaust.* New York, 1983.

Rudavsky, J. *To Live with Hope, to Die with Dignity.* Lanham, Md., 1987.

PESACH SCHINDLER

KIDDUSH HA-SHEM (lit., "sanctifying the Name [of God]"), Hebrew term that was used in postbiblical Jewish history to denote exemplary ethical conduct and that became applied to religious martyrdom. A Jew who consciously chose to offer his own life for the sake of his faith was considered a *kadosh* ("holy one"), sanctified as a martyr.

The long epoch of Jewish martyrdom emerged during the periods of Greek domination in the second century B.C. and the subsequent persecutions of the Roman era. The religious faith of the Jews was repeatedly tested during the Middle Ages under both Muslim and Christian rule. The chronicles of the period depict acts of *Kiddush ha-Shem* by entire communities in England, France, and Germany, especially in the wake of the Crusades. Acts of martyrdom punctuated Jewish history from the fifteenth to the nineteenth century in the precarious world of ghettos, inquisitions, expulsions, and pogroms in Europe. In most instances the choice of accepting *Kiddush ha-Shem* was voluntary, with various options made available by the hostile surrounding society and even by Jewish law.

The Holocaust eliminated the element of choice for the victim. Religious (conversion), ideological, or economic means could not influence the racial definitions and the fate of the Jews. Rabbi Shimon Huberband, a member of the secret ONEG SHABBAT group in the WARSAW ghetto, invoked the Jewish religious legal authorities Maimonides and Rabbi Moshe Sofer (the Ḥatam Sofer) in broadening the definition of *Kiddush ha-Shem*: a Jew murdered by non-Jews, whether from religious motives or for criminal reasons, is considered a *kadosh*.

Numerous eyewitness reports describe *Kiddush ha-Shem* scenes in which the *Viddui* (the confessional) and the final *Shema Yisrael* ("Hear O Israel"; Deuteronomy) were recited in public and death was faced with dignity, love, and even joy. Among the many rabbinic responsa emerging from the Holocaust was the answer of Rabbi Efraim Oshry in the Kovno ghetto concerning the proper text for the blessing traditionally recited by Jews about to undergo martyrdom: "Blessed are you, Lord, who has added holiness to our life through His commandments and commanded us the command to sanctify His Name in public." Among the many ritual artifacts discovered in the ghettos and camps were prayer books and notes inscribed with this text, evidently to be utilized prior to the expected moment of martyrdom.

Among the most remarkable eyewitness reports is the final plea by the eminent scholar of pre-Holocaust Jewry, Rabbi Elchanan Wasserman, sent to his death in Lithuania.

> Evidently they consider us righteous in Heaven, for we have been chosen to atone with our bodies for all of Israel. If so, we must repent now, at this very spot. Time is short. If we repent we shall be able to save our brothers and sisters in America. The NINTH FORT [where the Jews of Kovno were executed] is close. Let us remember to be faithful in sanctifying the Name. We shall walk erect. Let us not, Heaven forbid, inject impure thoughts that would invalidate our sacrifice. We are about to fulfill the most critical of all commandments: *Kiddush ha-Shem*. The very fires that shall consume our bodies will in turn spark the renewal of the Jewish people.   (quoted in Eliav)

BIBLIOGRAPHY

Eliav, M., ed. *I Believe: Testimonies of the Life and Death of Believers during the Holocaust.* Jerusalem, 1969. (In Hebrew.)

Gottfarstein, Y. *Kiddush Hashem over the Ages and Its Uniqueness in the Holocaust Period; Jewish Resistance during the Holocaust.* In Proceedings of the Conference on Manifestations of Jewish Resistance, pp. 453–482. Jerusalem, 1971.

Huberband, S. *Kiddush Hashem: Jewish Religious and Cultural Life in Poland during the Holocaust.* New York, 1988.

Schindler, P. "The Holocaust and Kiddush Hashem in Hassidic Thought." In *Religious Encounters with Death*, edited by F. E. Reynolds and E. N. Waugh, pp. 170–180. London, 1977.

PESACH SCHINDLER

KIELCE, district capital in southeast POLAND, situated north of Kraków and south of Radom. The Jewish community of Kielce was established in 1868, but it was only at the turn of the century that many Jews began moving there from the neighboring townships. By 1921 the Jews in the city numbered 15,550, about one-third of the total population. According to the 1931 census, the number of Jews in Kielce was 18,083; in 1939 it was estimated at 24,000.

The city was captured by the Germans on September 4, 1939, a few days after the outbreak of World War II, and anti-Jewish atrocities began immediately: expropriations, heavy fines, forced labor, the taking of hostages, beatings, and killings. The first head of the JUDENRAT (Jewish Council) was Dr. Moses Pelc, who was soon sent to AUSCHWITZ for refusing to cooperate with the Germans in the execution of their policies. He was replaced by the industrialist Hermann Levy, who served the Germans until the liquidation of the ghetto, when he was murdered by Hans Geier, an SS officer, in September 1942.

The Kielce ghetto was established early in April 1941 in accordance with an official order issued by Stadthauptmann Hans Drechsel, the German civilian administrator of the city. The number of Jews grew when 1,000 Jews deported from Vienna were brought to Kielce, as well as several thousand from neighboring small towns and more distant areas around Poznań and Łódź. By the end of 1941 there were 27,000 Jews in the Kielce ghetto. The able-bodied males were used by the Germans as laborers in the local stone quarries. Others worked in the ghetto

KIELCE

Administrative Divisions of Poland under German Occupation, 1939–1945

1 Pomerania   6 Warthegau
2 Brandenburg   7 Danzig (West Prussia)
3 Saxony   8 East Prussia
4 Lower Silesia   9 Generalgouvernement
5 Upper Silesia   10 Białystok Region

© Polish National Publishing House, Warsaw, 1979
(Państwowe Wydawnictwo Naukowe)

■ Camp

⊠ Extermination Center

as tailors, shoemakers, and carpenters, and at other trades. Between April 1941 and the mass *Aktionen* of August 20 to 24, 1942, some 6,000 Jews died of hunger, cold, and typhus within the ghetto confines.

In January 1942 seven Jews were shot for trying to leave the ghetto. Several other executions had taken place in the preceding summer, especially of activists and community leaders. Under the command of two SS officers, Hauptsturmführer und Kriminalkommissar Ernst Karl Thomas and Hauptmann

Hans Geier, the liquidation of the ghetto began, on August 20. It lasted until August 24, when all the Jews, with the exception of two thousand who were young and healthy, were loaded on freight trains and sent to TREBLINKA. The sick Jews and the children of the Jewish orphanage had been killed by the Germans before the deportation. Some five hundred Jews managed to escape.

The remaining two thousand Jews of Kielce were placed in three labor camps in Kielce: HASAG-Granat (quarries, workshops, and mu-

Jewish refugees, survivors of the Kielce pogrom, waiting to leave Poland (July 1946).

nitions), Henryków (carpentry), and Lud-wików (foundry). A projected revolt, to be led by David Barviner and Gershon Levkowitz, was aborted by an informer. In August 1944 the surviving inmates were sent to BUCHEN-WALD or Auschwitz. The last surviving group, consisting of forty-five Jewish children, was taken to the Jewish cemetery and killed there by the Germans.

When the Soviet army captured Kielce on January 16, 1945, only two Jews remained of what had once been a twenty-thousand-strong community. However, during the eighteen months that followed, about one hundred and fifty Jews—former residents who had survived the camps or were hiding in the forests, and Jews who had never lived in Kielce—gradually gathered in the former Jewish community building at No. 7 Planty Avenue. Most of them lived on funds sent by the JOINT DISTRIBUTION COMMITTEE, forming a kibbutz and waiting for an opportunity to go to Palestine.

The hatred of the Poles toward the Jews was so intense that whenever a former Jewish resident appeared in town he was greeted with the words: "What? You are still alive? We thought that Hitler killed all of you." Ru-

mors spread that masses of Jews would soon return to reclaim their former houses and belongings. The incitement culminated at the end of June 1946 when a woman ran through the streets shouting that the Jews on Planty Avenue were killing Polish children and drinking their blood. Another rumor was spread that a Polish boy had been killed in the basement of the community building and his blood used to make matzoth.

On July 1, mobs began gathering around the building. When the police were called in all they did was to confiscate the few licensed weapons that the Jews had. Appeals to the church dignitaries were dismissed with the excuse that they could not intercede for the Jews because the latter had brought communism into Poland. On July 4 the mob attacked and massacred forty-two Jews and wounded about fifty more. The central Polish authorities in Warsaw sent in a military detachment and an investigation committee. Order was quickly restored, and seven of the main instigators and killers were executed. The missing Polish boy was soon found in a nearby village.

Thus, the thousand-year history of the Jews of Poland came to an ignominious end with a medieval-style pogrom, an event that touched off a mass migration of hundreds of thousands of Jews from Poland and other countries of eastern and central Europe who had somehow survived World War II and the Holocaust.

In 1946 the tomb with the names of the forty-two victims that had been erected in the Kielce Jewish cemetery was destroyed by the local Poles. It was rebuilt in 1987, when the chairman of the Kielce Society in New York, William Mandel, also erected an iron fence around the cemetery. The monument for the forty-five children killed in 1944 was rebuilt as well.

BIBLIOGRAPHY

Citron, P. *The Kielce Book: The History of the Kielce Community from Its Foundation to Its Destruction.* Tel Aviv, 1958. (In Hebrew.)

Stockfisch, D. *About Our House Which Was Devastated.* Tel Aviv, 1981. (In Hebrew and Yiddish.)

SINAI LEICHTER

KIEV. *See* Babi Yar.

Manfred von Killinger.

KILLINGER, MANFRED VON (1886–1944), German diplomat; ambassador to ROMANIA from 1941 to 1944. In World War I, Killinger served as a torpedo boat commander. He joined the Nazi party in 1928 and rose rapidly in the SA (Sturmabteilung; Storm Troopers). Though he was made *Reichskommissar* for Saxony in 1933, he narrowly escaped execution during the bloody purge of leading SA men on June 30, 1934 (the "Night of the Long Knives").

Killinger began rebuilding his political career by joining the Foreign Office, and in 1940 was made a roving troubleshooter for eastern European affairs. In this capacity he visited the capitals of Germany's new eastern European allies, urging them to request German advisers and making no secret of the Third Reich's interest in the way they treated their Jews. His major success was in Slovakia, where he advised the ouster of the relatively independent-minded foreign minister, Ferdinand Ďurčanský, in favor of the pro-German Vojtech TUKA as foreign minister and Alexander (Saňo) MACH as interior minister. Subsequently, Killinger was made German ambassador to Slovakia, where he installed the system that brought in Dieter WISLICENY as adviser for Jewish affairs.

In December 1940, Killinger left Slovakia to become the German ambassador to Romania. Again German advisers quickly followed, including Gustav RICHTER as consultant for Jewish affairs. Given his SA background, it is not surprising that Killinger had numerous quarrels with the SS. His relations with Richter became especially strained when the latter, without keeping Killinger informed, reached an agreement with the Romanian government in July 1942 concerning the deportation of Romanian Jews to Poland. The ensuing squabble gained time for the Romanians, who eventually backed out of the deportation agreement. Killinger committed suicide in Bucharest in 1944 to avoid capture by the Russians.

BIBLIOGRAPHY

Broszat, H. "Das Dritte Reich und die rumänische Judenpolitik." *Gutachten des Instituts für Zeitgeschichte* 1 (1958): 102–183.

Browning, C. R. *The Final Solution and the German Foreign Office: A Study of Referat D3 of Abteilung Deutschland, 1940–1943.* New York, 1978.

CHRISTOPHER R. BROWNING

KISHINEV (Rom., Chişinău), capital of the Moldavian SSR. From 1918 to 1940 and again from 1941 to 1944 it was the capital of BESSARABIA, in ROMANIA. Jews lived in the town from the eighteenth century, and by the late nineteenth century they made up half its population. They fell victim to pogroms in 1903 and 1905. The community was a cultural center for the Jews of Bessarabia and Romania, with a rabbinical academy (yeshiva), a Yiddish newspaper, Hebrew and Yiddish schools, and Zionist and Socialist activities. In 1930 the 41,405 Jews living there constituted over 36 percent of a total population numbering 114,896. Under Soviet rule, from July 1940 to July 1941, the number of Jews in the city increased to an estimated 60,000.

On June 22, 1941, with the German invasion of the Soviet Union, Kishinev's town center was severely bombarded by German and Romanian planes. Thousands, including many Jews, died in the bombing and the resulting conflagrations. The disorderly flight of the Soviet authorities caused panic among the Jews, who were seen by the Romanian majority in the city as supporters of the Communist regime. There was no official evacuation of the Jews, although some fled to the east on their own initiative and at their own risk. Kishinev and the surrounding villages were inhabited mainly by Romanians who viewed the entry of the Romanian and German armies as a liberation and not as an occupation. Thousands of Jews from Kishinev and from nearby towns were cruelly slaughtered by Romanian farmers or executed by Romanian soldiers while attempting to flee.

The annihilation of the Jews of Kishinev was carried out in several stages. With the entry of the Romanian and German units, an

KISHINEV

Annexations from June to September 1940: (1) Bessarabia and (2) N. Bukovina to USSR; (3) N. Transylvania to Hungary; (4) S. Dobruja to Bulgaria.

unknown number of Jews, estimated by Matatias Carp (1946) at ten thousand, were slaughtered in the streets and in their homes. After the establishment of the ghetto, about two thousand Jews, mainly members of the liberal professions (doctors, lawyers, engineers) and local Jewish intellectuals, were systematically executed by Einsatzkommando 11a of Einsatzgruppe D. Members of the Romanian army and police force took part in some of these executions as auxiliaries.

After the wave of killings, the eleven thousand remaining Jews were concentrated in the ghetto, created on July 24, 1941, on the order of the Romanian district ruler and the German Einsatzkommando leader, Paul Zapp. The inhabitants of the ghetto were robbed, tortured, conscripted for forced labor, and executed. The Jews of central Romania attempted to assist their brethren in the ghetto, sending large amounts of money by illegal means. A committee was formed to bribe the Romanian authorities so that they would not hand the Jews over to the Germans.

On August 7, 500 Jewish men and 25 Jewish women were sent to work in the Ghidighici quarries; within a week about 325 of them had been killed by Romanian soldiers. That fall, on the Day of Atonement (October 4), the military authorities began deporting the remaining ghetto Jews to TRANSNISTRIA, by order of the Romanian ruler, Ion ANTO-NESCU. One of the heads of the ghetto, the attorney Shapira, managed to alert the leaders of the Jewish communities in Bucharest, but attempts to halt the deportations were unsuccessful. The first group was taken by the Orhei-Rezina road toward the Dniester River. The property of all the deportees was plundered by their escorts and by the representatives of the Romanian National Bank, and most of the Jews of the first group were murdered while crossing the river. The deportations continued throughout October. Hundreds of Jewish corpses littered the roadsides leading to the Dniester. On October 31, the last convoy of 257 deportees left the ghetto. The community was not completely liquidated, however, since some Jews had found places of concealment in Kishinev and its vicinity or elsewhere in Romania. In May 1942, the last 200 Jews in the locality were deported. Kishinev was liberated in August 1944. At that time no Jews remained in the locality.

BIBLIOGRAPHY

Carp, M. *Legionarii şi rebeliunea*. Vol. 1 of *Cartea Neagră*. Bucharest, 1946.
Istoriia Kishineva (1466–1966). Kishinev, 1966.
"Kishinev." In *Rumania*, vol. 2, edited by J. Ancel and T. Lavi, pp. 411–416. *Pinkas ha-Kehillot; Encyclopaedia of Jewish Communities*. Jerusalem, 1980. (In Hebrew.)
Mircu, M. *Pogromurile din Basarabia*. Bucharest, 1947. See pages 17–24.

JEAN ANCEL

KISTARCSA, camp located 9 miles (5.6 km) northeast of Budapest. Before the Nazis occupied Hungary, Kistarcsa was an internment camp. With the start of the DEPORTATIONS from Hungary in the spring of 1944, it became a transit camp from which Jews in the Budapest area were sent onward for annihilation, primarily to AUSCHWITZ.

During the 1930s, the regent, Adm. Miklós HORTHY, interned left-wing political opponents (among them Jews) in facilities at the Kistarcsa, Topolya, and Csepel camps. After the outbreak of World War II, Jewish refugees who managed to obtain legitimate papers were also held in these camps. The five buildings of the Kistarcsa camp, originally meant to house 200 prisoners, soon became overcrowded with 2,000 Jews.

When the Nazis occupied Hungary on

Jews rounded up by the SS and taken to the Kistarcsa camp (after 1944).

March 19, 1944, the ss began rounding up Jews. They were first held in railway stations in various Budapest suburbs, and from there transferred to the Kistarcsa camp. During the Nazi occupation, the SS took over the camp, but it was administered directly by the Hungarian police. By all accounts, the camp commandant, István Vasdenyei, was humane and did whatever he could to ease the plight of the Jews under his control. He cooperated with the Jewish relief organizations, the Magyar Izraeliták Pártfogo Irodaja (Welfare Bureau of Hungarian Jews), the Országos Magyar Zsidó Segito Akcio (National Hungarian Jewish Assistance Campaign), and the Orthodox Nepasztal (People's Table), which cared for the inmates.

The first transport of 1,800 Jews left the camp for Auschwitz on April 29, 1944. Adolf EICHMANN and his commando sent eighteen more trainloads of roughly similar size from Kistarcsa to Auschwitz before Horthy declared the cessation of deportations on July 7 of that year. Furious at Horthy's intervention, Eichmann attempted to dispatch another train on July 15. Acting on information from Vasdenyei, Horthy turned back the transport before it reached the Hungarian border. On July 19 Eichmann sent his underling Franz Nowak and a special team of deportation experts to the camp. Among the Hungarians present were László BAKY, the Hungarian secretary of state, and Pál Ubrizsi, the commandant of the Rokk Szillard jail. They sent 1,200 Jews to Auschwitz on what was the last deportation train from Kistarcsa. About 1,000 Jews remained in the Kistarcsa camp until it was dismantled on the Day of Atonement, September 27, 1944, and its inmates sent to various labor camps in Hungary.

BIBLIOGRAPHY

Braham, R. L. *The Politics of Genocide: The Holocaust in Hungary.* New York, 1981.
Lavi, T., ed. *Hungary.* In *Pinkas Hakehillot; Encyclopaedia of Jewish Communities.* Jerusalem, 1986. (In Hebrew.)

ROBERT ROZETT

KLAIPĖDA. *See* Memel.

KLAUSENBURG. *See* Cluj.

KLOOGA, subcamp of the VAIVARA camp in northern ESTONIA, near TALLINN. The Klooga camp was created in the summer of 1943, and was one of the large labor camps in Estonia. It held about two to three thousand male and female Jewish prisoners, most of whom arrived in August and September of 1943 from the VILNA ghetto; a minority came from the KOVNO ghetto and elsewhere. There were also about one hundred Soviet prisoners of war in the camp. The two camps at Klooga, the men's camp and the women's camp, were about 600 yards apart. Each had a large two-story building housing the Jewish prisoners. Barbed-wire fences enclosed the entire camp as well as the two internal camps, which were guarded by German and Estonian SS men.

The camps in Estonia, including Klooga, were created for exploitation of the local natural resources, assistance to the German war effort, and construction of fortifications against the advancing Soviet army. Three shifts of prisoners worked in the cement and brick works and in the sawmills at Klooga; part of the production was used for building fortifications, and part was sent to Germany. Other prisoners worked in a factory producing wooden clogs for the camp prisoners.

Conditions for the Jewish prisoners were extremely harsh, particularly for those transporting bags of cement from the factory to the train station. The prisoners received 7 to 9 ounces (200–250 g) of bread, a pint (0.5 l) of soup, and a limited quantity of water daily, and were obliged to work even when they were sick. The camp elder and most of the Jewish Kapos appointed by the camp commandant treated the other prisoners humanely and tried to help them. The Jewish underground in the camp had about seventy-five members, organized into groups of five. Most had belonged in the past to the underground in the Vilna ghetto. According to several accounts, the underground managed to obtain a few pistols, but failed in its attempts to establish contact with partisans and to organize an escape. In view of the frequent transfers of prisoners from camp to camp, the underground was unable to form a solid

Corpses of slain prisoners from the Klooga camp stacked for burning, as found by Soviet troops in September 1944.

core and leadership, hence the absence of organized resistance when the camp was liquidated. A number of escape attempts by individuals were successful; others failed, and the escapees were caught and executed.

As the Soviet army advanced through Estonia in July and August of 1944, the transfer of the prisoners in the Estonian camps to the STUTTHOF concentration camp in Germany began, via the Baltic Sea. In mid-September, while Jewish prisoners were still in the camps of Klooga and Lagedi, the German front in Estonia collapsed. On September 18, five hundred of the prisoners were shot at Lagedi.

Early on September 19, Klooga was surrounded by German and Estonian SS men. Toward midday they began to take groups of prisoners from the camp to a nearby forest for execution, beginning with the men's camp. Some of the men tried to hide inside the camp, but most were found and shot. Others tried to flee from the execution site. Approximately twenty-four hundred Jews and one hundred Soviet prisoners of war died in this slaughter. A few days later, on September 28, when the Soviet army liberated Klooga, they found the corpses of the slain stacked for burning. Eighty-five of the prisoners, who had managed to hide within the camp or escape to the nearby forests, survived.

BIBLIOGRAPHY

Dworzecki, M. *Jewish Camps in Estonia, 1942–1944.* Jerusalem, 1970. (In Hebrew.)

YITZHAK ARAD

KNOCHEN, HELMUT (b. 1910), SS and SD (Sicherheitsdienst; Security Service) officer. A native of Magdeburg, Knochen studied history and English at the universities of Leipzig and Göttingen and worked as a teacher and editor. He became a member of the Nazi party in 1932, joined the SS in 1936, and entered the SD administration. In 1937 he became an officer in the SS, rose rapidly in rank, and was promoted to *Standartenführer* in 1942.

In 1940 Knochen was appointed a senior commander of the Sicherheitspolizei (Security Police) and SD in Paris, and two years later, in 1942, his area of jurisdiction was extended to include all of occupied northern France, as well as Belgium. In this post he was in charge of rounding up French Jews and deporting them to concentration camps and extermination camps; he was also responsible for the execution of many Frenchmen. Following the liberation of France by the Allied forces, Knochen was posted to the Leibstandarte-SS "Adolf Hitler" (Adolf Hitler SS Bodyguard Regiment) of the Waffen-SS.

In June 1946 a British military court in the British zone of Germany sentenced Knochen to death for the murder of British pilots who had been taken prisoner. The sentence was not carried out, however. That October he was extradited to France, brought to trial there, and again sentenced to death, in 1954. In 1958 the sentence was commuted to life imprisonment. President Charles de GAULLE granted Knochen a pardon in 1962 and he was sent back to Germany, where he retired in Baden-Baden.

BIBLIOGRAPHY

Marrus, M. R., and R. O. Paxton. *Vichy France and the Jews.* New York, 1981.

SHMUEL SPECTOR

Erich Koch.

KOCH, ERICH (1896–1986), Nazi party functionary and governor of occupied territories. Born into a working family in Elberfeld, in the Rhineland, Koch graduated from a commercial secondary school and became a railway clerk. In World War I he served as a private, and when the war was over he fought in the ranks of the Freikorps—irregular volunteer units—against the French.

Koch was among the first to join the Nazi party (his membership card was No. 90). In 1928 he was appointed *Gauleiter* of East Prussia, and in 1930 was elected as one of East Prussia's Reichstag deputies. When the Nazis came to power he also became the *Oberpräsident* (governor) of the region.

In 1941 Koch was appointed *Reichskommissar* of the Ukraine and governor of the Białystok district over the objections of Alfred ROSENBERG, the minister of occupied territories in the east, who wanted exclusive jurisdiction in the area. Through these appointments Koch came to govern extensive territories, ranging from Königsberg on the Baltic to the shores of the Black Sea. His treatment of the inhabitants of these territories was exceedingly harsh and cruel; his aim was to implement the ideas of Hitler and Himmler regarding the total subjugation of the Slav peoples. Koch frequently went over Rosenberg's head, although Rosenberg was nominally his superior.

After the war, Koch lived for several years in Schleswig-Holstein, under an assumed name. He was arrested by the British occupation forces and extradited to Poland in 1950. In 1959 he was put on trial in Warsaw, and on March 9 of that year was sentenced to death by hanging. Owing to his poor state of health, however, Koch was not executed. He spent the rest of his life in a Polish prison until his death in November 1986.

BIBLIOGRAPHY

Orłowski, S., and R. Ostrowicz. *Erich Koch przed polskim sądem.* Warsaw, 1959.

Reitlinger, G. "Last of the War Criminals: The Mystery of Erich Koch." *Commentary* 27/1 (January 1959): 30–42.

SHMUEL SPECTOR

KOCH, ILSE. *See* Koch, Karl Otto.

KOCH, KARL OTTO (1897–1945), commandant of concentration camps. Koch was born in Darmstadt, where he attended a commercial secondary school and became a bank clerk. Toward the end of World War I he was wounded and captured by the British, and was a prisoner of war until October 1919. In 1930 he became a member of the Nazi party and a year later joined the SS. He held senior command posts in the Sachsenburg, Esterwegen, and Lichtenburg (Prettin) concentration camps in 1934, and the following year was appointed commandant of the notorious CO-LUMBIA HAUS, a prison in Berlin. In 1936 Koch was commandant of the Esterwegen and SACHSENHAUSEN concentration camps; in May 1937 he married Dresden-born Ilse Köhler (1906–1967). On August 1 of that year Koch was appointed commandant of the newly established BUCHENWALD camp, and promoted to SS-*Standartenführer*. His wife was made an SS-*Aufseherin* (overseer) in the camp commanded by her husband. Before long she became notorious for her extreme cruelty to the prisoners and for her nymphomania, which she vented on the SS guards in the camp.

In September 1941 Karl Otto Koch was appointed commandant of MAJDANEK, then a Soviet prisoner-of-war camp run by the Waffen-SS in Lublin. Under his tenure the camp was greatly enlarged, and civilian prisoners, including Jews, were brought in. Crematoria were constructed, and there was an enormous rise in the number of prisoners killed. In July 1942, after a mass outbreak from the camp, Koch was suspended and put on trial before an SS and police court in Berlin, but was acquitted in February 1943. He then held administrative posts in postal-service security units, only to be arrested again in August of that year on charges of embezzlement, forgery, making threats to of-

Karl Otto Koch, commandant of the Buchenwald concentration camp. From the album of Ilse Koch. [National Archives]

ficials, and "other charges." The last apparently referred to murders for which he was responsible that went beyond existing orders, and to his hobby of collecting patches of tattooed human skin and shrunken human skulls; Ilse was also arrested as an accomplice to her husband. It was she who selected the living prisoners whose skin she wanted, after they were killed, for her own collection and for use in making lampshades. In early 1945 Karl Otto Koch was sentenced by the Supreme Court of the SS (*Oberste SS- und Polizeigericht*) in Munich, and in April of that year he was executed.

Ilse Koch was acquitted and went to Ludwigsburg to live with her two children and her husband's stepsister. She was arrested by the Americans on June 30, 1945, tried in 1947, and sentenced to life imprisonment. In 1949 she was released under a pardon granted by Gen. Lucius D. Clay, the military governor of the American zone in Germany. Under pressure arising out of hearings held by a United States Senate committee, she was immediately re-arrested upon her re-

Ilse Koch ("the Bitch of Buchenwald"). [National Archives]

lease, and in January 1951 was again sentenced to life imprisonment, by the *Landesgericht* (State Court) in Augsburg. In September 1967 she committed suicide in her prison cell.

BIBLIOGRAPHY

Burney, C. *The Dungeon Democracy*. London, 1945.
Smith, A. L., Jr. *Die "Hexe von Buchenwald": Der Fall Ilse Koch*. Cologne, 1983.

SHMUEL SPECTOR

KOGON, EUGEN (1903–1987), journalist and political scientist; prisoner in the BUCHENWALD concentration camp. Kogon studied economics and sociology in his native Munich, as well as in Florence and Vienna, and earned a doctor's degree in law and political science. A Catholic, he was critical of the church, a view reflected in the articles he published in various (mostly Catholic) Austrian magazines; he also acted as adviser to the Christian trade unions in Austria.

Kogon's anti-Nazi positions led to his arrest when the Nazis marched into Austria in 1938, and, in 1939, to his imprisonment in Buchenwald. For several years he was on hard labor of different types. In 1943 he became the medical clerk in the camp, remaining in that post until April 1945. From this vantage point Kogon was able to gain insight into the MEDICAL EXPERIMENTS being performed on the prisoners. Prompted by the humane instincts that he retained throughout the years of his imprisonment, Kogon tried to use his position to alleviate sanitary conditions in the camp and save the lives of individual prisoners. He cooperated with the underground in the camp (most of whose leaders were German Communists). Kogon was one of forty-six Buchenwald prisoners whom the Gestapo planned to kill on the eve of liberation, but he managed to be smuggled out of the camp in a locked container on April 12, 1945. Once outside, he put pressure on the camp commandant, by means of a fabricated threatening letter, to behave properly. He also persuaded American troops who were approaching the camp to liberate it without delay.

After the liberation, Kogon drew up a report on Buchenwald for the Psychological Welfare Branch at the Allied Forces Headquarters. He later elaborated his report into a book that became the first comprehensive description of the Nazi concentration camps, *Der SS-Staat: Das System der deutschen Konzentrationslager* (1946; published in English as *The Theory and Practice of Hell: The German Concentration Camps and the System behind Them*, 1950). Containing the first fundamental analysis of the concentration camps, the book has since gone through several editions and has been translated into many languages. Among other things, it analyzes from sociological and psychological perspectives the means used by the SS to divide the prisoners into various groups and thereby facilitate control over them.

In 1946 Kogon helped found the journal *Frankfurter Hefte*, and he remained one of its editors and contributors until his death. His articles dealt mostly with the nature of Nazism and the development of the Federal Republic of Germany. From 1951 until his retirement in 1968, Kogon was a professor of political science at the College of Engineering in Darmstadt. Politically, he was active on behalf of the European Movement, which advocated a united Western Europe, serving as chairman of the German European Union from 1949 to 1953. He was also chairman of the German Political Science Association.

Basing his efforts on his idealistic humanist convictions, Kogon continued to call for the complete investigation and publicizing of the nature and meaning of Nazism and its racist ideology. As he stated in *Nationalsozialistische Massentötung durch Giftgas* (Nazi Mass Murder by Poison Gas; 1983), which he coedited, "Thought and action securely anchored in humanity provide the only protection against the racist mania and all its consequences; humanity is also the source of the right normative perceptions on which all existential decisions should be based. This applies to the individual, to society, and to the State."

BIBLIOGRAPHY

Des Pres, T. *The Survivor: An Anatomy of Life in the Death Camps.* New York, 1976. See pages 155–162.

FALK PINGEL

KOLBE, MAXIMILIAN (1894–1941), Polish monk, philosopher, priest, and Catholic saint. Kolbe was born in Zduńska Wola, in the Łódź district. His Christian name at birth was Raymond; at the age of seventeen he entered the Franciscan order and became Friar Maximilian. In 1912 he went to Rome to study theology and philosophy. He founded the Order of the Knights of the Immaculata in 1917, and was ordained a priest the following year; he returned home in 1919. In Poland, which by then had gained independence, Kolbe served as a priest; in 1927 he founded the City of the Immaculata (Pol., Niepokalanow), a center near Warsaw that was to disseminate the Catholic faith in the spirit of the Virgin Mary. By 1939 the number of the faithful at the center, followers of Kolbe, had grown to seven hundred. In 1930, in spite of being afflicted with tuberculosis, Kolbe went to the Far East, together with several assistants, to establish a Catholic mission. Located at Nagasaki, Japan, the mission was modeled on the Niepokalanow Center in Poland. Kolbe named it Mugenzai no Sono (Jpn.; Garden of the Immaculata). In 1936 Kolbe was summoned back to Poland, where he was appointed head of the Niepokalanow Center and its operations. His special interest was the center's publications network, which included a monthly, a youth magazine, and a popular newspaper, *Mały Dziennik* (Small Daily). Kolbe was very active in disseminating his religious views and his social ideas in speech and writing, and he gained a reputation for his piety and devotion.

Early in the German occupation, Father Kolbe was arrested and removed from Niepokalanow, but by December 1939 he was allowed back to his "city," where he set up an institution for the care of refugees from Poznań and its environs and, it was reported, also extended help to Jewish refugees. In February 1941 Father Kolbe was again arrested, and put into the PAWIAK PRISON. Three months later he was deported to the AUSCHWITZ extermination camp. According to eyewitness accounts by other prisoners, Father Kolbe remained true to his faith and sought to bring comfort to many other victims. In July 1941, a prisoner from Kolbe's block succeeded in escaping from the camp, and as punishment the SS decided to execute every tenth prisoner in the block. Standing in line next to Kolbe was a Polish workingman by the name of Gajowniczek, to whose lot it fell to be one of the victims. When the man cried out, "What will happen to my wife, to my children?" Kolbe stepped out of the line and declared that he wanted to take Gajowniczek's place. The Germans agreed, and Kolbe was moved to a starvation cell, where he was later put to death with a phenol injection.

In 1971 the Vatican proclaimed the beatification of Father Kolbe (a step below sainthood), and in October 1982 he was canonized as a saint of the Catholic church. Since 1971, and with greater intensity after his canonization, a debate has raged in Poland, Austria, the United States, and Britain concerning Kolbe's personality and work. It was claimed that while Kolbe was to be admired for what he did in his life and for his act of self-sacrifice, he had also been contaminated with antisemitic views, and the newspapers that he published had an anti-Jewish slant.

The ensuing examination of these claims showed that the newspapers published under Kolbe's supervision, and especially the daily, which had had a wide circulation, did indeed have a strong antisemitic flavor. While Kolbe had tried to restrain the daily's extreme antisemitism, his own letters and writings had an antisemitic tone, and he had justified the exclusion of the Jews from the Polish economy. Kolbe's brand of antisemitism was not racist, and he preached that the Jews should convert; some of his expressions against Jews and Freemasons, however, were quite extreme, and his writings contain references to the PROTOCOLS OF THE ELDERS OF ZION.

BIBLIOGRAPHY

Ricciardi, A. *St. Maximilian Kolbe: Apostle of Our Difficult Age.* Boston, 1982.

Saint Louis Center for Holocaust Studies. *Saint Maximilian Kolbe: An Interdisciplinary Interfaith Learning Project.* Saint Louis, 1984.

Treece, P. *A Man for Others: Maximilian Kolbe, Saint of Auschwitz, in the Words of Those Who Knew Him.* San Francisco, 1982.

ISRAEL GUTMAN

KOLDICHEVO, concentration camp established early in the summer of 1942 on a farm of the same name. It was located 11 miles (18 km) from BARANOVICHI, on the highway to Novogrudok, Belorussia (which in the interwar period belonged to Poland). In November 1942 a crematorium was constructed in the camp, and 600 corpses were incinerated there.

The Koldichevo camp was used for imprisoning Polish and Belorussian members of the underground and Jews from Gorodishche, Diatlovo, Novogrudok, Stolbtsy, and Baranovichi. The Jews were put into stables, in a separate part of the camp. The commandant of the camp was Fritz Jörn, an SS-*Hauptscharführer.* During the period from 1942 to 1944, twenty-two thousand persons—mostly Jews—were murdered in Koldichevo. One of the prisoners in the camp, Dr. Zelik Levinbok of Baranovichi, managed to supply medicines in large quantities to the parti-

KOLDICHEVO

sans, with the help of a local peasant who was his patient. Eventually, Levinbok himself, together with his wife and eight-year-old son, managed to escape and join the partisans. There was a Jewish underground in the camp, headed by Shlomo Kushnir, a shoemaker. Its members had two guns and four hand grenades, and a Jewish prisoner in the camp who was a chemist manufactured a quantity of acid, to be used in self-defense.

By means of tools that they obtained, the prisoners breached a wall. They practiced moving slowly and crawling on all fours, sewed cloth onto the soles of their shoes, and equipped themselves with knives. On March 17, 1944, a stormy night, they broke out from the camp, having first poisoned the watchdogs. Twenty-four prisoners were recaptured, but seventy-five escaped to the partisans; most joined the unit of Tuvia BIELSKI.

BIBLIOGRAPHY

Baranowicze Memorial Book. Tel Aviv, 1953. (In Hebrew.)

SHALOM CHOLAWSKI

KOLOMYIA (Ger., Kolomea; Pol., Kołomyja), city in the western part of the Ukrainian SSR, on the Prut River. Jews lived in Kolomyia from the sixteenth century. Between 1772 and 1918 it was part of Austrian-held Galicia, and in the interwar period it belonged to Poland. At the beginning of 1939 the city's Jewish population was about fifteen thousand; they were joined in September 1939 by thousands of Jewish refugees from the German-occupied parts of Poland. On September 17, 1939, Kolomyia was occupied by the Red Army and incorporated into the Soviet Union.

When the Germans invaded the Soviet Union, in June 1941, several hundred Kolomyia Jews fled to the east. On June 30 the Soviet army withdrew from the city, and three days later, on July 3, Hungarian troops entered (Hungary was an ally of the Germans). In those three days Ukrainian nationalists staged a pogrom against the Kolomyia Jews; when the Hungarians took over, the Hungarian military governor managed to restrain the Ukrainians. In the first half of July many anti-Jewish measures were imposed; for example, the Jews had to wear a badge with a Star of David (*see* BADGE, JEWISH), their property was confiscated, their freedom of movement was restricted, and they were put on forced labor.

The city came under direct German administration on August 1, and the anti-Jewish policy became more severe. On August 19 the Jews were ordered to pay a large ransom and to hand over their valuables. Also in August, a JUDENRAT (Jewish Council) was set up, headed by Mordechai Horowitz, who stayed in that post up to the end of 1942. Opinions of Horowitz are contradictory: many survivors stress his devoted efforts on behalf of the community, while others point out that he complied with all the demands made by the Germans for payments in money or in kind.

On October 12, the first large-scale *Aktion* took place in Kolomyia. The Germans and the Ukrainian police rounded up some 3,000 Jews, jailed them, and a few days later killed them in huge ditches that were located in a grove near Sheparovtse, a village 5 miles (8 km) from the city. Again, on November 6, hundreds of Jews were seized and murdered in the same place. On December 23, all the Jews who had foreign passports were ordered to report

to the Gestapo; 1,200 Jews responded to the order, and they were all taken to Sheparovtse and killed there. On January 24, 1942, the Germans arrested 400 Jewish intellectuals. They were first tortured and then killed.

A ghetto was established in Kolomyia on March 25, and over 18,000 persons were crowded into it. Many succumbed to the intolerable conditions, starvation, and disease. Despite all the difficulties, however, educational and cultural activities were organized for the ghetto inhabitants. On April 3 and 4 approximately 5,000 people were deported from the ghetto to the BEŁŻEC extermination camp, and another 250 were killed in the ghetto alleys. At the end of April more Jews were brought into the ghetto from a number of neighboring towns, including Kuty, Kosov, and Zabolotov. In an *Aktion* on September 7, 1942, 7,000 Jews were taken to Bełżec and another 1,000 were murdered inside the ghetto. Sporadic killing went on up to October of 1942. On October 11 another *Aktion* was undertaken, in the course of which children were removed from the orphanage and included among another 4,000 persons deported to Bełżec. In the latter half of that month the chairman of the Judenrat, Mordechai Horowitz, committed suicide. In an *Aktion* on November 4, 1,000 Jews were driven to Sheparovtse and shot to death there. On January 20, 1943, the remnants of the community, numbering some 2,000 persons, were rounded up and concentrated in a few houses in the ghetto; on February 2 the ghetto was definitively liquidated and the last of its inhabitants murdered at the Sheparovtse killing ground.

On March 29, 1944, Kolomyia was liberated by the Soviet army, and several dozen survivors came out of their hiding places. A few days later the Germans launched a counterattack and came so close to the city that the survivors had to flee; they were not able to return until August. Some of the surviving Jews of Kolomyia crossed the border into Romania in order to make their way from there to Palestine. Others went west, to Poland, and from there continued on to Palestine and other destinations.

BIBLIOGRAPHY

Bickel, S., ed. *Kolomyia Record*. New York, 1957. (In Hebrew.)

Noy, D., and M. Schutzman, eds. *Kolomeyer Memorial Book*. Tel Aviv, 1972. (In Hebrew.)

AHARON WEISS

KOLOZSVÁR. *See* Cluj.

KOMMISSARBEFEHL (Commissar Order), order issued by the German army to kill the political commissars in the Red Army who fell into German hands. The guidelines that Hitler gave the Wehrmacht for the attack on the Soviet Union (Operation "Barbarossa") ordered it to plan the attack not only from its military aspects but from the ideological aspect as well. Thus, the attack was to include the physical destruction of the bearers of the Communist idea and the political activists of the Soviet state establishment.

On June 6, 1941, two weeks prior to the invasion of the Soviet Union, the Oberkommando der Wehrmacht (Armed Forces High Command; OKW) issued the *Kommissarbefehl*.

It must be expected that the treatment of our prisoners by the political commissars of all types, who are the true pillars of resistance, will be cruel, inhuman, and dictated by hate. . . . Therefore, if captured during combat or while offering resistance they must on principle be shot immediately. This applies to commissars of every type and position, even if they are only suspected of resistance, sabotage, or instigation thereto.

According to the Directive for the Conduct of the Troops in Russia, . . . in their capacity as officials attached to enemy troops, political commissars . . . will not be recognized as soldiers; the protection granted to prisoners of war . . . will not apply to them. After having been segregated they are to be liquidated. . . .

Commissars seized in the rear area of the army group . . . are to be handed over to the Einsatzgruppen or Einsatzkommandos of the Sicherheitspolizei [Security Police].

The order was signed by Gen. Walter Warlimont and its issue was authorized by Gen. Wilhelm KEITEL, the OKW chief of staff. It was based on the Order on Jurisdiction in the Operation "Barbarossa" Area of May 13, 1941, which gave the army and the SS wide powers and facilitated the establishment of a regime of terror and tyranny in the Soviet territories occupied by the Germans.

The *Kommissarbefehl* and the order of May 13 were both in violation of international conventions on the treatment and rights of prisoners of war and civilians in occupied territories. Together with other orders of the same type, it made the Wehrmacht an accomplice in the Nazi war crimes committed in the Soviet Union. A few days after the *Kommissarbefehl* was issued, Field Marshal Walther von Brauchitsch, chief of the Oberkommando des Heeres (Army High Command), issued guidelines giving every officer the authority to decide on the execution of commissars who had been made prisoners of war. Commissars were executed as soon as they were identified as such, whether on the front, when they were taken prisoner, or in prisoner-of-war camps in the rear. In the summer of 1941 Keitel ordered that all copies of the *Kommissarbefehl* that had been distributed to the various army headquarters be destroyed, in an effort to remove evidence implicating the army in war crimes.

BIBLIOGRAPHY

Dallin, A. *German Rule in Russia, 1941–1945: A Study of Occupation Policies*. New York, 1957.

Jacobsen, H. "The Kommissarbefehl and Mass Executions of Soviet Russian Prisoners of War." In *The Anatomy of the SS State*, edited by H. Krausnik et al., pp. 505–535. New York, 1968.

Reitlinger, G. *The SS: Alibi of a Nation*. New York, 1981.

YITZHAK ARAD

KOMOLY, OTTÓ (also Nathan Kahn; 1892–1945), Hungarian Jewish leader. Komoly was born in BUDAPEST and studied engineering. During World War I, he became a highly decorated officer. An active Zionist, he was elected deputy chairman of the Hungarian Zionist Federation late in 1940. Toward the end of 1941, he was drawn to the activities of Rezső (Rudolf) KASZTNER, who was trying to form a committee around Social Democrats and Liberal Jews to help Jewish refugees arriving in HUNGARY. Although the committee did not really coalesce, Komoly, Kasztner, Samuel Springmann, Joel BRAND, and several other Zionists continued to proffer aid to the refugees.

Following a suggestion by the YISHUV's recently organized rescue committee under Itzhak GRUENBAUM, the RELIEF AND RESCUE COMMITTEE OF BUDAPEST was formally established, with Komoly and Kasztner at its head, early in 1943. In his capacity as a leader of the committee, Komoly took part in relief work and in attempts to smuggle Jewish refugees into Hungary. In the committee's major achievement, about eleven hundred Polish Jews were brought to Hungary through the Tiyyul ("Excursion"; the code name for the operation of smuggling Polish Jews into Hungary) from Poland. With the help of Orthodox Jewish elements, Zionist youth movement members, and the PRACOVNÁ SKUPINA (Working Group), the Relief and Rescue Committee began to send messengers to Poland in the spring of 1943 to locate surviving Jews. Once found, they were smuggled to safety in Hungary, usually by way of Slovakia. This rescue work gained momentum in the autumn of 1943 and continued until the German occupation of Hungary in March 1944.

After the Germans entered Hungary, Komoly focused on efforts to convince the more moderate elements of the Hungarian leadership to protect the Hungarian Jews. As a head of the Relief and Rescue Committee, he also played a role in the Brand mission, the "Kasztner train," and other negotiation attempts between Hungarian Jews and the Nazis.

From the summer of 1944 until his death in January 1945, Komoly strove to help Jews through his contacts with neutral diplomats in Budapest. In September of that year, Friedrich Born, the representative of the International RED CROSS in Hungary, appointed Komoly head of Section A, the Red Cross department established to help Jewish children. Together with Born and members of the Zionist youth movement, Komoly set up children's houses under international protection, beginning in the summer of 1944 and continuing more intensively after the ARROW CROSS PARTY coup of October 15, 1944. After that month, Section A expanded its activities to include provision of food and other supplies for the Jews of Budapest. As head of the Relief and Rescue Committee and Section A, and because of his contacts, Komoly emerged as a central figure in the rescue activities in Budapest during the Arrow Cross reign of terror.

Apparently because of his rescue activities, the Arrow Cross executed Komoly, shortly before the conquest of Budapest by the Red Army. He was posthumously awarded the Hungarian Order of Freedom. In Israel, Moshav (cooperative settlement) Yad Natan was named after Komoly.

BIBLIOGRAPHY

Cohen, A. *The Halutz Resistance in Hungary, 1942–1944*. New York, 1986.

Rozett, R. "Child Rescue in Budapest, 1944–1945." *Holocaust and Genocide Studies* 2/1 (1987): 49–59.

Vago, B. "Budapest Jewry in the Summer of 1944: Otto Komoly's Diaries." *Yad Vashem Studies* 8 (1970): 81–105.

ROBERT ROZETT

KOPPE, WILHELM (1896–1975), a senior SS commander in occupied POLAND. Born in Hildesheim, Koppe served in the German army in World War I and then was a merchant and shopkeeper.

In August 1930 Koppe became a member of the Nazi party, and in 1932 he joined the SS. The following year, he was elected to the Reichstag. Rising rapidly in the SS, he was made a *Brigadeführer* in August 1934 and a *Gruppenführer* in September 1936.

On October 26, 1939, Koppe was appointed *Höherer SS- und Polizeiführer* (Higher SS and Police Leader; HSSPF) in the WARTHEGAU (the Poznań region), a post he held until November 9, 1943. Koppe was one of the leading figures in the establishment of the CHEŁMNO extermination camp, where 320,000 people were killed, and in the liquidation of the ghettos in the Warthegau. In January 1942 he was promoted to *Obergruppenführer*, and in November 1943 he became the HSSPF in the GENERALGOUVERNEMENT.

After the war, Koppe lived in West Germany under an assumed name (Lohmann) and worked as a factory manager. His real identity was discovered in 1961, and he was arrested and brought to trial in West Germany. The proceedings against him were discontinued in 1966, and he was released on medical grounds.

BIBLIOGRAPHY

Datner, S. *Wilhelm Koppe: Nieukarany zbrodniarz hitlerowski.* Warsaw, 1963.
Hilberg, R. *The Destruction of the European Jews.* 3 vols. New York, 1985.

SHMUEL KRAKOWSKI

KORCZAK, JANUSZ (pen name of Henryk Goldszmit, 1878 or 1879–1942), physician, writer, and educator. Korczak was born in Warsaw, the son of an assimilated Jewish family. His father was a successful attorney who became mentally ill when Korczak was eleven; this was a heavy blow to the family's financial situation, and a trauma that cast its shadow over Korczak throughout his life.

Even while still a student of medicine at Warsaw University, Korczak was drawn to circles

Janusz Korczak and some of his young wards.

of liberal educators and writers in Poland. When he entered medical practice, he did his best to help the poor and those who suffered the most; at the same time he began to write. His first books, *Children of the Streets* (1901) and *A Child of the Salon* (1906), aroused great interest. In 1904 he was drafted into the Russian army as a doctor, and was posted to East Asia.

Both as doctor and as writer, Korczak was drawn to the world of the child. He worked in a Jewish children's hospital and took groups of children to summer camps, and in 1908 he began to work with orphans. In 1912 he was appointed director of a new and spacious Jewish orphanage in Warsaw, on Krochmalna Street. Throughout his life, his partner in his work was Stefania Wilczyńska, a superb educator, the daughter of a wealthy Jewish family who dedicated her life to the care of orphans and greatly influenced Korczak and his career as an educator. In the orphanage, Korczak studied the secret depths of the child's soul, and it was in the orphanage that he made practical application of his educational ideas.

Korczak called for an understanding of the emotional life of children and urged that children be respected. A child was not to be regarded as something to be shaped and trained to suit adults, but rather as someone whose soul was rich in perceptions and ideas, who should be observed and listened to within his or her own autonomous sphere. Every child, he maintained, has to be dealt with as an individual whose inclinations and ambitions, and the conditions under which he or she is growing up, require understanding. In several of his books—such as *King Matthew the First* (1923), *When I Am Small Again* (1925), and the short theoretical work *The Child's Right to Respect* (1929)—Korczak stressed the social conflict between child and adult in a situation when power and control are in the hands of the adult, even when the adult does not understand or refuses to understand the child's world, has no respect for the child, and deliberately deprives the child of his or her due. In Korczak's view, "to reform the world" meant "to reform the educational system."

In 1914 Korczak was again called up for military service in the Russian army, and it was in military hospitals and bases that he wrote his important work *How to Love Children*. After the war he returned to Poland—now independent—and to his work in the Jewish orphanage, but he was also asked to take charge of an orphanage for Polish children and to apply there the methods he had introduced in the establishment on Krochmalna Street. The 1920s were a period of intensive and fruitful work in Korczak's life. He was in charge of two orphanages (where he also lived), served as an instructor at boarding schools and summer camps and as a lecturer at universities and seminaries, and wrote a great deal. In the late 1920s, he was able to put into effect his longtime plan to establish a newspaper for children as a weekly added to the Jewish daily in the Polish language, *Nasz Przegląd*; it was written by children, who related their experiences and their deepest thoughts.

In the mid-1930s, Korczak's public career underwent a change. Following the death of the Polish dictator, Józef Piłsudski, political power in the country came into the hands of radical right-wing and openly antisemitic circles. Korczak was removed from many of the positions in which he had been active, and he suffered great disappointment. As a result, he took a growing interest in the Zionist effort and in the Jewish community in Palestine. He visited Palestine twice, in 1934 and 1936, showing particular interest in the state of education, especially the cooperative educational achievements of the kibbutz movement; but he was also deeply impressed by the changes he found in the Jews living there. On the eve of World War II, Korczak was considering moving to Palestine, but his idea failed to reach fruition.

From the very beginning of the war, Korczak took up activities among the Jews and Jewish children. At first he refused to acknowledge the German occupation and heed its rules; he refused to wear the yellow badge (*see* BADGE, JEWISH) and as a consequence spent some time in jail. When, however, the economic situation took a sharp turn for the worse and the Jews of Warsaw were imprisoned in the ghetto, Korczak concentrated his efforts on the orphanage, seeking to provide the children there with food and the basic conditions of existence. He was now an elderly and tired man and could no longer keep track of the changes that were taking place in the world and in his immediate vicinity, and he shut himself in. The only thing that gave him the strength to carry on was the duty he felt to preserve and protect his orphanage, where old rules continued to apply: it was kept clean, the duty roster was observed, there were close relations between the staff and the children, an internal court of honor had jurisdiction over both children and teachers, every Sunday a general assembly was held, there were literary evenings, and the children gave performances. Polish friends of Korczak's reported that they went to see him in the ghetto and offered him asylum on the Polish side, but he refused, not prepared to save himself and abandon the children.

During the occupation and the period he spent in the ghetto, Korczak kept a diary. At the end of July 1942, when the deportations were at their height—about ten days before he, the orphans, and the staff of the orphanage were taken to the UMSCHLAGPLATZ—Korczak wrote the following entry: "I feel so soft and warm in the bed—it will be hard for me to get up. . . . But today is Sabbath—the day on which I weigh the children, before they have their breakfast. This, I think, is the first time that I am not eager to know the figures for the past week. They ought to gain weight (I have no idea why they were given raw carrots for supper last night).''

On August 5, the Germans rounded up Korczak and his two hundred children. A witness to the orphans' three-mile march to the deportation train described the scene to the historian Emanuel RINGELBLUM as follows: "This was not a march to the railway cars, this was an organized, wordless protest against the murder! . . . The children marched in rows of four, with Korczak leading them, looking straight ahead, and holding a child's hand on each side. . . . A second column was led by Stefania Wilczyńska; the third by Broniatowska (her children bearing blue knapsacks on their backs), and the fourth by Sternfeld, from the boarding school on Twarda Street." Nothing is known of their last journey to TREBLINKA, where they were all put to death.

After the war, associations bearing Korczak's name were formed in Poland, Israel, Germany, and other countries, to keep his memory alive and to promote his message and his work. He became a legendary figure, and UNESCO named him "Man of the Year." Books and plays have been written about Korczak, and his own writings have been translated into many languages.

BIBLIOGRAPHY

Arnon, J. "The Passion of Janusz Korczak." *Midstream* 19/5 (May 1973): 32–53.
Korczak, J. *Ghetto Diary.* New York, 1978.
Lifton, B. J. *The King of Children: A Biography of Janusz Korczak.* New York, 1988.
Olczak, H. *Mister Doctor.* London, 1965.
Perlis, Y. *Janusz Korczak: Exemplary Life.* Naharia, Israel, 1982. (In Hebrew.)

ISRAEL GUTMAN

KORCZAK-MARLA, ROZKA (1921–1988), underground fighter and partisan. Korczak-Marla was born in Bielsko, Poland, and until the outbreak of World War II lived in Płock. At that time she went to VILNA, where she joined the leadership of the left-wing Zionist

Rozka Korczak (left) with Abba Kovner and Vitka Kempner (later Mrs. Kovner) as partisans after the liberation of Vilna in July 1944.

movement Ha-Shomer ha-Tsa'ir, with Abba KOVNER and Vitka Kempner. When Vilna's Ghetto No. 1 was liquidated and forty thousand Vilna Jews were killed, Korczak-Marla agreed with Kovner that the surviving Jews should offer armed resistance in the ghetto. Kovner made this proposal at a meeting of the movement's activists that Korczak-Marla attended. His proposal was approved at the meeting, and was followed by a manifesto drafted by him and published on January 1, 1942. Korczak-Marla was active in the FAREY-NEGTE PARTIZANER ORGANIZATSYE (United Partisan Organization). After Yitzhak WITTEN-BERG's self-surrender to the Germans, when a decision was made to leave the ghetto for the forests, Korczak-Marla was among those who went to the Rudninkai Forest. There, the creation of autonomous Jewish partisan units was initiated.

In July 1944 Korczak-Marla returned to

Vilna, which by then had been liberated, and she immigrated to Palestine on December 12, 1944. She joined Kibbutz Eilon and reported to the Jewish leaders on the Jewish resistance movement and the atrocities committed during the war. Later, she moved to Kibbutz Ein ha-Horesh, together with a group of ex-partisans that also included Kovner and Kempner. Korczak-Marla took part in educational projects and in the work of MORESHET, the memorial museum named after Mordecai ANIELEWICZ. She helped to establish the Holocaust studies centers at Givat Haviva and Yad Mordecai.

A book by Korczak-Marla, *Lehavot be-Efer* (Flames in the Ashes), was published in 1964.

BIBLIOGRAPHY

Kowalski, I. *Anthology of Armed Jewish Resistance, 1939–1945.* Vol. 1. See pages 484–485. Brooklyn, N.Y., 1986.

NILI KEREN

KORETZ, ZVI (d. 1945), Chief Rabbi of Salonika. Born in Rzeszów, Galicia, Koretz graduated from the Vienna Rabbinical Seminary and later studied at the Berlin Hochschule für die Wissenschaft des Judentums, an academy for Jewish studies. His appointment as Chief Rabbi of Salonika in 1933 reflected the victory of modernizers who wanted a Western, liberal rabbi to represent their community. The resulting communal split never healed, and Koretz's first term was marked by open clashes. The government headed by Ioannis Metaxas urged his reappointment in 1938.

The Germans imprisoned Koretz in Vienna from May to December 1941 for alleged anti-German propaganda, but in December 1942 they made him president of the Salonika Jewish community. He presided efficiently, and perhaps naively, over the deportations in March and April 1943. Deported to Bergen-Belsen with the JUDENRAT (Jewish Council) in August, he died of typhus in May or June of 1945 and was buried in Tröbitz, in Germany.

BIBLIOGRAPHY

Ben, J. "Jewish Leadership in Greece during the Holocaust." In *Patterns of Jewish Leadership in Nazi Europe, 1933–1945.* Proceedings of the Third Yad Vashem International Historical Conference, edited by Y. Gutman and C. J. Haft, pp. 335–352. Jerusalem, 1979.

Eck, N. "New Light on the Charges against the Last Chief Rabbi of Salonica, Dr. Zvi Koretz." *Yad Vashem Bulletin* 17 (December 1965): 9–15.

Recanati, D. *Salonika Memorial.* Vol. 1. Tel Aviv, 1972. (In Hebrew.)

STEVEN B. BOWMAN

KORHERR, RICHARD (b. 1903), German statistician employed, in his professional capacity, in the destruction of the Jews. Born in Regensburg, Korherr graduated from his academic studies with honors, and before long began to publish statistical works that earned him high praise. In 1928 he joined the staff of the Reich Bureau of Statistics, transferring in 1930 to the Bavarian Bureau of Statistics. The Bavarian prime minister appointed him chairman of the board of Reich und Heimat (Reich and Home), a government-sponsored society. Korherr's book *Geburtenrückgang* (Decline in the Birth Rate) was well received; Benito MUSSOLINI personally translated it into Italian, and it also appeared in a Japanese translation. The 1936 edition of the book had a foreword by Heinrich HIMMLER.

For a time in the early 1930s, Korherr was unemployed; from 1935 to 1940 he was director of the Würzburg municipal bureau of statistics and also lectured at the local university. As of 1934, and thereafter concurrently with his job in Würzburg, Korherr was in charge of the section of statistics and demographic policy in the headquarters of Rudolf HESS, then the deputy Führer. In 1937 and 1938 Korherr published *Untergang der alten Kulturvölker* (Decline of the Historical Civilized Peoples), and in 1938 an atlas, under the title *Volk und Raum* (People and Space). In May 1937 Korherr joined the Nazi party, but he did not become a member of either the SA (Sturmabteilung; Storm Troopers) or the SS.

On December 9, 1940, Korherr was appointed chief inspector of the statistical bureaus of the *Reichsführer-SS und Chef der*

Deutschen Polizei and of the REICHSKOMMISSARIAT FÜR DIE FESTIGUNG DES DEUTSCHEN VOLKSTUMS (Reich Commissariat for the Strengthening of German Nationhood), both jobs under Himmler. Korherr wrote numerous memoranda on a variety of statistical problems. In December 1942 he began processing data for the "FINAL SOLUTION" of the "Jewish question" in Europe, a task in which he was assisted by a Dr. Simon, a Jew who was the statistician of the Reichsvereinigung der Juden in Deutschland (Reich Association of Jews in Germany). Korherr also availed himself of material supplied by Adolf EICHMANN's section in the REICHSSICHERHEITSHAUPTAMT (Reich Security Main Office; RSHA).

Korherr was the author of the document that came to be known as the *Korherrbericht* (Korherr Report), whose subject was the extermination of the Jews of Europe; in 1943 and 1944 he updated the report every three months. In his trial in Jerusalem, Eichmann stated that the *Korherr Report* had served him in the planning stages of the extermination. Information on the number of Jews enabled the Nazis to determine the size of the team they would need to organize the liquidation of the Jews in a specific place or specific country, the number of railway cars that would be required, and the final destination of the victims, the extermination camp. Korherr's acquaintances described him as a technocrat, totally dedicated to his job, who was always trying to become close to Himmler, an effort in which he was not always successful.

After the war Korherr tried to diminish the importance of the report that bore his name. In evidence that he gave on July 13, 1951, at the trial of Alfred Filbert, commander of Einsatzkommando 9, Korherr claimed that the statistical data in his report were false, because they had been based on inflated figures given in the Einsatzgruppen reports. Thanks to the recommendation he received from Dr. Simon—whose life he had saved—Korherr was given a post by the West Germany Ministry of Finance, but he was dismissed from his job following the publication, in 1961, of Gerald Reitlinger's book *The Final Solution,* in which the *Korherr Report* figured prominently.

BIBLIOGRAPHY

"The First Unabridged Publication of the Two 'Korherr Reports.'" In *The Holocaust and the Neo-Nazi Mania,* edited by S. Klarsfeld, pp. 165–210. New York, 1978.
Wellers, G. "The Numbers of Victims and the Korherr Report." In *The Holocaust and the Neo-Nazi Mania,* edited by S. Klarsfeld, pp. 139–161. New York, 1978.

HANS-HEINRICH WILHELM

KOŠICE (Hung., Kassa), city in southeastern Slovakia; part of the territory annexed by HUNGARY on November 11, 1938. The first thirty-two Jewish families reached Košice in 1843; in 1930 the Jewish population of the city was 11,191, and by 1944 it had increased to 11,830. The number of Jews rose owing to the arrival of refugees from Poland and Slovakia during the earlier years of World War II, but the increase was tempered by the loss of the significant number of Jewish men from Košice who were drafted into the MUNKASZOLGÁLAT (Hungarian Labor Service System) beginning in the summer of 1940.

On the day the Germans occupied Hungary (March 19, 1944), their troops entered Košice. The city was designated as part of the first anti-Jewish operation zone (for the purpose of deportations, Hungary was divided into six zones). Late that month the authorities took as hostages about one hundred prominent Jews to ensure the Jewish community's cooperation. In mid-April a ghetto was set up in Košice and surrounded by a fence built by the Jews. On April 28 there was a major drive to incarcerate the Jews in the ghetto, under the direction of the mayor of Košice, Sándor Pohl, and the chief of police, György Horvath. During the concentration and subsequent deportation, the police acted with brutality. Jews from nearby towns and villages, as well as some of Košice's Jews, were concentrated in two brickyards located at the edge of the city. Altogether, more than twelve thousand Jews were held in the brickyards and the ghetto.

During the deportations, which began on May 15, 1944, all the Jews were sent to the brickyards. From there they boarded trains headed for AUSCHWITZ. Three transports left Košice, each with about four thousand Jews, the last departing on June 2, 1944. Two-thirds of the deportees from the city—some eight thousand individuals—were gassed immediately upon their arrival in Auschwitz. On May 17, the Zsidó Tanács (Jewish Council), which included Dr. Dezső Berger, Jenő Ungar, Igniac Spira, and Dr. Akos Kolozs, tried to blunt the blow that had befallen the community. They asked the head of the Košice Jewish Women's Association, Mrs. Samuel Gotterer, who was the wife of a severely wounded World War I veteran, to address a plea to the wife of Adm. Miklós HORTHY, the Hungarian regent. Her letter beseeched the Horthys to exempt children under the age of eighteen, women over the age of fifty, and men over the age of sixty from the transports that were allegedly destined for labor centers in the east. Her plea fell on deaf ears. During the rest of the deportations from Hungary, which lasted until early July of 1944, Košice was the point where the Hungarian authorities handed over the Jewish deportees to the Germans.

After the war some four hundred fifty Jews returned to Košice from the camps; about three thousand survived the war in Hungarian labor units, in the underground, or in the Czechoslovak Eastern Army, which fought alongside the Soviet army. The city, along with the surrounding area, which had been annexed by Hungary, was incorporated into the reestablished Czechoslovakia. In the middle of the 1960s, only thirteen hundred Jews were left in Košice.

BIBLIOGRAPHY

Braham, R. L. *The Politics of Genocide.* New York, 1981.

ROBERT ROZETT

Zofia Kossak-Szczucka.

KOSSAK-SZCZUCKA, ZOFIA (maiden name, Szatkowska; 1890–1968), Polish Catholic writer. Kossak-Szczucka's novels were in the main historical, among them *Krzyżowy* (The Crusaders) and *Złota Wolność* (Golden Freedom). During the German occupation of Poland, she led the Catholic underground organization, Front Odrodzenia Polski (Polish Resistance Front), which conducted social and educational activities and, from 1942, assisted Jews. In September 1942, Kossak-Szczucka helped found the Tymczasowy Komitet Pomocy Żydom (Temporary Committee for Aid to Jews). That December the committee became the Rada Pomocy Żydom (Council for Aid to Jews), known as ZEGOTA. Kossak-Szczucka then moved to the Społezna Organizacja Samoobrony (Civic Self-Defense Organization), where she continued to care for Jews in hiding. In September 1943 she was arrested under an assumed name, and the Germans did not identify her. She was interned in AUSCHWITZ until July 1944, and wrote a chronicle of this period, *Z otchłani* (From the Abyss). After the war she settled in Great Britain, returning to Poland in 1957.

BIBLIOGRAPHY

Bartoszewski, W., and Z. Lewin, eds. *Righteous among the Nations: How Poles Helped the Jews.* London, 1969.

Prekerowa, T. "The Just and the Passive." *Yad Vashem Studies* 19 (1988): 369–378.

TERESA PREKEROWA

KOVEL (Pol., Kowel), town in Volhynia, now in the Ukrainian SSR; in the interwar period it belonged to Poland. On the eve of World War II Kovel had a Jewish population of 13,200, about half the total population of 27,677. After 1939 the number of Jews grew, since many Jews from the German-occupied parts of Poland took refuge in Kovel. The Germans entered the town on June 28, 1941. In the first few days of the occupation, 1,000 Jews were seized and killed. The local Ukrainian authorities were hostile to the Jews and harassed them by withholding food supplies, electricity, and water, among other measures. At the end of July the Jews had to surrender all their Torah scrolls, which were then burned in public. This was followed by the confiscation of valuables in Jewish possession and the imposition of a collective fine.

On May 21, 1942, two ghettos were established in Kovel. One, in the new part of the town, held eight thousand persons—people who were working and had special passes, as well as their families. The other was in the old part, where six thousand persons were billeted, none of them with passes in their possession. The second ghetto was surrounded by police on June 2, and in an operation that went on for three days, all the inhabitants were taken out and killed. The turn of the other ghetto, where the workers lived, came on August 19. Many of the Jews tried to flee and hide, but they were caught and forced into the Great Synagogue; on the synagogue walls they inscribed their last wills and their call for revenge. On October 6, 1942, the liquidation of the Kovel Jews was completed.

At the beginning of May 1942 two emissaries of the underground in Warsaw, Frumka PLOTNICKA and Tema Sznajdermann, had succeeded in entering Kovel. On their return to Warsaw, they reported on resistance groups in the Kovel ghetto who had smuggled out arms from warehouses and passed them on to Soviet partisans active in the area. The

hostile attitude of the partisan unit's commander foiled the resistance groups' efforts to leave the ghetto and go into the forests, and only a few succeeded in doing so.

Kovel was liberated on July 6, 1944, after a prolonged battle in which the town was destroyed. In the following days about forty Jews converged on Kovel, coming out of the forests and other hiding places.

BIBLIOGRAPHY

Belar, B. *Pincas Kowel.* Buenos Aires, 1951. (In Yiddish.)

Leoni-Tsuferfin, E. *Kovel: A Book of Testimonies and Memoirs for Our Community Which Was Mowed Down.* Tel Aviv, 1957. (In Hebrew.)

SHMUEL SPECTOR

KOVNER, ABBA (1918–1988), underground leader and partisan commander, one of the architects of the BERIHA, poet, and writer; influential figure in Israel's cultural and political life.

Kovner was born in Sevastopol, Russia, attended a Hebrew secondary school in VILNA, and studied plastic arts; from his youth he was a member of the Ha-Shomer ha-Tsa'ir Zionist youth movement. During the period when Vilna was the capital of the Lithuanian SSR (1940–1941), he was active in the underground. When the city was captured by the Germans at the end of June 1941, Kovner, together with a group of his comrades, found temporary refuge in a Dominican convent on the outskirts of the city. On returning to the ghetto he learned of the massacres of the Jews, came to the realization that resistance was the only response, and decided to apply himself to the creation of a Jewish fighting force. At a meeting of the He-Haluts movement in Vilna, held on the night of December 31, 1941, a manifesto that Kovner had drawn up was read out. It stated (in part): "Hitler plans to kill all the Jews of Europe . . . the Jews of Lithuania are the first in line. *Let us not go like sheep to the slaughter.* We may be weak and defenseless, but the only possible answer to the enemy is resistance!" This was the first time that the mass killing of Jews by the EINSATZGRUPPEN was analyzed as being part of a master plan for the destruction of European Jewry, and also the first time that Jews were urged to offer organized fighting resistance to the Nazis.

On January 21, 1942, a Jewish combat organization, the FAREYNEGTE PARTIZANER ORGANIZATSYE (United Partisan Organization; FPO), was founded in Vilna, made up of youth movements and the various political parties. Kovner was a member of the FPO leadership, and in July 1943, when its first commander, Yitzhak WITTENBERG, fell into the Nazis' hands, Kovner took his place (using the *nom de guerre* "Uri"). During the final deportation from Vilna in September 1943, he directed the FPO's operations and the escape of the ghetto fighters into the forests. In the Rudninkai Forest (*see* PARTISANS), Kovner commanded a Jewish unit made up of Vilna ghetto fighters, as well as the Jewish camp's "Revenge" battalion.

After liberation, Kovner became one of the architects of the Beriha escape movement and was the moving spirit in the Organization of Eastern European Survivors. This was a supra-partisan organization comprising various Zionist factions that called for the unity of all forces, a call based on "the lesson of the Holocaust" and the dangers still threatening the Jewish people. In July 1945 Kovner arrived at the JEWISH BRIGADE GROUP base camp at Treviso, Italy, where he addressed an assembly of Jewish soldiers and, in moving and penetrating words, described the Holocaust and the Vilna uprising.

Kovner arrived in Palestine in the second half of 1945, on a short visit, in order to solicit support and resources for revenge operations in Europe against persons who had carried out murders or had been responsible for them. On his way back to Europe he was arrested by the British and returned to Palestine, where he spent some time in jail. After his release in 1946, Kovner joined Kibbutz Ein ha-Horesh, together with his wife, Vitka Kempner (who was also his partner in the underground and in the fighting), and a

Abba Kovner in Vilna (July 1944).

Jewish partisans from Vilna who fought in the Rudninkai Forest return to Vilna after the city's liberation (July 14, 1944). Standing fourth from the left is Abba Kovner.

group of former partisans. During the Israeli War of Independence (1947–1949), Kovner was the education officer of the Givati brigade and produced the brigade's publication, *Battle Page*.

When the War of Independence came to an end, Kovner went back to his kibbutz and devoted his time to writing. He published two volumes of prose writings in the Panim el Panim (Face-to-Face) series and issued collections of his many poems, among them the partisan poems *Ad Lo Or, Mi-Kol ha-Ahavot,* and *Ahoti ha-Ketanna.* In 1970 he was awarded the Israel Prize in Literature. Kovner was chairman of the Israel Hebrew Writers' Association and the founder of MORESHET (the institute for Holocaust research in Givat Haviva, Israel) and of the Mordecai ANIELEWICZ Communities House. He shaped the character of the contents of Beth Hatefutsoth, the Nahum Goldmann Museum of the Jewish Diaspora, in Tel Aviv. A collection of his statements on current issues was published in the book *Al ha-Gesher ha-Zar* (1981).

BIBLIOGRAPHY

Arad, Y. *Ghetto in Flames: The Struggle and Destruction of the Jews in Vilna in the Holocaust.* Jerusalem, 1980.

Kovner, A. "A First Attempt to Tell." In *The Holocaust as Historical Experience: Essays and a Discussion,* edited by Y. Bauer and N. Rotenstreich, pp. 77–94. New York, 1981.

Kovner, A. "The Mission of the Survivors." In *The Catastrophe of European Jewry,* edited by I. Gutman and L. Rothkirchen, pp. 671–683. Jerusalem, 1976.

ISRAEL GUTMAN

KOVNO (Lith., Kaunas; Pol., Kowno), city in central LITHUANIA, situated at the confluence of the Neman and Neris rivers; founded in 1030 by Koinas, a Lithuanian prince, and named after him. In 1795 Kovno was part of the Polish-Lithuanian territory that was annexed by Russia, and from 1842 it was a district capital. Between 1920 and 1939 Kovno was the capital of independent Lithuania; in 1940 all of Lithuania was incorporated into the Soviet Union.

For the Jews of eastern Europe, Kovno was an important spiritual and cultural center. It was the site of the famous Slobodka yeshiva (Slobodka was a suburb of Kovno; its Lithuanian name is Vilijampole), and was also renowned for its extensive Zionist activities and for its Hebrew school system, ranging from kindergartens to teachers' training colleges.

In 1939 approximately forty thousand Jews lived in Kovno, constituting nearly one-quarter of the city's total population. During the Soviet rule, from 1940 to the German invasion in 1941, the Hebrew educational institutions were closed down and most of the Jewish social and cultural organizations were liquidated; of the city's five Yiddish dailies, only one remained in existence, becoming an organ of the Communist party. On June 14, 1941, a week before the German invasion, hundreds of Jewish families were rounded up and exiled to Siberia, among them factory owners, merchants, public figures, and Zionist activists and leaders.

Establishing the Ghetto. Kovno was occupied on the third day of the invasion, June 24, 1941. Several thousand Jews escaped from the city and made for the interior of the Soviet Union, some of them losing their lives during their flight. Even before the German entry into the city, bands of Lithuanians went on a rampage against the Jews, especially those living in the Slobodka suburb. The murder of Jews continued when the Germans occupied the city and took charge of

When the Germans occupied Kovno on June 24, 1941, they saw bands of Lithuanians seizing Jews in the streets and beating them to death. Here, Lithuanians beat Jews while German soldiers watch.

the killings. Thousands of Jews were moved from the city to other locations, such as the Seventh Fort (one of a chain of forts constructed around Kovno in the nineteenth century), where they were first brutally mistreated by the Lithuanian guards and then shot to death. A total of ten thousand Jews were estimated to have been murdered in June and July of 1941.

When a civilian administration was set up by the Germans, with SA-Brigadeführer Hans Kramer as city commissar, it issued a whole range of anti-Jewish decrees. The Jews were given one month to move into the ghetto that was being established. The area earmarked consisted of two parts (the "small ghetto" and the "large ghetto"), both situated in Slobodka, on either side of the main thoroughfare. A barbed-wire fence, with posts manned by Lithuanian guards, was put up around the ghetto, the gates of which were also watched by German police.

Aktionen and Punitive Decrees. When the ghetto was sealed off in August 1941, it contained 29,760 Jews. In the following two and a half months, 3,000 Jews—men, women, and children—were killed. On October 28 the "big *Aktion*" was staged, in the course of which 9,000 persons (half of them children) were taken to the NINTH FORT and murdered there. The *Aktionen* were then discontinued and a prolonged period of relative calm set in, which lasted up to March 1944. Of the 17,412 Jews now left in the ghetto, most of the adults were put on forced labor, mainly in military installations outside the ghetto. They were under constant, unbearable pressure and harassment. Two thousand Jews, most of them skilled artisans, were organized into "brigades" and put on jobs related to the war effort. Another 4,600 Jews worked in the ghetto workshops, where no Germans or Lithuanians were in attendance. Instead of wages, the Jews were given food rations, which in fact were on a starvation level. To stay alive, the ghetto inhabitants sold off their remaining possessions and used the proceeds to buy the food that was being smuggled into the ghetto at great risk.

During the so-called quiet period, there was a recovery of sorts among the Jews and their nourishment improved. This is not to say that the period was free of punitive measures and unpleasant surprises. In February 1942 the Jews were ordered to hand in all the books, other printed materials, and manuscripts in their possession; in August of that year the synagogues were closed down and public prayer services were outlawed. The bureau of education and the schools—which had continued to function—were now ordered closed (except for the vocational-training schools), and the bans on bringing food into the ghetto and being in possession of cash were strictly enforced. Hundreds of people were deported to RIGA or sent to work camps in various parts of Lithuania.

Internal Administration. Life inside the ghetto was administered by the Council of Elders of the Kovno Jewish Ghetto Community (Ältestenrat der Jüdischen Ghetto Gemeinde Kauen), chaired by Dr. Elhanan ELKES, a well-known physician and public personality, with Leib Garfunkel, a lawyer and veteran Zionist leader, acting as his deputy. Most of the members of the Kovno Ältestenrat were chosen for their posts through direct elections by the Jewish community members. Forced labor and the maintenance of public order were the responsibility of the Jewish police, which had a complement of about 150 men. Appointments to the police and supervision of the force were in the hands of the Ältestenrat. A department of health, welfare, culture, and the like was maintained by the Ältestenrat, providing various services to the ghetto population and running public institutions such as a hospital and medical clinic, a home for the aged, a soup kitchen, a school, and an orchestra. There were concerts, lectures, literary evenings, and other cultural events. After public education was prohibited, it was in fact kept up under the cover of the vocational-training schools. Even in the ghetto, Kovno Jews maintained their tradition of Torah study and of cultural and educational activities and mutual help, over and above the facilities and functions sponsored by the Ältestenrat. The political parties were also active, in the first instance by trying to locate their members and come to their aid. This led to the formation of Matsok (the Hebrew acronym for Zionist Center Vilijampole, Kovno), which was headed by several members of the Ältestenrat and its staff. They maintained contact with the anti-Nazi underground that existed in the ghetto. The Ältestenrat departments also provided substantive aid to the members of the under-

ground who left the ghetto to join the partisans in the forests. In this, as well as in other social and communal aspects, the Kovno ghetto was an unusual phenomenon that has no parallel in the annals of the behavior of Jews under Nazi occupation.

Ghetto into Concentration Camp. Under an order issued by Heinrich HIMMLER on June 21, 1943, it was decided to impose a concentration camp regime upon the surviving Jews of the REICHSKOMMISSARIAT OSTLAND ghettos. In the autumn of 1943, the Kovno ghetto became a central concentration camp, KL (for *Konzentrationslager*) Kauen. Four thousand inhabitants of the ghetto were transferred to small camps, situated in Kovno's suburbs or its vicinity, in places such as Aleksotas, Šančiai, Palemonas, KĖDAINIAI (Keidan), and Kaišiadorys. On October 26, 1943, 2,800 Jews were moved to work camps in Estonia. An exceptionally cruel blow was dealt to the ghetto on March 27, 1944, when 1,800 persons—infants, children, and elderly men and women—were dragged out of their homes and murdered. Also executed were 40 officers of the Jewish police, killed for having given direct aid to the anti-Nazi underground in the ghetto; among those put to death were Moshe Levin, the police chief, and his deputies Yehuda Zupovitz and Ika Grinberg. The remaining police became a JÜDISCHER ORDNUNGSDIENST (Jewish ghetto police) under the direct control of SS men. The Ältestenrat was abolished, and Dr. Elkes was appointed *Judenältester* (senior Jew), a position devoid of any real authority, although he retained his moral authority among the Jews.

Anti-Nazi Underground. Groups of young people belonging to the Zionist YOUTH MOVEMENTS, such as IRGUN BERIT ZION and especially Ha-Shomer ha-Tsa'ir, He-Haluts ha-Tsa'ir, and Betar, resumed their activities, with the emphasis on the struggle against the Nazis. A substantial impetus to their decision to engage in such underground activities was given by Irena ADAMOWICZ, a Polish woman who acted as an emissary for the underground movements in the Warsaw and Vilna ghettos and visited Kovno in July 1942. The Communists were also quite active in the anti-Nazi struggle, through the Antifascist Struggle Organization, which was headed by Haim YELIN. Members of this organization sought to acquire arms and also to establish contact with the Soviet partisans in the forests. In the summer of 1943 the Zionists and the Communists established a joint body, the General Jewish Fighting Organization (Yidishe Algemeyne Kamfs Organizatsye; JFO), whose purpose was to organize operational cells and facilitate their departure from the ghetto so that they could join the partisans. At its height, the JFO had about six hundred members. Some were given military training, including instruction in the use of arms, by officers of the Jewish police. In September 1943 the JFO established a direct link with the partisan movement in Lithuania thanks to the help of a Jewish woman parachutist, Gesja GLAZER ("Albina"), who made a secret visit to the ghetto. The new connection enabled the JFO to send armed teams of members to the Augustów forests to set up partisan bases there. The cost of this venture was heavy. Out of a hundred JFO members who took part, ten were shot to death, fifteen died in prison, and fourteen were taken to the Ninth Fort.

At the end of 1943, 170 JFO members, split into eight groups, left the ghetto in trucks that they had secretly obtained from their Lithuanian drivers, and made for partisan bases in the Rudninkai Forest, south of Vilna (which was nearer than the Augustów Forest). Most of them joined the Kovno battalions of the Lithuanian partisan movement. Altogether, some 350 Kovno Jews, most of them members of the JFO, left the ghetto in order to join the partisans. About 100 of them met their death en route or were killed in action.

Liquidation of the Ghetto. On July 8, 1944, as the Red Army was approaching Kovno, the German authorities embarked upon the transfer of the Jews to concentration camps inside Germany. Many Jews went into hiding, in underground bunkers that they had prepared for just this purpose. The Germans used bloodhounds, smoke grenades, and firebombs to force the Jews out into the open; in the process, some 2,000 Jews died, by choking or burning, or as a result of the explosions. Only 90 were able to hold out in the bunkers and live to see the Red Army enter Kovno (on August 1, 1944). About 4,000 Kovno Jews were taken to Germany, the ma-

jority going either to the KAUFERING or the STUTTHOF concentration camps. In October 1944 they were joined by a number of Kovno Jews who had been held in camps in Estonia. When the camps were liberated, nearly 2,000 Kovno Jews had survived; together with those who had held out in various hiding places in Kovno and the vicinity, they accounted for 8 percent of the 30,000 Jews who had made up the original population of the ghetto.

After the war, the survivors were joined by Kovno Jews who came back from the Soviet interior. In 1959, 4,792 Jews were living in Kovno, approximately 2 percent of the city's population. Until 1951, Kovno had a Jewish orphanage and a Jewish school (this was the last such school to exist in the Soviet Union). Many of Kovno's Jews emigrated to Israel.

BIBLIOGRAPHY

Arad, Y. "The Judenräte in the Lithuanian Ghettos of Kovno and Vilna." In *Patterns of Jewish Leadership*, pp. 93–112. Jerusalem, 1979.
Bar-on, Z. A., and D. Levin. "The History of an Underground." *In Dispersion* (Winter 1964–1965): 155–168.
Brown, Z. A., and D. Levin. *The Story of an Underground: The Resistance of the Jews of Kovno (Lithuania) in the Second World War.* Jerusalem, 1962. (In Hebrew.)
Garfunkel, L. *The Destruction of Kovno's Jewry.* Jerusalem, 1959. (In Hebrew.)

DOV LEVIN

KOVPAK, SIDOR ARTEMEVICH (1887–1967), Soviet partisan commander in World War II. Kovpak was born in the village of Kotelva, in the Poltava district. During the Civil War he was a partisan fighter for the Reds, and he subsequently fought under Vasily Chapayev in the Red Army. Between the two world wars, Kovpak was employed in party and administrative offices, and in 1940 he was the mayor of the Putivl municipality in Sumy Oblast (district).

As the Germans drew near to the Sumy district in late September of 1941, Kovpak and Semyon Rudnev organized a partisan battalion that developed into a division. On October 26, 1942, at the head of his fifteen hundred fighters, Kovpak set off on a combat expedition to the west, and in early 1943 he reached northern Volhynia; in the second half of that year he conducted combat expeditions through Volhynia and Polesye. On June 12, 1943, he went on an expedition to the Carpathian Mountains, with two objectives: to demonstrate a Soviet presence in Eastern Galicia, where the UKRAINSKA POVSTANSKA ARMYIA (Ukrainian Insurgent Army) was in power, and to blow up oil installations in the Drogobych region. On his way, Kovpak liberated Jews from the Skalat labor camp, and a group of young people joined the division as a Jewish company under the command of veteran Jewish partisans. After bloody battles, the division was obliged on its way back to split into small groups. Many died during the retreat, and only part of the division reached the assembly point in northeastern Volhynia.

In January 1944, Kovpak was wounded and flown to the hinterland. He was twice awarded the Soviet medal for heroism, and was promoted to the rank of major general. His division was named the "Kovpak First Ukrainian Partisan Division," and placed under the command of Lt. Col. Petro Vershigora. On January 5, 1944, it began a campaign through Volhynia, Eastern Galicia, the Lublin district, Brest-Litovsk, and Pinsk. At the end of the campaign it was dismantled. In 1947 Kovpak was appointed deputy chairman of the Supreme Soviet of the Ukrainian SSR. His account of his partisan activities was published in *Our Partisan Course* (1965).

BIBLIOGRAPHY

Armstrong, J. A. *Soviet Partisans in World War II.* Madison, Wis., 1964.

Vershigora, P. P. *Liudi s chistoi sovest'iu.* Moscow, 1966.

SHMUEL SPECTOR

KOWALSKI, WŁADYSŁAW (1895–1971), Pole who saved Jews during the Holocaust. A retired colonel in the Polish army at the time of the German occupation, Kowalski was the WARSAW representative of the Dutch-based Philips concern. Nazi Germany's interest in the Dutch-owned company facilitated the mobility of its foreign representatives, affording Kowalski freedom of circulation in all parts of Warsaw, including the closed-off Jewish ghetto. His first opportunity to help Jews took place outside the ghetto, on the "Aryan" side, when he encountered Bruno Borl, a ten-year-old boy wandering the streets of Warsaw in September 1940, seeking food and shelter. Taking the boy home, Kowalski fed him and provided him with a new identity and a home with friends.

This led to a series of bolder undertakings. Two brothers named Rubin, a lawyer and a dentist, were helped to find a new location after their hiding place was uncovered by an informer. Exploiting his freedom of movement, Kowalski smuggled seven Jews out of the Warsaw ghetto in February 1943 by bribing the Polish guards at the gates, and found safe havens for the Jews on the "Aryan" side. In November of that year he helped a family of four move from the Izbica area to a safer place with friends in Warsaw. He also offered refuge to twelve Jews in his Warsaw home. Roman Fisher, a construction worker whom Kowalski had rescued, built an underground shelter with material that Kowalski surreptitiously brought with him inside heavy suitcases. From late 1940 until August 1944, Kowalski paid for the upkeep of those of his charges for whom he had arranged hiding places. The group hiding in his home was kept busy manufacturing toys that Kowalski sold in the market, thus helping defray maintenance costs. After the suppression of the WARSAW POLISH UPRISING in October 1944, and the forcible evacuation of all the Warsaw residents by the Germans, Kowalski converted a basement in a ruined building into a bunker and hid there along with forty-nine Jews. Their daily ration consisted of three glasses of water, a modicum of sugar, and vitamin pills. They stayed hidden for 105 days; by the time they were liberated by the Russians in January 1945, they were reduced to eating fuel. More than fifty Jews benefited from Kowalski's help during the occupation period.

In 1947, Kowalski married one of the Jewish women he had rescued, and they emi-

Władysław Kowalski (standing), speaking at a special ceremony held at Yad Vashem in Jerusalem on October 30, 1967, for "Righteous among the Nations" living in Israel. From left to right: Apolonia Oldak (Poland), Kowalski, Katriel Katz, of the Yad Vashem directorate, and Supreme Court Justice Moshe Landau. At the far right: Malvina Czismadia (Hungary) and Stefan Raczyński (Poland).

grated to Israel in 1957. In 1963 he was recognized by YAD VASHEM as a "RIGHTEOUS AMONG THE NATIONS."

BIBLIOGRAPHY

Bartoszewski, W., and Z. Lewin, eds. *Righteous among Nations: How Poles Helped the Jews, 1939–1945.* London, 1969.

MORDECAI PALDIEL

KRAKÓW, city in southern POLAND; the third largest in the country and one of the oldest. Kraków is mentioned from the eighth century; in the eleventh century it became the residence of the Polish princes. Between 1320 and 1596 it was the capital of the kingdom of Poland.

From the early fourteenth century, Kraków was one of the most important Jewish communities in Europe. In 1495 the Jews of the city were expelled to Kazimierz, a new town being built nearby that eventually became a quarter of Kraków, and the history of the Jews in the two places became closely intertwined. In 1867 Jews were given the right of residing in every part of the city.

Beginning in the Middle Ages, Kraków was an outstanding center of Jewish learning and culture in Europe. During the Swedish invasion (1655–1657) the Kraków Jewish community underwent much suffering, but after the city was liberated the community gradually regained its strength. From 1815 to 1846 Kraków and its environs constituted a free republic, and the Jewish community flourished. Subsequently, in the period from 1846 to 1918, when the city was part of Austrian-ruled Galicia, the Jewish community grew and progressed further, with a thriving cultural and social life. In independent Poland (1918–1939) Jewish life flourished in Kraków

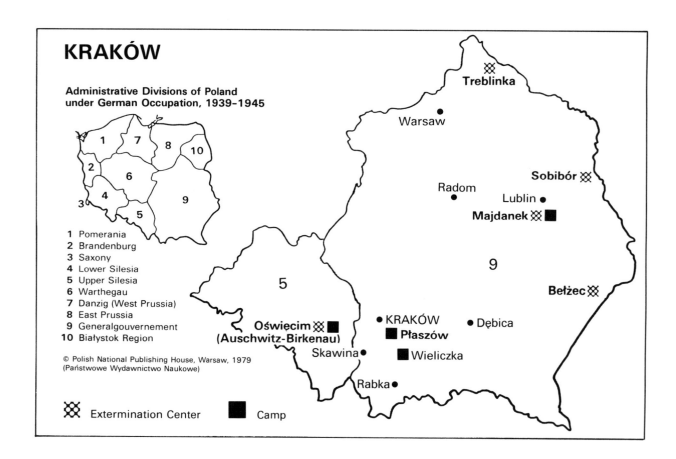

KRAKÓW

Administrative Divisions of Poland
under German Occupation, 1939-1945

1 Pomerania
2 Brandenburg
3 Saxony
4 Lower Silesia
5 Upper Silesia
6 Warthegau
7 Danzig (West Prussia)
8 East Prussia
9 Generalgouvernement
10 Białystok Region

© Polish National Publishing House, Warsaw, 1979
(Państwowe Wydawnictwo Naukowe)

✖ Extermination Center   ■ Camp

more than ever, although in the years preceding the outbreak of World War II the Jewish community suffered from the increase of antisemitism in the country.

In 1540, Kraków had a Jewish population of 2,100; in 1772, 4,000; in 1880, 20,000 (one-third of the total); in 1900, 25,000; and in 1921, 45,000. By 1939 the number of Jews had grown to 60,000, out of a total population of about a quarter of a million.

Nazi Occupation. Kraków was occupied by the German army on September 6, 1939, and the persecution of the Jews was launched without delay. It was organized mainly by Einsatzkommando 2 of Einsatzgruppe I, commanded by Obersturmbannführer Max Grosskopf. On October 26 the occupation authorities declared Kraków the capital of the GENERALGOUVERNEMENT (the territory in the interior of occupied Poland). As a result, the persecution of the Jews was intensified. It was in Kraków that the Generalgouvernement issued all its anti-Jewish decrees.

A Jewish committee was organized in the early stage of the occupation, and on November 28 it was declared a JUDENRAT (Jewish Council). The chairman of the Judenrat was Dr. Marek Bieberstein, with Dr. Wilhelm Goldblatt as his deputy. In the summer of 1940 both men were imprisoned by the Gestapo and Dr. Artur Rosenzweig was appointed chairman. On December 5 and 6, the Germans conducted a sweeping terror operation in the Jewish quarters, mainly to raid Jewish property. Several synagogues were burned down on this occasion.

On May 1, 1940, a decree was issued placing the city's boulevards and major squares out of bounds to Jews. That same month the expulsion of Kraków Jews to neighboring towns was launched; by March 1941, forty thousand Jews had been expelled and no more than eleven thousand were left in the city. While the expulsions were taking place, the victims were robbed of all their property.

The Ghetto. On March 3, 1941, the Kraków district governor, Otto Wächter, published a decree on the establishment of the ghetto, to be located in Podgorze, a section in the southern part of the city. The ghetto was

Moving into the Kraków ghetto.

sealed off on March 20, within a wall and a barbed-wire fence. It covered an area of no more than 656 by 437 yards (600 × 400 m), bisected by Limanowskiego Street. In addition to the Kraków Jews, several thousand Jews from neighboring communities were also packed into the ghetto, mainly from Skawina, Wieliczka, and Rabka. In late 1941, eighteen thousand Jews were imprisoned in the ghetto. The worst problems were the overcrowding (four to five persons to a room) and the poor sanitary conditions.

Several organizations were active in the ghetto in efforts to alleviate the plight of the population. The more important were the Jüdische Soziale Selbsthilfe (Jewish Social Self-Help Society), later called the Jüdische Unterstützungsstelle (Jewish Aid Agency), and the Centralne Towarzystwo Opieki nad Sierotami (Federation of Associations for the Care of Orphans; CENTOS).

The Germans established several factories in the ghetto to exploit the cheap manpower that was available among the imprisoned population. Several hundred Jews were also employed in factories situated outside the ghetto, and they were daily escorted to and from their work.

On March 19, 1942, the Germans launched what they called an *Intelligenz Aktion*, a terror operation directed at the intelligentsia in the ghetto. Some fifty prominent Jews were seized in this operation and were taken to AUSCHWITZ, where they were killed.

Deportations. At the end of May 1942, the Germans began deporting Jews from the ghetto to the extermination camps. On May 28 the ghetto was hermetically sealed off and the *Aktion* was launched. Taking part were special detachments of the Gestapo, the Schutzpolizei (regular uniformed police), and a Waffen-SS unit stationed at Dębica. The *Aktion* continued until June 8, and when it ended six thousand Jews were deported to the BEŁŻEC extermination camp; three hundred were shot to death on the spot. Among the victims were the poet Mordecai GEBIRTIG and the Judenrat chairman, Artur Rosenzweig, who had refused to carry out the Germans' orders. The Judenrat was liquidated, and in its place the Germans put up a Kommissariat, headed by David Guter.

Following this *Aktion* the ghetto area was reduced by half, although it still had a population of twelve thousand. In mid-October 1942 the Jewish Kommissariat was ordered to compile a list of four thousand ghetto inmates for yet another deportation. When the order was ignored, the Germans launched a second *Aktion*, on October 27 and 28, in which they employed their usual terror tactics to round up seven thousand Jews for de-

Jews of Kraków forced to dig a pit while under armed guard.

portation. In addition, they shot six hundred Jews on the spot. Most of the deportees were sent to Bełżec, and the rest to Auschwitz. In the course of this *Aktion* the hospital, the home for the aged, and the orphanage, all situated on Jozefinska Street, were liquidated. When the *Aktion* was over the ghetto area was further reduced, and what remained was cut in two. The first part, known as "A," contained the Jews who were working, and the second, "B," the rest of the ghetto prisoners.

On March 13, 1943, the residents of part "A," two thousand in number, were transferred to the PŁASZÓW camp; the following day, March 14, an *Aktion* took place in which part "B" was liquidated. Some twenty-three hundred Jews were taken to the Auschwitz-Birkenau extermination camp and killed there in the gas chambers, and seven hundred Jews were killed on the spot. Of the Jews who were transferred to Płaszów, only a few hundred survived.

The Resistance Movement. From its inception, the Kraków ghetto had underground organizations operating in it, of which the more prominent were the Akiva and Ha-Shomer ha-Tsa'ir Zionist YOUTH MOVEMENTS.

In the initial stage the underground operations concentrated on education and mutual help. The Jewish underground also published a newspaper, *He-Haluts ha-Lohem* (The Fighting Pioneer). In October 1942 the Żydowska Organizacja Bojowa (Jewish Fighting Organization), a united underground organization independent of the Warsaw ŻOB, was formed. It set itself the goal of conducting an armed struggle against the Nazi occupiers.

Heading the organization were Zvi BAUMINGER, Aharon LIEBESKIND, Gola Mira, Shimshon DRAENGER, and Gusta (Justyna) DRAENGER-Dawidson. The Jewish Fighting Organization decided not to prepare for an uprising inside the ghetto, whose restricted space offered no chance at all for an armed struggle, and instead to move the fighting to the "Aryan" side of Kraków. Some ten operations were launched outside the ghetto, the most famous being the attack on the Cyganeria café in the center of the city, which was frequented by German officers. Eleven Germans were killed in this attack and thirteen wounded.

Attempts were also made to engage in partisan operations in the vicinity, but these encountered difficulties caused by the group's isolation and the hostile attitude manifested by the local units of the ARMIA KRAJOWA (the Polish Home Army), which did not take kindly to Jewish partisan operations. The Jewish underground suffered heavy losses, and in the fall of 1944 its remnants decided to cross the border into Slovakia and from there to make their way into Hungary. This plan succeeded, and members of the Kraków Jewish Fighting Organization continued their resistance operations in Budapest, where they joined up with the Ha-No'ar ha-Tsiyyoni (Zionist Youth) organization.

On the "Aryan" side of Kraków, a branch of ZEGOTA (Rada Pomocy Żydom, or Council for Aid to Jews) was active from the spring of 1943. It was headed by Stanisław Dobrowolski, a Polish Socialist Party activist. The Jewish representative in the branch, Miriam Hochberg-Peleg (whose underground alias was Maria Marianska), made tireless efforts in behalf of the Jews in the ghetto. The Zegota branch aided several hundred of the Kraków Jews who escaped.

After the war about four thousand survivors of the ghettos and concentration camps, most of them former residents of Kraków and its vicinity, settled in the city, remaining there for a short while. In 1946 thousands of Jews who had fled to the Soviet Union at the beginning of the war and were now returning to Poland made their home in Kraków, whose Jewish population rose to ten thousand. Several Jewish institutions were established, including a branch of the Jewish Historical Commission (the forerunner of the Warsaw ŻYDOWSKI INSTYTUT HISTORYCZNY, or Jewish Historical Institute), which was headed by Josef Wulf and Michał Maksymilian Boruchowicz (Borwicz). Most of these Jews emigrated from Poland between 1947 and 1951, under the impact of the antisemitic waves that struck the country. After 1968 only a handful of Jews were left in Kraków.

BIBLIOGRAPHY

Dawidson, G. *Justina's Diary*. Naharia, Israel, 1978. (In Hebrew.)
Karol, Z. "Cracow." In vol. 2 of *Jewish Mother Cities*, edited by Y. C. Cohen-Fischmann, pp. 284–354. Jerusalem, 1948. (In Hebrew.)
Pankewicz, T. *The Cracow Ghetto Pharmacy*. New York, 1987.
Peleg, M., and M. Benzvi. *Outside the Walls of the Ghetto in Occupied Cracow*. Jerusalem, 1986. (In Hebrew.)

SHMUEL KRAKOWSKI

KRAMER, JOSEF (1906–1945), commandant of the BERGEN-BELSEN camp. Kramer was born in Munich. He joined the Nazi party in 1931, and a year later became an SS man. His concentration camp career began in 1934, in DACHAU, where he was at first a guard, but his advance was rapid and he held senior posts in a number of concentration camps, including SACHSENHAUSEN and MAUTHAUSEN. For several months in 1940 he served as aide-de-camp to Rudolf HÖSS, the commandant of AUSCHWITZ. From April 1941 to May 1944, Kramer was commandant of the NATZWEILER camp. He was promoted to the rank of *Hauptsturmführer* in 1942. In May 1944 he was again posted to Auschwitz, and was put in charge of the gas chambers and crematoria in Auschwitz II–Birkenau. On December 2 of that year he was appointed commandant of Bergen-Belsen. Following his arrival there, Bergen-Belsen officially became a concentration camp, and conditions deteriorated sharply.

When the camp was liberated, Kramer was arrested by the British and put on trial, together with forty-four other members of the camp staff, among them fifteen women. The trial, which took place in Lüneburg, lasted from September to November 1945. Kramer was sentenced to death, as were ten others of the accused, and was executed on December 12, 1945.

BIBLIOGRAPHY

Phillips, R., ed. *Trial of Josef Kramer and Forty-Four Others: The Belsen Trial*. London, 1949.

SHMUEL KRAKOWSKI

KRASNODAR, capital of Krasnodar Krai (territory) in Northern Caucasia, in the Russian Soviet Federated Socialist Republic. In 1926 the total population of Krasnodar was about 174,000 and its Jewish population was 1,746, which presumably had increased by 1941. By

KREMENCHUG, city in the central Soviet Ukraine; it is a port on the Dnieper, a railway junction, and a center of metal, machine, textile, and food industries. Kremenchug was founded in the sixteenth century, and Jews first settled there at the end of the eighteenth century. In 1926 it had a Jewish population of 28,969, out of a total of 60,000. On the eve of the Holocaust its Jewish population was 40,000, out of a total population of 90,000.

Kremenchug was occupied by the Germans on September 9, 1941. Many of the Jews had fled the city or had been evacuated by the Soviet authorities, and only nine thousand were left when the Germans came. Even in the first few days of the occupation, the Germans and Ukrainian police harassed and mistreated the Jews. The Jews had to wear on their sleeve a badge (*see* BADGE, JEWISH) with a Star of David, they were under curfew after 5:00 p.m., they were prohibited from making purchases in the shops, and they were put on forced labor, to clean and repair the city streets. When a church was reopened in Kremenchug, on September 25, Jews in large numbers sought to convert, and the mayor and two clerics extorted large sums of money from them in exchange for the con-

the time the city was occupied by the Nazis on August 9, 1942, thousands of refugees from the southern part of the Ukraine and the Crimea, Jews and non-Jews, had flocked into Krasnodar, in an effort to escape from the Germans.

In the wake of the German army, Sonderkommando 10a of Einsatzgruppe D entered the city. On August 16 an officer of that unit went to the home of a Jewish professor, Vilik, and put him in charge of the Jewish population of the city. The following day, Professor Vilik was told to inform the Jews that they must report for registration. A few weeks later the Jews were ordered to assemble at a certain point in Krasnodar. From there they were taken outside the city and killed, some by means of GAS VANS. Seven thousand persons, mostly Jews, were murdered by the men of Sonderkommando 10a.

Krasnodar was liberated by the Soviet army in February 1943. From July 14 to 17, 1943, a trial was held there of thirteen Soviet citizens who had served in a Sonderkommando 10a auxiliary unit and had participated in the mass murder (*see* TRIALS OF WAR CRIMINALS: KRASNODAR TRIAL).

SHMUEL SPECTOR

version. The following day the Jews were ordered to report for a roll call, but only thirty-five hundred Jews, together with one hundred families of mixed marriage, answered the call. On September 27 the Jews were ordered to move into a camp consisting of wooden barracks in Novoivanovka, a suburb. The conditions were hardly bearable, and the Jews were not even allowed to prepare cooked food.

The killing of the Jews of Kremenchug was launched on September 28. The Jews were taken from Novoivanovka to pits, previously dug by prisoners of war, on the way to the village of Peschanoye. On the first day sixteen hundred Jews were murdered, and by November 7 all those who had been concentrated in Novoivanovka were dead. Most of the remaining fifty-five hundred Jews who had gone into hiding were turned over to the Nazis by local Ukrainians and were also murdered. A small group of professional men, mostly doctors, were retained for a while, pending their replacement. They were killed in January 1942.

Kremenchug was liberated by the Soviet army on November 29, 1943.

SHMUEL SPECTOR

KRIMCHAKS, Jews who settled in the Crimean peninsula, apparently as early as the second century B.C. In their dress and housing the Krimchaks followed the customs of their Tatar neighbors, and for everyday conversation they used a Jewish-Tatar dialect. In the 1926 census the Krimchaks accounted for 6,383 out of a total Jewish population in the Crimea of 42,000. Before the October Revolution they were mostly merchants and artisans, and subsequently suffered in the Sovietization of the country's society and economy.

When Einsatzgruppe D arrived in the Crimea in the wake of the German army, it encountered the problem of the peninsula's heterogeneous population, in ethnic and religious terms. Not knowing whether to include the KARAITES and Krimchaks in the "FINAL SOLUTION," the Einsatzgruppe commander, Otto OHLENDORF, in September 1941 asked

KRIMCHAKS

the REICHSSICHERHEITSHAUPTAMT (Reich Security Main Office; RSHA) in Berlin to decide the issue. The problem went all the way up to Heinrich HIMMLER, who ordered that the Krimchaks be included in the murder program, while the Karaites were to be exempt.

Between October 30 and November 16, 1941, the German army completed the occupation of the Crimea, with the exception of Sevastopol, which held out until July 3, 1942. In the first few weeks following the conquest, Einsatzgruppe D men rounded up the Jews, including the Krimchaks, and killed them. The following are the data on the murder of the Krimchaks, derived from various sources, mostly German. In SIMFEROPOL, which had the largest concentration of Krimchaks (2,500 in the 1926 census), 1,500 Krimchaks were murdered, on December 9, 1941. In Karasubazar (now Belogursk), the ancient Krimchak center, the murder of Krimchaks took place on November 10, 1941. In Bakhchisarai, some 40 Krimchak families were killed on December 13, 1941. In Yevpatoriya, the Krimchaks were murdered on November 24, 1941, together with the other Jews in the town. In Feodosiya 1,052 Jews were murdered subsequent to November 16, 1941, among them all the Krimchaks who had been living there. In Kerch, 7,000 Jews, including Krimchaks, were murdered between December 1 and 3, 1941.

According to routine reports submitted by the Einsatzgruppen, 2,504 Krimchaks were murdered in the period from November 16 to December 15, 1941. It may be assumed that this does not include all the Krimchak victims, and that additional Krimchak Jews, in groups and individually, were murdered at a later date. About 70 percent of the Krimchak population appears to have been killed in the Holocaust. When the war was over, only about 1,500 Krimchaks were left in the Crimea.

BIBLIOGRAPHY

Loewenthal, R. "The Extinction of the Krimchaks in World War II." *American Slavic and East European Review* 10 (1951): 130–136.
Spector, S. "The Destruction of the Krimchak Jews during the Nazi Occupation." *Pe'amim* 27 (1986): 18–25. (In Hebrew.)

SHMUEL SPECTOR

KRIMINALPOLIZEI (Kripo), the German criminal police. In the Third Reich, punishable offenses with a political aspect were handled by the GESTAPO, rather than by the criminal police. Until 1936 the criminal police was part of the administration of the *Länder*, the territorial divisions making up the Reich. As part of the centralization of the police introduced that year by Heinrich HIMMLER, the criminal police of all the *Länder* were incorporated into the Prussian criminal police. The following year (1937), the latter became the Reichskriminalpolizeiamt (Reich Criminal Police Bureau). Together with the Gestapo, the bureau became part of the Hauptamt Sicherheitspolizei (Security Police Main Office), which in turn, with the SD (Sicherheitsdienst; Security Service), was incorporated into the REICHSSICHERHEITSHAUPTAMT (Reich Security Main Office; RSHA) in 1939, with Reinhard HEYDRICH as its first chief. Kripo became the RSHA's Section V, with Arthur NEBE as section chief.

Within the borders of the Reich, Kripo officers wore plain clothes, but when they were on duty in German-occupied countries they wore SS uniforms—including those among them who did not belong to the SS—and SS insignia corresponding to their civilian ranks. The duties they performed in the occupied countries related to nonpolitical crimes, as in the Reich, but from time to time they were called on by the Gestapo to assist it in its operations against Jews and political opponents.

BIBLIOGRAPHY

Best, W. *Die deutsche Polizei*. Darmstadt, 1941.
Krausnick, H., et al. *Anatomy of the SS State*. London, 1968. See pages 127–301.

ADALBERT RÜCKERL

KRISTALLNACHT ("Crystal Night" or "Night of the Broken Glass"), pogrom conducted throughout Germany and Austria on November 9 and 10, 1938. It was officially presented as a spontaneous outburst provoked by the assassination of the third secretary of the German embassy in Paris, Ernst vom Rath, by a seventeen-year-old Polish Jew, Herschel GRYNSZPAN. The name *Kristallnacht* comes from *Kristallglas* (beveled plate glass) and refers to the broken shopwindows of Jewish stores.

The riots came as the culmination of assaults made upon the Jews in Germany and Austria following the ANSCHLUSS in March 1938, in which almost all elements of the Nazi regime had participated. Hermann GÖRING, who was responsible for the implementation of the economic FOUR-YEAR PLAN, had made practical and legal preparations for the "Aryanization" (*see* ARISIERUNG) of Jewish property; other decrees and laws affected the Jews' public and personal status and increased their segregation from the general public. Using administrative "infractions" committed by Jews and "unemployment" of Jews as pretexts, the GESTAPO and the SS under Heinrich HIMMLER and Reinhard HEYDRICH launched massive arrests of Jews, who were imprisoned in the concentration camps of DACHAU, BUCHENWALD, and SACHSENHAUSEN. Beginning in July 1938, these camps were readied to receive an even greater number of Jews. Functionaries of the National Socialist party, the *Gauleiter*, and the SA (Sturmabteilung; Storm Troopers) instigated local assaults on Jewish businesses and synagogues.

The authorities increasingly took to coercing Jews to leave the German Reich, disregarding the obstacles to emigration that had become obvious through the meager results of the EVIAN CONFERENCE. More and more indi-

Ruins of the Fasanenstrasse synagogue in Berlin. [Leo Baeck Institute, New York]

vidual Jews and entire groups were forcibly expelled, mainly from Austria and from Czechoslovakia after the latter had been truncated by the MUNICH CONFERENCE. The catalytic development was the deportation of about 17,000 Polish Jews who were driven into a no-man's-land between the two countries on October 28, 1938, following a ploy of the Polish government intended to deprive Polish Jews of the right of return from countries under German rule. The greatest number of the deportees were left stranded near the border town of ZBĄSZYŃ. Herschel Grynszpan's parents were in this group, and news of their plight drove the desperate youth to his act of revenge.

Following his shooting of vom Rath on November 7, an inflammatory editorial appeared in the *Völkischer Beobachter*, the official Nazi organ, and sporadic anti-Jewish rioting started on November 8. On the afternoon of November 9, vom Rath died. The same evening, Joseph GOEBBELS harangued the "old fighters" of the party who had gathered in Munich at their annual commemoration of Hitler's abortive putsch of November 8 and 9, 1923. Apparently with Hitler's consent, Goebbels hinted that this was the hour for action against the Jews. That night, instructions were conveyed to all parts of the country. In accordance with the orders, the crowds were encouraged by the SA to participate in the atmosphere of outrage. Mass frenzy broke out: synagogues were destroyed and burned, shopwindows of Jewish-owned stores were shattered, the shattered glass covering the sidewalks, and the demolished stores were looted. Jewish homes were assaulted, and in many places Jews were physically attacked. About 30,000 Jews—especially those who were influ-

Aftermath of *Kristallnacht* on Potsdamerstrasse in Berlin.

ential and wealthy—were arrested, often with the help of previously prepared lists, and were thrown into the three above-mentioned concentration camps, where they were treated with great cruelty by the SS. This was the first time that riots against the Jews of Germany had been organized on such an extensive scale, accompanied by mass detention. Though the violent onslaught was officially terminated on November 10, in many places it continued for several more days. In Austria it started only on the morning of November 10 but was especially fierce; arrests were widespread, and 4,600 Viennese Jews were among those sent to Dachau.

Heydrich's orders for the arrests were dis-

The burning of the synagogue in Siegen, a city 49 miles (79 km) east of Cologne.

patched to the state police and the SS only after midnight, when the action was already in full swing. Heydrich, together with Himmler and Göring (who had not been present at the Munich celebration), were taken by surprise by Goebbels's initiative. Himmler ordered the SS to remain in their billets and not to take part in the rioting, while Heydrich forbade looting, but to no avail.

In a provisional assessment, Heydrich reported to Göring on November 11 that 815 shops, 29 department stores, and 171 dwellings of Jews had been burned or otherwise destroyed, and that 267 synagogues were set ablaze or completely demolished (in fact, this was only a fraction of the number of synagogues actually destroyed). The same report refers to thirty-six Jews killed and the same number severely injured, but later it was officially stated that the number killed was ninety-one; in addition, hundreds perished in the concentration camps.

The pogrom was followed by administrative and legal orders issued with a fourfold object: to complete the process of "Aryanization" to the benefit of the government's disrupted revenues; to expedite the Jews' emigration; to isolate the Jews completely from the general population; and to abolish the still quasi-autonomous organization of the REICHSVERTRETUNG DER DEUTSCHEN JUDEN (the representative body of German Jewry) and other official Jewish institutions. These proposed developments were inaugurated at a representative meeting on November 12 called and presided over by Göring, who announced that Hitler had charged him with the implementation of the Reich's Jewish policy. In the ensuing discussion, the damage to Jewish property was estimated at several hundred million reichsmarks, and the insurance payments due to owners of 7,500 demolished stores came to 25 million reichsmarks.

Decisions taken on economic issues included a fine of one billion reichsmarks imposed on the Jewish community under the pretext of reparation for the murder of vom Rath, and confiscation by the state of the insurance payments, while at the same time making the Jewish store owners liable for the repairs. "Aryanization" was to be implemented along the lines already practiced by Hans Fischböck, the Austrian minister of

Kristallnacht in Baden-Baden. On November 10, 1938, Jewish men were rounded up by the police and marched through the city.

commerce. On Heydrich's suggestion, it was decided to coordinate the Jews' emigration through a ZENTRALSTELLE FÜR JÜDISCHE AUS-WANDERUNG (Central Office for Jewish Emigration) to be established in Germany along the lines of the one developed by Adolf EICH-MANN in Austria. Some of the economic measures were announced the same day; additional steps, including those aimed at undermining the Jews' status, were promulgated during the following months. The Kristallnacht prisoners surviving in the concentration camps were released early in 1939 for immediate emigration or for the "Aryanization" of their property, often for both.

The sharp reaction to the Kristallnacht outrage that was expressed by the Western press and public did not affect the Nazis. When President Franklin D. ROOSEVELT recalled the United States ambassador, Hugh Wilson, as a protest and declared his deep shock, the German ambassador in the United States was recalled home as well, because of "American interference in internal German affairs." Public pressure did, however, force most of the western European governments to admit more refugees, especially children.

Göring, who had persuaded Hitler to put him in charge, now handled the Reich's Jewish policy together with Himmler, and Goebbels's aspirations to play a decisive part were thus thwarted. The methods of the SS and of the SD under Heydrich became policy. While this conclusion about the result of the outbreak is generally accepted, historians differ in their opinions about its cause. Some hold that Goebbels exploited circumstances by improvisation, and others maintain that the assault was premeditated; probably both methods were involved. In any case, Kristallnacht was a turning point. It was the Nazis' first experience of large-scale anti-Jewish violence, and opened the way to the complete eradication of the Jews' position in Germany.

BIBLIOGRAPHY

Graml, H. *Der 9. November "Reichskristallnacht."* Bonn, 1955.

Kochan, L. *Pogrom: 10 November 1938.* London, 1957.

Schleunes, K. *The Twisted Road to Auschwitz: Nazi Policy toward German Jews, 1933–1939.* Chicago, 1970.

Thalmann, R., and E. Feinermann. *Crystal Night, 9–10 November 1938.* London, 1974.

Yahil, L. "Jews in Concentration Camps in Germany prior to World War II." In *The Nazi Concentration Camps.* Proceedings of the Fourth Yad Vashem International Historical Conference, edited by Y. Gutman and A. Saf, pp. 69–100. Jerusalem, 1984.

LENI YAHIL

KRÜGER, FRIEDRICH WILHELM (1894–1945), senior SS commander in occupied Poland. Born in Strasbourg, Krüger served in the German army in World War I. He became a Nazi party member in 1929, joining the SA (Sturmabteilung; Storm Troopers) in 1930 and transferring to the SS in 1931. The following year he was elected to the Reichstag, and in January 1935 he was promoted to the rank of *Obergruppenführer.* From October 4, 1939, to November 9, 1943, Krüger was the *Höherer SS- und Polizeiführer* (Higher SS and Police Leader) in the GENERALGOUVERNEMENT. As such, he was responsible for the liquidation of all the ghettos in the Generalgouvernement and for the operation of the BEŁŻEC, SOBIBÓR, and TREBLINKA extermination camps, where 1,720,000 Jews were murdered.

In May 1942, Krüger was given the additional title of Secretary of State for Security (*Staatssekretär für das Sicherheitswesen*) in the Generalgouvernement administration, and also became "Himmler's Representative for the Strengthening of Germandom in the Generalgouvernement." In the latter function he was responsible for the expulsion of 110,000 Poles from the ZAMOŚĆ area and the settlement of Germans in their place.

In May 1944, Krüger was appointed commander of the "Prinz Eugen" Division of the Waffen-SS, which fought against the parti-

Friedrich Wilhelm Krüger. [National Archives]

sans in western Yugoslavia. On May 9, 1945, the day after Germany's surrender, he committed suicide.

BIBLIOGRAPHY

Birn, R. B. *Die Höheren SS- und Polizeiführer: Himmlers Vertreter im Reich und in den besetzten Gebieten.* Düsseldorf, 1986.

Krausnick, H., et al. *Anatomy of the SS State.* London, 1968.

SHMUEL KRAKOWSKI

KRUK, HERMAN (1897–1944), chronicler of the VILNA ghetto. Born in Płock, Poland, Kruk as a young man joined a Jewish socialist youth group that was close to the BUND. Under the influence of the Russian Revolution he joined the Polish Communist party, but was soon disillusioned by the party's stand on Jewish issues. In the 1920s, he found his way back to the Bund and was active in Tzukunft, the Bund's youth movement. Moving to Warsaw, he devoted himself primarily to educational and public activities, helped establish workers' libraries, contributed to *Volkstzeitung*, the Bund newspaper, and became one of the leaders of the movement in Poland.

In September 1939, when the Germans invaded Poland, Kruk fled from Warsaw and made his way to Vilna, which in October came under Lithuanian control. A large number of refugees from Poland had gathered there, and Kruk helped to organize their everyday life. Meanwhile, Lithuania was annexed by the USSR, in August 1940. With the help of the Bund, Kruk obtained a visa to the United States, but the Soviet authorities did not permit him to leave. In June of 1941, when the Soviet Union was invaded and German forces were approaching Vilna, Kruk decided to stay in the city under German rule and to record the events that were taking place. At the beginning of his diary, he wrote:

> I don't have the strength to become a wanderer once again. I am staying . . . and since I am staying and will be a victim of fascism, I will at least take up my pen and write the city's chronicle. There is no doubt: Vilna will be occupied, the Germans will make it fascist, the Jews will be put into a ghetto, and I shall record all these events.

Kruk's diary, written in Yiddish, is one of the most important documents relating to the Vilna ghetto. Not all of it has been saved—some pages are missing—but what survives gives an accurate description of the events in the ghetto and the lot of the Vilna Jews under Nazi occupation. The first entry in the diary is dated June 23, 1941, the evening of the German entry into Vilna; and the last, July 14, 1943, about two months before the ghetto's final liquidation. Kruk was active in the affairs of the ghetto and had a close relationship with its administration and its chairman, Jacob GENS. With a sharp eye for the developments unfolding before him, he recorded in his diary direct and undistorted information on the history of the ghetto, the deportation and extermination process, the ghetto's day-to-day life, the struggle for existence, the cultural activities, and the ghetto's underground and its relations with the JUDENRAT (Jewish Council). His own position faithfully reflected the Bund's attitude; at times he criticizes the Judenrat for its actions and at times he justifies it.

Kruk established and managed the ghetto library. He was also employed by EINSATZSTAB ROSENBERG, a Nazi agency that, among other activities, collected documentary material from the Vilna headquarters of YIVO, the Yidisher Visenshaftlikher Institut (Institute for Jewish Research), for transfer to Germany. Together with other Jewish employees of the agency, Kruk managed to smuggle into the ghetto valuable documents and thereby save them from being dispatched to Germany. His diary was typewritten, in three copies, and these were placed in different hiding places. One of the copies was discovered after the war by the poet Abraham SUTZKEVER, who gave it to YIVO in New York, where it was published as *Tagbuch fun Vilner Geto* (1960).

When the ghetto was liquidated, in September 1943, Kruk was deported to the KLOOGA concentration camp in Estonia. He continued to keep his diary in the camp. Some parts written during this period were eventually brought to Israel and handed over to MORESHET, a Holocaust research institute near Hadera, and were published. The last entry in the diary was made on September 17, 1944. The following day, Kruk was killed by the Nazis in the Lagedi concentration camp in Estonia.

BIBLIOGRAPHY

Arad, Y. *Ghetto in Flames*. New York, 1982.
Korczak, R. *Flames in Ash*. Merhavia, Israel, 1946. (In Hebrew.) Contains sections of Kruk's diary.

YITZHAK ARAD

KRUMEY, HERMANN (b. 1905), SS official. Born in Mährisch-Schönberg, Moravia, Krumey joined the SS after the ANSCHLUSS with Austria in 1938. From November 1939 to May 1940 he served in the Waffen-SS as an *Obersturmbannführer*, in the Posen (Warthegau) headquarters of the *Höherer SS- und Polizeiführer* (Higher SS and Police Leader). Between May 1940 and March 1944 he was a member of the Sicherheitspolizei (Security Police) in Łódź.

In the summer of 1941, Krumey was sent from Łódź to Croatia to take part in concentrating Jews in camps. In 1942 he helped

arrange at least six transports from the ZA-
MOŚĆ area to AUSCHWITZ. He also assisted in
deporting the Jews of Łódź to extermination
camps, and in deporting Poles farther east.

Krumey entered HUNGARY with the occupation forces on March 19, 1944, as a leading
member of Adolf EICHMANN's Sonderkommando (Special Commando). In this capacity,
he played an important role in organizing
Hungary's JUDENRAT (Jewish Council), the
Zsidó Tanács, and in laying the groundwork
for the destruction of Hungarian Jewry. In
June 1944, in the wake of negotiations between Eichmann and the RELIEF AND RESCUE
COMMITTEE OF BUDAPEST, close to twenty-one
thousand Jews were transferred to STRASS-
HOF, a concentration camp in Austria. Krumey became the head of the Sonderkommando assigned there. Most of these Jews survived the war.

He was arrested by the Allies in Italy in May
1945, but was not prosecuted. Rezső (Rudolf)
KASZTNER, the Zionist leader involved in the
negotiations with the SS in Hungary, signed
an affidavit on Krumey's behalf on May 5,
1948, and Krumey was released. He was again
arrested in 1960, and after a trial in Frankfurt
in 1965 was condemned to five years' hard
labor, on February 3. Following an appeal by
the prosecution, a new trial was held in
1968–1969, and Krumey was condemned to
life imprisonment on August 29, 1969. The
conviction was upheld by the Federal Court
(*Bundesgerichtshof*) of Karlsruhe on January
17, 1973.

BIBLIOGRAPHY

Biss, A. *A Million Jews to Save: Check to the Final
Solution.* Cranbury, N.J., 1975.
Brand, J., and A. Weissberg. *Desperate Mission: Joel
Brand's Story.* New York, 1958.

RANDOLPH L. BRAHAM

**KRUPP VON BOHLEN UND HALBACH,
GUSTAV** (1870–1950), German industrialist
and armaments manufacturer. Born into a
leading family of bankers, Krupp studied law
at Heidelberg before entering a diplomatic
career on the staff of a number of German
embassies. Through marriage he entered the

Gustav Krupp von Bohlen und Halbach.

Krupp family firm in 1906, becoming president in 1909. He was a member of the Prussian State Council between 1921 and 1933
and from 1931 was president of the Reich
Union of German Industry (Reichsverband
der Deutschen Industrie). Although initially
reputed to be an opponent of Hitler, Krupp
in May 1933 accepted office in the governing
body of the Adolf-Hitler-Spende (Adolf Hitler
Fund) in Berlin, which made generous contributions to the Nazi party and the SS. This
resulted in economic benefits for Krupp, particularly in the facilities offered to the firm's
enterprises in occupied eastern Europe,
where extensive use was made of the FORCED
LABOR of Jews, Poles, and Russian prisoners
of war. An estimated 70 percent to 80 percent
of the labor force of 100,000 died as a result
of the inhuman treatment. At a large fuse
factory at Auschwitz, Jews were worked to a
state of collapse and then gassed.

At the end of World War II, Krupp was
arrested as a major war criminal on charges

of complicity in preparing a war of aggression, but he was not brought to trial, on grounds of ill health. He was also found unfit to plead at the Krupp Case, held in 1947 and 1948 (the tenth of the twelve trials constituting the SUBSEQUENT NUREMBERG PROCEEDINGS), at which the defendants were accused of plundering and of exploiting forced labor.

BIBLIOGRAPHY

Batty, P. *The House of Krupp.* New York, 1967.
Ferencz, B. *Less than Slaves.* Cambridge, Mass., 1979.

LIONEL KOCHAN

KUBE, WILHELM (1887–1943), Nazi party functionary and governor of occupied territories. Born in Głogów (Ger., Glogau), Silesia, Kube was one of the earliest members of the Nazi party and held various posts in the party hierarchy. In 1928 he became *Gauleiter* of the east German province of Ostmark, and in 1933, *Gauleiter* of the west German province of Kurmark. From 1924 to 1928, and again in 1933, he was a Nazi deputy in the Reichstag and in the Prussian Landtag (provincial legislature); in the latter body he was also chairman of the Nazi caucus. In 1933 Kube was appointed *Oberpräsident* (governor) of the Brandenburg-Berlin district. Because of his quarrels with party leaders and suspicions of embezzlement on his part, he was removed from all his posts.

In 1941 Kube was appointed *Generalkommissar* (governor) of Belorussia, which formed part of REICHSKOMMISSARIAT OSTLAND. Headquartered in Minsk, he fell out with the senior SS and police commanders, and attacked them for their mass murder and "scorched-earth" actions against the local population. He also demanded that there be no more transports of Jews from the Reich to the Minsk ghetto. Kube's charges and complaints were not motivated by humanitarian considerations; rather, he felt that these actions by the SS and the police were being carried out over his head and therefore that they weakened his authority. He put his complaints and protests in writing, in a letter to the Führer's bureau.

Wilhelm Kube.

On September 22, 1943, Kube was killed by a bomb planted under his bed by his maid, a Soviet partisan who had been assigned to the post.

BIBLIOGRAPHY

Hilberg, R. *The Destruction of the European Jews.* New York, 1985.

SHMUEL SPECTOR

KULMHOF. See Chełmno.

KULTURBUND DEUTSCHER JUDEN (Cultural Society of German Jews), organization engaged in promoting culture and the arts among the Jews of GERMANY between 1933 and 1941. The idea of establishing a cultural society for German Jews was put forward in the spring of 1933; its purposes were to enable the Jewish population to maintain the

Dr. Kurt Singer conducting an orchestra and choir in a performance in Berlin of Handel's *Israel in Egypt* (February 1937). [Bildarchiv Abraham Pisarek, Berlin]

cultural life to which they were accustomed, and to alleviate the distress of the thousands of Jewish theatrical artists and musicians who had been thrown out of their jobs when the Nazis came to power. The concept of an organization of this kind was the brainchild of a young theater director, Kurt Baumann, but the moving spirit in planning and running it was Dr. Kurt Singer, a medical doctor and musician who had been the director of the Berlin Opera. Singer headed the Kulturbund during the first five years of its existence, its most flourishing period. Joining Singer in the organizing team, at his invitation, were Julius Bab, an expert on the theater, and Werner Levie, as administrator. After consultations with the representative bodies of German Jewry, the organizing team applied to the German authorities, and the Prussian Ministry of Culture appointed Hans Hinkel—the head of its theater committee and a veteran Nazi cultural-affairs activist—as the society's supervisor. The Gestapo, on the other hand, was hesitant about accepting the society's existence. It gave its approval only when the words *deutscher Juden* were eliminated from the title (the society instead became known as the Jüdische Kulturbund,

or Jewish Cultural Association), and it put the society's operations under surveillance.

In October 1933, the theater company organized by the Kulturbund in Berlin staged its first play, Gotthold Lessing's *Nathan der Weise* (Nathan the Wise). At about this time a symphony orchestra, an opera, a cabaret group, and a permanent lecture program were launched. The number of persons joining the society as members and subscribers was lower than the organizers had expected—some 18,000 out of the 160,000 Jews who made up the Berlin Jewish community.

On the model of the Berlin group, cultural societies on a regional and local level were established by Jewish communities all over the country. The more important of the regional organizations were the Rhein-Ruhr society, based in Cologne, which ran a regular theater; the Rhein-Main group, based in Frankfurt, which had an orchestra that also played outside its own region; and the Bavaria Cultural Society, based in Munich. The outstanding local societies were in Breslau, which ran an extensive program of musical activities; Mannheim, whose director, Karl Adler, managed to put all Jewish cultural and educational activities under one roof; and Hamburg, whose theater company also appeared regularly out of town. The membership of the societies in the medium-sized and small communities was proportionately much larger than in Berlin (indeed, usually twice as large).

In April 1935, thirty-six Jewish cultural societies, with seventy thousand members, were active in the Reich, and they organized themselves under an umbrella organization, the Reichsverband der Jüdischen Kulturbünde (Reich Association of Jewish Cultural Societies), centered in Berlin. This enabled the regional and local societies to improve their activities, facilitated the rational use of the existing artistic resources, and made possible the operation of a central professional training center that could influence the policies upon which the societies based their work. The German authorities also had an interest in the existence of a countrywide association, from both the administrative and the political aspects.

Hinkel, in the meantime, had been transferred to Joseph GOEBBELS's Ministry of Propaganda, from which he now supervised the Reich Association. The demand by the Nazis for overall supervision grew stronger, especially since the Gestapo, which also had a hand in the supervision, wanted a nationwide organization to be utilized for speeding up Jewish emigration.

Another organizational change was made in the wake of the November 1938 KRISTALL-NACHT pogrom. On orders of the authorities, the umbrella organization, which had been a federation of independent societies, was transformed into a centralized body in charge of all Jewish cultural activities, including those that the local and regional societies had been carrying out on their own. These included the remaining publishing houses (most of the Jewish publishing houses had been closed down) and the editorial offices of the one newspaper, the *Jüdisches Nachrichtenblatt*, that the Jews were allowed to publish. In its new form the Kulturbund maintained its operations, mostly in the field of entertainment, on a modest scale. These were important to the Jewish population, whose conditions of life had come increasingly to resemble life in a ghetto. This remained the situation until the Kulturbund itself was closed down, in September 1941, on the eve of the deportations of eastern Europe.

Among the institutions maintained by the cultural societies were the following: four theater companies (the central theater in Berlin, a youth theater that was also based in Berlin and became a traveling troupe, and companies in Cologne and Hamburg); four symphony orchestras; two opera companies (one in Berlin and the other a traveling opera, also based in Berlin); a number of choirs (the largest, at Mannheim, consisted of one thousand singers); many chamber orchestras; entertainment groups and lecturers; and mixed groups that visited even the smallest, most out-of-the-way communities and entertained them with song and music, recitations and games. All these activities—which also included exhibitions—gave moral support to the persecuted Jews and helped to sustain their spirits.

The question of the Jewish content of its activities preoccupied the Kulturbund from the very beginning. The point at issue was whether it should aim at maximum integration with the culture of the majority in the country—which was what most of the Jewish public expected and most of the organization's leaders demanded—or whether it should be an instrument for heightening Jewish consciousness and for Jewish spiritual regeneration. This latter was what the Zionists advocated and, in their view, was what the Jews of Germany desperately needed. Another significant factor was the ban on the use of German cultural resources that the supervising authorities were gradually imposing on the Jews. At first, the view that prevailed emphasized integration into German culture, although important cultural events of Jewish content also took place, such as the presentation of Stefan Zweig's *Jeremiah* by the Berlin Jewish Theater at the beginning of its second season. But this trend changed as time went on.

The growing hostility to which the Jews were exposed and the need to protect themselves from its debilitating moral effect, together with the realization that it was not a passing phase through which they were living, reinforced the view that it was the cultural society's task to enrich the Jewish population's Jewish experience. Efforts were made, beginning in 1936, to include in the program of theater performances the works of Jewish playwrights, especially from eastern Europe or Palestine; and the writing of original Jewish plays and musical works was encouraged and supported. As a result, the Jewish component in the programs rose steadily. These efforts, however, had only partial success, and did not always meet with a positive response from the Jewish public. The transformation of the organization from a "Jewish Cultural Society" into a "Society for Jewish Culture" could not be successfully accomplished under the conditions prevailing at the time it was undertaken. Moreover, the mounting difficulties that the Jews had to cope with just to keep alive did not serve to encourage their interest in matters of the spirit.

Nevertheless, at a time of persecution and despair, the Kulturbund was a spiritual support for the German Jews, strengthening the ties of individual Jews with the Jewish people and with their faith, and giving them pride in their Jewish identity. In that sense, the society's activities were a form of moral resistance to the hostile regime.

Elena Kutorgiene-Buivydaité.

BIBLIOGRAPHY

Cochavi, Y. *Armament for Spiritual Survival.* Naharia, Israel, 1988. (In Hebrew.)

Freeden, H. "A Jewish Theatre under the Swastika." *Leo Baeck Institute Yearbook* 1 (1956): 142–162.

Freeden, H. *Jüdisches Theater in Nazideutschland.* Tübingen, 1964.

YEHOYAKIM COCHAVI

KUTORGIENE-BUIVYDAITÉ, ELENA
(1888–1963), a "RIGHTEOUS AMONG THE NATIONS." Born in Šiauliai (until 1917, Shavli) in Lithuania, Kutorgiene completed her medical studies at Moscow University in 1912 and was then employed as an ophthalmologist in a hospital in Moscow. In 1922 she returned to Lithuania, worked in medical institutions in KOVNO, was active in the OEUVRE DE SECOURS AUX ENFANTS, a Jewish welfare organization for children, and established close relations with Jewish doctors.

During the German occupation of Lithuania, Kutorgiene concealed Jews in her home in Kovno and found other places of concealment for them as well. She established close ties with the underground movement of the Kovno ghetto; the meetings that both she and the local partisans held with the commander of the ghetto underground, Haim YELIN, took place in her home. Kutorgiene helped the underground to obtain arms, sought out hiding places for underground activity, and disseminated anti-Nazi literature. Her son Viktoras assisted her. She kept a diary, *Yoman Kovno* (Kovno Diary), sections of which have been published in the USSR and in Israel, in the journal *Yalkut Moreshet*. She also hid the writings of Yelin and of his brother Meir in her home in Kovno.

Following the city's liberation, in August 1944, Kutorgiene worked on the Special Government Commission for the Investigation of War Crimes. After the war she was awarded the Order of Lenin for her extensive social and medical activity, and the Medal for Work during the Great Patriotic War; in 1958 she received the honorary title of Outstanding Doctor of Lithuania. In 1982 she was awarded the title of "Righteous among the Nations" by YAD VASHEM in Jerusalem.

BIBLIOGRAPHY

Kutorgiene, E. "Kovno Diary." *Yalkut Moreshet* 17 (January 1974): 31–72.

HAYA LIFSHITZ